Counseling and Psychotherapy: A Behavioral Approach *by E. Lakin Phillips*

Dimensions of Personality *edited by Harvey London and John E. Exner, Jr.*

The Mental Health Industry: A Cultural Phenomenon *by Peter A. Magaro, Robert Gripp, David McDowell, and Ivan W. Miller III*

Nonverbal Communication: The State of the Art *by Robert G. Harper, Arthur N. Weins, and Joseph D. Matarazzo*

Alcoholism and Treatment *by David J. Armor, J. Michael Polich, and Harriet B. Stambul*

A Biodevelopmental Approach to Clinical Child Psychology: Cognitive Controls and Cognitive Control Theory *by Sebastiano Santostefano*

Handbook of Infant Development *edited by Joy D. Osofsky*

Understanding the Rape Victim: A Synthesis of Research Findings *by Sedelle Katz and Mary Ann Mazur*

Childhood Pathology and Later Adjustment: The Question of Prediction *by Loretta K. Cass and Carolyn B. Thomas*

Intelligent Testing with the WISC-R *by Alan S. Kaufman*

Adaptation in Schizophrenia: The Theory of Segmental Set *by David Shakow*

Psychotherapy: An Eclectic Approach *by Sol L. Garfield*

Handbook of Minimal Brain Dysfunctions *edited by Herbert E. Rie and Ellen D. Rie*

Handbook of Behavioral Interventions: A Clinical Guide *edited by Alan Goldstein and Edna B. Foa*

Art Psychotherapy *by Harriet Wadeson*

Handbook of Adolescent Psychology *edited by Joseph Adelson*

Psychotherapy Supervision: Theory, Research and Practice *edited by Allen K. Hess*

Psychology and Psychiatry in Courts and Corrections: Controversy and Change *by Ellsworth A. Fersch, Jr.*

Restricted Environmental Stimulation: Research and Clinical Applications *by Peter Suedfeld*

Personal Construct Psychology: Psychotherapy and Personality *edited by Alvin W. Landfield and Larry M. Leitner*

Mothers, Grandmothers, and Daughters: Personality and Child Care in Three-Generation Families *by Bertram J. Cohler and Henry U. Grunebaum*

Further Explorations in Personality *edited by A.I. Rabin, Joel Aronoff, Andrew M. Barclay, and Robert A. Zucker*

Hypnosis and Relaxation: Modern Verification of an Old Equation *by William E. Edmonston, Jr.*

Handbook of Clinical Behavior Therapy *edited by Samuel M. Turner, Karen S. Calhoun, and Henry E. Adams*

Handbook of Clinical Neuropsychology *edited by Susan B. Filskov and Thomas J. Boll*

The Course of Alcoholism: Four Years After Treatment *by J. Michael Polich, David J. Armor, and Harriet B. Braiker*

Handbook of Innovative Psychotherapies *edited by Raymond J. Corsini*

The Role of the Father in Child Development (Second Edition) *edited by Michael E. Lamb*

Behavioral Medicine: Clinical Applications *by Susan S. Pinkerton, Howard Hughes, and W.W. Wenrich*

Handbook for the Practice of Pediatric Psychology *edited by June M. Tuma*

Change Through Interaction: Social Psychological Processes of Counseling and Psychotherapy *by Stanley R. Strong and Charles D. Claiborn*

Drugs and Behavior (Second Edition) *by Fred Leavitt*

Handbook of Research Methods in Clinical Psychology *edited by Philip C. Kendall and James N. Butcher*

A Social Psychology of Developing Adults *by Thomas O. Blank*

(*continued on back*)

CLINICAL
RELAXATION
STRATEGIES

Clinical
Relaxation
Strategies

Kenneth L. Lichstein
Memphis State University

WILEY

A WILEY-INTERSCIENCE PUBLICATION

John Wiley & Sons

New York • Chichester • Brisbane • Toronto • Singapore

Library of Congress Cataloging-in-Publication Data:

Lichstein, Kenneth L.

  Clinical relaxation strategies.

  (Wiley series on personality processes)
  "A Wiley-Interscience publication."
  Includes bibliographies.
    1. Relaxation—Therapeutic use. 2. Relaxation.
I. Title. [DNLM: 1. Relaxation. 2. Relaxation
Technics. WM 425 L698c]

RC489.R45L54 1988   613.7'9   87–25296
ISBN 0–471–81592–6

Printed in the United States of America
10 9 8 7 6 5 4 3 2

To
Betty

Series Preface

This series of books is addressed to behavioral scientists interested in the nature of human personality. Its scope should prove pertinent to personality theorists and researchers as well as to clinicians concerned with applying an understanding of personality processes to the amelioration of emotional difficulties in living. To this end, the series provides a scholarly integration of theoretical formulations, empirical data, and practical recommendations.

Six major aspects of studying and learning about human personality can be designated: personality theory, personality structure and dynamics, personality development, personality assessment, personality change, and personality adjustment. In exploring these aspects of personality, the books in the series discuss a number of distinct but related subject areas: the nature and implications of various theories of personality; personality characteristics that account for consistencies and variations in human behavior; the emergence of personality processes in children and adolescents; the use of interviewing and testing procedures to evaluate individual differences in personality; efforts to modify personality styles through psychotherapy, counseling, behavior therapy, and other methods of influence; and patterns of abnormal personality functioning that impair individual competence.

IRVING B. WEINER

Fairleigh Dickinson University
Rutherford, New Jersey

Preface

Some time has passed since my fateful conversation with a practitioner colleague. Intending to present relaxation to her client, she asked me to recommend a book that displayed the available relaxation alternatives, as this practitioner did not have broad expertise on the subject. No such book existed.

Although the practice of relaxation dates back thousands of years, the salient scientific and professional literature on this subject has emerged only recently. Early in this century, the pioneering efforts of Jacobson with progressive relaxation and Schultz with autogenic training failed to generate broad interest. It was only in the late 1950s that the unplanned union of cultural, professional, and scientific forces created a veritable explosion of interest in relaxation. In the past few decades, an enormous, but somewhat invisible, body of knowledge on relaxation has accumulated within diverse disciplines, cultures, and philosophical contexts.

The need to organize a broad sampling of relaxation procedures under one cover stimulated my initial interest in writing this book. Thereby, students and practitioners could enjoy convenient access to the variety of relaxation techniques heretofore scattered in the literature of this and other countries.

Although the pragmatics of relaxation therapy implementation are an important focus of this book (Chapters 4 and 5), the scope of this book is broader than this. I wanted to produce a truly comprehensive accounting of relaxation so that one volume would present the multifaceted aspects of this subject. Thus, I have drawn upon some 1800 references in providing an encyclopedic treatment of the history (Chapter 1), theory (Chapter 2), basic research (Chapter 3), and clinical outcome research (Chapter 7) of relaxation, as well as an extended discussion of the integration of relaxation with other therapy techniques and systems (Chapter 6). This book is designed to serve three masters—the student, the scholar, and the practitioner. Related techniques, principally hypnosis and biofeedback, have generated vast literatures in their own right. They are accorded a small amount of space in the present text and are discussed only to the extent that they increase our understanding of nonhypnotic and nonbiofeedback relaxation. Many of the same relaxation methods are discussed in different chapters, but consistency was not observed in ordering the presentation of relaxation methods from one chapter to the next. Historical chronology, weight of evidence, amount of salient literature, and other factors dictated different coherent sequences for each chapter.

Scores of people, most of whom shall go unnamed, have made a valued contribution to this book. Chief among these are students who have in sum spent thousands of hours in retrieving library materials, performing word processing, and executing sundry other tasks: Donna Brooks, Thane Dykstra, Terry Eakin, Jim Edwards, Suzanne Fischer, Linda Hensley, Ron Johnson, Deborah O'Laughlin, John Sanders, and Jeff Wright. Marlin Moore provided invaluable consultation on the mechanics of word processing and on how to make computers behave. Deborah Brackstone executed her responsibilities as director of the interlibrary loan office with unfailing perseverance. Faye Wright, my past research assistant, past secretary, and present friend, is much deserving of my gratitude for her patience, industriousness, and superior (to my own) grammar. The manuscript was completed under the watchful care and dedicated efforts of my present secretary, Ms. Eula Horrell.

Numerous individuals have graciously consented to critique this manuscript, in part or whole and at various stages of development, and the book has benefited from their careful reading and willingness to be candid with me. Recognition is most strongly due Ed Blanchard, Jack Rachman, and Carolyn Johnson, and to these generous and talented people I am truly indebted. No less have I profited from the good counsel and encouragement of my esteemed colleague, Will Shadish.

A few special people have made an indirect contribution to this book. As a young assistant professor, I was wanting in many professorial skills and in need of a mentor. Ted Rosenthal ably and gently functioned in this role and provided me parts of the graduate education I never got in graduate school. The most satisfying aspect for me of serving on a university faculty is sharing in the personal and professional growth of graduate students. Two of my students, Jim Sallis and Tim Hoelscher, have grown remarkably well, and I have been enhanced by participating in their education.

During the many years I worked on this project and before, I have enjoyed the generous support and encouragement of my parents, Max and Sarah, and my wife's parents, David and Florence. I hope this acknowledgment makes up for the many times I forgot to say thanks. And lastly, I wish to thank my wife, Betty, and my children, Benjamin, Jeremy, and Jennifer. They bring joy to my life and give meaning to activities such as book writing, which would otherwise be trivial.

KENNETH L. LICHSTEIN

Memphis, Tennessee
January 1988

Contents

CLINICAL
RELAXATION
STRATEGIES

CHAPTER 1

A Historical Perspective

"The importance of relaxation as a preventive and therapeutic measure in this age of hypertension, maladjustment, and neurosis is being very slowly, perhaps rather too slowly, recognized." Thus wrote Professor Bagchi of the University of Iowa in 1936 (p. 424). The wisdom of this cautionary note has suffered little in the half century since its writing. No less impressive, it may have captured the spirit driving the visionaries of several millennia past who invented relaxation, namely, Eastern meditation.

Over time, relaxation in its many forms has been practiced by millions. Contrasting modern scientific methods of relaxation with their ancient counterparts, the similarities far outweigh the differences. The 20th century's primary contribution to the history of relaxation is that the scientific community discovered and decreed legitimate that which ordinary folk had known for thousands of years. Specifically, there are various methods of quiescent self-inquiry that lead to states of well-being not otherwise obtainable. These methods are collectively referred to as relaxation, and their practice likely predates the beginning of recorded history.

MEDITATION

The basis of modern relaxation techniques—most notably progressive relaxation, autogenic training, and guided imagery—lies in the meditation heritage of Eastern religions. Most 20th century "discoveries" are direct duplications or simple variations of time-honored meditative approaches (Malhotra, 1963).

Meditation is the generic name given to religious study in the numerous Eastern religions. For the most part, these religions were not divinity centered. Instead, religious study emphasized introspection. Thus, in its pure form, meditation serves a purpose roughly analogous to prayer and devotion in the Judeo-Christian systems.

Meditation has been used to achieve three primary goals: (a) contemplation and wisdom, (b) altered states of consciousness, and (c) relaxation. As Shapiro (1980) pointed out in the preface to his monograph on meditation, Eastern religions have emphasized the first two goals, Western culture the third. The Westernization of meditation has involved stripping the method of its philosophical/religious adornment, and then embellishing those aspects relevant to relaxation. The results are secular relaxation techniques that allow those burdened by 20th century stress to achieve inner peace, as did the Hindu peasant who longed for meaning and tranquility 5000 years ago.

Hinduism and Yoga

The earliest evidence of formal relaxation comes from the origins of Hinduism in India between 3000 and 4000 B.C. (Berry, 1971; Chan, Faruqi, Kitagawa, & Raju, 1969; Feuerstein, 1975). Its religious rituals were largely devoted to animal veneration and sacrifice, but they also included some interest in meditation. This meditation aspect represented the beginning of yoga, one of the subdisciplines of Hinduism, and was composed initially of loosely defined instructions to assume a comfortable posture, fix one's attention on a single object, and suppress respiration. Early devotees who achieved superior mastery of yoga introduced the familiar lotus sitting position—legs crossed and intermeshed. By the early Buddhist period, approximately 200 B.C., the philosophy and practice of yoga matured into a comprehensive, systematic body of knowledge as recorded by the sage Patanjali (Rama, 1979), although new developments and elaborations continued for at least another thousand years.

The contribution of yoga to the evolution of meditation cannot be overestimated. Not only was it the first formal meditation system, but it remains to this day the most heterogeneous body of meditative approaches organized under a single name (Feuerstein, 1975). Indeed, the derivation of most other forms of meditation can be traced directly to yoga.

Yoga philosophy endorses an ascetic life style and prescribes advancement through numerous levels of knowledge and experience in quest of *samadhi,* the ultimate altered state of consciousness. Samadhi is characterized by a feeling of peacefulness and a sense of transcending one's corporal limits. Similar experiential states are a vital part of most other meditative systems such as Buddhism (*nirvana*) and Zen Buddhism (*satori*). Also, it may be noted that an important feature of the currently popular Transcendental Meditation (transcendence) owes its origin to yoga.

There are six primary schools of yoga (Chaudhuri, 1975; Douglas, 1971; Feuerstein, 1975; Rama, 1979; Rieker, 1971), each emphasizing distinctive points of view and procedure. *Hatha* Yoga is typified by numerous gestures and postures (calisthenics) conducted within a symbolic, reflective atmosphere, the goal being to unite body and mind harmoniously. On the opposite end of the spectrum is *Raja* Yoga, which prescribes body immobility and thought expression until *samadhi* naturally emerges. Some writers, including Rama, also used the term *Raja* Yoga as a generic label encompassing all other yoga forms. *Jnana* Yoga places greatest value on acquisition of knowledge of the yoga scriptures and lore. *Kundalini* Yoga prescribes a variety of exercises to tap *chakras,* seven pools of energy within our body. *Bhakti* Yoga stresses loving devotion to God through prayer, song, and various rituals (as in the Hare Krishna movement, Goleman, 1977). *Karma* Yoga encourages enactment of yoga principles through active participation in mundane matters; in other words, adherents strive to become model citizens. A seventh school, *Tantric Yoga,* was the last to develop (between 600 and 1200 A.D.), and is a synthesis of the other schools infused with magic and 'mysticism. Its contribution to meditative technique include the use of a *mantra,* silent repetition of a sacred word, the use of a *yantra,* an object for gaze meditation, and the reliance on imagery exercises to vivify desired realities.

Hinduism and its meditation component, yoga, failed to gain broad acceptance as formal disciplines outside of India. However, yoga exerted a powerful influence on the development of Buddhist meditation forms, and the dissemination of the latter throughout Asia reflected yoga traditions.

Buddhism

Six hundred B.C. marks the birth of the Buddhist religion (Layman, 1976; Ling, 1973). Buddhist interest in meditation can be traced to the spiritual enlightenment and sense of tranquility first achieved by the Buddha himself while meditating under the sacred *bodhi* (enlightenment) tree. At first, Buddhist meditation was primarily an intellectual experience. Sitting quietly amid peaceful surroundings, in the lotus position inherited from yoga, the meditator dwelled on philosophical/religious themes in search of increasingly nobler truths. The method took numerous forms depending upon one's sect and personal preferences, but it often involved some form of respiration mindfulness (Swearer, 1971). The general purpose was to attain an advanced level of concentration aimed, in part, at ridding the mind of tangential thoughts. With practice, one can advance through levels of consciousness until reaching peaceful intellectual clarity accompanied by a diminished sense of individuality (Goleman, 1972a).

At about the time of the birth of Christ, Buddhism was fragmenting within India into two major sects, Theravada and Mahayana, and numerous minor ones (Conze, 1959). Also by this time, and for some 1000 years hence, the Buddhist influence was spreading to most Asian countries. Each new culture that assimilated Buddhism introduced revisions in religious belief and practice. Similarly, the original meditative practice also saw modification. Some versions emphasized respiration or imagery, others emphasized repetition of words or phrases (mantras), and so forth.

Perhaps the most influential of the newer meditative forms is Zen Buddhism, which first emerged in China and subsequently in Japan (Legate, 1981; Phillips, 1973). Zen identified the Buddha's enlightenment experience as the distinctive, precious contribution of Buddhism. Thus, the meditative method was elevated to a position of focal importance in Japanese religious rituals.

By approximately the year 1300 A.D., the expansion of Buddhism in Asia was complete. Over the next 500 years, the popularity and influence of Buddhism varied greatly from one Asian country to the next, mostly as a function of political and military transitions.

THE FIRST HALF OF THE 20TH CENTURY

During the period 1890–1930, the three major forms of current relaxation practice—meditation, progressive relaxation, and autogenics—emerged in the Western world. During this time, meditation achieved its first noteworthy exposure outside of the Orient, and the latter two methods were invented.

Meditation

Two Buddhist scholars addressed the World Parliament of Religions in Chicago in 1893, and they enjoyed a positive reception (Layman, 1976). This was a historic occasion in that it concretely led to the promulgation of meditation in the West. Enthusiastic accounts of the Chicago conference filtered back to Japan and encouraged a small but steady stream of Buddhist teachers to emigrate to the United States. The first Zen center in the United States was founded in San Francisco in 1909. Overall, though there were pioneering advances of meditation in America during the first half of this century, they were few in number and registered little impact.

Slow dissemination persisted despite meditation endorsement by luminary figures. In the professional sphere, William James (1902, pp. 391–397) called attention to several meditation systems within the context of a discussion of altered states of consciousness, and Franz Alexander (1922/1931) commented on the compatibility between meditation and psychoanalysis. In the public domain, the heroic political efforts of Mahatma Gandhi catapulted Hinduism and its meditative rituals into public awareness throughout the world (Morgan, 1953), but this also failed to stimulate Western adoption of meditation.

By 1950, virtually every major American city had at least one Zen center. However, meditation attracted only a small following until a combination of factors resulted in a sharp increase in its popularity in the 1950s.

Progressive Relaxation

Edmund Jacobson was born in Chicago in 1888 (Jacobson, 1977, 1979) and died in the same city in January, 1983 (McGuigan, 1986; Oken, 1983). A childhood experience in a traumatic fire stimulated his interest in the subject of anxiety, which was to remain a primary focus throughout his life. Jacobson pursued this interest in his undergraduate studies at Northwestern and as a graduate student at Harvard, where he earned a Ph.D. in psychology at the young age of 22. Although he studied with the most eminent psychologists of the time—James, Royce, and Munsterberg—and with the renowned physiologist Cannon, Jacobson grew dissatisfied with the modest level of scientific rigor typifying the psychologists' work. Therefore, in 1910 he declined a Harvard fellowship and undertook study with Titchener at Cornell. Unfortunately, here, too, the experimental methods fell short of Jacobson's standards. After one year, Jacobson left Cornell to begin medical school at the University of Chicago.

Jacobson earned an M.D. in 1915 (McGuigan, 1978). He joined the physiology department at the University of Chicago a few years later and remained there till 1936, devoting much of his time to research (Oken, 1983). For more than 50 years, Jacobson advanced progressive relaxation in his clinical research reports, supported by his private practice and the sponsorship of foundations.

Jacobson's interest in methods of relaxation began at Harvard in 1907, prompted in part by his desire to remediate his own insomnia (Jacobson, 1938a; McGuigan, 1978). He first published on the topic of relaxation in 1912, when he asked experimental subjects to achieve greater relaxation through their own efforts in a basic research study on perceptual processes. He commenced clinical applications of progressive relaxation around 1918 (Jacobson, 1920b, 1924), and first published an account of the clinical method in two 1920 articles that included case histories treating anxiety, insomnia, and tics.

Of particular historical interest in these two articles was the versatility and flexibility Jacobson encouraged in the use of progressive relaxation. Although Wolpe (1958) is credited with devising the condensed format for progressive relaxation that is currently popular, and Goldfried (1971) is credited with introducing the sophisticated self-control format, both of these variations on the standard method were delineated and endorsed by Jacobson in 1920. However, in his major work (Jacobson, 1929) and subsequent publications, Jacobson gave primary emphasis to a meticulous procedure and a plodding pace in progressive relaxation.

Jacobson was most productive between 1925 and 1940. His efforts focused on cognitive and physiological processes in progressive relaxation (see Chapters 2 and 3 for an in-depth treatment of this research). The technical requirements of this line of research led Jacobson to invent instrumentation to measure muscle activity (electromyography) and eye movements (electro-oculography) (Jacobson, 1973a). This period witnessed the publication of his classic text, *Progressive Relaxation* (Jacobson, 1929), and the layman's version, *You Must Relax* (Jacobson, 1934c). Beginning in this period, Jacobson also maintained an active clinical practice. As enumerated in the second edition of his classic text (Jacobson, 1938a), progressive relaxation was applied to a broad array of disorders, exemplified by anxiety, insomnia, tics, headaches, and depression.

Under his tutelage, Jacobson's wife used progressive relaxation to achieve natural childbirth with their first child in 1930 (Szirmai, 1980), and he later wrote a book on this subject (1959). Jacobson's observation that the "eyes are active" (1938b, p. 144) during dreaming occurred 15 years before the *official* discovery of rapid eye movements by Aserinsky and Kleitman (1953). Indeed, Jacobson (1973a) recounts that Kleitman, an internationally renowned sleep researcher, was uninterested at first in Jacobson's finding but eventually directed Aserinsky, Kleitman's graduate student, to go to Jacobson's lab to learn about these eye movements.

During the course of his career, Jacobson has made a prolific contribution to the scientific literature, including more than a dozen books. Yet, his views on anxiety processes and treatment did not gain a wide audience until Wolpe (1958) adopted progressive relaxation as a key ingredient in systematic desensitization (Goldfried, 1980). The reasons for this 40-year delay of professional acceptance of Jacobson's views are no doubt numerous and complex. Stoyva (1973) and Goldfried (1977) cite incompatibility with the psychoanalytic model, which dominated mental health during these years, and I strongly concur. Other factors will be discussed later in this chapter. For the moment, let it suffice to say that the fields of psychosomatic treatment and behavioral medicine are deeply indebted to the courageous and inspired work of Edmund Jacobson.

Autogenic Training

Around 1900, while engaged in the practice of clinical hypnosis, Berlin neurologist Oskar Vogt observed that a number of his patients spontaneously self-induced hypnotic-like states after a period of conventional training (Schultz & Luthe, 1959). These patients consistently reported sensations of heaviness and warmth to be particularly prominent in their experience. Perceiving the potential usefulness of this self-induced hypnosis, Vogt and his collaborator, Korbinian Brodmann, encouraged the systematic use of autohypnosis because of its therapeutic effects on headaches, tension, fatigue, etc.

Revising and elaborating upon Vogt's seminal ideas, Johannes Schultz (born 1884, died 1970) developed the system known as autogenic training during the second and the third decades of this century (Lindemann, 1973; Luthe, 1965b; Schultz, 1954–1955). Trained initially as a dermatologist, Schultz shifted to neurology and psychiatry early in his career. He began practicing hypnosis around 1905 and later devoted most of his attention to autohypnotic processes. Schultz observed that his subjects regularly experienced sensations of heaviness and warmth, as previously reported by Vogt, as well as other sensations including calming of the heart and cooling of the forehead. These emergent sensations, six in number, formed the core of the relaxation-induction method Schultz developed.

Schultz emphasized self-induction in order to decrease patient dependency on the therapist, and he encouraged the patient to assume an active role in the therapeutic process (Luthe, 1962a). Based primarily on his research work on hallucination induction with normal subjects and clinical experience in the treatment of anxiety and psychosomatic disorders, Schultz first described autogenic training in 1926 and his major book, *Das Autogene Training* appeared in 1932.

Following a series of academic and clinical appointments, Schultz devoted himself to the full-time practice of psychiatry in Berlin in 1924. During the course of his career he published more than 400 articles and several books. Much like progressive relaxation, autogenic training was slow to attract the attention of health professionals. Wolfgang Luthe (1965b), Schultz' main disciple and principal expounder of autogenics in the Western hemisphere, pointed out that fewer than 50 articles on autogenic training appeared between 1930 and 1945. With respect to American usage, the language barrier was a major delimiting factor.

1950-1970

In the decade following 1950, several independent factors converged to spark the popularity of all relaxation approaches. Perhaps the most critical of these factors was the attenuation of psychiatry's control over the delivery of mental health services. During the first half of this century, psychiatry dominated mental health services primarily through the modality of psychoanalysis. During World War II and its aftermath, an enormous need for mental health services thrust psychologists and, to a lesser extent, social workers into the position of primary caregivers, in contrast to their accustomed duties as testers and psychiatric assistants (Brieland, 1977; K. A. Kendall, 1982; P. C. Kendall & Norton-Ford, 1982; Korchin, 1983; Reisman, 1976). This influx of new professionals and orientations created a dynamic (not necessarily psychodynamic) atmosphere receptive to existing approaches that had previously achieved only marginal recognition within the psychoanalytic-psychiatric establishment (e.g., relaxation). This same process stimulated the development of new therapeutic systems (e.g., behavior therapy).

A second factor, which simultaneously undermined established psychotherapeutic approaches and elevated (perhaps exaggerated) the value of a wide variety of nontraditional approaches including relaxation, was the social unrest that erupted in the 1960s. Psychotherapy was certainly not a highly visible target of this phase of world history, nor was it affected as much as were other institutions. Yet, the impatience with slow change and the contempt for existing practices that marked the cultural revolution also invaded the field of psychotherapy. This was a time when exotic forms of individual and group psychotherapy and a potpourri of "growth experiences" appeared in rapid succession (e.g., Schultz, 1967) and were often embraced by seasoned professionals and uninitiated laymen alike. This same cultural process encouraged self-exploration and experimentation with altered states of consciousness. Attitudes such as these, which placed increasing value on knowledge of self, were congruent with diverse forms of relaxation and facilitated the broad dissemination of this class of techniques.

There were other narrow forces that helped popularize particular relaxation approaches. With regard to meditation, there were numerous triggers. Respected accounts of extraordinary physiological feats performed by yogis (Vakil, 1950) began attracting attention soon after World War II. Shapiro

(1980) pointed out that rigorous scientific accounts of meditation masters' admirable control over their physiology began appearing in respected scientific journals in the late 1950s (e.g., Anand, Chhina, & Singh, 1961a; Bagchi & Wenger, 1957; Kasamatsu et at., 1957). Similarities between the LSD state and various forms of meditation (Gellhorn & Kiely, 1972; Layman, 1976) stimulated interest in Eastern meditation approaches as an offshoot of the ascendancy of recreational drug use. There was a large spurt in the oriental population of the United States following World War II due to American servicemen returning to the United States with oriental wives, and this influx stimulated oriental culture, including meditation (Layman, 1976). Lastly, Maharishi Mahesh Yogi, in his genius for marketing be it intentional or accidental, began influencing millions of people in 1958 with his brand of yoga relaxation, Transcendental Meditation (TM) (Forem, 1974; Yogi, 1975, 1976).

By 1958, Jacobson had published a substantial amount of basic research and clinical data in support of progressive relaxation. However, excepting for an occasional, isolated reference (e.g., Garmany, 1952; Hadley, 1938; Jones, 1953; Kubie, 1943; Neufeld, 1951; Pascal, 1947; Read, 1944; Traut, 1932), the health professions virtually ignored his contribution, perhaps due in part to the impracticality of the lengthy treatment course Jacobson advocated (Goldfried & Trier, 1974). Wolpe's publication of *Psychotherapy by Reciprocal Inhibition* in 1958 swiftly remedied this condition. As an integral part of his method of imaginal exposure to graduated anxiety (systematic desensitization), Wolpe prescribed an abbreviated format of progressive relaxation to serve as the anxiety antagonist. Typically, Wolpe employed five to seven sessions, and only one half of each session was used to teach progressive relaxation. Compare this protocol to the orthodox one composed of 10 to 20 times this number of sessions, often extending over half a year or longer by Jacobson's (1929) own account.

Systematic desensitization had a tremendous impact on psychology and psychiatry in the years that followed and focally illuminated progressive relaxation before the mental health professions. As pointed out earlier, Jacobson (1920a, 1920b) early on endorsed the usefulness of abbreviated progressive relaxation to the point of condensing the entire procedure down to one or two sessions. The distinction properly due Wolpe on the matter of abbreviated progressive relaxation is one of emphasis, not invention.

Autogenic training was virtually unknown in this country before Schultz published a short article in the *British Journal of Medical Hypnotism* (1954–1955), followed by a brief chapter in Masserman and Moreno's (1957) edited survey of psychotherapy. By this time, utilization of autogenic training in Europe (particularly in Austria, Germany, and Spain) and Japan had begun to accumulate momentum (Fromm-Reichmann & Moreno, 1956; Luthe, 1965a). However, it was the publication of Schultz and Luthe's book *Autogenic Training* (1959) that prompted serious interest in the United States. This book included 600 references on autogenic training published mostly since 1950 and drawn from countries around the world, primarily Germany. Up until 1960, only one percent of the autogenic literature appeared in English (Schultz & Luthe, 1961). Although to the present day the language barrier continues to be a formidable obstacle in disseminating information on this method, the exposure of autogenic training in English-speaking countries has sharply increased.

During the approximate period 1960–1970, the varieties of relaxation therapy became entrenched in the mainstream of American psychotherapy as more and more professionals were exposed to these methods and used relaxation in their clinical practice. Maupin's review of Zen Buddhism and its relationship to psychotherapy, appearing in 1962 in a prominent conservative journal, is illustrative of this trend. Following are some developments of historical import during this period.

Shapiro (1980) cites a Gallop poll indicating that by the mid 1970s, nearly eight percent of Americans had some involvement in Eastern philosophy and/or meditation. Timothy Leary and the TM movement may be cited as major facilitators of this extraordinary growth.

The deluge of publicity Timothy Leary attracted during the 1960s exerted a strong positive influence on the dissemination of meditation (Flagler, 1967; Weil, 1963). This effect was congruent with Leary's philosophy that preached the virtues of altered states of consciousness and the adoption of alternative lifestyles and unconventional solutions to problems. Even more to the point, Leary's Harvard colleague and cosponsor of these views, Richard Alpert, changed his name to Baba Ram Dass and explicitly prescribed eastern meditation as an integral part of the lifestyle they favored (Ram Dass, 1971).

TM began to flourish in the mid-1960s (Forem, 1974). The Students International Meditation Society, the TM organization specifically targeting college students, was formed in 1965 and a network of centers on college campuses sprang up throughout this country. In 1971, Maharishi International University was created with campuses in several countries. Currently, the American campus is in Fairfield, Iowa. By about 1970, Forem reports, TM was practiced in 60 countries. The TM organization claims to have trained more than one million individuals by the mid-1970s (Domash, 1977a). Benson's secular version of TM first appeared in 1974 in *Psychiatry* (Benson, Beary, & Carol). He then educated a vast general audience in meditation through his best-selling book, *The Relaxation Response* (1975).

Progressive relaxation became a household word by 1970, particularly in the homes of behavior therapists. Scores of published accounts of systematic desensitization helped certify progressive relaxation as one of the key techniques of behavior therapy. Also, by about this time therapists had begun to employ progressive relaxation independent of systematic desensitization to treat such disorders as interview anxiety (Zeisset, 1968), migraine headaches (Lutker, 1971), phobic anxiety (Mathews & Gelder, 1969), excitedness in autistic children (Graziano & Kean, 1968), and test anxiety (Laxer, Quarter, Kooman, & Walker, 1969). Late in his career Jacobson published seven books on progressive relaxation (1959, 1963, 1964a, 1964b, 1967a, 1967c, 1970), followed by the highly referenced text by Bernstein and Borkovec (1973).

Mostly through the efforts of Wolfgang Luthe, autogenics achieved high visibility in the 1960s. In addition to publishing numerous articles, Luthe edited a multilingual, international text (1965a) and an exhaustive six-volume series (1969–1973) on autogenic therapy. An English translation of a German monograph on clinical procedures in autogenics also appeared during this period (Kleinsorge & Klumbies, 1962/1964). In 1969, the Oskar Vogt Institute was created at Kyushu University, Fukuoka, Japan, for the study and training of autogenic therapy (Schultz & Luthe, 1969).

1970–PRESENT

In recent years, we have witnessed the emergence of three significant, relatively novel trends in psychotherapy (broadly defined) that have had a major impact on the varieties of relaxation therapies. These are biofeedback, self-control, and behavioral medicine, and they will now be reviewed with regard to their connection with relaxation therapy.

Biofeedback

Biofeedback may be defined as (a) the use of instrumentation to monitor ordinarily imperceptible biological processes, and then (b) feeding back information on changes in these processes to the subject through simple, convenient displays for the purpose of (c) teaching greater voluntary control over these biological processes. The first major surge of interest in biofeedback occurred about 1965 when Miller and his associates began publishing a series of articles describing remarkable control achieved by rats over aspects of their own physiology through operant conditioning training. Miller (1969) described how rats learned to change their own heart rate, blood pressure, intestinal contractions, kidney function, etc. It should be noted that, by his own admission (Miller, 1978), some of these fascinating research findings have since fallen into disrepute. Nevertheless, this and other research obviously generated possibilities for clinical applications with humans, and by 1970 clinical biofeedback was well established. More thorough accounts of the history of biofeedback are available for the interested reader (e.g., Blanchard & Epstein, 1978; Gatchel & Price, 1979).

Indications of the growth of biofeedback activity may be gleaned from *Psychological Abstracts* and *Index Medicus,* the primary indexing sources for the psychological and medical literatures, respectively. The key word "biofeedback" was introduced in *Psychological Abstracts* in 1974 and in *Index Medicus* in 1977. By the late 1970s, a large number of biofeedback studies were reaching the journals reflecting both clinical and scholarly interest in the subject. In the period 1977–1980, there was an average of 186 and 137 biofeedback citations per year in the psychological and medical indexes, respectively.

The growth of biofeedback had a positive influence on relaxation therapies in general. Whereas in the past, relaxation approaches did not enjoy acceptance among physicians, now segments of the medical community endorsed biofeedback for the treatment of traditional medical disorders such as headache and essential hypertension (for comprehensive accounts of clinical biofeedback, see Blanchard & Epstein, 1978; Gatchel & Price, 1979). Thus, the enthusiasm generated by biofeedback penetrated medical settings and won increased exposure for other psychological interventions as well. Further, as it became apparent that biofeedback and nonbiofeedback relaxation techniques were interchangeable in many cases (Silver & Blanchard, 1978; Tarler-Benlolo, 1978), the instrumentation cost of the former often resulted in the selection of relaxation as the preferred treatment.

Self-control

The concept of self-control closely relates to issues such as motivation, will, and determination that have captivated psychology since its inception. Around 1970, an empirically derived notion of self-control coalesced from the intermingling of numerous, relatively independent sources.

Consensual agreement does not exist regarding the definition of self-control. I drew upon some of the major writers in this area to evolve a definition that encompasses most of the usage given the term. Self-control refers to episodes in which an individual performs in a self-enhancing way that contradicts sound prediction (Goldfried & Merbaum, 1973; Kanfer, 1971; Kanfer & Karoly, 1982; Thoresen & Mahoney, 1974). The three key ingredients in this definition are episodes, self-enhancing, and sound prediction.

The term *episodes* implies that a given individual will exert self-control at some times and not at others. Specifically, self-control is viewed as a planned, effortful state, as opposed to an embedded, enduring personality trait. Describing self-control as *self-enhancing* reflects conventional practice. When persons behave in ways that are self-defeating, this, too, could conceivably be the result of self rather than external control, but the term *self-control* is rarely invoked in this negative context. *Sound prediction* entails the following. There occurs deceleration of undesirable behavior (including motor expression, thoughts, or emotions) or acceleration of desirable behavior following a relatively stable baseline, and most importantly, external constraints or encouragement are not present to a sufficient degree to account for the change. Conversely, behavior may continue relatively unchanged despite the presentation of temptations or obstacles. Some perceive negative attributes of self-control, including rigidity and interpersonal detachment (Shapiro, 1983a).

This definition implicitly stipulates that the individual, that is, the self-system (Bandura, 1978), deserves primary credit for generating certain operations that account for the behavior in question. The dimensions and range of these operations are complex and extend beyond the realm of this book. The reader is referred to the recent text by Karoly and Kanfer (1982) for a comprehensive treatment of this matter.

The self-control movement was formally christened in a landmark paper by Kanfer (1971), following a decade of interest in cognitive factors in the clinical domain. Albert Bandura's research (1969) emphasizing multifaceted cognitive processing variables mediating behavior was undoubtedly a crucial influence. Other innovations that contributed to the development of a well-rounded self-control orientation were (a) theoretical and clinical advances in covert conditioning (Cautela, 1966b; Homme, 1965), (b) the potential for self-regulation suggested by biofeedback, (c) demonstrations of the clinical utility of individuals actively manipulating their own environment, in other words, stimulus control procedures (Goldiamond, 1965), and (d) initial evidence indicating individuals can restructure their conscious thoughts to promote behavioral improvement, in other words, cognitive behavior modification (Meichenbaum, 1969).

With specific import for relaxation therapy, Goldfried's (1971) historic paper restyled the cognitive and relaxation components of systematic desensitization into a self-control format. Goldfried focally addressed the critical issue of clinical discontinuity between deep, static relaxation cultivated in a peaceful, protected environment, and utilization of that relaxation method in the tumult of normally occurring stress.

The self-control reformulation of progressive relaxation emphasized the learning of a highly-abbreviated, portable version of relaxation that could be applied as a "general anxiety-reducing skill" (Goldfried, 1971, p. 228), which the client could conveniently summon up in the natural course of events as needed. Thus, the role of the client was redefined as an active therapeutic agent working in his/her own behalf when confronted with noxious stimuli.

As a historical note, I must again add that Jacobson (1920a) used the terms *relative relaxation* and subsequently (1929) *differential relaxation* to describe a brief, unobtrusive version of progressive relaxation employed to extend the benefits of progressive relaxation from the therapy office to the natural environment. Wolpe (1958) also acknowledged the usefulness of differential relaxation, although he did not routinely encourage its use. He concluded that unplanned encounters with intense anxiety-provoking situations rendered differential relaxation therapeutically inert.

In the past decade, self-control relaxation has generated considerable interest and stimulated a new surge of enthusiasm concerning the potential usefulness of relaxation. Variations on Goldfried's prescription have evolved under such names as cue-controlled relaxation, coping relaxation, and applied relaxation (see Chapter 5 for elaboration). Recent reviews (e.g., Deffenbacher & Suinn, 1982) cite progress in the technology of teaching self-control relaxation and amplifications of the basic method, including the use of breath manipulations and conditioned cognitive prompts. Self-control relaxation formats have also proved highly amenable to integration with cognitive restructuring approaches, resulting in comprehensive strategies for combating anxiety and tension. Alternately termed stress inoculation training, anxiety management training, and self-control desensitization, these conjoint approaches fall under the popularized class of strategies termed *stress management* (see Chapter 6 for elaboration).

Behavioral Medicine

Although controversy persists as to the precise definition of behavioral medicine, the consensus view holds that it consists of a multidisciplinary approach to the prevention and treatment of medical disorders (Gentry, 1978). Others focus on the application of behavior therapy techniques to illness and to health risk behaviors (Pomerleau, 1979). Marked by experimental methodology and conservative scientific scrutiny, behavioral medicine may be contrasted with the psychoanalytically dominated field of psychosomatic medicine first popularized by Franz Alexander in the 1930s (Laman & Evans, 1980).

The term *behavioral medicine* did not even exist in 1970. Some major landmarks giving impetus to the development of this new field were the 1974 conference, "Applying Behavioral Science to Cardiovascular Risk," Seattle, Washington (Laman & Evans, 1980), and the Yale Conference on Behavioral Medicine in 1977 (Schwartz & Weiss, 1978). The Academy and Society of Behavioral Medicine and the *Journal of Behavioral Medicine* grew out of the Yale Conference. Weiss (1980) pointed out that formal training programs in behavioral medicine and research activity in the area have sharply increased since 1975.

The rise in popularity of biofeedback was one of the pivotal forces giving impetus to the fledgling field of behavioral medicine in the early 1970s (Blanchard, 1982; Shapiro, 1979). With each new application of biofeedback, opportunities materialized to apply collateral interventions as well. Over time, comprehensive behavioral medicine treatment packages evolved in such areas as heart disease, pain management, and essential hypertension. Most often, some form of relaxation is a mainstay of the therapeutic regimen. This conclusion is supported by the substantial amount of space dedicated to relaxation therapy in behavioral medicine texts (e.g., McNamara, 1979; Pomerleau & Brady, 1979; Prokop & Bradley, 1981). A special issue of the *Journal of Consulting and Clinical Psychology,* 1982, Volume 50(6), was devoted to behavioral medicine and provided further evidence of the substantial role of relaxation in this area. The issue included 13 articles reviewing particular disorders (e.g., smoking, obesity, and hypertension) that have attracted the attention of behavioral medicine practitioners. Twelve of these articles specifically recommended relaxation as an independent or adjunctive therapeutic modality.

PRESENT STATUS

More than 50 years have passed since Jacobson (1929) lamented that a scientific method of relaxation did not previously exist. Medical and psychiatric treatment often included exhortations to relax but, typically, instructions on how to accomplish this, short of "take a vacation," were not forthcoming. This state of affairs has since undergone drastic alteration. By now, a variety of relaxation techniques are widely known and have earned the respect of health professionals. For example, the American Psychiatric Association (1977) issued a position statement on meditation, recognizing the potential contribution of this form of relaxation in psychiatric regimens and encouraging further research to more clearly delineate the clinical utility of meditation.

For millions of people, relaxation is much more than a vague concept with fuzzy details on how to attain it. Recent books and audiotapes for professionals (e.g., Bernstein & Borkovec, 1973; Goldfried, 1976; Schultz & Luthe, 1969; Woolfolk & Lehrer, 1984) and laymen (e.g., Benson, 1975; Budzynski, 1974; Davis, Eshelman, & McKay, 1980; Rosen, 1977; Smith, 1985) make a variety of scientifically documented relaxation techniques readily available. Further, there is a substantial accumulation of basic and clinical research testifying to the validity of many of the applications of these techniques.

One way of gauging the visibility and importance of a treatment approach is to monitor publication trends. We compared the number of articles published on relaxation therapy with publications on social skills training, a well recognized and highly regarded treatment mode. In this analysis, relaxation therapy was defined as treatment package interventions that included a relaxation component, as well as interventions exclusively composed of relaxation. A parallel definition was applied to social skills training. For the years 1985 and 1986, we surveyed two premier journals, *Behavior Therapy* (BT) and the *Journal of Consulting and Clinical Psychology* (JCCP). Table 1.1 presents our findings.

Considering the behavioral journal (BT) first, relaxation therapy appeared in 13.4 percent of the published articles in the years 1985 and 1986 considered jointly, compared to an incidence of 17.1 percent for social skills training. The occurrence of both relaxation and social skills research was proportionately smaller in JCCP, which serves a broader readership. For the two years in this journal, both relaxation and social skills research were represented in 8.2 percent of the articles. Interestingly, research in relaxation therapy was reported at about three-fourths the incidence of research in social skills in BT but at the same rate as social skills research in JCCP. To summarize, relaxation is a highly visible technique in the clinical literature, and although it is well repre-

TABLE 1.1. Number (And Percent) of Published Articles on Relaxation Therapy and Social Skills Training

Journals	Relaxation Therapy		Social Skills Training	
	1985	1986	1985	1986
Behavior Therapy	6 (14.3%)	5 (12.5%)	8 (19.0%)	6 (15.0%)
Journal of Consulting and Clinical Psychology	12 (9.8%)	7 (6.3%)	11 (9.0%)	8 (7.2%)

sented within general clinical psychology (as reflected in JCCP), its main stronghold is in behavior therapy.

The remainder of this book presents a comprehensive account of relaxation therapy. Chapter 2 summarizes the underlying theories supporting the three major forces in relaxation therapy: meditation, progressive relaxation, and autogenic training. Chapter 3 reviews basic research, organized by relaxation techniques, to determine the effects of the major relaxation methods. Approximately 10 specific relaxation techniques, varying along the dimensions of procedural style and depth of effect, are described in great detail in Chapters 4 and 5. Chapter 6 discusses the integration of relaxation methods with traditional psychotherapeutic approaches and describes the contribution of relaxation in multifaceted treatment packages for particular disorders. The final chapter reviews the clinical outcome literature that evinces a diverse range of target symptoms for effective relaxation application.

The purview of this book is limited to methods of relaxation requiring neither special equipment nor highly specialized expertise. The techniques reviewed and taught herein can be mastered easily by psychologists, counselors, psychiatrists, social workers, and the like, having general psychotherapy training. Other mature intervention systems, particularly biofeedback and hypnosis, though bearing substantial overlap with relaxation therapy, will be afforded only minimum coverage.

FUTURE TRENDS

Interesting developments are beginning to emerge that hold considerable promise for improving relaxation therapy. Data in these areas are not sufficiently developed at the present time to justify firm conclusions or strong recommendations. In drawing attention to the following subjects, my goal is to stimulate efforts among clinicians/researchers to further explore these areas.

Relaxation Techniques Used by Nonpsychotherapists

To date, psychologists, counselors, and to a lesser extent psychiatrists have been the major users of relaxation techniques. Two other groups of professionals who might profitably employ methods of relaxation, particularly the highly condensed forms (Chapter 5), are social workers and medical caregivers.

Social workers are often employed by governmental and private institutions to provide direct client services or to assist clients in obtaining appropriate services elsewhere. In either case, there may be a disproportionately large percentage of economically disadvantaged and bureaucratically frustrated clients. All too often, clients will exhibit emotional eruptions born of chronic discouragement and acute crises (Levy, 1981).

The presentation of simple relaxation techniques can be expected to improve the quality of life for the above clientele in two ways. First, anxiety reduction as an end in itself is a far more desirable state than is emotional distress. Second, the individual would be able to operate more efficiently in interactions with the environment and would be more likely to secure potential opportunities. It is encouraging to observe that relaxation therapy is gaining greater acceptance among clinical social workers, as evidenced by the endorsement of this approach by current social work texts (e.g., Schinke, 1981; Wodarski & Bagarozzi, 1979) and recent published research (Thyer, 1983).

Medical caregivers, including physicians and nurses, are a second group for whom the increased use of brief relaxation methods may prove fruitful (Morris, 1979). The medical health practitioner frequently encounters patients exhibiting acute anxiety symptomatology, which interferes with medical evaluation and treatment. The accurate recording of blood pressure, routine gynecological examinations, and minor outpatient surgery are examples of medical procedures that are hampered by patients' elevated anxiety. In these instances, the anxiety often could be subdued easily by the impromptu presentation of one of the convenient relaxation methods described in Chapter 5, particularly guided imagery and deep, slow breathing. (Clinical data relevant to this assertion are presented in Chapter 7, *Preparation for Medical and Dental Treatment.*)

The case of conditioned nausea associated with cancer chemotherapy serves as a dramatic illustration of this point. Despite the use of antiemetic drugs, nausea and vomiting may be so severe in this context that some patients will actually terminate treatment and risk dire consequences (Lyles, Burish, Krozely, & Oldham, 1982; Redd, Rosenberger, & Hendler, 1982–1983). Various forms of relaxation have proven helpful in abating this side-effect and in permitting the chemotherapy course to continue more easily (Redd & Andrykowski, 1982), although the problem of nausea may return when formal relaxation therapy is discontinued. Lyles et al. (1982) recommend training the oncology nurse in brief relaxation methods so that once progress in overcoming nausea has been established, the nurse can maintain these benefits through the periodic administration of booster relaxation.

In cases of refractory, persistent anxiety, the medical practitioner is advised to refer the patient to a colleague well versed in anxiety management therapies for a more systematic intervention. However, the primary medical caregiver can conveniently apply relaxation to mitigate transitory, situation-specific anxiety manifesting in individuals who are otherwise well adjusted.

Empirical Assessment of Relaxation Practice

In most clinical situations, a relaxation method is taught in the therapy session, and the client is instructed to practice at home on a regular basis, usually daily. [Surprisingly, Glaister (1982) and Hillenberg and Collins (1982) presented survey data that suggests clinical researchers often do not emphasize home relaxation practice.] The question of compliance to the home practice instruction is supposedly critical since the home is the primary arena of treatment exposure, yet this matter has been neglected.

A voluminous amount of relaxation therapy clinical outcome research has been conducted (see Chapter 7), and researchers have, of course, credited the relaxation procedure when treatment outcomes were favorable and discounted the technique when outcomes were unfavorable. However, the absence of specific knowledge of home relaxation practice precludes drawing firm conclusions as to the usefulness of relaxation therapy with particular disorders regardless of therapy outcome. The interested reader is referred to Lichstein and Hoelscher (1986) for an extended discussion of this point.

Further complicating these issues is the likelihood that the amount of relaxation practice that constitutes a therapeutic dose varies as a function of several factors, including type of relaxation method, client characteristics, and target symptom. In some circumstances, one relaxation practice per week in the therapist's office may be sufficient to produce desired goals, and at other times, less than seven or more practices a week would have little therapeutic value.

Heretofore, therapists and researchers have employed three strategies to assess the amount of home relaxation practice. Most often, according to Hillenberg and Collins (1982), they have simply assumed that the amount of home relaxation practice conforms to therapeutic instructions (e.g., Goebel, Viol, Lorenz, & Clemente, 1980; Gray, Lyle, McGuire, & Peck, 1980; Mathews & Gelder, 1969). Alternatively, clients may supply self-report data to document practice times (e.g., Bali, 1979; Lewis, Biglan, & Steinbock, 1978; Woolfolk & McNulty, 1983) or, least often, other household members may submit observational accounts of clients' practice (e.g., Andrasik, Blanchard, Neff, & Rodichok, 1984; Lichstein & Eakin, 1985). These three strategies represent an ascending sequence along a validity continuum, but all suffer from two major drawbacks. First, they can be easily falsified. Demanding therapists and therapeutic or familial contingencies tied to relaxation practice would increase the occurrence of this source of error. Second, these methods are all obtrusive measures at risk for producing an unknown amount of transient reactivity.

Initial inquiries to identify the controlling variables of home relaxation practice relied almost exclusively on self-report data to determine level of compliance. Some data mildly suggest that amount of self-reported home relaxation practice may be, in part, a function of the type of relaxation technique being used (Borkovec, Grayson, & Cooper, 1978; Lehrer, Atthowe, & Weber, 1980; Silver, Blanchard, Williamson, Theobald, & Brown, 1979; Simpson, Dansereau, & Giles, 1972; Zuroff & Schwarz, 1978) and the personality characteristics of the trainee (Delmonte, 1980, 1984c; Lewis, Biglan, & Steinbock, 1978; Smith, 1978), although strong predictor variables have yet to be found. Bennett and Millard (1985) provided some data suggesting a taped message that explains the rationale behind relaxation and emphasizes the importance of practice decreases the rate of treatment drop out, but does not elevate level of home practice. Other subject and setting variables relevant to relaxation practice levels are a matter of conjecture. Moreover, little confidence can be placed in the extant results, due to the unreliability of self-reported relaxation levels (Lichstein & Hoelscher, 1986).

A group of researchers recently reported a strategy for assessing relaxation practice that improves on existing methods (Collins, Martin, & Hillenberg, 1982; Hillenberg & Collins, 1983; Martin, Collins, Hillenberg, Zabin, & Katell, 1981). The client is given a series of relaxation tapes for home practice use. A 1-second tone is dubbed onto approximately one half of these tapes. The client is instructed to listen to the relaxation tapes in a specified order and then to report to the therapist at their weekly meeting which tapes had a tone and the approximate location (i.e., beginning, middle, or end) on the tape. Although this approach suffers from the same drawbacks afflicting past procedures—namely, that it can be easily falsified and it is an obtrusive measure— it was a bold first step toward an adequate solution to this problem. Jacob, Beidel, and Shapiro (1984) have since introduced a variation on the above procedure wherein subjects are asked to monitor the occurrence of relaxation cue words instead of tones. However, this does not represent a methodological advance over the original approach.

Recently, Taylor, Agras, Schneider, and Allen (1983) reported on the first major advance in this area. Hypertensives were given a conventional, portable tape recorder and a relaxation tape to guide their home practice. Unbeknownst to the subjects, a computer chip embedded in the tape recorder was activated by an inaudible 60 Hz tone dubbed onto the relaxation tape. The computer chip rendered a real time accounting of time spent playing the *marked* tape. Presumably, this time pattern perfectly matches actual relaxation practice, assuming subjects do not play the relaxation tape for other purposes. Though disadvantaged by substantial complexity and cost, this system does assess relaxation compliance accurately and unobtrusively.

Our own research program (Hoelscher, Lichstein, & Rosenthal, 1984) independently developed a device similar to that of Taylor et al. (1983). Our relaxation assessment device (RAD) is composed of a digital watch concealed in the battery compartment of a conventional, portable tape recorder. The battery compartment and the tape compartment housing a relaxation tape are both sealed. Subjects are informed that these compartments are sealed to ensure the safekeeping of the tape and recorder. The circuitry is designed so that the cumulative time function of the watch is actuated only when the play mode is in force. For a total price of about $100 per unit, the RAD will permit the unobtrusive monitoring of naturally occurring rates of relaxation practice for purely clinical purposes, as well as the systematic evaluation of compliance induction strategies and of salient client characteristics. I should note that still another unobtrusive method of monitoring relaxation has appeared (Riley, Berry, & Kennedy, 1986), which operates by counting the number of times the rewind button is depressed. Future research employing devices such as these should clarify the clinical status of relaxation therapy and identify the controlling variables of high relaxation practice rates.

Compliance stands as one of the major health care challenges, and this is no less true in the area of relaxation therapy. Technological advances such as those mentioned above hold great promise for stimulating progress in this domain.

Relaxation as a Life-style Commitment

In the numerous avenues by which Western therapists have approached the relaxation experience, one theme is shared by them all: We don't need religion and philosophy. Benson (1975), in describing the *relaxation response,* most forthrightly and articulately endorses this assumption. This view holds that there is a technology of relaxation which may be extracted from the highly adorned and embellished practices of the East. Further, regardless of whether we are testing revered systems or creating novel approaches, careful scrutiny and experimentation will lead us to shape relaxation procedures toward more potent and efficient forms.

In principle, I have no quarrel with this Western philosophy of being anti-philosophical, except that it may foster a serious problem. Clients tend to prematurely discontinue their practice of relaxation.

Even a superficial survey of the broad spectrum relaxation literature leads to an obvious dichotomy of the Eastern and Western approaches on numerous dimensions, two of which relate to the present discussion. First, there are a host of studies evaluating Eastern meditation practitioners having several decades of relaxation experience. Studies of individuals practicing Western relaxation techniques for a period of time even remotely similar to the above are extremely rare. Second, it is commonplace for the Eastern *master, teacher,* or *priest* to practice the same relaxation procedure that he[1] is disseminating. Indeed, the Eastern literature is replete with *masters'* personal accounts of the importance of relaxation (meditation), and many of the scientific evaluations of long-term meditation practitioners are of masters. It is rare to find a Western writer who advocates by self-reference the helpfulness of relaxation (Jacobson & Carlson, 1925, being one such case).

The above two points illustrate the usefulness of incorporating relaxation into one's philosophy of life, rather than seeing relaxation as an isolated route to gain symptomatic relief. In Eastern cultures, meditation is an inseparable part of the person's values and religious beliefs that are retained for as long as a lifetime, and as a result, there is a heightened likelihood that meditation will be practiced for years at a time, if not in perpetuity. In Western cultures, our insistence on denuding relaxation of its religious/philosophical context also creates a discontinuity between the individual's normal life-style and values, and the relaxation task. This point of view leads to sporadic patterns of relaxation practice precipitated by intermittent symptomatic flare-ups. This

[1]In this case, the male pronoun referring to Eastern masters, teachers, and priests is not an instance of sexist language. Females have only rarely occupied such positions.

pattern is bound to be discouraging, and sooner or later the client will permanently discard relaxation practice. Survey data from Ganguli (1982) is consistent with the above views. This author observed that long-term meditators were motivated by an interest in personal growth. In contrast, those who discontinued meditation were interested initially in correcting a deficiency.

Evidence is beginning to accumulate from the relaxation treatment of such disorders as hypertension (Benson, Marzetta, & Rosner, 1974; Martin & Epstein, 1980; Patel, 1977), Raynaud's disease (Glueck & Stroebel, 1978), and headaches (Blanchard, Theobald, Williamson, Silver, & Brown, 1978; Epstein, Hersen, & Hemphill, 1974) that treatment effects accruing to relaxation therapy are sustained only as long as relaxation practice continues. When psychophysiologic disorders benefit from relaxation therapy, this is likely due to correction of pathophysiological processes or improvement of the client's ability to cope with the large and small injustices of life that occur daily. However, it is paramount to understand that the pathophysiological processes were *probably not* permanently corrected and life's injustices were *definitely not* permanently smoothed over by a successful relaxation course. Clients run the risk of inviting the return of pretreatment symptomatic distress when they discontinue relaxation practice.

Future research has a dual task in this domain. First, the actual relationship between duration of relaxation practice and symptom return needs to be more clearly explicated. Second, methods of promoting long-term lifestyle commitment to relaxation practice deserve serious attention.

The Blessed Irritant

Reviewing relaxation, from its Eastern beginnings to current practice, yields the inescapable conclusion that the period of relaxation is shrinking. Originally, meditation could comprise several hours, if not several days, of quiet dedication. The dawn of the 20th century witnessed progressive relaxation and autogenic training structured within 1-hour doctors' sessions and requiring perhaps half a year to attain full mastery. In 1958, Wolpe contrived a six-session format for progressive relaxation. Eight years later, Paul (1966a) popularized a one-session progressive relaxation induction. Goldfried (1971) stimulated interest in self-control relaxation, whereby the relaxation experience could be summoned up almost instantly in the course of everyday events. Research on paced respiration (Harris, Katkin, Lick, & Habberfield, 1976, described in Chapter 3) documents how naive subjects can elicit relaxation after a few minutes of instruction in breath slowing.

The momentum of history has forced relaxation into as small a capsule as possible. I cannot envision greater procedural condensation, save for discarding technique altogether, and this is not likely to occur. Instead, procedural aspects of relaxation may suffer diminished emphasis, as the *attitude of relaxation* ascends in importance over the technique.

A relaxed attitude may be fostered by the practice of relaxation, even when physiological relaxation is the primary goal. This attitude may arise from several different aspects of the relaxation process. Perhaps the most common and interesting avenue for the creation of a relaxed attitude is the almost universal, *unwanted* presence of wandering thoughts during relaxation. If the trainee can adopt a tolerant, relaxed attitude concerning this irritant, then the essence of what will germinate into an enduring trait may be established. A relaxed attitude holds the potential of pervading one's life to a far greater extent than could somatic mechanisms in relaxation. Indeed, inclination toward a relaxed attitude sustains somatic relaxation and diminishes the importance of the latter as a goal state.

The occurrence of mind wandering, this blessed irritant, will potentially serve the cause of relaxation most handsomely. A relaxed approach to life is routinely prescribed for stress-laden individuals (see discussion of Type A behavior, Chapter 6), but the technology for grasping Type B, or a relaxed attitude, is elusive. For some, the practice of relaxation offers such a technology. Therapists would do well to emphasize the value of the fortuitous opportunity afforded by mind wandering and thereby nurture a relaxed attitude in their clients. Future research should assess the attitude of relaxation separate from assessing physiological, behavioral, and experiential states of relaxation. For some disorders, clinical outcome in relaxation therapy may be partly due to adoption of a relaxed attitude independent of the traditional relaxation markers.

CHAPTER 2

Theoretical Foundations

This chapter describes the theories that explain the underlying mechanisms of the major relaxation techniques. The discussion will focus primarily on the deep methods of relaxation comprising Chapter 4, as these have been the focus of most of the theorizing. An overriding concern of this writer is to avoid the use of language that is highly complex and confusing for the general readership. A chapter discussing physiological mechanisms is particularly at risk for this pitfall. I will try to limit the use of technical terms and clearly define those that are central to the discussion.

AUTOGENIC TRAINING (AT)

The AT procedure combines pleasant nature scene imagery with somatic focusing. Subjects direct their attention to a series of six bodily sensations, such as, warmth in limbs and breathing calm, while simultaneously enjoying, in imagination, the relaxing environment of a familiar lake, meadow, etc. This procedure is described in detail in Chapter 4.

The effects of AT are attributed to the influence of the diencephalon (defined below) and proximal brain structures in promoting diffuse relaxation. This brain process is elicited primarily by periods of reduced afferent stimulation and secondarily by two other elements of AT, repetitive mental phrases and passive concentration (Luthe, 1970a; Luthe, Jus, & Geissmann, 1965; Schultz & Luthe, 1959). AT theory and supportive research will now be discussed in greater detail.

Reduced Afferent Stimulation

AT theory rests mainly on the work of Hess (1957), who studied brain functions during several decades of meticulous animal research, mostly with cats. His research focused on the diencephalon. This is composed principally of the thalamus and hypothalamus and sits atop the brainstem. Hess's method involved direct electrical stimulation to narrowly specified brain locations and observation of the resulting physiological and behavioral changes. Hess found that stimulation of the diencephalon and adjacent brain structures, such as the septum, preoptic area, and midbrain, produces changes in a wide range of bodily functions, including pupil size, heart rate, blood pressure, respiration, and sleep. The hypothalamus proved to be the most influential structure controlling these functions. Further, it may be apparent to the reader that these phenomena are associated with emotionality. Indeed, Hess was able to create states such as fear or aggression by systematically evoking particular physiological patterns.

In effect, Hess diagrammed the anatomy of the autonomic nervous system, confirming the earlier observations of Cannon (1929) and others. Hess labeled the collection of excitatory processes (e.g., heart acceleration, increased blood pressure, and pupil dilation, previously termed sympathetic arousal) as *ergotropic responses*. Similarly, he used the term *trophotropic* to refer to the quiescent state defined by parasympathetic functioning (e.g., heart deceleration, decreased blood pressure, and pupil constriction).

AT theorists (Luthe, 1962a; Luthe, Jus, & Geissmann, 1965) have inferred from Hess's research the mechanism by which the trophotropic response is evoked, that is, diffuse relaxation. When the individual fashions an environment emitting minimal stimulation, the low sensory input (i.e., diminished afferent stimulation) is coded by the reticular system and thalamus, which in turn instruct the hypothalamus to mitigate ergotropic activity (i.e., arousal and vigilance). Trophotropic functioning emerges by default as ergotropic signals subside.

Alternatively, others (summarized by Gellhorn, 1967) have documented a more direct process in which stimulation of the anterior hypothalamus elicits the trophotropic response. Repeated elicitations (i.e., relaxation practice) results in what Gellhorn (1967, p. 48) calls "trophotropic tuning"—a lower elicitation threshold and a stronger response. Initially, Gellhorn developed this model with progressive relaxation in mind, but it is equally applicable to AT and other relaxation techniques.

Repetitive Mental Phrases

The content of the reiterated mental phrases (e.g., limb warmth and heaviness, heart slowing) mimics trophotropic responses and is said to reinforce the trophotropic state. Some mild evidence (discussed in Chapter 3) suggests that the content of these phrases promotes corresponding physiological changes (Lehrer, Atthowe, & Weber, 1980; Shapiro & Lehrer, 1980). Only one study has directly tested the question of similarity between autogenic phrase content and physiological response. Blizard, Cowings, and Miller (1975) trained normal young adults in the first two standard exercises, heaviness and warmth. Subsequently, hand focusing with "warm and heavy" suggestions was alternated with the opposite suggestions of "cool and light." The cool and light suggestions produced reliable heart and respiratory rate increases, but affected neither EEG alpha nor, more importantly, finger temperature. Warm and heavy suggestions had no significant effect on any measure. Inadvertent muscle tensing and not the cool and light imagery may have been responsible for the observed arousals. In brief, repetition of the AT hand-warming phrase did not evoke a parallel somatic response.

Subsequent research by one of the above investigators (Cowings, 1977a, 1977b) examined the combination of AT and heart rate biofeedback. She demonstrated that directional cardiovascular changes, consistent with either warmth or cold instructions, could be induced.

There is no strong, direct evidence to substantiate the claim that the content of autogenic phrases is any more powerful or focal than the phrases used in other forms of relaxation and mantra meditation. This subject is discussed further in this chapter's section considering Benson's relaxation response approach. Two areas of research stemming from hypnosis and Peter Lang's imagery work bear indirectly on this question of AT content, and these will now be overviewed.

Barber (1978) summarized hypnotic literature documenting self-induced physiological alterations (e.g., control of skin rash, inducing skin inflammation) through suggestions of same. Barber concluded that suggestions of "physiological instructions," once assimilated into one's cognitive set, can alter blood flow patterns and thereby produce an isomorphic response. The degree to which the subject believed in the suggestion emerged as an important mediating factor. As vascular processes are highly relevant to many of the autogenic phrases, this body of research is confirmatory of autogenic claims.

A brilliant series of studies by Lang and his colleagues (Lang, Kozak, Miller, Levin, & McLean, 1980) lends indirect support to the assertion by AT theorists that self-referent physiological descriptors may alter physiological functioning. Normal student volunteers listened to scripts depicting neutral, action, or fear themes. Subjects were trained to focus their attention on propositions emphasizing either the stimulus properties of the imagined scene (e.g., a black spider with thick body and long legs) or the response properties inherent in the scene (e.g., my heart raced and I began sweating profusely). Subjects having prior training in attending to response propositions, when subsequently exposed to imagery scripts emphasizing self-referent physiological descriptors (i.e., response propositions), manifested greater self-report and physiological arousal than subjects attending to stimulus propositions. A follow-up study described in the same article utilized a variation of the basic design reported above. It found moderately strong support for the hypothesis that focusing on a specific response proposition (e.g., heart rate or sweating) will provoke an isomorphic visceral response.

More recently, Lang and his associates (Lang, Levin, Miller, & Kozak, 1983) reported two more studies, the second of which replicated and extended the above findings. Snake or speech phobic student volunteers received two imagery training sessions cultivating stimulus or response propositions. During a third session of fearful imagery trials, elevations in heart rate and muscle tension, but not skin conductance and respiration, reflected the superior impact of response training. Further, there occurred a shift in the pattern of physiological response activation that paralleled specific scene content. Other laboratories (e.g., Bauer & Craighead, 1979) have also tested Lang's propositional structures and obtained confirmatory data.

This research stems from Lang's (1977, 1979) theory, which holds that the brain integratively codes emotional imagery in terms of a network composed of the perceptual characteristics of the stimulus array and the efferent outflow (i.e., somato-visceral responses) associated with previous experience. Lang's model is compatible with the belief that autogenic phrases promote concordant physiological changes. However, there are important dissimilarities between the circumstances defining AT and Lang's research which prevent a simple equation. AT is primarily used with a clinical population, whereas Lang's work has been limited to undergraduate volunteers. More importantly, Lang has focused on arousing imagery and autogenics is concerned with the opposite, and there are data to suggest that dissimilar processes and effects are associated with arousing and relaxing imagery (Carroll, Baker, & Preston, 1979; Dugan & Sheridan, 1976; Grayson & Borkovec, 1978).

A group of investigators in England conducted two tests of Lang's theory with reference to relaxing imagery, but flaws in experimental design seriously limit the import of these studies. Carroll, Marzillier, and Watson (1980) asked normal subjects to imagine lying peacefully in bed preparing to fall asleep. Imagery scripts emphasized either response propositions (e.g., your whole body feels warm and comfortable) or stimulus propositions (e.g., it is quiet and dark). A third group served as a control and was asked to imagine a relaxing scene without further instructions. The outcome of this experiment was somewhat disappointing in that neither self-reports of sleepiness nor heart rate changes distinguished one group from another. Indeed, all groups showed heart rate acceleration during imagery compared to baseline. However, the study may be faulted for not clearly differentiating baseline and trial periods. Imagery training was conducted prior to a 5-minute baseline. Then, five imagery trials of only 30 seconds duration were presented in rapid succession. Ironically, subjects were afforded a greater opportunity to become absorbed in the relaxing imagery during baseline than during imagery trials.

In the second investigation, Carroll, Marzillier, and Merian (1982) compared relaxing imagery (content not specified) and arousing imagery in scripts emphasizing either response or stimulus propositions. They replicated the findings of Lang et al. (1980) in that the arousing imagery produced greater psychophysiological reactivity when it contained response propositions than with stimulus propositions. However, Carroll et al. (1982) observed that the particular physiological function depicted in the script was not necessarily synchronous with the actual physiological response. More salient to current concerns, relaxing imagery did not produce physiological effects that significantly diverged from baseline. Unfortunately, this experiment also conflicts with some of the key characteristics of AT. Normal subjects were again employed and, as the authors pointed out, they were already quite relaxed as they reclined in the experimental chamber prior to imagery exposure. Finally, the experimental regime militated against attaining substantive relaxation effects: Standard scripts of relaxing and arousing imagery were presented in an alternating sequence, and subjects were allotted only 50 seconds to dwell on each imagery script.

Lang's theory of emotional imagery is highly promising, although its current status is not without question, particularly in light of other laboratories' (e.g., Anderson & Borkovec, 1980; Hermecz & Melamed, 1984) difficulties in achieving robust replications of Lang's results. Specifically, its applicability to AT and other forms of imaginally mediated relaxation (e.g., guided imagery) is largely unknown. There is a small amount of clinical data on the subject of guided imagery which disproves Lang's predictions (see *Relaxation Comparisons* under *Migraine Headache*, Chapter 7). Lang's pioneering efforts in the empirical study of imaginal processes have generated considerable scientific interest which may, in time, spark research that verifies the alleged significance of AT phrases.

Passive Concentration

The autogenic state resides on the continuum between wakefulness and sleep at a point close to sleep labeled "predrowsiness." The appearance of slow brain waves (theta, usually occurring in the early sleep stages) in the EEG records of awake autogenic trainees supports this contention (Luthe, 1962a). Passive concentration is credited with securing the stability of the autogenic state on this continuum (Jus & Jus, 1965c; Luthe, Jus, & Geissmann, 1965), particularly during the first two standard exercises of heaviness and warmth (Jus & Jus, 1969). A more active form of concentration would lead to normal alertness and diminution of relaxation effects. Greater passivity on the other hand would allow the individual to slip into sleep. It is further hypothesized (Schultz & Luthe, 1959) that passive concentration is the cognitive style indigenous to and facilitative of trophotropic functioning. Thus, teachers of AT and other relaxation approaches (e.g., Benson, 1977) emphasize the importance of adopting the proper attitude and attentive set denoted by passive concentration.

To date, one basic research study (Harano, Ogawa, & Naruse, 1965) has tested the above assertions. Twenty normal volunteers dwelled upon the first two standard formulas (heaviness and warmth) while instructed either to actively strive for relaxation or to passively permit relaxation to emerge. Digital skin temperature and blood volume pulse increased during passive concentration, indicating relaxation, and decreased during active concentration. Expectancy and experimenter bias were poorly controlled in this study, but it nevertheless deserves applause as one of the few attempts to experimentally analyze AT processes. A clinical trial (Reed & Meyer, 1974) pitted an active orientation in AT against a passive one in treating test anxiety and found these seemingly incompatible approaches equally effective (discussed further in Chapter 7).

Final Comments on Autogenic Training

In general, the theory offered to explain AT effects is reasonably sound. However, empirical demonstrations of specific aspects of this theory are wanting. Process research to separate out the contributions of the components of this approach is needed. The basic method recommended herein has been termed the dismantling treatment strategy (Agras, Kazdin, & Wilson, 1979) or component control comparisons (O'Leary & Borkovec, 1978). This methodology consists of a group design experiment with each condition featuring one or more elements of the aggregate procedure. Some of the studies cited above (Blizard et al., 1975; Harano et al., 1965) represent starting points, consistent with this methodology, in the process of isolating the active ingredients in AT and testing its underlying assumptions.

PROGRESSIVE RELAXATION (PR)

When practicing PR, the subject sequentially tenses and then releases the major skeletal muscles. In this process, the subject concentrates on the contrasted sensations and attempts to achieve more complete muscular relaxation. See Chapter 4 for complete procedural details on this technique.

From his earliest studies, Jacobson (1920b) held that there exists a state of reciprocal influence between the brain and peripheral structures of the body. He described a harmonious, egalitarian relationship whereby the peripheral physiology and the brain simultaneously stimulate each other. The level of arousal or activity in either of these partners is controlled, in part, by the amount of signal received from the other. Thus, the brain can be quieted by diminishing sensory input to it. So influenced, the brain in turn tranquilizes the autonomic nervous system. Jacobson (1967a) endorsed the term *neuromuscular* to emphasize the integration of neurological and muscular processes. This model is consistent with the role ascribed to afferent stimulation in autogenic training. While they are similar in important respects, the two theories do differ in their emphases. PR focuses more on striate musculature and autogenics focuses on diverse involuntary functions.

Jacobson considered the skeletal musculature (also called striate or voluntary musculature) as the most effective means of manipulating brain activity from among the numerous sources of brain input. This conclusion had two bases: (1) the muscles are plentiful and therefore account for a considerable portion of brain input, and (2) they are readily responsive to intentional control. Thus, PR cultivates low muscular arousal to facilitate parasympathetic dominance through brain mediation (Jacobson, 1938a).

The neuromuscular theory of PR gives rise to two testable predictions based on the critical premise of reciprocity. First, mental activity (thoughts) will produce efferent signals that are reflected in concomitant muscular activity and vice versa. Second, there occurs a dulling of neurologic reflexes when the muscles are relaxed and brain activity is thereby quieted. These hypotheses were tested through experimentation, mainly by Jacobson.

Mental and Muscular Activity

Jacobson began his studies on the correspondence between cognitions and striate muscle activity in the early 1920s (1925a) and employed instrumentation to assess muscle tension a few years hence (1927a). Jacobson's efforts culminated in a series of seven reports (1930a, 1930b, 1930c, 1930d, 1931a, 1931b, 1931c). Before summarizing his findings, I should point out that Jacobson pioneered major advances in psychophysiological instrumentation to obtain clear records of minute muscle potentials in this line of research. With the collaboration of two engineers from the Bell Telephone Laboratories, Jacobson modified the conventional string galvanometer to attain greater precision in muscle assessments (1930a, 1931c) and was the first to measure eye movements by the method of electro-oculography (1930c).

The research series referred to above explored the extent and nature of the relationship between three types of cognitions and muscle activity: motion, visualization, and linguistics. The first group of studies focused mainly on the skeletal muscles of the arms. Initially, Jacobson (1930a, 1930b) asked subjects to imagine right arm movements. This instruction was associated with an approximate average increase of more than 400 percent in the right bicep muscle potential compared to resting levels. Further, the right bicep was unaffected by experimental control imagery (e.g., imagine left arm movement or imagine no movement in the right arm). Imagery relating to diffuse body movements, such as sweeping with a broom, increased right bicep activity, though not as much as when the image was wholly devoted to right arm movement. Later in this series, Jacobson (1930d) detected actual right arm movements with a sensitive lever during imagery only with matched content.

Two studies examined cognitive effects of muscle status. Normal subjects with extensive prior training in PR could not produce an image of right arm movement while maintaining complete relaxation of their right arm (Jacobson, 1930d). The second study (Jacobson, 1931b) evaluated a 40-year-old amputee whose left arm was severed just above the elbow at age 8. Measurements of the left bicep remnant and right bicep correlated with the subject's report that he was unable to imagine only left hand movement. The image of left hand movement always included right hand movement and, unlike the trials conducted on normal subjects, instructions to imagine either left or right hand movement induced tension in both arms. Apparently, one of the conditions necessary for producing the left hand image was compensatory muscle action of the right hand. Over time, left and right hand imagery became fused with synchronous muscle action.

The second cognitive form this series considered was visualization of static objects and scenes as distinguished from imagined body movement. In these trials, reactivity of the ocular muscles resulted in eye movements that conformed to the shape of the object being visualized, as though the subjects were actually looking at it (Jacobson, 1930c). In a follow-up experiment (Jacobson, 1931a), differential muscular involvement was observed when subjects were instructed to imagine bending the right arm or *visually* imagine bending the right arm. With the former, most subjects showed increased muscle action in the right arm but not the eyes. This pattern was reversed when the instructions directed the subject to "visually imagine." Some subjects exhibited simultaneous reactivity in ocular motility and bicep tension. Every subject exhibited reactivity in at least one of these regions.

The last cognitive form involved verbal imagery (Jacobson, 1931c). Electrodes were attached to the tip of the tongue, the cheek, and/or the lower lip. A sharp rise in muscle activity in these sites (collectively called the speech musculature) coincided with the initiation of verbal imagery, for example, counting or recalling a poem. Control imagery of either motoric or pictorial themes did not provoke the speech musculature.

The major conclusions of these seven experiments may be summarized as follows. First, motoric, pictorial, and linguistic imagery occur in cooperation with striate muscle activity. Second, the location and pattern of the muscle activity are specific to the type and composition of the imagery. Third, peripheral muscle action should not be viewed as an epiphenomenon of cognitions but rather as a necessary component of the cognitive experience.

Though Jacobson's research did not stimulate broad interest, some of Jacobson's contemporaries did provide corroborative research (e.g., Shaw, 1940) and theory (Freeman, 1931). More recently, the relationship between mental and muscle activity (and general arousal) has attracted greater attention. Gellhorn (1958a, 1958b, 1964, 1969), in referring to a proprioception model of arousal, marshalled (mostly animal) research data consistent with the above. Of particular interest was Gellhorn's (1958a, 1958b) observations of tranquilized experimental subjects. Cats stripped of muscular innervation by curare exhibited diminished excitability of the hypothalamus and reduced sympathetic arousal. Further, Jacobson's findings have been generally confirmed and extended to include muscular elements in affective imagery (Cacioppo, 1982; Cacioppo & Petty, 1981), although the results are not uniformly supportive of Jacobson.

Davison (1966) presented conflicting data in his review of curare experiments. Curare is a drug that blocks neural impulses (efferent messages) to muscles, thus temporarily rendering the subject totally paralyzed. Jacobson emphasized the role of afferent messages from the muscles to the brain, which are indirectly reduced to zero by curare. Under these conditions, Jacobson would predict parallel nullification of cognitive activity. However, Davison cited data other than Gellhorn's indicating that various forms of cognitive activity, including anxiety, persist in curarized animals and humans.

Davison offered two alternative explanations to account for PR effects. First, the procedure generates pleasant sensations which neutralize noxious thoughts and emotions. Second, the method by which the muscles are relaxed may shed light on the underlying process of PR. Self-generated muscle flaccidity is attained through diminution of efferent impulses, and reduction of afferent messages to the brain may be an unimportant consequence. Curare does not influence efferent activity at its source. It merely blocks its muscle effect, and the persistence of neural outflow may account for cognitive activity during the curare state.

Neurologic Influence

If there exists a condition of reciprocal influence between the brain and the striate musculature, then different degrees of afferent activity derived from the musculature should prompt comparable levels of neurologic activity. Jacobson focused on the knee-jerk reflex to test this theory. The knee jerk seemed an appropriate choice as it is a common index of neurologic functioning and lends itself to accurate quantification by the measurement of leg displacement.

His first experiment to demonstrate neurologic control through muscle relaxation, however, examined spasms of the esophagus. Jacobson (1925b) reported on the treatment of three severe cases of this disorder. In all three, esophageal spasm was virtually eliminated following the client's mastery of general body PR. Of particular interest for present concerns is the fact that the esophagus contains both voluntary and involuntary (smooth) muscle. Spasming had occurred in both types of muscle and was now absent in both. Jacobson concluded that smooth muscle spasm subsided secondary to lowered brain activity brought about by PR.

In the first knee-jerk study (Jacobson & Carlson, 1925), seven subjects—including the two authors—submitted to knee-jerk tests delivered by automated hammers. Subjects comfortably reclined and engaged in either PR, in which they were pretrained, or ordinary rest. During the rest phase, a normal knee-jerk reflex occurred initially and gradually diminished as relaxation naturally evolved from the quiet situation. In contrast, the knee jerk was completely absent most of the time during PR. The authors compared these results to those of Tuttle (1924), who found that the knee jerk was absent during deep sleep but present, though weak, during light sleep. Jacobson and Carlson concluded, therefore, that PR can produce a level of neuromuscular relaxation deeper than that obtained during light sleep. Miller (1926), while working in Jacobson's lab, published data on muscular response to electric shock consistent with the above. In a within-subject analysis, shock response was attenuated during relaxation. Freeman (1933) published similar data on PR suppression of shock response.

A follow-up study (Jacobson, 1928) evaluated the knee-jerk reflex during differential relaxation, the selective use of certain muscles at a minimal level of exertion after attaining general relaxation (see Chapter 5 for a more complete definition of differential relaxation). Twenty-one medical students, unfamiliar with PR, engaged in simple writing tasks for 1 hour. Repeated knee-jerk tests gradually diminished in magnitude during this period, replicating the findings obtained during the ordinary rest phase in the previous study (Jacobson & Carlson, 1925). Five neurotic patients were then exposed to the same procedure and only two showed the customary decline in the reflex, suggesting that the other three individuals had a diminished capacity to relax. Lastly, 14 subjects having extensive prior training in PR engaged in simple reading or writing tasks during ordinary rest, differential relaxation, or postrelaxation. To summarize the results, the strength of the knee-jerk reflex closely matched the relaxation state. Specifically, the deeper the level of relaxation, the weaker the reflex. During the postrelaxation periods, about half the subjects showed a strong carry-over effect in that the absence of the reflex persisted, and about half showed some recovery.

Final Comments on Progressive Relaxation

Jacobson's clever studies to evaluate neurologic effects of PR confirmed his predictions based upon the theory of striate muscle control of neurologic processes. Jacobson's research was systematic and convincing, though shortcomings can be noted. Jacobson rarely conducted statistical analyses to estimate the probability of obtained results. He provided scant details on how subjects were recruited, and it often appeared that individuals enchanted with Jacobson's work volunteered for the research. Randomization was usually not employed in assigning subjects to treatment and control conditions. Lastly, the inclusion of more thoughtful control conditions would have helped illuminate PR processes. For example, it would have been instructive to compare imaginal focus on muscle relaxation, imaginal focus on relaxing scenes unrelated to the muscles, and standard PR to more clearly define the role of the musculature in the relaxation process. Recent studies of this sort wherein PR is compared to passive relaxation are reviewed in Chapter 3 and, in brief, yield inconsistent results. In all fairness to Jacobson, general practices in experimental methodology have improved considerably in the many years that have passed since Jacobson's research. By the standards of his day, Jacobson's studies were meticulous and sophisticated.

At the heart of Jacobson's theory is the assumption that experiential anxiety will vary as a function of aggregate or particular muscle tension levels. Current research addressing this issue has cast doubt on a unitary causation (muscular) model of anxiety. There is a substantial amount of clinical research, reviewed in Chapter 7, testifying to the usefulness of PR in anxiety treatment. However, in dispute with Jacobson's assertion are fine-grained analyses of other basic and clinical research reports which find little or no correlation between muscle tension and anxiety level (e.g., Janda & Cash, 1976; Lichstein & Lipshitz, 1982; Mathews & Gelder, 1969; Raskin, Bali, & Peeke, 1980). Indeed, Jacobson himself occasionally reported such incongruous findings (e.g., Jacobson, 1942). More likely, muscle status is but one factor that interacts with cognitive and biochemical factors to determine anxiety and other emotional states.

MEDITATION

The term meditation connotes a class of techniques spanning a broad diversity of procedures. This section will consider two main approaches: mantra and breath meditation. Both involve sitting passively while directing one's attention to a repetitive, monotonous stimulus. In mantra meditation, the repetition in one's mind of a word or short phrase serves as the focus, and in breath meditation, attention is focused on respiratory processes. Chapters 4 and 5 provide complete procedural details on these methods.

A major obstacle in understanding the theoretical bases of various meditation approaches is that the original theories were derived thousands of years ago from religious philosophy. Most often, these views are metaphorical and poetic and are cast in terms unsuitable for scientific testing. Fair coverage of these ancient theories is beyond the scope of this book. The present section will emphasize contemporary theories of meditation effects.

Mantra Meditation

Some writers (e.g., Shapiro, 1978c; Washburn, 1978) conceptualize the variety of meditative forms within two main categories: concentrative and receptive or open meditation. In receptive meditation, the individual minimally structures the meditation experience. The meditator assumes an attitude of goalless-ness and remains open to whatever thoughts or sensations occur. Some of the more unstructured forms of Zen breath awareness exemplify this class. Alternatively, the concentrative approach is structured and involves directing attention to a stimulus. The stimulus may be external, as in fixing one's gaze on a flower or some religious/philosophical symbol, or it may be internal, as in the captivating puzzle of a Zen koan (e.g., what is the sound of one hand clapping?). Not atypically, a single individual will employ both receptive and concentrative techniques in different combinations and sequences (e.g., Schulte & Abhyanker, 1979). At present, the most common form of concentrative meditation utilizes a mantra.

As originally conceived, a mantra was a portion of a religious text designed to uplift the soul of the meditator (Morgan, 1953). The mantra may consist of anything from a syllable to a paragraph. In Kundalini Yoga, the role of the mantra was to excite one of the neglected energy centers, called chakras. In Transcendental Meditation (TM), the mantra allegedly is fitted to the individual's personality in order to nurture psychological growth, awareness, and peacefulness (Yogi, 1975). I should add that reports indicate there are 16 TM mantras assigned solely according to the meditator's age (Carrington, 1978a; Goleman, 1977; Morse, Martin, Furst, & Dubin, 1979; Stroebel & Glueck, 1978). The little research available on the subject of comparative effectiveness of secular and sanskrit mantras finds no differences. (See discussion of this subject in Chapter 3.)

Herbert Benson, noted Harvard physiologist, has most seriously investigated the subject of mantras. He began his studies of TM around 1970 as part of his ongoing research on the self-regulation of essential hypertension (e.g., Benson, Herd, Morse, & Kelleher, 1969; Benson, Shapiro, Tursky, & Schwartz, 1971). The TM research program proved highly successful and sparked Benson's interest in the general subject of relaxation. Finally, comparisons between numerous meditation and relaxation methods led to Benson's concluding that the differences between the variety of approaches were nothing more than stylistic nuances reflecting a core set of four universal ingredients (Benson, Beary, & Carol, 1974).

These four procedural elements comprising Benson's (1975) popular secular method of relaxation are: (1) a quiet environment, (2) an object to dwell upon, (3) a passive attitude, and (4) a comfortable position. The usefulness of elements (1), (3), and (4) are obvious, and they are present in virtually all relaxation techniques. The role of element (2) is somewhat more complex.

In recommending an object to dwell upon, Benson is simply prescribing a mental device that will lure one's attention away from worldly concerns. Benson most often employs the emotionally neutral word *one,* which is silently repeated in the same way that devotees of TM use a mantra. According to personal preferences, one may substitute another word or phrase, breath focus, or fixed gaze on an external object. From Benson's point of view, it is crucial that the mind be consumed by a repetitive, monotonous stimulus, and the exact form of the mental device is unimportant. Benson disagrees with claims by other schools of thought that the *meaning* of the mantra contributes to meditation effects.

Benson asserts that some form of repetitive, monotonous stimulus (mantra) is universally present in relaxation methods; this is not at issue. Besides those techniques that manifestly rely on a specified mantra, other approaches that involve dwelling on one's muscles, as in progressive relaxation, or silently chanting the phrases of autogenic training will readily satisfy the definition of a mantra as a mental device. What is at issue is the extent of the mantra's influence, beyond that already obtained by the other three ingredients identified by Benson, and the mechanism of its action.

Benson and his colleagues (Beary & Benson, 1974; Benson, Beary, & Carol, 1974; Benson, Kotch, Crassweller, & Greenwood, 1977) refer mainly to the work of Hess (1957) discussed earlier in this chapter. Indeed, the term *relaxation response,* coined by Benson to describe the effects of his and other relaxation procedures, is a synonym for Hess's term *trophotropic response* (parasympathetic functioning). However, there is no evidence that repetition of a mantra exerts any direct or indirect influence on that aspect of the brain credited with trophotropic control (anterior hypothalamus). In an attempt to isolate the active ingredients in Benson's relaxation procedure, Beary and Benson (1974) presented physiological data showing that Benson's technique was superior to two control conditions: sitting quietly while reading neutral material or sitting quietly with eyes closed. Unfortunately, two components of Benson's procedure were not controlled for: instruction in adoption of a passive attitude and the mantra. We must therefore refrain from attributing the obtained results to the mantra, particularly when Benson (1975) believes that the passive attitude is the most important element in the relaxation procedure.

Lastly, Benson, Beary, and Carol (1974) acknowledge that the mantra helps us to relax by diverting our attention away from worldly concerns. This valid point is discussed further under the heading *Cognitive Diversion* later in this chapter.

Final Comments on Mantra Meditation

In discovering the four essential ingredients necessary to elicit the relaxation response, Benson (1975) reviewed the technical characteristics of many relaxation methods. Included among these were yoga, Zen, TM, progressive relaxation, autogenic training, Sentic cycles, and Judeo-Christian prescriptions. The four ingredients identified above were common to all these approaches. Surely, these four elements must represent some basic, universal human phenomenon. Were this not the case, there would be a small likelihood that they would appear in methods separated by enormous periods of time and marked cultural dissimilarities. It is likely that Benson has hit upon a procedural combination that does reliably produce relaxation, as Benson claims. However, the relative contribution of the components and the mechanisms of influence remain largely unknown.

Breath Meditation

Some methods of breath meditation require only minimal concentration on breathing processes. The meditator assumes a nonfocal, nonlingual state wed more closely to feelings and images. With respect to this shift in consciousness, the theory has been advanced that there occurs a correlated shift in brain processes.

Earle (1981) provided an excellent accounting of the view that meditation cultivates right brain hemisphere functioning. Were this the case, traits such as global perspective, inductive reasoning, and artistic inclination would profit. As these traits manifest in interpersonal functioning, the practitioner would appear more calm, tolerant, and flexible—characteristics often associated with meditation. However, as Earle also pointed out, psychological evidence bearing on this theory is equivocal. The most telling evidence concerning brain functioning and possible lateralization would, of course, derive from EEG studies. Here, too, studies of EEG synchronization and wave amplitude and frequency fail to provide convincing evidence of right-brain dominance. Others inquiring into lateralization effects in meditation (Delmonte, 1984b; Pagano & Warrenburg, 1983) concurred that existing data do not warrant such assertions.

In approaching breath meditation from an entirely different perspective, some devotees of Eastern breath techniques attribute the relaxation effects produced by these methods to two key ingredients: air flow through the nose and movement of the diaphragm. As such, most breath meditation methods prescribe the combination of nasal breathing, as opposed to mouth breathing, and diaphragmatic breathing, also called abdominal breathing.

Ballentine (1976) described the warming and humidifying of inhaled air as it passes through the nose, thereafter exerting a soothing influence. He also claimed that shifting patterns of airflow currents through the nasal passages stimulate nerve endings there which have a calming effect on the nervous system.

The diaphragm is a sheet of muscle spanning the horizontal plane separating the thorax and abdomen. When at rest, it is dome shaped and protrudes into the thorax. To instigate inhalation, the diaphragm contracts, causing it to flatten and descend and resulting in expansion of the thoracic cavity and compression of the abdomen. Exhalation occurs as the diaphragm naturally recoils to its resting state (Comroe, 1965).

Ballentine (1976) pointed out that diaphragmatic breathing is highly efficient and requires less energy expenditure in contrast to chest breathing, wherein enlargement of the thoracic cavity is accomplished by the expansion and upward shift of the rib cage. Clinical experience in the treatment of patients with chronic obstructive pulmonary disease supports this view (Sackner, 1975). Further, Ballentine stated that chest breathing is effortful and associated with states of sympathetic arousal.

There is a small amount of experimental data on this matter, which have yielded inconsistent results. Leischow and Chornock (1985) tested some of these assertions with male student volunteers. Breathing methods, diaphragmatic versus thoracic, were crossed with innate breathing styles. Contrary to Ballentine's prediction, thoracic breathing was associated with a slower respiration rate. It should be pointed out that this study was not conducted within the context of relaxation training. A second study on this same subject (Bacon & Poppen, 1985) also isolated breathing patterns from the meditation context. Within-subject comparisons on two of three normal volunteers revealed that digital skin temperature, a relaxation correlate, stabilized or increased during diaphragmatic breathing, while hand cooling accompanied uninstructed (normal) breathing and thoracic breathing periods.

Hirai (1975) contended that parasympathetic dominance is fostered by stimulating the nerves that supply the abdominal viscera. He is referring to the vagus nerve, which supplies many visceral organs, including the heart, lungs, and stomach (Carpenter, 1972). Hirai claimed that the diaphragmatic motion causes the contents of the abdomen to gently stimulate the vagus nerve which in turn promotes parasympathetic functioning. Others (Ajaya, 1976; Rama, 1979) also pointed to vagal stimulation as the route to parasympathetic dominance, but they identified the lungs as responsible for providing the needed stimulation. In this scheme, it is the regularity of lung action achieved through intentional breathing that influences the vagus nerve.

These theories on nasal breathing, the role of the diaphragm, and the effects of vagal stimulation are plausible but unvalidated. On the subject of clinical practice, I am inclined to agree with Harvey (1978) in recommending adoption of these suggestions. On a theoretical level, judgment must await additional data.

I would like to offer an explanation of breath meditation processes that is more firmly grounded in current research. This view also identifies two factors: carbon dioxide and cognitive diversion.

Carbon Dioxide

To state the obvious, breathing techniques alter normal breathing patterns, and a rudimentary understanding of respiratory physiology will partially explain the relaxation effects achieved through these methods. Respiration is the process of exchanging inhaled air for blood gases remaining after oxidation of nutrients. The exchange takes place in the lungs. Air flow in and out of the lungs is a mechanical process accomplished through the action of the intercostal muscles acting on the rib cage, action of the diaphragm, and several other muscles of lesser importance. One of the main distinguishing features between inhaled and exhaled air is the carbon dioxide (CO_2) content in the latter, which is highly relevant to present concerns.

CO_2 is a product of internal combustion. Exhaled air has roughly a three percent CO_2 content (Consolazio, Johnson, & Pecora, 1963) compared to virtually no CO_2 in inhaled air (Otis, 1964). A certain level of CO_2 is normally maintained in venous blood, as it carries the products of combustion to the lungs and other organs for elimination. However, only part of the CO_2 is passed in exhalation, resulting in a tonic level of CO_2 in arterial blood as well. This level is measured in terms of CO_2 pressure (PCO_2) and is about 40 mm Hg in the arteries (Roughton, 1964; Slonim & Hamilton, 1976).

PCO_2 is an important factor in regulating blood pH, involuntary respiratory stimulation, and other bodily processes. In large doses, as when CO_2 is added to inhaled air, marked elevation of bodily stores of CO_2 (hypercapnia) will eventually lead to diffuse analgesia, convulsions, and unconsciousness (Meduna, 1950; Woodbury & Karler, 1960). Hypocapnia (insufficient PCO_2), which may be induced by hyperventilation (rapid deep breathing), brings on dizziness and will lead to unconsciousness if persistent. Mild hypercapnia has particular implications for the study of relaxation.

When PCO_2 is increased by a small amount (some 10 percent or 2-5 mm Hg), complex central and peripheral bodily processes are set in motion. The overall net effects include heart rate slowing, dilation of the peripheral vasculature, stimulation of gastric secretions, depression of cortical activity, and a global sensation of mild somnolence (Price, 1960; Schulte & Abhyanker, 1979; Slonim & Hamilton, 1976; Sokoloff, 1960; Tenney & Lamb, 1965).

The transition from wakefulness to drowsiness or light sleep preparatory to sound sleep illustrates the symptomatology of mild hypercapnia (in cooperation with other biobehavioral changes). Increased PCO_2 averaging 5 mm Hg routinely accompanies this transition (Birchfield, Sieker, & Heyman, 1958; Naifeh, Kamiya, & Sweet, 1982). In brief, mild hypercapnia exhibits parasympathomimetic properties. These effects vanish in favor of sympathetic dominance if hypercapnia advances by another 10-20 mm Hg, forming the second stage of hypercapnia (Woodbury & Karler, 1960). The third and final stage is massive central nervous system depression, unconsciousness, and, if sustained, death.

The relaxing effects of mild hypercapnia have long been established. Indeed, Wolpe (1958) and others (e.g., Haslam, 1974; Slater & Leavy, 1966) have obtained anxiolytic effects in nervous subjects by administering limited amounts of CO_2 via inhaled air. These results have been duplicated recently with normal subjects in designs that controlled for placebo effects (Griez & Van Den Hout, 1982; Van Den Hout & Griez, 1982b). However, not all the findings in this area have been positive. Van Den Hout and Griez (1982a) obtained mixed results in evaluating the anxiolytic properties of CO_2 treatment of neurotic patients when neutral expectancies for improvement prevailed, and this same laboratory (Griez & Van Den Hout, 1983) observed both parasympathetic and sympathetic responses in normal subjects following a single CO_2 inhalation. Ley and Walker (1973) found no advantages of a 65 percent CO_2 mixture of air compared to normal air on several physiological and subjective measures with nervous subjects and normals. It appears that the response to artificial administration of CO_2 is determined by a complex interaction of subject expectancy and amount of CO_2 exposure. These latter studies may have induced too high a level of PCO_2.

Mild hypercapnia is easily induced by two simple forms of insufficient breathing: breath holding and hypoventilation (Slonim & Hamilton, 1976). PCO_2 rises to about 45-50 mm Hg within a minute when adults hold their breath under ordinary circumstances (Fowler, 1954; Kellogg, 1964). The accumulation of PCO_2 roughly approximates a linear function, although there is somewhat greater acceleration initially (Lanphier & Rahn, 1963). As a result, 5-10 seconds of breath retention may yield a PCO_2 increase of 2-5 mm Hg, that is, mild hypercapnia, although the specific values of this equation have not yet been established. Similarly, one may voluntarily depress respiration (hypoventilation) by invoking slow, shallow breathing. This breathing style does not eliminate CO_2 as rapidly as it is produced and will give rise to the same mild hypercapnic state as does breath holding, although the method of hypoventilation takes longer. Both forms of insufficient breathing normally lead to a respiratory urge that defies resistance but is easily satisfied by a deep breath and/or temporary resumption of normal breathing.

The two methods of breath relaxation presented in Chapter 5 closely resemble these forms of insufficient breathing. It is likely that at least part of the relaxation experience resulting from these two breath manipulations is due to the drug effect of CO_2 elevation.

Cognitive Diversion

One of the basic premises of psychoanalytic theory is that diminished attention to troubling thoughts produces temporary and incomplete anxiety reduction

(Sullivan, 1953; Wolberg, 1954), as exemplified by repression and selective inattention. From a contemporary point of view, methods of seducing one's attention away from internal or external noxious stimuli promise anxiety relief. Evidence of the virtues of cognitive diversion is plentiful in research and in common experience. Rosenthal (1980) has most eloquently summarized a large body of research evincing the clinical utility of tasks which lure one's attention away from troubling thoughts. Others (Bahrke & Morgan, 1978; Boals, 1978; Burish & Lyles, 1979; Ellis, 1984; Redd, Rosenberger, & Hendler, 1982–1983; Rosenthal & Rosenthal, 1983; Turk, Meichenbaum, & Genest, 1983) have specifically considered cognitive diversion mechanisms inherent in a wide variety of relaxation techniques.

Volitional alteration of one's breathing pattern requires attention, and it is surprisingly demanding of cognitive resources for so simple an act. Furthermore, somewhat unfamiliar bodily sensations abound when breathing is altered, and these also compete for a share of awareness, as do all novel stimuli. Much like any other emotionally neutral act capable of consuming attention, breath manipulations fill our mind with unprovocative content. Lastly, it is interesting to note that breath manipulations, particularly breath mindfulness, satisfy all of the requisites for evoking the relaxation response as described by Benson. The repetitive, neutral stimulus of repeating the word *one* in Benson's method is replaced by dwelling on one's breath.

If cognitive diversion does explain part of the effect of methods of breath relaxation, then more difficult or complex breathing patterns that naturally command more careful attention should prove to be more powerful relaxation techniques (Hirai, 1975). This is particularly true when highly intrusive, noxious thoughts are a presenting problem.

There is some data to support this theoretical prediction. Undergraduate female volunteers were trained either in the complex light panting and pant-blow breathing patterns of the Lamaze (1956/1970) natural childbirth method or in a simple deep breathing procedure (Worthington & Martin, 1980). Tolerance of hand immersion in ice water and self-report measures were employed before and after training to evaluate these breathing strategies and other factors. Subjects employing the Lamaze breathing method exhibited significantly greater pain tolerance than subjects using the deep breathing method. Subjects using either of these breath methods surpassed untrained subjects. Self-report estimates of pain did not discriminate groups. Although this experiment did not evaluate relaxation per se and therefore did not precisely address the issue of present concern (i.e., cognitive diversion advantages and attendant increments in relaxation effects correlated with increased breathing pattern complexity), it does lend indirect support to this hypothesis.

Final Comments on Breath Meditation

Much research remains to be done to clarify breath meditation processes, and this research may lead to more effective relaxation procedures. The effect of manipulating bodily stores of carbon dioxide (PCO_2) is a particularly promising area of inquiry. Respiration potentially represents an efficient and potent means of altering biochemical mechanisms salient to relaxation. Slow, shallow breathing (hypoventilation) characterizes not only breath meditation but virtually all other relaxation techniques as well. Thus, methods of relaxation that do not ostensibly or primarily seek to adjust respiratory patterns may do so inadvertently, and PCO_2 research may also illuminate these other methods. Attempting to specify with precision what amount of PCO_2 elevation optimizes relaxation and identifying the breathing patterns best able to obtain this effect are avenues of research strongly warranted by the present reasoning.

GENERAL RELAXATION MECHANISMS

Any explanation of a particular relaxation technique increases our understanding of other relaxation methods as well. The two sections that follow will discuss facets of relaxation mechanisms that have not been owned by any one relaxation school but that are salient to most.

Restricted Environmental Stimulation

Most forms of relaxation are practiced while the subject is comfortably reclined in a quiet, dimly lit room. Distracting stimuli, such as tight clothing or jewelry, are often adjusted or removed. The obvious similarities between these setting conditions and those that govern restricted environmental stimulation techniques (REST, popularly known as sensory deprivation) have been discussed at length by Suedfeld (1980; Suedfeld & Kristeller, 1982) and noted by others (Boals, 1978; Carrington, 1978a; Woolfolk, 1975). Indeed, there are so many commonalities between relaxation and REST, the two may be used simultaneously for mutual enhancement (Borrie & Suedfeld, 1980; Jacobs, Heilbronner, & Stanley, 1984; Suedfeld, Roy, & Landon, 1982). The concept of diminished afferent stimulation is certainly of major prominence in REST, and knowledge of REST effects may shed light on the role of diminished afferent stimulation in relaxation techniques.

Unfortunately for present purposes, the bulk of the deprivation research has examined prolonged periods (Suedfeld, 1980; Zubek, 1973) rather than shorter ones more closely matched to the length of relaxation sessions. Most of the research considers periods ranging from 2 days to 2 weeks. The techniques employed are highly diverse, ranging from social isolation in a minimally furnished room to complete immersion in body temperature water. The impact of such experiments is usually neutral or negative, including the occurrence of hallucinations, irritability, impaired functioning on certain cognitive tasks, and perceptual deficits. Autonomic changes during prolonged deprivation are equivocal. Normal subjects rarely exhibit positive effects of prolonged REST, although some health practitioners advocate "rest cures" for emotionally disturbed individuals (Suedfeld, 1980).

Some information relevant to present concerns may be gleaned from the few short-duration REST studies. During 24 hours of sensory deprivation, the subjective experiences of 20 females were varied, ranging from relaxation to fright (Suedfeld & Borrie, 1978). To explain the idiosyncratic pattern of responses, the authors suggested that the impact of sensory deprivation is, in part, determined by the individual's history of related experiences and the way in which the individual cognitively structures the ambiguity of the sensory deprivation situation. Bexton, Heron, and Scott (1954) invited normal males to spend several days in isolation, and these researchers observed a more consistent pattern in the initial part of the study. During this period, subjects were characteristically relaxed, they slept frequently, and they exhibited feelings of elation. In one of the very few REST studies devoted to evaluating relaxation effects, Turner and Fine (1983) observed significant decreases in biochemical stress indicators after normal subjects received four sessions of flotation REST (combined with autogenic phrases).

Lilly (1956) reported data on two subjects who submitted to extreme sensory restriction in an isolation tank, almost totally immersed in body temperature water with visual, auditory, tactile, and kinesthetic stimulation sharply curtailed. After about 45 minutes, both subjects began to experience a pleasant sense of relaxation. Over the next hour, however, the experience assumed a more noxious quality. Most interestingly, Lilly reported that repeated training sessions in this environment resulted in unplanned, positive, psychological changes: increased self-tolerance, decreased fear, and increased personal integration.

More recently, Lilly (1977) recounted the experiences of hundreds of individuals in the isolation tank. These were almost all positive experiences typified by relaxation, personal growth, and meditative self-inquiry. Lilly explained the sharp contrast between his subjects' experiences and the negative reports characterizing the customary REST experiments in terms of expectancy. Pointing to the commonly-used term *sensory deprivation* which betrays the experimenters' negative set, Lilly argued that his subjects never complained of being deprived. Rather, they used the opportunity offered by a distraction-free environment to cultivate enhanced enlightenment and expanded awareness. However, we should also remember that the student volunteers recruited for most REST research differed in many important respects from the mature, sophisticated individuals who sought out Lilly.

Two experiments conducted in my laboratory bear upon the present discussion, although they were not originally construed as REST research. We were interested in discovering which relaxation effects, if any, would occur if the setting conditions for relaxation were created but if no relaxation techniques were presented. In the first study (Sallis & Lichstein, 1979), 17 undergraduate volunteers were instructed to close their eyes and refrain from body movements while comfortably reclining in a quiet, dimly lit room for 15 minutes. Note the strong similarity between this experimental situation and REST. The sole dependent measure, frontalis muscle tension, revealed significant reductions during this short period of time.

The second study (Lichstein, Sallis, Hill, & Young, 1981) replicated and extended the findings of the first. Twenty undergraduate volunteers received the same instructions, except that the session was now 30 minutes in length. Heart rate, skin resistance level, and frontalis muscle tension showed significant changes in the relaxation direction. These changes, indicating a global parasympathetic effect, leveled off in approximately 15 minutes. It is interesting to compare the above findings with those of a similar experiment (Meyers & Craighead, 1978) which failed to find such relaxation changes. One of the main differences between the studies was uncertainty, present in the latter, regarding equipment safety and session length. Also, Meyers and Craighead afforded subjects a longer period to recline as electrode placement occurred in the reclining chair, compared to a separate chair in our studies. It is also unclear as to whether Meyers and Craighead created an expectancy or social atmosphere conducive to relaxation.

Ornstein (1971), impressed by the presence of repetition in most forms of meditation, described a REST variant to help explain the function of repetition. Subjects were confined to a uniform visual field, called Ganzfeld, either by washing their retinas with light (Cohen, 1957) or covering their eyes with halved table-tennis balls (Hochberg, Triebel, & Seaman, 1951). In either case, some subjects reported the experience of blindness. It is not as though they had difficulty seeing or focusing; they had lost the ability to see. Ornstein (1971) draws an analogy between the repetitive, fixed stimulus of a mantra or an object to dwell upon in gaze meditation and the reaction of these REST subjects to a severely constrained perceptual environment. To a lesser degree, meditation subjects also withdraw from (or lose the capacity to perceive) the impinging environment about them and seem bound to inner passions, much like the subjects in Hochberg et al. (1951) who generated hallucinations while deprived of a dynamic visual field. Piggins and Morgan (1977, 1978) argue that visual and cognitive distortions (altered states of consciousness) are likely to arise when the perceptual environment is limited to a single object, as in gaze meditation, or a single cognition, as in mantra meditation.

It is difficult to draw firm conclusions about the role of diminished afferent stimulation in the relaxation process based upon REST research. However, several avenues for future research merit attention. Our research suggests that optimal relaxation benefits are obtained in about 15 minutes. It is quite possible that, at some point beyond this, autonomic effects are reversed. Such critical period phenomena have been reported in the prolonged deprivation research (Zubek, 1973). The role of instructions, expectancy, etc., may be important in creating an attitudinal set which physiologically primes the subject for a certain course. Thus, when an individual reclines in a stimulus-impoverished environment for the defined purpose of relaxing, we may find different results compared to framing the situation as basic research in restricted environmental stimulation.

Relaxation by Volition

I believe that a fifth factor should be added to Benson's (1975) list of elements common to the varieties of relaxation techniques. All methods of relaxation enlist the cooperative volition of the participant. The significance of this ingredient becomes readily apparent when one considers the absurd notion of administering relaxation to an uncooperative inductee.

When the subject comfortably reclines in readiness for the relaxation experience, in most cases this demonstrates a willful commitment to attaining a deeper level of relaxation. This commitment also implies the subject possesses some knowledge or conception of the goal state of the task at hand, in other words, the relaxation experience. Barber and Calverley (1964, 1965a) provided some data supporting the contention that the intent to relax, or a preparedness to relax, will facilitate attainment of this goal. Subjects informed that they will be exposed to a hypnotic induction achieved deeper levels of hypnosis and relaxation than subjects receiving the identical induction under the guise that these were nonhypnotic "control" procedures. Similarly, subjects allotted 5 minutes to place themselves under hypnosis without prior training produced roughly equivalent hypnotic effects as subjects who were given a formal hypnotic induction, and superior hypnotic effects compared to subjects simply instructed to rest for 5 minutes (Barber & Calverley, 1969). Thus, self-hypnosis and no-hypnosis groups, differing only with respect to expectations and intent, exhibited a differential response on multiple measures including behavioral indices of relaxation. In addressing this same issue, Onda (1967) points out that the Zen meditator must "assume an attitude of looking forward to the intended outcome" (p. 135).

In order to maintain a relaxed atmosphere, the task orientation in relaxation must not be time limited. Green, Green, and Walters (1970) introduced the term *passive volition,* which I think captures the key process here. The intentional, goal-directed nature of the relaxation process should be framed in a low-effort, unpressured context.

Perhaps, for some people, the exercise of will alone is sufficient to evoke a relaxation response. For others, will is included within a set of conditions which must all be met in order to further relaxation. At the least, some investment of therapy time to instill the belief that the client has the capability to attain relaxation should prove useful. The will to relax may be the only factor that distinguishes the REST setting, which affords little or no relaxation effects, from relaxation therapy. Further, within the REST domain itself, we can cite volition (a mixture of intention, expectancy, and preparedness) as the prime mover of the bliss visited upon users of Lilly's (1977) isolation tank versus the psychopathology flare-ups threatening many REST research volunteers.

Relaxation research finds that placebo (therapeutically inert) treatments, particularly those that are highly credible, sometimes produce substantive relaxation effects. Perhaps one explanation for this phenomenon lies in the notion of the will to relax. The potential power of relaxation by volition was dramatically revealed in a series of studies on the relaxing effects of inhaling elevated levels of carbon dioxide (Griez & Van Den Hout, 1982; Van Den Hout & Griez, 1982b). Although the relaxation effects obtained with carbon dioxide generally surpassed those of normal air, on some measures (e.g., heart rate), subjects who thought they were receiving carbon dioxide but actually received air attained significant decreases comparable to the true carbon dioxide group. However, subjects administered air did not show heart rate decreases when informed that carbon dioxide often causes increased tension (Van Den Hout & Griez, 1982b). True carbon dioxide subjects showed the same heart rate reductions whether they were led to expect positive or negative effects. Thus, subjects receiving air manifested substantive heart rate slowing (which averaged seven beats per minute) only when they believed that carbon dioxide promotes relaxation. The credit belongs to the subject's intent.

From a narrow perspective, the operation of autogenic phrases may be viewed as relaxation by volition. More generally, however, the exercise of one's will appears to be a requisite ingredient in achieving relaxation with any method.

CONCLUSIONS

This chapter summarized the leading theories of relaxation, but it is not an exhaustive account. Shapiro (1980) listed some 20 different explanations for meditation effects, including hypo-oxygenation, cognitive restructuring, social influence, ego regression, cortical lateralization, and habituation. These views boast varying degrees of empirical support and remind us of the seemingly insurmountable complexity of relaxation theory.

There is considerable similarity among the theories associated with relaxation methods, although differences in terminology and emphasis sometimes obscure these similarities. Hypothalamic action is strongly implicated in producing relaxed states, but the mechanisms for recruiting hypothalamic involvement have not been clearly specified. I heartily endorse Benson's (1975) conclusions that certain ingredients common to most relaxation approaches account for the observed effects. I have added greater emphasis on the role of cognitive diversion and restricted environmental stimulation (already noted in Benson's scheme), and have drawn attention to the mechanisms of blood CO_2 and volition in relaxation. Muscular processes in relaxation boast the largest amount of scientific support, but Jacobson's view lacks conviction as a unitary model of relaxation. A relaxed attitude may ultimately emerge as one of the most important relaxation components, yet this is an elusive experimental entity, and there exists little research in its behalf.

No single theory of relaxation reigns superior. Indeed, an adequate theory of relaxation could not be constructed without summoning most of the views reported herein. Each captures a unique, indispensable facet of this multivariate phenomenon, and the entire relaxation enterprise is threatened when any one element is wanting.

CHAPTER 3

Basic Research

There is by now a voluminous literature on the subject of relaxation. The present chapter will focus on a subset of the research that explores the basic processes associated with particular techniques. The primary purpose of this chapter is to assess the current status of the major methods of relaxation from a laboratory perspective. The second purpose of this chapter is to evaluate basic research findings comparing methods of relaxation.

Reports included herein have studied normal volunteers or clinical subjects exposed to a subtherapeutic dosage of relaxation for basic research purposes. The decision to categorize research as basic, in contrast to clinical, is often difficult and arbitrary. Nevertheless, research deemed more heavily clinical is reported in Chapter 7. Emphasis will be given to those studies that possess some degree of experimental control more clearly isolating and evaluating treatment effects.

MEDITATION

There is a large diversity of meditation approaches. I will cover the two disciplines that have gained the greatest recognition, Transcendental Meditation and Benson's relaxation response procedure, as well as review other approaches.

Transcendental Meditation (TM)

Since its inception around 1960, TM has spawned several hundred studies. Although the results of TM research have generally been favorable, most of the studies contain serious methodological flaws, which cast suspicion over the validity of these results. A surprisingly large proportion of the TM research admits a subject-selection bias, and this is the most damaging methodological problem. TM subjects are usually individuals who entered TM training on their own initiative. Typically, these individuals have been practicing TM from a few months to a few years, and often they are TM teachers. In some studies, the TM subjects serve as their own controls as dependent measures are collected before, during, and after TM practice (e.g., Barwood, Empson, Lister, & Tilley, 1978; Gash & Karliner, 1978; Wallace, Benson, & Wilson, 1971).

Most other studies compare TM practitioners with naive subjects who are instructed simply to rest while dependent measures are collected. These measures are then compared to measures taken on the TM group (e.g., Frumkin & Pagano, 1979; Jevning, Pirkle, & Wilson, 1977; Lintel, 1980). In both designs, we must consider the highly plausible possibility that individuals who seek out, successfully master, or stick with TM possess unspecified personality and somatic characteristics predisposing them to high TM achievement, and that these characteristics are not evenly distributed in the general population. Therefore, studies of self-selected TM practitioners may inflate the magnitude of TM effects we would otherwise find with most people.

Consider level of initial values of dependent measures, which exemplifies selection-bias effects. Several studies (e.g., Ferguson & Gowan, 1976; Kanas & Horowitz, 1977; Rogers & Livingston, 1977; West, 1980; Williams, Francis, & Durham, 1976) reveal that subjects who seek out TM training [and other methods of meditation (Ganguli, 1982; Rivers & Spanos, 1981)] exhibit elevated levels of anxiety, depression, etc., compared to randomly selected controls. Wilder's (1957) research on initial value effects demonstrated that treatments produce the most change in those measures that are initially most divergent from the population mean. Kinsman and Staudenmayer (1978) convincingly demonstrated in biofeedback treatment that failure to equate by matching on physiological measures at pretest or failure to correct for inequalities statistically (analysis of covariance) can yield spurious results. Therefore, improvement in the TM group may sometimes be due to initial value effects and not to the influence of TM itself. A related confound arises from high attrition rates, often exceeding 50 percent, in all forms of meditation and relaxation (e.g., Delmonte, 1980; Patel et al., 1985; Rivers & Spanos, 1981). Psychological and physiological attainments of long-term meditators attributed to cumulative practice effects might better be ascribed to self-selection of gifted individuals who persist in training.

A series of studies on TM conducted by Frumkin and Pagano (1979) graphically demonstrated the importance of methodological rigor. In the first study, the authors employed an experimental design modeled after much of the TM research. Practitioners of TM, recruited from the local chapter of the Students International Meditation Society (an organization officially sanctioned by the TM movement), were compared with randomly selected college students in a memory of digits task. Meditators and controls were tested on their recall (pretest). They then meditated or rested quietly, respectively, and were retested (posttest). The results indicated that the TM subjects had significantly better memory than the controls at posttest, contrasted to no difference between the groups on the pretest. One might reasonably conclude from this study that TM has beneficial effects on memory and concentration.

The same article goes on to report two follow-up studies that attempted to replicate the first with the addition of a series of methodological improvements incorporated into the design. For example, subjects in the two groups were matched on age, sex, handedness, and visual acuity (digits were presented visually). Further, monetary rewards were offered for superior memory perform-ance to ensure that both groups enjoyed high motivation to perform correctly. In both of the latter two experiments, the controls actually outperformed the TM subjects. Overall, these authors concluded that TM benefits ap-parently demonstrated in the first study are best viewed as an artifact of methodological inadequacy.

Another issue raised by Frumkin and Pagano (1979) is experimenter-bias effect. In experiment one, the experimenter was himself a TM practitioner. In experiments two and three, the experimenter was neutral. He was uninformed as to the TM or control group status of each subject, and all data were scored by research assistants who were also blind to the group identity of each sub-ject. As several design features were altered in this research series, the contri-bution of experimenter bias to the favorable outcome of the first experiment cannot be determined. Potentially, the influence of experimenter bias (be it intentional or inadvertent) in research is formidable (see extended discussions by Barber, 1976; Rosenthal, 1966). Recently (Segreto-Bures & Kotses, 1982), potent experimenter-bias effects were experimentally isolated in a form of re-laxation training, electromyographic biofeedback. The issue of experimenter bias in TM research is particularly salient, as much of the scientific data on TM has been published by researchers who are themselves devotees of TM, employed by Maharishi International University or by other components of the worldwide TM organization.

A volume of collected studies on TM (Orme-Johnson & Farrow, 1977), published by the TM organization, provides further basis for concern about experimenter bias in TM research. The book presents 104 basic and applied studies on TM of which about 50 percent are reprints of previously published articles. The research spans a broad range of psychological, physiological, and sociological topics. About 10 percent of the studies were conducted by faculty and students at TM institutions. At least another 20 percent of the studies were conducted by individuals with close ties to the International Association for the Advancement of the Science of Creative Intelligence. With the exception of four studies, all of the reports in this volume suffer from the subject-selection bias discussed above. The four random assignment studies (Brauti-gam, 1977; Miskiman, 1977b; Wilson, Honsberger, Chiu, & Novey, 1975; Za-marra, Besseghini, & Wittenberg, 1977) will be discussed in Chapter 7, as they are all clinical investigations.

Every article in this volume obtained an outcome favorable to TM, and this consistency is troubling. It is rare to find such consistency in experimental findings when conditions of unbiased scientific endeavor prevail, even when testing potent psychological variables. At least 10 negative outcome studies of TM (Curtis & Wessberg, 1976; Michaels, Huber, & McCann, 1976; Otis, 1974; Simpson, Dansereau, & Giles, 1972; Smith, 1976; Treichel, Clinch, & Cran, 1973; Walrath & Hamilton, 1975; Williams & Herbert, 1976; Williams & Vick-erman, 1976; Williams & West, 1975) were published prior to the publication of the 1977 TM volume, but they were omitted from the TM collection. Similarly, this volume omitted any reference to reviews on meditation (Davidson, 1976; Kanellakos & Lukas, 1974) that described additional unpublished negative outcome data on TM. Since 1977, numerous studies have reported negative TM effects (see Tables 3.1, 3.2, and 3.3), which raises the question of why did most of the early TM research favor TM? There is no explicit evidence that experimenter-bias effects impregnated these studies. However, prudent weighing of this and other factors that threaten the validity of most of the TM research recommends caution in relying too heavily on this body of research. For a further discussion of the methodological problems detracting from TM research, see the excellent review by Smith (1975).

Tables 3.1, 3.2, and 3.3 summarize studies of the physiological, psychological, and biochemical effects of TM. Selection criteria for inclusion in these tables gave preference to recently conducted research and frequently referenced older studies. Research comparing TM with other treatments (e.g., progressive relaxation) was omitted from these tables and will be discussed later in this chapter. All of the research in these tables is contaminated by the subject-selection bias discussed earlier in this chapter. Indeed, all basic research on TM is blemished by this methodological weakness excepting for seven studies (Beiman, Johnson, Puente, Majestic, & Graham, 1984; Otis, 1974; Puente, 1981; Puente & Beiman, 1980; Simpson, Dansereau, & Giles, 1972; Yuille & Sereda, 1980; Zuroff & Schwarz, 1978). The first and latter five studies will be described in detail later in this chapter in the division on comparisons of relaxation treatments. Of these six studies, four yielded negative results on TM (Beiman et al., 1984; Puente & Beiman, 1980; Simpson et al., 1972; Yuille & Sereda, 1980), and two were equivocal (Puente, 1981; Zuroff & Schwarz, 1978). The second study (Otis, 1974) was presented with insufficient clarity to permit detailed discussion. However, it appeared that Otis was unable to discern differential effects between the TM and control subjects based upon questionnaire, interview, and physiological data.

These tables reveal a remarkably diverse array of effects arising out of the practice of TM. However, scanning of the columns reveals that positive outcomes for TM on a particular variable are usually counterbalanced by a negative outcome for that variable in another study. Thus, conclusions about TM effects must be tempered by this inconsistency.

The thrust of Tables 3.1, 3.2, and 3.3 suggests that TM produces a spectrum of effects reflecting parasympathetic dominance and experiential calm. Wallace and associates (Wallace, 1970; Wallace & Benson, 1972; Wallace, Benson, & Wilson, 1971) contend that the constellation of physiological and psychological characteristics associated with TM define a state that is distinct from either wakefulness, sleep, or other induced states. Others (Barwood et al., 1978; Fenwick et al., 1977; Younger, Adriance, & Berger, 1975) have argued that TM simply brings the individual into a state of light (stage 1) or deeper sleep (Pagano, Rose, Stivers, & Warrenburg, 1976), and that there is nothing unique about the TM experience. Both sides have marshalled supportive data, leaving this question in a state of ambiguity.

A series of experiments by Jevning, Wilson, and associates on biochemical effects of TM strongly suggests that at least some effects occur independently of sleep. Their standard research protocol consisted of studying a group of about 15 experienced TM practitioners and a control group on several dimensions. The control group was subsequently retested after several months of TM practice. The main findings of these studies were that, during and immediately following TM practice, significant changes occurred in biochemical indicators of relaxation—phenylalanine (Jevning, Pirkle, & Wilson, 1977), cortisol (Jevning, Wilson, & Davidson, 1978), and prolactin (Jevning, Wilson, & Vander-Laan, 1978). The TM groups and the quiet rest control groups both slept about 30 percent of the experimental sessions as determined by polysomnographic recordings, though the changes listed above did not occur in the control groups. Further, the magnitude of these changes was not significantly correlated with amount of time slept within the TM group. Other labs (Wolkove, Kreisman, Darragh, Cohen, & Frank, 1984) have also observed that sleep accounts for no more than a small amount of TM effects.

Benson's Procedure

The method of secular or noncultic meditation introduced by Herbert Benson (Benson, Beary, & Carol, 1974) is virtually identical to TM, with the exception that an emotionally neutral word (Benson recommends "one") is silently repeated in place of the sanskrit mantra.

In comparison to TM, there is little basic research available on Benson's approach and the results are inconsistent. However, the methodological sophistication of the studies in this area are generally superior to that found in the TM literature.

In the first published study of Benson's method (Beary & Benson, 1974), 17 subjects with no prior relaxation experience received 1 hour of training in Benson's procedure. During the next hour of experimental evaluation, 12 minutes of relaxation were embedded within a series of four resting control phases. Significant declines in oxygen consumption (13 percent), carbon dioxide elimination (12 percent), and respiration rate (29 percent) accompanied the relaxation practice only. These changes observed by Beary and Benson are roughly comparable to those found with TM (Wallace, 1970; Wallace, Benson, & Wilson, 1971). It should be noted that the changes in oxygen and carbon dioxide were calculated by the continuous measurement method (Benson, Steinert, Greenwood, Klemchuk, & Peterson, 1975), which is more conservative than the sparse sampling procedure previously employed by TM researchers.

A second study by Benson (Benson, Dryer, & Hartley, 1978) monitored eight subjects riding a stationary bicycle for 30 minutes. During the middle 10 minutes, they simultaneously practiced *either* TM or Benson's method. Half the subjects showed an 8 percent decrease in oxygen consumption during this period. Respiratory quotient and heart rate were unaffected. Unfortunately, the authors did not identify which relaxation technique the four reactive sub-

TABLE 3.1. Physiological Effects of Transcendental Meditation: Basic Research Having a

Study	EEG Slowing[a]	Decreased Alpha or Theta Blocking	Heart Rate Slowing	Increased Cardiac Output	Decreased Blood Pressure	Decreased Electro-dermal Activity[b]
Allison, 1970						
Badawi et al., 1984	×		NEG			NEG
Banquet, 1973		×	×			
Barmark & Gaunitz, 1979			NEG			
Barwood et al., 1978	NEG					
Bennett & Trinder, 1977	NEG					
Benson, Steinert, et al., 1975			×			
Dillbeck & Bronson, 1981	×					
Farrow & Hebert, 1982	×		×			×
Fenwick et al., 1977			×			
Gash & Karliner, 1978			NEG		NEG	
Goleman & Schwartz, 1976			NEG			
Hebert & Lehmann, 1977	×					
Heide, 1986		NEG				
Holmes et al., 1983			NEG		NEG	NEG
Jevning et al., 1976				×		
Jevning et al., 1977	×					
Jevning, Wilson, Smith, & Morton, 1978			NEG	×	NEG	
Lang et al., 1979			×			
Lintel, 1980						NEG
McEvoy et al., 1980	×					
Morse et al., 1977	NEG		NEG		NEG	NEG
Orme-Johnson, 1973						×
Orme-Johnson & Haynes, 1981	×					
Puente, 1981	NEG		NEG			×
Travis et al., 1976	NEG		NEG			
Treichel et al., 1973						
Wallace, 1970	×	NEG	×			×
Wallace et al., 1971	×		×		NEG	×
Wallace et al., 1983					×	
Walrath & Hamilton, 1975			NEG			NEG
Williams & West, 1975	NEG	NEG				
Wolkove et al., 1984						×
Wood, 1986			NEG		NEG	

[a]This variable subsumes several EEG indices including increases in alpha or theta patterns, decreases in evoked potentials, and increased EEG coherence.

[b]This variable subsumes several electrodermal indices including skin resistance level and spontaneous skin resistance fluctuations.

[c]This variable subsumes several temperature indices including surface hand temperature and rectal temperature.

× = Significant changes in this variable can be attributed to TM effects in either within- or between-subject comparisons.

NEG = Significant changes in this variable did not occur in within-subject comparisons in the TM group, or changes in the TM group did not exceed those occurring in the control group.

Subject-selection Bias

Increased Temperature[c]	Quicker Autonomic Recovery	Decreased Respiration	Decreased Muscle Activity	Decreased Eye Movements	Decreased O$_2$ Consumption	Decreased CO$_2$ Elimination	Decreased Liver Blood Flow	Decreased Kidney Blood Flow
		×						
		×						
			×	×				
NEG		×						
				×				
					×	×		
		×			×			
					NEG	NEG		
	×							
		NEG						
							×	NEG
		×					×	NEG
	NEG							
		NEG	NEG					
	×							
		×	NEG					
			NEG					
		NEG				NEG		
					×			
NEG		×		NEG	×	×		
		NEG						
		×						
			NEG					

TABLE 3.2. Psychological Effects of Transcendental Meditation: Basic Research Having a

Study	Increased Relaxation	Decreased Anxiety	Decreased Depression	Decreased Aggression	Decreased Neuroticism
Appelle & Oswald, 1974					
Aron & Aron, 1982					
Barmark & Gaunitz, 1979	×				
Carsello & Creaser, 1978					
Delmonte, 1980					NEG
Delmonte, 1981a					
Dillbeck, 1977		×			
Ferguson & Gowan, 1976		×	×	NEG	×
Frumkin & Pagano, 1979					
Goleman & Schwartz, 1976		×			×
Hanley & Spates, 1978					
Hjelle, 1974		×			
Holmes et al., 1983	NEG				
Jedrczak et al., 1985					
Jedrczak & Clements, 1984					
Kanas & Horowitz, 1977		NEG			
Martinetti, 1976					
Mills & Farrow, 1981					
Morse et al., 1977					
Nidich et al., 1973					
Nystul & Garde, 1977					
Nystul & Garde, 1979					
Orme-Johnson & Haynes, 1981					
Otis, 1974					
Pagano & Frumkin, 1977					
Pelletier, 1974					
Sabel, 1980					
Schwartz et al., 1978		×			
Seeman et al., 1972					
Spanos et al., 1979					
Travis, 1979					
Wallace et al., 1982					
Warrenburg & Pagano, 1982–1983					
Williams & Herbert, 1976					
Williams & Vickerman, 1976					
Williams et al., 1976					×
Wood, 1986					

× = Significant changes in this variable can be attributed to TM effects in either within- or between-subject comparisons.

NEG = Significant changes in this variable did not occur in within-subject comparisons in the TM group, or changes in the TM group did not exceed those occurring in the control group.

Increased Self-Actualization	Improved Academic Performance	Improved Memory	Improved Auditory or Visual Perception	Improved Fine Motor Coordination	Improvement In Miscellaneous Self-Report and Performance Measures
				×	
					×
					×
	NEG				
					×
×					
		NEG			
					×
×					×
					×
					×
					NEG
			×		
					×
					NEG
×					
×					
NEG					
					×
					NEG
			×		
			×		
					NEG
×					
					NEG
					×
			×		
	NEG	NEG			NEG
				NEG	
				NEG	
				NEG	

TABLE 3.3. Biochemical Effects of Transcendental Meditation: Basic Research Having a

Study	Decreased Catecholamines	Decreased Dopamine	Increased Serotonin	Decreased Cortisol	Increased Testosterone
Bujatti & Riederer, 1976	×	NEG	×		
Jevning et al., 1977					
Jevning, Wilson, & Davidson, 1978				×	NEG
Jevning, Wilson, Smith, & Morton, 1978					
Jevning, Wilson, & VanderLaan, 1978					
Lang et al., 1979	NEG				
Michaels et al., 1976	NEG				
Michaels et al., 1979				NEG	
Wallace et al., 1971					
Werner et al., 1986				NEG	

×   = Significant changes in this variable can be attributed to TM effects in either within- or between-subject comparisons.

NEG = Significant changes in this variable did not occur in within-subject comparisons in the TM group, or changes in the TM group did not exceed those occurring in the control group.

jects employed, thus precluding further understanding of the distinct properties of TM versus Benson's method. Using a similar design and employing only relaxation response training, Gervino and Veazey (1984) found relaxation during exercise produced significant reductions in oxygen uptake, respiration, and systolic blood pressure.

A partial replication and extension of the Beary and Benson (1974) study obtained equivocal results (Christoph, Luborsky, Kron, & Fishman, 1978). Mild/moderate hypertensive subjects participated in one laboratory evaluation composed of four alternating 12-minute periods of quiet reading and Benson's relaxation method. Significant decreases occurred in respiration rate (17 percent) and heart rate (3 percent) during the relaxation periods in contrast to levels during quiet reading. There were no differences in blood pressure. The authors emphasized the importance of individual response patterns, as exemplified by some of the subjects who actually increased respiration rate during relaxation.

Several studies pitted Bensonian meditation against biofeedback. In one of these, normal volunteers submitted to four weekly training sessions involving pulse transit time biofeedback, Benson's meditation training, or a reading/rest control group (Steptoe & Ross, 1982). A complex series of effects during rest and task periods on numerous physiological measures may be summarized as follows. The biofeedback and meditation groups consistently exhibited relaxation markers, and the control group did not. The meditation subjects did par-

Subject-selection Bias

Decreased Blood Lactate	Decreased Blood pH	Increased Plasma Amino Acids	Increased Plasma Phenyl-alanine	Increased Prolactin	Increased Growth Hormone	Decreased Thyroid Function
		NEG	×			
×						
				×	NEG	
NEG						
NEG						
×	×					
				NEG	NEG	×

ticularly well on measures of respiration, transit time, and skin conductance. Hurley (1980) randomly assigned college students to hypnotic training, electromyographic biofeedback, Benson's technique, or no treatment. Psychological questionnaires were administered before and after eight weekly treatment sessions. Unlike hypnosis and biofeedback, Benson's method did not differ from no treatment on measures of anxiety and ego strength. None of the treatment groups performed better than the no-treatment group on a measure of locus of control.

The final study in this meditation versus biofeedback series is distinguished by its sophisticated methodology and confusing results. A single, complex article by Cuthbert, Kristeller, Simons, Hodes, and Lang (1981) reported a series of studies illustrating the impact of the subject-experimenter relationship on Bensonian meditation effects. Student volunteers engaged in computer-instructed heart rate biofeedback or meditation over three sessions. Meditation subjects attained greater reductions in heart rate, skin conductance, and self-rated relaxation, while respiratory slowing favored the biofeedback group. Frontalis muscle tension data were insignificant.

The study that followed replicated the above comparison and added a quiet-rest control group and a monetary incentive factor. The incentives exerted little influence, but more importantly, between group heart rate and skin conductance differences did not materialize.

The last study of Cuthbert et al. (1981) attempted to isolate the unintended factor accounting for the differential results of the previous two efforts. In the first study, all subjects were trained by one experimenter, whereas a team of experimenters conducted the second study and unintentionally fostered a weaker experimenter-subject interpersonal bond. To isolate this factor, the last study crossed type of treatment (biofeedback versus meditation) with type of relationship (supportive and involved versus minimal formal contact). A third factor, presence or absence of periodic knowledge of results, was also added.

The most interesting data from this third study occurred in the heart rate measure, and I will describe only these results. A complex and somewhat puzzling interaction emerged. When subjects had knowledge of heart rate changes, meditation subjects receiving high experimenter support obtained significantly greater heart slowing than biofeedback subjects, duplicating the findings of the first experiment, which also informed subjects of progress. However, when knowledge of results was absent, minimal contact meditation subjects attained the lowest heart rate.

Amid their concluding remarks, Cuthbert et al. (1981, p. 539) lament, "We might well wish for less complexity!" These data at once tempt our desire to tease out the clinical implications of relationship variables and frustrate attempts at closure on this matter.

Two studies compared Benson's approach with treadmill exercises. Bahrke and Morgan (1978) examined how anxiety was affected by one session of treadmill exercise, Benson's relaxation method, or rest. Normal adult male volunteers were randomly assigned to one of these treatments. Questionnaire data on state anxiety registered significant pre to postsession decreases in all three groups. No group differences occurred. Modest changes in skin temperature occurred for both the rest and relaxation groups. No heart rate changes occurred beyond that expected due to the exercise contrast. Measures of oxygen consumption also failed to differentiate the rest and relaxation groups. In brief, this well-designed study found no advantage of Benson's method over simple rest. Similar results were reported by Sime (1977). Test-anxious undergraduates received exercise training, Benson's technique, or placebo medication. Significant reductions in heart rate and electrodermal responses occurred in the exercise group only. Significant reductions in muscle tension and blood pressure occurred in all groups following a simulated stress test, though no between-group differences materialized. Self-reported anxiety also failed to distinguish the groups.

Two studies evaluated this form of meditation during physical exertion. Hoffman et al. (1982) randomly assigned volunteers to a month's practice of meditation or a daily resting period control. During pre-post handgrip isometric tests, elevated plasma norepinephrine emerged in the posttest of the meditators only. Heart rate and blood pressure effects did not materialize. The investigators then replicated these results by training the control subjects in Bensonian meditation and providing a third handgrip test. These data were interpreted as reflecting lower physiological tone and diminished stress reactivity following meditation. In a near identical design replication, Morrell and

Hollandsworth (1986) observed a pattern of results similar to that of Hoffman et al., but the differences in this second study did not reach statistical significance. Further, Morrell and Hollandsworth interpreted the norepinephrine trend to reflect heightened arousal in the meditation subjects.

Klepac, Hauge, Dowling, and McDonald (1981) evaluated the role of the relaxation response in a component analysis of Meichenbaum's (1977) stress inoculation method of pain control. Dental phobic students were equipped with (a) Bensonian relaxation, (b) cognitive restructuring, (c) practice in arm shock exposure, and/or (d) no treatment in a complete factorial design. Pre-post evaluations revealed that the combination of relaxation and exposure (treatments a and c) and cognitive restructuring alone (treatment b) increased duration of arm shock tolerance. However, generalization to tooth shock tolerance did not occur. Data from secondary dependent measures were inconsistent.

Overall, the basic research on Benson's relaxation response has found it to be equal to or moderately better than control groups. No other lab has replicated the profound relaxation effects Benson reported in his initial studies.

Other Meditation Approaches

There are, of course, a multiplicity of meditation techniques beyond the popular, standardized methods of TM and Benson's approach. To achieve a clear but concise summary presentation of the wide array of meditation literature, I grouped diverse techniques according to common elements to form three categories: breath meditation, mantra meditation, and mixed approaches.

Breath Meditation

The breath meditation methods mostly involve either passive breath mindfulness, training in breath holding, or, less frequently, some form of rapid breathing. These techniques derive from yoga and Japanese Zen traditions.

In a within-subject, pre-post design, Dwivedi, Gupta, and Udupa (1977) found significant reductions in blood pressure, heart rate, and respiration rate following training in breath meditation and body awareness. In a similar design testing the same meditation technique, Sinha, Prasad, and Sharma (1978) observed reductions in reaction time, increases in attention span, and increases in relaxation as indicated by skin resistance level. Goyeche, Chihara, and Shimizu (1972) presented breath meditation, cotention (ocular concentration), and simple rest periods in a randomized sequence to eight student volunteers. Superior effects were produced during the meditation period with respect to decreases in heart rate and respiration rate and increases in abdominal breathing and self-reported feelings of well-being. Udupa, Singh, and Settiwar (1975) monitored normal subjects who practiced a series of yoga breathing exercises daily for 6 months. Over the course of this period, improved physiological functioning was noted in several areas, particularly breath-holding time and pulse rate. Biochemical benefits were registered in serum lipids, plasma cortisol, and serum steroids. Other physiological and biochemical measures showed no change.

Contrary to O_2 findings in other forms of meditation, Miles (1964) recorded an average *increase* of 22 percent in O_2 consumption while an experienced meditator practiced three yoga breathing exercises. Comparable findings to these were also reported by Rao (1968). Similarly, no CO_2, O_2, or blood pH changes occurred with experienced Pranayama (slow breathing through alternate nostrils) meditators (Pratap, Berrettini, & Smith, 1978). Others (Stanescu, Nemery, Veriter, & Marechal, 1981) have reported a variety of respiratory benefits accruing to the regular practice of yoga deep breathing.

In a well-controlled group design study (Goldman, Domitor, & Murray, 1979), university student and employee volunteers were randomly assigned to a Zen breath treatment, an antimeditation control group (vigorous cognitive exercises), or no treatment. Treatment sessions were conducted for 5 consecutive days. Overall, the results did not reflect strong meditation effects. The meditation and antimeditation groups produced comparable ratings of the pleasantness of their techniques. Ratings on level of altered state of consciousness and relaxation favored the meditation group. Pre-post anxiety questionnaires and measures of visual perception revealed significant reductions for all groups, but differences between groups did not materialize. Lastly, the groups did not differ on their reaction to a posttreatment stress test (a demanding intellectual task), as assessed by the state form of the State-Trait Anxiety Inventory (Spielberger, Gorsuch, & Lushene, 1970). Another study of college students practicing Zen (Shapiro, 1978a) found some small improvements in self-percepts compared to a control group.

Malec and Sipprelle (1977) evaluated one session of the same method with student volunteers and observed significant physiological effects (decreased frontalis muscle tension and respiration rate, but no change in heart rate or electrodermal activity) compared to a quiet sitting control group. Attempts to manipulate meditation outcome expectations (relaxed, aroused, or neutral) proved ineffective. In a longer trial (Kolsawalla, 1978), pre-post questionnaires sandwiching 75 days of practice indicated that decreased dogmatism and tension and increased emotional maturity attended practitioners of breath meditation, but not control subjects.

Kubose (1976) reported a methodologically rigorous study somewhat similar to that of Goldman et al. (1979) above. One of the main differences was that Kubose presented treatment for 3 weeks versus only 1 week by Goldman et al. Kubose randomly assigned 27 undergraduate volunteers to a meditation, control, or no-treatment group. The meditation procedure was the common Zen method of breath counting. Although this is primarily a form of breath meditation, it also includes attending to a mantra (numbers). The control group simply remained seated during their sessions duplicating the meditation task in all respects except they were not instructed to count breaths. The no-treatment group met on two occasions to complete questionnaire data only. The treated groups met daily for 3 weeks. The dependent measures included two innovative indices. First, subjects were equipped with a convenient response key that they depressed to signify each instance of distracting thoughts. Second, the experimenter entered the training session on selected days after a variable duration had elapsed. The subjects' task was to estimate how much time had passed since the beginning of the session without the aid of a watch.

Analyses of the cognitive intrusion measure described above revealed that distracting thoughts were more likely to occur as the 15-minute sessions wore on but that such thoughts diminished across sessions. As wandering thoughts are a frequent problem for novice meditators, the ameliorative effects of time and/or practice on this disruptive trait are a useful finding. The time estimation task did not reveal significant differences between the two treated groups, although the meditation group tended to be more accurate.

Other findings of this study were as follows. Meditation subjects showed larger within-session decreases in pulse rate than control subjects. This comparison approached significance. Two measures of creativity, the Remote Associations Test and perception of embedded figures (Witkin, 1950), revealed a small advantage for the meditation group. Lastly, a questionnaire measure of self-actualization (Shostrom, 1966) did not distinguish any of the three groups. Increased self-actualization for Zen meditators has been reported in another investigation (Compton & Becker, 1983), but this effect emerged after a year's practice.

Paced respiration, a secular parallel to Zen, teaches subjects to slow their breathing to about 50 percent of baseline rate (Harris, Katkin, Lick, & Habberfield, 1976). This approach represents a seemingly small but noteworthy variation on traditional meditation. Instead of instructing subjects in breath mindfulness and then gauging success by respiration decrements, paced respiration teaches the goal behavior directly.

Harris et al. (1976) employed the on-off cadence of a light bulb to guide the slowing of student volunteers' respiration. Also included were a light bulb attention control group (counting the number of on-off changes) and a rest control group. The paced respiration group exhibited less anticipatory anxiety (as measured by electrodermal responding) than the other two groups, and a smaller response to actual shock than the attention control group. Heart rate changes did not distinguish the groups. These results are impressive considering that paced respiration subjects received only 10 minutes of training. A related study (Westcott & Huttenlocher, 1961) examining different rates of respiration in normal subjects found that shallow, slow (six breaths per minute) breathing did produce heart rate deceleration.

Clark (1979) also conducted an interesting test of paced respiration. Women high in dental fear viewed a film depicting dental work after (a) 8 breaths per minute (bpm) paced training, (b) 16 bpm training, (c) 24 bpm training, (d) attention control training, or (e) no treatment. Respiration rate and subjective discomfort were lower in the 8 bpm group than any other during the film showing. Electrodermal and heart rate indices were nondiscriminatory. Finally, data from Holmes' lab demonstrated that paced respiration is an effective strategy in coping with threatened shock (McCaul, Solomon, & Holmes, 1979), and that rapid (2 second) inhalation paired with slow (8 second) exhalation is the most effective phasic pattern (Cappo & Holmes, 1984).

Mantra Meditation

A number of basic research studies have examined forms of mantra meditation in group design comparisons. Elson, Hauri, and Cunis (1977) studied 11 practitioners of Ananda Marga, a type of yoga meditation similar to TM. Control subjects, matched to the meditators by age, height, weight, and sex, submitted to the same physiological measurements and experimental procedure as did the meditators, except the former group was told to remain "wakefully relaxed" without further meditation instructions. Using the criterion of onset of stage 2 sleep, not one meditator slept while 6 of 11 control subjects showed some sleep. Several comparisons between the groups on amount of alpha-theta activity showed stronger effects for the meditators. For example, pre-post comparisons of the meditators revealed that alpha-theta productivity nearly doubled, though no changes were observed in the control subjects at these same points. Skin resistance level increased 21 percent for the meditators during the session denoting increased relaxation, while the control subjects registered significant decreases on this measure. Small changes occurred for both groups in heart rate, skin temperature, and respiratory rate. Studying practitioners from this same school of meditation, another study (Corby, Roth, Zarcone, & Kopell, 1978) observed evidence of autonomic arousal, though not unpleasant, during states of deep meditation.

Delmonte (1981b) compared a TM-like form of meditation with rest in a within-group design. The primary dependent measure, hypnotic suggestibility (Barber, 1965), showed significant increases only following meditation (see Chapter 6 for an expanded discussion of this article). Others (Heide, Wadlington, & Lundy, 1980) have failed in their attempt to produce the same effect, but did observe that preexisting high hypnotic suggestibility predicted successful meditation.

Credidio (1982) randomly assigned normal, middle-aged female volunteers to meditation, a combination of skin temperature and electromyographic biofeedback, or a quiet-rest control group. The meditation method was that of Carrington (1984), termed Clinically Standardized Meditation. This technique is also very similar to TM. All subjects were administered seven treatments at weekly intervals, and were instructed to practice daily at home. Meditation produced significantly greater decreases in forehead muscle tension compared to both of the other groups, though these differences did not occur until the last two sessions (sessions six and seven). Analyses of digital skin temperature revealed some changes occurring in the biofeedback group, but no significant effects for meditation. The Eysenck Personality Inventory (Eysenck, 1963) failed to predict the pattern of treatment effects.

A second study on Clinically Standardized Meditation (Muskatel, Woolfolk, Carrington, Lehrer, & McCann, 1984) rated undergraduates volunteering for meditation training as high or low on a Type A behavior subset, time urgency (according to the questionnaire of Jenkins, Zyzanski, & Rosenman, 1979). Subjects were randomly assigned to 3 1/2 weeks of meditation or no treatment. Pre-post evaluations on ability to estimate elapsed time and ability to tolerate an enforced waiting manipulation revealed that treated subjects achieved superior gains on both these measures of time urgency. Oddly, treatment gains were independent of pretest level of time urgency.

Morse and his colleagues (Morse, Schacterle, Furst, Brokenshire, et al., 1981; Morse et al., 1982) tested a secular mantra meditation technique with dental students. Salivary analyses and performance on dental examinations documented anxiety reduction benefits of meditation in within- and between-subject designs.

This same research group has conducted a series of studies on mantra content, yielding the most scientifically rigorous data on this subject. The first study (Morse, Martin, Furst, & Dubin, 1977) compared subjects experienced in TM with neophyte meditators who selected any one of the following as mantras—one, om, flower, garden, river, or sail. TM did not prove to be superior on measures of skin resistance, respiratory rate, heart rate, blood pressure, electroencephalography, or electromyography. Self-report data were equivocal.

In a within-subject comparison, Morse, Martin, Furst, and Dubin (1979) exposed 48 subjects to a sequence of six phases, each lasting 3-5 minutes: a) alert, b) resting relaxation, c) meditation on the word "love," d) meditation on the word "hate," e) meditation on the word "one," and f) silent rest while repeating a series of unrelated numbers. A 3-minute break separated each phase. Skin resistance spontaneous fluctuations, a measure of anxiety, were significantly higher during the alert phase compared to any of the three meditation phases, which did not differ from each other. This pattern of results was also obtained for respiratory rate, heart rate, and skin resistance level. With few exceptions, no other significant differences were found between phases on physiological measures. When asked to choose their favorite phrase, 25 subjects elected "love" meditation ($p < .01$), 11 elected "hate," and only 6 of 48 cited "one," the word preferred by Benson (1975). Stimulation of tangential thoughts were more strongly associated with "hate" and "love" meditation than with "one" meditation. These self-report data support Benson's (1975) contention that "one" is a neutral word, but the assertion that neutral mantras are superior to emotionally laden mantras was contradicted.

In their most recent effort, Morse and Furst (1982) introduced 40 different mantras to 72 healthy volunteers. The mantras represented a diversity of themes, as exemplified by Sanskrit (aum), common (man), positive (love), negative (vomit), and sensation (cool) terms.

When mantras evoked thoughts or sensations, these usually faded within a couple of sessions. When sensations were perceived, these were positive about 80 percent of the time and were associated with neutral or positive mantras. Typical sensations were tingling, warmth, heaviness, lightness, and floating.

Negative sensations (20 percent) were usually associated with negative words such as vomit, icepick, and coronary. The most common negative sensations were pain, cold, and itching. The absolute impact of aversive mantras should not be overstated. Not only does aversiveness decline rapidly with repeated exposure, but the most frequently cited negative mantra (vomit) was deemed unpleasant by only 60 percent of the subjects.

Subjects' ratings of mantras identified "love," "aum," "shirim," "sky," and "fly" as the most desirable when rated according to dimensions such as ease and depth of meditation state. Not surprisingly, rated lowest on these scales were the negative words enumerated above. The word "love" received the largest number of endorsements for favorite mantra. The Sanskrit mantra "aum" and "sky" were also frequently picked. Benson's "one" was the eighth most popular mantra.

West (1979b) conducted still another test of types of mantras. Subjects were trained in a method of meditation that closely paralleled TM. Half of these subjects were given an actual TM mantra, i-ing, and half were given a mantra invented for this study, mantram, which is the Sanskrit singular form for "mantra" (White, 1976). An untreated control group was compared with the two meditation groups on measures of skin conductance taken prior to relaxation training and at 3-month and 6-month follow-ups. Meditation subjects, considered jointly, showed a significant decrease in spontaneous skin conductance responses over 6 months, with the bulk of the improvement occurring within 3 months. The control group did not exhibit changes on this measure. A second measure of electrodermal activity, skin conductance level, did not distinguish the experimental and control groups in any session. Finally, no differences emerged between the two meditation groups, although TM devotees would argue that the TM mantra was not assigned on an individual basis according to the undisclosed TM guidelines. Smith's (1976) clinical study (discussed in Chapter 7) also failed to demonstrate superiority of the TM mantra over "bogus" mantras.

Mixed Meditation Approaches

The meditation studies that follow are classified as mixed approaches, either because the methods employed were combinations of techniques, the meditation procedures were not described in sufficient detail to permit a more precise definition, or the technique studied could not be included under the headings of breath or mantra meditation.

Some of the earliest scientific data on meditation come from Bagchi and Wenger's (1957) travels across India with a portable physiograph in search of authentic yogis whose meditative achievements could be objectively verified. They recorded 98 sessions on 45 yogis who claimed up to 30 years of experience with various meditative styles. The results were reported in anecdotal form. Briefly, the heart rate, blood pressure, and electroencephalographic (EEG) effects were unremarkable. The main changes occurred with respiration (slowing to four breaths per minute in some instances) and skin resistance (reaching a 70 percent increase). A subsequent report on the same data (Wenger & Bagchi, 1961) indicated that the depression of respiratory and electrodermal functions were significant compared to control groups. This later report also described the unusual ability of one yogi who learned to generate body heat in defending against the cold Himalayan cave where he sometimes meditated. As a result, "he could perspire from the forehead on command within 1 1/2 to 10 minutes," (p. 313).

Deikman (1963) conducted one of the earliest (quasi) experimental investigations of meditation and one of the few tests of gaze meditation. Four middle-aged subjects, naive as to meditation, were invited to spend 12 sessions in gaze meditation, focusing upon a vase. Deikman interviewed subjects after each session to obtain qualitative data. Subjects experienced the exercise as generally pleasant. Further, subjects reported perceptual distortions of the vase and gradually diminishing awareness of music and other distractors. Two of the subjects, who participated in the above experiment, continued gaze meditation for some 100 sessions (Deikman, 1966), and their experience during the extended period was consistent with their early experience.

A more recent study of gaze meditation (DiNardo & Raymond, 1979) found that decreased cognitive intrusions were associated with an internal, rather than external, locus of control (q.v., Rotter, 1966) and an actual, rather than imaginal, object of meditation (a lit candle). Employing the rate of signaled cognitive intrusions as a marker of depth of meditation, two studies found that high hypnotizability predicted successful gaze and/or breath meditation (Spanos, Rivers, & Gottlieb, 1978; Van Nuys, 1973). However, a different view of the hypnotizability-meditation relationship found that practicing gaze meditation did not increase hypnotizability (Spanos, Gottlieb, & Rivers, 1980). This study also found that the rate of intensive thoughts declined over eight sessions, but not significantly so.

In one of the most detailed investigations of meditation ever reported, Kasamatsu and Hirai (1966) studied 48 Zen priests and disciples. The method of meditation was Zazen or Zen sitting meditation. "During the Zen sitting, the disciples' eyes must be open and look downward about one meter ahead and his hands generally join" (p. 315). EEG and several other measures of physiological functioning were collected, but only the EEG data were reported.

The subjects ranged in age from 24 to 72 years old, and their experience in Zazen ranged from 1 to over 20 years. In interpreting the following findings, the reader should note that all recordings were conducted with the eyes opened, and it is particularly difficult to depress EEG functioning when the eyes are not closed. All of the subjects showed long intervals of unusually high amplitude alpha. This finding was compared with the resting performance of age-matched, untrained control subjects who primarily exhibited the expected beta pattern with brief periods of low amplitude alpha. It was noted that the degree of EEG effects produced by the meditators correlated with their years of practice. For example, sustained theta patterns were seen only in subjects having more than 20 years experience.

A series of trials assessing response to auditory clicks were performed on three Zen masters and four control subjects. Both groups manifested the predicted alpha blocking response, that is, interruption of alpha waves for about 2 seconds following a click. However, the alpha blocking response continued unabated in the meditation subjects, whereas habituation in the form of diminished alpha blocking occurred in the controls in the same time frame. This suggests strong, persistent concentration prevailed among the meditation subjects.

Lastly, these authors claim that the state of consciousness attained in Zazen is distinct from hypnosis or sleep. The reader may recall that Wallace (1970) advanced a similar assertion for TM a few years later. Kasamatsu and Hirai pointed out that the prominent alpha pattern in Zazen did not occur in hypnotic subjects they examined. Sleep is distinguished from Zazen in that practitioners of the latter manifest heightened alertness and EEG (alpha and theta) blocking to auditory stimuli that do not occur in sleep. Further, EEG sleep spindles and other characteristic waveforms of sleep do not emerge in Zazen. These results were replicated on a similar but larger sample of subjects reported by Hirai (1974).

Approximately a decade earlier, Kasamatsu et al. (1957) investigated similar phenomena to that explored by Kasamatsu and Hirai (1966). This first study produced a brief report on two Zen and yoga experts and two control subjects. The meditation subjects generated more EEG alpha than did the controls during meditation or quiet rest, respectively. Quizzically, the meditation subjects did not exhibit alpha blocking in response to hand clapping or bells, in contrast to persistent alpha blocking observed by Kasamatsu and Hirai.

A series of studies by an Indian research group examined the effects of 6 months of intense, comprehensive training in Hatha Yoga on healthy, young, adult male volunteers. In the initial report, Udupa, Singh, and Settiwar (1972) presented data on 20 physiological and biochemical indicators. Overall, statistically significant improvement occurred in about half of these, while changes in the remaining measures were generally in a therapeutic direction. To summarize the most important findings, respiratory capacity and efficiency showed marked benefits. Endocrine analyses, changes in metabolic functions, and the physiological effects of an exercise tolerance test all showed an inconsistent pattern. The second report (Udupa, Singh, & Yadav, 1973) described large improvements in numerous psychological measures on pre-post comparisons. These included performance (it was implied that this was on some academic task), IQ, memory, neuroticism, and mental fatigue. The Cornell Medical Index (Brodman, Erdmann, & Wolff, 1949) registered substantive decrements in physiological and psychological complaints. Significant decreases in biochemical indices of arousal, plasma acetylcholine and serum cholinesterase, were also noted. The final study (Gode, Singh, Settiwar, Gode, & Udupa, 1974) found that urinary testosterone levels increased significantly over the 6-month period, suggesting improved functioning of the endocrine system.

Other laboratories have also investigated yoga meditation. Gopal, Bhatnagar, Subramanian, and Nishith (1973) conducted physiological assessments on two groups of subjects before and after calisthenics. One of the groups was composed of 14 young adult males, all of whom had been practicing yoga for at least 6 months. The second group of males was untrained in yoga and was matched to the first group on age, height, and weight. The yoga subjects exhibited significantly better functioning than the control group on three of eight measures of respiration (tidal volume, vital capacity, and respiratory rate). Heart rate and blood pressure measures favored the trained subjects, but were not statistically significant. Banquet and Lesevre (1980) presented a visual choice, reaction time task to a group of subjects experienced in yoga meditation and to a control group. The task was repeated after these groups practiced yoga or rested quietly, respectively. Continuous EEG recordings were taken to elucidate brain processing mechanisms. Significantly faster reaction times by the yoga subjects in the pretest suggest long-term advantages with such training. There was no evidence for short-term effects, as the interventions had no differential impact on reaction time performance. Analyses of evoked potentials tentatively suggested that yoga training enhances selective attention and vigilance skills.

Individuals attending a 3-month Buddhist retreat engaged in the extraordinary sum of 16 hours of meditation daily (Brown, Forte, & Dysart, 1984). The meditation regimen began with breath awareness, and was extended to include awareness of all mind and body sensations while walking and sitting. A control group consisted of retreat staff who were experienced meditators but nonparticipants in the current retreat experience. Tachistoscope-delivered tests of visual acuity registered gains for the retreat subjects, but not the controls. Other data from this same meditation program (Shapiro, Shapiro, Walsh, & Brown, 1982) indicated that feminine traits were more prevalent in this sample of men and women than in the general population, and that femininity increased over the 3-month period.

Leung (1973) examined the effects of meditation on interviewing skills. Undergraduate volunteers, trained in breath meditation and a verbal cue form of mantra meditation, next viewed videotapes of mock client interviews, as did untreated control subjects. Performance measures of empathy and accurate listening favored trained over untrained subjects, suggesting that meditation may be useful in counselor preparation.

There is a small amount of basic research on sleep effects of meditation. Reed (1978) collected correlational data from 110 individuals, many of whom practiced some variety of meditation. Meditation practice predicted significant improvement in dream recall the following day. A second study of a hybrid meditation technique (Cartwright, Butters, Weinstein, & Kroeker, 1977) tested meditation effects on REM sleep, and found no effect.

Osis, Bokert, and Carlson (1973) factor analyzed questionnaires given to practitioners of varied meditation techniques, and Kohr (1977) replicated this analysis with individuals practicing mantra meditation. We should keep in mind that these two investigations employed nonrandom samples composed of individuals belonging to parapsychology organizations.

To summarize the results and communicate a sense of which meditation effects reliably occurred, I will briefly describe the three factors that materialized in both studies. The first factor referred to general status during the day, independent of the meditation session. It reflected contentment toward life and positive self-evaluation. The second factor may be termed intensification of consciousness. Increased clarity of thought, increased concentration, and greater meaningfulness of life were the main themes here. Lastly, there was a negative experience factor indicating that frustration, intrusive thoughts, and fatigue were sometimes present in meditation. Additional analyses on the Kohr (1977) data (reported in Kohr, 1978 and Puryear, Cayce, & Thurston, 1976) revealed that meditation benefits grew over the 1-month evaluation period, global benefits were more likely to occur among individuals disposed toward low anxiety and few personal problems, and anxious individuals experienced anxiety reduction.

Brown and Engler (1980) described five stages occurring in Vipassana, or mindfulness, meditation from Buddhist tradition. The practitioner is said to pass through these stages as meditation skills advance. These researchers administered Rorschachs to American and Asian meditators of this school in an attempt to document cognitive shifts accompanying these stages. The subjects varied in meditative skill from neophyte to master, roughly reflecting length of practice. The method basically involves sequentially centering one's attention on breath, other bodily sensations, selected cognitions, etc. A major drawback of this study was that Rorschach interpretations were not done blind to the subjects' meditation status, admitting the possibility that experimenter preconceptions were superimposed on the unstructured data leading to biased results. Therefore, it is not surprising that these authors found the Rorschach data closely matched the cognitive characteristics postulated for each stage: I. normal protocols, II. barren protocols reflecting disinterest in external stimuli, III. profuse associations indicating rapidly expanding range of consciousness, IV. perceptions of energy and space as transcendent expressions of the self, and V. an integrative superstructure, reflecting a harmony between the subject's world view and the disparate elements of the stimulus material.

Data supportive of this idea of advancing levels of experience in meditation were also forthcoming from a cross-sectional study of varied meditation methods (Davidson, Goleman, & Schwartz, 1976). Three psychological instruments were administered to four groups of individuals defined as: (a) not practicing meditation, (b) beginning meditation, (c) practicing meditation for up to 2 years, or (d) practicing meditation for more than 2 years. Longevity of practice correlated with increased hypnotizability (Shor, Orne, & O'Connell, 1962) and absorption (Tellegen & Atkinson, 1974), and decreased trait anxiety (Spielberger, Gorsuch, & Lushene, 1970).

Brief mention is due a study by Woolfolk and Rooney (1981), in which student volunteers submitted to one session of meditation—mantra and breath regulation combined. Robust physiological (skin conductance, systolic blood pressure, and heart rate) and self-report indicators of relaxation did occur, but instructions to expect either relaxed or energized effects exerted no influence.

In a rare test of meditation with children, Linden (1973) taught third graders a combination of breath and gaze meditation and obtained impressive results. Matched groups received group therapy or no treatment. Pre-post evaluations revealed that the meditation group achieved superior gains on field independence [as measured by a child version of Witkin's (1950) Embedded Figures Test] and test anxiety compared to both remaining groups. Improved reading ability did not occur in any group.

Unlike devotees of other relaxation disciplines (excepting for hypnosis), practitioners of meditation have shown a fascination for performing astonishing feats that have even included magically appearing and disappearing (Bagchi, 1969). The meditation lore abounds with such wondrous accounts (e.g., Eliade, 1954/1969; Sivananda, 1971; Vajiranana, 1962).

In recent times, an airtight box has served as the most common medium to document extraordinary achievements. Vakil (1950) was the first to carefully verify this sort of phenomenon. He recounts that a yogi priest "entered an airtight subterranean concrete cubicle on one of the main highways of Bombay city. The act was witnessed at close quarters by well over 10,000 spectators" (p. 871). All six interior walls of the box were studded with thousands of 3-inch long nails. Fifty-six hours after the vault was sealed, a small hole was bored into the lid, 1400 gallons of water were poured in, and the orifice was sealed again. Six and one half hours later, the yogi was removed from the box, having spent over 62 hours encased. The subject was at first stuporous and manifested a pulse of 80 beats per minute, a blood pressure of 112/78 mm Hg, and a respiratory rate of about nine breaths per minute. With the aid of smelling salts, the subject rapidly regained normal functioning. Except for a few minor scratches, there was no evidence of tissue damage incurred from the nails. The author added that there was sufficient air in the box to sustain human life for about 80 hours, though he still viewed this accomplishment as extraordinary. Other accounts of such public demonstrations are also available (Bagchi, 1969; Hoenig, 1968).

Karambelkar, Vinekar, and Bhole (1968) studied a similar achievement in the laboratory. Four subjects spent between 12 and 18 hours in an air-tight box, 6.75' × 4' × 3.5'. One subject (designated A) was described as a yoga professional. A second subject (B) had 3 years of yoga experience. The remaining subjects (C and D) did not practice yoga. Physiograph leads and other assessment devices were contained in the box. Subject A lasted 18 hours. Subjects B, C, and D lasted between 12.5 and 13.75 hours. Subject A exhibited the lowest oxygen consumption and the highest tolerance to air carbon dioxide levels accumulating from expiration. Subjects did not differ on measures of skin resistance level, blood pressure, heart rate, or respiratory rate. Other laboratory evaluations of yogis in sealed boxes have yielded comparable results (Anand, Chhina, & Singh, 1961b).

Claims of "heart stopping" among long-term meditation practitioners have also been investigated. Wenger, Bagchi, and Anand (1961) cite a series of accounts dating back to 1935 describing yogis who can depress heart functioning to the point of temporary cessation. The present study identified four experienced yogis who made such claims. Each was studied with precision by using physiological instrumentation. To summarize the findings, these individuals could not directly control heart functioning, but they could exert considerable influence on the heart through a combination of breath and muscular manipulations, though not to the point of cessation. The basic strategy involved what is commonly referred to as the Valsalva maneuver, breath holding while exerting muscular tension in the thorax and abdomen. Under these conditions, the pulse grows faint and the heartbeat is difficult to detect. The possibility still exists that other meditators can stop the heart through nonmechanical means, as such a feat has been documented in an untrained individual who employed a self-styled method of relaxation (McClure, 1959).

Pelletier and Peper (1977) presented three case descriptions of unusual pain tolerance. The third case involved an individual who employed meditation for this purpose, and only this case will be reported. The subject, "a 50-year-old Dutch meditator" (p. 365), was prepared for a full complement of physiological assessments during all laboratory sessions. Of particular interest to the present discussion was a session in which the subject exhibited a normal stress and bleeding response prior to meditation. Subsequently, during a combination of meditation and alpha biofeedback, the subject pushed a 26-gauge steel needle through his left upper arm on three separate occasions. In contrast to the unambiguous pain response in the premeditative state, there was no evidence of brain wave reactivity to these self-inflicted wounds and, most noteworthy, no bleeding occurred. Further, neither respiratory rate nor muscle tension registered evidence of reactivity. Contradictory findings in two other measures were reported. Heart rate showed significant decreases while electrodermal arousal rose significantly.

In concluding this section on extraordinary feats, we would do well to heed the caution of Dalal and Barber (1969). Such public displays are inimical to the training procedures and philosophy of Eastern schools of meditation, and claims of unnatural attainment routinely bow to mundane explanations when subjected to careful scrutiny.

Final Comments on Meditation

Looking back over the wealth of basic research data on the variety of meditation approaches, some conclusions do emerge which summarize the thrust of this literature. I should add that most of the conclusions proffered herein apply equally well to the realm of relaxation in its entirety. In general, there can be no doubt that the variety of meditation approaches are legitimate techniques that often lead to deeper states of phenomenological and physiological relaxation. Most other comprehensive reviews in this area reach the same conclusion (Shapiro, 1980; West, 1979a; Woolfolk, 1975). Nevertheless, we do find negative outcome studies, and individual failures do occur within studies showing an overall positive outcome. Two explanations for these contradictory findings, both based on the principle of individual differences, can be offered.

There are some people who cannot profit from meditation. Research has not revealed clearcut personality predictors of successful meditation, although such distinguishing features surely exist within a complex matrix. Predisposing characteristics might include a certain reactive quality in one's autonomic makeup, an innate capacity for expanding one's cognitive processes and perceptual attention, and an attitudinal set compatible with meditation procedures and goals. I have cited some data suggesting hypnotic susceptibility as one such prognostic factor. A second explanation for why meditation is sometimes unsuccessful is that some individuals may find only particular meditation methods suitable. In most research protocols, people are not given the opportunity to sample and select the method that holds the greatest personal appeal. As a result, individuals who might have exhibited strong meditation effects will sometimes find themselves practicing a technique that does not suit them well. Here again, research has not systematically evaluated which technique/ person characteristics are salient for deciding on this matchup. Chapter 4 offers some thoughts on this subject to help guide clinical decisions.

One of the principal factors determining the strength of meditation effects is practice. The importance of practice cannot be overstated. Numerous studies of diverse meditation techniques demonstrate increments in meditation effects along the continuum bounded by neophyte trainees on one end and practitioners of many years' duration on the other (e.g., Brown & Engler, 1980; Compton & Becker, 1983; Davidson, Goleman, & Schwartz, 1976; Dillbeck, 1977; Elson, Hauri, & Cunis, 1977; Ferguson & Gowan, 1976; Hanley & Spates, 1978; Hjelle, 1974; Karambelkar, Vinekar, & Bhole, 1968). Further, the emergence of more profound relaxation effects is slow to asymptote. This point was dramatically illustrated by Kasamatsu and Hirai (1966). Zen practitioners with over 20 years' experience exhibited deeper relaxation than those with 15 years' experience, who in turn surpassed those having 10 years' meditation experience, and so on. Although some studies have not found a correlation between length of practice and magnitude of meditation effects (Cauthen & Prymak, 1977), the bulk of the evidence points strongly to the importance of this factor.

As a variation on his hypnosis research findings, Barber (1970) argued that meditation (and hypnosis) does not produce unique states or abilities. Citing what little data were available at the time, Barber concluded that nonpractitioners can duplicate achievements otherwise attributed to meditation prowess, given the presence of task-specific experiences and motivation. Since Barber's writing, a critical analysis of the research does not contradict his conclusions (Holmes, 1984). Pre-post evaluations of meditation and casual comparisons with control groups claim unique potency for meditation, but the more rigorous studies (e.g., Frumkin & Pagano, 1979; West, 1979b), controlling for nonmeditation variables deemed salient from Barber's perspective, find scarce differences between practitioners and naive subjects. However, here, too, conclusions are not without qualification. Studying those practitioners who are willing to submit to scientific scrutiny in an unfamiliar setting may fail to detect much of what meditation has to offer.

Some writers would object to this entire section on meditation, arguing that the paradigms fostering Eastern meditation and Western science are sufficiently incongruous as to render inadequate and misleading scientific attempts to understand and evaluate meditation (Shimano & Douglas, 1975; Walsh, 1980; Walsh, Goleman, Kornfield, Pensa, & Shapiro, 1978). Shapiro (1983b) articulately argued that, for some, the primary (and substantive) impact of meditation is in the spiritual and phenomenological realms that defy quantification in scientific parlance (reductionistic terms). As my own views and that of the bulk of the above research have been soaked in Western thought and scientific practice, the analyses and conclusions presented in this chapter may be constrained by an inappropriate paradigm. Although I am at a loss to assess the validity of this criticism, I am not reluctant to admit its plausibility.

PROGRESSIVE RELAXATION (PR)

Two time periods have witnessed a flurry of basic research activity on PR. The first extended from 1925 to 1940, wherein Jacobson himself published a considerable amount of data. The second period began around 1965 and continues to the present. The current era has investigated briefer PR formats in more diverse contexts. Let us begin with a review of Jacobson's work.

Basic Research by Jacobson

Much of Jacobson's research consisted of direct tests of theoretical assumptions relating to the interrelationship between striate muscle tension, reflexes, and cognitions. These theoretical tests supported the view that the brain and the musculature act in concert through a reciprocal, egalitarian relationship. This research was presented in detail in Chapter 2. The bulk of the remainder of Jacobson's basic research efforts focused on the effects of PR on muscular tension and on blood pressure. These two lines of research are outlined below.

Muscle Tension

One of the major obstacles to the serious study of muscle activity was the limited capability of available physiological instrumentation. Jacobson began his muscle studies in 1927 (Jacobson, 1943c), employing a string galvanometer to obtain measures of muscles. By 1930, Jacobson introduced refinements in this technique permitting accurate measurement of a fraction of a microvolt (a millionth of a volt abbreviated as μV), a level of sensitivity rivaling current standards. However, analysis of data from this instrument proved burdensome

(1930a, 1939a, 1940b). The vibrating string was filmed at regular intervals, and then painstaking measurement of string deflections was performed under magnification.

The substance of Jacobson's contributions to electromyography rests on improvements on the string galvanometer he pioneered (1940b, 1940c, 1941b). A major breakthrough occurred in 1937 through rectification of the raw muscle signal. This device, called a neurovoltmeter, was developed by Jacobson in collaboration with engineers from Bell Telephone Laboratories. It portrayed muscle activity levels on a needle meter that lent itself to convenient visual inspection. A year later, another major advance was accomplished by averaging the raw muscle signals per unit of time. This revision, called the integrating neurovoltmeter, resulted in improved convenience and accuracy in the quantification of muscle activity. This last instrument has at times been called an action potential integrator, an integrating microvoltmeter, and a myovoltmeter. By any name, this instrumentation launched modern electromyography.

The basic approach followed by Jacobson contrasted muscle activity in normal adults, without benefit of relaxation training, with normal adults or chronically nervous patients before and after such training. This paradigm was applied to examine tonic muscle tension (Jacobson, 1934b, 1943b) and latency to relax (Jacobson, 1934a, 1936a).

Jacobson (1934b) monitored the right biceps of normal college student volunteers while they reclined during two separate sessions on one day, and two more sessions on a second day, scheduled a week later. These subjects were explicitly instructed to relax only in the second session on each of these two days. A second group of students participated in only one session on these two days and were instructed to relax in both sessions. For the first group, a slight trend toward greater muscular relaxation occurred in the second session of each day. Noteworthy changes between days or between these two groups did not occur. The overall mean muscle tension level of these subjects was 0.9 μV. Six anxious patients submitted to similar evaluations prior to PR training. Their records were considerably more erratic than the students' records and averaged 3.63 μV. Following 4 to 9 months of relaxation training that included 1–2 hours of home practice daily, these same patients registered an average of 0.26 μV in the laboratory, which was considerably below the level attained by the students.

Jacobson (1943b) conducted a second experiment of a somewhat similar nature several years later. Seven adult female volunteers underwent about 3 months of PR training. Before and after training, assessments were made of the right thigh (quadriceps femoris) while the subjects read quietly. The average tension level dropped from 0.83 μV in the pretest to 0.15 μV in the posttest. Ten control subjects tested at matched points in time, but with no intervening relaxation training, showed a rise from 1.58 μV to 2.57 μV. Thus, it appears that normal adults, as well as anxiety-ridden individuals, gain substantial muscular benefits from Jacobson's technique. As indicated below, studies of latency to relax yielded comparable results.

Jacobson (1934a) invited 14 normal students and 16 nervous patients to participate in a latency experiment. Two signal clicks, spaced at about 2 seconds, were presented to subjects whose right biceps were monitored. At the first click, subjects bent their right arms. At the second click, they were to relax. Latency to relax was defined as the interval from the second click to attaining complete relaxation. Jacobson did not supply a clear, operational definition of "complete relaxation," but he usually employed the criteria of falling below 1.0 μV. Thirteen of the students and 12 of the patients required more than 1 second to relax. The students averaged 3 μV at the 1-second mark, as did 10 of the patients. Six patients were particularly tense, averaging about 7 μV at this same point. This latter subgroup of highly tense patients was retested subsequent to relaxation training and then averaged 1.5 μV at the 1-second mark. To control for a possible trials effect, five other highly anxious patients were not given a pretest. Following relaxation training, their performance on this same task mirrored the posttraining performance of the six patients reported above.

In a follow-up experiment (Jacobson, 1936a), the same latency task was administered to normal college students, collegiate athletes, and patients with extensive prior training in relaxation. On two measures of muscular relaxation, depth and latency, the trained patients manifested greater relaxation than the athletes, who in turn surpassed the students.

Jacobson's later work considered the additional advantages of PR beyond simple rest. In a convention paper abstract, Jacobson (1940f) referred to data on four individuals who had the longstanding habit of taking daily rest periods. In laboratory evaluations, these individuals showed considerable muscle activity during rest. In a subsequent, more complete report (Jacobson, 1942), data were presented on seven middle-aged volunteers who were chronically tense and accustomed to resting 1 or more hours a day. Right arm recordings during rest revealed tension levels in the 1 to 15 μV range, which was generally higher than recordings obtained from 17 normal controls. Four of the tense subjects underwent 2 to 3 months of PR training. Thereafter, three of these individuals showed substantive improvement, averaging about 0.25 μV, which was far below the level of the control group. The fourth patient's pretest level averaged a fraction of a μV and no additional benefits occurred as a result of relaxation training.

In the late 1930s, a conflict arose between Jacobson and P.F.A. Hoefer. Hoefer claimed that untrained individuals routinely displayed zero muscle tension in resting muscles (1941; Hoefer & Putnam, 1939). Jacobson (1935, 1943d) asserted that the instrumentation employed in Hoefer's and other laboratories was insufficiently sensitive to detect low but enduring muscle tension during rest, and that complete muscle inactivity could be attained only through training in PR. Jacobson (1943c) replicated Hoefer's procedure in the hope of resolving the existing disagreement. Continuous recordings were secured from the right leg (tibialis and gastrocnemius muscles) of 10 normal subjects in successive 6-minute periods of lying at rest, standing motionless, and lying at rest again. As Jacobson predicted, readings of about 5 μV, 18 μV, and 2 μV were obtained at the gastrocnemius site during these three periods, respectively. A similar pattern occurred for the tibialis muscle. In a related study testing whether or not resting subjects generated zero muscle action (Jacobson & Kraft, 1942), recordings of the right thigh were taken as 100 normal, middle-aged adults of both sexes sat quietly and read. Subjects were not medicated and were naive as to relaxation techniques. Most of the subjects produced average muscle potentials in the 0.5 μV to 2.5 μV range.

Blood Pressure

Jacobson conducted a series of studies that monitored time-correlated variation in muscle tension and blood pressure. In his first report on this subject, Jacobson (1936b) briefly described the resting experience of 15 normotensive and 7 hypertensive subjects. Blood pressure decreases were observed in both groups over an hour rest period only in those cases when arm and abdominal muscle activity approached zero. Subsequently, Jacobson (1939b) provided more details on this research strategy. Blood pressure was monitored in subjects before and after half an hour of quiet rest that followed a 15-minute adaptation-rest period. Muscle recordings were derived from the right arm and, in some cases, the abdomen. Data from 17 normal, young adults with no prior PR training revealed that low levels of muscle tension (generally in the 1–2 μV range) persisted during the session, and blood pressure was fairly constant. Normal and hypertensive subjects experienced in relaxation showed blood pressure drops of about 10 mm Hg (systolic and diastolic) and 20 mm Hg, respectively, over the course of a session in which they practiced relaxation. Hypertensive individuals untrained in PR, or who were unsuccessful in achieving relaxation in a particular session, did not show blood pressure reductions. Subsequent analyses of heartbeat overlays on the electromyogram records (Jacobson, 1940e) revealed that the force and rate of heart function closely mapped muscle and blood pressure variations.

In a subsequent study, Jacobson (1939c, 1940d) instructed subjects to induce muscle tension by vigorously tensing the right fist for 5 to 10 minutes in the midst of a rest period. Sharp rises in systolic and diastolic blood pressure accompanied this muscle tension, and blood pressure returned to its baseline level when the arm exercise was discontinued. Parallel findings were obtained with four hypertensive subjects. They averaged about 10 mm Hg blood pressure increase during the tension phase. One of the purposes of this study was to isolate the role of muscle activity in hypertension from that of the more widely recognized global factor of emotional distress. By conducting the experiment under emotionally neutral conditions, Jacobson showed that blood pressure is reactive to muscular variations independent of emotionality.

Final Comments on Jacobson's Research

Some overall conclusions can be derived from Jacobson's basic research program. The findings were strong and clear, pointing to direct effects of PR on the striate musculature and indirect effects on cognitions (see Chapter 2), blood pressure, and heart function. From a methodological point of view, there are important strengths and weaknesses. On the positive side, it is obvious that Jacobson conducted his research with care and precision. Dependent measures were thoughtfully selected, and valid, innovative methods of measurement were employed. Appropriate control conditions and manipulations were also employed.

Alternatively, two shortcomings were apparent. First, Jacobson never conducted statistical analyses. Although the results he reported usually permitted unambiguous interpretation simply by inspection, statistical analyses (assuming they proved favorable) would have increased the level of confidence that could be justifiably placed in his conclusions. Second and of great concern are the issues of experimenter bias and subject-selection bias. Jacobson himself was the primary experimenter in the vast majority of relevant research conducted during this period. Trained subjects were usually selected from among his private patients. Control subjects were volunteers and the method of recruitment was usually not specified. Random assignment of subjects to conditions was not observed. In sum, the same criticisms levied against the TM research earlier in this chapter apply with equal strength to Jacobson's research on these latter two sources of bias.

Contemporary Progressive Relaxation Research

Since Wolpe's (1958) adoption of PR as a component of systematic desensitization, interest in PR has rapidly ballooned. As a result, a considerable amount of basic research has since accumulated on Jacobson's technique. However, it is important to bear in mind that the method under study at present is a highly condensed version of the method espoused by Jacobson. Most often, current usage of the term PR refers to a technique involving less than 20 muscle groups that is administered in its entirety in one or two sessions. The procedure described by Bernstein and Borkovec (1973) and the one presented in the following chapter fairly reflect the practice of the past several decades.

Two basic paradigms have been used to evaluate PR. In the first, subjects are evaluated before and after a relaxation session and may be compared to no-relaxation controls. The second paradigm involves the presentation of a stressful stimulus to trained and untrained subjects, and the evaluation of their response.

Pre–post Evaluations

In the late 1960s, Gordon Paul (1969c) stimulated the current wave of PR basic research with a celebrated study contrasting PR and hypnosis. The few studies that preceded Paul yielded inconsistent findings: Some observed improved state anxiety following PR (Grings & Uno, 1968; Johnson & Spielberger, 1968; Meldman, 1966), while another failed to find physiological effects (Grossberg, 1965). Although these papers attracted little attention, the clever methodology employed by Grings and Uno (1968) is noteworthy. Separate neutral stimuli were conditioned to evoke either arousal or relaxation (through PR training). Subsequently, the electrodermal response to the arousal stimulus was significantly diminished when paired with the relaxation stimulus.

Paul (1969c) conducted two sessions of PR, hypnosis, or quiet rest with normal female student volunteers. The sessions were scheduled a week apart, and subjects were instructed to practice their method twice daily in the interim. Within-session physiological monitoring found that the three groups were equal on all measures at the outset of session one. Pre-post, within-session comparisons between the PR group and the hypnosis and control groups yielded identical results for each session. PR produced significantly greater relaxation effects on heart rate and forearm muscle tension than either of the other two groups. PR surpassed only the control group in depressing respiration rate. All groups produced significant but comparable reductions in skin conductance derived from the dominant foot. Self-report anxiety (Anxiety Differential; Husek & Alexander, 1963) revealed comparable improvement in the PR and hypnosis groups that exceeded improvement experienced by the control subjects. In sum, this well-designed study strongly supported the efficacy of PR and argued for its superiority over hypnosis. Another group (Anderson, Lubetkin, Logan, & Alpert, 1973) also found PR to be superior to a low demand form of hypnosis (and self-relaxation control) in depressing heart rate during a relaxation period. However, PR and hypnosis proved equivalent with this sample of inpatient alcoholics during a stress test.

A second report published by Paul in the same year (1969a) described an attempt to predict treatment response in the above experiment. The same subjects completed questionnaires on extraversion, emotionality, and honesty prior to the first treatment session. This data failed to correlate with the magnitude of treatment response during the two training sessions. It also failed to predict physiological responses to fearful imagery presented at the beginning of the first session and the end of the second session.

Less encouraging findings were obtained by other investigators conducting similar research contemporaneous with Paul's efforts. Edelman reported two methodologically sophisticated studies in a 1970 article. In the first study, 40 undergraduate volunteers were randomly assigned to one taped session of either PR, suggestions of relaxation only (passive relaxation), instructions only to tense, or soothing music. Over the course of the session, subjects in the PR and music conditions registered greater decreases in systolic blood pressure than did subjects in the two piecemeal PR groups. No significant changes occurred in diastolic blood pressure or heart rate.

The follow-up study examined PR effects as a function of the subject's anxiety status. The trait scale of the State-Trait Anxiety Inventory (STAI; Spielberger, Gorsuch, & Lushene, 1970) was used to select high or low anxious student volunteers. One session of taped PR had no differential effect on these two subject types for the three physiological measures cited above. Both groups showed a significant decline in systolic blood pressure only. Comparably significant anxiety improvement occurred for groups on pre-post administrations of the STAI-State scale, but greater gains were made by the high anxious subjects on the STAI-Trait scale. This second study suggests that the disappointing performance of PR in the first study cannot be attributed to the claim that nonanxious subjects respond less favorably to PR than anxious subjects. However, this series did not consider the larger issue of the efficacy of a tape-recorded PR format. More recently, negative outcomes in PR trials with student and nonstudent volunteers have also been reported in comparisons with biofeedback (Bowles, Smith, & Parker, 1979; Delman & Johnson, 1976) and hypnosis (Bullard & DeCoster, 1972).

Two studies by Mathews and his colleagues also produced modest results at about this same time. In their first study (Mathews & Gelder, 1969), 10 phobic psychiatric outpatients submitted to an assessment session, then were randomly assigned to a 6-week treatment course in either PR or supportive psychotherapy. PR began with the customary tensing and relaxing techniques and advanced to differential relaxation requiring attentiveness to somatic cues but no tensing. After treatment was concluded, a second assessment session was conducted. None of the physiological measures (forearm muscle tension, forearm blood flow, and palmar skin conductance) or psychological measures (Taylor Manifest Anxiety Scale, Taylor, 1953; neuroticism scale of the Eysenck Personality Inventory, Eysenck, 1963) differentiated the two groups on prepost analyses.

The second experiment reported in the same article employed a within-subjects design, conducted physiological evaluations during actual relaxation practice, and employed a revised set of measures. Fourteen patients received two sessions of PR training and then submitted to two assessment sessions while they practiced relaxation or simply rested in counterbalanced order. Tonic frontalis electromyography (EMG) and the number of spontaneous skin conductance fluctuations were significantly lower during the relaxation session than the control session. Relaxation session skin conductance change scores exceeded those of the control session. Heart rate and respiration rate failed to distinguish the treatments. Patients' self-report ratings favored the relaxation experience. These ratings strongly correlated with the number of skin conductance fluctuations, somewhat less with heart rate, respiration rate, and skin conductance level, and very little with EMG. The authors concluded that PR decreased sensory input to the central nervous system by dampening several modalities including, but not limited to, the striate musculature and thereby induced a global suppression of arousal.

The second study by this group (Lader & Mathews, 1970) compared effects of a barbiturate drug (Brietal, methohexitone sodium), PR, and a control condition. Eighteen anxious psychiatric patients received all three treatments in counterbalanced order in a single session. A major drawback to this study was that PR was delivered via a 5-minute tape recording. This was likely an inadequate exposure to the method. Not surprisingly, several physiological and psychological measures indicated no significant relaxation effects occurred during the PR and control (a nondemanding, pleasant audio tape) phases. For reasons unrelated to present concerns, drug effects were also of no consequence.

More recently, Janda and Cash (1976) reported significant decreases in heart rate, frontalis muscle tension, and self-report anxiety during the course of one PR session with 10 student volunteers. However, there was little correlation among these measures. Fox and Oitker (1980) also observed self-reported anxiety reduction among student volunteers after one PR session. Other data (Gordon, 1976) indicated that PR effects are increased when student volunteers are afforded the opportunity to select the procedure. Schandler and Grings (1976) observed that a single taped PR session yielded significantly greater effects than listening to soft music, as evidenced by forehead and forearm muscle tension, skin conductance level, and anxiety (Anxiety Differential; Husek & Alexander, 1963), but not by systolic blood pressure, respiration rate, or heart rate. Comparisons with biofeedback were also conducted, but will not be reported herein.

A single group, pre-post design was used to evaluate PR effects on six heart patients (Davidson, Winchester, Taylor, Alderman, & Ingels, 1979). All of these patients had undergone open heart surgery within the previous 5 years, and all had metallic myocardial markers implanted to permit fluoroscopic viewing of heart function. An indwelling intravenous line permitted the convenient collection of blood samples before and after PR, and blood pressure was taken by conventional means. Following PR training, subjects submitted to one PR test session. Significant decreases occurred in plasma norepinephrine but not plasma epinephrine or dopamine. Several measures of heart function (e.g., velocity of myocardial circumference shortening) exhibited changes consistent with a relaxed state. Cardiac output, heart rate, and blood pressure were unaffected. Plasma norepinephrine level correlated with resting systolic blood pressure and heart rate changes during relaxation. Based primarily upon the norepinephrine data, the authors concluded that PR effects are mediated by the sympathetic nervous system.

Elkins, Anchor, and Sandler (1978) exposed volunteers to 10 sessions of PR supplemented with autogenics. Significantly greater reductions in frontalis muscle tension and anxiety (State-Trait Anxiety Inventory, STAI; Spielberger, Gorsuch, & Lushene, 1970) were attained by these individuals than by untreated subjects. Reinking and Kohl (1975) tested an abbreviated form of PR—facial relaxation only—and found forehead muscle tension decreases in this group exceeded that of untreated subjects, but were less than decreases attained through biofeedback (see Chapter 6 for further discussion). All groups reported equivalent decreases in self-reported tension.

Several studies have featured PR effects on blood pressure. Tasto and Huebner (1976) and Schandler and Grings (1976) observed no effect of PR on the blood pressure of normotensives, whereas Fey and Lindholm (1978) did obtain significant systolic and diastolic effects with normotensives (see Chapter 6 for continued discussion of this study). Trivial PR effects during laboratory manipulations of the blood pressure of hypertensives have also been reported (reported in duplicate: Redmond, Gaylor, McDonald, & Shapiro, 1974; Shapiro, Redmond, McDonald, & Gaylor, 1975).

Utilizing a clever gastric acid telemetry device, Sigman and Amit (1982) found no evidence of stomach acidity change in taped PR and control comparisons among healthy young adults. As an obvious clinical implication, these data do not recommend PR for peptic ulcer patients. In a replication (Sigman & Amit, 1983), quiet reading induced gastric acidity suppression, but there was no change during PR.

In a brief report that unfortunately omits important details, Stoudenmire (1973) conducted the only study to address the important issues of the length and the frequency of PR sessions. Normal undergraduate female volunteers received three taped PR sessions. Session length was either 15, 30, or 45 minutes. The sessions were scheduled within 3, 9, or 15 days. Three anxiety questionnaires administered before and after the treatment course produced spotty results. The scheduling factor yielded no significant results. One of the questionnaires (STAI-State) favored the 45-minute session length. A replication of this study using clinical subjects certainly appears warranted. Other studies by Stoudenmire (1972, 1975) found state but not trait anxiety improvement subsequent to taped PR training. Other basic (Johnson & Spielberger, 1968) and clinical (Counts, Hollandsworth, & Alcorn, 1978; Thompson, Griebstein, & Kuhlenschmidt, 1980) research has also found that relaxation effects on anxiety are confined to state changes. Further, introverts showed a greater response to PR than extroverts (Stoudenmire, 1972), when categorized by the Eysenck Personality Inventory (Eysenck, 1963), and soothing music produced comparable changes to that of PR with anxious undergraduates (Stoudenmire, 1975).

Nakamura and Broen took an interesting approach to the question of relaxation-induced behavioral change. Motivated by Hull-Spence theory (Spence, 1956), Nakamura and Broen (1965a) tested the assumption that relaxed states simultaneously diminish the response priority of well-learned behaviors and increase the response priority of weaker behaviors, that is, relaxation facilitates behavior change. Undergraduate volunteers were trained in competing simple motor tasks to different levels of strength criteria. Those subjects subsequently given PR produced the less preferred task at higher rates than subjects not trained in PR. Nakamura and Broen (1965b) employed a similar design in a follow-up experiment and replicated their previous findings. However, the relaxation-facilitation effect did not hold up when there was great disparity in strength between the competing responses.

Interested mainly in testing the relaxation effects of brief restricted environmental stimulation (REST), Jacobs, Heilbronner, and Stanley (1984) compared a relaxation package (PR, breath regulation, and imagery) practiced in a conventional setting, with the same package practiced under flotation REST.

Physiological indicators strongly favored the relaxation effects of the latter, with modest relaxation effects accruing to conventional relaxation. However, multiple sources of uncontrolled expectancy bias and limited home relaxation practice may have mediated against robust relaxation effects in the conventional group.

A few studies have examined the important issue of relaxation effects on imagery. Clinicians have endorsed the use of relaxation as a facilitator of imagery (contrary to Jacobson's data, see Chapter 2), but there is little evidence to directly substantiate this claim. In studies not designed primarily to study relaxation-imagery relationships, but rather physiological effects of imagery, negative correlations have been reported between physiological arousal and imagery (Anderson & Borkovec, 1980; Haney & Euse, 1976; Weerts & Lang, 1978), lending indirect support to the notion that relaxation aids imagery. However, other studies in this genre have observed little or no relationship between these variables (Bauer & Craighead, 1979; Grayson & Borkovec, 1978). On a more positive note, speech phobic individuals treated with systematic desensitization, including PR, reported more imagery vividness and displayed greater initial heart rate reactivity during hierarchy visualization than subjects working through the hierarchy without the aid of PR (Borkovec & Sides, 1979a). Rehm, Mattei, Potts, and Skolnick (1974) presented preliminary data of a direct test of effects of an unspecified relaxation technique on imagery vividness and latency. Unexpectedly, relaxation proved to have deleterious effects on imagery.

More recently, Lohr and his colleagues studied relaxation effects on imagery controllability, which involves ability to alter the form, position, color, and motion of mental images. Student volunteers were given five training sessions of either taped PR or a taped academic discussion about relaxation (Hamberger & Lohr, 1980). EMG and self-report analyses found superior relaxation effects among the PR subjects. Unfortunately, the Gordon Test (Richardson, 1969) evaluating the controllability of emotionally neutral imagery failed to distinguish the two groups. A subsequent study (Lohr & Rookey, 1982) employed a similar design to evaluate PR effects on high and low speech phobic subjects' ability to control neutral and phobic imagery. Anxious subjects showed greater gains on image controllability than nonanxious subjects, but analyses indicated this was not due to PR effects. Repeated measures and other nonspecific factors were cited as alternative explanations for these results.

Seven studies addressed the question of PR effects on short-term memory. Pascal (1949) tested Jacobson's (1932) assertion that short-term memory, as well as all cognitive functions, suffers as relaxation deepens (see related research by Jacobson in Chapter 2). Normal subjects recalled nonsense syllables while sitting upright as usual or while reclined after 5 minutes of relaxation in a between-subjects design. The method of relaxation was PR without the tensing component, in other words, passive relaxation (see Chapter 5). Contrary to prediction, recall was significantly better following passive relaxation. Moreover, empirical analyses suggested a positive relationship existed between depth of relaxation and amount recalled.

Chaney and Andreasen (1972) also obtained encouraging results. Student volunteers were placed under stress by a threat to penalize their course grade contingent upon poor performance on a short-term random digit recall task. Students trained in PR outperformed placebo pill and irrelevant training control groups. Raising somewhat analogous issues to those of Chaney and Andreasen, Straughan and Dufort (1969) found that PR aided memory in high anxious subjects, but actually hampered memory in low anxious subjects. Yesavage (1984) taught healthy elderly volunteers mnemonic techniques for recalling people's names and faces. In addition, half the subjects received PR training and half engaged in a discussion group. The PR subjects demonstrated significantly greater recall than the control subjects, and improvement was correlated with anxiety reduction. A previous study by this same author (Yesavage, Rose, & Spiegel, 1982) found a strong, positive correlation between anxiety level and memory benefits for elderly receiving PR.

The last two studies obtained negative results. Volunteer patients at a VA hospital were categorized as either high, medium, or low anxious (Wilson & Wilson, 1970). Subjects received one session of PR, light exercise to increase muscle tension, or no treatment immediately before taking a paired-associate learning test. The performance of the tension exercise subjects was superior to the PR subjects, who in turn surpassed the untreated controls. In addition, PR afforded no special memory benefits to the high anxious subjects. Finally, elementary age children were tested in their recall of word lists (Bartlett, Burleson, & Santrock, 1982). Learning and recall were conducted under conditions of congruent or incongruent induced affect. The presence of relaxation (passive relaxation and deep breathing) produced no memory benefits compared to the absence of relaxation.

Braud (1981) tested relaxation enhancement of parapsychological (psi) skills by contrasting PR with quiet rest in a within-subject design (another portion of this study is also discussed in the *Autogenic Training* section of this chapter). Self-rated relaxation and skin resistance level both evinced PR effectiveness, but psi enhancement on a guessing task did not materialize in group comparisons. Subsequent analyses revealed psi improvement for moderately relaxed individuals, exceeding the psi performance of either unrelaxed or deeply relaxed subjects (see further discussion in Chapter 6). Earlier work by Braud and Braud (1973, 1974) and by Stanford and Mayer (1974) suggested that PR increases one's ability to describe a picture not within sight.

Wilson (1985) tested PR effects on social attraction at three levels of expectancy instructions. PR did enhance positive evaluations of others, but this was strongly correlated with instructions as to PR potency.

Langevin, Stanford, and Block (1975) evaluated sexual response to male, female, and neutral slides by heterosexual and homosexual men. Sexual arousal to preferred sexual stimuli was greater following PR than when PR was absent.

Several studies have examined the ability of PR to increase hypnotic susceptibility, and these have generally yielded negative results (e.g., Radtke, Spanos, Armstrong, Dillman, & Boisvenue, 1983). These studies are discussed at greater length in Chapter 6.

Stress Tests

Studies in this section propose to evaluate the practical usefulness of PR by creating laboratory analogues of stress involving anxiety, pain, etc. Paul (1969b) was the first to assess advantages accruing to subjects equipped with PR training when challenged by stress. He randomly assigned normal female student volunteers to two sessions of instruction in either PR or hypnosis or to a quiet rest control group as described in Paul (1969c) above. At the beginning of the first training session, subjects imagined an emotionally neutral scene and a stressful scene as determined by the Fear Survey Schedule (Wolpe & Lang, 1964) for selected periods within a 2-minute span. Subjects later spent parts of 2 minutes imagining the same stressful scene at the conclusion of the second session. Analyses were performed on composite, physiological stress response scores that reflected reactivity to the final imagery test in relation to reactivity displayed during the pretest. PR and hypnosis subjects exhibited significantly smaller responses than did the control subjects, but the former two groups did not differ from each other. Van Egeren, Feather, and Hein (1971) employed speech phobic subjects in imagery tests of PR. Relaxed subjects exhibited less reactivity (as evidenced by skin conductance responses, but not by respiration, heart rate, or vasomotor responses) to phobic and neutral scenes than nonrelaxed subjects.

Davidson and Hiebert (1971) evaluated subjects' reactions to 10 showings of a stressful movie; a violent woodshop accident. Subjects' preparation involved either training in taped PR, practice in self-styled relaxation, or no treatment. Over the course of these trials significant decreases in skin conductance level occurred in the PR and self-relaxation groups, but not the no-treatment group. PR subjects also exhibited fewer spontaneous skin conductance responses than did the no-treatment subjects. Self-report anxiety as measured by the Affect Adjective Check List (AACL; Zuckerman, 1960) did not differentiate the groups. In brief, taped PR did better than nothing, but only a little better than nonspecific instructions to relax in this repeated exposure stress test. A second study (Folkins, Lawson, Opton, & Lazarus, 1968) evaluating tolerance of this movie also reported moderate benefits accruing to PR subjects.

More recently, Lehrer (1978) evaluated tonic and stress inhibitory effects of PR. Alpha biofeedback was assessed with one group of subjects, but this aspect of the study will not be reported herein. Anxious patients and normal adults were randomly assigned to either four or five sessions of PR training or no contact. Test sessions were conducted with all subjects before and after the 3-week PR training period. Subjects were instructed to relax as best they could in the test sessions. They were then exposed to a series of aversive tones, followed by auditory reaction time trials. A state anxiety questionnaire (Spielberger, Gorsuch, & Lushene, 1970) and approximately a dozen physiological measures were employed to evaluate subjects' resting and reactive levels. PR had a greater effect on self-report anxiety than no treatment, but surprisingly the effects were greater on nonpatients than patients. To summarize the complex physiological outcomes, most measures of resting levels on the physiological variables proved negative. Superior effects of PR occurred in reducing reactivity among patients to intrusive stimuli on measures of heart rate, skin conductance, and EEG alpha. Physiological effects of PR on nonpatients were less pronounced.

Burish, Hendrix, and Frost (1981) employed normal college students in a design similar to Lehrer (1978), and obtained a similar pattern of results. Passive relaxation (tense phase omitted from PR) was more effective than instructions to relax in controlling physiological (skin temperature, heart rate, and finger pulse volume, but not muscle tension) and experiential (AACL) reactivity to threatened electric shock. The groups did not differ when stress was absent. Connor (1974) found that one session of taped PR afforded little advantage to student volunteers' stress coping.

Six studies examined the utility of PR in aiding individuals to tolerate physical pain. Lehrer (1972) tested a procedure that appeared to be taped passive relaxation and found some small benefits associated with it in tolerating electric shock. Cogan and Kluthe (1980) introduced pain to normal student volunteers by overinflating a blood pressure cuff about their arm. Taped PR significantly reduced perceived pain intensity compared with no treatment. A subsequent study (Cogan & Kluthe, 1981) expanded the above paradigm by adding patterned breathing and patterned finger tapping groups to evaluate the distraction factor. PR again surpassed no treatment in pain control effects. The two control groups fell between PR and no treatment.

An ice water immersion test (reported in duplicate, Stevens, 1977; Stevens & Heide, 1977) found PR effectively prolonged pain tolerance with less effect on pain experience. Adding visual attention focusing to PR further suppressed pain perception. Hackett and Horan (1980) conducted a component analysis of a pain management treatment package that also tested ice water tolerance. A combination of PR and deep breathing exerted the largest beneficial effect on student volunteers' ability to withstand ice water, but nevertheless this had little effect on perceived discomfort, as in the Stevens study. Mental distraction techniques were less effective than PR-deep breathing, but more effective than training in coping self-instructions.

Grimm and Kanfer (1976) earlier reported a pattern of results opposite to that of Hackett and Horan (1980). Student volunteers trained in distracting imagery withstood hand immersion in ice water longer than PR-trained subjects (despite the fact that PR subjects attained significant within-subject improvement). There was no significant difference between PR and two control groups, placebo and no treatment, on this measure. Other pre-post treatment comparisons revealed that the two treated groups, imagery and PR, registered significant decreases in heart rate and perceived discomfort, but the control groups did not.

Strickler and his associates published two studies examining passive relaxation effects in the domain of alcoholism. The first study (Strickler, Bigelow, Wells, & Liebson, 1977) trained diagnosed alcoholics in passive relaxation and observed lower frontalis muscle tension among them than in a neutral training control group during training and subsequent exposure to a tape recording describing temptations to drink.

The second study (Strickler, Tomaszewski, Maxwell, & Suib, 1979) employed college students identified as heavy social drinkers. All subjects were informed that they would be delivering a speech to a group later in the experiment. Subjects next received a tape recording describing (a) further details on public speaking anxiety, (b) passive relaxation, or (c) neutral content. Electrodermal levels during taping confirmed the arousing, relaxing, or neutral effects of the three tapes, respectively. Of particular interest was the next phase when subjects had free access to beer while waiting for their expected speech. Alcohol consumption among passive relaxation subjects was significantly lower than that of subjects in both other groups. Dobbs, Strickler, and Maxwell (1981) employed a design very similar to Strickler et al. (1979) to study cigarette smoking behavior. They, too, found passive relaxation (combined with breath relaxation) to be associated with physiological and experiential relaxation and with smoking suppression.

One study (Philipp, Wilde, & Day, 1972) tested the contribution of PR in aiding asthmatic subjects to tolerate inhalation of an asthma-inducing drug. Following five training sessions in PR that emphasized breathing and abdominal exercises, these subjects showed improved postinhalant respiration on several indicators of respiratory function relative to their own baseline levels and to untrained asthmatics. Relaxation effects were more pronounced for psychogenic than biogenic asthmatic subtypes.

Final Comments on Progressive Relaxation

The most striking conclusion that leaps from the large PR basic research literature concerns the dissimilarity of findings between Jacobson's data and that of current researchers. Jacobson obtained consistent, robust, unambiguous PR effects, and present-day researchers do not.

Lehrer (1982) claimed that the lengthy, painstaking original method of PR is well worth the effort, and is strongly superior to the abbreviated method that replaced it. Two unpublished dissertations (Snow, 1977; Turner, 1978) comprise the entire literature of head-on comparisons between orthodox and abbreviated PR, and neither method has emerged superior. Nevertheless, Lehrer may be correct, but researchers and clinicians have uniformly opted for the modern version for a variety of pragmatic reasons, and this preference probably would not be swayed even if clearcut demonstrations of orthodox PR superiority were plentiful.

Other reasons may contribute to the weaker PR effects in the *modern era*. Current studies have generally controlled for subject-selection biases and placebo effects better than Jacobson did. A broader range of physiological and subjective dependent measures are now routinely employed, and this invites a more varied pattern of effects, compared to Jacobson's emphasis on muscular effects of his muscular procedure. Lastly, I concur with Borkovec and Sides' (1979b) conclusions that PR has suffered from greater reliance on taped inductions and from employing scanty few training sessions, compared to many sessions of live training alone employed by Jacobson.

The modern era of PR boasts a methodologically sophisticated literature that has examined PR in diverse contexts. Paul's (1969c) data still stand as the most convincing evidence of PR efficacy with normal subjects. Subsequent research on tonic effects of PR has yielded highly inconsistent findings. Studies testing PR utility in attenuating responses to stress tests have generally found positive, though not very powerful, effects. PR clinical research (presented in Chapter 7) has yielded stronger findings than PR basic research. A floor effect and fewer training sessions characterizing the latter may partially explain these differences.

The absence of basic research on self-control relaxation (see Chapter 5 for description of this method) is noteworthy. This method grew out of PR and has gained broad clinical popularity. A small amount of data on self-control relaxation is presented below in the relaxation comparisons section.

Data on clinical applications of self-control relaxation (see Chapter 7) are generally positive. Potentially fruitful avenues of basic research on this approach include the development of more effective self-monitoring strategies that signal the activation of self-control relaxation, and the assessment of the relative efficacy of breath, imagery, and cue word components routinely employed in the technique.

AUTOGENIC TRAINING (AT)

The language barrier places us at a decided disadvantage in studying basic effects of AT. The bulk of the research in this area hails from non-English-speaking countries. Shortly after AT was introduced in this country, Luthe (1962b) estimated that only 1 percent of AT articles were written in English. To further document this point, we reviewed the citations on AT in *Psychological Abstracts* and *Index Medicus* for the 3-year period 1980–1982. *Psychological Abstracts* contained 69 articles on AT, 39 of which (57 percent) were written in a foreign language. *Index Medicus* contained 46 articles on AT during this period, and 37 of these (80 percent) were in a foreign language. Moreover, most of the English language articles are treatment studies, resulting in there being very few basic studies on AT that are conveniently available. Therefore, my knowledge of basic research on AT is based primarily on Luthe's (1970a) comprehensive review, comprising the fourth volume of the six-volume autogenic series edited by Luthe (1969–1973).

At least two important disadvantages arise from this situation. First, Wolfgang Luthe has devoted a major portion of his career to advocating the autogenic approach and cannot, therefore, be considered an unbiased observer. In all fairness to Luthe, however, his works are characterized by a critical attitude in appraising research and a respect for deliberate scientific judgment. Second, without direct access to the original scientific documents, I am unable to conduct my own methodological critique, which might lead me to more conservative conclusions than those reached by Luthe.

What follows then, in large part, is my summary of Luthe's (1970a) review of European and Asian basic research on AT. In those instances where original material is available to me, this will be so indicated by direct reference.

Passive Concentration

Obviously, the autogenic trainee must attend to the task at hand in order to produce the fairly complex series of mental operations comprising AT. Nevertheless, autogenic trainers place great emphasis on the attitude with which the subject approaches this experience. An attitude of "passive concentration" or "passive attention" is prescribed, wherein the subject's awareness is characterized by a nondemanding tone, neutral affect, and marginal clarity. In brief, the subject is instructed to create a vague, relaxed atmosphere preparatory to initiating the particulars of the autogenic method. Some data cited by Luthe suggest that it is important to substitute a sense of "passive striving" for the customary attitude of goal-directed, active striving engendered in routine activities. For example, increased skin temperature and peripheral vasodilation were associated with the passive concentration of one subject, while this same subject exhibited decreased skin temperature and peripheral vasoconstriction during active concentration. The less one forces or commands relaxation to occur, the more relaxed one is likely to become, and this advice seems well-suited to virtually any method of relaxation.

The next section will consider effects of the six standard AT exercises. These effects are organized according to their physiological, biochemical, or psychological nature.

Effects of Autogenic Training

Luthe (1970a) cited about a dozen studies in support of the conclusion that AT, particularly the "heavy" exercises, promotes general muscle relaxation throughout the body. It is not clear whether muscle relaxation would accompany any autogenic phrase administered early in the induction sequence, or whether this phrase exerts a special influence on the muscles. Luthe admits the occurrence of an "occasional paradoxical increase of muscle action potentials" (p. 19). Such unwanted effects are termed autogenic discharges, and their cause is largely unknown.

To summarize about two dozen studies, the typical electrodermal response involves a gradual, consistent increase in skin resistance for the duration of the six standard exercises, although one study (Jus & Jus, 1965b) did observe a distinct electrodermal "shift" immediately following the completion of the heaviness and warmth exercises. Uherik and Sebej (1978) also observed a shift in skin resistance bilateral asymmetry that occurred after 10 AT sessions. During periods of autogenic concentration, highly trained subjects are electrodermally unresponsive to noises that would usually be distracting. Across studies, approximately 10 percent of the subjects exhibited a paradoxical decrease in skin resistance, signaling increased arousal.

Braud and Masters (1980) randomly assigned volunteers from the community to one session of taped training in the six standard autogenic exercises or one session of "opposite" autogenic exercises (e.g., light and cool extremities, warm forehead). Significant relaxation responses occurred for the autogenic group in two of three electrodermal indices, but not for the opposite group. Self-report ratings of imagery helpfulness and pleasantness did not distinguish the two groups. These encouraging results are particularly noteworthy in light of an admirable experimental design feature. At the outset of the session, when the experimenter introduced the subject to the general procedure and placed electrodes, the experimenter did not know which treatment the subject was to receive. After leaving the subject chamber, the experimenter opened an envelope revealing which training tape was to be played. This strategy offers strong protection against inadvertent experimenter-bias effects (Rosenthal, 1966). The results of this experiment may be contrasted with those of Blizard, Cowings, and Miller (1975), in which opposite autogenic exercises exerted an arousal effect, but autogenic exercises had no effect (see Chapter 2 for a more complete discussion of the Blizard et al. study).

Radiographic tests and physiological assays of patients experiencing gastrointestinal distress (e.g., ulcer, duodenitis) revealed slowing and increased regularity in the pattern of peristalsis following AT. Improved coordination and efficiency were also noted in other muscular actions along the gastrointestinal tract, as well as decreased stomach acidity. There is some evidence to suggest that the heaviness formulae exerted particular influence in calming gastric motility, and ironically, "My abdomen is warm" stimulated gastric motility. Luthe (1970a) recommended omission of this latter phrase when working with patients complaining of stomach discomfort. Nakagawa, Ishida, Dobeta, and Kimura (1966) observed that AT may stimulate peristalsis, following their observation of three subjects.

Based upon some 80 studies, we may conclude that increases in surface skin temperature and peripheral blood flow reliably occur with AT. These effects begin to emerge during the "heaviness" phrases and become more pronounced during the "warmth" exercises. The location in which these physiological effects appear often parallels the content of the "warmth" exercises (Ikemi, Nakagawa, Kimura, et al., 1965). The magnitude of temperature and blood flow changes often correlates with the degree of warmth that subjects experience. When increased skin temperature occurs, it is always equally bilateral, even when perceived warmth is unbalanced (Langen, 1969). The remaining four standard exercises, including "My forehead is cool," produce much less consistent effects in these two variables.

Gillespie and Peck (1980) evaluated AT-like imagery—feel the warmth of the fireplace on your hands. They observed paradoxical effects and significant hand cooling. A second study (McDonagh & McGinnis, 1973) found similar AT-like suggestions ineffective. Kelton and Belar (1983) tested AT with children (ages 9–11 years) and also obtained disappointing results. Normal children received four sessions on consecutive days of either AT or AT/skin temperature biofeedback combined. AT was limited to the first two training exercises for heaviness and warmth. Neither treatment group successfully cultivated hand warming.

Seven other well-designed studies examined AT effects on finger temperature. All (Keefe, 1978; Kluger, Jamner, & Tursky, 1985; Sheridan, Boehm, Ward, & Justesen, 1976; Surwit & Fenton, 1980; Vasilos & Hughes, 1979) but two (Freedman & Ianni, 1983; King & Montgomery, 1980) observed significant temperature increases associated with AT, usually in the 0.5° to 1°C range. Training effects were usually greatest during the first 5 or 10 minutes of the session (Kluger et al., 1985; Surwit & Fenton, 1980; Vasilos & Hughes, 1979), sometimes declining to below baseline levels thereafter. When compared to the AT/skin temperature biofeedback combination, AT proved comparable (Keefe, 1978; Sheridan et al., 1976; Vasilos & Hughes, 1979) and inferior (Surwit & Fenton, 1980).

A large amount of data from approximately 35 studies indicate that the "heaviness" exercise promotes heart rate deceleration in 5 percent of normal subjects and 10–15 percent of tachycardia patients. When autogenic concentration is interrupted by such factors as wandering thoughts or distracting noises, heart rate increases of about 5 percent are generally observed. Interestingly, consistent cardiac effects do not occur during the third standard exercise, "Heartbeat calm and regular." Much less information is available on blood pressure effects. A handful of studies reveal a 5–25 percent decrease in systolic and diastolic pressure usually occurs in hypertensive subjects exposed to the first three standard exercises. In one study of normotensives, 4 weeks of "heaviness" training exerted no reliable influence on blood pressure. A few of these subjects did, however, manifest paradoxical blood pressure changes. Additional data on the blood pressure effects of abbreviated AT is available in a study focusing on Raynaud's phenomenon (Surwit, Allen, Gilgor, & Duvic, 1982). Four weeks of abbreviated, taped AT training had no effect on the blood pressure of these normotensives. Erbeck, Elfner, and Driggs (1983) reported positive effects of AT with normotensive student volunteers. Subjects averaged about a 5 mm Hg decrease in both systolic and diastolic readings, although biofeedback subjects achieved even greater decreases.

Numerous studies of normal subjects' respiration patterns during AT reveal substantive effects. Respiratory indicators, such as rate, amplitude, and duration, gradually alter in the direction of relaxation during the first three standard exercises, and a marked deepening of these effects accompanies the fourth exercise, "My breathing is calm." Some loss of respiratory benefits occurs during the last two standard exercises. One group (Jus & Jus, 1965a) observed that while respiration slowed, the style of breathing shifted from the abdomen to the thorax, which is the reverse of the usual Eastern meditation prescription.

A wealth of data exists in EEG evaluations of AT. There is good consistency in the data across laboratories, and the findings may be summarized as follows. Long-term trainees with a minimum of 6 months' practice manifest EEG changes in the form of increased synchronization of EEG waveforms immediately upon assuming an attitude and posture consistent with passive concentration. As the standard exercises unfold, alpha activity predominates with a mixture of theta activity (slow waves characteristic of stage 1 sleep). Theta activity is probably due to drowsiness, which often emerges during AT, as opposed to being a direct effect of AT itself. EEG indicators of stage 2 sleep, K complexes and sleep spindles, are infrequently observed. Some authors note spells of alpha blocking during AT. Others report paroxysmal activity, intermittent bursts of high frequency rhythms. Alpha blocking and paroxysmal activity are apparently due to lapses in attention to the AT prescription and occur more often in novice trainees. In general, long-term trainees exhibit more stable and profound EEG effects than short-term trainees. Degossely and Bostem (1977) presented data consistent with the above, but Jus and Jus (1977a) reported conflicting data. Jus and Jus observed that the first two standard exercises— heaviness and warmth—yielded an EEG pattern characteristic of drowsiness, but this reverted to alert wakefulness (including beta waves) when the last four standard exercises followed.

A modest amount of research on biochemical effects of AT suggests that beneficial changes in serum iodine (Luthe, 1965c) and serum cholesterol (Luthe, 1965d) follow practice of this technique. Cortisol findings have been much more variable. Subjects practicing only the heaviness and warmth chant did not show decreases in cortisol, ACTH, or luteinizing hormone over four practice sessions (Turner & Fine, 1983). Luthe (1970a) reviewed pilot data suggesting that AT enhances physical exercise performance and, when practiced during the postexercise period, hastens recovery to the resting state as indicated by O_2 consumption levels.

More than any other relaxation discipline, AT researchers have taken the question of paradoxical (adverse) training effects seriously. One type of paradoxical effect is called autogenic discharges. These are defined as cognitions, affects, or bodily sensations that spontaneously appear during an AT session and that are unrelated to the themes of the AT exercises. The content of auto-genic discharges may be completely novel, or they may be related to the past experiences of the trainee. Autogenic discharges are usually experienced as unpleasant, and the degree of associated distress ranges from extremely mild to terrifying. Luthe (1970a) presented some pilot data he had collected that indicated that individuals who are sexually deprived as a result of their reli-gious convictions, produce far more sexually-oriented autogenic discharges of varied types than do individuals reporting satisfactory sexual outlets. This re-search implies that the autogenic state facilitates the release of personal mate-rial not usually aired.

The remaining portion of this section will be devoted exclusively to AT stud-ies published in English. These studies were not integrated into the above por-tion of this section because (a) they investigated multiple dependent measures and do not fit neatly into the above organization, or (b) they address effects different from those reported above.

There is one basic research study on pain control with AT, and its design admits numerous weaknesses. Raikov (1978) trained subjects in hypnosis and documented induced anesthesia. Among those who could not be hypnotized, 12 were trained next in AT. Half of these reported reduced anxiety when pricked with a pin, but none reported decreased pain.

Hollandsworth, Gintner, Ellender, and Rectanus (1984) exposed graduate student volunteers to a series of five experimental periods in one session—three quiet rest periods alternating with AT and auditory stress periods. The experimental session was conducted after 8 days of AT training. The main intent of this study was to replicate decreased O_2 consumption reported in the Transcendental Meditation literature. This did not occur, despite subjective ratings reflecting successful relaxation induction. Heart rate effects were also insignificant, but reductions in respiratory rate and volume did occur.

To test the incremental value of electrodermal biofeedback to AT-like re-laxation (suggestions of heaviness and warmth), Steptoe and Greer (1980) em-ployed a crossover design with healthy young adults in two sessions composed of taped AT only and taped AT/biofeedback combined. Both treatments proved effective in reducing electrodermal arousal, heart rate, and self-rated tension during rest and cognitive tasks, and only minor differences between the treatments emerged.

One study (Tebecis, Ohno, Takeya, et al.,1977) selected the uncommon de-pendent measure of fine body movement while sitting still to evaluate AT ef-fects. Clever instrumentation (described in greater detail in Sugano & Takeya, 1970), sensitive to weight shifts, was employed for this purpose. Over the 4 1/2 month training period, normal high school students demonstrated significant reduction in body movement compared to untrained, matched controls. Three scales (extraversion–introversion, neuroticism, and lie) of the Maudsley Per-sonality Inventory (Eysenck, 1959) revealed no within- or between-group dif-ferences. The physiological results of this study were presented separately (Tebecis, Ohno, Matsubara, et al., 1977). Finger temperature increases and increased occurrence of EEG slow waves obtained only for AT subjects. Neither group demonstrated changes in finger pulse amplitude, respiration, or hand microvibration.

Jessup and Neufeld (1977) randomly assigned 20 psychiatric inpatients, mostly depressives, to four relaxation groups: taped autogenic training, frontalis EMG biofeedback, quiet rest, or a variation of placebo biofeedback treatment. This last group received the same tone delivered to the biofeedback group, except it varied in pitch noncontingently. The tone was not deceptively portrayed as a biofeedback tone, as is customarily the case, but instead it was described as a relaxation aid whose sound qualities would help promote relaxation. This condition produced the best results. Skin resistance level, EMG, and hand skin temperature manifested no treatment effects. Within-session heart rate change scores were significantly lower in the placebo group than any of the other groups, which did not differ from each other. An inconsistent pattern of forehead skin temperature changes emerged. Pre-post changes on the 11 scales of the Mood Adjective Check List (Nowlis, 1965) were also inconsistent, but they favored the placebo group.

There is little data available on the *psychological* effects of AT on normals. Ruggieri and Mazza (1980) trained normal high school volunteers in AT over a 3-month period. Pre-post administrations of Witkin's (1950) Embedded Figures Test revealed significantly greater gains on field independence for these subjects compared to matched, untreated controls.

Braud (1981) conducted an interesting test of another psychological trait, parapsychological (psi) ability. (Another portion of this study is discussed in the *Progressive Relaxation* section of this chapter.) One group of community volunteers received conventional, taped AT, and a second group received an arousal version consisting of instructions to have active concentration, lightness and coolness of limbs, heartbeat increasing, etc. Not surprisingly, three electrodermal indices demonstrated relaxation only among conventional AT subjects. The main hypothesis of the experiment, relaxation enhancement of psi abilities, proved correct at moderate levels of relaxation but not above or below this range (see further discussion in Chapter 6).

A series of studies by Cowings and Toscano (1977) examined the effects of a combination of biofeedback and AT on artificially induced motion sickness. The treatment package included biofeedback training to control three modalities: (a) peripheral vasodilation (as indicated by the blood volume pulse measure), (b) respiration rate, and (c) heart rate. The AT component involved instruction in the first four standard autogenic exercises. In sum, the treatment package was termed autogenic feedback training (AFT). The reader is reminded that the independent contributions of biofeedback and AT cannot be isolated in the research reported below.

The first test of AFT was reported in duplicate (Cowings, Billingham, & Toscano, 1977; Cowings & Toscano, 1977). Normal subjects were secured in a chair that was rotated up to 30 rpm. At regular intervals, subjects executed a specific series of head movements. The resulting experience is termed the

Coriolis effect, which mimics motion sickness symptoms. Coriolis reactivity was gauged by the number of motion sickness symptoms exhibited by subjects, as quantified on the Coriolis Sickness Susceptibility Index (CSSI; Graybiel, Wood, Miller, & Cramer, 1968). Subjects receiving AFT posted significantly lower scores on the CSSI than untrained subjects, reflecting differential frequency of such indicators as sweating, drowsiness, and nausea during Coriolis trials.

Follow-up research has since replicated and extended the above findings. In one study (Cowings & Toscano, 1982), subjects were screened for moderate or high susceptibility to motion sickness. This factor did not prove to be important, as both levels of subjects made significant gains on Coriolis tests (as measured by the CSSI) subsequent to AFT, while moderate and high susceptible subjects who did not receive AFT showed no change over six trials. A second study (Toscano & Cowings, 1982) compared the effects of AFT, a cognitive distraction treatment, and no special preparation on tolerance for Coriolis acceleration. The AFT group surpassed both others, suggesting that the mechanism of AFT influence is not cognitive distraction from worry or maladaptive monitoring of bodily sensations. Rather, learned control of autonomic processes emerges as the most likely explanation.

Final Comments on Autogenic Training

There can be no doubt that AT is a legitimate method of relaxation induction. For clinical purposes, more fine-grained scrutiny of AT may not be required. However, critical questions relevant to the expansion of our basic understanding of AT do persist.

AT research typically finds that relaxation effects appear very early in the induction sequence and level off about midway through. Coincidentally, this is the same pattern one would expect to find as active subjects begin to rest in a quiet environment. Luthe's (1970a) presentation does not give adequate information regarding the presence or absence of an adaptation period. Our research (Lichstein, Sallis, Hill, & Young, 1981; Sallis & Lichstein, 1979), presented in detail in Chapter 2, has clearly shown that the process of accommodating to a restful environment produces substantive relaxation effects in the absence of any relaxation technique. Relaxation research that does not provide an adaptation period prior to relaxation assessment is subject to a serious methodological confound.

Assuming that adaptation influences have been ruled out, it is not clear that the standard exercises contribute much beyond the "passive concentration" attitude. AT therapists emphasize the importance of this attitude, and rightfully so. However, the trainee deeply absorbed in such a state is essentially engaged in nonfocal meditation and may derive small additional benefit from the standard exercises.

When Schultz invented AT, he constructed the content and sequence of the method to track a physiological and experiential course already observed among hypnotic subjects (see Chapter 1). Over the years, AT researchers have come to believe that the AT formulae induce similar physiological changes. This contention has profound theoretical implications for the potential power of self-control strategies and, most fortunately, can be readily tested, although this has yet to be done. If we were to vary the sequence of the six standard exercises, we could test whether the isomorphism between psychophysiological changes and self-instruction content holds up. Further, a sequence analysis would begin to shed light on the relative contributions of passive concentration versus the autogenic formulae in contributing to the AT effect.

Researchers (and clinicians) routinely employ incomplete AT inductions, often confining themselves to the heaviness and warmth exercises. In light of this common practice to further abbreviate AT, research to assess what, if any, relaxation cost is associated with AT shortening would be helpful in guiding induction decisions.

IMAGERY

Imagery for relaxation represents a small proportion of the varied applications of imagery (q.v., Sheikh, 1983; Singer & Pope, 1978). Selecting imagery material to include in this book was difficult because it was sometimes unclear, for example, whether a particular study employed imagery as a cognitive distractor, a self-reward, or a relaxation device. When the authors did not make their intentions clear, I was guided by the content of the imagery and the type of measures chosen to evaluate it. Also excluded from this section are imagery themes closely related to autogenic training, even when standard autogenic procedures were not employed.

Horan and Dellinger (1974) employed a method called "in vivo" emotive imagery, which instructs subjects to use relaxing imagery as they are confronted by noxious stimuli. In this study, undergraduate volunteers immersed their hands in ice water for as long as possible while imagining a pleasant nature scene ("in vivo" emotive imagery), counting backwards (cognitive distraction control group), or with no preparation or coaching at all. The groups' ability to tolerate ice water immersion was, in ascending sequence, no treatment, distraction, and imagery, but only the no treatment-imagery comparison was significant.

In a series of studies, Worthington further explored the role of imagery in pain control. Worthington used imagery themes mainly composed of engaging in activities in pleasant nature scenes (E. L. Worthington, personal communication, July 7, 1982) to extend tolerance of ice water immersion. His first study (Worthington, 1978) found that enhanced perceptions of being in control and coping self-statements were effective, but pleasant imagery was not. A subsequent report (Worthington & Shumate, 1981) reversed this outcome pattern: imagery proved effective and coping self-statements did not. Lastly, Worthington and Feldman (1981) contrasted three styles of presenting the imagery and obtained effects for perceived pain, but not for actual pain tolerance. A direct manner with clear, straightforward instructions was significantly better than written instructions, but not significantly better than a collaborative nondirective manner.

Sim (1980a) reported on a somewhat novel imagery strategy. Subjects practiced "body visualization" for 2 weeks, which involved reviewing in imagination one's body and clothing from top to bottom. This was followed by 10 weeks of imagining a "silent void" in front of the forehead. Weekly monitoring of digital skin resistance revealed a fivefold increase in these student volunteers over the 3-month period, compared to no change in untreated controls.

In the final study in this section, subjects stressed by mental arithmetic next received soothing instructions in relaxing imagery, heard an irrelevant didactic presentation, or rested quietly (Katz, 1974). Electrodermal activity confirmed lower arousal for the imagery group than the other two.

Final Comments on Imagery

Relaxing imagery, often called guided imagery, is commonly employed in clinical practice, but basic researchers have not exhibited comparable interest. Little is known of the physiological and psychological effects of imagery. Lang's research (discussed in Chapter 2) systematically examined the components and effects of arousing imagery. This could serve as an excellent model to guide future research on relaxing imagery.

COMPARISONS OF RELAXATION TECHNIQUES

This section will consider studies that have contrasted methods of relaxation within the realm of basic research. The bulk of the comparative research has pitted Transcendental Meditation against progressive relaxation. Fewer studies involved evaluations of other meditation techniques, progressive relaxation, and autogenics.

Comparisons Among Meditation Techniques

Two studies evaluated Transcendental Meditation (TM) and Benson's method, and both found no differences between the two. These pre-post, nonrandom assignment studies found no changes on a battery of creativity tests (Domino, 1977) or a locus of control questionnaire (Zaichkowsky & Kamen, 1978). Significant but comparable reductions in frontalis muscle tension occurred in the two treatments, but not in a no-treatment control (Zaichkowsky & Kamen, 1978).

A third study (Beiman, Johnson, Puente, Majestic, & Graham, 1984) randomly assigned community volunteers to TM, Benson, stress management, or no treatment. Five questionnaires and four physiological measures failed to distinguish the groups. A strong internal locus of control favored a strong relaxation effect. A fourth study (Puente, 1981) also employed random assignment (to TM, Benson, or no treatment), and yielded equivocal results on five physiological measures. On respiration and percent of EEG alpha, the two treated groups were equivalently superior to no treatment. On heart rate and skin conductance, *untreated subjects* were least aroused. On frontalis muscle tension, Bensonian subjects were more relaxed than the other two groups. This study also boasts two uncommon methodological ingredients worthy of mention. First, uninformed raters listened to tapes of actual TM and Benson sessions, and determined that treatment delivery was biased in favor of TM. Second, the majority of the participants preferred to receive TM treatment, a second biasing factor usually left unassessed.

TM was also one of the treatments in each of the two remaining studies comparing meditation techniques. The first was a highly rigorous, true random assignment study (Yuille & Sereda, 1980). Students responding to announcements of a meditation study were randomly assigned to TM, Savasana Yoga (a method of body focusing akin to passive relaxation), a pseudomeditation control group (a self-directed meditative experience), or a no-treatment control. TM was presented by a "certified TM teacher" and Savasana was taught by an "experienced Hatha Yoga instructor." A series of 10 cognitive tests (e.g., memory, intelligence, reading skills) were administered prior to initiating treatments and again after 3 months of practice. The results were disappointing. Dropout rate, a powerful indicator of treatment influence, surpassed 40 percent in both true meditation groups. With minor exception, neither TM nor Savasana produced significant changes in any of the broad array of cognitive abilities tested.

The second study (Becker & Shapiro, 1981) addressed a fine point in the meditation literature concerning alpha blocking in response to auditory distraction. Clicks were presented every 15 seconds during 15 minutes of treatment. Experienced practitioners of either Zen, yoga, or TM meditated during treatment, and two attention-manipulation control groups rested quietly. All groups exhibited normal EEG alpha and skin conductance habituation patterns, and significant differences between groups did not emerge. These results cast doubt on claims of heightened awareness alleged to occur during meditation.

Progressive Relaxation versus Passive Relaxation

Passive relaxation is identical to PR except that the muscle tense-release part is omitted. Subjects are instructed to sequentially review in their mind the muscles of their body and focus their attention on pleasant sensations. The procedure is described in detail as level 3 relaxation in Chapter 5. If the tense-release procedure were not an active ingredient of PR (i.e., PR and passive relaxation were equally effective), PR's status would suffer. In this case, PR would be judged an unnecessarily ornate procedure, and passive relaxation could be viewed as a simple variant of autogenic training. Unfortunately, existing data do not lead us to a resolution of this matter.

Haynes, Moseley, and McGowan (1975) conducted the first basic research study of this comparison. Normal undergraduates were randomly assigned to one session of taped PR, taped passive relaxation, electromyographic (EMG) biofeedback, false feedback, or no treatment. Only biofeedback and passive relaxation resulted in significant EMG reductions comparing baseline and the end of treatment. Similarly, EMG comparisons conducted at the end of treatment showed biofeedback and passive relaxation to be similar, and both to be significantly lower than PR and the no-treatment control, which did not differ from each other. The false feedback condition fell in the midrange of the five groups.

This study, in essence, indicated that the tense-release component actually detracts from the effectiveness of PR. However, our faith in this conclusion must be substantially tempered by three serious methodological shortcomings in this study. First, PR involves more complex operations than passive relaxation and, therefore, may require more than one session to attain a level of mastery comparable to that of one session of passive relaxation. Two or three treatment sessions would have provided a more adequate comparative test. Second, some research (to be reviewed in the following section) reveals taped PR to be inferior to live PR. Parallel research on passive relaxation does not exist. It is possible that PR suffers more in a taped format than does passive relaxation. The results of live presentations of these two treatments would have been more convincing. Third, the results of this study rest on a single dependent measure—frontalis electromyography. As is apparent from the majority of the studies presented in this chapter that collected multiple dependent measures, the between-group pattern of other physiological and experiential indices likely would disagree with the EMG pattern.

All of the remaining data on the relative merits of PR and passive relaxation derive from clinical research, primarily from the laboratories of Borkovec and Haynes. Borkovec conducted clinical trials with insomniacs (Borkovec, Grayson, O'Brien, & Weerts, 1979; Borkovec & Hennings, 1978; Borkovec, Kaloupek, & Slama, 1975) and anxious individuals (Borkovec, Grayson, & Cooper, 1978; Borkovec & Hennings, 1978). These findings strongly point to the opposite conclusion from that derived by Haynes, Moseley, and McGowan (1975). Specifically, Borkovec has repeatedly observed that tensing-releasing is *the* key factor in PR, and physiological attention-focusing (passive relaxation) is an inactive ingredient. Conversely, in clinical outcome research with insomniacs (Haynes, Sides, & Lockwood, 1977; Haynes, Woodward, Moran, & Alexander, 1974) and muscle-contraction headache sufferers (Haynes, Griffen, Mooney, & Parise, 1975), Haynes has uniformly shown passive relaxation to be therapeutically effective. Chapter 7 provides more in-depth coverage on Borkovec's and Haynes' clinical research.

Data from other laboratories have not helped clarify this issue, as findings consistent with those of both Borkovec (Warrenburg, Pagano, Woods, &

Hlastala, 1980) and Haynes (Woolfolk & McNulty, 1983) have been reported. One study (Rickard, Crist, & Barker, 1985) found that PR was more effective than passive relaxation with low hypnotic suggestible subjects, but the two techniques were equivalent with high suggestible subjects, based upon self-ratings of relaxation. Further, Edelman (1970) found that neither the tense-release technique nor passive relaxation achieved a noticeable relaxation effect. The sharp divergence in the findings in this domain cannot be readily explained. One possibility that merits future attention calls for a component analysis of the passive relaxation method. The research cited above does not provide sufficient detail on the method of passive relaxation to permit identification of the distinguishing characteristics of the successful and unsuccessful attempts. The potential variations here are numerous and deserve careful study.

Progressive Relaxation versus Self-control Relaxation

Harris et al. (1984) provided scant details on a research study on this subject. Coronary heart disease patients exhibited lower frontalis muscle tension during math and anagram problems when armed with cue-controlled relaxation than with progressive relaxation. Other dependent measures (blood pressure, skin conductance, and heart rate) did not separate the groups. A second study also favored the self-control format. Cue-controlled relaxation suppressed muscle reactivity during shock trials more than progressive relaxation in a within-subject analysis (Ewing & Hughes, 1978).

Live versus Taped Progressive Relaxation

Paul and Trimble (1970) first raised the question of whether a PR induction delivered by audiotape is as effective as PR presented in the customary "live" manner. The results of their inquiry provided an unambiguous endorsement of live administration. Undergraduate volunteers taught PR by taped instructions achieved significantly inferior relaxation effects on measures of muscle tension, heart rate, and composite physiological stress response, compared to matched subjects who received live PR inductions reported in earlier studies (Paul, 1969b, 1969c). Respiratory rate and an anxiety questionnaire, the Anxiety Differential (AD; Husek & Alexander, 1963) did not distinguish the two modes of PR delivery. Further, comparisons between taped PR, taped hypnosis, and a quiet-rest control group revealed that taped PR no longer achieved superior results over the other two groups, in contrast to the outcome of the live presentation series.

A similar pattern of results with student subjects has since been obtained in other laboratories (Quayle, 1980; Russell, Sipich, & Knipe, 1976). A blood pressure study (Brauer, Horlick, Nelson, Farquhar, & Agras, 1979) found no difference between taped and live PR at the end of treatment, but systolic pressure was significantly lower in the live group at 6-month follow-up. Cancer patients receiving chemotherapy tolerated live PR, but four of five receiving taped PR became nauseous while listening to the tape (Morrow, 1984).

Israel and Beiman (1977) compared three treatment sessions of live PR, taped PR, and unspecified self-relaxation with anxious volunteers from the community, and obtained a pattern of results opposite to those of Paul and Trimble (1970). None of the physiological measures (i.e., heart rate, respiration rate, and frontalis muscle tension) revealed differences between any of the groups. The sole self-report measure, the AD, indicated the live PR group achieved superior experiential relief.

A subsequent, expanded version of this same study (Beiman, Israel, & Johnson, 1978) added subjects, conditions, and treatment sessions to those reported in the Israel and Beiman (1977) article. In this later publication, five treatment sessions and a sixth unassisted generalization session were conducted to evaluate live PR, taped PR, electromyographic biofeedback, and meditation. Data from the first five sessions were analyzed separately for the two PR groups and the biofeedback/meditation groups. Only the former part will be reported herein. The form of PR delivered in these five sessions followed the recommendation of Bernstein and Borkovec (1973), in that the procedure was gradually abbreviated until only relaxation by recall was conducted in session six. Within-session reductions in heart rate and skin resistance response (this dependent measure was omitted from the earlier report in this series) were greater for the live group than for the taped PR group. By sessions four and five, the superiority of live PR also extended to frontalis muscle tension. Respiratory rate and the AD did not distinguish the groups, duplicating the response of Paul and Trimble's subjects on these measures.

In the sixth session (generalization), all four groups were contrasted. All groups improved in trait anxiety, as measured by the Affect Adjective Check List (Zuckerman, 1960) and the State-Trait Anxiety Inventory (STAI; Spielberger, Gorsuch, & Lushene, 1970), from the first to the sixth session, as well as in state anxiety (AD) and muscle tension during the sixth session. On the measure of skin resistance response, live PR was superior to the other three treatments, which did not differ from each other. Surprisingly, live PR and self-relaxation did not differ from each other on respiration rate during this session, but both surpassed taped PR and biofeedback. In summary, the results of Beiman et al. (1978) should be interpreted as overriding the premature findings of Israel and Beiman (1977), leaving the data, so far, in unanimous support of live over taped PR.

A study by Riddick and Meyer (1973) contradicted the early findings of Paul and Trimble. Neither physiological (heart rate and skin conductance), behavioral (spontaneous movement), nor self-report data favored live or taped PR. However, a placebo-tranquilizer-pill condition did not do as well as live PR on movement or taped PR on heart rate. The only unusual characteristic of this study was that a soft sound signal was triggered by a movement detection device and thus alerted subjects in the taped PR condition to discontinue their movements. Two recent studies employing college students also found taped PR equivalent to live PR (Hamberger & Schuldt, 1986; Stefanek & Hodes, 1986). Low statistical power and floor effects probably detracted from both of these studies. Two additional features of the Hamberger and Schuldt study, though also undermined by these methodological flaws, deserve mention. This investigation failed to find a difference between therapist presence versus therapist absence in taped presentations, or between a fixed versus a contingent pace in live presentations.

The superiority of live over taped PR may derive from two factors: pacing and social influence. The latter factor in a live induction will, of course, never be matched by taped presentation, and its importance will vary according to the context in which relaxation is presented and the strength of the client's preferences. On the other hand, pacing involves repeated tensing-releasing of each muscle group until it exceeds subjective relaxation criteria before proceeding to the next muscle group, and this can be accomplished in a taped presentation. Lang, Melamed, and Hart (1970) described an automated systematic desensitization system with subject-controlled switches that enabled the subject to repeat muscle groups during the taped PR protocol. Borkovec has since employed a similar self-pacing automated PR procedure and has had success with anxious subjects (Borkovec, Grayson, & Cooper, 1978) and insomniacs (Borkovec, Grayson, O'Brien, & Weerts, 1979). However, the most meaningful test of self-paced taped PR would be a direct comparison with live PR. The only available test of this sort was conducted in an unpublished dissertation (Godsey, 1980), and self-paced, taped PR still proved inferior to live PR.

Data from the biofeedback literature suggests that the social influence factor alluded to above may contribute little to the relaxation effect. Several studies (Borgeat, Hade, Larouche, & Bedwani, 1980; Hamberger & Lohr, 1981; Wolfe, 1977) found that biofeedback training was not enhanced by therapist presence compared to therapist absence (similar to the findings of Hamberger & Schuldt, 1986, reported above). Reasoning by default thus implies that self-regulated pacing may be needed to equate taped and live PR (and other relaxation) inductions. There is no data on the question of live versus taped presentations of other relaxation methods.

Meditation versus Progressive Relaxation

One study published in triplicate (Gilbert, Parker, & Claiborn, 1978; Parker, Gilbert, & Thoreson, 1978a, 1978b) compared Benson's approach with progressive relaxation (PR). Patients in an inpatient alcohol treatment program were randomly assigned to 3 weeks of treatment in either Benson's method, PR, or quiet rest. All treatments were presented via tape recorder. Within-session changes were analyzed for session one only, in which systolic and diastolic blood pressure reductions favored Benson's technique. All groups showed significant within-session improvement in state anxiety (STAI; Spielberger, Gorsuch, & Lushene, 1970), heart rate, and spontaneous skin conductance fluctuations. Assessments conducted at the beginning and end of the 3-week program revealed significant improvement in systolic blood pressure occurred in the Benson group only, whereas diastolic improvement occurred in the Benson and PR groups. All groups improved on heart rate and state anxiety, and no group showed skin conductance changes. Decreased tension accrued to the meditation and PR subjects, while decreased depression accrued only to the latter. Generalization measures taken during the treatment course, at times distinct from the treatment sessions, revealed reduced state anxiety in all groups and no heart rate or skin conductance changes in any group. Significant increases in systolic and diastolic blood pressure occurred in the rest group, while significant decreases in diastolic pressure occurred only in the Benson and PR groups.

Other Benson-PR contrasts found trivial differences between the methods when subjects are exposed to a stressful film (Bradley & McCanne, 1981) or cold pressor and reaction time tasks (English & Baker, 1983). Testing subjects' responses to slides depicting mutilation, PR proved somewhat superior to relaxation response training based upon self-report and electrodermal indices (Green, Webster, Beiman, Rosmarin, & Holliday, 1981).

Ten studies contrasted TM and PR. The research designs in this group are of three types: pre-post group design comparisons, postgroup comparisons only, and a group design response to stress.

Six studies evaluated subjects before and after TM and PR treatment. Simpson, Dansereau, and Giles (1972) conducted a highly rigorous study. Fifteen undergraduate volunteers from the Army ROTC program were randomly assigned to 2 weeks of training in TM (administered by a qualified instructor), PR, or to a no-treatment, quiet-rest control condition. Five pretraining and eight posttraining experimental sessions were conducted to gather data on a wide range of physiological and psychological variables. Measures of heart rate, respiration rate, and blood pressure failed to reliably discriminate the groups. PR subjects consistently exhibited higher skin resistance levels than the other two groups, though these data were not submitted to statistical analyses. A variety of psychological tasks, including reaction time, arithmetic, and letter counting, did not reveal any advantages accruing to either relaxation group. Similarly, global self-report ratings of daily functioning yielded comparable scores for the three groups. An anxiety questionnaire (IPAT; Cattell, 1957), administered before and after relaxation training, found no significant differences. In attempting to explain the highly consistent negative results of this study, the authors indicated that most of the subjects did not practice their relaxation method twice daily as instructed. Indeed, four of five TM subjects found it philosophically objectionable, and they were particularly disgruntled.

Zuroff and Schwarz (1978) ran a similar study with a larger number of undergraduate subjects (60) and more extensive treatment (9 weeks). All groups registered significant improvement on ratings of general life adjustment, pulse rate, and two measures of anxiety—behavioral indicators of anxiety during an analogue social interaction and an anxiety questionnaire (S-R

Inventory; Endler, Hunt, & Rosenstein, 1962). A third measure of anxiety (Affect Adjective Check List; Zuckerman, 1960) favored TM. Self-reports on drug use before and after treatment did not reveal any significant changes. TM subjects reportedly practiced their method more than the PR subjects, but correlation analyses failed to find a link between levels of practice and the effect on the S-R questionnaire. Two and a half years later, few subjects in either treatment group were still practicing their treatment method (Zuroff & Schwarz, 1980).

Throll evaluated PR and TM, and separately reported the psychological (Throll, 1981) and physiological (Throll, 1982) effects at posttreatment and up to 4 months follow-up. It is not clear if random assignment to groups was observed. This study provides the strongest data suggesting the superiority of TM over PR. Two scales (neuroticism and extraversion) of the Eysenck Personality Inventory (EPI; Eysenck, 1963), state anxiety (STAI), and heart rate evinced greater improvement in TM subjects at posttreatment, while only oxygen consumption favored PR at this same point. At long-term follow-up, the same two scales of the EPI, trait (rather than state) anxiety, and respiration rate supported TM, and PR maintained its lower oxygen consumption. One possible explanation for the strength of the TM showing was that the ratio of amount of home practice among TM and PR subjects was about 6:1 respectively.

A fourth study (Thomas & Abbas, 1978) found both TM and PR to be effective, but not differentially so, in decreasing anxiety among nonclinical subjects. Drennen and Chermol (1978) observed these two techniques to be equally ineffective in altering self-actualization. The last study in this series offered TM, PR, or no treatment to students for extra credit, and students selected the group that most interested them (Davies, 1977). Pre-post comparative assessments with the control group revealed that, for those who practiced regularly, significant reductions in trait anxiety (STAI) occurred in the TM group, and significant increases in self-actualization (Personal Orientation Inventory; Shostrom, 1966) occurred in the TM and PR groups. However, noncompliance was a major feature of this study. The 76 percent of TM subjects and 48 percent of PR subjects who practiced irregularly did not attain significant change.

Three studies, using a posttest group design, examined resting levels of subjects already experienced in relaxation. Warrenburg, Pagano, Woods, and Hlastala (1980) found disappointing results in their study of long-term TM, long-term PR, and short-term PR practitioners. Each subject participated in two sessions, divided into periods of practice of their respective techniques alternating with quiet rest and quiet reading control periods. The PR technique involved body focusing on relaxed sensations without first tensing (passive relaxation). Reductions for all groups were found in O_2 consumption and respiration rate. Tonic heart rate levels in the long-term PR group were significantly lower than the TM group. Theta EEG analyses did not reveal any significant differences. This study merits distinction for two reasons. First, it is one of the few basic research, O_2 consumption studies of PR, and it is one of the few attempts to replicate Wallace's (1970) O_2 findings on TM. Oxygen consumption dropped about 4 percent in all groups in the present study, which is far less than the 16 percent reported by Wallace. [Incidentally, a clinical trial with hypertension (Cottier, Shapiro, & Julius, 1984) documented nearly a 7 percent average O_2 decrease during PR.] Second, this and the study reported below are the only two studies of recent vintage that evaluated PR practitioners with several years experience.

Curtis and Wessberg (1976) monitored TM and PR practitioners, all having 2 years of experience, together with a third group of naive subjects in one session during which the first two groups practiced their accustomed method and the third group rested. Surprisingly, no between- or within-group changes occurred in any of the dependent measures: electrodermal activity, heart rate, and respiration rate. Lastly, Cauthen and Prymak (1977) compared subjects having three levels of experience in TM with individuals exposed to 1 week of PR practice and another group instructed in a pseudomeditation technique. TM practitioners had either 5 years, 1 year, or 1 week experience. The results offered modest support for the efficacy of these relaxation techniques. No respiration rate effects occurred at all. During the one session of monitoring, there were no within-group changes in skin conductance level, although the 5-year TM group manifested a lower tonic level than the pseudomeditation group. Skin temperature warming occurred among the PR and 1-week TM subjects. Heart rate decreases were registered by the PR and 5- and 1-year TM subjects.

The final study (Puente & Beiman, 1980) in the TM-PR series randomly assigned anxious volunteers from the community to one of four conditions. One group was trained in a combination of the self-control form of PR (see Chapter 5 for a description of this method) and cognitive restructuring techniques. This group was contrasted with subjects trained in TM, a self-styled relaxation group, and a no-treatment group. Each group received seven training sessions. An experimental evaluation session was conducted before and after the treatment series. This session evaluated the subject's reactions to six stressful slides depicting medical-surgical stimuli. The PR and self-relaxation groups showed superior treatment gains on measures of cardiovascular responsivity, but not in self-reported distress. The fact that PR did not outperform self-relaxation suggests the presence of nonspecific treatment effects in this study.

Heide and Borkovec (1983) conducted a unique study featuring the systematic analysis of unwanted relaxation effects. Anxious volunteers from the community submitted to two laboratory sessions on consecutive days. All subjects received one session of taped progressive relaxation (PR) and one session of mantra meditation (the mantra "ah-nam" was employed) in counterbalanced sequence. By their own account, tension occurred in 30.8 percent of subjects during PR and 53.8 percent during meditation. Only one subject reported tension during both techniques, which suggests that idiographic preferences determine technique superiority. Interestingly, clinical data also indicate greater anxiety peaks in meditation than in PR (Lehrer, Woolfolk, Rooney, McCann, & Carrington, 1983).

Considering a total of 10 questionnaire and physiological measures, a large percentage of subjects exhibited changes in a direction contrary to relaxation on at least one subjective and one physiological measure in the PR (35.7 percent) or meditation (57.1 percent) sessions. Fear of losing control, high absorption (Tellegen & Atkinson, 1974), and sensory alteration were mild-moderate predictors of paradoxical relaxation effects. It should be emphasized that few subjects manifested prominent relaxation-induced anxiety. Rather, most changes in the arousal direction were small and might be viewed more accurately as a failure to attain relaxation uniformly in all measures.

Relaxation enhancement was also evaluated. PR proved superior to meditation on the following measures: Anxiety Differential (Husek & Alexander, 1963), heart rate, skin conductance responses, and self-ratings of mental and bodily tension. No measure evinced superiority of meditation. Overall, PR was more acceptable than meditation when judged by the occurrence of either negative or positive effects.

Three studies reported below will conclude this section. They share a common feature in that PR was compared with a TM-like treatment. All three studies include random assignment of subjects to conditions and other admirable methodological controls. However, TM advocates would argue that these "TM" procedures are less effective than the orthodox method. Unfortunately, there is no data on which to resolve this question.

Two of these studies (Boswell & Murray, 1979; Fee & Girdano, 1978) presented tape-recorded treatments to normal undergraduates, and both obtained disappointing results. Boswell and Murray assigned the same sanskrit sounding mantra to their TM subjects and compared the performance of this group with groups receiving PR, pseudomeditation, or no treatment. All groups exhibited significant decreases on the STAI-Trait scale. Three physiological measures—spontaneous skin resistance responses, skin conductance level, and heart rate—failed to discriminate the groups in within-session changes. Further, these same measures plus a fourth, STAI-State, did not reveal any group differences in ability to cope with stress as indicated by an anxiety-provoking intelligence test. Fee and Girdano presented 10 training sessions of (a) electromyographic (EMG) biofeedback, (b) meditation (TM-like mantra and breathing combined), (c) PR enhanced with autogenic phrases, imagery, and cognitive strategies, or (d) a placebo treatment (tapes discussing academic issues in mental health). A fifth group receiving no treatment was also included. Laboratory assessments conducted before and after the treatment period found no effects for skin potential level, heart rate, or skin temperature. The biofeedback and meditation groups showed significant decreases on frontalis EMG. The PR and meditation groups showed significant decreases on respiration rate.

The third study involved live treatment presentation by highly experienced clinicians, but this also obtained disappointing results. The anxiety theory of Davidson and Schwartz (1976) motivated a comparison of meditation and PR by Lehrer, Schoicket, Carrington, and Woolfolk (1980). This theory posits partially independent somatic and cognitive anxiety subsets that are reactive to variables that provoke anxiety (i.e., threatening situations) or attenuate anxiety (i.e., relaxation techniques). The individual's anxiety experience is primarily determined by idiographic response tendencies, whereas relaxation effects are governed by the nature of the technique. Thus, mantra meditation, which captivates the individual's attention, mainly addresses cognitive anxiety, while PR focuses on somatic anxiety reflected in the musculature.

Lehrer, Schoicket, Carrington, and Woolfolk (1980) presented four training sessions of Clinically Standardized Meditation (CSM; Carrington, 1978a), PR, or no treatment to anxious subjects from the community. CSM is a secular method of mantra meditation that is similar to TM. Effects were evaluated by questionnaire data, physiological indicators during rest, and physiological responses to sound and light stressors. As predicted, forearm and frontalis EMG were lower in the PR group than in the CSM group. Surprisingly, the no-treatment group also registered significantly lower muscle tension than the CSM group. An identical pattern occurred with heart rate. The authors hypothesized that the EMG and heart rate elevations in the CSM group were due to heightened preparedness for the stress tests. However, in the aftermath of the stress stimuli, the CSM subjects showed the greatest cardiac deceleration. Skin conductance, the primary measure of cognitive anxiety, did not distinguish the groups. EEG alpha, another indicator of cognitive anxiety, produced mild evidence in favor of CSM. The IPAT Anxiety Scale and the STAI-State scale yielded inconsistent results. Self-report scale ratings suggested that subjects receiving the cognitive treatment (CSM) derived stronger cognitive benefits (e.g., less worry about problems) and subjects exposed to the somatic treatment (PR) derived stronger somatic benefits (e.g., increased feeling of heaviness). Overall, this study appears to offer very modest support for the Davidson-Schwartz theory, although Lehrer et al. were more enthusiastic than I in their conclusions. Further, the main differences between PR and CSM occurred when CSM was associated with seemingly paradoxical EMG and heart rate effects. On most measures, neither CSM nor PR outperformed the no-treatment group.

Autogenic Training versus Progressive Relaxation

Five studies have conducted such a comparison, and two of these came out of Lehrer's laboratory. None of these reports revealed a clearcut advantage of one method over the other.

In Lehrer's first study, normal volunteers were randomly assigned to five training sessions of AT or PR, or no treatment (Shapiro & Lehrer, 1980). Pre-post measures of tonic skin conductance and heart rate were negative, as were physiological indices of stress response to aversive tones. State anxiety (STAI) and subjective relaxation ratings also proved negative. Subjects trained in AT reported somewhat greater awareness of warm and heavy sensations in their limbs than did subjects trained in PR. A symptom questionnaire (SCL-90; Derogatis, Lipman, & Covi, 1973) revealed that only the treated groups made gains in anxiety, depression, number of symptoms, and mean symptom intensity.

Lehrer, Atthowe, and Weber (1980) replicated the above study with some methodological changes. The most important change was that highly anxious individuals now served as subjects. A sham biofeedback group was also added. Heart rate decrease occurred in the AT group only. Finger temperature and respiration rate did not distinguish any of the groups. Here again subjective ratings identified experiences consonant with the autogenic themes occurring in the AT group only. The IPAT Anxiety Inventory registered significant decreases for both treated groups. Hypnotizability as measured by the Stanford Hypnotic Susceptibility Scale (Weitzenhoffer & Hilgard, 1959) did not predict response to relaxation.

To study aspects of taped relaxation that might influence outcome, Nathan, Nathan, Vigen, and Wellborn (1981) presented PR and AT tapes to undergraduate students. Within method of relaxation, the tapes were equally divided between male and female therapist voice and between the presence or absence of a musical background. Subjects admitted preferences for tapes spoken by the opposite sex and containing background music. Self-ratings of relaxation were higher for AT than PR (though the absolute margin was not great) and higher for the background tapes.

Students attending a continuing education class on creativity were taught PR or AT (Borgeat, Stravynski, & Chaloult, 1983). Further, half the subjects in each treatment were told to expect particularly strong effects with regard to sleepiness and the generation of mental images. Subjective ratings on 10 relaxation indices were employed to evaluate treatment effects. Unfortunately, pretreatment ratings were not obtained. Outcome suggestions exerted negligible influence on reported effects. Six of 10 measures revealed no significant difference between the two relaxation methods. AT earned higher ratings for mental relaxation, presence of imagery, and presence of emotions. PR was judged to be more boring.

The last study in this section randomly assigned normal male undergraduates to eight treatments of either electromyographic biofeedback, taped PR, or taped AT (Staples, Coursey, & Smith, 1975). The AT subjects registered significantly higher frontalis muscle tension throughout the program. All groups showed decreases in state anxiety questionnaires (Affect Adjective Check List, Zuckerman, 1960; Mattsson scale, Mattsson, 1960) associated with individual sessions, but trait anxiety (Manifest Anxiety Scale; Taylor, 1953) did not vary over the treatment course. Subjects' ratings of their attitudes toward the treatment techniques favored PR. In sum, none of the methods produced powerful relaxation effects, and strong differences between the treatments did not emerge.

Imagery versus Progressive Relaxation

Bellack (1973) adapted the conditioning paradigm of Grings and Uno (1968), discussed earlier in this chapter, to contrast progressive relaxation and pleasant imagery. These approaches proved equally effective in abating shock-conditioned anxiety. A second test of progressive relaxation and pleasant imagery also found them comparably effective (Miller & Bornstein, 1977). This latter study included soothing music with half the subjects, but detected no relaxation increment therefrom.

Final Comments on Relaxation Comparisons

Live presentations of progressive relaxation are usually more effective than taped presentations, and this is the only relaxation contrast that identifies disparity. The remainder of the extant basic research literature fails to reach a consensus that recommends one or several relaxation techniques above others. The bulk of the studies find no significant differences between relaxation treatments. Isolated studies favor particular approaches with respect to particular variables, but results such as these do not hold up against the test of replication. The only relaxation comparison to receive substantive attention, TM versus PR, did not reveal clear advantages consistently associated with either one of these methods. Indeed, nine of the 10 studies found, with minor exceptions, no significant differences between TM and PR on a host of psychological and physiological variables.

Overall, I am in agreement with the conclusion drawn by other reviewers on this subject (Shapiro, 1982). Specifically, claims of unique attributes advanced by some schools of meditation [particularly Transcendental Meditation (e.g., Orme-Johnson, 1977)] and relaxation are unjustified.

It seems safe to conclude that bias in group responses to a series of relaxation techniques cannot be predicted. Yet, *individual* preferences for particular relaxation techniques clearly do exist. To date, we have not begun to systematically investigate the important question of which factors are salient to an optimal subject-relaxation technique match. For the present, tentatively stated clinical guidelines, with little empirical support, will have to suffice in making these decisions (see Chapter 4 for further discussion).

CONCLUSIONS

This chapter reviewed several hundred basic research studies on relaxation. Surprisingly, this formidable body of information does not give rise to a string of firmly supported conclusions, because contradictory outcomes are pervasive. Several possibilities may explain this unfortunate state of affairs.

First, the number of methodologically corrupt studies far outnumber those boasting strong methodological integrity. Thus we should expect spurious outcomes and inconsistent results across studies.

Second, excepting for the highly standardized procedures of TM, there is great procedural variation in relaxation method among studies of any particular relaxation technique. This point is dramatically illustrated by the history of progressive relaxation (PR). When Edmund Jacobson was virtually the only person doing PR research, there was extraordinary consistency in findings across studies. During the past 20 years, no two researchers (nor clinicians) can agree on the procedural details of the method, and there is much less consistency in PR research findings. Although other factors have also contributed to this shift in PR research outcome, procedural variability is likely one of them.

Third, as occurs in all cases of acquiring new skills or conditioning effects, regular practice sustained over an ill-defined but substantial period of time is indispensable to achieving relevant gains. Jacobson argued that months of practice were needed to benefit from PR, and most current studies in any Western relaxation discipline rarely train beyond several weeks. I can cite the meditation literature to support this point. The several studies of highly experienced trainees generally reported more profound effects than studies of relatively novice trainees. A related point concerns the frequency and quality of unsupervised practice. Most studies present instruction in once-a-week sessions, and subjects are asked to practice once or twice daily at home. Based upon recent data on hypertensive subjects (Taylor, Agras, Schneider, & Allen, 1983) and anxious subjects (Hoelscher, Lichstein, & Rosenthal, 1984), much of the prescribed practice never gets done.

Despite the above obstacles to firm conclusions, the extant literature does justify summary observations. These are offered in descending order of confidence.

1. When a randomly selected person practices a randomly selected method of relaxation, one of three outcomes with differential degrees of certainty may result. The individual may be harmed, but there is little chance of this occurring. No detectable changes may occur, and there is a fair likelihood of this happening. Lastly, some measure of experiential and/or biological benefit will emerge in the majority of trainees, but these desirable changes are highly variable from one individual to the next with respect to their magnitude, generality, longevity, and the amount of practice required to bring them about.

2. Relaxation processes may be viewed on a temporal continuum delineated by predisposition to relaxation (before), state effects (during), and trait or long-term effects (after) (Davidson & Goleman, 1977). Relaxation basic research has focused on state effects. Little is known about person and setting variables affecting receptivity to relaxation, and even less is known about long-term effects, particularly with Western techniques.

3. The particular type of relaxation technique employed may evoke a spe-

cific experiential and/or biological pattern. This conclusion is drawn mainly from data on autogenic training. However, the more likely outcome of relaxation is best described as global parasympathetic effects. The specific pattern of emphases will vary from one individual to the next, primarily as a function of subject vulnerabilities and response tendencies.

4. As research designs become more sophisticated, alternative explanations for relaxation effects become more abundant. In other words, not unlike other areas of psychological research, the general tendency throughout this literature reflects an inverse relationship between methodological rigor and magnitude of treatment effects (Holmes, 1984). However, I would be remiss if I failed to explicitly point out that notable exceptions to this trend do exist (e.g., Beary & Benson, 1974; Gopal, Bhatnagar, Subramanian, & Nishith, 1973; Jevning, Pirkle, & Wilson, 1977; Lehrer, 1978; Paul, 1969c). I do not believe that relaxation traditions will succumb under the challenge of sophisticated methodologies. To the contrary, I expect relaxation effects will thrive as there develops greater technique refinement and greater selectivity in technique application. Some promising areas of relaxation research include: (a) the study of subject characteristics and subject-technique pairings; (b) component analyses to identify subsets of procedural features that are instrumental to treatment outcome; (c) the assessment, prediction, and manipulation of unsupervised relaxation practice; (d) empirically derived guidelines for effect-specific relaxation dosages with respect to the frequency, duration, and longevity of relaxation practice, and (e) long-term relaxation effects.

CHAPTER 4

Deep Relaxation Methods

This chapter is devoted to instruction in the use of the three most frequently employed methods of inducing deep relaxation—autogenic training, meditation, and progressive relaxation. The descriptor "deep" (a) signifies that the method may produce a large magnitude relaxation effect, as evidenced by physiological and experiential markers, and (b) implies that the subject must assume a static position, that is, comfortably seated or recumbent in a peaceful environment conducive to relaxation. Deep relaxation methods are the traditional relaxation strategies and in both respects noted above, are dissimilar to the more recently popularized brief relaxation methods presented in the following chapter.

AUTOGENIC TRAINING (AT)

AT is largely an imaginal method of relaxation in which the subject adopts a passive attitude, and creates a peaceful environment and comforting bodily sensations in his/her mind.

The standard exercises of AT are composed of six relaxation themes.

   I. Heaviness
  II. Warmth
 III. Cardiac Regulation
 IV. Respiration
  V. Abdominal Warmth
 VI. Cooling of the Forehead

The first two standard exercises, heaviness and warmth, have seven parts each.

1. Right arm
2. Left arm
3. Both arms
4. Right leg
5. Left leg

6. Both legs

7. Arms and legs

In total, the six standard exercises have 18 components, seven for the first, seven for the second, and one each for exercises III through VI. Schultz and Luthe (1959, 1969) recommended one or two training sessions for each of these relaxation components. At this pace, approximately 6 months are required to master the standard exercises of AT. Although this may be the practice of AT's European orthodoxy, its American usage is markedly more compact (Pikoff, 1984a).

I have developed a 25-minute induction for the six standard exercises. The procedure fairly reflects common practice among American therapists, and apparently induces a deep relaxation state. The essential difference in procedure between the compact version, to be described, and the orthodox version is the elimination of prolonged repetition present in the latter. A deeper state of relaxation may be achieved by the orthodox procedure, but the cost in time is enormous. Therapists interested in mastering the original form of AT are referred to Schultz and Luthe (1959, 1969). The following presentation is adapted from these two books.

In a quiet, dimly lit setting, the client is asked to take a comfortable position. Schultz and Luthe (1969, pp. 7–11) recommended lying down on a couch or bed, with a comfortable pillow supporting the head and sometimes the knees as well. AT may also be conducted successfully while reclining in a padded chair or slumping forward in a hard chair, but Schultz and Luthe consider the sitting posture less adequate. With eyes closed, the client assumes a *passive* and *casual* attitude. This attitude is said to be "one of the most important factors" (Luthe, 1963, p. 177) in AT and may be suggested to the client as follows:

> It is important that throughout this procedure you adopt a relaxed, passive, and casual attitude. You cannot force relaxation to occur. Just give up conscious control over your body, and allow your bodily processes to flow naturally. If the relaxation experience does not evolve exactly as you wish, do not become concerned but rather maintain your passive attitude. This will most likely ensure that you will eventually achieve the desired relaxation effect.

To commence the standard exercises, the therapist continues by explaining the role of imagery in AT.

> Autogenic training relies upon your ability to focus on your body and imagine you are getting relaxed. An essential part of this process involves your picturing yourself in a comforting, peaceful environment. Most people choose a scene that is familiar to them, such as lying on the sand at a beach, or sitting in a meadow on a summer day. Take the next few seconds to choose your peaceful scene. (Perhaps some discussion is needed to assist the client in making a selection. This

same scene should be used whenever autogenics are employed. Have the client briefly describe the relaxation scene.) I'm going to help you achieve relaxation by suggesting relaxing sensations for different parts of your body. I will repeat the feelings you are to focus on, and then you are to continue on your own until I suggest a new focus—imagining you are actually experiencing your relaxation scene, focusing on the identified body part, and sensing the identified feeling. To repeat, maintain a relaxed, casual, and passive attitude toward the procedure at all times. If your thoughts wander, or the relaxation is slow to come on, do not be concerned. Maintaining a casual attitude will hasten the eventual emergence of relaxation. (If the client does not find the relaxation scene imagery pleasing, it can be dispensed with entirely or introduced at a later date [Schultz & Luthe, 1969, p. 24].)

The following phrase (standard exercise I.1) is spoken by the therapist in a calm, soothing voice for about 30 seconds.

I am at peace . . . My right arm is heavy . . . My right arm is heavy . . . My right arm is heavy . . . I am at peace . . . My right arm is heavy . . . My right arm is heavy . . . My right arm is heavy. (For left handers this first chant may refer to the left arm. At this point the therapist should repeat the following instructions.) Now continue on your own, imagine you are on the beach (or wherever), and think about the heavy feeling in your right arm.

After about 30 seconds of silence, standard exercise I.2 is introduced. This phrase, as well as all ensuing ones, begins with a call for attention by saying, "Now focus on another image . . . ," or, "The next phrase is . . . ," or, "Let's continue with a new focus . . . ," etc. Exercise I.2 mirrors the format of I.1.

I am at peace . . . I am at peace . . . My left arm is heavy . . . My left arm is heavy . . . I am at peace . . . My left arm is heavy . . . My left arm is heavy . . . My left arm is heavy.

Another 30 seconds are allowed for unassisted meditation. If needed, this may again be prompted by the instruction, "Please continue to imagine heaviness in your left arm as you lie on the peaceful beach."

The first standard exercise, heaviness, continues in this same manner with I.3 (both my arms are heavy) through I.7 (my arms and legs are heavy). In identical fashion, the therapist guides the client through the seven parts of exercise II (warmth). Suggestions of heaviness should be interspersed in exercise II. Exercise II.7 is exemplified.

I am at peace . . . My arms and legs are warm . . . My arms and legs are heavy and warm . . . My arms and legs are warm . . . I am at peace . . . My arms and legs are heavy and warm . . . My arms and legs are warm. (As is always the case, this phrase is followed by the client's silent meditation for a period approximately equal to the duration of the therapist's presentation of the exercise.)

Standard exercise III adds the formula, "Heartbeat calm and regular," to suggestions of heaviness and warmth.

I am at peace . . . My arms and legs are heavy and warm . . . Heartbeat calm and regular . . . Heartbeat calm and regular . . . I am at peace . . . Heartbeat calm and regular . . . Heartbeat calm and regular . . . My arms and legs are heavy and warm . . . Heartbeat calm and regular . . . Heartbeat calm and regular.

This chant is the entirety of standard exercise III, since multiple parts occur only in standard exercises I and II. Standard exercise III takes about 45 seconds to present, and the client is allowed comparable time to meditate.

Standard exercise IV builds on the previous three and is now presented verbatim.

I am at peace . . . My arms and legs are heavy and warm . . . I am at peace . . . Heartbeat calm and regular . . . My breathing is calm . . . My breathing is calm . . . I am at peace . . . My breathing is calm . . . My arms and legs are heavy and warm, heartbeat calm and regular . . . My breathing is calm . . . My breathing is calm . . . My breathing is calm.

Standard exercise V continues to add to the autogenic foci already established.

I am at peace . . . My arms and legs are heavy and warm, heartbeat calm and regular . . . My breathing is calm . . . My breathing is calm . . . My abdomen is warm . . . I am at peace . . . My abdomen is warm . . . My abdomen is warm . . . I am at peace . . . My arms and legs are heavy and warm . . . Heartbeat calm and regular . . . My breathing is calm . . . My abdomen is warm . . . My abdomen is warm . . . My abdomen is warm. (This chant is delivered in about 70 seconds, and equal time is afforded the client for self-reflection.)

The final exercise (VI) is as follows.

I am at peace . . . My arms and legs are heavy and warm, heartbeat calm and regular . . . I am at peace . . . My breathing is calm . . . My abdomen is warm . . . My forehead is cool . . . My forehead is cool . . . I am at peace . . . My breathing is calm . . . My abdomen is warm . . . My forehead is cool . . . My forehead is cool . . . I am at peace . . . My forehead is cool . . . My forehead is cool . . . My forehead is cool.

The combined therapist presentation and client quiet meditation of standard exercise VI lasts about 2 1/2 minutes.

Special Exercises

In the treatment of nonspecific anxiety, or when a global relaxation effect is otherwise desirable, the six standard exercises prove satisfactory. However, when dysfunction or distress is localized, variations on the standard exercises may be invoked to more precisely serve individual needs. Such variations are termed special exercises by Schultz and Luthe, and they fall under two general categories: organ-specific formulae and intentional formulae. Special exercises should be employed only after the standard exercises are well practiced.

Organ-specific Formulae (OF)

OF utilize the same themes comprising the standard exercises, heaviness, warmth, calm and regular, and coolness. These are now tailored to the particular needs of the client. For example, an individual suffering from lower back pain may find the following phrase helpful: "My back is warm." Another person exhibiting a muscular tic on one side of the mouth may profit from "My mouth is calm and regular." Creation of an individualized phrase should be guided by the psychophysiological process associated with the key term, for example, muscular relaxation (heaviness), vasodilation (warmth), and vasoconstriction (coolness). Schultz and Luthe caution against using the formulae of heaviness or warmth in relation to the head, for fear of causing excessive blood flow to that region. Schultz and Luthe (1959) list some 20 disorders with which OF have been effectively employed. Some examples are: "My nose is cool" for hay fever, "My feet are warm" for blushing, "My bladder is warm" for nocturnal enuresis, and (I kid you not) "My anus is heavy" for hemorrhoids.

Intentional Formulae (IF)

These are phrases designed to increase the occurrence of deficient psychological functions or to diminish excessive psychological functions. IF may take one of several different forms. A *neutralizing* formula may be employed to deflate an exaggerated concern or preoccupation. It takes the form "_____ does not matter." *Reinforcing* formulae are utilized to stimulate action or motivation in the face of unproductive inertia. An example is "I am alert and will study longer," employed by a reluctant student. Asserting one's disinterest in a desired object is a method of achieving self-discipline. Termed *abstinence* formulae, one inserts the name of the controversial object or situation into the chant, "I know that I avoid _____." For example, the words cake or alcohol might complete this sentence for obese or alcoholic individuals, respectively.

IF should be practiced daily while in a state of deep relaxation or when confronted with a relevant situation. Although Schultz and Luthe refer to psychoanalytic and hypnotic explanations underlying the operation of IF, a more parsimonious understanding is available. The resemblance of IF to Wolpe's (1958) systematic desensitization and more recent forms of self-control desensitization are inescapable. Physiological relaxation and assertive cognitions are substituted for conditioned anxiety in relation to the stimulus in question.

Autogenic Meditation

Seven meditative exercises comprise an autogenic strategy designed to develop visual imagery. Schultz and Luthe recommended their use only after mastery of the standard exercises. If a client is experiencing difficulty in an imagery-based therapy, then the meditative exercises may be utilized to enhance visual imagery skills and thereby promote therapeutic progress. The training of imagery skills is an important, neglected area of research, and AT is to be commended for its contribution here. The seven exercises are arranged in order of difficulty and complexity. They should be taken in order and successful practice of each should precede advancement. Schultz and Luthe reported that about a month of effort is typically required to produce the visual phenomena associated with each of the following levels, but I have seen clients attain mastery in a fraction of this time. Indeed, clients already possessing moderate imagery facility could proceed through all seven levels in one or two sessions.

1. *Spontaneous experience of colors.* During periods of prolonged relaxation up to 60 minutes, vivid colors will spontaneously occur in imagination. Statistically, the first colors to appear cannot be predicted, although personal preferences do exist.

2. *Experience of selected colors.* The colors that most frequently appeared during level 1 are now produced on demand. The chromatic range may be extended until most colors are under control.

3. *Visualization of concrete objects.* The client is instructed to persevere with a passive attitude until an image of a concrete object spontaneously occurs. Training is continued until a variety of concrete objects can be imaginally generated with clarity on demand.

4. *Visualization of abstract objects.* The focus is now placed on abstract words, for example, truth, justice, friendship. Representations of this material often take a dreamlike form accompanied by auditory imagery.

5. *Experience of a selected state of feeling.* Emotions, desires, or moods having personal meaning to the client supply the imagery themes. The resulting imagery may take a realistic or symbolic form.

6. *Visualization of other persons.* At the beginning, the imagery subjects are people who are emotionally neutral to the client. Ultimately, clear, vivid imagery of personally significant people can be generated.

7. *Answers from the unconscious.* Here clients pose psychodynamically rich questions to themselves such as "Who is the one I love?" While in a state of meditation, the client awaits spontaneous emergence of the answer. This psychoanalytic preference in Schultz and Luthe's thinking need not limit the potential usefulness of the creative state attained in level 7. The attributes of

unencumbered thinking and receptivity to diverse possibilities characterizing this level may also be effectively applied to pragmatic current concerns and problem-solving tasks.

Final Comments on Autogenic Training

The core of AT is the six standard exercises. This basic method of relaxation induction is extended to produce the variations of special exercises and autogenic meditation. Autogenic therapy, which is essentially a comprehensive therapy approach, is distinguished from autogenic training by the addition of further elaborations of the standard exercises and the introduction of nonrelaxation therapeutic techniques. A full presentation of autogenic therapy is beyond the scope of this book. The reader interested in mastering autogenic therapy is referred to the six volume collection, *Autogenic Therapy,* edited by Luthe (1969–1973).

MEDITATION

Several theorists (Goleman, 1972b; Naranjo, 1971; Shapiro, 1980) have advanced the notion that the multitude of meditation techniques fall into a few procedurally defined categories. Despite inconsistency in nomenclature, three types are most prominent: focal, diffuse, and mixed. The most common genre, focal meditation, involves mentally or visually dwelling on a single stimulus. The focus of attention may be a word, a phrase, a concept, an image, or an object. In contrast, diffuse meditation methods prohibit repetitive or constant absorption in a restricted range of stimuli, and instead they encourage nonselective openness and expanded breadth of awareness. Mixed types integrate both focal and diffuse aspects without emphasis on either.

Herein I will present a sampling of focal methods involving only a repetitive word or fixed gaze on an object. These approaches typify meditation methods which have won popularity in Western cultures. The breath meditation methods taught in Chapter 5 are best conceptualized as mixed types. Diffuse types of meditation or, more accurately, open lifestyles typified by the philosophies of Gurdjieff (Ouspensky, 1957) and Krishnamurti (1960/1967) have attracted relatively little interest, do not fit well into the meditation for relaxation model, and will not be presented.

For those interested in further reading on noncultic or secular relaxation, Benson (1975) and Carrington (1978a) provided a comprehensive discourse on this subject. For individuals contemplating study of more orthodox Eastern styles of meditation and their accompanying philosophies, I recommend the following books for embarkation: Ram Dass (1971, 1978), Devi (1963), Singh (1970), and Goleman (1977).

Mantra Meditation

During their ongoing program studying the processes and effects of high blood pressure, Herbert Benson and his colleagues considered several relaxation techniques as a treatment for this disorder. In the late 1960s they undertook a series of investigations of Transcendental Meditation (TM), the results of which convinced them of the procedure's psychophysiological potency (Benson, Marzetta, & Rosner, 1974; Benson, Rosner, Marzetta, & Klemchuk, 1974a, 1974b; Wallace & Benson, 1972; Wallace, Benson, & Wilson, 1971). Over the next several years, the meditation procedure was stripped of its religious/philosophical meaning and ornament, as Benson sifted out what he perceived to be the active ingredients responsible for the relaxation effects.

Thus, Benson produced a secularized, efficient meditative technique capable of eliciting *the relaxation response* (Benson, 1974b, 1975; Benson, Beary, & Carol, 1974). This response is claimed to be an innate human relaxation potential triggered by the conjoint operation of four key ingredients. Benson was able to specify these four factors by reviewing the history of relaxed altered states of consciousness and identifying shared characteristics among them (Benson, 1975). These are:

1. *A quiet environment.* The relaxation setting should provide little or no stimulus impingement. Distractors of either a pleasant or noxious sort will impede the emergence of relaxation.

2. *A mental device.* Attention should be consumed by a benign stimulus. A mantra, as prescribed by TM, adequately serves this purpose. So, too, does the repetition of any other convenient word or phrase. Focus on a tactile sensation or fixed gaze on an object accomplish this same end. The basic strategy is to preoccupy oneself with an emotionally neutral, repetitive, monotonous stimulus.

3. *A passive attitude.* This refers to an attitude of unconcerned acceptance. One cannot expedite relaxation by pressured concentration on its achievement. This hard-driving attitude is the perfect opposite of the relaxation prescription and will prevent the emergence of the intended state. The reader will recall that a passive attitude is emphasized in autogenic training and also appears in other types of therapies (e.g., Masters & Johnson, 1970).

4. *A comfortable position.* A comfortable reclined, seated, or even standing position is required. An uncomfortable position will cause distraction.

These four components do seem to grasp the essence of most relaxation strategies and may surprise the reader with their simplicity. Benson recommended creating these conditions, which reliably produce the relaxation response, once or twice daily for 10–20 minutes each. The following verbatim instructions typify an induction.

Please close your eyes and find a comfortable position in your chair. Let your body relax simply by allowing it to be limp. Review your muscles and let them relax. Most importantly, try to create a relaxed attitude in your mind. You cannot force relaxation to occur. Just relax and let it happen. Breathe through your nose at an easy, calm pace, and say the word *one* to yourself with each exhalation. Every time you breathe out, slowly repeat *one* silently to yourself. This word serves to focus your attention on internal feelings of relaxation and will help the relaxation grow. Should your mind wander, do not be concerned. Return your attention to the word "one" in a calm, untroubled manner. Please continue for about 15 minutes.

Benson recommends the word *one* in this procedure because of its neutral, unremarkable qualities. It is interesting to note, however, the similarity between the words *one* and *om*. The latter is one of the most significant yoga mantras representing the deity Brahma (Eliade, 1954/1969; Morgan, 1953). Benson points out that any other simple, euphonic, nonemotionally charged word would do as well as *one*. Benson's view is supported by the small amount of existing research addressing this issue (see Delmonte, 1983 and Chapter 3 herein). According to yoga beliefs, the sound of the mantra and vibrations generated throughout the body during silent meditation mobilize physical and spiritual resources including Kundalini energy (Douglas, 1971; Singh, 1970; Yogi, 1975). Some schools of meditation, including TM, advance the unsupported claim that only a master teacher can select the mantra perfectly suited to the personality and physiology of the aspirant.

I encourage clients to select a special word or mantra that feels comfortable for them. Clients usually find words such as *peace, calm,* or *relax* to their liking. The innumerable meditation sects offer other possibilities that some clients find appealing. Examples are the Hare Krishna chant of Bhakti Yoga (Prince, 1978), common Sanskrit mantras such as *Ah-nam, Shi-rim,* or *Ra-mah* recommended by Carrington (1978a), repeating the sequence of counting from 1 to 10 as in Zen Buddhism (Chang, 1959), or any of the Sanskrit mantras listed in Table 4.1.

To extend the influence of meditation beyond the boundaries of the actual practice sessions, most schools of meditation encourage the trainee to become what amounts to being obsessed with their mantra during all waking moments (Kapleau, 1966; Ram Dass, 1978). Though more extreme, this practice parallels the use of a cue word in self-control relaxation (see Chapter 5).

Traditionally, Eastern meditators have emphasized the importance of bodily positions during meditation, although Benson and most other Western experts (e.g., Shapiro, 1980) do not share this view. The supreme goal is the lotus position, with each foot perched upon the opposing thigh, and the back and head held straight (see Kapleau, 1966, pp. 315–320, for a picture of this position and several variations). However, even the half lotus with only the left foot raised thusly poses a grievous mechanical problem and should not even be attempted by most people. The best position for a client is the one that seems right to him or her. Sitting American Indian style on the floor or

TABLE 4.1. Eastern Mantras

Source	Mantras
Buddhism	
Ram Dass, 1971	Om
	Rama
	Gate Gate Paragate
	Parasamgate Bodhi Swaha
	Om Mani Padme Hum
	Om Tat Sat
	Om Namah Shivaya
Yoga	
Singh, 1970	Aham Braham Asmi
	Ayam Athma Brahman
	Soham
	Sohang
	Hansa
	Aham-sah
Feuerstein, 1975; Govinda, 1959	Om (brain)
(A mantra for each of six energy	Ham (respiratory system)
centers in Kundalini Yoga.)	Yam (circulatory system)
	Ram (stomach)
	Vam (secretion and reproduction)
	Lam (sexuality)
Transcendental Meditation	
Morse & Furst, 1982	Eng
(There are allegedly a total	Enga
of 16 TM mantras.)	Shirim
	Hirim

on a pillow is comfortable to many. Meditation may also be done while reclining, sitting in a chair, standing, or walking (Dhammasudhi, 1968, p. 53; Kapleau, 1966, p. 33; Sivananda, 1971, p. 82). If one is moved to shift posture during the meditation, this need not be avoided but should be done slowly and with awareness.

Similarly, there are classical guidelines for what one should do with the hands during meditation. One may rest the palms in the lap, one upon the other, face upward, and touch the thumbs to form an ellipse as in Zen Buddhism (illustrated in Kapleau, 1966), or place each hand on the ipsilateral knee, palm up and fingers outstretched, with the thumb and forefinger forming a circle, as in Kundalini Yoga (pictured in Sivananda, 1971). Ultimately, here, too, personal preference should guide decisions.

Detailed personal accounts of progressive relaxation and autogenic training are unavailable. Not so with meditation. The interested reader might find it facilitative of his/her own meditation experience to share that of others (Kapleau, 1966; Luk, 1964; Walsh, 1977, 1978).

Gaze Meditation

This method substitutes a visual point of focus for the mantra to occupy one's attention. The above discussion, concerning sitting postures and hand placement in mantra meditation, applies equally to gaze meditation.

Gaze meditation was first emphasized in Tantra Yoga and the object of focus was termed a *yantra* (Douglas, 1971; Feuerstein, 1975). Typically, yantras were complex, colorful abstract designs relying heavily on geometric shapes to represent deities and elements of nature. The most common yantra was the circular pattern called *mandala*. Alternatively, one may employ the picture of a revered individual, such as the Buddha (Chang, 1963), a flower (Carrington, 1978a), a fruit (Humphreys, 1935/1970), a lit candle (Ram Dass, 1971), a dot on a blank wall (Singh, 1970; Sivananda, 1971), and so on. With eyes opened or closed, one may gaze upon or imagine a part of one's own body. As prescribed in the classic writings, the body part selected would usually be a *chakra* or "energy" point, e.g., navel, heart, point between eyebrows (Singh, 1970).

Gaze meditation may be performed in a special part of the home decorated to create a peaceful, conducive environment employing rugs, art objects, special books, etc. (Ram Dass, 1971). Incense and other fragrances can also enhance the meditation experience. There is no consensus on the exact positioning of the object of focus. Typically, it would be a few feet away from the meditator at about eye level or no more than some 30 degrees above or below this plane, usually below. The room should be dimly lit, by natural light if convenient, and the eyelids should be comfortably situated, perhaps half-closed. It is most important to avoid eye strain in gaze meditation (Mishra, 1959, p. 66). When such discomfort appears, the practitioner should close his/her eyes for a time and continue the focus on the object in imagination.

In this manner, one simply sits motionless and gazes at the yantra. As in any other form of meditation, a passive, accepting attitude is a key ingredient. The mind will wander, more at the beginning than at an advanced level, and this must be patiently tolerated.

Over time, the appearance and meaning of the yantra will shift in one's mind (Deikman, 1963). As with a kaleidoscope or a Rorschach card, the meditator will provide structure for ambiguous forms and will create ambiguity where structure existed. The yantra will stimulate images, thoughts, and feelings eventually leading to deeper states of meditation.

PROGRESSIVE RELAXATION (PR)

In its original form (Jacobson, 1929), PR involved relaxing two or three muscle groups per session till some 50 groups covering the entire body had been relaxed. Oftentimes, several sessions would be devoted to a single resistant muscle group before advancing to the next. Typically, a client required 3 to 6

months to achieve complete mastery of the technique. However, unlike autogenic training, PR has undergone systematic revision and abbreviation over
the years, though this was not prompted by Jacobson himself. Jacobson
(1964b) did alter the PR procedure in his method of self-operations control,
but this did not serve to condense the format. Self-operations control trains
the client in the philosophy of self-control through minimal expenditure of
muscular energy. Thus, this procedural variation of PR emphasizes efficiency
in the engineering of movement. However, this method is no less cumbersome
than the original.

As indicated in Chapter 1, from the very first, Jacobson recognized the
value of shorter PR formats and practiced such with a certain number of his
patients. Indeed, some 50 years after his initial inquiries into relaxation, Jacobson (1967b) still prescribed condensed versions. These notable exceptions
notwithstanding, a lengthy, cumbersome PR procedure has rightly been associated with Jacobson, and has deterred professionals otherwise inclined toward
employing relaxation therapy.

As outlined in Chapter 1, Wolpe (1958) introduced the first major overhaul
of PR, so that it could be conveniently employed as an incompatible response
to inhibit anxiety. Wolpe thinned Jacobson's procedure down to about six
sessions, primarily by omitting many of the small muscle groups included in
the original format. By the mid 1960s the procedure had been streamlined
further, in the interest of time economy, by the disciples and adherents of
Wolpe. This latter form successively relaxes about 15 muscle groups in about
20 minutes. Current usage of the term, progressive relaxation, refers to this
20-minute format. King (1980) recommended the formal term "abbreviated
progressive relaxation" to distinguish it from the original, but this nomenclature has not gained wide use.

It should be added at this point that even further abbreviations of PR have
been popularized in the last several years, though these probably do not
achieve a depth of relaxation comparable to the deep relaxation methods. The
condensed versions are more appropriately considered self-control strategies
and are discussed in detail in the following chapter.

Current PR practice basically involves tensing and then relaxing the major
muscle groups of the body. Lehrer, Batey, Woolfolk, Remde, and Garlick
(1983) remind us that Jacobson employed only a small amount of muscle tensing during the preliminary stages of training, and that for the most part,
Jacobson simply asked clients to focus their attention on muscle sensations as
in what is now called passive relaxation. Unfortunately, standardization does
not exist on key procedural variables. This point is illustrated by decisions
such as which muscle groups should be included, in what order they should
be presented, and what type and amount of verbal suggestion should be provided by the therapist (Hillenberg & Collins, 1982). For example, Jacobson
(1940a, 1970) insisted that the therapist not supply verbal suggestions of relaxation, and some current practitioners strictly adhere to this recommendation (Lehrer, Atthowe, & Weber, 1980; McGuigan, 1984; Shapiro & Lehrer,

1980). However, other current researchers of comparable regard endorse the use of relaxation patter (Bernstein & Borkovec, 1973; Rosen, 1976). What little data exist on the relative merits of orthodox Jacobsonian relaxation versus current practice find no significant difference (Snow, 1977; Turner, 1978). Wolpe (1973) introduced still other innovations. Unlike most therapists, he models some of the tense-release operations to help clients master proper procedure.

Similar disagreement exists as to whether each muscle group needs to be tensed once (Cautela & Groden, 1978; Rimm & Masters, 1979; Taylor, 1978), or several times (Paul, 1966a; Rosen, 1976). The only study to address this issue, albeit indirectly, trained mouse-phobic students in two taped PR sessions with either one tense-release cycle per muscle group or repeated cycles on an as-needed basis (Linder & McGlynn, 1971). All subjects next went through the systematic desensitization procedure. Pre-post behavioral avoidance tests revealed that both groups made significant gains and outperformed no-treatment and placebo groups, but were no different from each other.

Issues such as these lend themselves to empirical test, but adequate trials have not yet been conducted. The hypnosis literature can serve to illustrate the type of research needed to clarify some of these PR issues, and also can provide some insight into their resolution. For example, Barber and Calverley (1965a, 1965b) found that suggestions of relaxation (i.e., relaxation patter) did enhance subjects' relaxation experience during hypnotic inductions.

Following is an induction that fairly reflects common practice. The client should be comfortably seated or reclined with eyes closed in a dimly lit room.

Please keep your eyes closed throughout the following procedure. I am going to ask you to tense the different muscles of your body, and when I do, tense them as much as you can until I say "relax." Then let your muscles return to the resting state immediately. Throughout the tensing and relaxing phases, it is most important to focus all of your attention on the sensations coming from your muscles.

Each of the following 16 muscle-group cycles is composed of a muscle tension phase lasting about 7 seconds, followed by a 45-second relaxation phase. The therapist ought to be providing tension patter in a crisp voice, followed by relaxation patter in a soothing tone, during the tension and relaxation phases, respectively. The tension phases are initiated by the instruction "When I say 'now' go ahead and . . . ," or "at the signal, please. . . . " Each tension phase is terminated with the cue "relax."

1. "Tense the muscles of your right hand and forearm by clenching your fist." Following is a verbatim account that will be given only for this first tense-relax cycle.

When I say "now," go ahead and tense the muscles of your right hand and forearm by clenching your fist. Now. Keep it tight, feel the strain, the tension, the muscles are working so hard, and relax (7 seconds). Relax completely, relax immediately. Just give up control of the muscles and let them lie there quietly. Compare in your mind the feelings of tension you were feeling just a few seconds ago in your right hand and forearm to the restful relaxation that is gradually emerging now. The more carefully you focus your attention on the feelings of serenity and tranquility, the greater the relaxation effect you will enjoy. Feel the peaceful, calm sensations growing more and more (45 seconds).

The therapist may vary the particular content of the tension-relaxation patter for each cycle. The amount of relaxation patter should gradually decrease both within and across phases to minimize the client's dependence on the therapist's voice. Thus, there should be longer periods of therapist silence at the end of each relaxation phase than at the beginning, and less patter during relaxation phases occurring later in a session than earlier ones. Gradual diminution of therapist patter also continues across training sessions.

2. "Tense the large muscle in your right upper arm, the biceps, by bending your arm at the elbow and flexing." At this point, it may be appropriate to point out that the client is also generating unnecessary tension in the right hand and forearm. With the intent of optimizing the client's ability to discriminate subtle body phenomena and minimize total muscle expenditure, instruct the client to relax the hand and forearm while tensing the biceps. You will usually notice the hand going limp at this point. This creates a good opportunity for the therapist to suggest the following. "Hereafter, always try to maintain the greatest amount of relaxation by tensing only those muscles that you intend to tense." At several points later on, make comments such as "While you were tensing your back, your face appeared nice and relaxed. That was done very well."

3. "Tense the muscles of your left hand and forearm by clenching your fist."

4. "Tense the muscles of your left biceps in the same manner that you did your right."

5. "Tense the muscles of your forehead by raising your eyebrows as high as they will go and wrinkling your forehead."

6. "Tense the muscles in the middle portion of your face by closing your eyes tightly and wrinkling your nose."

7. "Tense your lower face by pressing both your lips and teeth together, and pressing your tongue against the roof of your mouth."

8. "Tense your neck. There are many muscles there that act to pull your neck in different directions. You can tense all of these at the same time by trying to move your neck in four directions simultaneously. Doing this, your neck will not be able to move in any direction, although you may feel a shaking or tremor there since all the muscles are tugging against each other." Some clients have difficulty with this one. Several cycles in separate left, right, forward, or back positions may be required, particularly if neck tension is a chronic problem for the client.

A breathing exercise should be interposed at this point if the therapeutic goal is an abbreviated self-control format of PR as described in Chapter 5. "Before going on, to help deepen the relaxation, I want you to take five deep breaths and hold each one for about 5 seconds. Softly say the word 'relax' as you exhale slowly and quickly scan your body to seek out and deepen the feelings of relaxation." Ultimately, the breathing technique will help cue relaxation in the natural environment and will be explained in complete detail in the next chapter. If self-control relaxation is not the desired goal, then the breathing exercise can be omitted.

9. "Tense the large muscle groups in your upper back by pulling your shoulders back as though you were trying to touch them behind you."

10. "Tense the muscles of your chest and abdomen by simultaneously pulling your shoulders in front of you and tensing your stomach."

11. "Tense the muscles in your right upper leg. Similar to the neck, the thigh has many muscles that work in opposition. You can tense all of these at the same time by raising your right leg about an inch and making your thigh hard."

12. "Tense your right calf by pointing your foot and toes forward. Don't strain too hard as this muscle has a tendency to cramp." (This tension phase should last only about 3 seconds.)

13. "Tense your right ankle and shin by pointing your foot and toes toward your face."

14. "Tense your left thigh by raising your left leg about an inch and making it rigid."

15. "Tense your left calf by pointing your foot and toes forward." (Tense for 3 seconds.)

16. "Tense your left ankle and shin by pointing your foot and toes toward your face."

This completes the PR induction. The following list can be drawn upon to assist the therapist in varying the relaxation patter.

smooth muscles	quiet	pleasurable	tightness decreasing
loose muscles	placid	pleasant	strain diminishing
soft muscles	limp	peaceful	tension leaving
slack muscles	calm	tranquil	soothing
motionless	warm	comfortable	restful
stillness	serene	heavy	

As was the case with the organ-specific formulae in autogenic training, it is common practice to revise these 16 muscle groups to accommodate individual needs. If any of these 16 sites are already strained or otherwise subject to aggravation, then that cycle or those cycles should be omitted to avoid further insult. For example, omit the back, stomach, and possibly thigh muscles with a client experiencing lower back pain. On the other hand, if there exists a particular need for relaxation in a body zone, then it should receive special attention. The cycles for the face, neck, and shoulders might be repeated two or three times in treating a tension headache sufferer. Instead of routinely tensing and relaxing each muscle group several times, which, in my opinion, creates a laborious procedure yielding little additional benefit to most clients, the therapist can simply ask the client if a muscle group is relaxed before going on to the next. Alternatively, the therapist can identify troublesome muscle groups by questioning the client before beginning the relaxation induction and can plan to selectively repeat these groups.

Marchetti, McGlynn, and Patterson (1977) employed a clever strategy to address this concern. Subjects were conveniently outfitted with a telegraph key, which they depressed to signal the therapist to repeat the prior muscle group. To exemplify the idiographic approach recommended herein, only a few muscle groups might be relaxed for economy in treating a client who is experiencing clearly delimited tension in a relatively small body zone, and who would not derive any particular benefit from a global relaxation effect. On the other extreme, the 20-minute PR procedure presented above may be inadequate for clients experiencing massive anxiety. For these individuals, entire sessions may be devoted to several repetitions of just a few muscle groups (Lehrer, 1982), thus emulating the original pace of PR.

DEEP RELAXATION PROCEDURAL ELEMENTS IN COMMON

The three relaxation strategies presented in this chapter exhibit similar procedural features. Beyond the mechanics of administration which distinguish one from the other, there are numerous therapeutic concerns that require attention irrespective of induction method. These elements in common will now be discussed.

Therapist Preparation

Whether relaxation is a small part of a broadly defined, long-term therapy or the primary focus of a time-limited therapeutic contact, the general standards of ethical conduct and interpersonal sensitivity governing conventional therapies apply equally to relaxation therapy. Clients' trust in and respect for the therapist serve to encourage clients' willingness to close their eyes, relinquish bodily control, and submit to intense self-exploration. The techniques presented in this chapter are intended for use by graduate students and therapists already schooled in one or more of the widely recognized, interpersonally based therapies: psychodynamic, behavioral, client-centered, emotive/experiential, etc. A "therapist" equipped solely with an arsenal of relaxation techniques will fail to meet the complex challenge posed by clients. Individuals are sometimes cast in the therapist role without having broad, formal psychotherapy training. This may occur, for example, in hospital settings. These therapists should at least be alerted to the fact that relaxation therapy is not a panacea. A narrowly-defined relaxation therapy can bring unexpected emotional problems to the surface that must either be dealt with by the therapist or referred to an appropriate colleague.

Speaking on the subject of who is qualified to administer autogenics (and by implication other relaxation methods), Luthe (1970a, p. 150) advocated what I believe to be an extreme, untenable, and unenforceable position. He would restrict the practice of autogenics to physicians and, when *closely supervised,* psychologists. I respect the able skills nurtured in the many helping professions. I think the public's best interests are served by encouraging practitioners from diverse professions to draw upon autogenics (and other methods of relaxation), constrained only by prudent judgment and the limits of their individual training.

There is little data speaking to the question of how much training is needed to conduct relaxation therapy successfully. Clinical trials that have included comparisons of experienced and inexperienced therapists have found superior relaxation effects occurring with the former (Holroyd & Andrasik, 1978; Turner & Ascher, 1982) and no difference between the two (Blanchard, Andrasik, Neff, et al., 1983; Lick & Heffler, 1977; Russell & Wise, 1976).

There has been no research on ways of training relaxation therapists. Some authors (e.g., Cox & Meyer, 1978) have employed such plausible training devices as readings, viewing videotapes of inductions, and practice with nonclients, but there is no data to demonstrate the necessity of any of these. The following suggestions likewise have not been subjected to scientific scrutiny.

I recommend two steps prior to the clinical use of relaxation. First, the therapist should have thorough academic and personal knowledge of the relaxation experience; in other words, the therapist should invite a colleague to perform a relaxation induction on him or her and then practice relaxation daily for several weeks. In this way, the therapist will become aware of procedural and experiential nuances of relaxation that are difficult to convey in prose. If the therapist could arrange to receive a relaxation induction by more than one colleague, all the better. This can only enhance one's ability to effectively conduct relaxation therapy.

Second, the relaxation methods should be practiced on friends, family, or other volunteers until the therapist's style achieves a smooth, professional quality. Some therapists may sort out helpful information from audiotapes of their own inductions leading to self-improvement. While quiescent and attentive to the therapist's voice, clients will readily detect a halting, unsure therapist who is struggling to communicate a method of relaxation. The clinical setting is not the time for the therapist to obtain needed practice.

Client Characteristics

The inclusion of relaxation in therapy may be suggested by either the therapist or the client. There are important client characteristics that should be considered by the therapist before suggesting relaxation or acquiescing to the client's proposal. At this stage, the therapist should not be weighing the comparative merits of relaxation method particularities, but should be assessing medical and psychological factors that may preclude any form of relaxation for a period of time.

Medical or quasi-medical disorders often provide the reason for employing relaxation therapy. Essential hypertension, headache, chronic pain, acute anxiety attacks, and stomach ulcers are examples. The therapist should secure medical clearance before the presentation of relaxation or any other psychotherapeutic approach for such disorders. If the client is currently under a physician's care for the disorder in question, then the client may be receiving medication that would require adjustment as the relaxation therapy exerts an impact. As a case in point, biofeedback training with diabetics can alter metabolic processes and necessitate reduction of daily insulin dosage (Fowler, Budzynski, & VandenBergh, 1976; Seeburg & DeBoer, 1980). Others (Benson, 1977; Hartman & Reuter, 1983; Schultz & Luthe, 1969, p. 116) have reported a similar insulin response with diabetic relaxation practitioners (see also *Diabetes* section, Chapter 7).

Alternatively, if a client is not under a physician's care for a particular symptom that might plausibly have an organic basis, then a medical screening is in order. Relaxation therapy is a major component within the burgeoning field of behavioral medicine (Pomerleau & Brady, 1979), and therapists who advocate relaxation will frequently encounter medically-oriented symptoms in their practice. Such therapists would do well to heed the cautions offered above, as well as establish an ongoing relationship with a physician who stands ready to consult.

Some clients will balk at the mention of relaxation and add, "I've tried it and it doesn't work." Turk, Meichenbaum, and Genest (1983, p. 261) recommend that the therapist thoughtfully respond to such an assertion.

> It is important for the therapist to understand exactly what the patient means by the judgment 'tried relaxation' and also by 'it did not work.' The therapist is listening for such parameters as the type of relaxation, timing, criteria for success, duration of efforts, how and when the patient was trained, and the nature of the patient's self-statements about the utility of relaxation and his or her reactions following failure.

Following exploration of issues such as these, this matter may be resolved in a variety of ways: (a) relaxation will not be pursued, (b) the method of relaxation with which the client is familiar will be presented with modifications to correct past problems, or (c) a different method of relaxation will be presented.

Certain psychiatric types have proved to be difficult relaxation subjects. Fewtrell (1984) presented some data suggesting that individuals with feelings of depersonalization may not respond well to relaxation. Persons who are actively schizophrenic or exhibit a paranoid view of life will usually be resistant to relaxation, although there are reports of successes with the psychoses using TM (Stroebel & Glueck, 1978) and autogenics (Luthe & Schultz, 1969b; Shibata & Motoda, 1967a). In the case of paranoia, the issue of trust may become a major preoccupation when clients are asked to close their eyes and follow the relaxation instructions. Yorkston and Sergeant (1969) reported that some 3 percent of their psychiatric sample of 92 subjects refused to close their eyes and could not relax. Indeed, merely dimming the lights may suffice to precipitate a flood of paranoid ideation. Individuals who are relaxation phobic (Hallam & Jakes, 1985; LaFemina, 1979), due to a negative association, and who display an aversion to internal focusing, etc., would respond similarly.

A substantial number of therapy sessions may have to be designated for developing a relationship prior to attempting relaxation with such individuals. This "courtship" may eventually lead to the client's comfortable acceptance of relaxation. In accordance with the logic of in vivo desensitization (Craighead, Kazdin, & Mahoney, 1976) and operant shaping procedures (Morris, 1973), the therapist can permit paranoid clients and others to keep their eyes open, with lights at normal setting initially, but gradually introduce and extend periods with eyes closed and dim light. The social phobic client will require a treatment protocol similar to that given the paranoid individual. In this case, the client may be so bound by sympathetic arousal and cognitive distress that the initial potency of relaxation would appear feeble by comparison. Relaxation should be introduced when the client is psychologically acclimated to therapy. Once mastered in the clinic and home settings, relaxation may then be applied to symptomatic concerns.

For many individuals, the lack of structure characterizing mantra meditation is somewhat unsettling. This is particularly true of those who stand to profit the most from relaxation, people who are highly structured and time pressured, namely, the Type A personality (Matthews, 1982). Therefore, the method of mantra meditation and other relatively unstructured methods of relaxation possess value as an assessment tool. Clinical experience supports this view. I have observed an inverse correlation between a client's ability to tolerate breath mindfulness meditation and prominence of Type A personality pattern.

The sexual element may surface as the therapist is softly presenting the relaxation scenario in a dimly lit room (Benson, Kotch, & Crassweller, 1978; Bernstein & Given, 1984; Langevin, Stanford, & Block, 1975). The therapist is advised to take precautionary measures if the nature of the therapist-client relationship is receptive to such suggestion.

The above comments on subject characteristics are born of clinical experience and conjecture. Very little systematic research has been conducted on the subject of what kinds of individuals can profit most from relaxation (notable exceptions to this statement occur in the headache and insomnia literatures discussed in Chapter 7), as distinct from the question of what types of symptoms are amenable to relaxation therapy. To the extent that restricted environmental stimulation techniques (REST, Suedfeld, 1980) overlap with methods of relaxation (see discussion in Chapter 2), some hypotheses on clients' response to relaxation could potentially be generated by the results of parallel REST research. The REST literature contains numerous attempts to identify subject characteristics that correlate with tolerance of REST (Suedfeld, 1980), examining such variables as age, sex, occupation, hearing capacity, anxiety level, and introversion-extraversion. To summarize the considerable amount of literature in this area, no strong, consistent relationships have been found between any of these, or other variables studied, and reaction to REST. Although the outcomes of the REST investigations do not encourage analogous ventures in relaxation research, questions of this sort in the area of relaxation are highly important, and continued efforts along these lines are needed.

Relaxation Procedure Selection

Research has not demonstrated powerful advantages of one relaxation technique over another. Except in a few cases, the decision to employ a particular relaxation technique is a matter of clinical discretion. Administering relaxation can become very boring for the therapist, and the therapist may wish to alternate relaxation procedures with successive clients to preserve his/her concentration and alertness. By virtue of one's training, perceived client responsivity, or comments by colleagues, preferences for one of the relaxation methods may be reinforced (either causatively or superstitiously) over time. Although there probably are optimum matches between particular relaxation techniques and clients' characteristics, empirical rules do not exist to guide such decisions.

The client may express a preference, directly or implicitly, for a relaxation method. Previous exposure to relaxation from actual experience, reading, conversation, etc., may negatively or positively predispose the client to a particular relaxation approach. The client's knowledge of relaxation methods should be ascertained by interview, and the relaxation procedure selection decision should follow accordingly. In support of this policy is one piece of research (Gordon, 1976) suggesting that allowing clients to exercise choice in relaxation procedure selection enhances clients' perceived value of the procedure and perceived relaxation effect. If a client preference does not exist, as is typically the case, the choice again reverts to clinical discretion.

Circumstances will sometimes arise that suggest one method over another. Siegal and Lichstein (1980) have raised the possibility that progressive relaxation might prove unsuitable for the elderly, due to the physical strenuousness of the procedure. These concerns led Yesavage (1984) to delete the neck and back components of progressive relaxation training for his elderly subjects.

Similarly, physical ailments such as arthritis or muscle sprain would partially or entirely preclude this method. Alternatively, a focal symptom requiring localization of relaxation effect might particularly benefit from progressive relaxation. For example, clients distressed by a "heaviness on the chest" (commonly reported by highly anxious clients) or by tension headache, could repeat tense-relax cycles in the affected body regions until relief appears. Such localization of effect is also possible with the organ-specific formulae of autogenic training, but meditation is not well suited to deal with focal distress.

Procedural complexity may at times be a relevant factor. The simplicity of Benson's procedure may enable it to succeed with a client of modest intellectual ability, where the multiplicity of steps involved in progressive relaxation and autogenic training would overwhelm and befuddle the same client. Conversely, some clients may be disappointed by the ritualistically barren relaxation response technique (Goldstein, Shapiro, Thananopavarn, & Sambhi, 1982). To them it appears as merely the remains of what used to be a robust procedure. From a slightly different point of view, individuals disposed to an obsessive-compulsive personality style will have diminished tolerance for relaxation techniques residing on the lower end of the procedural complexity dimension (meditation). Conversely, individuals who endorse a "free" lifestyle and revel in ambiguity tend to be uncomfortable with approaches that are high on this continuum (e.g., progressive relaxation).

In extracting the key elements of relaxation, Benson may have overlooked what may have seemed to him a superfluous ingredient—ritual for ritual's sake. The importance of therapeutic ceremony in raising client expectations and enlisting clients' active cooperation has been discussed at length elsewhere (Torrey, 1972). An elaborate ritual is important to some clients, and Benson's meditation method will not be readily accepted by these individuals.

Introducing Relaxation Therapy

Some clients will select a therapist because of that person's reputed expertise in relaxation therapy. Prior to the first therapy session, these clients have already diagnosed their disorder and prescribed relaxation. In these cases, the therapist must resist the temptation to hastily apply a relaxation technique, in favor of conducting his/her own assessment in accordance with current professional standards. Indeed, the therapist may have to exert considerable restraint to resist the zeal with which some clients seek the rapid relaxation cure of their malady.

The more typical case involves a client who seeks therapy with only a global, vague, media-induced notion of Freud and dream interpretation defining his expectations of therapy. Many of these clients have little or no prior knowledge of relaxation. Expecting therapy to consist primarily of childhood reminiscences, the client may react with surprise or negativism to the suggestion of relaxation. Such a situation calls for educating the client as to the existence of many different therapy approaches, with particular reference to the rationale and merits of short-term therapy (see Small, 1971, for an extended discussion of this subject), and symptom-specific therapy (this primarily derives from learning theory-based therapies and numerous survey texts are available on this subject, e.g., Craighead, Kazdin, & Mahoney, 1976; Rimm & Masters, 1979; Wilson & O'Leary, 1980). A substantial amount of time may have to be invested to orient the client as to the common use and potential effectiveness of relaxation in order to promote receptivity and cooperation in the client. This didactic approach to global attitude change is followed up with an analysis of the role of stress in the client's problem and the natural role relaxation can play in treatment.

The typical kind of reasoning offered here to the client raises the issues of chronicity, automaticity, and response stereotypy in a given individual's pattern of responding to stress. Psychogenic ulcer may serve as an example. A woman exposed to marital stress, work-related stress, etc., over a long period of time (chronicity), may now find herself to be tense and anxious in these settings even when an immediate threat is absent (automaticity), and characteristically suffers stomach upset (response stereotypy), which may or may not be accompanied by other stress symptoms. Therefore, effective treatment includes (but is not limited to) neutralizing the automaticity and response stereotypy features by substituting relaxation for tension. The presence of an environmental stressor encourages but does not preordain an individual's self-destructive anxiety response. Mastery of relaxation increases the probability that the client will be able to maintain a calm, adaptive posture in the face of stressors.

Elements of Induction Procedure

The induction procedures for the three relaxation methods presented in this chapter may be broken down into similar components. These will now be discussed.

Rationale

While the introduction of relaxation therapy can take numerous sessions, the rationale is usually brief. I define the rationale as the relaxation procedure's summary justification, including a historical overview and mode of physiological operation. It is presented after the introduction has convinced the client of the general usefulness of relaxation and immediately before the actual relaxation induction.

At one time, it was my practice to deliver long-winded, scientifically sophisticated rationales, until I realized that the majority of clients did not understand and/or were not interested in this information. Little data are available on the usefulness of relaxation rationales, but it appears that there is little or no advantage to presenting a particularly thorough one (Bennett & Millard, 1985; Riley, Berry, & Kennedy, 1986). Therefore, I arrived at a concise rationale that basically communicates two bits of information: (a) this is a legitimate, well-established procedure, and (b) it works. Should a more detailed rationale be required, it can be constructed from Chapter 2 of this text or derived from Bernstein and Borkovec (1973).

Typically, the lights are dimmed, and the client is asked to close his/her eyes and assume a comfortable position. At this point, the rationale commences the first induction and need not be repeated in future sessions. Following is a verbatim rationale.

> The relaxation procedure you're about to learn was developed about 50 years ago and has since undergone several revisions and refinements. The relaxing effects of the procedure have been well documented in controlled research, and it is a method commonly employed by psychotherapists. It will likely produce a substantial physiological relaxation in you, including decreases in heart rate, perspiration, respiration, etc., and experientially you will feel very calm and at ease. This is not hypnosis. You will not lose consciousness or be psychologically controlled in any way. Let's begin.

The entire rationale takes less than a minute. The hypnosis disclaimer is routinely included to dissipate any concerns or suspicions clients sometimes have in confusing hypnosis with relaxation therapy (Hendler & Redd, 1986). Indeed, the disclaimer succeeds in avoiding the occasional inadvertent creation of a trance state.

The above rationale is equally suited for autogenic training or progressive relaxation. It satisfies the curiosity of most clients and rarely invites questioning. However, a lengthier rationale may be required for Benson's meditation procedure. In view of the absence of elaborate ritual in this method, the client may require some additional information to compensate for low face validity. The extended rationale would review the logic employed by Benson by briefly discussing the four key ingredients found in most relaxation techniques: a quiet environment, a mental device, a passive attitude, and a comfortable position.

Setting

Creating the proper atmosphere for relaxation can be useful. Eyeglasses, particularly contact lenses, should be removed. Tight fitting clothing, such as belts, neckties, and shoes, should be loosened. Jewelry that might possibly provide tactile distraction for the client should also be removed. A quiet, dimly lit room, outfitted with a comfortable couch, bed, or chair, is an obvious asset. Many relaxation therapists advocate the supine position, and this was also popular in yoga under the name shavasana or corpse position (Hoenig, 1968). The presence of soothing background music may facilitate relaxation (Nathan, Nathan, Vigen, & Wellborn, 1981; Reynolds, 1984).

By creating a comfortable, quiescent setting, relaxation effects are virtually ensured with most clients, even if the relaxation procedure is itself ineffectual. This phenomenon is termed adaptation and has been well documented in our laboratory (Lichstein, Sallis, Hill, & Young, 1981; Sallis & Lichstein, 1979).

Persons comfortably reclined, with eyes closed in a dimly lit room, will exhibit unambiguous physiological relaxation effects over the next 15 minutes or so, even when no relaxation procedure is presented. In psychophysiology research, adaptation effects are an obstacle to the valid evaluation of relaxation procedures and must be controlled in some manner. For treatment purposes, however, adaptation effects are allied with the goal of producing deep relaxation and are welcome.

Some relaxation therapists (e.g., Clarke & Jackson, 1983, p. 133; Smith, 1985; Thompson, Griebstein, & Kuhlenschmidt, 1980) have suggested that relaxation training be conducted under suboptimal conditions, namely, a moderately comfortable chair in a somewhat noisy environment, to facilitate generalization of treatment effects, inasmuch as stressful situations are highly dissimilar to most training settings. Relative to this point, Freedman, Ianni, and Wenig (1983) presented dramatic data documenting the advantages of training biofeedback under stressful conditions (discussed in greater detail in Chapter 7, *Raynaud's Disease* section).

I think this is a valid hypothesis, and is even more so with the brief relaxation methods intended for use in challenging situations (see Chapter 5). However, a suboptimal environment may pose an insurmountable obstacle to some clients, particularly during the early practice sessions, and thereby deny them a successful relaxation experience. As a guiding principle appropriate for some clients, the relaxation setting should be the least conducive to relaxation without sacrificing the relaxation effect. This principle cannot be more specific as the ability to tolerate relaxation distractors varies greatly across clients, and will increase in a given client with relaxation practice. Similarly, clients should not restrict their relaxation practice to a single location, so that generalization of relaxation skills to other settings is not inhibited (Marquis, Ferguson, & Taylor, 1980).

Therapist's Induction Style

While presenting the relaxation procedure, the therapist should model a casual, passive attitude. Creating a casual atmosphere will itself promote relaxation. Extrapolating from the biofeedback literature (Bregman & McAllister, 1982), it is counterproductive for clients to try too hard to relax.

The therapist should remain seated, enabling the client to become accustomed to a stationary auditory signal. The therapist's voice should be soft, slow, and relaxed. The therapist need not be concerned if some errors occur in the relaxation induction. For example, if one of the muscle groups in the progressive relaxation procedure is mistakenly omitted, then the therapist must casually accept this. If the flow of the relaxation induction is altered and the therapist compulsively goes back to administer the omitted cycle, the therapist risks disruption of the client's relaxation.

Little research has been conducted to test the above or similar assumptions on the best presentation style for relaxation. Some data suggest that no advantages are gained by a direct, persuasive manner versus a collaborative, nondirective manner, but the former is superior to written instructions (Worthington & Feldman, 1981). Data bearing on the advantages of a warm, supportive therapist versus a more formal, matter-of-fact therapist in meditation inductions are equivocal (Cuthbert, Kristeller, Simons, Hodes, & Lang, 1981; see Chapter 3, *Benson's Procedure* part of *Meditation* section for detailed discussion). On the other hand, Corah, Gale, Pace, and Seyrek (1981) found that delivering taped, passive relaxation with a slow, soothing voice was more effective than the same method presented in a conversational tone (see Chapter 7, *Preparation for Medical and Dental Treatment*). Generalizations from the above research must be limited until replications and extensions to varied techniques and subject populations warrant their broad endorsement. At present, therapists must be content to be guided mainly by experience and judgment in this area.

Some individuals are comforted by being touched (Drescher, Whitehead, Morrill-Corbin, & Cataldo, 1985). Although this has not been experimentally tested in the relaxation domain, a reassuring touch on the arm, for example, could facilitate relaxation in clients experiencing difficulty. Therapists inclined to employ this tactic should be cautious not to arouse erotic responses.

Taped Induction

Some therapists employ a homemade or commercial tape recording of a relaxation induction in place of or in addition to a live induction (e.g., Ferguson, Marquis, & Taylor, 1977; Martin, 1970; Sherman, 1982). I do not recommend the use of tape recordings. The existing research on taped versus live inductions (reviewed in Chapter 3) favors the clinical superiority of the latter. On the matter of home practice, employing a tape is inconsistent with the ultimate goal of client self-reliance. Existing research comparing taped and unassisted home relaxation practice found that insomniacs (Lick & Heffler, 1977), anxious individuals (Mayer, Frederiksen, & Scanlon, 1984), and hypertensives (Hoelscher, Lichstein, Fischer, & Hegarty, 1987) derive no advantage from the addition of the tape recording. With a minority of clients, however, taped home practice for a limited time only may be helpful in establishing successful relaxation routines.

Client's Self-administration

Schultz and Luthe (1969) estimated that 40 percent to 60 percent of their clients incorrectly practiced autogenic training at home. In this and other relaxation procedures, errors of content, sequence, and timing are quite common. Asking the client to self-administer the relaxation technique in the therapist's presence permits error detection and constructive feedback on the client's performance.

Here again, the passive, casual attitude is paramount, and absolute adherence to all technique details is not desirable. One feature that is often handled incorrectly, and that cannot be compromised, is timing. This is particularly critical with progressive relaxation and autogenic training because of their segmentation. Clients tend to rush each cycle. While quietly focusing on internal states, a minute feels like an hour. I discourage clients from looking at a clock to establish timing, because this is incompatible with a passive attitude. Rather, the therapist should time the cycles and give appropriate feedback until the client has established natural rhythms approximating the prescribed intervals. Client self-administration of all or part of the relaxation procedure in the office can be done at the end of the first or second relaxation sessions. This is all that is usually needed to assure proper home technique.

Number of Training Sessions

Universal standards do not exist on this subject, but general guidelines have emerged. Transcendental Meditation training requires about six sessions. Progressive relaxation studies usually involve about five sessions and infrequently more than 10 (Borkovec & Sides, 1979b). I think about six sessions should suffice in teaching and refining most techniques. In a related vein, session length and time between sessions may influence relaxation efficacy, but there is little data on variables such as these (Stoudenmire, 1973).

In the clinical endeavor, client feedback dictates much of the decision on when to discontinue training. A related question of greater clinical import is the longevity of client relaxation practice. Presumably, practice outlives training, and the necessity of continued practice cannot be overemphasized to clients. The importance of relaxation practice and related issues are discussed in Chapters 1 and 7.

Terminating Induction

Just before ending the relaxation induction, the therapist should ask, "Is there disturbing tension left in any part of your body?" An affirmative response is countered with additional progressive relaxation cycles, organ-specific autogenic formulae that directly address the specific tension, or other similar measures. One of these methods may be applied even when the original relaxation procedure was Benson's or another meditation technique.

To conclude the induction, the therapist instructs, "Whenever you are ready, open your eyes, and sit up." Some therapists advocate gradualness in the termination, and for example, ask the client to count backwards from 10 to 1 and then sit up, but I have not found any advantage to this. Autogenic training sometimes employs a rousing conclusion by energetically flexing the arms and taking several deep breaths (Luthe, 1963), but the desirability of this is also not apparent to me. During the first few minutes subsequent to the relaxation, clients may feel a little lethargic. The client should remain seated during this time, as physical exertion may bring on dizziness. If the client fell asleep during the relaxation exercises, he/she would be particularly disoriented in the postinduction period.

Besides allowing clients time to readjust to normal functioning, the postinduction period should be used for clients to reflect on their relaxation experience. Most clients will report that they felt relaxed and that it was an enjoyable experience. Others will identify minor difficulties, such as the therapist spoke too fast or too softly, the room was too cold, the client was distracted by bathroom needs, etc.

A common complaint of relaxation novices is mind wandering, the unwanted surfacing of negative and positive thoughts and fantasies unrelated to the relaxation task. The problem of mind wandering is indigenous to virtually all methods of relaxation and has been a central issue in meditation from its inception. For example, Goleman and Epstein (1983) described the Buddhist view of "five hindrances" to concentration in meditation: lust, ill will, sloth, agitation, and doubt. The harder clients try to eliminate mind wandering, the more intrusive the unwelcome thoughts become. Clients should be instructed to maintain a relaxed, tolerant, and nonjudgmental attitude about mind wandering and to refrain from effortful attempts to discipline their thoughts during relaxation. With continued relaxation practice, the tendency for the mind to wander will diminish naturally (Kubose, 1976; Walsh, 1977). Further, as clients learn to be accepting of this frustrating predicament, a more tolerant attitude will generalize to other aspects of their life, and this is a significant, beneficial side-effect of relaxation. Indeed, these psychological changes may generalize more readily to nonrelaxation settings than physiological effects and may represent a principal benefit of relaxation. (See discussion in Chapter 1, *The Blessed Irritant*.)

Clinical Assessment

Relaxation effects may occur in the behavioral, physiological, and/or experiential domains, and effects may emerge early in the induction process. Thus, assessment and induction should occur simultaneously, and their respective implementation benefits from reciprocal influence.

Individuals will sometimes become so relaxed, they will fall asleep in the midst of a relaxation induction or self-practice (e.g., Jones, 1953). If this occurs occasionally, it is probably of little concern. If it occurs regularly, then it may or may not be undesirable. For example, insomniac clients practicing relaxation at bedtime welcome relaxation abbreviated by sleep. Conversely, anxious individuals employing relaxation within a coping skills or self-control framework are deprived of a learning opportunity by sleep. When needed, we have found simple remedies suffice in shielding relaxation from sleep: (a) instruct the client not to fall asleep, (b) add light to the room, or (c) decrease the comfort of the relaxation position.

Experiential Assessment

Self-ratings are perhaps the most common means of assessing relaxation, because they are easily learned and convenient, and because the experiential component of the relaxation process is of crucial importance.

Typically, the therapist describes a 1 to 10 or 1 to 100 scale [as in Wolpe's (1973) subjective units of disturbance (suds)], and the client rates his/her level of relaxation pre-post induction to summarize the experience. Such ratings are routinely used in the office, as well as at home (see Figure 4.5), to gauge relaxation progress. Though convenient, global ratings such as these invite criticism of low sensitivity and reliability.

Webster, Ahles, Thompson, and Raczynski (1984) proposed an interesting self-report variation that may prove useful. They employ a tension mannequin, a simple drawing of the human body mapped off into 16 segments corresponding to muscle clusters customarily employed in progressive relaxation. Segments are separately rated on 5-point scales. These authors presented data to indicate that relaxation is unequally distributed in body zones and that this method distinguishes clinical states, such as head and back pain. Similar use of a human figure drawing to assess autogenic training has also been reported (Luthe, Trudeau, Mailhot, & Vallieres, 1977).

Behavioral Assessment

Easily observable changes in posture, behavior, and overt physiological functions, most notably respiration, are correlated with experiential and physiological indices of depth of relaxation. Figures 4.1 and 4.2 are the most sophisticated instruments available to monitor behavioral indicators of relaxation.

The Relaxation Checklist (Figure 4.1) lists nine relaxation markers that are rated on 5-point scales, anchored by high arousal indicators on the high end and low arousal on the low end. The inventors of this instrument (Luiselli, Steinman, Marholin, & Steinman, 1981) employed it to evaluate the effects of progressive relaxation on conduct-disordered children. They report strong interobserver reliability but no validity data.

The Behavioral Relaxation Scale (Figure 4.2) consists of 10 observable markers and shows considerable content overlap with this other instrument. The therapist or observer rates each dimension 0 (relaxed) or 1 (unrelaxed), depending on the presence of relaxation or tension criteria (briefly outlined in the figure), in each of five consecutive 1-minute intervals. Its originators (Poppen & Maurer, 1982; Schilling & Poppen, 1983) provided strong reliability and validity data supporting its use. Interestingly, they employed this list both as an assessment tool and a relaxation induction strategy (see *Anxiety* and *Children's Problems,* Chapter 7 for further discussion).

While presenting relaxation training, the therapist should be actively scanning all of the relaxation signs enumerated in these two scales, and should allow the information gleaned from this process to govern verbal feedback given to the client as the induction unfolds. Thus, the therapist is monitoring the degree of success of the presentation and giving both encouraging and corrective feedback to the client.

To illustrate, a decrease in the depth and rate of respiration is one of the most convenient, reliable, and universal bodily signs of relaxation. At the beginning of the relaxation induction, the therapist should observe the client's respiratory flow. After several minutes the therapist might say to the client, "I see that your breathing has become slow, shallow, and regular. This indi-

Relaxation Checklist

1. Forehead		
Deeply furrowed or wrinkled	5 4 3 2 1	Smooth
2. Eyes		
Deeply wrinkled, squeezed tightly	5 4 3 2 1	Loosely closed, almost fluttering
3. Neck		
Veins or muscles visible, extended	5 4 3 2 1	Smooth
4. Head		
Held straight, centered	5 4 3 2 1	Tilted to one side or forward
5. Arms		
Closed to body or shoulders raised	5 4 3 2 1	On chair arms or lap or away from body, shoulders forward
6. Hands		
Closed fist, clenching chair, tapping	5 4 3 2 1	Open, palms up, resting on lap or chair arms
7. Legs		
Close together swaying, wiggling	5 4 3 2 1	Apart, knees out, no movement
8. Feet		
Together, flat on floor, tapping	5 4 3 2 1	Apart, resting on heels, toes pointing out
9. Breathing		
Rapid, uneven	5 4 3 2 1	Slow, even

Figure 4.1. Scale of behavioral markers of relaxation developed by Luiselli, Steinman, Marholin, and Steinman (1981). (Reproduced by permission of the publisher, Haworth Press, © 1981.)

cates that a general relaxation effect is already occurring. Were we to monitor your heart rate, sweat gland activity, brain waves, etc., we would find that your entire body is slowing down into a comfortable relaxation." If respiration does not slow down, that alerts the therapist to some difficulty. The therapist might ask the client, "How are you feeling now," and the client could identify some interference with the induction.

Physiological Assessment

While sophisticated physiological instrumentation defines the standard for relaxation assessment, this approach is not available in most clinical settings. There are, nevertheless, convenient and feasible means by which physiological effects may be tracked, and these may provide useful information.

An indisputable, hard sign of relaxation is heart rate slowing, which can be measured simply by taking a pulse. A pre-post pulse assessment will almost always show a pulse decrement due to a combination of adaptation and relaxation effects. This tactic will convince even the most skeptical client of the therapist's wizardry. Morse, Schacterle, Furst, and Bose (1981) reported that increased salivation, sometimes to the point of drooling, is correlated with depth

Behavioral Relaxation Scale

relaxed		*unrelaxed*
	1. Breathing	
below baseline rate		above baseline rate
	2. Quiet	
no vocalization		some vocalizations
	3. Body	
no body movement		body movement present
	4. Head	
in midline and at rest		raised, tilted, or moving
	5. Eyes	
closed and smooth		open, eyeball movement, or eyelids wrinkled
	6. Jaw	
slightly parted		tight or open wide
	7. Throat	
no movement		swallowing or twitching
	8. Shoulders	
sloped, motionless, and in midline		raised, uneven, or moving
	9. Hands	
comfortably curled fingers		clenched, extended, or moving
	10. Feet	
pointing away from each other at about 90° and motionless		verticle, horizontal, or moving

Figure 4.2. Scale of behavioral markers of relaxation developed by Poppen and Maurer (1982).

of relaxation, and may be obvious to the therapist and/or the client. Along these same lines, Hiebert, Dumka, and Cardinal (1983) demonstrated that subjects can accurately assess their own heart rate, respiration rate, and finger temperature (using a simple thermometer, see Figure 4.5 and text discussion). Such data may be helpful in convincing clients of the efficacy of their home practice efforts, or these data may alert the therapist that some modification of procedure is needed.

Negative Effects of Relaxation

The question of adverse relaxation side effects may first arise during the post-relaxation debriefing. Clients may describe unsettling thoughts, emotions, or sensations that unexpectedly appeared during the relaxation (West, 1980).

Such threats to relaxation are known as unstressing in Transcendental Meditation (Goleman, 1971), autogenic discharges in autogenic training (Luthe, 1970a), and *makyo* in Zen (Ikemi, Ishikawa, Goyeche, & Sasaki, 1978). However, an alternative point of view does not see these effects as necessarily adverse. The various annoying and unsettling experiences that frequently visit the early stages of autogenics (and other methods of relaxation) may be interpreted as a positive indicator that relaxation is beginning to impact on an individual unaccustomed to the relaxation experience (Schultz & Luthe, 1969). Pensinger and Paine (1977–1978) advanced a theory of autogenic discharges consistent with the view that such phenomena evidence therapeutic processes. These authors argued that these atypical experiences arise from shifts between primitive and mature psychophysiologic processes (analogous to primary and secondary thought processes in psychoanalysis), instigated by autogenic practice.

Previously repressed, noxious thoughts are a common source of unwanted intrusions into relaxation (also discussed in Chapter 6). The experience of relaxation leaves the mind calm and uncluttered and increases the likelihood that uncensored thoughts and emotions will spontaneously erupt into consciousness. When these have a negative quality and show some persistence, the client may naturally develop a fear of relaxing (Martin, 1951). This serves primarily to prolong the stay of these unwelcome thoughts and to intensify the client's alarm.

A diversity of individualized, largely unpredictable sensations also may occur as a result of the in-depth, undistracted, self-inspection constituting relaxation. The client may be hypersensitive in any of the perceptual modalities and may sense perceptual distortion. Sounds, visual images, odors, etc., may assume a dreamy, hallucinatory quality. Bodily lightness or heaviness, a sense of floating, and awareness of heartbeats and blood flow are other phenomena commonly reported. Slight, involuntary muscle twitches may also become a source of concern.

Whatever information clients provide on their relaxation experience is important, and the therapist should respond with constructive suggestions. Some revision of the presentation style, sequence, or content of the relaxation procedure may be indicated. Occasionally, the client will perceive the basic nature of the relaxation procedure as grating, in which case switching to a completely different procedure may be the solution.

There are sporadic reports of relaxation-induced emotional disturbances dating from the practice of Zen Buddhism (Kapleau, 1966, pp. 38–41). The extant meditation literature (Benson, Rosner, Marzetta, & Klemchuk, 1974a; Carrington, 1978a; French, Schmid, & Ingalls, 1975; Glueck & Stroebel, 1975; Kennedy, 1976; Lazarus, 1976; Shimano & Douglas, 1975; Vahia et al., 1972) cites numerous instances of psychiatric disturbance precipitated or exacerbated by meditation, including depression, depersonalization, psychosis, and suicide attempts, but such serious side effects are not routinely encountered. Benson (1974b) and Walsh and Roche (1979) observed that extended periods of meditation are a common cause of meditation-induced emotional disturbance.

When daily meditation reaches several hours, withdrawal, insomnia, and hallucinations may occur. Carrington (1978a) also cautioned against "overmeditation," indicating that initially the period of meditation should be very brief for some, and this can be gradually extended with experience.

French and Tupin (1974) reported two instances in which pleasant imagery led to disturbing thoughts. There are numerous, isolated reports of paradoxical relaxation effects in the AT literature (e.g., Schultz & Luthe, 1969), and such unwanted effects have been documented with children as well (Luthe, Trudeau, Mailhot, & Vallieres, 1977). In his practice involving a variety of relaxation approaches, Smith (1985) has observed "paranormal" experiences, typified by visions of the future. There are also reports of negative side effects associated with progressive relaxation (Cohen, Barlow, & Blanchard, 1985; Cotanch, 1983a; Delman & Johnson, 1976; Fewtrell, 1984; Geer & Katkin, 1966; Horan, 1973; Jacobsen & Edinger, 1982; Morrow, 1984; Sherman, 1975; Waddell, Barlow, & O'Brien, 1984). In the only study to systematically evaluate noxious relaxation effects, Heide and Borkovec (1983) found unwanted effects (e.g., increased physiological arousal and self-reported tension) with both meditation and progressive relaxation, but such effects were more common with the former (see Chapter 3 for an extended discussion of this study). These same authors (Heide & Borkovec, 1984) have also provided an excellent, extended discussion of this subject which they term relaxation-induced anxiety.

To estimate the incidence of adverse relaxation side effects, Edinger and Jacobsen (1982) surveyed 200 psychologists listed in the membership directory of the Association for Advancement of Behavior Therapy. Of the 138 respondents, 116 claimed experience with some kind of relaxation therapy and completed a questionnaire on observed side effects. The reported data are nonspecific with regard to relaxation method and patient population. The most common side effect noted was intrusive thoughts, occurring in 15 percent of clients. The remaining side effects were, in descending order of frequency, fear of losing control (9.3 percent), disturbing sensory experiences (3.6 percent), miscellaneous (2.5 percent), heterosexual arousal (2.3 percent), muscle cramps (2.1 percent), spasms (1.7 percent), homosexual arousal (0.9 percent), and psychotic symptoms (0.4 percent). Reported occurrence of side effects was unrelated to therapists' years of experience. Relaxation therapy was prematurely discontinued in about 4 percent of cases due to the presence of side effects.

Schultz and Luthe (1969, p. 21) reported that intruding thoughts and anxiety were the most common early complaints, occurring respectively in 69 percent and 40 percent of their clients receiving autogenic training. Reporting on 100 novice autogenic training trainees (mostly individuals receiving treatment for psychosomatic disorders), Luthe (1962c) observed 53 different types of side effects (termed autogenic discharges), and at least one of these occurred in nearly all subjects. The most common sensations were a tingling feeling (reported by 76 percent of the subjects), muscle twitches (55 percent), gastrointestinal sensations (52 percent), circulatory sensations (51 percent), numbness (41 percent), tautness (38 percent), and visual phenomena (33 percent).

In general, the relaxation beginner may encounter unfamiliar experiences causing confusion or fear. The therapist's reassurance that these are common experiences will assist the client in redefining them in acceptable terms. Clients reporting even intense distress can usually tolerate a few minutes of relaxation. The relaxation period can be gradually increased over time according to whatever pace is comfortable for the client. Clinical experience complemented by some research data (Cohen, Barlow, & Blanchard, 1985; Kubose, 1976) indicate that for some, the disturbing thoughts, sensations, etc., will fade in a few weeks, never to return. For others, persistent novel feelings will become familiar and pleasant.

Homework

Every known method of relaxation exhorts clients to practice regularly. The necessity of home practice is such that if the client is obstinately non-compliant in this matter, continued relaxation therapy is futile and should be discontinued.

Most relaxation techniques require one or two 15-minute practice sessions daily. The client should try to produce a relaxation setting resembling that of the therapy office—comfortable, quiet, and unpressured. A time of day should be selected when there is ample time for relaxation, a comfortable sitting or reclining position is available, and environmental distraction is minimal. It is of no particular importance exactly when or where this is, provided the above conditions are approximated. Creating a highly conducive structure for relaxation practice is particularly important during the novice period, but it becomes less so as relaxation skills mature and the challenge posed by distractors and stressors can be managed.

In discussing generalization of biofeedback effects, Luiselli (1981) made a point that equally applies to relaxation. The setting parameters—time, place, position, etc.—should be varied so that the relaxation experience does not adhere singularly to one setting. If the client becomes accustomed to achieving relaxation under varying conditions, the ability to produce relaxation when confronted with novel, stressful situations will likely be increased. See also the related discussion under *Setting* earlier in this chapter.

The meditation literature (Benson, 1975; Carrington, 1978a; Ram Dass, 1971; Sivananda, 1971) insists that digestive processes may interfere with relaxation and cautions against practice within 2–3 hours following a meal. Smith (1985) alerts us to the fact that tobacco smoke and caffeinated foods are stimulants, and relaxation practice should not occur immediately after use of these products. Alternatively, Schultz and Luthe (1959) recommend practice immediately after lunch and supper. I have simply allowed the client to experiment with different times and arrive at his or her own conclusions on scheduling.

The assignment of relaxation practice homework may bring to focus the issue of resistance. Unlike psychodynamic therapies, many other therapies (particularly learning theory-based, symptom-specific therapies) ignore, deny, or minimize the importance of client resistance to therapeutic progress (Jahn & Lichstein, 1980). However, a client's repeated failure to practice regularly must be squarely addressed.

Psychodynamic therapists have given a great deal of attention to the subject of resistance. Typically, resistance is cast as an unconscious dilemma arising from instinctual drives (Wolberg, 1954). This reasoning leads to prolonged, in-depth investigation of resistances to uncover the hidden motivations and thereby achieve curative insight. However, this approach will greatly delay therapeutic progress when simple, problem-solving analyses offer reasonable solutions. In such instances, it is useful to define resistance as the psychotherapy counterpart of patient noncompliance in medical settings (Haynes, Taylor, & Sackett, 1979). This view holds that resistance can materialize for many different reasons (Jahn & Lichstein, 1980).

Some of the common factors promoting relaxation practice noncompliance are presented below. They are listed in their approximate descending order of frequency of occurrence.

1. *Not enough time.*   Clients will lament about their inability to find the time to practice, due to their very busy schedule. A careful review of the client's daily routine will usually reveal at least one 15-minute period at home or at work when practice could occur. A 15-minute appendage before or after one of the meals, or just before bedtime, is another opportunity to consider. From another perspective, the client is saying that at any point in time, relaxation is competing with preferred activities. Capitalizing on this predicament, some of these activities may be placed on contingency for relaxation practice in accordance with the Premack Principle (Danaher, 1974).

2. *Forget.*   This is a convenient and sometimes overworked excuse that can be readily tested. Family, friends, or co-workers may be enlisted to supply reminders. Notes or other stimuli can be conspicuously displayed at key locations, such as on the refrigerator or a pillow, as memory prompts (Surwit, Pilon, & Fenton, 1978). The client also can carry a portable timer as a reminder cue (Sirota & Mahoney, 1974). Naturally occurring stimuli, such as a telephone ring or each instance one checks the time, can be defined as reminder cues to prompt relaxation practice (Patel, 1977). Budzynski (1973) recommended the use of a small piece of colored tape on the wristwatch dial as a reminder.

3. *Unsure of relaxation procedure.*   This is a legitimate difficulty usually limited to the first week or two of training with progressive relaxation or autogenic training. I give a skeleton outline of the training procedure, so that the client may review it prior to practice. These outlines are prepared on index cards for convenient carrying and are presented in Figures 4.3 and 4.4. Friends or family may be trained by the client to assist in relaxation homework by reading from these cue cards during the relaxation to guide the client. In addition, assistants can give feedback on timing if this is a stubborn problem for

```
          Progressive Relaxation

  1.  Right hand and forearm
  2.  Right biceps
  3.  Left hand and forearm
  4.  Left biceps
  5.  Forehead
  6.  Middle Face
  7.  Lower Face
  8.  Neck
  9.  Upper back
 10.  Chest and abdomen
 11.  Right thigh
 12.  Right calf
 13.  Right ankle and shin
 14.  Left thigh
 15.  Left calf
 16.  Left ankle and shin

      Tense for about 7 sec.

      Relax for about 45 sec.
```

Figure 4.3. Progressive relaxation homework cue card.

```
          Autogenic Training

  I.1  Heaviness–right arm
  I.2  Heaviness–left arm
  I.3  Heaviness–both arms
  I.4  Heaviness–right leg
  I.5  Heaviness–left leg
  I.6  Heaviness–both legs
  I.7  Heaviness–arms and legs
 II.1  Warmth–right arm
 II.2  Warmth–left arm
 II.3  Warmth–both arms
 II.4  Warmth–right leg
 II.5  Warmth–left leg
 II.6  Warmth–both legs
 II.7  Warmth–arms and legs
III.   Heartbeat calm and regular
 IV.   Breathing calm
  V.   Abdomen warm
 VI.   Forehead cool
```

Figure 4.4. Autogenic training homework cue card.

the client. Relaxation tape recordings might also prove useful in this situation for a week or two.

4. *Unsuccessful relaxing.*   It is unlikely that clients will be able to reproduce the same depth of relaxation by self-administration as was attained in the therapy session. This contrast is greatest during the first few weeks of therapy because the therapist is better at relaxation administration than the client. Also, the client loses the benefit of the hypnotic influence of the therapist's voice when practicing relaxation. Therefore, this problem is normal and predictable and will vanish with continued training.

Most clients are accepting of this explanation and will not allow this contrast effect to prevent their home practice. To demonstrate that a relaxation effect is being produced at home, clients can self-monitor heart rate, respiration rate, and skin temperature, as recommended by Hiebert, Dumka, and Cardinal (1983). Self-assessment of muscle tension can be conducted accurately by some individuals (Batey, Lehrer, & Woolfolk, 1984), but these data are probably less reliable than heart rate and the like.

Figure 4.5 reproduces the home record form we employ with our clients. Relaxation practices are evaluated pre-post on experiential and index finger temperature indices (a) to convey relaxation progress (quantity and quality) to the therapist, and (b) to produce immediate feedback reinforcement for the client via temperature change. We employ an inexpensive miniature finger thermometer (available from the Conscious Living Foundation, P.O. Box 9, Drain, Oregon 97435). Most clients will produce at least a 1° or 2° rise (due to adaptation effects if nothing else), and this *hard* biological evidence encourages regular practice. The client is asked to bring the form to weekly therapy sessions. The form may serve the additional function of a practice reminder prompt (see paragraph 2, above).

5. *No quiet place.*   Inasmuch as a quiet environment is facilitative of relaxation, it is desirable. However, if a client's work and home settings are absolutely devoid of quiet interludes, then a noisy setting will suffice. Practicing relaxation under adverse conditions is preferable to no practice at all. To minimize noise distraction, the client can resort to ear plugs or a white noise generator, which is commercially available as a sleep aid.

6. *Declining interest in relaxation.*   The client may gradually or suddenly lose interest in relaxation therapy, and will discontinue home practice because he/she simply doesn't want to do relaxation any more. Non-assertive clients will continue to cooperate during within-session training, but will communicate declining interest in their avoidance of home practice. According to the reasoning behind the client's decision, relaxation training may resume at full speed or may be terminated indefinitely. Three reasons are most commonly encountered.

First, the client's expectations for rapidity of symptom relief may exceed the normal pace of relaxation influence, and the client prematurely concludes that the method is ineffectual. This "normal pace" is, in part, a function of

Relaxation Practice Record

Name _____ Relaxation Method _____

		Practice 1						Practice 2				
			Rating		Temp				Rating		Temp	
Day	Date	Time	Pre	Post	Pre	Post		Time	Pre	Post	Pre	Post
Mon	_____ 198__	___ am ___ pm						___ am ___ pm				
Tues	_____ 198__	___ am ___ pm						___ am ___ pm				
Wed	_____ 198__	___ am ___ pm						___ am ___ pm				
Thur	_____ 198__	___ am ___ pm						___ am ___ pm				
Fri	_____ 198__	___ am ___ pm						___ am ___ pm				
Sat	_____ 198__	___ am ___ pm						___ am ___ pm				
Sun	_____ 198__	___ am ___ pm						___ am ___ pm				

Rating

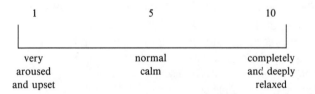

1	5	10
very aroused and upset	normal calm	completely and deeply relaxed

PLEASE RECORD PRACTICE INFORMATION
IMMEDIATELY FOLLOWING EACH PRACTICE

Figure 4.5. Form for recording home relaxation progress.

symptom type, intensity, and longevity, and therefore general guidelines are not possible. Reference to the research literature on a particular symptom (see Chapter 7) may be helpful in generating reasonable relaxation expectations. When client expectations are excessive, the client must be taught appropriate goals.

Second, when a client is convinced of the efficacy of relaxation or any therapy approach, the prospect of symptom removal may evoke both delight and regret. There is threatened loss of reinforcers (secondary gain) contributing to current symptomatology when symptoms are discarded. Greater responsibility and pressure may come to bear on the individual once relieved of a symptom's burden. In general, according to the centrality a given symptom achieved in the client's psychological ecology, symptom relief may herald broad, profound psychological change. When clients juggle issues of this magnitude, their ambivalence deserves serious attention, and relaxation therapy should be suspended until the conflict is resolved.

Third, relaxation practice may elicit negative sensations, emotions, beliefs, etc. When this occurs at home, uncomfortable relaxation effects will likely result within therapy sessions as well and are best addressed then, as discussed above. In this case, defer home practice until relaxation is positively experienced under therapist supervision. Clients sometimes require a period of acclimation to comfortably accept the relaxation experience.

CHAPTER 5

Brief Relaxation Methods

Chapter 4 presented several methods of relaxation. These were grouped in one chapter because they produce deep states of relaxation. To successfully attain such a state, several conditions must be met.

1. The subject must assume a comfortable seated or reclined position.
2. There should be minimal sensory distractions.
3. Somewhere between 5 and 30 minutes are required for relaxation induction.

In sum, a leisurely, nondemanding setting is required to achieve deep relaxation. Furthermore, while in a state of deep relaxation, the individual's ability to efficiently and effectively interact with the environment is impaired. Although there are many situations in which the above characteristics pose no problem, these same characteristics become highly inconvenient or create insurmountable obstacles in other situations.

Consider the case of a man wishing to approach a woman at a party. Unfortunately, the man pauses in acting on this desire because he is tense. Even if he were highly skilled in deep relaxation and had practiced his method earlier in the day, the benefits of deep relaxation are not available to him in this situation, and his nervousness will persist. The methods presented in Chapter 4 are too obvious and would attract unwanted attention from others. Further, the requisite setting characteristics are not available in this predicament. If, nevertheless, he were to successfully practice his relaxation at the party, he would be *too deeply relaxed* to launch a conversation. Lastly, having initiated the conversation, what if a surge of anxiety erupted in its midst? Obviously, it would not be practical to excuse himself for 20 minutes to prepare for the conclusion of the social interaction.

The plausible situation, just described, is offered as a case in point to illustrate the limitations of deep relaxation methods. Innumerable other social situations would present the same difficulties. Other situations which may be described as crisis intervention or sudden acute anxiety attacks might also render deep relaxation methods inapplicable. Deep relaxation methods would be inappropriate in other circumstances because the symptomatology would be too mild to justify this approach. For example, in cases of transient mild anxiety, restlessness, and distractability, utilization of deep relaxation would amount to overkill.

The present chapter will teach brief methods of relaxation that are well-suited to the demands of the situations described above. The term *brief* is used as a summary referent because most of these methods require much less time to learn and much less time to implement than the deep relaxation methods. Other characteristics defining most of the brief methods are as follows.

1. They will induce a mild to moderate level of relaxation. Deep relaxation usually does not result.

2. They are highly portable. These methods do not depend on specific setting characteristics. They can be rapidly and conveniently employed in most situations.

3. They are unobtrusive. The subject may employ many of these methods while actively engaged in social interaction or complex motor functions, without either alerting others as to the presence of relaxation practice or interrupting the task at hand.

SELF-CONTROL RELAXATION

Overview

In Chapter 1, I outlined the significance of Goldfried's (1971) reformulation of systematic desensitization as a method of self-control. The present section is an elaboration of Goldfried's position, based upon further developments that have since occurred.

The term *self-control relaxation* does not reflect a specific set of procedures in the extant literature, but rather a number of procedural variations that share some common elements. This term was selected because it best reflects the guiding philosophy governing these interventions.

The core procedure is usually progressive relaxation. It then undergoes substantial revision to incorporate features from applied relaxation, cue-controlled relaxation, and differential relaxation. These variations will now be briefly described as extensive reviews are available elsewhere (Barrios & Shigetomi, 1979; Deffenbacher & Suinn, 1982; Denney, 1980; Grimm, 1980).

Applied Relaxation

This procedure grew directly out of Goldfried's (1971) reconceptualization. After training in standard progressive relaxation, emphasis is placed on educating the client in the rationale of relaxation as an active coping skill by utilizing relaxation skills in everyday life. Some training in differential relaxation (described below) is usually included. Early demonstrations of the usefulness of applied relaxation (also called self-control relaxation and coping relaxation) were conducted with subjects displaying public speaking anxiety (Goldfried & Trier, 1974) and test anxiety (Chang-Liang & Denney, 1976).

Cue-controlled Relaxation

This consists of first training the client in progressive relaxation. While relaxed, the client silently repeats a cue word such as "relax" or "calm" with each exhalation. The cue word will come to evoke a mild relaxation effect approximating the relaxation experience with which it was associated. When faced with a threatening situation, the client may begin to slowly chant the cue word to counteract the impending tension. The method was introduced in the mid-1960s by Paul (1966b), who called it conditioned relaxation, and by Cautela (1966a), who called it relaxation with covert verbal response. But the method was later popularized in a series of clinical trials by Russell and his colleagues as cue-controlled relaxation (Russell & Matthews, 1975; Russell, Miller, & June, 1974, 1975; Russell & Sipich, 1973, 1974).

It is fitting to add that in 1946, a psychologist named Dorothy Yates published a brilliant rendition of cue-controlled relaxation that has since been forgotten in the expanse of history. Under the rubric of "association-set technique," a pleasing word was paired with abbreviated progressive relaxation and guided imagery. Further, she instructed her clients to self-monitor in stressful situations, so that they may recruit their relaxation skills during the early onset of stress therein.

Differential Relaxation

Early on, Jacobson (1929) strongly advocated differential relaxation, and others (Gurdjieff, 1973, pp. 161–163) recommended similar procedures. More recently, several investigators have revived interest in it (Bernstein & Borkovec, 1973; Lazarus, 1971; Sherman & Plummer, 1973). The procedure is initiated after the client has mastered progressive relaxation. It involves training in interoceptive monitoring, that is, directing the client's attention to subtle internal cues that discriminate tense and relaxed states. The client's task is twofold: (1) Maintain body awareness during normal activities, and (2) employ muscles necessary for a particular task at a minimal level of exertion and allow unneeded muscles to stay relaxed.

Procedure

It may be apparent to the reader that there is little standardization in the area of self-control relaxation. The method presented below is a synthesis of the several versions most frequently cited. It is most similar to the hybrid approach taken by Deffenbacher and his colleagues (Deffenbacher, Mathis, & Michaels, 1979; Deffenbacher & Payne, 1977; Deffenbacher & Snyder, 1976).

Self-control relaxation is divided into four levels. The sequence of levels reflects increments in brevity and portability, culminating in a completely self-control format in level 4. The procedure may be initiated at either level 1 or

2 (as discussed under *Level 2*) but should not otherwise be presented out of sequence.

Level 1

This consists of standard progressive relaxation as described in Chapter 4. The following modifications are needed to smoothly integrate level 1 with levels 2–4.

1. The self-control rationale should be discussed at length with the client. The essential ingredients of this rationale emphasize that the client must take an active role in this therapy by practicing the skills taught in the session, by critically analyzing his or her routine experiences, and by enacting the skills acquired in self-control relaxation when needed. This view of the client's role in psychotherapy is in sharp contrast to the traditional, passive role of the client and may be difficult for some clients to understand and accept at first.

2. A brief overview of the self-control program should be outlined. This would include a description of the four level process and its ultimate goals.

3. The actual technique of standard progressive relaxation is altered in level 1 in that five deep breaths and a cue word, such as "relax," "calm," or "peace," are interposed after the eighth muscle-tension cycle, the neck. This is done to begin training in the cue-controlled aspect of the intervention. In this level, the cue word is softly said aloud with the five exhalations. In subsequent levels, this will be changed to a nonvocal self-statement.

Level 2

This level accomplishes two things: The progressive relaxation procedure is condensed into four tense-relax cycles, and the cue word is subvocalized. Level 1 can be skipped over entirely, and training in self-control relaxation may be initiated at level 2 if the client is contending with only mild anxiety. In this case, level 2 relaxation usually proves adequate. In addition, level 2 relaxation (with or without the cue-controlled component) may be extracted from the self-control sequence and employed as an independent, rapid induction relaxation technique for clients presenting mild anxiety or irritability.

For most clients, presentation of level 2 presupposes mastery of level 1 following 1–3 weeks of daily home practice. To present level 2, the client is asked to assume a comfortable position with eyes closed, as in level 1. The general format of tensing for 7 seconds and relaxing for 45 seconds accompanied by the therapist's relaxation patter is unaltered.

The beginning instruction is "Today I am going to abbreviate the relaxation procedure in order to work toward the goal of your producing a comfortable relaxation very rapidly. I am going to ask you to tense several groups of muscles at one time, so that your entire body will be covered in just four cycles." The actual instructions are as follows.

1. "Tense both arms by making fists, and rigidly extend your arms." (Frequently I will comment during the relaxation cycle that the subject has either succeeded or failed to maintain relaxation in other parts of the body during the tension phase.)

2. "Tense most of the muscles of your face and neck by closing your eyes tightly, pressing your lips and teeth together, and tensing your neck at the same time." (The forehead is omitted. This muscle is sometimes problematic and for such individuals, a separate cycle for the forehead should be added.)

At this point, the breathing exercise is again interjected with one small variation. The subject should say "relax" or whatever cue word he or she prefers, silently with each exhalation. The selection of the cue word is, of course, the responsibility of the client, and may be guided by the discussion of selecting a mantra in Chapter 4. The client should be told to use the word as a cue or self-instruction to scan body tensions and "let go" of any tensions that are detected.

3. "Tense your upper back, chest, and stomach. Imagine you are trying to move your shoulders forward and backward simultaneously, which will enable you to tense the front and back of your upper body. Tense your stomach at the same time."

4. "Tense most of the muscles in both your legs by making your legs straight and rigid, raising them about an inch, and pointing your feet and toes forward."

Level 3

Clients who began self-control relaxation with level 1 usually need no more than 1 week at level 2, if they are diligent in their practice, before progressing to level 3. Clients who began the sequence at level 2 will require as many as 3 weeks before they are ready to advance to the next level.

Level 3 dispenses with the tensing portion entirely, asking clients to simply focus their attention on their bodies and recreate the sensations of relaxation with which they have become very familiar. The procedure is sometimes called relaxation by recall (Bernstein & Borkovec, 1973) or passive relaxation (Haynes, Moseley, & McGowan, 1975). Occasionally, clients will be disconcerted by the omission of muscle tensing, and after a week at level 3, temporary resumption of level 2 may be desirable. Also in level 3, the five deep breaths associated with the cue word are changed to *moderately* deep breaths, so that others could not perceive the altered breathing pattern. Finally, the first step toward differential relaxation is introduced by asking the client to sit erect with eyes opened during the procedure. If opening the eyes greatly detracts from the relaxation effect, this revision can be delayed till level 4.

Following is a verbatim introduction to level 3.

As you have become very skillful in relaxation and can now detect subtle body sensations, of which you were previously unaware, the tensing part of the relaxation process can now be eliminated. I will assist you by directing your attention to your body in stepwise fashion. Whenever you detect tension, simply let go by bringing on the sensations of relaxation with which you are very familiar. In essence, if you think about relaxing feelings, your body will follow. Of course, since you are erect and some amount of physical exertion is required to maintain your posture, it would be impossible for you to attain the same depth of relaxation that you have achieved in the past. The muscles you do not have to use can be completely relaxed, and the other muscles should be exerted to the least extent to maximize relaxation.

Each of the 16 muscle groups are now reviewed, using the same relaxation patter recommended in Chapter 4. About 30 seconds is spent on each. A verbatim presentation is provided for the first muscle group only.

1. "Focus all of your attention on your right hand and forearm. Recall the feelings of relaxation there. Try to feel a warmth, a heaviness flowing from these muscles as they become soft and tranquil. Feel the relaxation starting to emerge."
2. Right biceps
3. Left hand and forearm
4. Left biceps
5. Forehead
6. Middle face
7. Lower face
8. Neck

Interject the cue-controlled procedure at this point as follows. I now want you to take five moderately deep breaths, hold each one for about 5 seconds, and give yourself the instruction to relax as you exhale. I use the term "moderately" to indicate that your breaths should be somewhat deeper than they are normally, so that you know they are special breaths, but not so deep as to attract the attention of people nearby.

When the client completes the breathing component, continue with the remaining muscle groups.

9. Upper back
10. Chest and stomach
11. Right thigh
12. Right calf
13. Right ankle and shin
14. Left thigh
15. Left calf
16. Left ankle and shin

Level 3 relaxation takes about 8 minutes. In the time remaining in this session and the next, two additional matters of great importance need be discussed.

The first issue concerns longevity of relaxation practice, as was discussed at some length near the end of Chapter 1. In the self-control relaxation system, level 3 is the last level in which relaxation retains its static form. I strongly urge clients to continue practicing level 3 (or if they prefer, levels 1 or 2) relaxation on an indefinite basis for at least 5–10 minutes daily. This serves a dual purpose. It ensures a relaxation break during the day that dispels accumulated tensions, and it maintains a fresh awareness of the relaxation experience. The latter enables the client to rapidly call forth a relaxation effect in the actual use of self-control relaxation (level 4). Similarly, King (1980) pointed out that conditioned stimuli such as special words will gradually lose their relaxation-evoking properties upon discontinuation of the practiced association between themselves and deep relaxation (unconditioned stimulus).

The second issue that must be introduced in detail in level 3 (or earlier) is self-monitoring. Ultimately, the success or failure of self-control relaxation will depend on the client's effectiveness in self-monitoring. The successive levels of the self-control format attain increments in brevity and portability at the cost of depth. Finally, in level 4, we arrive at an extremely compact method capable of producing only mild relaxation. Thus, self-control relaxation will effectively combat emotional distress only if the coping strategy is enacted when emotional distress is in its early, low arousal stages. The importance of timing in applying level 4 relaxation cannot be overemphasized, and self-monitoring collects the information that governs the timing decision.

I usually begin training the client in self-monitoring during level 3 and continue this topic for the duration of level 4. What is monitored derives from the tridimensional model of emotional arousal (Borkovec, Weerts, & Bernstein, 1977; Lang, 1978). This empirically derived view conceives of anxiety—or emotional distress in general—as having three loosely correlated components: cognitive, physiological, and motoric. The presence of emotional arousal is signaled by disturbance in one or more of these modes. These three dimensions comprise a horizontal definition of emotional arousal. Vertically, each dimension may be seen as an emergent process ranging from low to high disturbance. Further, in identifying environmental stress triggers, we emphasize routine, daily irritants which claim a heavier loading on health status than do major life events (DeLongis, Coyne, Dakof, Folkman, & Lazarus, 1982). Figure 5.1 presents a form I use to elucidate this model of emotional arousal. Further, homework assignments with this form assist the client in refining self-monitoring skills.

The Emergence of Emotional Distress form presents the three modes of emotional experience (horizontal analysis) at each of four levels of arousal (vertical analysis). In session, I will explain and discuss the form by emphasizing the following points.

Thoughts (e.g., "I can't face my boss"), sensations (e.g., funny feeling

Emergence of Emotional Distress

Name _____ Date _____

	Thoughts	Sensations	Behaviors
100% ___ Extreme Out of Control			
75% ___ Excessive Inappropriate Conduct			
50% ___ Moderate Public Events			
25% ___ Mild Private Events			
0% ___ Normal Calm			

Briefly describe situation _____

Figure 5.1. Form used to train self-monitoring of arousal cues. These cues are ultimately employed as self-control prompts instigating self-control relaxation.

in stomach, heart pounding), and behaviors (e.g., clenching fist, staring) are different dimensions of emotional expression. The extent of distress varies along a continuum in each of these dimensions. The continuum is divided into fourths for purposes of convenient analysis. The first quarter (0–25 percent) encompasses the early warnings of emotional distress. Taking the example of an executive who is displeased with his secretary, a prototypical thought in this quartile may be, "She misspelled my customer's name again." Sensations that might plausibly accompany this are funny feelings in the stomach. Typically, overt behaviors are not manifested in the 0–25 percent range, and that is why it is labeled *private events*. So far, no one except the employer knows that he is beginning to get upset, and even he likely would not realize he has initiated the emergent process of emotional distress unless he is skilled in the method of attentively self-monitoring. This is particularly true of the cue function of visceral sensations, which usually escape awareness until they are pronounced (Adam, 1978). If this individual recognized the significance of these thoughts and sensations, they would lead him to immediately commence self-control relaxation at this ideal time.

Unfortunately, most people are not aware of the emotional difficulty they are in until they are more advanced along this vertical continuum to a point where it is far more difficult to calm down. Jacobson (1970) employed a method he called *autosensory observation* to train self-monitoring skills. While imagining feared situations, the subject scrutinizes sensory experiences to cultivate awareness of early, subtle somatic cues. However, there is no data to support the utility of this approach. One study (Luborsky et al., 1976) demonstrated that biofeedback training can improve individuals' ability to estimate their own blood pressure. Another study (Sime & DeGood, 1977) also found improved internal discrimination of muscle tension following biofeedback, but little improvement following progressive relaxation.

Overall, little empirical progress has been made in the area of training skills in internal self-monitoring (Boice, 1983), which variously comes under the names *visceroception* (Adam, 1978), *autosensory observation* (Jacobson, 1970), and *interoception* (Brener, 1977). This area has been neglected despite the presence of some data suggesting such skills aid the therapeutic effectiveness of relaxation (Blanchard, Jurish, Andrasik, & Epstein, 1981). Brener (1977) eloquently outlined the potential significance for improved self-control of individuals learning to make fine interoceptive discriminations, but the methods of achieving the goal and the limits to learning in this area have yet to be outlined.

In fostering visceroceptive self-monitoring skills, we have found the Stress Inventory-5 (SI-5) questionnaire to be very helpful (Smith & Seidel, 1982). The SI-5 is composed of some 100 sensation descriptors ranked on 9-point Likert scales and organized into 18 physiologically homogeneous subsets presented in descending order of prevalence. For example, the first (and most frequently endorsed) factor is *gastric distress* which is composed of 10 items, some of which are pressure in the stomach, nausea and sinking feelings, and butterflies in the stomach. Other high frequency factors are *cardiorespiratory activity, restless activity,* and *self-conscious tense activity.*

We administer the SI-5 to clients experiencing difficulty in identifying salient arousal cues to educate them as to what sensations might be occurring and to focalize their internal scanning. Pennebaker and Skelton (1981) present convincing experimental data indicating that visceroception is facilitated by instructions of the sort we are suggesting. Their positive findings on what they term *hypothesis-guided selective search* are consistent with our clinical experience.

In the 25–50 percent range, one or more of the dimensions are escalating. Staying with this same example, perhaps the executive is now thinking, "I can't believe how many times she makes this mistake." He is experiencing greater somatic arousal and, in the behavioral mode, is sighing with an annoyed expression on his face. Not only is this individual more energized now in two of these dimensions (i.e., thoughts and sensations) than he was just a very short time earlier, but he has visibly aired his displeasure (behaviors) and must also potentially contend with an adverse reaction from his secretary. These two aspects of the second quartile make it more difficult for self-control relaxation to be beneficial at this level of arousal.

The last half of the emergent continuum (50–100 percent) is of little interest from a self-control standpoint. Arousal in this range is not likely to respond to self-control relaxation. Figure 5.2 presents an example of the Emergence of Emotional Distress form, as the fictitious client may have completed it for homework. This example is typical of the pattern clients exhibit. Note that in the 75–100 percent range, the client's thoughts are highly exaggerated and catastrophic, physiological sensations are substantive, and the behaviors have a wild character. Contrasting this quartile to the first, there is little or no dysfunction present in the latter. The first quartile usually serves to identify the concern and warn the individual that he or she must activate coping skills immediately. Clients are advised that if they are remiss in employing their coping skills early, or if the coping skills failed to stabilize their state, and emo-

Emergence of Emotional Distress

Name _____ Date _____

	Thoughts	Sensations	Behaviors
100% ___ Extreme Out of Control	My business is going down the drain and my life is ruined.	headache; heart throbbing; stomach cramps	shouting insults
75% ___ Excessive Inappropriate Conduct	She is constantly wasting my time with her errors.	heart beating faster	criticizing secretary in loud voice; hands on hips
50% ___ Moderate Public Events	I can't believe how many times she makes this mistake.	mild chest and shoulder tension	sigh; annoyed expression
25% ___ Mild Private Events	She misspelled customer's name.	stomach discomfort	none
0% ___ Normal Calm			

Briefly describe situation ___Secretary made error_____

Figure 5.2. Example of completed homework assignment in self-monitoring of arousal.

tional distress enters the 50–100 percent range, they should remove themselves from the situation and draw upon level 1 or level 2 relaxation.

Level 4

One to two weeks practice at level 3 is usually sufficient. Level 4, however, typically requires at least 2 weeks. Level 4 squarely tackles the question of transferring relaxation effects to the natural environment. The client must now self-monitor, recall relaxation by silently chanting "relax," and utilize breaths with cue words, all while ambulatory and engaged in sundry activities. It is important to emphasize that a substantive relaxation effect is neither possible nor desirable at this level. Clients may become discouraged by their inability to produce a deep relaxation experience unless they are forewarned. Level 4 relaxation is a fragile, subtle form of relaxation that will prove exceedingly useful only if it is skillfully applied.

Level 4 is introduced by asking the client to sit erect in a chair with eyes open and to maintain an interpersonal orientation in body posture and eye contact. No one observing should be able to detect that the client is actively engaged in self-control relaxation. The therapist continues with the following.

> Your task now is to *avoid* disruptive anxiety by: (1) self-monitoring and (2) invoking your self-control relaxation skills when your self-monitoring detects *early* signs of emotional distress. While you are engaged in this twofold process, you are also attending to the people and things in your environment and appropriately interacting with them. You may be wondering if it is possible to carefully attend to dissimilar internal and external events simultaneously, that is, to do two things at once. The answer is emphatically yes. Self-control relaxation is simply a skill that requires practice. At first it may feel awkward, but within a week or two, you should be able to manage these two functions smoothly. To begin learning this skill, let us start with a conversation while you actively review your internal sensations, body posture, and thought content.

For the next 5 minutes or so, the therapist and client may engage in light conversation. Every 30–60 seconds, the therapist should interject queries such as "Are you able to self-monitor?," "Have you detected any signs of nervousness?," etc. These prompts, bolstered by reassuring comments, are the key teaching devices at this point.

Most clients develop a sense of how to do this initial stage of self-control relaxation within 5 or 10 minutes. The next step involves increasing the demands of the environment. Typically, I will ask clients to undo and tie their shoelaces, dial the telephone, search out an item in a purse, etc. Now, interaction with the environment requires more muscular exertion and more cognitive attention. Again, the therapist's primary role is one of coach and consultant, as the client must maintain clarity in self-awareness. The therapist may offer such reminders as "Are you allowing unneeded muscles to stay relaxed?," "Is there any tension coming on?," and so on. If at any time during these practice exercises, the client does perceive unwanted sensations, posture, or thoughts, the therapist should guide the client in the application of self-control relaxation, as in the example below.

> Continue to tie your shoelace while you take your slow breaths and begin your chant of "relax." Thoroughly scan your body with each exhalation and recall or recreate comfortable feelings of relaxation. Try to *feel* a gentle wave of relaxation flowing through your body. Let go of any tensions you still feel. Let your body loosen up.

In this and future sessions, the complexity and demands of the environment are gradually increased, as the client becomes more adept at self-control relaxation. The nature of the environmental task at hand may be styled to reflect problem areas for the client. For example, if the client gets particularly uptight when interacting with a supervisor, then this situation can be role-played in the session (the role of the employer taken by the therapist) to allow the client to manage a high probability threat under controlled, therapeutic conditions.

It is crucial that the importance of self-monitoring continues to be strongly emphasized as an indispensable ingredient in self-control relaxation. In addition to the points made under level 3, self-monitoring makes a valuable contribution as a therapeutic intervention in its own right. It is a well-documented phenomenon (see review by Nelson, 1977) that self-monitoring alone can alter the characteristics being monitored in a therapeutic direction. Indeed, the therapeutic effects of self-monitoring alone sometimes closely approximate those of relaxation or biofeedback (Hiebert & Fox, 1981). Use of the cue word, "relax," (or whatever word the client prefers) should also be strongly encouraged. There is some evidence to support the conclusion that the cue word can acquire conditioned stimulus properties by having been repeatedly associated with deep levels of relaxation (Delmonte, 1979). Thus, recalling the cue word may automatically evoke aspects of the relaxation experience.

The therapist should review the client's homework assignments using the Emergence of Emotional Distress form (Figure 5.1) and assist the client in identifying easily discernible cues that reliably occur in the 0–25 percent range. Level 4 relaxation can only produce a mild state of relaxation that will exert little or no impact on well-developed emotional distress. Referring to the model of emergent emotional distress presented in level 3 relaxation, the 50 percent point serves as a rough upper limit for using self-control relaxation. Ideally, the client should be alerted to the impending threat of emotional distress by cues in the 0–25 percent range. If the client responds with self-control relaxation in the 25–50 percent range, the arousal process still can be controlled and emotional equilibrium reinstated. However, the likelihood of successfully applying self-control relaxation drops sharply in the 25–50 percent range, and success is highly improbable beyond 50 percent.

Final Comments On Self-control Relaxation

Self-control relaxation is a versatile, effective relaxation intervention. Once mastered, clients have four relatively independent methods of relaxation at their disposal. They may now select a particular method which best fits the joint demands placed by the setting and symptom. As presented herein, progressive relaxation forms the basis upon which self-control relaxation is developed, but this need not be the case. Self-control relaxation could just as easily be formed from any other static relaxation method, as illustrated by Shapiro's (1978b) adaptation of Zen meditation and Woolfolk's (1984) adaptation of mantra and breath meditation. Were a client disposed toward any particular method of relaxation (including the Lamaze childbirth technique, which I have used as a base), I would not hesitate to capitalize on this preference and shape toward the self-control goal.

The tridimensional model of emotional distress (horizontal view) poses a formidable challenge for any method of relaxation, including the self-control approach. Relaxation focuses on the physiological dimension of emotional disturbance. Secondarily, relaxation channels one's thoughts to soothing, monotonous content and reduces tension in postural expression, thereby addressing the cognitive and motoric dimensions, respectively. For subjects whose primary mode of experiencing emotional distress is in the cognitive or motoric dimensions, relaxation alone will not be sufficient to ameliorate the anxiety, anger, frustration, etc. The introduction of specific interventions designed for disturbing cognitions (e.g., rational emotive therapy, Ellis, 1973) and maladaptive motoric expression (e.g., behavioral rehearsal procedures, Lange & Jakubowski, 1976) bring us closer to a comprehensive stress management program. Although an in-depth presentation of stress management is beyond the scope of this book, Chapter 6 further discusses the integration of relaxation with other therapy techniques in this realm.

ABBREVIATED AUTOGENIC TRAINING (AT)

Overview

As described in Chapter 4, common practice of AT involves a shorter version of the method than was originally devised. However, even the more compact form, presented in the previous chapter, is too complex to be considered a brief form of relaxation. Many clinical reports (e.g., Nicassio & Bootzin, 1974; Sargent, Green, & Walters, 1972; Surwit, Pilon, & Fenton, 1978) employ only the first two standard exercises, heaviness and warmth throughout the body, to accomplish a relatively rapid relaxation induction. This method will be taught in the section below titled *procedure 1*. A second procedure will be presented that is modeled after self-control relaxation. *Procedure 2* begins with the six standard exercises of autogenic training, and then gradually moves toward a very brief form, through revisions instituted over several sessions.

Procedure 1

The first two standard exercises of AT have not been shown to be clinically superior to the last four. Despite this lack of documentation, clinicians have exhibited a strong preference for suggestions of heaviness and warmth. Following is an AT-styled procedure reflecting this preference that we have found to be useful as a simple, rapid induction technique in our clinical research (Lichstein & Sallis, 1981), and for which we have preliminary evidence recommending its effectiveness as a method of relaxation (Lichstein & Sallis, 1982).

> I am going to help you relax with a procedure that relies upon your ability to focus on your body and imagine you are becoming relaxed. An essential part of this procedure involves you picturing yourself in a comforting, peaceful environment. Most people choose a scene that is familiar to them, such as lying on the sand at the beach, or lying in a meadow on a summer day. Take the next few seconds to choose your peaceful scene. (Perhaps some discussion is needed to assist the subject in selecting the scene.) Please keep your eyes closed throughout the following exercise. I am going to suggest two sensations, heaviness and warmth, for different parts of your body. I will repeat the feelings you are to focus on, and then you are to continue on your own for 30 seconds, imagining you are actually experiencing your relaxation scene, focusing on the identified body parts, and trying to feel the identified sensations. It is very important that at all times you maintain a relaxed, passive, and casual attitude towards the procedure. You cannot force relaxation to occur.

The following phrases are chanted four times in a slow, calm, soothing voice at a pace of about 5 seconds per repetition. This results in a 20-second therapist presentation for each phrase, followed by 30 seconds of silent meditation by the client. Thus, the entire induction takes about 4 minutes.

1. "My arms are heavy and warm." (After presenting this phrase four times, the therapist should add the following after this presentation only, "Now go ahead and imagine that you are in your relaxation scene and focus on these feelings emerging in your arms." Pause about 30 seconds.)
2. "My face is heavy and warm."
3. "My chest is heavy and warm."
4. "My legs are heavy and warm."

Procedure 2

AT may be converted into a self-control technique in a similar manner to the process undergone by progressive relaxation. Clients for whom progressive relaxation is inappropriate (e.g., arthritic pain precludes muscle tensing), now have a comparable alternative available to them.

Below is the summary list of AT presented in Chapter 4.

  I. Heaviness
      1. Right arm
      2. Left arm
      3. Both arms
      4. Right leg
      5. Left leg
      6. Both legs
      7. Arms and legs
 II. Warmth
      1. Right arm
      2. Left arm
      3. Both arms
      4. Right leg
      5. Left leg
      6. Both legs
      7. Arms and legs
III. Cardiac Regulation
 IV. Respiration
  V. Abdominal Warmth
 VI. Cooling of the Forehead

After a week or two of practicing the above method, most clients are ready to begin the abbreviation process. Cue-controlled relaxation, breaths with a relaxation cue word, can be added to the AT procedure early in training. Differential relaxation, introduced at level 3 of self-control relaxation, can be incorporated during the last few sessions of AT as a self-control procedure. Lastly, the significance of ongoing relaxation practice and self-monitoring, detailed for self-control relaxation, apply equally to this version of AT and should be discussed at length with the client.

Five sessions, occurring at weekly intervals with the client practicing daily at home, are needed to complete the abbreviation process. This involves systematically deleting portions of the standard AT phrases, while incorporating vestiges of the omitted phrases into surviving phrases. Eventually, we arrive at a single phrase which combines key elements of all six themes.

The schedule for revision of the format is outlined below. This scheme uses the Roman numeral labels for the standard exercises.

Session 1: Standard exercises I–VI
Session 2: Omit I.1–I.6 and II.1–II.6
Session 3: Omit I.7 and II.7
Session 4: Omit III
Session 5: Omit IV
Session 6: Omit V

To exemplify the abbreviated formats, the inductions for sessions three and six are provided in their entirety.

SESSION 3.   The therapist begins in the customary manner:

Please get comfortable in your chair, close your eyes, and allow yourself to relax with a passive, casual attitude. (After pausing 15 seconds or so, the therapist continues.) I am at peace . . . My arms and legs are heavy and warm . . . My arms and legs are heavy and warm . . . Heartbeat calm and regular . . . Heartbeat calm and regular . . . I am at peace . . . My arms and legs are heavy and warm . . . Heartbeat calm and regular . . . I am at peace . . . My arms and legs are heavy and warm . . . Heartbeat calm and regular . . . Heartbeat calm and regular. (Pause about 45 seconds and commence IV.) I am at peace . . . My arms and legs are heavy and warm . . . My arms and legs are heavy and warm . . . Heartbeat calm and regular . . . I am at peace . . . My breathing is calm . . . My breathing is calm . . . My breathing is calm . . . I am at peace . . . My breathing is calm . . . My arms and legs are heavy and warm, heartbeat calm and regular . . . My arms and legs are heavy and warm, heartbeat calm and regular . . . My breathing is calm . . . My breathing is calm. (Pause about 60 seconds and begin V). I am at peace . . . My arms and legs are heavy and warm . . . Heartbeat calm and regular . . . My breathing is calm . . . My abdomen is warm . . . My abdomen is warm . . . I am at peace . . . My abdomen is warm . . . My abdomen is warm . . . I am at peace . . . My arms and legs are heavy and warm . . . My arms and legs are heavy and warm . . . Heartbeat calm and regular . . . My breathing is calm . . . I am at peace . . . My abdomen is warm . . . My abdomen is warm . . . My abdomen is warm. (Pause about 90 seconds and begin VI.) I am at peace . . . My arms and legs are heavy and warm, heartbeat calm and regular . . . My arms and legs are heavy and warm, heartbeat calm and regular . . . My breathing is calm . . . My abdomen is warm . . . I am at peace . . . My forehead is cool . . . My forehead is cool . . . My forehead is cool . . . I am at peace . . . My breathing is calm . . . My abdomen is warm . . . My forehead is cool . . . My forehead is cool . . . My forehead is cool . . . I am at peace . . . My arms and legs are heavy and warm . . . Heartbeat calm and regular . . . My forehead is cool . . . My forehead is cool. (After about 2 minutes of silence, terminate the induction.)

SESSION 6.   The relaxation setting is created (comfortable position, eyes closed, passive attitude), and the therapist begins:

I am at peace . . . My arms and legs are heavy and warm . . . My arms and legs are heavy and warm . . . Heartbeat calm and regular . . . Heartbeat calm and regular . . . I am at peace . . . My breathing is calm . . . My breathing is calm . . . My abdomen is warm . . . My abdomen is warm . . . I am at peace . . . My forehead is cool . . . My forehead is cool . . . My forehead is cool . . . I am at peace . . . My arms and legs are heavy and warm . . . Heartbeat calm and regular . . . My breathing is calm . . . My abdomen is warm . . . My forehead is cool. (This therapist presentation takes about 100 seconds, and the client should be allowed about 3 minutes to meditate. If desirable, the induction may be truncated even further by deleting the repetitions and chanting each of the key phrases only once.)

By the time the one autogenic formula presented in session six constitutes the entire induction, over a month of therapist coaching and daily practice have developed most clients' ability to create a moderate relaxation quite rapidly. This conclusion is based upon clinical experience only.

Final Comments on Abbreviated Autogenic Training

Procedure 1 of the abbreviated autogenic method is roughly comparable to level 3 of self-control relaxation in terms of procedural requirements, duration of induction, and level of relaxation produced. Procedure 2 bears a similar relationship to self-control relaxation. Reliable guidelines for selecting progressive relaxation versus autogenic format do not exist. The reader is referred to the section entitled *Relaxation Procedure Selection* in Chapter 4 for a discussion of some relevant issues.

BREATH MANIPULATIONS

Overview

Relaxation may be induced rapidly and with great procedural simplicity by altering one's breathing pattern. Two methods of ancient origin (Chang, 1959; Dhammasudhi, 1968; Dwivedi, Gupta, & Udupa, 1977; Karambelkar, Vinekar, & Bhole, 1968; Rama, 1979; Rieker, 1971; Stanescu, Nemery, Veriter, & Marechal, 1981; Swearer, 1971) will be described. The first, called *breath mindfulness,* is intended for practice on a regular basis. The second, *deep breathing,* is particularly useful for rapidly calming down individuals in an agitated state.

Breath Mindfulness

This approach is based primarily on yoga and Zen practices, but its application has even been embraced by such as Edmund Jacobson (1921). The method simply requires the meditator to focus attention on his breathing and allow the natural breathing process to emerge. As a result, respiration usually slows down and becomes shallower, a wide range of bodily functions follows suit, and experientially the meditator feels very peaceful.

The cross-legged lotus position was recommended, but even in early times, the novice was cautioned to refrain from this sitting position if it caused strain. Any comfortable seated or reclined position is acceptable. (See Chapter 4 for an extended discussion of this and related issues.)

The basic procedure of breath mindfulness was adopted by numerous other oriental religions, most notably Zen Buddhism. Here, awareness of respiratory sensations in the nasal passages and lungs was also emphasized. A mantra, counting, fixed gaze on an external object, or a relaxation cue word can be added in synchrony with the breathing at the discretion of the therapist or client (Owens, 1975; Shapiro, 1978c).

Following is a verbatim transcript of a secularized relaxation induction through breath mindfulness. Although the research on diaphragmatic (abdominal) versus chest (thoracic) breathing is mixed (see Chapter 2), most schools of thought endorse the former, and this should be encouraged if it feels comfortable to the client. The therapist should present these instructions in a relaxed tone.

Please close your eyes (some schools of meditation keep the eyes open) and take a comfortable position. Allow your body to relax and try to adopt a peaceful, calm attitude. Let your attention drift to your chest and abdomen. Notice the rising and falling of your chest or abdomen with each breath. Breathing is, of course, one of your natural functions, and it will continue without any effort on your part. Observe your own breathing, as though you were watching the breathing of another. Give up all voluntary, conscious control of your breathing. Let your bodily processes take over, so that your breathing flows naturally and smoothly. As you give up control of your breathing, your body will begin to function more efficiently, and you will notice your breathing slowing down, becoming shallow and regular. This indicates that less oxygen is coming into your body, reflecting diminished bodily need. In fact, your whole body is slipping into a state of diminished functioning: Your heart, brain, blood pressure, and so forth, are slowing down into a natural rhythm of peaceful relaxation. As you continue to dwell on your respiration, you may become aware of other bodily sensations you do not usually notice, such as the gentle throbbing of your heart, air passing through your nose and lungs, and the flow of blood in your body. Please continue to focus on your breathing and other comforting bodily sensations. If your mind wanders to other subjects, that is no matter for concern. Your attention will soon drift back to breath mindfulness. Now please continue on your own.

In the therapy session, the client should be given a few minutes to enjoy the relaxation experience. For homework, the length of practice should vary between 5 and 30 minutes, once or twice daily, according to what the client can comfortably tolerate.

A modern version of breath meditation has simply taught clients to breathe slow (a 50 percent rate reduction to about eight breaths/minute) and regularly when anxiety threatens (e.g., Clark, Salkovskis, & Chalkley, 1985; Harris, Katkin, Lick, & Habberfield, 1976; McCaul, Solomon, & Holmes, 1979). This method is sometimes called *paced respiration* and employs some sort of timing device (functionally comparable to a metronome) as a guide in training relaxed breathing. Paced respiration appears to be effective and easy to learn.

Deep Breathing

Deep breathing, as presently construed, consists of three operations: taking a deep breath, retaining the breath, and exhaling slowly. The method is designed to produce a rapid, mild state of relaxation. The technique is particularly well-suited to ameliorating intense states of emotional distress (e.g., anger and anxiety) in individuals who have had no prior exposure to relaxation procedures. As such, it may be usefully employed to intervene in a crisis situation or to curtail transitory anxiety states. This method of deep breathing will also curtail hyperventilation, a common and unsettling development in acute anxiety states (Suess, Alexander, Smith, Sweeney, & Marion, 1980). The method usually is not intended for regular practice on a daily basis.

Each of the operations in the deep breathing procedure contributes to the overall usefulness of the technique. Taking a deep breath requires some amount of volition and attention, thus creating a diversion from troubling thoughts. Breath retention increases blood carbon dioxide content beyond normal levels, which in turn promotes a state of mild lethargy (see Chapter 2 for further explanation). Slow exhalation naturally resembles the culmination of a tense-relax cycle in progressive relaxation, leading to tension reduction in body musculature and accompanying benefits.

The procedure is versatile in that it can be done virtually anywhere. Deep breathing has no requirements as to necessary setting conditions. Similarly, subjects need not be seated nor have their eyes closed, though at times these may be helpful.

The simple induction procedure is as follows.

> Take a deep breath. Now hold it for 5 to 10 seconds, and when you exhale, let it go slowly. (Pause till exhalation begins.) Feel the tension flowing out from your whole body as you breathe out. (Pause until subject is ready for next deep breath.) Again, take a deep breath and hold it. (Pause till exhalation begins.) Feel yourself becoming more relaxed as you slowly exhale. (Saying cue words, such as relax or calm, may be added to the slow exhalation.)

Two to five deep breaths should be taken as needed. The entire procedure takes about a minute.

Final Comments on Breath Manipulations

The two procedures of breath control share several advantages. First, they focus on a physiological function, respiration, that is often affected during emotional states. If control can be established over this key function, the entire arousal syndrome may be short circuited, particularly in individuals showing a tendency toward hyperventilation. Second, I have found clients to be generally receptive to these breath strategies. Lastly, neither of these procedures involve mental imagery. Clients having difficulty forming pictures in their mind would probably respond better to these breath methods than to techniques requiring this mental skill. Further, because the breath methods do not involve imagery, keeping one's eyes closed is no longer highly requisite. Some clients are resistant to closing their eyes and would, therefore, be more accepting of the breath methods. Although I usually recommend closing the eyes because it cuts down on distracting stimuli, both breath methods have been employed successfully with eyes opened.

Most methods of relaxation seek autonomic control through indirect routes such as the musculature, imagery, austere cognitions, and so forth. Respiration relaxation is the only convenient direct entry point in the autonomic nervous system. Thus, paced respiration presents strong potential as a relaxation method, combining features of ease of learning and effectiveness, and deserves more research and clinical attention than it has received so far.

GUIDED IMAGERY

Overview

Imagery has long been employed in yoga (Feuerstein, 1975) and Zen (Chang, 1959) methods of meditation to complement other strategies. The use of imagery as a method of relaxation induction is widely endorsed by contemporary therapists, but supportive basic research has been neglected. Pleasant nature scenes were common imagery themes in Tantra Yoga some 2000 years ago (Feuerstein, 1975, p. 157), and presently they are the most frequently used subjects for adults in guided imagery (e.g., Bellack, 1973; Horan & Dellinger, 1974; Kretschmer, 1969; Leuner, 1978; Singer, 1974; Taylor, 1978; Wolpe, 1973).

Daydreaming has long been recognized as a restful retreat from routine activities (Singer, 1975). Guided imagery as a relaxation technique (also called positive imagery, Crits-Christoph & Singer, 1981) may be viewed as planned daydreaming as it has a reminiscent quality. Content sometimes found in daydreaming that is inappropriate for guided imagery includes a future orientation, a desire to attain goals not yet achieved, and desires that are irrational, unrealistic, or socially inappropriate. The content of guided imagery is usually devoted to a situation that the individual has already experienced that is quiet, pretty, and restful. A pleasant nature scene is ideal. For example, as part of his psychoanalytically styled method of guided affective imagery, Leuner (1978) reports the ease with which his clients can generate the image of a peaceful meadow and the pleasant experience this imagery usually creates. In any case, the client's task is to revive a former pleasant experience in imagination analogous to the process of relaxation by recall (see above, *Self-control Relaxation, level 3*).

Procedure

The rationale for guided imagery can be presented very quickly, as it is obvious to most clients.

> I would like to help you become more relaxed by imagining a tranquil, comforting experience. As you become more involved in the image, your mind will be freed of troubling thoughts, and your bodily processes will conform to the peaceful atmosphere you create in your mind.

If possible, the image selected should be one that the client has actually experienced and that is relatively fresh in memory. Some discussion between the therapist and client is needed to make a proper selection. Research has not been conducted to compare the efficacy of relaxing imagery themes. Therefore, the combined judgment of the therapist and client will have to suffice in selecting an image having relaxation induction properties. Following is the image I have used most often in therapy.

> Please find a comfortable position and close your eyes. I will assist you in imagining the scene you have selected by directing or guiding your imagery to different aspects of the scene. Try to recall the sounds and odors of the experience to make the image as realistic as possible. Try to feel as though you are actually *living* your imagined scene right now. Imagine you are lying on the beach in your bathing suit. Feel the warm sand on your back and the sun gently warming your body. You are feeling very peaceful and relaxed. It is a quiet day. You can hear birds in the distance and the hushed sound of voices. The smell of the ocean (or lake) is intoxicating. Your muscles seem to be melting from the warm glow of the sun. Please continue to enjoy this serene experience on your own.

The reader will note that the therapist is speaking as though describing a scene that is being observed to promote a vivid, realistic imaginal experience. The client is encouraged to assume a participant role by imagining actually experiencing the situation, as opposed to viewing the image as you would a movie. Although therapists routinely advocate the superiority of the participant role in enhancing imagery vividness and effects (e.g., Cautela, 1970; Elkins, 1980; Shipley, 1979), experimental evidence (Bauer & Craighead, 1979) only mildly supports this contention. The inclusion of particulars in the image (e.g., "feel the warm sand" and "hear birds") helps secure the client's attention in the image and away from competing troublesome thoughts. Following the implications of Lang's (1979) views, the therapist should also include descriptions of what the client is supposed to be experiencing, such as "muscles seem to be melting," to elicit the corresponding physiological event.

Final Comments on Guided Imagery

Guided imagery, more than any other relaxation technique, relies on visual imagery skills. This trait is not uniformly present in the general population,

and individuals having difficulty creating an absorbing image would not benefit from this method.

The extant literature contains suggestions for improving the imagery of individuals exhibiting deficits in this skill, although the effectiveness of these
training strategies have not been experimentally demonstrated. Indeed, some
discouraging data along these lines are presented in Chapter 3 in trials with
progressive relaxation. Nevertheless, relaxation has been recommended to
overcome the client's anxiety and distractability, which may detract from image clarity (Cautela & McCullough, 1978; Crits-Christoph & Singer, 1981;
Hershey & Kearns, 1979; Jaffe & Bresler, 1980; Kolvin, 1967; Lang, Kozak,
Miller, Levin, & McLean, 1980), but when the imagery is intended as a relaxation strategy, it makes little sense to employ another method of relaxation to
aid the imagery.

Other exercises recommended to enhance imagery or develop imagery skills
include describing the mental image of an object just seen in the room (Cautela
& McCullough, 1978; Woolfolk & McNulty, 1983), imaging emotionally neutral but distinctive stimuli, for example, the taste of a lemon, a tennis volley
(Phillips, 1971), mentally manipulating the color and motion of geometric
shapes before moving on to more complex imagery (Gaarder & Montgomery,
1977), describing multiple sensory modalities in the scene (Cautela & Wisocki,
1971), using tape-recorded imagery instructions to aid home practice (Cautela
& Wisocki, 1971), or viewing oneself performing in an emotionally neutral
situation (Shipley, 1979). Convenient methods of assessing imagery include
having clients estimate the clarity of their image on a rating scale (Cautela &
McCullough, 1978; McCullough & Powell, 1972) or asking clients to provide
an ongoing verbal narration of their imagery (Kazdin, 1975).

Guided imagery is perhaps the best relaxation approach to use with children. The content can be tailored to fit whatever imaginal preferences the child
may have, including the use of favored television programs, games, characters
in novels, and heroes (Hall, 1983; Lazarus, 1971; Lazarus & Abramovitz,
1962). Indeed, such personalizing has been reported with adults as well
(Horan, 1973). The restrictions usually operative with adults (a realistic scene,
previous experience, etc.) do not necessarily apply to children. The interested
reader should consult Rosenstiel and Scott (1977) for more details on presenting imagery to children. Though their remarks are not limited to relaxation
imagery, they provide some useful clinical guidelines.

OCULAR RELAXATION

Overview

Early in his career, Jacobson (1929) began to study the use of ocular techniques, composed of the same kind of tense-relax procedure as the rest of his
method. He observed that eye movements were diminished by this procedure

and, more importantly, there was a concomitant reduction in mental activity. Jacobson (1929, 1938b) recommended the ocular method, in addition to full body progressive relaxation, to aid insomniacs in falling asleep faster, and he presented some case history material testifying to the sleep benefits of his approach. Jacobson (1938a) also emphasized the role of the speech musculature in stimulating cognitive activity, although our recent research has investigated ocular motility only.

Jacobson's own efforts in the laboratory documented the impact of cognitive activity on striate musculature including the oculomotor system (see Chapter 2). Contemporary research has expanded this view to include skeletomuscular, as well as diverse physiological functions, as manifestations of cognitive and affective imagery (see reviews by Cacioppo, 1982; Cacioppo & Petty, 1981; Lang, 1979). Of particular salience to the present discussion are numerous studies demonstrating the correspondence of eye movements with various cognitive tasks (e.g., Klinger, Gregoire, & Barta, 1973; Nakano, 1971; Singer, Greenberg, & Antrobus, 1971; Weiner & Ehrlichman, 1976). However, a related area of research that has been neglected involves the reciprocal influence of peripheral musculature on imaginal processes. Specifically, can we gain influence over cognitive processes by manipulating ocular motility as Jacobson suggested?

We (Lichstein & Sallis, 1982) studied eye exercises, similar to those used by Jacobson, in a laboratory evaluation of two subjects. Ocular relaxation was compared to autogenic phrases of warmth and heaviness throughout the body in four sessions. Each session alternated the sequence between ocular relaxation and autogenics, with baseline periods sandwiching the two treatments. Ocular relaxation and autogenics produced comparable decreases (about 40 percent) in forehead muscle tension, compared to the average baseline level. Ocular relaxation resulted in very modest heart rate reductions contrasted to greater heart rate effects occurring with autogenics. In the measure of greatest interest, eye movements, ocular relaxation produced a 40 percent reduction, which was nearly twice as much as the autogenic effect. Self-report measures of sleepiness, mental activity, and body relaxation favored autogenics by a small but consistent margin. Overall, ocular relaxation produced mild to moderate general relaxation effects and large reductions in ocular motility with these normal subjects. Effects on emotionally aroused subjects have not yet been assessed.

Clinical applications of ocular relaxation so far have been limited to insomnia (Lichstein, 1983; Lichstein & Blew, 1980), where the results have been moderately strong. These studies will be discussed in greater detail in Chapter 7.

Procedure

The procedure involves tensing and relaxing the eyes in much the same manner as progressive relaxation is done. Following is a verbatim introduction.

Please find a comfortable position and close your eyes. Keep your eyes closed for the duration of the procedure. The method I am going to teach you involves tensing and then relaxing your eye muscles with the goal of reducing eye movement. This has the overall effect of relaxing both your mind and body. (The therapist continues by describing the procedural format.) I am going to ask you to move your eyes in different directions, and when I do, please hold your eyes in that position, tensing them as much as you can, until I say "relax," and then let your eyes return to the resting state immediately. Throughout the tensing and relaxing cycles, it is most important to focus all of your attention on the sensations coming from your eyes.

As with progressive relaxation, the six eye positions are tensed for 7 seconds and relaxed for 45 seconds. Nearly continuous patter is provided by the therapist to accompany the two phases. Below is a verbatim presentation of the first cycle only, followed by the basic tensing instructions for the remaining five positions.

1. "When I say 'now,' I want you to raise your eyes as high as they will go, as if you were trying to look out of the top of your head. Okay, now. Keep it tense, feel the muscles tugging, focus on the tension (tense for 7 seconds), and relax. Let your eyes return to a comfortable resting position. Just give up control of your eyes and let them lie there quietly. Keep your attention clearly focused on the sensations coming from your eyes. Compare in your mind the feelings of tension that you were feeling just a few seconds ago to the feelings of restful relaxation gradually coming on now. Try to focus in on the feelings of calm and quiet (relax for 45 seconds)."

2. "Move your eyes downward as if you were trying to look out of your chin."

3. "Move your eyes all the way to the right as if you were trying to look out of your ear."

4. "Move your eyes all the way to the left as if you were trying to look out of your other ear."

5. "Rotate your eyes in a great big circle."

6. "Roll your eyes in a circle the other way."

In reviewing the procedure with the client following its administration, some clients will report difficulty in detecting ocular sensations. For these individuals, I suggest gently placing their fingertips over their eyelids during several practice sessions to help them key in on the eye movements.

Final Comments on Ocular Relaxation

Ocular relaxation is a new, relatively untested technique. Future research is needed to more clearly specify the cognitive and somatic effects accruing to the procedure. The critical question that deserves particular attention is the claim by some of Jacobson's (1929) subjects that the exercises made their minds go blank. If this effect can be reliably produced, then ocular relaxation promises to have a strong therapeutic influence on individuals disturbed by problems such as worrisome thoughts and obsessions.

CHAPTER 6

Relaxation Integrated with Other Treatments

Relaxation therapy, as defined in this book, refers to the therapeutic use of relaxation as the sole or primary intervention. However, the role of relaxation in many therapeutic contexts does not satisfy this definition. Often, relaxation is enlisted to facilitate another therapeutic technique or system, wherein relaxation is clearly not functioning as the principal intervention.

Generally, when relaxation is not the central intervention, it assumes one of two subordinate roles: adjunct or component. Relaxation may function as a helper or assistant (adjunct) to the primary strategy on a regular or intermittent basis. Whether or not relaxation is recruited into this auxiliary role may be determined as much by the personal preferences of the therapist as by theoretical percepts or client needs. Thus, the utilization frequency of relaxation as a therapeutic adjunct for a particular technique (e.g., free association, covert sensitization, hypnosis) will vary both within and between therapists. In its second role, relaxation has roughly equal but minority status among several treatment components orchestrated to form a treatment package. This is most often done to address multifaceted problems, such as addictive behaviors or chronic pain, wherein it is feared that neglect of any aspect of the syndrome would undermine the overall therapeutic impact or durability of therapy gains.

SOME GENERAL CONSIDERATIONS

Relaxation enjoys a unique set of characteristics in comparison to all other psychotherapy techniques.

1. The effects of the procedure can be *reliably predicted*. The psychophysiological influences of relaxation on human functioning have been well established, and variation of effects from one person to the next is usually confined within the relaxation range.

2. The *majority* of psychotherapy clients are suitable for and can successfully achieve relaxation. Contraindications for use and negative side effects are atypical. Most outpatient psychotherapy clients can achieve some level of unambiguous relaxation on the first attempt.

3. Relaxation effects are *demonstrable and readily perceived*. Unlike other psychotherapy approaches whose benefits accrue slowly over time by small increments, relaxation effects occur simultaneously with application. Any observer may ascertain the presence of relaxation effects by visual inspection or by complex instrumentation, and at the same time, their presence is unequivocally known to the client.

No other psychotherapy method can reliably produce *immediate, substantive effects with most clients*. Indeed there are very few psychotherapy techniques that may legitimately lay claim to any one of these characteristics.

The variety of forms and symptom applications of relaxation are numerous. However, one very important use, which the existing literature has ignored, capitalizes on the three impressive characteristics listed above. Typically, a client seeking psychotherapy enters with the expectation of lengthy treatment and slow change. In addition to whatever specific experience or information a client may possess regarding therapy, most therapeutic approaches to a greater or lesser extent are marked by longevity and slow change. Media portrayal emphasizes these notions, and clients' perceptions are accurate in this matter. Imagine what delight and wonder must infuse the client when confronted with a therapy procedure (relaxation) whose immediate effects, both profound and pleasant, are accurately described prior to its administration. By virtue of this experience, client-therapist rapport will be facilitated, and the client's respect for and confidence in the therapist will be enhanced. In essence, relaxation can create a generalized positive set toward therapy, benefiting the subsequent use of therapy procedures unrelated to relaxation. For this reason, relaxation is indicated even in the absence of a specific, compelling symptomatic need. If the therapist can detect a mild, albeit therapeutically inconsequential justification for relaxation, then therapy will ride the wave of client optimism generated by the procedure. This rationale encourages the use of relaxation in more forms of psychotherapy and with more client types than has traditionally been the case. Therefore, relaxation should be applied far beyond its obvious use for symptom relief (see Chapter 7).

Over the past several thousand years, religious and spiritual leaders have developed systems of meditation to be used by normal, healthy individuals for growth experiences. Physicians developed progressive relaxation and autogenic training to be prescribed to individuals seeking relief from physical and emotional distress. As originally conceived, meditation is thus distinguished by its being (a) indifferent to medical/scientific standards, (b) embedded within a broad philosophical context, (c) geared towards enhancing valued attributes rather than remediating unwanted attributes, and (d) intended for adoption by a large segment of the population. These four distinguishing characteristics obtain for the yoga of the earliest Hindu visionaries, as well as the extraordinarily successful pop Transcendental Meditation (TM) of the past two decades.

However, these same strengths of meditation, which have fostered its 5000 year life, may be drawbacks in the clinical domain of Western culture. The lack of scientific grounding, philosophy, growth orientation, and simplicity of most meditation methods may offend clients seeking treatment. Therapists are therefore obliged to assess their clients' inclination in these matters, prior to selecting the method of relaxation to serve as adjunct or component. When confronted by a biased client, the therapist may elect to offer progressive relaxation or autogenic training to avoid conflict, or the therapist may revise the packaging of a meditation technique to make it more acceptable, best exemplified by Benson's (1975) relaxation response. Torrey (1972) and others have discussed at length the critical importance of congruence between clients' expectations and the therapy technique's form and rationale. The force of this principle is no less potent in relaxation therapy.

RELAXATION AS A THERAPEUTIC ADJUNCT

Behavior Therapy

Systematic Desensitization

Systematic desensitization was one of the earliest entries of the behavior therapy movement when it emerged around 1960 (Kazdin, 1978). The method involves constructing a hierarchy of feared situations around a particular theme, and then asking the client to imagine the hierarchy items in ascending sequence while engaging in a response incompatible with anxiety (Wolpe, 1973). The purpose of systematic desensitization is to reduce the client's fearfulness of the target situation.

At present, progressive relaxation most often serves as the incompatible response (Wolpe, 1984). In his historic 1958 clinical treatise, Wolpe introduced a condensed version of progressive relaxation, compared to the laborious method of Jacobson (1929). The early systematic desensitization researchers (e.g., Lang & Lazovik, 1963; Paul, 1966a) established progressive relaxation as the standard anxiety inhibitor in systematic desensitization, primarily because it proved convenient and effective (P. J. Lang, personal communication, May 23, 1984; G. L. Paul, personal communication, May 22, 1984), although hypnosis was also employed during this seminal period (Lang, Lazovik, & Reynolds, 1965; Wolpe, 1958).

Some (Levin & Gross, 1985; Mathews, 1971) have suggested a second route by which relaxation can contribute to systematic desensitization. These observers assert that relaxation enhances image vividness, which in turn may potentiate systematic desensitization effectiveness (Dyckman & Cowan, 1978). However, as indicated in Chapter 3, the evidence for relaxation imagery effects is weak and inconsistent. Further, Jacobson's own studies in this area (reviewed in Chapter 2) suggest that deep (muscular) relaxation is incompatible with cognitions and imagery.

Other relaxation methods, as well as nonrelaxation anxiety inhibitors, have been employed on occasion, including vigorous muscular action (Farmer & Wright, 1971), anger (Goldstein, Serber, & Piaget, 1970), laughter (Ventis, 1973), and respiratory relief (Longo & Vom Saal, 1984). Wolpe (1982) endorsed the use of such alternative forms of relaxation in systematic desensitization as autogenic training, Transcendental Meditation (TM), yoga, and electromyographic biofeedback. Examples of successful utilization of other relaxation methods in systematic desensitization include autogenic training (Kondas, 1967), emotive imagery (Jackson & King, 1981; Lazarus & Abramovitz, 1962), slow breathing (Clark, 1963), TM (Boudreau, 1972), and Bensonian meditation (Kirsch & Henry, 1979).

To what extent does progressive relaxation (or any method of relaxation) contribute to the therapeutic outcome in systematic desensitization? Beginning in the late 1960s, this question has been heavily researched. Arguably, one could dispense with the formalities of progressive relaxation and have the client imaginally work through the anxiety hierarchy while resting calmly, without suffering a loss of therapy benefits. Conversely, perhaps progressive relaxation is the main therapeutic ingredient in systematic desensitization and the hierarchy is a frill. A component dismantling strategy (discussed in greater detail later in this chapter) has been enlisted to address this question. The prototypical design contains at least two of the following treatment groups: standard systematic desensitization, systematic desensitization with progressive relaxation omitted (hierarchy only), and progressive relaxation alone.

To date, this issue has not yet been resolved. The extant literature abounds with well-controlled studies that carefully document that the efficacy of systematic desensitization suffers significantly when progressive relaxation is omitted (e.g., Borkovec & Sides, 1979a; Davison, 1968; Lomont & Edwards, 1967), or that the efficacy of systematic desensitization is unaffected by the absence of progressive relaxation (Folkins, Lawson, Opton, & Lazarus, 1968; Gillan & Rachman, 1974; Yulis et al., 1975). Similarly, when progressive relaxation alone is pitted against standard systematic desensitization (which, of course, includes progressive relaxation), the two are found to be equal (Howard, Murphy, & Clarke, 1983; Ribordy, 1976; Zeisset, 1968), or systematic desensitization is found to be superior (Davison, 1968; Johnson & Sechrest, 1968; Rachman, 1965).

This literature domain is nearly hopelessly confused. Nevertheless, some consistencies do emerge (Mathews, 1971; McGlynn, Mealiea, & Landau, 1981). First, relaxation makes an important therapeutic contribution to systematic desensitization with some individuals and not others. Some parameters that favor the inclusion of relaxation are fewer number of therapy sessions, briefer imaginal exposure to the hierarchy, more severe anxiety, and therapist-determined hierarchy pacing. Second, the more in vivo exposure is utilized in the treatment plan, the less important relaxation and imaginal hierarchy are to the ultimate treatment outcome. Lastly, the comments by Rachman (1968) some years ago still stand as probably the most valid summary observation on this subject. Rachman concluded that training in progressive relaxation (and by implication any other formal relaxation method) served a facilitative but nonessential role in most cases of systematic desensitization. Minimal verbal instructions to assume an ordinary state of calm usually would suffice.

Suinn (1972a, 1972b) introduced a technique called visuo-motor behavior rehearsal (VMBR), a closely related variant of systematic desensitization. The method calls for the client to imagine situations while relaxed (with progressive relaxation), and may be used to reduce noxious emotions associated with these situations. VMBR differs from systematic desensitization primarily in that the former is recommended for facilitating complex skill development, as in sports, when the reduction of noxious emotions is not necessarily the primary goal. More recent clinical data (Suinn, 1976) support the utility of this technique, but the contribution of the relaxation component has not been addressed. Another systematic desensitization variant is rational stage-directed therapy (Tosi & Reardon, 1976). This approach pairs relaxation with a series of imaginal exercises drawing on themes from rational emotive therapy, but little efficacy data is available.

Covert Conditioning

J. R. Cautela is primarily responsible for developing a family of techniques attempting to manipulate actual behaviors, by imagining those behaviors with either reinforcing or punishing imaginal contingencies (Cautela & Baron, 1977). Relaxation has become a frequently employed adjunct with one of these techniques, covert sensitization, but not with any of the others (Upper & Cautela, 1979). Instances of the infrequent use of relaxation with other covert conditioning techniques include the covert reinforcement treatment of public speaking anxiety (Daniels, 1975b) and snake phobia (Marshall, Boutilier, & Minnes, 1974). Covert sensitization (Lichstein & Hung, 1980) was the first covert conditioning technique to be introduced, and it has achieved, by far, the most popularity. When Cautela (1966b, 1967) introduced the procedure, he recommended teaching clients progressive relaxation preparatory to the aversive imagery training, but he gave no specific rationale for including relaxation. Cautela implied that relaxation facilitated treatment by reducing the anxiety that was partly responsible for triggering the undesirable target behaviors.

Cautela (Cautela & McCullough, 1978) has since claimed that relaxation enhances the clarity and impact of the covert sensitization imagery. Although relaxation effects on imagery are plausible and may occur with some individuals, the thrust of what little research exists on this subject (reviewed in Chapter 3) challenges the assertion that relaxation benefits imagery. Several authors have called attention to the need for visualization training for some clients to increase their therapeutic response to covert sensitization (Ashem & Donner, 1968; Janda & Rimm, 1972; Snowden, 1978; Stuart, 1967). Unfortunately, little systematic work has been undertaken to develop such a technology.

Chapter 5 of the present text discusses other methods of imagery enhancement recommended by clinicians. Related issues on the important subject of imagery in covert conditioning are discussed in greater detail by Kazdin (1977).

The use of relaxation, most often progressive relaxation, in covert sensitization has become routine. Examples of this adjunctive role of relaxation in covert sensitization occur in the treatment of cigarette smoking (Lawson & May, 1970; Lichstein & Sallis, 1981; Sipich, Russell, & Tobias, 1974), drug abuse (Anant, 1968; Elkins, 1980), homosexuality (Callahan & Leitenberg, 1973; McConaghy, Armstrong, & Blaszczynski, 1981), obesity (Elliott & Denney, 1975; Stuart, 1967), and sexual deviancy (Barlow, Leitenberg, & Agras, 1969; Cautela & Wisocki, 1971).

A contrast between covert sensitization with and without relaxation would elucidate the contribution of relaxation to this behavior therapy technique. Unfortunately, such tests have not been conducted. The study closest to this goal (Snowden, 1978) compared an unspecified method of relaxation (intended as a placebo control group) with covert sensitization (which included the same relaxation) for heroin abuse. From the present perspective, this was a test of the incremental value of covert sensitization to relaxation, and this proved to be substantial. Covert sensitization significantly depressed heroin use, but relaxation alone did not. Based upon the absence of data, other reviewers (Kazdin & Smith, 1979) and I must conclude that the role of relaxation in covert sensitization and other covert conditioning therapies remains unknown.

Thought Stopping

This technique requires the therapist to shout "stop" while the client is engaged in unwanted, persistent ruminations (Cautela & Wisocki, 1977). With practice, the client learns to disrupt these ruminations by silently invoking the instruction "stop." There are many examples of relaxation employed in collaboration with thought stopping (Cautela, 1977; Cautela & Baron, 1973; Daniels, 1975a; Flannery, 1972; Leger, 1978; Mathews & Shaw, 1977). However, no attempt has been made to assess the contribution of relaxation with this technique.

Assertiveness Training

Individuals handicapped in their ability to communicate thoughts, feelings, and intentions may profit from a collection of techniques housed under this rubric. Common constituents of assertiveness training are cognitive restructuring, modeling, rehearsal, feedback, and relaxation (Lange & Jakubowski, 1976). One study (Hock, Rodgers, Reddi, & Kennard, 1978) contrasted assertiveness training with assertiveness training plus relaxation (progressive relaxation and pleasant imagery), permitting a view of the additive effects of relaxation.

This study treated asthmatic children (see Chapter 7, *Asthma* section for further details) and obtained significant improvement in respiratory function in the combined group, but found assertiveness training alone to be ineffective.

In their discussion, the authors raise an interesting point with implications for other populations as well. Those who might benefit from assertiveness training are likely to be anxiety prone, and while aiding skill development, assertiveness training may itself be anxiety enhancing. Therefore, dual sources of anxiety, symptomatic and iatrogenic, invite supplemental relaxation in assertiveness training.

Modeling

Bandura's brilliant studies of modeling (also called imitation, observational learning, and vicarious learning) began in the early 1960s and are summarized in Bandura (1969). In its simplest terms, modeling is defined as the increased likelihood of producing particular behaviors having observed others engage in those behaviors. Modeling effects may be acquired by direct observation of a model, or by seeing other observers enacting modeling effects (symbolic modeling). Relaxation may potentiate modeling effects by decreasing inhibitory anxiety or by facilitating cognitive rehearsal of the modeled behaviors, and there is good evidence to warrant the incorporation of relaxation into modeling therapies.

Snake phobic volunteers, recruited from the community, were randomly assigned to several conditions evaluating fear reduction treatments (Bandura, Blanchard, & Ritter, 1969). Two of these conditions are of interest to this discussion: progressive relaxation and symbolic modeling combined (group *a*), and symbolic modeling alone (group *b*). Both groups proved to be effective treatments, although group *a* had a small edge. The groups did not differ in rate of treatment progress during vicarious extinction trials, snake approach behavior, or generalized anxiety, but superior gains were made by group *a* on perceived fear arousal during snake approach behavior and changed attitudes toward snakes.

A second study published in the same year (Spiegler, Liebert, McMains, & Fernandez, 1969) provided more convincing evidence of the usefulness of relaxation in symbolic modeling. Snake phobic volunteers from the community were treated with either a film that modeled nonphobic interactions with snakes, taped progressive relaxation, or the film and taped progressive relaxation combined. Although all three groups showed significant pre-post gains in snake approach tests, the combined group was clearly superior, relaxation alone second, and film alone third.

More recently, individuals claiming dental fear were administered modeling plus progressive relaxation, modeling only, or placebo treatment (Wroblewski, Jacob, & Rehm, 1977). The modeling relaxation group surpassed the treatment effects obtained by the modeling and placebo groups on behavioral but not self-report measures. This pattern of results is the reverse of that in Bandura et al. (1969) where only self-report measures distinguished the group receiving relaxation.

Arguing against incorporating relaxation into modeling therapy are data by Rimm and Medeiros (1970). Snake phobic students receiving one session of progressive relaxation-participant modeling combined attained significant pre-post improvement on self-report and behavioral avoidance measures, but no more so than students trained in participant modeling only. Further, those receiving only relaxation exhibited little improvement.

Autogenic Behavior Therapy

Luthe (Luthe & Blumberger, 1977) and others (Ohno, Takeya, & Matsubara, 1977) have proposed the term *autogenic behavior therapy* to encourage the integration of autogenics with behavior therapy techniques. As an example, one application of autogenic behavior therapy involves the use of autogenic training in systematic desensitization (e.g., Kondas, 1967). In a related vein, more than any other relaxation method, autogenics has become wed to biofeedback, most often skin temperature biofeedback. This combination was first popularized by Elmer Green of the Menninger Foundation (Green, Green, & Walters, 1970), who coined the term *autogenic feedback training* (AFT). AFT has gained wide audition, particularly in the area of migraine treatment (see Chapter 7).

Luthe argues that autogenics is more effective than the more common choice of progressive relaxation when employed in behavior therapy, and he advocates the use of the former. However, data addressing the comparative effectiveness of these two relaxation methods as behavior therapy adjuncts are not available.

Psychodynamic Therapies

Meditation

For more than half a century, psychoanalytic (Alexander, 1922/1931; Malhotra, 1961), neoanalytic (Fromm, 1963), and Eastern (Suzuki, 1963; Watts, 1957) theorists have commented on the potential usefulness of incorporating Eastern religious philosophy into psychodynamic therapies. Some obstacles to this goal, born of friction between these two systems, have been noted. For example, Suzuki (1963) pointed out that Western philosophy and values are "analytical, inductive, objective" (p. 5), whereas the Eastern orientation is "nondiscriminative, deductive, intuitive" (p. 5). On the other hand, there are areas of congruence between Eastern philosophy and psychodynamic psychotherapy that likely would have a mutually reinforcing influence when the two systems interact. Fromm (1963) identified several compatible zones, such as cultivation of personal discipline and ethics, liberation from external sources of control, and emphasis on systematic self-inquiry.

Jung (1969) typifies the above group. Well versed in Eastern philosophy, Jung integrated aspects of this view into his therapy. For example, he routinely analyzed mandalas produced by his patients in the same manner that orthodox analysts dissected dreams. Jung (1969) believed that mandalas were "genuine creations of the unconscious" (p. 304) and tapped archetypal structures.

The question of Eastern philosophy contributing to psychodynamic therapies is tangential, however, to the main interests of this book. The use of Eastern methods of meditation in these therapies is more to the point.

There are numerous isolated examples of different forms of meditation employed within the context of an otherwise conventional psychodynamic therapy (e.g., Carrington & Ephron, 1975; Deatherage, 1975; Gersten, 1978; Glantz, 1981; Kutz, Leserman, et al., 1985; Nurnberg, 1978; Peerbolte, 1967; Shafii, 1973a). Beyond feeling more relaxed, with concomitant anxiety reduction and other closely related psychophysiologic changes (insomnia and blood pressure reduction), directly attributable to the meditation technique, what broader personality changes might occur subsequent to the insertion of meditation into psychotherapy? Kornfield (in Walsh, Goleman, Kornfield, Pensa, & Shapiro, 1978) and others (Carpenter, 1977; Shafii, 1973a) observed that with meditation comes greater insight into one's conflicts and motivations, as we gain greater clarity in perceiving our own feelings and thoughts, but supportive data have not been forthcoming.

Some therapists (Carrington, 1978b; Kondo, 1958; Kutz, Borysenko, & Benson, 1985; Welwood, 1980) have pointed out that the benefits of meditation tend to be more global than those of psychotherapy, and that meditation prepares the individual to address focal psychological problems in therapy. Carrington and Ephron (1975) observed decreased paranoid tendencies and increased self-confidence resulting from TM practiced while in psychotherapy. They also noted decreased depression and increased positive affects. According to Shafii (1973a, 1973b), the shift in attention from external (secondary process) to internal (primary process) reality is one aspect of meditation that fosters psychosexual regression. When this occurs within an ongoing psychoanalysis, early childhood experiences previously lost to awareness are unearthed for analytic work. Other salient aspects are the silence and immobility during meditation. Both of these reduce attention to and reliance on verbal and motoric dimensions of functioning and thereby facilitate further regression to preverbal, motorically primitive developmental stages. Along similar lines, there are some data (Reed, 1978) to suggest that meditation enhances dream recall, which may then be employed for psychoanalytic work.

According to Fromm-Reichman (1950, pp. 10–11), one of the main reasons Freud originally situated the patient on a couch was to induce relaxation to facilitate the unencumbered flow of thoughts. Speaking more specifically on meditation and other methods of relaxation, theorists since have offered rationales on how adjunctive relaxation aids free association and the psychoanalytic process in general. The main reason given is that it frees creative energy and fosters primary process thinking (Carrington & Ephron, 1975; Kutz, Borysenko, & Benson, 1985). In so doing, repressed material is more likely to surface when the client is comfortably relaxed during free association (Glueck & Stroebel, 1978; Ikemi, Ishikawa, Goyeche, & Sasaki, 1978; Peerbolte, 1967).

Although verifiable documentation is meager, numerous personal accounts of therapy experiences expose some possible benefits that might be obtained from the union of meditation and psychotherapy. Walsh (1976) described the effects of informal meditation occurring during an ongoing psychotherapy (which was followed by rigorous, systematic meditation subsequent to psychotherapy termination, described in Walsh, 1977, 1978). Walsh reported that if he focused his attention on slow inhalations while dysphoric, the intensity of the emotion was unaffected but its valence changed to positive. If he focused his attention on exhalation during dysphoria, the intensity of the dysphoria waned as the valence changed. Walsh also used the term *meditative perception* to describe increased self-awareness and self-acceptance during his routine daily experience, a generalization from the attitude trained in breath mindfulness meditation.

Several theorists (Kondo, 1952; Kretschmer, 1969; Rachman, 1981; Schuster, 1979; Walsh, 1979; Welwood, 1980) have claimed that therapy enhancement will result if the therapist practices meditation. Carrington (1978b) listed five specific benefits to her own practice of psychotherapy resulting from her meditation experiences: more discerning of clients' unconscious conflicts, improved dream interpretation, greater alertness over successive hours of psychotherapy, less threatened when clients have negative reactions, and better able to give advice on clients' meditation practice. Keefe (1975) noted similar benefits accruing to the therapist: enhanced self-awareness, sharper perception, and increased focus on the present.

The little experimental data available on the question of therapist as meditator support the above observations. Lesh (1970) observed increased empathy, openness to experience, and self-actualization in masters' counseling students following practice of Zen counting meditation for 1 month. Leung (1973) trained undergraduate volunteers in Zen meditation and found subsequent increases in the basic psychotherapeutic skills of empathy and accurate perception (see Chapter 3 for further discussion of this article).

Shafii (1973a) raised an interesting point (reiterated by Carrington, 1978b, above) in noting that, with the rising popularity of meditation, therapists will be treating increasing numbers of clients for whom meditation is an important part of their past or present experience. Therapists ignorant of meditation will be ill-equipped to appreciate the meaning of this experience and to advise their clients accordingly.

Despite the successful trials noted above, meditation is poorly represented among current psychodynamic practitioners. Perhaps organizing the scattered data on this subject in the present discussion will serve to heighten the awareness of psychodynamic therapists about the availability of this adjunctive strategy and will stimulate its increased usage.

Progressive Relaxation (PR)

In the early part of this century, there was some psychoanalytic discussion of muscular relaxation, though these endorsements exerted little impact. Ferenczi

(1925/1960, p. 282), a central psychoanalytic figure, recommended muscular relaxation to aid free association. Ferenczi probably did so without knowledge of Jacobson's work. Later, Ferenczi (1930) and Alexander (1933) noted that relaxed patients dealt more effectively with resistance blockages than did tense and frustrated patients, but such patients did not employ any formal technique of relaxation.

To date, PR has stimulated little theoretical or pragmatic interest among psychodynamic therapists, and, accordingly, there are few instances of its use in that context (e.g., Kendall, 1967; Kubie, 1943). Other examples include a case history describing the application of PR (as part of systematic desensitization) to refractory anxiety within an ongoing psychodynamic therapy (Chesni, 1980). Pascal (1947) presented case studies to document the usefulness of a form of passive relaxation in stimulating recall of repressed material and in strengthening the therapist-client relationship. Lazarus (1961), primarily interested in testing group systematic desensitization, employed a control condition composed of psychodynamic group therapy plus PR that proved ineffectual.

Drawing upon the counterconditioning rationale fueling systematic desensitization, Wilson and Smith (1968) instructed neurotic clients to free associate while under the influence of progressive relaxation and a "light to moderate hypnotic trance" (p. 475). The authors viewed this treatment method as desensitizing anxiety-laden thoughts unsystematically as they occur in unplanned sequence. Good clinical results were reported.

Autogenic Training (AT)

More than any other method of relaxation, AT claims a kinship with psychodynamic therapy. AT and psychoanalysis share a common heritage in that both emerged around 1900 from schools of hypnosis (Hoppe, 1961). From the outset, AT therapists presented their method of relaxation within a broader psychotherapeutic context, which relied heavily on psychoanalytic theory and has included attention to such processes as transference in AT (Lapierre, 1977). With respect to AT contributions to psychoanalysis, Rorschach analyses suggest that the heaviness exercises in AT promote expression of repressed information and greater receptivity to social influence (Saraceni, Ruggeri, & Cagossi, 1977). Stephanos, Biebl, and Plaum (1976) provide an example of AT integrated into psychoanalysis in much the same way that meditation has been incorporated (see above).

Schultz and Luthe (1969) reported that in the late 1950s the association between AT and psychoanalysis was formalized by the introduction of methods of autogenic neutralization (Luthe, 1970b, 1973). This approach sought to dispel conflictual emotions through the combination of AT and psychodynamic interpretation. Functionally, these methods amount to guided free association while in a deeply relaxed autogenic state. Therefore, this approach is reserved for clients who have thoroughly mastered AT. A brief overview follows.

Autogenic neutralization is composed of two techniques: autogenic abreaction and autogenic verbalization. Autogenic abreaction involves encouraging the client to produce the diversity of relaxation side effects termed *autogenic discharges* (see discussion in Chapter 4). These are now experienced more intensely and for prolonged periods, as they are presumed to represent emotional conflicts that may be released in this manner. Psychodynamic interpretation and discussion of their meaning may follow the experience. Autogenic verbalization refers to exploration of a particular emotional conflict while relaxed. It differs from autogenic abreaction in that it is focal and structured. Dream interpretation is often woven into the neutralization process. It should be clear that both aspects of autogenic neutralization draw heavily upon psychodynamic theory and practice. Conversely, an ongoing psychodynamic psychotherapy could readily incorporate AT and these methods of neutralization to expedite the analytic process or to achieve a breakthrough at a therapeutic impasse.

Imagery

Leuner's (1978) method of guided affective imagery utilizes imagery to reveal psychoanalytic conflicts. Leuner relies mainly on a dozen standard themes that tend to evoke thoughts and emotions related to key psychoanalytic concepts. Several nature themes, such as a meadow, a brook, and a mountain, are among the standard themes, as they are said to tap such key issues as oral drives and masculine identity. The method thus acts to facilitate unearthing of psychodynamic conflicts and further the analysis of such.

Humanistic Therapy

Several authors (e.g., Forem, 1974; Goleman, 1971; Keefe, 1975; Sallis, 1980, 1982; Sato, 1958; Walsh, 1980) have drawn attention to parallels in theory, process, and goals between meditation and schools of humanistic psychotherapy, particularly the systems of Maslow (1968) and Jourard (1968). Most schools of meditation and humanistic psychotherapy begin with the basic belief that, in essence, people are good, and when personality obstacles are removed, this goodness materializes. As this process approaches its ultimate development, terms such as *satori* or *samadhi* are applied by Easterners and *self-actualization* by Westerners. Several studies (Ferguson & Gowan, 1976; Hjelle, 1974; Seeman, Nidich, & Banta, 1972) have documented increases in self-actualization after practicing meditation, thereby providing evidence of the similarity between Eastern and Western growth experiences.

   Meditation is said to promote a higher level of personality integration, thus increasing accurate perception and transcendent, other-oriented values, as in Maslow's "Being-Cognition" and "Being-Values," and Jourard's transcendent behavior. Unleashing ourselves from the past and the future, and thus freeing our psychological energies to wholly invest attention in the here and now characterizes both meditation and Jourard's transcendent perception. Indeed, both Maslow and Jourard emphasized desirable goals more than the means by which to attain them, and meditation presents as one possible vehicle by which these valued humanistic traits can be realized.

Psychodrama

Rothman (1961) discussed the utilization of relaxation (autogenics) within psychodrama. Based upon her clinical experience, Rothman asserted that autogenics diminishes stage fright that sometimes impedes psychodrama, stimulates the communication process, and aids dream recall.

Group Therapy

Despite my efforts, I was unable to locate a single instance of relaxation incorporated into psychodynamic group therapy other than the Lazarus (1961) trial cited above. Relaxation in group therapy usually occurs in structured, problem-focused behavior therapy groups (Upper & Ross, 1979). Virtually every type of relaxation method has been presented successfully in a group setting to treat such disorders as insomnia (e.g., Woolfolk, Carr-Kaffashan, McNulty, & Lehrer, 1976), chronic pain (Turner, 1982), Raynaud's disease (Keefe, Surwit, & Pilon, 1980), cigarette smoking (Schinke, Blythe, & Doueck, 1978), hypertension (Hoelscher, Lichstein, & Rosenthal, 1986), phobias (Spiegler, Liebert, McMains, & Fernandez, 1969), and general anxiety (Brown, 1980; May, House, & Kovacs, 1982).

The size of the group usually numbers three to six members, although effective inductions have occurred with groups as large as 80 (Shelton, 1973), and even 300 (Neufeld, 1951). Orme and Snider (1964) observed that larger groups (about 15 members) were more effective than smaller groups (about five members) in their autogenics treatment of alcoholics, although Luthe (1963) and Arcan (1977) recommend a maximum of 10 in autogenics groups.

The critical question in this domain concerns the relative efficacy of individual versus group relaxation inductions. Efficacy will be determined by at least two factors: the power of the relaxation induction, and the level of home relaxation practice. Plausibly, either of these could suffer in the group format.

Anecdotal data suggest that some people can profit from individual relaxation training sessions, but they feel uncomfortable when there are others besides the therapist present. Others require individualized instruction and do not respond well in a group (De Rivera, De Montigny, Remillard, & Andermann, 1977; Geer & Katkin, 1966; McDonagh & McGinnis, 1973).

There are a few studies that have contrasted individual and group relaxation inductions. Paul and Shannon (1966) provided some data bearing indirectly on this question. They found individual and group systematic desensitization (both of which included progressive relaxation training) to be equally effective with speech phobic students, suggesting the relaxation component was not undermined in the group setting. In treating alcoholics, Miller and Taylor (1980) also contrasted treatment packages (which included progressive relaxation) in individual and group formats, and obtained results identical to those of Paul and Shannon (1966).

More direct tests have also pointed towards therapeutic equality between individual and group relaxation training. Studies pitting individual against group inductions have obtained no significant difference in the treatment of dysmenorrhea (Heczey, 1980) and hypertension (Hoelscher, Lichstein, & Rosenthal, 1986; Nath & Rinehart, 1979).

In brief, virtually all available data support the view that there is little or no therapeutic loss in moving from individual to group relaxation formats. Thus, the attractiveness of group relaxation therapy resulting from its cost effectiveness is untempered by clinical considerations.

Hypnosis

There are many procedural and outcome features common to both hypnosis and relaxation. Indeed, one thrust of T.X. Barber's prodigious research contributions (summarized in Barber, 1969) was to explicate the overlap between these two systems. The main question of current concern asks: What is the contribution of relaxation in an adjunctive role in hypnosis? Anecdotal evidence suggests a substantial contribution. Autogenic training was born of hypnotic practice and refined as a variant thereof. Contemporary hypnotic inductions often begin with some form of relaxation (Coe, 1980), such as progressive relaxation (e.g., LaBaw, Holton, Tewell, & Eccles, 1975) or imagery (Kohen, Olness, Colwell, & Heimel, 1984). A successful hypnotic trance derives in part from a relaxed state, and the deliberate induction of relaxation may heighten the subject's receptivity to hypnosis and ability to attend to hypnotic instructions (Gruen, 1972). Further, relaxing imagery and other relaxation techniques may be recruited to deepen the hypnotic trance (Clarke & Jackson, 1983).

Barber (1984, p. 144) delineated eight reasons why hypnotherapists often employ various relaxation techniques:

(1) They define the situation as "hypnosis." (2) They are "easy" suggestions that most subjects can "pass." (3) They can help reduce critical and analytical thinking. (4) They can change the situation so that imagining and fantasizing is appropriate. They can also provide a "calm mind," which has several important uses: (5) thinking through solutions to life problems; (6) mentally practicing tasks or performances such as delivering a speech or taking a test; and (7) mentally rehearsing overcoming addictions, such as smoking and alcoholism. Finally, (8) they can help produce peace of mind or calmness, which is useful for overcoming stress-related disorders, such as migraines, headaches, asthma, insomnia, and hypertension.

Research on relaxation influences in hypnosis has focused on changes in hypnotic susceptibility attendant to relaxation practice. Delmonte (1981b) conducted a prototypical study. Volunteers were trained in a standardized form of TM, ostensibly in preparation for a study on imagery processes. Subjects were then measured for hypnotic suggestibility with Barber's (1965) scale, following either TM or simple rest, presented in this sequence to half the subjects and in the reverse sequence to the other half. Suggestibility was significantly higher following TM than after rest. With minor exception, this effect held among subjects who had correctly guessed the true purpose of the study, as well as among those who did not claim such knowledge, thus ruling out with reasonable certainty the influence of demand and placebo effects. Data consistent with the results of this experiment, but less rigorously controlled, have been reported for the hypnotic effects of TM (Walrath & Hamilton, 1975), for progressive relaxation (Leva, 1974), and for a mixture of relaxation techniques (Springer, Sachs, & Morrow, 1977).

Negative data on the effect of relaxation on hypnotic susceptibility have also been forthcoming. Radtke, Spanos, Armstrong, Dillman, and Boisvenue (1983) submitted normal volunteers to 10 sessions of progressive relaxation, biofeedback, or no treatment. Two hypnotic susceptibility scales (Shor & Orne, 1962; Weitzenhoffer & Hilgard, 1962) were administered at pre-post points. No increases in susceptibility occurred, despite (muscle relaxation) evidence of successful relaxation inductions in both treated groups. The interested reader is directed to other data also arguing against relaxation as a hypnotic aid (Banyai & Hilgard, 1976; Heide, Wadlington, & Lundy, 1980; Katz, 1979; Simon & Salzberg, 1981; Spanos, Gottlieb, & Rivers, 1980; Spanos, Radtke-Bodorik, & Stam, 1980; Spanos, Steggles, Radtke-Bodorik, & Rivers, 1979).

A more direct test of the degree to which relaxation aids hypnosis can be readily conducted by comparing hypnosis with relaxation preparation to the same hypnotic procedure without relaxation. Unfortunately, such trials have not been conducted and, at present, the use of relaxation in hypnosis depends mainly on the persuasive influence of theory and the therapist's personal experience.

Biofeedback

Biofeedback bears a similar relationship to relaxation as does hypnosis. At times, relaxation and biofeedback are competing interventions for the same target behavior; on other occasions, relaxation is used in partnership with biofeedback to extend the effectiveness of the latter.

More data are available on the several relationships between relaxation and biofeedback than was the case with hypnosis. Here again, the relative efficacy of biofeedback and relaxation is tangential to the focus of this book. The interested reader is directed to excellent reviews bearing on this question (Sharpley & Rogers, 1984; Silver & Blanchard, 1978; Tarler-Benlolo, 1978). To summarize the extant literature, the effects of biofeedback and relaxation are indistinguishable much of the time.

Several studies have compared biofeedback alone to the combination of relaxation and biofeedback, permitting evaluation of the contribution of relaxation as a therapeutic adjunct in biofeedback. Herzfeld and Taub (1977) assigned normal volunteers to 10 sessions of finger temperature biofeedback, which alternated between instructions to increase or decrease. Half of these sessions were augmented by slides and verbal suggestions (similar to autogenics) of either warmth or cold consistent with the direction of feedback for that day. Mean skin temperature change in suggestion enhanced sessions was significantly greater than change during nonsuggestion sessions. Herzfeld and Taub (1980) have since replicated this effect in a between-groups design. The combined thermal imagery/skin temperature biofeedback group averaged 2.01° F increase, nearly triple that of subjects receiving skin temperature biofeedback alone (0.73° F). Similar data have emerged from other labs (Bregman & McAllister, 1982; Sheridan, Boehm, Ward, & Justesen, 1976) arguing for the facilitative role of warmth imagery in skin temperature biofeedback. Related data, indicating the addition of autogenics does not increase skin temperature biofeedback effects, have also been reported (Keefe, 1978; Vasilos & Hughes, 1979).

Qualls and Sheehan (1981) did find that when enhanced with pleasant nature imagery, EMG biofeedback (frontalis electromyography) produced significantly lower levels of muscle tension than biofeedback alone. The imagery effect was strongest in those student volunteers evincing high absorption capacity (Tellegen & Atkinson, 1974). Burish's lab (Burish, Hendrix, & Frost, 1981) produced some negative data on this question. Studying student volunteers at rest and during threatened shock stress, they observed no physiological or experiential advantages of adding passive relaxation to EMG biofeedback. Reinking and Kohl (1975) obtained negative results in attempting to enhance EMG biofeedback. Using an abbreviated form of progressive relaxation, facial relaxation only, their student volunteers derived no added benefits from supplementing frontalis biofeedback with relaxation, as measured by frontalis and self-reported tension. Negative data on the incremental value of combined progressive relaxation and autogenic training to EMG biofeedback were also obtained by Hutchings and Reinking (1976) in their headache treatment.

Two studies contrasted direct blood pressure biofeedback with and without progressive relaxation. Glasgow, Gaarder, and Engel (1982) treated hypertensives and found the combination of relaxation and biofeedback to be more effective than biofeedback alone, although the difference was not statistically significant. Fey and Lindholm (1978) did observe statistically greater effects with relaxation/biofeedback combined over biofeedback alone (systolic and diastolic blood pressure, heart rate, and self-rated relaxation) with normotensive subjects. Interestingly, relaxation only was equally as effective as relaxation/biofeedback combined at most comparison points.

Several isolated studies tested various other relaxation-biofeedback combinations. Data from Cowings (1977a, 1977b) indicate that autogenics significantly increases the cardiovascular effects of heart rate biofeedback. The unusual union of progressive relaxation and skin temperature biofeedback had a greater effect on handwarming than biofeedback alone (King & Montgomery, 1980).

It should be remembered that adding relaxation to biofeedback constitutes an increment in treatment time and therapeutic exposure. A conservative way of judging the benefits of supplemental relaxation is to include a contrast with a group receiving extra biofeedback so that the total biofeedback exposure equals the time consumed by biofeedback and relaxation combined. Such trials have not been conducted.

Parapsychological (psi) Phenomena

Braud (1981) articulately presented the argument that low autonomic arousal is a psi conducive state, and therefore, psi enhancement should follow relaxation inductions. There have been numerous tests of this notion, and although the results are not uniformly supportive, corroborating data do exist.

In the early 1970s, a series of reports (Braud & Braud, 1973, 1974; Stanford & Mayer, 1974) employing the same paradigm yielded consistent, remarkable results. In brief, subjects trained in progressive relaxation and pleasant imagery could accurately describe pictures exhibited in a separate room at a "hit" rate far greater than chance.

A more recent study by Braud (1981) produced qualified results. Community volunteers were trained in either autogenic training or progressive relaxation. (Further details on this and other studies in this section are presented in the *Progressive Relaxation* and *Autogenic Training* sections of Chapter 3.) He evaluated psi ability by asking autogenics subjects to discern the thoughts of another viewing a series of pictures and by asking progressive relaxation subjects to manipulate a variable voltage generator to match a target voltage unknown to the subject. The results stemming from both relaxation inductions were identical. There occurred a curvilinear pattern wherein individuals attaining either no further relaxation (by electrodermal criteria) or deep relaxation evinced no psi enhancement. Moderately relaxed individuals did perform significantly better than those falling above or below this range.

Others have obtained less encouraging findings. Meditation subjects registered moderate improvement on a task involving reproduction of a picture from an adjoining room, but no improvement when asked to select a target tile among a matrix of tiles (Osis, Bokert, & Carlson, 1973). In a test of a variation of the Lozanov (1971/1978) method—a combination of progressive relaxation, slow breathing, imagery, suggestion, and music—Quider (1981, 1984) observed no benefits accruing to relaxation on a clairvoyance task—forced choice, guessing numbers.

Final Comments on Relaxation as a Therapeutic Adjunct

Obviously, many schools of therapy, some quite distinct from others, have seen the need to incorporate relaxation, and have perceived benefits accruing therefrom. However, experimental demonstrations of relaxation-produced incremental value have been less plentiful.

Behavior therapy employs relaxation (primarily progressive relaxation) more often than do other schools of therapy, the largest amount of salient research has occurred here, and the strongest supportive data exist in this domain. However, ambiguity, concerning the contribution of relaxation persists even in behavior therapy, particularly concerning the method of systematic desensitization. This is no small irony, since systematic desensitization was pivotal in popularizing relaxation.

Meditation has won an enthusiastic following in some circles of psychodynamic therapy, but the overall impact of meditation in this realm is small. Longstanding cogent arguments in behalf of meditation in psychodynamic therapies have not exerted substantive influence. Even autogenic training, which partly defines itself in psychodynamic terms, has failed to attract more than a whimper of interest.

The data supporting relaxation in group therapy are strong and consistent. These applications mostly involve behavior therapy treatments, and therapists should not hesitate to avail themselves of the efficient group format when delivering relaxation.

More equivocal data are found when examining the role of relaxation in biofeedback and hypnosis. One may argue there is only small cost associated with adding relaxation to the treatments, and some clients undoubtedly derive benefit from the relaxation supplement. The data recommending autogenic training in skin temperature biofeedback are strongest, but negative results occur here as well.

Adequate methodology for testing the incremental value of relaxation adjuncts is readily available. A given treatment presented by itself versus the same treatment with relaxation added will illuminate the relaxation contribution. This is a rudimentary version of the dismantling design discussed in greater detail in the section below. Controls for placebo and treatment credibility influences can be added to rule out competing outcome explanations. Conservative judgments on relaxation as a therapeutic adjunct, with different therapies and for different disorders, await further evidence from such methodologies.

RELAXATION AS A TREATMENT PACKAGE COMPONENT

The sections which follow are concerned mainly with describing and evaluating the role of relaxation as one member of a treatment package. Related issues, such as the relative efficacy of the treatment components and the efficacy of the treatment package as a whole, cannot be totally ignored, but they are deemed tangential to the central theme of this book and will not be emphasized.

In order to isolate the contribution of relaxation from package effects, what has been termed a dismantling design is required. For present purposes, this involves at least two treatment conditions—one which presents the package in its entirety, and one which presents the package minus one component, relaxation. Assuming the former group makes superior gains, outcome discrepancies may then be attributed to the presence of relaxation save for one qualification: nonspecific treatment effects.

Consider the example of treatment one constructed of components x, y, and z, and treatment two constructed of x and y. The superiority of treatment one may just as likely be due to elevated placebo power, therapist enthusiasm, etc., generated by the larger, more complex, and more demanding treatment protocol, as due to the therapeutic potency of component z. In discussing the dismantling of systematic desensitization, Kazdin and Wilcoxon (1976) eloquently draw our attention to the importance of controlling for and assessing such extraneous forces: "Showing differences between groups receiving portions of the package compared to a group receiving the complete package does not necessarily mean that the package constitutes the specific ingredients required for change. The groups may differ in the expectancies for improvement that they generate" (p. 739). As none of the research described below heeds this caution, their conclusions are subject to this alternative explanation.

There is some data (Hynd, Chambers, Stratton, & Moan, 1977; Hynd, Stratton, & Severson, 1978) to suggest that, relative to competing interventions, relaxation is viewed as a highly respected and credible treatment for smoking. Therapists employing relaxation are justified in being delighted with this information, but it also underscores the concerns raised by Kazdin and Wilcoxon.

Stress Management

Stress management training involves tension reduction through improved coping skills. The term *stress management* refers to a general approach, not a specific technique. Although there is no single standard method, there are important commonalities among the most widely accepted systems (Hamberger & Lohr, 1984; Meichenbaum & Jaremko, 1983; Novaco, 1977; Rosenthal & Rosenthal, 1983; Suinn & Richardson, 1971; Woolfolk & Lehrer, 1984) that convey the main ingredients of the approach as follows.

1. Some form of relaxation is employed to target the physiological arousal component of noxious emotions (e.g., anxiety, anger). The method of relaxation may be a static form, but it is increasingly more often a type of self-control relaxation.

2. Some form of cognitive restructuring is employed to combat self-defeating thought patterns by reordering the client's perceptions, values, and attitudes.

3. Some form of social skills training is employed to modulate motoric

(speech, posture) expressions of tension and to enhance interpersonal functioning.

4. Some form of instruction in self-monitoring is employed so that the individual can readily detect early somatic, cognitive, or motoric arousal cues. Such harbingers of serious emotional distress alert the client to invoke the newly acquired coping skills.

Chronic Anxiety

Most current anxiety theories (Barlow & Wolfe, 1981; Borkovec, Weerts, & Bernstein, 1977) endorse a model wherein cognitive, physiological, and motoric factors operate to produce the anxiety experience. Numerous factors (e.g., degree of arousal and setting demands) govern the level of stress response synchrony. The stress profile will vary accordingly within and between individuals (Hodgson & Rachman, 1974). Stress management treatments mirror this trichotomy, and treatment components are applied with unequal emphasis to match the relative intensity of the anxiety factors in an individual's stress profile (Davidson, 1978; Hugdahl, 1981).

Numerous clinical examples of stress management programs for chronic anxiety utilize progressive relaxation (e.g., Hamilton & Bornstein, 1977; Jannoun, Oppenheimer, & Gelder, 1982; Sarason, Johnson, Berberich, & Siegel, 1979), self-control relaxation (Barlow et al., 1984; Forman, 1982), and meditation (Lester, Leitner, & Posner, 1984). Not uncommonly, more than one relaxation method is taught within a program (Charlesworth, Murphy, & Beutler, 1981; Shaw & Blanchard, 1983).

There is little information available that isolates the relaxation component per se. Hillenberg and Collins (1986) recently presented some salient data. Anxious volunteers were randomly assigned to progressive relaxation treatment, cognitive restructuring treatment, their combination, or no treatment. The three active treatment groups produced anxiety relief superior to the control group, but they differed little from each other. It is noteworthy that either component of the successful package (the combination group) was as effective as the package.

A procedure called *induced anxiety* (Sipprelle, 1967) combines features of stress management and systematic desensitization. In a series of four 10-minute stages, clients first practice hypnosis or progressive relaxation, then focus on noxious thoughts and related affects and sensations, relax again, and discuss the experience with the therapist. Ollendick and Nettle (1977) tested the contribution of only the second relax stage on anxious undergraduates. One group received five sessions of the standard sequence as above (employing progressive relaxation), and a second group received this sequence except that the second stage, noxious thoughts, was extended and the third stage (second relax) was omitted. Both treated groups exhibited significantly lower heart rate than a no-treatment control group. Trait anxiety (State-Trait Anxiety Inventory, STAI; Spielberger, Gorsuch, & Lushene, 1970) and fears (Fear Survey Schedule; Wolpe & Lang, 1964) did not distinguish the groups. The no-second-relax group obtained lower STAI-State anxiety than the other two groups, which did not differ from each other. In sum, these results moderately support the conclusion that the second relax stage is gratuitous or even counter-productive.

Phobias

There have been several instances of stress management applied to focal anxiety, as exemplified by treatments of mathematics (Suinn & Richardson, 1971), speech (Fremouw & Harmatz, 1975; Weissberg, 1975), test (Deffenbacher, Michaels, Michaels, & Daley, 1980), and social (Butler, Cullington, Munby, Amies, & Gelder, 1984) phobias. Deffenbacher and Hahnloser (1981) dismantled a prototypical stress management program in presenting test anxious students with (a) cognitive techniques, (b) self-control relaxation, (c) treatments a and b combined (stress management), or (d) no treatment. All three treated groups (a, b, and c) fared better than the untreated group. The combination treatment (c) proved somewhat superior to the univariate treatments on self-report and performance measures, at posttreatment and follow-up. With respect to the main interests of this book, these data argue that self-control relaxation is effective as a unitary phobia treatment and does contribute to the overall impact of a phobia treatment package.

Type A Behavior

Jacobson (1955) and others have called attention to a cluster of personality traits highly correlated with coronary heart disease, predating the same pattern termed *Type A behavior* by Friedman and Rosenman (1959). In brief, this pattern is characterized by a high need for achievement, a sense of time urgency, and excessive proneness to hostility (see reviews by Margolis, McLeroy, Runyan, & Kaplan, 1983; Matthews, 1982).

There have been several attempts to diminish Type A behavior through stress management (Friedman et al., 1982, 1984; Hart, 1984; Levenkron, Cohen, Mueller, & Fisher, 1983; Ornish et al., 1983; Suinn, 1975; Suinn & Bloom, 1978), and these have met with good success. However, the role of relaxation in altering Type A behavior remains unclear. No clinical study has tested this component separate from others (see also *Heart Disease and Dysfunction,* Chapter 7). There is some basic research (Muskatel, Woolfolk, Carrington, Lehrer, & McCann, 1984) to suggest that the time urgency component responds to meditation. Further, Meyer Friedman (personal communication, November 23, 1983) indicated that even in their highly effective stress management intervention (Friedman et al., 1982), relaxation practice compliance was low and contributed little to the outcome.

One study (Krampen & Ohm, 1984) executed a design that roughly addressed questions salient to this section. Recovering myocardial infarction patients received a "standard" rehabilitation program (content unspecified), or the same program supplemented with relaxation training (autogenic training and progressive relaxation combined). Posttreatment evaluations revealed that the relaxation-enhanced group surpassed the other on physicians' ratings of general health, ergometric performance, arrhythmia improvement, and self-rated psychological and physical improvement. Several other measures showed no difference between the groups, and no measure revealed superiority of the non-relaxation group. Enthusiasm for these impressive results should be tempered by these facts: (a) We do not know the extent of Type A presence in these samples, (b) We do not know the nature of the basic rehabilitation program, and (c) We do not know the method by which patients were assigned to groups. Most importantly, this study did not assess the clinically crucial question of long-term effects.

Aggression

Primarily two forms of aggression have attracted stress management interventions: anger and child abuse.

Multicomponent stress management programs have incorporated self-control relaxation to control anger in adults (Deffenbacher, Demm, & Brandon, 1986; Novaco, 1977, 1980), combined self-control, breath, and progressive relaxation for acting-out adolescents (Feindler, Marriott, & Iwata, 1984; Lichstein, Wagner, Krisak, & Steinberg, 1987), used unspecified relaxation to manage aggression in adolescents (Schlichter & Horan, 1981), and applied breath relaxation for assaultiveness in a hearing-impaired, borderline-intelligent adolescent (Luiselli, 1984).

Although the trials above were successful, an earlier report by Novaco (1976) diminishes the status of the relaxation component in anger control. In the 1976 study, adults claiming anger problems were assigned to one of four groups: the combination of cognitive restructuring and an unspecified method of relaxation (probably self-control), relaxation only, cognitive restructuring only, and placebo. Treatments were evaluated by self-report and by responses to laboratory analogue challenge. The pattern of results ordered the groups in a descending sequence of efficacy: (a) cognitive restructuring/relaxation, (b) cognitive restructuring only, (c) relaxation only, and (d) placebo. Relatively small differences occurred between treatments a and b, and between treatments c and d, suggesting that relaxation made only a small contribution to the package (treatment a).

Sandler and his associates (Denicola & Sandler, 1980; Wolfe, Sandler, & Kaufman, 1981) treated child-abusing parents with a stress management package and parenting skills training, while Nomellini and Katz (1983) obtained a positive outcome targeting this same problem using a stress management program alone. However, the contribution of relaxation in these packages has yet to be isolated.

Other Applications

Stress maintains and exacerbates a wide array of human problems. Thus stress management, including relaxation, has been employed (sometimes in cooperation with other, more symptom-specific interventions) to address such problems as depression (Sallis, Lichstein, Clarkson, Stalgaitis, & Campbell, 1983; Steinmetz, Lewinsohn, & Antonuccio, 1983), panic disorder (Barlow et al., 1984), test anxiety (Lowenstein & Robyak, 1979; Thyer et al., 1981), drug-dependent insomnia (Kirmil-Gray, Eagleston, Thoresen, & Zarcone, 1985), headaches (Credidio, 1980), asthma (Ikemi, Nagata, Ago, & Ikemi, 1982), hypertension (Charlesworth, Williams, & Baer, 1984; Denicola, Furze, & O'Keeffe, 1982), and diabetes (Hartman & Reuter, 1983; Rose, Firestone, Heick, & Faught, 1983). Data are not available on the independent contribution of relaxation in most of these applications.

Anderson, Lawrence, and Olson (1981) did conduct a component analysis in their treatment of muscle contraction headache. They evaluated autogenics alone, cognitive coping training alone, and the two treatments together. The joint treatment proved to be more effective than either of its components, suggesting relaxation does make a therapeutic contribution in this package. Treating three individuals with panic disorder, Waddell, Barlow, and O'Brien, (1984) tested cognitive restructuring alone and combined with self-control relaxation. The addition of relaxation was correlated with both positive and negative symptomatic change, leaving the value of this component still in doubt.

Drug Abuse

For many individuals, anxiety is a potent factor in the causation, maintenance, and recidivism stages of drug abuse (Deardorff, Melges, Hout, & Savage, 1975; Miller, Hersen, Eisler, & Hilsman, 1974; Spoth, 1980). As numerous other factors also contribute to the drug abuse syndrome, relaxation for anxiety reduction is often one of several coordinated interventions in drug abuse treatment packages (exemplified by Foy, Nunn, & Rychtarik, 1984; Hall, Loeb, & Kushner, 1984; Kumaraiah, 1979; O'Brien, Raynes, & Patch, 1972). Other components commonly employed are social skills training, stimulus control procedures, cognitive restructuring, and various forms of aversion.

The justification for using relaxation in drug abuse treatment packages rests on several assumptions: (a) Relaxation can effectively allay anxiety among drug abusers, (b) Anxiety reduction leads to decreased drug use, and (c) Anxiety reduction will increase the therapeutic impact of other components of the treatment package.

On the first assumption, some basic and clinical research (discussed in greater detail in Chapters 3 and 7) has evaluated drug abusers' response to relaxation. Parker and his associates (Gilbert, Parker, & Claiborn, 1978; Parker, Gilbert, & Thoresen, 1978a, 1978b) found Benson's (1975) meditation method and progressive relaxation to produce greater blood pressure effects and mood improvement with alcoholics than quiet rest, but were not superior to the quiet rest control on other physiological and psychological indices. Strickler et al. (1977, 1979) presented some interesting data (described in detail in Chapter 3) suggesting that passive relaxation effectively relaxes alcoholics and attenuates alcohol consumption. The second assumption can also be addressed by correlating relaxation practice compliance and anxiety change scores with changes in drug consumption. More directly, the influence of relaxation may be evaluated when this is the sole treatment. These data are reported in Chapter 7.

The joint operation of the second and third assumptions can be tested in clinical trials by the dismantling design discussed above, and a few studies have done so. In a series of reports, Blake (1965, 1967) described an experiment that adequately isolated the contribution of progressive relaxation in electrical aversion therapy for alcoholism. Electrical aversion therapy with progressive relaxation was contrasted with electrical aversion alone. At 12-month follow-up, both proved effective with no significant difference between them when the success criteria of abstinence and reduced drinking were combined, thus casting doubt on the therapeutic role of relaxation. On a more positive note, the group receiving relaxation achieved a rate of abstinence more than twice that of the aversion only group, while the less respected measure of reduced drinking was more prevalent in the latter.

Miller and Taylor (1980) employed a similar design to study alcoholism treatment, and their effort also yielded disappointing effects for progressive relaxation. Problem drinkers were assigned to (a) bibliotherapy, (b) individual self-control training, (c) training as in b supplemented with relaxation, or (d) training as in c conducted in small groups. At posttreatment and 12-month follow-up, all groups boasted significant reductions in alcohol consumption and related dependent measures, with no difference between them.

As is apparent from the above research, data bearing on the contribution of relaxation in drug treatment are weak. Recent reviewers (Klajner, Hartman, & Sobell, 1984) reached the same conclusion. This group and others (Marlatt & Marques, 1977) have also pointed out that when relaxation is helpful, the mechanism may be increased perceived social competence or control rather than anxiety reduction. Klajner et al. (1984) also suggested that anxiety assessment may identify a substance abuser subset that is responsive in whole or part to relaxation therapy.

Smoking

Cigarette smoking is a form of drug abuse, but was not included in the preceding section because it is distinguished by its ubiquity and absence of prominent psychotropic effects. The three main theories advanced to explain smoking are that it produces desired changes in affect (primarily anxiety reduction), it is a socially reinforced, automatic habit, and it is maintained by nicotine addiction (Leventhal & Cleary, 1980; Lichtenstein & Danaher, 1976). In a given individual, one or more of these factors may be operative and, theoretically, relaxation therapy addresses only the first type.

Indirect evidence of the anxiety factor in smoking and the usefulness of relaxation in smoking treatments derives from several sources. In experimental settings, smoking increases during anxiety-eliciting tasks (Dobbs, Strickler, &

Maxwell, 1981; Rose, Ananda, & Jarvik, 1983). Dobbs et al. (1981) further demonstrated that passive relaxation can reverse this trend (see Chapter 3). Flaxman (1979) reported encouraging but quizzical follow-up data. Smoking treatment successes made more constructive use of progressive relaxation than failures, though relaxation benefited subjects driven more by habit and addiction than by affect. These results suggest that, for some individuals, relaxation may serve as a competing response, rather than as an instrument for anxiety reduction.

Chapter 7 presents the mediocre results of several studies treating smokers with relaxation only. Most often, an intervention package is assembled to reduce cigarette smoking, and relaxation (typically progressive or self-control relaxation) is a standard ingredient (examples are Best, Owen, & Trentadue, 1978; Brockway, Kleinmann, Edleson, & Gruenewald, 1977; Danaher, 1977; Elliott & Denney, 1978; Glasgow, 1978; Hackett & Horan, 1979; Marston & McFall, 1971; Shipley, 1981). Other frequently included components are rapid smoking, covert sensitization or some other form of aversion, stimulus control strategies, contingency contracting, social support, assertiveness training, and health education.

Three studies tested the independent contribution of the relaxation component. One compared (a) rapid smoking, (b) rapid smoking and progressive relaxation, (c) rapid smoking, progressive relaxation, and contingency contracting, and (d) contingent rapid smoking (Poole, Sanson-Fisher, & German, 1981). All groups produced significant smoking decrements at posttreatment, but more modest results at 12-month follow-up. At no point did groups b, c, or d outperform the basic treatment, group a, recommending the conclusion that relaxation (and the other treatment components) does not produce a therapeutic increment with at least one smoking treatment, rapid smoking. However, an earlier study supports the opposite conclusion (Sutherland, Amit, Golden, & Roseberger, 1975). This group found that the combination of progressive relaxation and rapid smoking was significantly more effective with smokers than either treatment singly. Lastly, we (Lichstein & Stalgaitis, 1980) added self-control relaxation to contingency contracting between spouses, both of whom were in smoking treatment, and it did not increase treatment efficacy. In light of these conflicting results and the common presence of relaxation in smoking packages, further component analyses are warranted.

Some 80 percent of smokers (and abusers of other drugs likewise) who succeed in quitting, after participation in psychological treatments, will resume baseline levels of smoking within about 6 months (Hunt, Barnett, & Branch, 1971). Theories claiming recidivism is partly anxiety controlled (Pomerleau, Adkins, & Pertschuk, 1978) have emphasized the role of relaxation as a therapy maintenance strategy. In support of this view, investigations of smoking recidivists (Ashenberg, Morgan, & Fisher, 1984; Shiffman, 1982) have identified stress as a potent factor in this process. Despite this cogent reasoning, Shiffman's (1984) data reveal problems in enactment. Of subjects trained in relaxation and other smoking control techniques, only 11 percent employed relaxation after treatment to cope with temptations to smoke. Some form of relaxation often occupies a position in relapse prevention programs (Marlatt & Gordon, 1985), but data in defense of relaxation's inclusion are not plentiful.

In principle, relaxation could serve several different avenues in the complex area of smoking control. Unfortunately, however, documentation of the relaxation influence is weak.

Pain Management

Pain management (from a psychological point of view) usually targets chronic pain states with two goals in mind: pain reduction and effective coping with refractory pain. There are, of course, many different kinds of pain and some of these, most notably head pain, are responsive to unitary relaxation interventions as described in Chapter 7.

Pain management packages (typified by Turk, Meichenbaum, & Genest, 1983) are similar to stress management packages and include such components as pain medication reduction, selective social reinforcement, increasing activity level, cognitive restructuring, and social skills training, as well as relaxation or biofeedback. This approach has been tested with the relaxation component in laboratory analogue studies (Horan, Hackett, Buchanan, Stone, & Demchik-Stone, 1977), and has been clinically applied to pain emanating from the lower back (e.g., Cinciripini & Floreen, 1982), upper back (Swanson, Maruta, & Swenson, 1979; Swanson, Swenson, Maruta, & McPhee, 1976), masseter muscle (Rosenbaum & Ayllon, 1981), temporomandibular joint (Olson & Malow, 1985; Stam, McGrath, & Brooke, 1984), and abdomen (Levendusky & Pankratz, 1975; McGrath, 1983). This model has been applied to chronic pain problems in children as well (Masek, Russo, & Varni, 1984).

Basic research, component analyses (discussed at greater length in Chapter 3) have identified additive contributions of relaxation to pain management packages (Hackett & Horan, 1980; Klepac, Hauge, Dowling, & McDonald, 1981). Sanders (1983) employed a sophisticated component analysis design that documented the important contribution of progressive relaxation to the treatment of back pain. Linton and Melin (1983) compared self-control relaxation and conventional rehabilitation combined to rehabilitation only in treating primarily back pain patients, and observed that the addition of relaxation secured incremental therapeutic benefits. We, therefore, conclude that the extant data recommends the inclusion of relaxation in pain treatment protocols.

Habit Control

Azrin and Nunn (1977) described a multifaceted program for control of such common habits as nail biting, hair pulling, stuttering, and tics. Examples of the program's components include motivation enhancement, competing behaviors, preventive actions, social support, and symbolic rehearsal. A simple relaxation strategy—slow, deep breathing and relaxed posture—is also usually included in the package. Two articles by these authors (Azrin & Nunn, 1974;

Azrin, Nunn, & Frantz, 1979) suggest that relaxation plays a particularly useful role in the treatment of stuttering. However, none of their publications clearly isolates the contribution of relaxation to their habit control program. Ladouceur and his colleagues (Ladouceur, Boudreau, & Theberge, 1981; Ladouceur, Cote, Leblond, & Bouchard, 1982; Ladouceur & Martineau, 1982) have since replicated the effectiveness of this treatment package with stutterers, but have obtained about 50 percent symptomatic relief compared to near 100 percent reported above.

Eating Disorders

Applications of relaxation within this area have most often targeted obesity. Amidst multiple interventions, most notably diet, exercise, stimulus control, and social support, constituting package treatments for obesity, relaxation is a common member (e.g., Foreyt et al., 1982; James & Hampton, 1982; Kirschenbaum, Harris, & Tomarken, 1984; Perri, Shapiro, Ludwig, Twentyman, & McAdoo, 1984; Wollersheim, 1970). However, little data exist on the amount of influence exerted by relaxation in these programs. One study (Romanczyk, Tracey, Wilson, & Thorpe, 1973) compared seven treatment groups, each adding a new treatment component. Neither relaxation nor any of the other treatment components increased the effectiveness of merely self-monitoring caloric intake.

Recently, bulimia (also called the binge–purge syndrome) has begun to attract the interest of behavior therapists. Kirkley, Schneider, Agras, and Bachman (1985) incorporated relaxation (method unspecified) into a package treatment for this disorder, emphasizing mainly stimulus control strategies, and obtained encouraging results. Similarly, Yates and Sambrailo (1984) integrated progressive relaxation with cognitive restructuring, assertion training, and other ingredients, and secured significant decreases in binge-purge episodes. To date, the role of relaxation in the bulimia treatment package is undetermined.

Final Comments on Relaxation as a Treatment Package Component

Many of the comments offered to conclude the section on relaxation as a therapeutic adjunct apply with equal force here. In brief, the available data do not, for the most part, justify the current level of usage of relaxation as a treatment package component. More dismantling design research is required to evaluate the relaxation component.

Among the areas that commonly employ relaxation, the strongest data supporting the inclusion of relaxation exist in the pain management area, and the weakest data exist in the area of drug abuse and smoking. By appearances, stress management is the most plausible arena of relaxation application, but the few attempts to isolate the relaxation component herein have yielded inconsistent results.

CHAPTER 7

Clinical Outcome Research

The present chapter outlines the areas of application of relaxation therapy and summarizes the results of these interventions. These areas of application are composed mainly of clinical disorders, such as anxiety and headache, but also include nonpathological situations in which relaxation can facilitate coping, as exemplified by childbirth and athletic performance. Unlike Chapter 6, which reviewed the use of relaxation as a therapeutic adjunct or as a component of a treatment package, this chapter will consider only those studies that satisfy the definition of relaxation therapy, that is, when relaxation is the sole or primary treatment. Ambiguity sometimes exists in classifying an investigation as clinical versus basic research. In some cases, difficult and partly arbitrary decisions led me to include studies in this chapter rather than in Chapter 3.

The therapeutic application of relaxation may be guided by one of three intervention strategies: (a) as a setting event, (b) with response-independent cueing, and (c) with response-dependent cueing (Luiselli, 1980). Employing relaxation as a setting event usually involves training in one of the deep relaxation methods (Chapter 4). The intention is to create an improved emotional and physiological tonus boasting longevity that will help defend against health threats. Response-independent and response-dependent cueing usually involve one of the brief relaxation techniques (Chapter 5). In the former case, relaxation is practiced as a preventive strategy on a fixed or variable schedule during symptom-free periods. The latter approach employs relaxation when prompted by the discovery of early danger signals of impending distress. There is no incompatibility between these three methods, and clinical prudence will often dictate their simultaneous use.

Most of the research can be adequately dichotomized in accordance with the gross methodological descriptors of case reports and group design studies. Case reports characteristically involve treatments applied to a very few number of subjects without benefit of outcome evaluation with reliable dependent measures. Baseline and follow-up data are often inadequate. Conjoint treatments also may be present, as well as confounding sources of social influence. In brief, case reports are poorly defended against threats to internal validity and, to a lesser extent, external validity (Campbell & Stanley, 1963), thus undermining the confidence associated with their findings.

At a minimum, group design studies are composed of one group: treatment. Complex group designs may include groups that test alternate treatments, evaluate the influence of subject characteristics, or control for nonspecific therapy effects such as placebo, expectancy, passage of time, and therapist demands. Applicability of the term *group design study* does not of itself guarantee major improvement over case studies with respect to the validity of research findings, there being considerable variability in design rigor under this rubric. This chapter will include comments on the salient methodological features of the studies reviewed, to facilitate the goal of drawing valid summary conclusions. A third, distinct methodological approach, single-case experimental designs (Hersen & Barlow, 1976), rivals the sophistication of group design studies, but will receive relatively little attention in this review due to their infrequent use with relaxation treatments.

The present chapter will be organized by specific disorders or situations. Several different schemes were considered in grouping or ordering the disorders presented below. Homogeneous subsets of disorders, clinical disorders versus challenging situations, applications with well-documented support versus poorly supported applications, as well as other schemes were considered and abandoned, as each resolved some difficulties but introduced others. In the end, no general principle guided the sequence.

The primary goal of this review is to assess the current therapeutic status of relaxation therapy in each area. When a treatment regimen combines more than one relaxation technique, the article will be cited under the subheading of the relaxation technique claiming the greatest proportion of training time. An attempt also will be made to address the relative efficacy of relaxation treatments when data salient to this question exist. In keeping with the boundary conditions established for this book, biofeedback and hypnotic treatments will not be closely examined, even though they have been tested with many of the same disorders.

To aid the reader in locating specific material in this chapter, below is a list of the disorders and situations covered. The sequence, though arbitrarily determined, reflects the order in which the conditions are presented.

1. Anxiety
2. Phobias
3. Depression
4. Phantom limb pain
5. Essential hypertension
6. Heart disease and dysfunction
7. Raynaud's disease
8. Diabetes
9. Hemophilia
10. Muscle-contraction headache
11. Migraine headache
12. Chronic pain
13. Dysmenorrhea

14. Preparation for childbirth
15. Preparation for medical and dental treatment
16. Cancer
17. Drug abuse
18. Athletic performance
19. Insomnia
20. Muscular dysfunction
21. Seizures
22. Sexual dysfunction
23. Asthma
24. Children's problems
25. General well-being
26. Social field effects
27. Miscellaneous applications

ANXIETY

Chapters 5 and 6 include discussions of this disorder. Briefly, current theory conceives of anxiety as an emotion comprising three sources of distress: physiological, cognitive, and motoric. Their aggregate influence produces an unpleasant experience in the affected individual, who then endorses self-descriptors such as uneasy, tense, nervous, tied up in knots, etc. Anxiety may disrupt normal life functions, sleep, eating, bowel movements, and concentration, serving as examples. Further, this disorder may instigate, maintain, or exacerbate other disorders such as ulcers, headaches, seizures, and essential hypertension.

The most adequate treatment strategy for anxiety is to ameliorate all contributing factors. When relaxation is employed as the sole anxiety intervention, the treatment focus will likely be unevenly distributed among the three factors that are potentially active in any given case. The pattern of treatment influence will vary as a function of the style of the particular relaxation technique (Davidson, 1978; Davidson & Schwartz, 1976). To illustrate, progressive relaxation mainly emphasizes the physiological mode, but also diverts attention away from troubling thoughts, so that secondary benefits are obtained in the cognitive mode as well. Alternatively, the numerous varieties of mantra meditation (e.g., Transcendental Meditation and Benson's procedure) zero in on thought control (the cognitive factor) and secondarily, global physiological relaxation also emerges. Lastly, the diverse forms of self-control relaxation (see Chapter 5) come the closest in mounting a tridimensional assault on anxiety by teaching brief, portable forms of relaxation (physiological mode), using relaxation cue words (cognitive mode), and helping the client to avoid anxiety producing postural styles (motoric mode).

Not included in this section are special subtypes of anxiety, for example, phobias and anxiety associated with medical and dental procedures. The reader is referred to the appropriate sections in this chapter for coverage of these areas.

Progressive Relaxation (PR)

Several of the studies in this section evaluated PR and other interventions with individuals seeking outpatient treatment who satisfy the essential requirements for the diagnosis of generalized anxiety disorder (American Psychiatric Association, 1980). Early on, Jacobson (1943a) discussed the role of chronic, excessive muscular tension in stimulating adverse brain patterns and other somatic sequelae eventually leading to "nervous breakdowns," and he provided some case study material to illustrate his point (Jacobson, 1941a). Jacobson (1970) and others (Dawley, 1975; Fox, Joy, & Rotatori, 1981; Haugen, Dixon, & Dickel, 1958; Kibler & Foreman, 1983; Sultana & Siddiqui, 1983) have since provided plentiful anecdotal data on PR treatment of a wide variety of anxiety disorders.

Motivated by Jacobson's theory, one group of investigators (Turin, Nirenberg, & Mattingly, 1979) combined taped PR with abstinence from caffeine to control psychological and chemical sources of unwanted activation. These authors employed a single-subject reversal design that included a music relaxation placebo phase to test this intervention. All six scales on the Profile of Mood States (POMS; NcNair, Lorr, & Dropplemen, 1971) reliably manifested improved functioning only during the two treatment phases. A recent group design study also found PR to be helpful in treating anxiety, but not as effective as rational emotive therapy (Lipsky, Kassinove, & Miller, 1980).

We (Hoelscher, Lichstein, & Rosenthal, 1984) conducted four live PR training sessions with 20 anxious volunteers from the community, while unobtrusively monitoring their taped relaxation practice at home via a cumulative stopwatch concealed within the recorder (see Chapter 1 for further description of this device). There occurred a significant pre-post reduction on one trait anxiety questionnaire (State-Trait Anxiety Inventory, STAI; Spielberger, Gorsuch, & Lushene, 1970), and a significant correlation between a second anxiety questionnaire (Eysenck Personality Questionnaire; Eysenck & Eysenck, 1975) and amount of empirically determined relaxation practice ($r = .43$). Self-reported relaxation practice levels were not correlated with the anxiety questionnaires. Actual relaxation practice occurred at an average of 71 percent of the once-daily prescription, although clients' self-report data suggested enthusiastic compliance by overestimating actual practice by 126 percent. Others have also reported success with PR for anxious volunteers from the community (Hillenberg & Collins, 1986, discussed in Chapter 6).

Hillenberg and Collins (1983) conducted the only experimental test of the homework practice contribution in PR. Anxious volunteers from the community trained in PR were instructed to practice daily or to refrain from all home practice. These two training groups yielded comparable treatment credibility ratings. A no-treatment group was also included.

The clinical results were marginal. Physiological measures in repeated laboratory evaluations revealed small differences between the three groups. Daily self-reported anxiety favored the effectiveness of the two treated groups over the third, with a small edge accruing to the home practice condition. Rate of home practice, monitored by the marked tape method (described in Chapter 1), occurred at only 60 percent of the prescribed level, which may have attenuated between-group differences. Indeed, since the client is cognizant of this method of monitoring relaxation, actual practice may have fallen short of this 60 percent mark.

PR treatment of nonspecific anxiety in college student volunteers has produced mixed results. Electromyographic (EMG) biofeedback and taped PR training were both more effective than no treatment in reducing anxiety, as reflected in students' grades (Stout, Thornton, & Russell, 1980). Biofeedback was superior to no treatment with respect to reduced muscle tension and school attendance, but PR was not. Lewis, Biglan, and Steinbock (1978) observed comparable anxiety reduction benefits accruing to students employing a self-administered PR manual (Rosen, 1976) and students using a manual that instructed them to devise their own method of relaxation.

A few studies obtained encouraging results in testing PR to reduce anxiety and other symptomatology with psychiatric inpatients having a range of diagnoses. Relaxation (combined EMG biofeedback and taped PR) was compared with group psychotherapy in treating patients manifesting marked anxiety problems (Townsend, House, & Addario, 1975). Significant reductions in muscle tension, state and trait anxiety (STAI), and disturbing moods (POMS) occurred in the relaxation group but not in the group psychotherapy patients. Hawkins, Doell, Lindseth, Jeffers, and Skaggs (1980) randomly assigned schizophrenic patients to four conditions; no-treatment rest, taped PR, thermal biofeedback, or taped PR/thermal biofeedback combined. Several self-report and physiological measures failed to discriminate training effects produced by these four groups. A subset of 10 patients did show significant anxiety improvement, and these patients were comparably distributed among the three treated groups. They also exhibited significantly higher pretreatment anxiety levels than the other patients. These results suggest either that a subset of schizophrenic patients manifesting acute anxiety are good prospects for relaxation treatment, or the natural tendency of extreme initial scores to gravitate toward the mean (Wilder, 1957) would have occurred just the same had a nonviable treatment been offered.

Gaber, Arieli, and Merbaum (1984) conducted a well-designed study with psychiatric outpatients, mostly diagnosed as neurotic or personality disorder. Patients were randomly assigned to 16 sessions of taped PR, taped assertiveness training, or quiet rest placebo. A no-treatment group was also included.

Assessments at posttreatment and 5-month follow-up yielded identical results. A psychopathology index composed of a subset of items from the Minnesota Multiphasic Personality Inventory (Hathaway & McKinley, 1943) found PR to be more effective than the other three groups, which did not differ from each other. This pattern also obtained with patients' self-ratings of distress. On the Global Symptom Index of the Symptom Check List-90 (Derogatis, Lipman, & Covi, 1973), the only significant effect found PR to be superior to no treatment.

Several studies have treated special forms of anxiety or special populations with PR. Taylor, Kenigsberg, and Robinson (1982) compared PR, diazepam, placebo medication, and no treatment for individuals with a diagnosis of panic disorder. The PR condition surpassed all other groups on self-report measures of state anxiety (STAI) and depression (POMS). Significant heart rate reductions were obtained only by the diazepam group. Nursing students screened for elevated death anxiety exhibited significant decreases on this variable following PR (White, Gilner, Handal, & Napoli, 1983). Fairbank, DeGood, and Jenkins (1981) presented a case study of a woman manifesting a posttraumatic startle response subsequent to a serious automobile accident. Over a 3-week period, three sessions of taped PR and autogenic training combined substantially reduced average anxiety ratings while driving, but had little effect on the frequency of startle responses. The next treatment phase, in vivo exposure to driving under circumstances similar to those of her accident, did depress the incidence of startle responses. Six-month follow-up indicated this symptom was virtually extinguished.

Taped PR training with inpatient alcoholics has produced mild to moderate anxiety relief benefits, with the strongest effects occurring in those individuals manifesting intense anxiety (McFarlain, Mielke, & Gallant, 1976; Page & Schaub, 1978). Similar results were reported on the use of PR to alleviate acute anxiety experiences of prison inmates (Kennedy, Wormith, Michaud, Marquis, & Gendreau, 1975). Bassett, Blanchard, and Estes (1977) also treated prison inmates. They contrasted taped PR with music sessions at three levels of expectancy for improvement in a factorial design. Subjects received three sessions on consecutive days. Anxiety questionnaires documented state, but not trait, anxiety decrements for the relaxation groups. Anxiety changes did not occur in the music groups. Expectancy was successfully manipulated but did not impact on treatment response.

Anxiety occurs more often in the elderly than in younger groups, but it has attracted surprisingly little interest from psychological investigators (Sallis & Lichstein, 1982). Due to numerous factors, including mounting constitutional frailty and social isolation, some elderly are hypervigilant with respect to anxiety cues and are prone toward an exacerbation cycle. DeBerry has published the only data on relaxation for anxiety in the elderly, and his results are very consistent. DeBerry (1981–1982, 1982) tested a combination of PR and imagery with female volunteers, and observed significant (STAI) anxiety improvement compared to untreated controls. Gains in collateral areas such as headaches, insomnia, and depression also were noted. Continued relaxation practice during the follow-up period promoted therapeutic longevity.

Self-control Relaxation (SCR)

Cautela (1966a) was the first to report on an SCR format with general anxiety. Cautela described three clinical cases to illustrate the benefits of cue-controlled relaxation (CCR), in combination with assertiveness training, systematic desensitization, and thought stopping. Only one study (Spoth & Meade, 1981) has since focused on CCR for general anxiety. These researchers evaluated six sessions of CCR with anxious college students. At treatment end, they found significant pre-post reductions on one state (STAI) and three trait (STAI; IPAT-General and IPAT-Covert Anxiety, Cattell, 1957) anxiety questionnaires. Modest evidence was found to support the advantages of a sophisticated, complex training format versus a more simplistic one.

An early test of differential relaxation pitted this against standard desensitization and two control groups to diminish anxiety manifested during interviews among inpatient psychiatric patients (Zeisset, 1968). Behavioral and self-report anxiety indices registered equivalently significant gains for the two treated groups, but not the control groups.

The remaining studies targeting general anxiety employed more broadly construed forms of SCR that often included training in self-monitoring, breath awareness, and imagery, and they targeted anxious female college students (Thompson, Griebstein, & Kuhlenschmidt, 1980), outpatients in a family medical practice (Cragan & Deffenbacher, 1984), and community volunteers (McCready, Berry, & Kenkel, 1985). Thompson et al. contrasted anxiety management training (AMT), Suinn's (Suinn & Richardson, 1971) abbreviated version of systematic desensitization, and stress management, composed principally of broad-spectrum SCR. Both treatments were supplemented by extra sessions delivering either additional practice with tape-recorded instructions or electromyographic (EMG) biofeedback. All treated subjects improved on STAI-State anxiety and ratings of anxiety severity, surpassing the same measures produced by matched, untreated controls. STAI-Trait anxiety, anxiety frequency ratings, and forearm EMG activity did not distinguish the treated and untreated subjects. At 3-month follow-up, anxiety severity ratings were obtained, indicating therapeutic gains had been maintained. The supplementary treatment sessions had no discernible effect on any of the above measures. However, during the treated semester, the AMT and SCR groups, supplemented with taped training, attained significantly higher academic grades than the untreated subjects. Inexplicably, the following semester only the AMT group, supplemented with biofeedback, surpassed the grades of the untreated subjects. Faulty matching procedures between treated and untreated subjects, and the absence of any controls for nonspecific treatment effects, urge caution in interpreting the results of this study.

Cragan and Deffenbacher (1984) randomly assigned stressed but nonpsychiatric patients from a general medical outpatient practice to AMT, SCR, or no treatment, thus approximating the design of Thompson et al. (1980). With minor exception, AMT and SCR produced comparable, significant reductions in state (STAI) and trait (STAI; Multiple Affect Adjective Check List–Anxiety Scale, MAACL; Zuckerman, Lubin, Vogel, & Valerius, 1964) anxiety, and in self-ratings of situation-specific anxiety and physiological arousal at posttreatment and 1-month follow-up. Resting blood pressure was unchanged throughout the study. Resting heart rate reductions occurred in the SCR group at follow-up only. Treatment generalization effects extending to depression and hostility (MAACL) also occurred in the two treated groups. The untreated subjects did not exhibit change in any measure. Unlike Thompson et al., this study found far-reaching psychological effects associated with these self-control interventions (e.g., trait anxiety, anger, hostility), but it, too, did not include any controls for nonspecific treatment factors.

McCready et al. (1985) employed a combination of therapist training and treatment manuals to treat worksite and community volunteers. Not only did state and trait anxiety (STAI) improve in these groups, but blood pressure and stress indices in a human figure drawing test also registered significant gains. An untreated control group showed little change.

Passive Relaxation

This form of PR omits actual muscle tensing, only requiring the subject to focus attention on relaxing muscle sensations (see Chapter 5 for a more thorough description of this method). One study (Canter, Kondo, & Knott, 1975) tested passive relaxation for nonspecific anxiety. A mixed group of in- and outpatient subjects were randomly assigned to training in EMG biofeedback or passive relaxation. The number of treatment sessions ranged from 10 to 25. Both groups attained significant reductions in muscle tension. Self- and therapist-ratings of anxiety agreed that about half the relaxation subjects manifested substantial improvement, whereas gains were made by some 80 percent of the biofeedback subjects.

Meditation

Many of the meditation approaches to anxiety treatment involve some sort of mantra—the quiet repetition of a word, phrase, or sound. In probably the most methodologically sophisticated effort in this area, Smith (1976) reported two experiments testing Transcendental Meditation (TM).

In the first experiment, college students were recruited for free anxiety treatments, without indication of what treatments were involved. Subjects were randomly assigned to (a) TM taught by authorized instructors, (b) a control treatment that attempted to mimic most of the ingredients of TM, except that subjects sat quietly twice daily without really meditating, or (c) a no-treatment group. Subjects were unaware of the existence of the other two groups. A pretreatment assessment battery was readministered 5½ months later for the no-treatment subjects, and 6 months later for the two treated groups. Attrition for both TM and control meditation were in the 50–60 percent range. Posttest scores for the two treated groups, analyzed by analysis of covariance, did not differ on measures of state anxiety (STAI), or symptoms of striate muscle tension and autonomic arousal (Fenz & Epstein, 1965), but both were lower than the no-treatment group on all three measures. A subsequent report on these same subjects (Smith, 1978) identified pretest variables that moderately correlated with anxiety improvement (no prior interest in psychotherapy, introversion, absorption in own thoughts, anxiety) and premature termination (psychoticism and low self-critical attitudes).

The second experiment replicated most of the design features of the first, except that one group was trained in a TM-like procedure and the second was instructed to engage in active, positive mentation while meditating, in contrast to the cognitive tranquility that most meditation approaches encourage. At the 3-month posttest, both groups made significant improvement on trait anxiety and autonomic arousal, and the active mentation group also improved on symptoms of muscle tension. However, there were no between-group differences.

The results of the first experiment argue against the special influence of the TM mantra, and those of the second experiment question the utility of tranquil thoughts. It may be that simply taking a daily rest break, the content of which is immaterial, serves the same purpose as TM and other meditation approaches. Support for this conclusion is found in other investigations with nonclinical subjects (Griffiths, Steel, Vaccaro, & Karpman, 1981; Peters, Benson, & Porter, 1977). As Smith (1976) conducted one of the few TM studies that combines the admirable methodological features of random assignment, credible control condition, and competent analyses, thoughtful observers are obliged to take its findings seriously. However, it is premature to generalize its conclusions to other dependent measures or to clinical populations.

Brooks and Scarano (1985) reported a methodologically impressive test of TM. Vietnam veterans presenting with multifaceted anxiety complaints, namely, posttraumatic stress disorder, were randomly assigned to either TM (taught by a certified instructor) or eclectic individual, group, or family therapy as deemed appropriate. At the end of 3 months of treatment, TM subjects registered significantly greater improvement than psychotherapy subjects on electrodermal reactivity and several self-report measures such as depression (Beck Depression Inventory; Beck, Ward, Mendelsohn, Mock, & Erbaugh, 1961), anxiety (Manifest Anxiety Scale; Taylor, 1953), insomnia, and alcohol consumption.

Benson, Frankel, et al. (1978) applied hypnosis or Benson's mantra meditation approach to anxious clients. Both groups made significant but equal gains on psychiatric evaluations and self-ratings of anxiety symptoms. Only the hypnosis group showed diastolic blood pressure (BP) reductions. Neither group improved on systolic BP, oxygen consumption, or heart rate. A control group generally did not do as well as the Benson and hypnosis patients, although the statistical analyses on this point were unclear. High hypnotizability seemed to facilitate the therapeutic response to hypnosis treatment as well as Bensonian meditation. TM has also proved useful in combating state anxiety (STAI), but not trait anxiety, in a group of seven individuals seeking treatment primarily for hypertension (Blackwell et al., 1976). Girodo (1974) reported that mantra meditation was helpful with five of nine of his anxious clients.

Benson's method was also applied to fifth grade children in Lebanon (Day & Sadek, 1982). Presumably experiencing heightened stress from living in a war-torn country, children were randomly assigned to meditation or reading control groups. Self-reported anxiety at posttreatment was lower among the meditating children.

An attempt to aid infertile couples through stress reduction proved difficult to evaluate (Harrison, O'Moore, O'Moore, & McSweeney, 1981). Only two of 10 couples assigned to TM completed the basic training course. Prior to treatment, these 10 couples did exhibit heightened anxiety compared to fertile controls, and the two completing couples did appear to benefit from TM.

A complex meditation approach, referred to as that of Patanjali (yoga), was applied to a mixed group of 200 patients (Vahia et al., 1972). Two months of daily training included instruction in postures, breathing, disciplining thoughts, visual imagery, and unfocused concentration. The patients mostly exhibited anxiety disorders, but individuals presenting with depression, asthma, and diabetes were also included. Significant improvement occurred on measures of severity and duration of symptomatology. These results were subsequently replicated with patients presenting mostly anxiety symptomatology (Vahia et al., 1973).

Autogenics (AT)

Two studies tested AT with special populations: student nurses and infertile couples. Motivated by the hypothesis that stress fosters absenteeism among nurses, Bailey (1984) trained one group of student nurses in AT and exposed a control group only to discussions of stress issues. Subsequent absenteeism was indeed less in the AT group. Unfortunately, this study contained no direct measure of stress, anxiety, or the like, leaving the mechanism of effect unknown.

AT produced modest effects on infertile couples (O'Moore, O'Moore, Harrison, Murphy, & Carruthers, 1983). Both the male and female partners decreased on STAI-State, but not trait anxiety. No pre-post improvement occurred for these couples on other questionnaires (Sixteen Personality Factor Questionnaire, Cattell, Eber, & Tatsuoka, 1970; Eysenck Personality Questionnaire, Eysenck & Eysenck, 1975; Manifest Anxiety Scale, Taylor, 1953). Plasma prolactin, a stress indicator, did drop significantly among the women, and this is noteworthy.

The last study in this section was also the most vigorous. Banner and Meadows (1983) randomly assigned 63 anxious volunteers from the community to nine sessions in one of five groups: (a) electromyographic biofeedback, (*b*) skin temperature biofeedback, (*c*) *a* and *b* combined, (*d*) taped AT, and (*e*) soothing music (intended as placebo control). Subjects also were assigned to a sixth condition, no treatment. Numerous dependent measures, two physiological (muscle tension and skin temperature) and some nine self-report, failed to distinguish the groups, including the no-treatment group, at posttreatment. This study stands as an indictment of AT for anxiety, but the uniform consistency of its negative results are somewhat puzzling in light of successes reported by other biofeedback and AT investigators.

Imagery

Chappell and Stevenson (1936) described perhaps the earliest of modern relaxation imagery applications. A group of peptic ulcer patients were trained in the use of positive imagery (content unspecified) to counteract anxiety that aggravated their condition. At 3-year follow-up, 26 of 28 patients still enjoyed marked symptom reduction. Ulcers continued unabated in untreated control subjects.

Schandler and Dana (1983) conducted clinical analogue research with undergraduate volunteers, preselected for high anxiety and other personality deficits (e.g., hostility). Subjects received three weekly sessions of either (*a*) relaxing imagery, as in pleasant nature scenes, combined with training in cognitive coping strategies, (*b*) frontalis electromyographic (EMG) biofeedback, or (*c*) self-devised relaxation accompanied by restful music (control group).

Only group *a* registered significant anxiety (Anxiety Differential; Husek & Alexander, 1963) decreases within and between sessions. Self-rated changes in nine other personality dimensions (e.g., hostility, depression) favored group *a* over *b,* which in turn surpassed *c.* Imagery subjects exhibited significant heart rate decreases in sessions 2 and 3, and EMG reduction in session 2 only. No group achieved significant finger temperature change, and the control group failed to attain significant physiological change on any measure. In sum, the imagery treatment, in combination with cognitive techniques, exerted moderate physiological and more pronounced psychological influence.

Other Relaxation Techniques

Twenty anxious outpatients, undergoing 4 weeks of electromyographic biofeedback and taped relaxation (method unspecified) training, exhibited decreased platelet MAO activity (previously implicated in other psychiatric disturbances) and decreased state (STAI) anxiety (Mathew, Ho, Kralik, Weinman, & Claghorn, 1981). Trait anxiety showed a smaller treatment response.

Brunson (1983) published an interesting short report that, unfortunately, was data poor. A series of six relaxation tapes, including progressive relaxation, autogenics, imagery, and breath focusing, were made available in a university counseling center office reserved for self-administered relaxation therapy. This strategy permitted delivery of these services to a large number of people, with very little demand on professional time. Center staff screened applicants to this program and stood ready to consult as needed.

Hodgson, Rachman, and Marks (1972) employed an unspecified method of relaxation as a treatment control with obsessive-compulsive individuals, preparatory to the treatments of primary interest—modeling and flooding. According to patient ratings, psychiatrist ratings, and performance indices, relaxation did little to abate the main symptomatology, but did benefit secondary symptomatology, depression and panic.

Rapee (1985) described an interesting case of a woman experiencing about seven panic attacks a week. Motivated by the assumption that hyperventilation plays an instrumental role in panic attacks, Rapee trained his client to reduce her rate of respiration to about eight breaths per minute when anxious (see discussion of paced respiration, Chapters 3 and 5). Panic attacks were occurring at about one per week at treatment end, and were absent at 6-month follow-up. Clark, Salkovskis, and Chalkley (1985) employed the same method with 18 panic attack sufferers and obtained uniformly positive results in uncontrolled trials.

Relaxation Comparisons

Schilling and Poppen (1983) trained anxious community volunteers in behavioral relaxation training, taped progressive relaxation, electromyographic biofeedback, or soothing music placebo. Behavioral relaxation training takes a somewhat novel approach in that the client is taught to produce 10 observable signs of relaxation (e.g., slow breathing, slack jaw, and feet pointed outward). These same markers serve as an assessment tool, the Behavioral Relaxation Scale, to gauge the depth of relaxation effect (see Chapter 4 for a more complete presentation of this assessment instrument).

Of present interest is the comparison of behavioral relaxation training (BRT) and taped progressive relaxation (PR). BRT was superior to PR on two measures: the Behavioral Relaxation Scale (which is not too surprising, since this also served as the BRT training guide) and frontalis muscle tension. There were no differences on the three remaining measures: skin conductance level, finger temperature, and self-rated relaxation.

Raskin, Bali, and Peeke (1980) treated anxious volunteers with biofeedback, progressive relaxation, or Transcendental Meditation (TM). Although it was not explicitly stated, group assignments were apparently done on a random basis, making this one of the few TM trials boasting this methodological feature. Several questionnaire, symptom, and physiological measures evinced the effectiveness of these treatments, but there were no between-group differences. Carrington, Lehrer, Woolfolk, and their associates (Carrington et al., 1980; Lehrer, Woolfolk, Rooney, McCann, & Carrington, 1983; Woolfolk, Lehrer, McCann, & Rooney, 1982) also contrasted progressive relaxation and a method of meditation similar to TM (clinically standardized meditation;

Carrington, 1984). Physiological and clinical markers with anxious volunteers documented the robust effectiveness of both techniques, though differences between them were inconsistent. One of the above studies (Carrington et al., 1980) also included a Bensonian (1975) meditation group, and it also fared well.

Beiman, Israel, and Johnson (1978) contrasted Bensonian relaxation with live and taped courses of self-control relaxation (also discussed in Chapter 3). Reductions in self-report measures of anxiety were equivalently significant in all groups, but somewhat greater reductions in physiological arousal attended live self-control relaxation training.

Hutchings, Denney, Basgall, and Houston (1980) conducted a five-condition experiment, but only two of these conditions are of current interest. Anxious students were trained in static formats of six relaxation techniques, for example, progressive relaxation, autogenic training, guided imagery, etc., or were trained in the same set of techniques styled into a self-control format. Subjects in these two conditions exhibited moderate treatment gains, but neither orientation (static versus self-control) proved superior.

A second contrast of progressive and self-control relaxation with psychiatric inpatients found a small edge for the self-control group (Hoshmand, Helmes, Kazarian, & Tekatch, 1985). An interesting and unique aspect of this study compared relaxation effects on patients also given minor tranquilizers versus unmedicated patients. Surprisingly, greater decreases in subjective stress occurred in the unmedicated patients.

As noted in Chapter 3, numerous studies have contrasted progressive and passive relaxation. In one such contrast with anxious college students, Borkovec, Grayson, and Cooper (1978) found progressive relaxation to be significantly more effective than no treatment, and passive relaxation proved to be of intermediary effectiveness relevant to these two groups.

Final Comments on Relaxation Therapy for Anxiety

Practicing relaxation diminishes anxiety. The extant literature supports this conclusion strongly for progressive relaxation and, to a lesser degree, for self-control relaxation and meditation. Well-controlled experiments have documented clinically significant effects in diverse populations and with varied dependent measures.

Anxiety effects tend to be setting specific; in other words, state anxiety changes more readily than trait anxiety. This is not always the case, but when only state-anxiety changes result, the clinical potency of the intervention is diminished. Clinicians should be wary of this pitfall and plan with clients to promote treatment generalization. Such efforts may include practicing relaxation in varied settings, practicing under increasingly less conducive circumstances (see relevant discussion in Chapter 4), and emphasizing the client's responsibility in producing and maintaining relaxation when anxiety threatens.

Two studies (Hillenberg & Collins, 1983; Hoelscher, Lichstein, & Rosenthal, 1984) alert us to the importance of high levels of home relaxation practice. As stated in Chapter 1, this is a crucial issue that will attract more attention in the future.

In the final pages of Chapter 1, I referred to thoughts wandering during relaxation as the blessed irritant, and I explained how this obstacle to relaxation posed an excellent opportunity to nurture a tolerant attitude. This attitude, should it persist during the day, promises lower levels of anxiety and other noxious emotions. Two other investigators, Goleman and Hendricks, have posited additional processes by which this same phenomenon, wandering thoughts, serves beneficial purpose.

In analyzing the therapeutic mechanisms of TM, Goleman (1971) reasoned that while practicing TM—or by logical extension, most other methods of relaxation—fantasies and concerns spontaneously surface in one's mind and are counterposed by the state of physiological relaxation. Thus, generalized anxiety reduction may be the product of this unplanned process paralleling systematic desensitization (see Chapter 6 for a description of systematic desensitization). It would be difficult to contrive a clean experimental test of this cognitive view of relaxation effects on anxiety, but the theory is nevertheless plausible, and supported by some data (Kirsch & Henry, 1979).

Hendricks (1975) advanced another cognitive rationale. During meditation and other methods of relaxation, the practitioner is constantly diverted by extraneous thoughts until sufficient self-discipline develops, wherein the practitioner maintains his/her mind on task. Were such cognitive control skills to generalize, the individual could readily constrain self-defeating thoughts that previously fostered anxiety and depression.

PHOBIAS

Phobias are a form of anxiety controlled by a relatively narrow set of stimulus characteristics, such as a particular object or a specific situation. A fear reaction is termed phobic if it is disproportionate to the threat posed by the stimulus. A phobia may represent an isolated area of anxiety dysfunction within an otherwise well-adjusted personality, or it can exert a pervasive influence on personality, as in some cases of agoraphobia. Phobic individuals are sometimes spared the social pressure of being viewed as abnormal, due to the high incidence of some types of phobias in the general population (e.g., spider or height phobias). In recent years, some form of exposure, actual being more effective than imaginal, has achieved the greatest success in phobia treatment (Barlow & Wolfe, 1981; Marks, 1978).

Progressive Relaxation (PR)

Speech phobic college students were randomly assigned to four conditions: taped PR, heart rate biofeedback (HRB), PR/HRB combined, or false HRB

(Gatchel, Hatch, Watson, Smith, & Gaas, 1977). Subjects delivered contrived speeches before and after the treatment course of four sessions. All four groups manifested significant pre-post reductions in self-reported and observed anxiety during these speeches. However, skin conductance and HR measures during the post speech favored the PR/HRB group over all others, and the PR and HRB groups over the false HRB group. Questionnaire data on speech anxiety collected at 1-month posttreatment did not distinguish the groups. The authors speculated that low basal anxiety levels may have led to comparability between groups on the anxiety measures, due to a floor effect.

A second study targeting speech phobic college students (Gross & Fremouw, 1982) pitted cognitive restructuring against PR, and included a no-treatment control group. Four measures of self-report anxiety showed the two treatments to be equivalent and superior to the control group. Analyses of the interaction between subject characteristics and treatment type yielded mild evidence in support of the theory that cognitive or physiological (PR) treatments are maximally effective when the client experiences stress in a parallel response mode. An earlier study very similar to Gross and Fremouw (1982) obtained less encouraging results. Speech phobic college students were randomly assigned to four sessions of rational-emotive therapy (RET), PR (defined as a placebo group), or no treatment (Trexler & Karst, 1972). Self-rated anxiety revealed stronger gains for the PR group than the other two. However, two anxiety inventories favored RET. Measures of electrodermal responding and behavioral observations were inconclusive. These results held up well at 6-month follow-up. This study is noteworthy in that it was one of the earliest to demonstrate expectancy equivalence in the placebo group through subjects' therapist and treatment credibility ratings.

A study of rat phobic college students produced disappointing results (Cooke, 1968). Devised to isolate the active ingredients in systematic desensitization, the study included a PR only group, a hierarchy only group, a systematic desensitization group, and two control groups. The outcome pattern did not lead to definitive answers, except that PR only was clearly ineffective. Similar designs have been executed with snake (Davison, 1968; Lang & Lazovik, 1963) and spider (Rachman, 1965) phobic students, and PR again proved ineffectual.

Another common focal anxiety concerns the taking of tests. To address this problem, Reed and Saslow (1980) assigned test anxious college students to three treatment conditions: EMG biofeedback/taped PR combined, taped PR only, or no treatment. Only the combined group posted significant pre-post gains on the Achievement Anxiety Test (AAT; Alpert & Haber, 1960). The combined and the PR only groups both registered reductions in state and trait anxiety (STAI; Spielberger, Gorsuch, & Lushene, 1970), and in muscle tension. Only the PR group showed significant increases in internal locus of control (I-E scale; Rotter, 1966). No significant changes occurred in the no-treatment group. Some positive (Bedell, 1976; Ryan, Krall, & Hodges, 1976), but more often negative (Allen, 1973; Freeling & Shemberg, 1970; Johnson & Sechrest,

1968) data on PR for test anxiety have been reported by other labs. Laxer applied PR to test anxious high school students, and observed that it benefited test anxiety but did not improve school grades (Laxer, Quarter, Kooman, & Walker, 1969; Laxer & Walker, 1970). A substantial amount of research exists on self-control formats of PR for test anxiety, and this material is presented below.

As should be apparent by now, the bulk of the clinical trials on relaxation for phobias has employed college student subjects. Much less data exist on relaxation therapy for nonstudent phobic clients. PR is sometimes included in exposure treatments for agoraphobia (e.g., Frame, Turner, Jacob, & Szekely, 1984), but the contribution of relaxation herein is indeterminate. In the few studies available on PR with nonstudent phobics treated in a clinical setting, the results do not recommend PR for this class of disorders (Gillan & Rachman, 1974; O'Brien, 1979). Howard, Murphy, and Clarke (1983) evaluated four different treatments (including a PR-meditation combination) and no treatment with subjects who fear flying. With minor exception, all five groups showed improvement. A unique feature of this study was that treatment effectiveness was determined, in part, by actual in-flight assessment.

Self-control Relaxation (SCR)

Goldfried (1971), credited with originating SCR, was one of the earliest contributors to phobia applications. One study (Goldfried & Trier, 1974) presented in the *Relaxation Comparisons* section below contrasted SCR against PR with speech anxious students. A second study (Goldfried & Goldfried, 1977) examined the role of SCR in systematic desensitization for speech phobics.

Speech anxiety was the target of another early SCR trial (Sherman, Mulac, & McCann, 1974). Student volunteers were randomly assigned, within stratified blocks, to SCR (akin to that of Bernstein & Borkovec, 1973), speech skills training, SCR/skills training combined, or no treatment. There was little difference between SCR, skills training, and no treatment on pre-post evaluations of subjective and behavioral indices of speech anxiety. However, the SCR/skills training group surpassed all others on these same measures. Further, the combined group and, to a lesser extent, the SCR group made greater gains on questionnaires assessing general anxiety unrelated to speech phobia (IPAT Anxiety Scale, Cattell, 1957; Willoughby Neuroticism Schedule, Wolpe, 1958; Fear Survey Scale, Wolpe & Lang, 1964). Fremouw and Zitter (1978) have partially replicated the interventions of Sherman et al. (1974) by using somewhat more comprehensive speech skills training and by adding cognitive restructuring to SCR. They found both independent treatments to be effective for speech anxious students.

The volume of research on SCR for phobias, most often examining test and speech anxiety among college students, began to increase sharply in the mid-1970s. This was partly due to the independent efforts of two research groups led by Deffenbacher and Russell, whose contributions will now be reviewed. In both cases, part of their research program strongly emphasized the contribution of SCR to systematic desensitization treatment of phobias, and this material is deemphasized herein.

Deffenbacher's first effort in this area appeared in 1976 and involved training four test anxious subjects in broad-spectrum SCR, which included progressive relaxation, cue-controlled relaxation, and breathing and imagery techniques, as well as training in self-monitoring of anxiety cues. All subjects registered significant pre-post improvement on test anxiety questionnaires (Achievement Anxiety Test, AAT, Alpert & Haber, 1960; Test Anxiety Scale, TAS, Sarason, 1972) and self-ratings of anxiety. More importantly, at post-treatment, two of the subjects retook civil service tests they previously had failed and now passed these tests by a large margin. The other two subjects, college students, posted substantial increases in grade point average of 0.8 and 0.6 following treatment. Deffenbacher and Rivera (1976) provided 6-month follow-up data on the two civil service workers described above. Both were still employed in civil service positions, and one had already received a promotion. In addition, both subjects reported diminished anxiety in situations unrelated to the original target setting, namely, social interactions at work and at home.

Subsequent efforts replicated the utility of SCR for test anxious college students in a single group, pre-post design (Deffenbacher & Snyder, 1976), and for students complaining of test anxiety (Deffenbacher & Hahnloser, 1981; Deffenbacher, Mathis, & Michaels, 1979; Snyder & Deffenbacher, 1977) and speaking anxiety (Deffenbacher & Payne, 1977) in comparison group designs that included a delayed treatment group and one or more conditions providing a self-control version of systematic desensitization, training in cognitive coping skills, or no treatment. One-year follow-up data (Deffenbacher & Michaels, 1980) on the Deffenbacher, Mathis, and Michaels (1979) study revealed that treatment gains held up well over this extended period. Moreover, these studies further illuminated the spillover benefits of SCR for general anxiety that had not been specifically targeted by the treatment.

Russell and his associates have focused their efforts on a particular SCR strategy: cue-controlled relaxation (CCR). Their initial publications were individual case studies illustrating the utility of CCR for test anxiety (Russell & Sipich, 1973, 1974) and snake phobia (Russell & Matthews, 1975). An uncontrolled study also revealed this approach to be effective for test anxiety, when training is presented in a small group format (Russell, Miller, & June, 1974).

This work was followed by group design research contrasting CCR, systematic desensitization, and no treatment for test or speech anxiety among college students. The first study (Russell, Miller, & June, 1975) found CCR and systematic desensitization to be no different from each other, but more effective than no treatment on test anxiety questionnaires (S-R Inventory, Test Form, Endler, Hunt, & Rosenstein, 1962; TAS). School grades were unaffected and neither treatment reduced nontargeted trait (STAI) or speech (S-R Inventory) anxiety. The second study (Russell, Wise, & Stratoudakis, 1976) also targeted test anxiety. Systematic desensitization again proved effective on the same test anxiety questionnaires, but the CCR group made significant gains on one measure only (TAS). Both groups improved on state anxiety (Husek & Alexander, 1963) associated with analogue testing situations, but not on the tests themselves. In contrast to their previous findings, STAI-Trait anxiety also responded to both treatments. The no-treatment group improved only on state anxiety.

The final study in this series targeted speech anxiety (Russell & Wise, 1976). Here, too, CCR and systematic desensitization made comparable gains that exceeded the no-treatment group on the primary measures: two speech anxiety questionnaires (Paul, 1966a; S-R Inventory). Spillover benefits to nontargeted anxiety were the same in all three conditions according to questionnaires of trait anxiety (Taylor, 1953) or test and contest anxiety (S-R Inventory). A final feature of this study found that experienced therapists did not produce greater improvement than inexperienced therapists.

Other researchers' experience with CCR has netted inconsistent results with designs that improved on Russell's approach by adding placebo groups. Three studies by McGlynn and his colleagues (Marchetti, McGlynn, & Patterson, 1977; McGlynn, Bichajian, Giesen, & Rose, 1981; McGlynn, Kinjo, & Doherty, 1978) found, with minor exception, CCR to be no more effective than placebo treatments, or even no treatment, with test anxious and shy college students. Peterson and Greathouse (1983) also reported negative data on CCR for test anxiety. A fourth test anxiety study (Counts, Hollandsworth, & Alcorn, 1978) did document positive CCR effects. CCR and CCR/electromyographic biofeedback together produced greater improvement than soothing music placebo and no-treatment control groups on measures of test (TAS) and state (STAI) anxiety, and test performance (Otis & Lennon, 1967), but not on trait (STAI) anxiety. CCR did not differ from CCR/biofeedback on any measure, indicating that the addition of biofeedback did not therapeutically enhance CCR.

Sweeney and Horan (1982) evaluated CCR for musical performance anxiety. Undergraduate music majors claiming such distress were randomly assigned to CCR, cognitive restructuring, CCR/cognitive restructuring combined, music skills training, or delayed treatment. Although CCR effects did not uniformly emerge on all dependent measures, questionnaire, physiological, and performance indicators suggested that CCR, cognitive restructuring, and their combination were equally effective and superior to music skills training and no treatment. Surprisingly, combining CCR and cognitive restructuring proved no more potent than the two interventions presented singly.

Some of the most important work in this area has been contributed by Ost and his colleagues. The first and prototype study (Ost, Jerremalm, & Johansson, 1981) screened clinic outpatients to identify socially phobic individuals. Volunteers were invited to engage in an analogue social interaction, which included behavioral and physiological monitoring. These data dichotomized clients as primarily physiological or behavioral reactors. Half of each reaction group were treated with social skills training (behavioral focus) and half with

SCR (physiological focus). A series of self-report, behavioral, and physiological indices revealed that client reaction style-treatment focus synchrony produced the best therapeutic results. This study stands as one of the best examples of the important treatment choice implications of differential anxiety assessment.

A subsequent study (Ost, Johansson, & Jerremalm, 1982) used a similar design to treat claustrophobic clients and closely replicated the results of their previous effort. Further, this second effort found that both treatments were more effective than no treatment, and treatment gains were well maintained at 1-year follow-up. A third study (Ost, Lindahl, Sterner, & Jerremalm, 1984) examined blood phobic subjects and dispensed with blocking by subject response bias. Exposure treatment was pitted against SCR, and both proved equally effective.

This same group has since published subject-treatment matched trials with agoraphobic (Ost, Jerremalm, & Jansson, 1984), social phobic (Jerremalm, Jansson, & Ost, 1986a), and dental phobic (Jerremalm, Jansson, & Ost, 1986b) volunteers. They failed to replicate their previous findings, in that SCR was effective for these disorders, but not differentially so among individuals tagged for physiological reactivity. Inadequate methods of assigning subjects to physiological versus behavioral or cognitive deficit categories and unreliable dependent measures were cited as possible explanations of the failure to replicate. Further, the cognitive-physiological distinction may be less valid therapeutically than the behavioral-physiological contrast, and for some disorders, such as agoraphobia, the differentiation of client subtypes simply may not yield therapeutic advantage.

Autogenics (AT)

Kondas (1967) tested children (age 11–15 years) having stage fright and college students having test anxiety. Subjects received AT only, systematic desensitization (including AT), only the systematic desensitization hierarchy (stage fright subjects only), or no treatment. Systematic desensitization produced the strongest, most stable effects, but this condition is not of primary interest in the present text. AT alone effected significant reductions in self-reported stage fright, but subjects receiving AT for test anxiety and untreated subjects showed no change. Five-month follow-up was conducted with the children exhibiting stage fright. At that time, benefits in the AT subjects had reversed to baseline level, while desensitization subjects maintained their gains. Snider and Oetting (1966) presented a more successful, uncontrolled trial of AT for college students with test anxiety. The results were poorly documented, but the subjects were said to improve their grades from C+ to B+ after this treatment. Case histories suggesting the usefulness of AT for elevator phobias and fear of flying, using mainly the fourth standard exercise, calm breathing, have also been reported (Morris, 1977).

Reed and Meyer (1974) conducted a study of AT that is distinguished by its comparison of passive and active orientations. Female college student volunteers were trained in AT as a tool for combating test anxiety and were instructed in either the customary passive AT attitude or its opposite. Both groups achieved significant reductions on a test anxiety questionnaire (Osipow & Kreinbring, 1971), but surprisingly they did not differ from each other.

Other Relaxation Techniques

Weinstein (1976) employed an unspecified method of relaxation in combination with emotive (positive) imagery to successfully treat fear of bathing and nightmares in a case study presentation of a 10-year-old burn patient.

Relaxation Comparisons

Test or speech anxiety was studied in most of the comparisons that follow. Three studies (Chang-Liang & Denney, 1976; Goldfried & Trier, 1974; Osberg, 1981) pitted versions of self-control relaxation against progressive relaxation with test or speech phobic college students, and all three found self-control relaxation to be superior. This convincing pattern was born of a variety of self-report and performance indices.

Kirkland and Hollandsworth (1980) found both cue-controlled relaxation and mantra meditation to be inadequate treatments for test anxiety. Lastly, test anxiety served as a vehicle to contrast three forms of self-control relaxation: applied relaxation without a special cue word, cue-controlled relaxation using a meaningful cue (e.g., calm), and cue-controlled relaxation using a meaningless cue (e.g., veg) (Barrios, Ginter, Scalise, & Miller, 1980). There were no between-group differences, but the applied relaxation group attained the largest within-group improvement.

Norton and Johnson (1983) conducted an interesting study of snake phobics. Agni Yoga, consisting of visualization of an expanding point of light, or progressive relaxation were tested with subjects claiming primarily cognitive or somatic anxiety relating to snakes. Subjective and behavioral indices indicated that progressive relaxation was more effective with somatic phobics and meditation with cognitive phobics.

Final Comments on Relaxation Therapy for Phobias

Self-control relaxation (SCR) emerges as a powerful intervention for phobias. In its broad-based form, typified in Deffenbacher's research program, it yielded stronger and more consistent results than did the more narrow form of SCR, cue-controlled relaxation. In planned contrasts with progressive relaxation, SCR consistently registered greater gains. Further, broad-based SCR often provoked gains in general anxiety beyond the boundaries of the targeted anxiety, as would be expected when training clients in a general coping skill.

The bulk of the SCR research treated college students, but Ost's brilliant efforts stand as a prominent exception to this. Future applications of SCR to nonstudent phobics should, nevertheless, bear in mind that greater difficulties may be encountered with this population.

There is not sufficient data to recommend other relaxation forms for phobia treatment. A good deal of progressive relaxation research does exist on this subject, and the results are disappointingly consistent. Progressive relaxation is ineffective in treating phobias.

Computer phobias have so far eluded relaxation therapy, but this promises to be a fertile area of relaxation application. The computer satiation of our society has precipitated anxiety both in young workers preparing for the technological challenges of the future and in older workers confronted with retraining to keep abreast of a sometimes harried technological pace. For many individuals, overcoming their computer phobia will be a difficult but rewarding effort.

DEPRESSION

Depression may arise from multiple sources, including biochemical, genetic, characterological, and environmental anomalies (Whybrow, Akiskal, & McKinney, 1984). Although diminished activity and lack of energy are routinely present in depression, calming treatments such as tranquilizers and relaxation have proven useful, particularly with mild to moderate depression when instigated by environmental demands (Lewinsohn, Munoz, Youngren, & Zeiss, 1978). In these instances, depression may be viewed as a passive form of anxiety or as a response to anxiety. In either case, depression may be responsive to relaxation treatments aimed at neutralizing distressing thoughts and reducing tension.

Progressive Relaxation (PR)

Reynolds and Coats (1986) tested PR, cognitive behavior therapy, or no treatment with depressed adolescents. Depression and anxiety questionnaires, and interview ratings revealed PR to be superior to no treatment at posttreatment and 5-week follow-up. PR was equal to or superior to cognitive behavior therapy on these measures as well.

Meditation

Yoga meditation consisting of breath awareness, but also including stretching exercises, was tested with depressed volunteers from the community (Klein et al., 1985). Running exercise and interpersonal/cognitive group therapy conditions were also tested. After the 12-week treatment course and at 9-month follow-up, meditators showed significant improvement in subjective depression and several questionnaire subtest measures of the same (SCL-90, Derogatis, Lipman, & Covi, 1973; Cornell Medical Index, Brodman, Erdmann, & Wolff, 1949). Similar gains were made by the other two treatment groups. This study left uncontrolled, plausible alternative explanations of change, such as passage of time and placebo.

Autogenics (AT)

Haward (1965) treated depressed outpatients with (*a*) medication and psychotherapy, (*b*) behavior therapy (details unspecified), or (*c*) behavior therapy and slow, methodical AT. Therapeutic impact was assessed by a battery of respiratory tests shown to be correlated with stress sensitivity. Only groups *a* and *c* registered significant improvement, and the group receiving AT was superior to the other two.

Final Comments on Relaxation Therapy for Depression

There is surprisingly little work available in this area, despite indicators of relaxation usefulness herein. The few available studies are positive. Further, there is mounting evidence of substantial overlap between anxiety and primarily unipolar depression (Dobson, 1985), and successes attained in the anxiety realm bode well for relaxation applications to depression.

PHANTOM LIMB PAIN

Following loss of a limb, about 35 percent of amputees (Melzack, 1971) report initial pain, and about 10 percent perceive persistent pain located at an extremity site that is no longer part of their body, in other words, phantom limb pain. More recent surveys indicate that the incidence of phantom limb pain among amputees may exceed 90 percent (Sherman & Tippens, 1982). The pain sensation is usually described as burning or cramping, and such reports may be interactive with psychological disposing factors, such as anxiety and depression (Sherman, Sherman, & Gall, 1980). Melzack (1971; Melzack & Loeser, 1978) has argued that the source of this pain lies not in the nerve endings at the amputation site. Rather, he proposes a "central biasing mechanism" due to dysfunction in the brainstem reticular formation. Commonly employed treatments include chemotherapy, surgery, physical therapy, etc., although no single treatment for this disorder has won broad acceptance (Sherman, 1980).

Progressive Relaxation (PR)

An interesting case report (McKechnie, 1975) involved a young adult male with a 10-year history of perceived pain in his amputated arm and hand. PR training, which included imaginally tensing and relaxing his phantom limb, markedly reduced phantom pain reports and this effect held up at 6-month follow-up.

Sherman (1976) reported that only one session, which presented PR and electromyographic (EMG) biofeedback from the leg stump, was needed to eliminate phantom limb pain in five subjects. More recently, Sherman, Gall, and Gormly (1979) presented case study data on 16 subjects treated with a combination of taped PR and EMG biofeedback derived from the forehead or the amputation stump. Of this group, 14 individuals reported complete or substantial pain relief after about half a dozen treatment sessions. None of the subjects reported recovery of pain at follow-ups, which ranged from 6 months to 3 years. The authors speculated that treatment effects occurred secondary to anxiety reduction, but this theory was not specifically tested. Placebo effects and reduced afferent stimulation from the amputation site persist as alternative explanations.

Final Comments on Relaxation Therapy for Phantom Limb Pain

Phantom limb pain is a high frequency problem that has attracted multiple medical treatments, though none have proved completely adequate. Uncontrolled tests of progressive relaxation have registered auspicious results. This domain strongly warrants further research efforts that are more highly controlled to isolate the viability of relaxation therapy.

ESSENTIAL HYPERTENSION

The great majority of all diagnosed cases of high blood pressure (BP) are not associated with an identifiable cause and are thus labeled essential hypertension (Shapiro & Goldstein, 1982; Surwit, Williams, & Shapiro, 1982). Chronic hypertension increases the individual's risk for serious illness, including heart and kidney disease, and stroke. The customary treatment for essential hypertension is chemotherapy, although the necessity of taking antihypertensive medication on a long-term basis sometimes poses problems: namely, low patient medication compliance and adverse drug side effects (Bulpitt & Dollery, 1973). Stress is a likely contributor to many cases of essential hypertension, as suggested by epidemiologic and experimental data (Benson, Kotch, & Crassweller, 1978; Patel, 1977). Relaxation can neutralize the stress factor and thereby serve as a safe alternative or adjunct to chemotherapy.

Progressive Relaxation (PR)

Not surprisingly, the earliest applications of PR to essential hypertension were conducted by Edmund Jacobson. Jacobson (1940a) presented a detailed case history to illustrate his contention that this disorder is primarily caused by chronic tension of the smooth vascular musculature and skeletal musculature

(Jacobson, 1948, 1957). Later, this same author (Jacobson, 1947) presented further case study data on PR for over 100 hypertensives.

Some four decades later, interest was aroused again in PR treatment of high BP. In one of the most intensive studies (Agras, Taylor, Kraemer, Allen, & Schneider, 1980), five hypertensive subjects submitted to 24-hour BP surveillance during 1-week of hospitalization. The first 2 days were reserved for baseline data. Three PR sessions were administered each day for the next 3 days, and relaxation practice was discontinued during the last day as a control for effects due to the passage of time. Throughout the study, BP was taken at short intervals in each 24-hour period to evaluate treatment-generalization effects. Diet, exercise, and antihypertensive medication were controlled to rule out their confounding influence.

Within-session decreases in systolic blood pressure (SBP) ($M \simeq 8$ mm Hg) and diastolic blood pressure (DBP) ($M \simeq 6$ mm Hg) occurred in about 75 percent of the treatment sessions. Treatment effects usually endured for 30–90 minutes following each PR treatment before BP returned to baseline levels. The best evidence for generalization of PR effects came from BPs taken during the nightly sleep period. For the three (of five) subjects who attained the largest within-session BP decreases, " . . . the mean difference in BP between nights following relaxation training and nights following no treatment is $-12.5/-7.3$ mm Hg, a lowering of clinical significance despite the brevity of relaxation training" (p. 862). Somewhat comparable generalization effects have been observed by others (Martin & Epstein, 1980; Wadden, 1983).

More recently, Agras and his colleagues examined the role of expectancy for improvement in PR treatment of essential hypertension (Agras, Horne, & Taylor, 1982). Subjects were randomly assigned to two groups that differed only in that one was told to expect immediate and the other delayed treatment effects. In both groups, treatment began with a detailed description of the treatment procedures, accompanied by an explanation of why BP changes should occur immediately after the first treatment session or only after all three treatment sessions were completed. Three PR treatments were then administered in 1 day. BPs were taken before and after each administration. By the end of the day, subjects in the immediate expectancy group showed a significantly greater decline in SBP (17.0 mm Hg) compared to the delayed expectancy subjects (2.4 mm Hg). DBP did not distinguish the groups. Treatment credibility ratings and perceived relaxation effects were comparable in the two groups. This study dramatically exposes the instrumental role of expectancy on systolic BP level, as has been shown previously (Goldring, Chasis, Schreiner, & Smith, 1956), although the mechanism of influence of this psychosocial factor remains unknown.

We (Hoelscher, Lichstein, & Rosenthal, 1986) conducted PR trials with the goal of examining home relaxation practice compliance. Hypertensives were randomly assigned to (a) individual PR training, (b) small group PR training, (c) the same as b plus contingency contracting (mainly with spouses) to induce high compliance, or (d) no treatment. Home relaxation practice was independently monitored by self-report records and unobtrusive accumulation of relaxation tape play time (Relaxation Assessment Device, RAD, described in Chapter 1).

Significant and comparable SBP/DBP reductions (averaging about 13/6 mm Hg) occurred at 6 weeks posttreatment in groups *a, b,* and *c,* compared to little change in *d.* Only one third of the subjects (in groups *a, b,* and *c*) practiced the prescribed one time a day (as per the RAD data) and subjects' self-report of relaxation practice nearly doubled, on the average, actual time spent practicing. Some amount of compliance decay occurred in all groups, but this stabilized at about a month. Surprisingly, compliance was lowest among subjects contracting for high compliance (group *c*). Relaxation practice significantly correlated with systolic but not diastolic change, reminding us that hypertension is a multidetermined phenomenon. In sum, we failed to identify powerful compliance induction strategies, but we did demonstrate large cost-effective advantages of group over individual treatment with no therapeutic loss (in the noncontingency group *b*).

Other, less tightly controlled studies may be cited that also support the usefulness of PR for high BP. One study (Brauer, Horlick, Nelson, Farquhar, & Agras, 1979) observed that treatment effects first surfaced at 6-month follow-up. At that point, live PR training exerted the greatest SBP effect (-17.8 mm Hg) compared to a taped PR group ($+0.7$ mm Hg) and individuals receiving psychotherapy (-1.6 mm Hg). DBP changes in these three groups of -9.7, -4.3, and -1.1 mm Hg, respectively, were not significantly different. Our own efforts (Hoelscher, Lichstein, Fischer, & Hegarty, 1987) found PR to be effective compared to no treatment, but we observed no differential effects between individuals given a PR tape to aid home practice and individuals practicing at home without tape assistance. Bali (1979) also found PR (combined with mantra and breath meditation) to be superior to psychotherapy on measures of SBP and DBP and self-reported anxiety (Manifest Anxiety Scale, MAS; Taylor, 1953). BP treatment effects were maintained at 12-month follow-up. Wadden (reported in duplicate, 1983, 1984) also employed a cluster of relaxation techniques (PR, meditation, passive relaxation, and imagery) and tested the usefulness of incorporating spouses into the training and practice regimens. Spouse participation did not enhance BP change. Basler, Brinkmeier, Buser, Haehn, and Molders-Kober (1982) presented obese hypertensives with one of four treatments: (a) behavior therapy for obesity, (b) behavior therapy for obesity, plus self-monitoring BP and social skills training, (c) behavior therapy for obesity plus PR, and (d) general information counseling on high BP. All treatments exerted a comparable, significant impact on BP compared to no treatment at 6-month follow-up.

Several studies have combined or contrasted PR and different biofeedback methods. One brief report (Sherman, Hayashi, Gaarder, Huff, & Williams, 1978) observed no hypertensive benefits for pregnant women treated with PR/electromyographic (EMG) biofeedback combined. PR proved to be an effective treatment for high BP in the remaining studies (Glasgow, Gaarder,

& Engel, 1982; Goebel, Viol, Lorenz, & Clemente, 1980; Hatch et al., 1985; Shoemaker & Tasto, 1975; Walsh, Dale, & Anderson, 1977). PR effects were comparable to direct BP biofeedback (Glasgow et al., 1982; Goebel et al., 1980; Hatch et al., 1985), to EMG biofeedback (Goebel et al., 1980), and to pulse-wave velocity biofeedback (Walsh et al., 1977). Taped PR proved superior to direct BP biofeedback in one study (Shoemaker & Tasto, 1975). Glasgow et al. (1982) found PR/biofeedback combined tended to be more effective than PR or biofeedback alone, but others (Goebel et al., 1980; Walsh et al., 1977) have not obtained superior effects for combined treatments. Follow-up on the Glasgow et al. (1982) study at 6-months posttreatment (Engel, Glasgow, & Gaarder, 1983) found no treatment deterioration.

The relative efficacy of chemotherapy and PR has been the subject of two studies. Taylor, Farquhar, Nelson, and Agras (1977) found PR/chemotherapy combined to be superior to chemotherapy or psychotherapy/chemotherapy at posttreatment for SBP effects, although these differences faded by 6-month follow-up. A brief reference to further follow-up to the Taylor et al. (1977) study appeared in Blanchard and Ahles (1979). At 3-years posttreatment, the PR group was worse than the other two. Presumably, this surprising (and somewhat alarming) finding resulted from decreased medication compliance among the PR patients, an anomaly also observed by others (Martin & Epstein, 1980). The second study (Luborsky et al., 1982) represents the only true PR-chemotherapy comparison, as the PR subjects were unmedicated. This study used a passive form of PR and found it to be inferior to chemotherapy. This research will be presented in greater detail in the passive PR section below.

Within the large PR for hypertension literature, there are few negative outcome trials. Cottier, Shapiro, and Julius (1984) reported such a one. They compared PR and no treatment, and found no difference in office BPs and clinically trivial differences in home BPs over a 5 month course. This study contained a methodological idiosyncracy, the effect of which on relaxation practice and outcome is indeterminate. It involved informing all subjects that, in addition to relaxation treatment, they would receive periods of active and placebo medication. In fact, all subjects were administered placebo only until the study's end. A second negative outcome study tested the combination of PR and other relaxation techniques, weight loss, and restricted salt intake. This package yielded significant SBP reduction, but no greater than that of a BP monitoring only group (Jacob, Fortmann, Kraemer, Farquhar, & Agras, 1985).

Self-control Relaxation (SCR)

Graham, Beiman, and Ciminero (1977) were the first to report on SCR for hypertension. They trained an unmedicated hypertensive, who also manifested generalized anxiety, in seven sessions of SCR emphasizing relaxation by recall (see description in Chapter 5). BPs were recorded in the therapy session by the therapist, and also at a medical clinic independent of the SCR therapy, to evaluate generalization effects. In-session BP reductions occurred as expected. More important, extra-session SBP/DBP decreased from about 155/95 mm Hg during baseline to 125/75 at posttreatment. Follow-up at about 1 year documented stable normotension.

This same group (Beiman, Graham, & Ciminero, 1978a) next trained two unmedicated hypertensives during seven and eight sessions of SCR. BP readings were taken at the beginning of the treatment sessions and twice daily by the subjects themselves. Natural environment systolic/diastolic BP readings revealed posttreatment decreases of 15/16 and 18/19 mm Hg for the two subjects. Within-session measures closely tracked the self-monitored BPs. Treatment gains were well maintained at 2 to 6-month follow-up. Beiman, Graham, and Ciminero (1978b) followed up on one of the above subjects, who persisted in manifesting high BP during medical examinations. A course of systematic desensitization successfully reduced his BP, bringing it in line with his BP in other settings.

More recently, another research group (Southam, Agras, Taylor, & Kraemer, 1982) also explored this question of generalization of BP treatment effects. Volunteers from the community were assigned either to a treatment group (SCR as in Graham et al., 1977) or to a no-treatment group. BP was measured by the researchers in the clinic sessions and by the subjects during the course of the day at 20-minute intervals, using a self-administered, ambulatory BP recorder. After eight sessions, significant differences between these groups in the clinic occurred only for DBP, -12.6 and -2.5 mm Hg for the treated and untreated groups, respectively. However, in the natural environment, the SBP/DBP decreases for the SCR group, 7.8/4.6 mm Hg, were both significantly greater than the corresponding changes for the control group, $-0.1/+1.7$ mm Hg. At 6-month follow-up, in-clinic measurements indicated the SCR group was $-6.0/-12.1$ mm Hg compared to baseline, and the control group was $+1.3/-2.2$ mm Hg. Only the diastolic findings were significant. Analyses of medication, weight, salt intake, and exercise changes during the study ruled out the contribution of these factors to the results. A follow-up report (Agras, Southam, & Taylor, 1983) documented excellent maintenance of therapeutic gains in the clinic and worksite at 15 months posttreatment, the longest follow-up of any kind of relaxation for BP yet obtained.

This group (Taylor, Agras, Schneider, & Allen, 1983) has since applied the same procedure and cleverly monitored relaxation practice compliance. Subjects were outfitted with relaxation tapes and recorders that contained hidden electronics (described in Chapter 1) to objectively measure home relaxation practice. Pre-post SBP/DBP changes were $-8.3/-5.4$ mm Hg. As revealed by the unobtrusive monitoring system, only 39 percent of subjects practiced relaxation at or above the prescribed level, five times per week, although self-report of practice suggested 71 percent adherence. For reasons that were not clear, actual relaxation time was uncorrelated with BP change (perhaps a truncated distribution suppressed the correlation). Employing the method of identifying a cue word at the end of the relaxation tape to monitor adherence (described in Chapter 1), another group also found no significant correlation between relaxation and BP (Jacob, Beidel, & Shapiro, 1984).

Agras and his associates (Agras, Schneider, & Taylor, 1984) recently brought a quizzical phenomenon to our attention. Subjects who showed an initial positive response to SCR, but who subsequently reverted to baseline BP levels, received the complete SCR training protocol a second time or routine follow-up group discussion of BP progress. Unobtrusive monitoring of relaxation practice documented good compliance. No differences ensued between these two groups, suggesting that once BP gains from SCR are lost, they cannot be recaptured.

Blanchard et al. (1984) applied SCR to hypertension and compared it to skin temperature biofeedback. The biofeedback also included autogenic phrases, but the autogenics appeared not to be a major part of the treatment. This study is distinguished by its use of more severe hypertensives than is usually the case in relaxation therapy. To qualify, subjects had to be maintained on at least two medications.

SCR did not perform well in this trial. Home and clinic SBP/DBP pre-post change was not significant for this group, whereas significant decreases did obtain in the biofeedback group. Similarly, laboratory stress tests failed to reveal robust SCR effects. On the positive side, following posttreatment medication withdrawal, SCR subjects' BPs did not exceed pretreatment medicated levels. A more recent report on this same study (Blanchard et al., 1986) finds little to recommend SCR at 1-year follow-up.

Passive Relaxation

Three studies are available in this section, and two of them utilized Brady's (1973) method, termed *metronome-conditioned relaxation* (MCR). The technique involves rhythmically chanting passive relaxation instructions (e.g., relax, let go) in synchrony with a metronome. The author claimed that the sound and rhythm of the metronome enhance the relaxation effect. Clients are typically assisted in their home practice of the method by a tape recording.

Initial antihypertensive trials of MCR employed a single subject withdrawal design (Hersen & Barlow, 1976), utilizing one treatment phase with two subjects (A-B-A) and a second treatment phase (A-B-A-B) with two others (Brady, Luborsky, & Kron, 1974). Three of four subjects showed an excellent DBP response to MCR; SBP was not reported. For these three subjects, pre-post diastolic changes averaged −8 mm Hg. Recently, this method has been submitted to a more rigorous test, with less profound results (Luborsky et al., 1982). Unmedicated patients having mild to moderate essential hypertension were randomly assigned to four conditions: chemotherapy, MCR, SBP biofeedback, or placebo exercise. At posttreatment, all four groups registered significant systolic decreases and, except for the exercise group, diastolic decreases as well. The average SBP change for the MCR group (−6.3 mm Hg) was significantly less than that for the chemotherapy group (−18.8 mm Hg), although the DBP changes (−5.4 mm Hg for the MCR group and −10.3 mm

Hg for the chemotherapy group) were not significantly different between these groups.

The third study (Goldstein, Shapiro, & Thananopavarn, 1984) is one of the few to evaluate relaxation with unmedicated hypertensives, and it obtained encouraging results. The relaxation method in this study combined passive relaxation, slow breathing, and pleasant imagery. Mild to moderate hypertensive volunteers were assigned to (a) relaxation plus medication, (b) relaxation, electromyographic biofeedback, plus medication, (c) self-monitoring of blood pressure control plus medication, or (d) relaxation only (unmedicated).

Home blood pressure morning self-assessments found the three treatment groups (a, b, and d) to be equivalently superior to group c on SBP and DBP. At night, however, a and b were superior to c and d on SBP, and on DBP, a and b were superior to c with unmedicated relaxation subjects (d) falling in the middle. Lab assessments found small but significant SBP/DBP decreases in all groups. Gains were well maintained at 1 year.

Meditation

One of the first meditative approaches applied to high BP was Transcendental Meditation (TM), and this has since been tested in several studies. Herbert Benson, later of relaxation response fame, conducted the earliest trials with TM, and these were all single group, pre-post designs with hypertensive individuals seeking TM training. The first report (Benson & Wallace, 1972a) found significant SBP (9 mm Hg) and DBP (6 mm Hg) decreases. The second report (Benson, Marzetta, & Rosner, 1974) found significant decreases only for SBP (15 mm Hg) after 9 weeks of TM practice. This study also revealed that subjects with the highest BPs attained the largest BP decreases. This initial values effect (Wilder, 1957) for BP has been observed in other investigations of meditation for BP as well (Peters, Benson, & Peters, 1977; Seer & Raeburn, 1980). Further studies of this same sort by Benson and his associates found significant decreases for both SBP and DBP among hypertensive individuals taking no antihypertensive medication (Benson, Rosner, Marzetta, & Klemchuck, 1974a) or on continuous antihypertensive medication regimens (Benson, Rosner, Marzetta, & Klemchuk, 1974b).

Mixed results were obtained in the TM treatment of seven hypertensives by another research group (Blackwell et al., 1976). At the end of the 12-week treatment course, six of these subjects exhibited a significant decrease in both SBP and DBP in either the clinic, their natural setting, or both. However, at 6-month follow-up, only three subjects had maintained their progress.

Pollack, Weber, Case, and Laragh (1977) reported the only negative results on TM for hypertension. Twenty patients trained in TM exhibited significant SBP reductions of about 9 mm Hg during the first 3 months of training, but during months 4 through 6, SBP was not significantly lower than the baseline level. DBP did not change during the course of the study.

None of the TM hypertension studies included a control group of any kind.

To correct this and other methodological weaknesses in the extant literature, Seer and Raeburn (1980) randomly assigned unmedicated hypertensives to a TM-like treatment (a single standard mantra was employed with all subjects), a placebo treatment (meditation without a mantra), or no treatment. The meditation and placebo groups made significant gains in DBP at the end of treatment and 6-month follow-up of about -10 mm Hg, compared to erratic fluctuation in the untreated subjects. SBP did not distinguish the groups. The implications of this study for TM are ambiguous, as these authors have not established that their TM simulation is equally as effective as the original. However, it is interesting to note that a simple rest break (the placebo group) did provide some benefits.

Benson's (1975) noncultic version of TM has also been tested with hypertension. Benson and his associates (Peters, Benson, & Peters, 1977; Peters, Benson, & Porter, 1977) conducted the first of these studies in addressing worksite stress (Schwartz, 1980). The Benson program offered relaxation training to all employees of a manufacturing firm and subsequently evaluated four groups of some 200 participants, mostly normotensive. Volunteers were randomly assigned to receive training in Benson's method of meditation, a quiet-rest control group, or no treatment. A fourth group of individuals, who also received no treatment, were selected from among those employees who initially elected not to volunteer for treatment. Training and evaluation were conducted over a 12-week period.

To compute the mean BP decrease, the mean of three baseline BP measures taken over a 5-week period was compared to the mean of three BP measures taken over the last 5 weeks of training. SBP/DBP decreases in this contrast were 6.7/5.2, 2.6/2.0, and 0.5/1.2 mm Hg for the meditation, quiet rest, and volunteer no-treatment groups, respectively. For both SBP and DBP, the meditation group achieved significantly greater decreases than the two control groups, which did not differ from each other. Less data were available on the fourth group composed of nonvolunteer individuals who received no treatment, permitting only pre-post BP point contrasts as opposed to comparisons between means. This group showed virtually no BP change and this was significantly less than that of the meditation group. In evaluating these results, we cannot ignore the potential influence of differential expectancies for improvement that may have distinguished the meditation and quiet rest groups.

Surwit and his associates conducted two studies testing Benson's method and biofeedback with borderline hypertensives, and obtained disappointing results. Surwit, Shapiro, and Good (1978) assigned subjects to eight sessions of SBP/heart rate biofeedback, electromyographic biofeedback, or Benson's relaxation technique. All treatments produced significant within-session SBP decreases averaging about 4 mm Hg (DBP data were not reported). Differences across sessions or between groups did not emerge. Follow-up data collected at 6-week and 1-year posttreatment were of the same order.

Hager and Surwit (1978) instructed subjects in the use of a portable SBP biofeedback device or Benson's method, and then prescribed home practice twice daily for 4 weeks. Subjects measured their own BPs before and after each home session. There were significant average within-session changes for both groups on SBP (-4.1 mm Hg) and DBP (-1.6 mm Hg). SBP did not decrease from baseline to treatment end, but DBP (mean change $= 2.0$ mm Hg) did drop in the two groups combined. None of the analyses revealed differences between biofeedback and Benson's technique. In sum, the Surwit studies found statistically significant but clinically trivial changes accruing to Bensonian relaxation (and biofeedback) for high BP. The authors suggested that increased treatment exposure may have resulted in larger treatment gains. Goldstein, Shapiro, Thananopavarn, and Sambhi (1982) also obtained a negative outcome with Benson's procedure. Antihypertensive drugs proved very effective and direct blood pressure biofeedback mildly effective, but meditation exerted no effect on lab or home SBP/DBP.

Over the past decade, Chandra Patel has forged a clinically impressive contribution in the domain of meditation for hypertension. Patel's (1973) first report drew a great deal of attention. Twenty hypertensives, most of whom were medicated, received three relaxation treatments a week for 3 months. The treatment protocol blended several different techniques: skin resistance level biofeedback, passive relaxation, autogenic phrases, and breath and mantra meditation. This research is included in the meditation section to reflect the prominence of this component in the protocol. By the end of 3 months, five patients discontinued antihypertensive medication, and the group as a whole reduced their drug consumption by 41 percent. The average SBP at baseline, 160 mm Hg, fell to 134 mm Hg, and DBP changed from 102 to 86 mm Hg.

A subsequent article (Patel, 1975a) reported 1-year follow-up data for these subjects, who were now practicing relaxation on their own and compared them to 9 months of data from age and sex-matched patients with comparable hypertensive symptoms. The controls submitted to three "treatment" sessions a week of quiet rest for 3 months to mimic the attention received by the treated subjects. Treated subjects now registered SBP/DBP averaging 144/87 mm Hg, still about 16/15 mm Hg below their baseline level. Medication reductions were largely maintained from the end of treatment. There was virtually no change in the BPs of control subjects. Patel (1975b) presented additional short-term data evaluating her treatment package. Herein, the SBP/DBP reductions were 11/10 mm Hg, and five patients decreased their antihypertensive medication by an average 28 percent. Patel (1976) reported similar BP data, as well as significant cholesterol reduction following the treatment package.

Patel (1975b) also presented data on this treatment protocol's effect on stress tolerance. Hypertensive patients were randomly assigned to 6 weeks of treatment or quiet rest control sessions. Exercise and cold pressure stress tests were presented before and after the 6-week period. The treated group exhibited significant improvement on all four BP indices for both tests, and the control group improved on none.

Patel and North (1975) presented further clinical trial data. Hypertensive subjects were randomly assigned to 12 treatment or quiet rest control sessions.

A second form of biofeedback, electromyography, was added to the extant treatment package, as was salient health education. Let me briefly comment on the education component. Treated subjects in Patel and Carruthers (1977) also received health education, but the therapeutic potency of this factor was called into question by a still more recent study (Patel, Marmot, & Terry, 1981). In this latter study, both treated and untreated subjects received health education, but BP decreases among the treated subjects were significantly greater than in the untreated subjects at posttreatment and 8-month follow-up. These differences were maintained at 4-year follow-up (Patel et al., 1985).

The results of Patel and North (1975) are as follows. Comparing pretreatment and 3-month follow-up levels, the treated subjects manifested average SBP/DBP decreases of 26/15 mm Hg compared to 9/4 mm Hg for the controls. Subsequently, the controls were given the same treatment used in the first phase. These individuals now exhibited decreases of 28 mm Hg systolic and 15 mm Hg diastolic, thus replicating the response of the first group of treated subjects. Additional confirmation of this approach has since been reported in treating hypertensives recruited within the employee pool of a large company (Patel et al., 1981).

Patel and Carruthers (1977) recruited volunteers from among the patients of a private medical practice. Four groups evolved: (*a*) individuals receiving treatment to quit smoking (smoking data are reported in the *Drug Abuse* section of this chapter), (*b*) normotensives receiving treatment, (*c*) normotensives not receiving treatment, and (*d*) hypertensives receiving treatment. Treatment in this study departed somewhat from Patel's customary approach in that there was a deliberate attempt to economize on professional time expenditure. There were only six treatment sessions presented once a week, and the nonbiofeedback portion was delivered by tape only. The three treated groups (*a, b,* and *d*) all showed significant pre-post reductions in SBP averaging about 12 mm Hg (including 19 mm Hg in the hypertensive group). Groups *b* and *d* exhibited significant DBP decreases of 7 and 11 mm Hg, respectively. The control group (*c*) did not show significant change in these or any other dependent measure. Particular groups also manifested significant decreases in heart rate (*a* and *d*), weight (*b*), cholesterol (*a* and *d*), triglyceride (*b* and *d*), and free fatty acids (*b*).

Overall, Patel's approach consistently has obtained larger and more durable BP reductions than any other nonpharmacological intervention for hypertension, averaging drops in SBP/DBP on the order of 20/15 mm Hg. There are two distinctive features of Patel's approach that might account for her results. First, she employs the most varied relaxation treatment package. Patel (1977) pointed out that numerous elements contribute to the manifestation of high BP, and the several components of her treatment package are styled to separately target these partially independent causal elements. I would like to propose an alternative explanation. The influence of diverse relaxation techniques is not as dissimilar as Patel suggests. The dissimilarities lie in the subject's idiosyncratic technique preferences, not in the technique. In presenting a smorgasbord of relaxation possibilities, the subject is afforded the opportunity of selecting for home practice the method of greatest personal appeal. This may exert a beneficial influence on relaxation depth achieved and consistency of practice. Second, most of Patel's subjects were recruited from within her on-going private medical practice. Most of these individuals were already engaged in hypertensive treatment. Their level of motivation, intelligence, self-discipline, etc., factors that may enhance an individual's ability to profit from relaxation therapy, may have exceeded those of subjects recruited from the general population or hypertensive clinics, as is the case in most other studies.

Little et al. (1984) recently conducted a partial replication and component analysis of Patel's work. Little et al. assigned pregnant, borderline hypertensive women to (a) meditation (as in Patel & North, 1975), (b) meditation plus skin conductance biofeedback, or (c) no treatment. Groups a and b did not differ on any measure. The treated groups (a and b) had significantly fewer hospital admissions and significantly lower DBP than the untreated group. Only group a achieved a significantly lower SBP than c. Lastly, the three groups did not differ on any of several pregnancy outcome indicators, for example, Apgar score, hours of labor, and babies' birth weight. Hafner (1982) employed a similar design to replicate Patel's findings, and although the meditation and meditation/biofeedback groups obtained substantial BP gains, these did not differ significantly from untreated subjects.

Various other meditation methods have also been used to treat hypertension. Datey, Deshmukh, Dalvi, and Vinekar (1969) employed Shavasan Yoga, a combination of slow breathing and body focusing. They instituted a clever control procedure with those hypertensives not previously maintained on drug therapy. These individuals were given 1 month of placebo medication before initiating Shavasan training. Comparing postplacebo with post-Shavasan BP levels, this group achieved extraordinary SBP/DBP reductions averaging 37/23 mm Hg (my computation from their table of raw data). The authors did not report the duration of yoga training nor any follow-up data. A second group of 22 patients all had their BP well controlled by medication. The average BP of this group did not change, but 13 of these individuals reduced their antihypertensive medication by an average of 68 percent over the training period. A third group of subjects whose BP was poorly controlled on medication showed a highly variable response to Yoga.

Stone and DeLeo (1976) evaluated a Buddhist method of breath counting meditation. Over 6 months, treated subjects reduced SBP by about 12 mm Hg and DBP by 10 mm HG. Untreated controls did not change. This study has attracted a great deal of attention because it also found, among treated subjects, significant reductions in dopamine-beta-hydroxylase, a plasma dopamine enzyme. To a somewhat lesser extent, it also found reductions in plasma renin, all indicators of sympathetic arousal. There are confirming biochemical data on the role of sympathetic arousal in hypertension from another study (Patel et al., 1981), but disconfirming data from two others (Brauer et al., 1979; Pollack et al., 1977).

Finally, Roberts and Forester (1979) compared 10 sessions of group mantra meditation (the Ananda Marga school) with 10 classes of health education. Over the 2-month treatment period, meditation subjects achieved significant decreases in both SBP (8 mm Hg) and DBP (4 mm Hg), while the control subjects achieved a significant decrease in SBP (6 mm Hg) but not DBP (1 mm Hg). Between-group differences did not reach significance.

Autogenics (AT)

A small amount of data are available on AT for hypertension. Klumbies and Eberhardt (1966) observed a drop in SBP/DBP from 165/100 to 130/80 after 4 months of AT practice in their 26 hypertensives. Others (Green, Green, & Norris, 1980) have reported positive anecdotal data on the combination of AT and skin temperature biofeedback. In a methodologically more sophisticated study (Luborsky, Ancona, Masoni, Scolari, & Longoni, 1980–1981), small groups of hypertensives (five patients each), received (a) pharmacological treatment only, (b) AT only, or (c) both. Only group a achieved significant blood pressure reductions. AT proved ineffectual, and quizzically, AT and pharmacotherapy combined (group c) also was ineffective.

Imagery

Crowther (1983) conducted the only study of imagery effects on hypertension and obtained impressive results. She prepared tapes describing each subject's self-selected relaxing imagery, and added suggestions of deep breathing, warmth, and muscle relaxation. Subjects received eight treatment sessions composed of (a) relaxing imagery as above, or (b) imagery as in a, plus stress management training. A no-treatment group (c) was included. Only the treated groups (a and b) made significant gains at posttreatment and 6-month follow-up, but they did not differ from each other. SBP/DBP for groups a and b combined were about 155/98, 132/85, and 139/88 mm Hg at pretreatment, posttreatment, and follow-up, respectively. Home blood pressures closely tracked experimental recordings. For most subjects, antihypertensive medication either was unchanged or decreased during the course of the study.

Other Relaxation Techniques

Hypertensive college students received about 20 sessions of an unspecified method of taped relaxation and skin temperature biofeedback (Bertilson, Bartz, & Zimmerman, 1979). SBP decreased about 12 mm Hg from the first to the last treatment session, and about half that much outside the therapy setting. DBP was unaltered.

A preliminary report evaluating an unspecified method of relaxation with moderate hypertensives obtained a clinically small but statistically significant blood pressure reduction of about 1.5 mm Hg for SBP and DBP both (Jacob,

Shapiro, McDonald, & Beidel, 1984). Relaxation effects did not generalize to an untreated setting, and when combined with effective chemotherapy, relaxation did not produce incremental effects.

Uncontrolled trials with Quieting Response training (Ford, Stroebel, Strong, & Szarek, 1983a) achieved success with only 5 of 15 essential hypertensives (for further details, see *Other Relaxation Techniques, Muscle-Contraction Headache* section). I should point out that conservative criteria were applied, 15 percent BP drop, in determining success.

Relaxation Comparisons

Cohen and Sedlacek (1983) conducted the seemingly unfair comparison of five sessions of relaxation response training (Benson, 1975) with 20 sessions of multimodal relaxation training (electromyographic and skin temperature biofeedback, progressive relaxation, autogenic phrases, and guided imagery). A no-treatment group was included. Not surprisingly, significant BP reductions and improved field independence occurred in the multimodal group only. A second study (O'Neill & Schafer, 1982) compared the relaxation response and progressive relaxation on an even basis, and found them to be equivalently effective.

Final Comments on Relaxation Therapy for Essential Hypertension

To echo conclusions drawn by reviewers of relaxation for hypertension (Frumkin, Nathan, Prout, & Cohen, 1978; Jacob, Kraemer, & Agras, 1977; Wadden, Luborsky, Greer, & Crits-Christoph, 1984), this is a methodologically sophisticated area evincing good therapeutic results. When used in cooperation with a chemical regimen, relaxation is associated with reductions of about 10 systolic and 5 diastolic mm Hg with moderate hypertensives, and changes of this magnitude are clinically important (Health and Public Policy Committee, American College of Physicians, 1985). These changes generalize to non-treated settings, maintain well over time, and probably are not attributable to placebo factors. Indeed, relaxation therapy has carved a role for itself in a broad spectrum of cardiovascular disorders (Barr & Benson, 1984).

There are several issues that deserve further attention. The majority of studies treated medicated hypertensives exhibiting mild to moderate hypertension. The usefulness of relaxation with unmedicated and severe hypertensives has not received sufficient attention. Seer (1979) raised the point that practicing relaxation may prompt lifestyle changes in areas such as diet and exercise, which are also active hypertensive factors. Very few studies have monitored and controlled for this threat to internal validity.

Several authors have commented on the importance of continued relaxation practice after therapeutic effects have been attained (Benson, Marzetta, & Rosner, 1974; Datey et al., 1969; Patel, 1977). They have observed that BPs will return to baseline levels within a few weeks of discontinuing relaxation, but that therapeutic gains can be recaptured readily if regular relaxation practice is resumed. Because the health impact of hypertension emerges from a slow, cumulative, extended process, the clinical utility of relaxation for hypertension can only be measured by long-term effects. Therefore, issues such as those above assume critical importance. More research is needed in these and related areas, as exemplified by long-term health benefits of relaxation for hypertension, identification of the hypertensive subset particularly responsive to relaxation, utility of booster treatments and more cost-effective means of facilitating long-term practice, and the possibilities of permanent regularization of BP following long-term practice.

HEART DISEASE AND DYSFUNCTION

Coronary heart disease or heart attack is the leading cause of death in this country (Surwit, Williams, & Shapiro, 1982). Relaxation therapy, though not affecting the coronary arteries directly, has focused on risk factors for heart disease. As such, a separate section of this chapter reviews the large amount of work done in hypertension. In Chapter 6 and below, I discuss relaxation for Type A or coronary prone behavior pattern. Also below, I discuss relaxation treatment aimed at reducing cardiac arrhythmias.

Progressive Relaxation (PR)

As personality factors have proved salient for heart disease, Bohachick (1984) trained cardiac patients in PR and assessed psychological effects. Compared to a matched control group, PR patients attained significant improvement in state anxiety (State-Trait Anxiety Inventory; Spielberger, Gorsuch, & Lushene, 1970) and in four scales of the Hopkins Symptom Checklist (Derogatis, Lipman, Rickels, Uhlenhuth, & Covi, 1974): somatization, depression, anxiety, and interpersonal sensitivity. Unfortunately, benefits did not occur in the two scales most relevant to cardiac disease: obsessive-compulsive and hostility. Further, tests of cardiac function were not conducted, leaving the question of cardiac benefits untested. Another group (Langosch et al., 1982) treated postinfarction patients with relaxation (a mixture of PR, autogenics, and breath awareness) or cognitive oriented stress management, and garnered modest support for the efficacy of both these approaches.

Roskies and her associates (1978, 1979) recruited healthy, Type A males, and administered either psychodynamic group therapy or PR with added self-control features. Both groups registered significant improvement on two physiological (systolic blood pressure and serum cholesterol) and a variety of psychological indicators. Small differences between the groups arose. To their credit, the investigators also monitored other health habits, such as smoking and exercise, and ruled out their causal influence. At 6-month posttreatment, treatment gains were well maintained, although serum cholesterol approached baseline levels in the psychotherapy group. Some data was also presented on a third group, coronary heart disease patients receiving relaxation. This clinical sample replicated the gains made by the asymptomatic subjects. Although the data of this study are impressive, failure to control for threats to internal validity (e.g., passage of time, placebo, etc.) preclude drawing firm conclusions.

Self-control Relaxation (SCR)

Coronary patients trained in cue-controlled relaxation did not show diminished reactivity when exposed to laboratory stressors (Cole et al., 1985). Subsequently, relaxation training was conducted in the presence of one stressor. Diminished cardiovascular response now occurred when this stressor was presented, but therapy benefits did not generalize to the second stressor. This study graphically portrays the importance of planning for generalization across settings and the potential drawbacks of relaxation training conducted under relaxation conducive circumstances.

Meditation

Angina pectoris (heart pain) patients were trained in Transcendental Meditation or received delayed treatment (Zamarra, Besseghini, & Wittenberg, 1977). Following 8 months of treatment, meditation subjects outperformed controls on three of eight exercise performance measures.

Benson, Alexander, and Feldman (1975) presented impressive data on the effects of Bensonian relaxation on heart disease patients exhibiting premature ventricular contractions (PVCs). Ambulatory monitoring (48 hours) before and after 4 weeks of meditation practice documented reduced PVCs in 8 of 11 subjects, this effect being strongest during sleep. Similar data has been reported by others (Voukydis & Forwand, 1977).

Recently, however, a replication controlling for baseline monitoring effects discounted the efficacy of meditation for this disorder (Weiss, Cheatle, Rubin, Reichek, & Brady, 1985). Ambulatory monitoring, as in Benson et al., was conducted at two points, separated by 1 month with no intervening treatment, to assess the effects of repeated monitoring. Patients were instructed in Bensonian relaxation after the second monitoring, and a third ambulatory assessment occurred after a month's practice. A significant reduction in PVCs occurred from assessment 1 to assessment 2, but no further reduction occurred at assessment 3 after meditation practice.

Final Comments on Relaxation Therapy for Heart Disease and Dysfunction

Stress responses, especially hostile ones, have been isolated as predictors of heart disease (Barefoot, Dahlstrom, & Williams, 1983; Dembroski, MacDougall, Williams, Haney, & Blumenthal, 1985). To the extent that relaxation can attenuate hostility, relaxation therapy may make a useful contribution in the treatment of coronary heart disease. The development of a relaxed attitude as a product of relaxation practice (discussed in Chapter 1), may claim particular salience in this domain.

The findings presented in the section above are optimistic, but preliminary. Therapeutic value in heart disease can be judged only by long-term influence, and such trials of relaxation therapy still wait to be conducted.

RAYNAUD'S DISEASE

Named after the author of its discovery, Raynaud's disease is a circulatory disorder defined by constricting vasospasms of the fingers and toes (Spittell, 1972). This pathophysiological response is most often triggered by cold temperature or emotional stress. Manifest symptoms include cold feeling in the digits, a series of local skin color alterations reflecting the changing vascular state, and, in extreme cases, gangrene. The term Raynaud's phenomenon is invoked when this process occurs secondary to another disease (e.g., lupus).

The most common medical treatments are preventative, such as dressing warmly, or chemical (Surwit, 1982). Untoward side effects associated with most of the chemical agents have made the development of psychological approaches for this disorder highly desirable. Skin temperature biofeedback, alone or in combination with other relaxation methods, has been frequently employed to warm the hands and thereby indirectly increase circulation in the fingers. There is good data to support the efficacy of this approach as indicated in recent reviews (Surwit, 1981, 1982). Below are reviewed relaxation approaches, used singly or in combination with biofeedback, for Raynaud's disease or phenomenon.

Progressive Relaxation (PR)

The one study available on PR for Raynaud's disease compared PR to PR-skin temperature biofeedback combined (Jacobson, Manschreck, & Silverberg, 1979). During training, both groups produced hand warming, but quizzically the PR only group attained significantly warmer levels than the combined group. Two thirds of both groups rated significant symptomatic improvement at posttreatment. Maintenance over time appeared to be related to longevity of relaxation practice.

Autogenics (AT)

Surwit, Keefe, and their colleagues, initially at Harvard and then at Duke University, have been most productive in this area over the past decade. Early case study successes using a combination of AT and skin temperature biofeedback for handwarming (Surwit, 1973) spurred further interest. In their first controlled effort to evaluate AT (Surwit, Pilon, & Fenton, 1978), women with Raynaud's disease were randomly assigned to conditions within a sophisticated multifactorial scheme. The design permitted contrasts between (a) taped AT and taped AT/skin temperature biofeedback combined (hereafter referred to as AFT, autogenic feedback training), (b) treatment and no treatment, and (c) professionally guided and unassisted home training. The results were fairly consistent across dependent measures. Treated subjects (AT and AFT) showed significant finger temperature improvement in within-group contrasts before and after treatment, and in between-group contrasts with untreated controls during a cold challenge stress test. Temperature increases were positively correlated with psychological stability and confidence, and age (Surwit, Bradner, Fenton, & Pilon, 1979). Parallel data, though not quite as strong, were obtained on self-reported frequency and intensity of Raynaud's attacks. No measure in the study revealed advantages of adding biofeedback to AT, nor of laboratory over home training. At 1-year follow-up (Keefe, Surwit, & Pilon, 1979), subjects reported no diminution of therapeutic benefits, but a repetition of the cold challenge stressor revealed that finger temperature had reverted to baseline levels. The authors cited reductions in self-reported relaxation practice over the year to explain the poor laboratory performance.

More recently, this group has collected data on the utility of AT for Raynaud's phenomenon secondary to other diseases. A case history of a woman suffering from mixed connective tissue disease (collagen vascular disease) depicted marked clinical improvement, matched by warmer finger temperature, during laboratory cold challenges after taped AFT (Keefe, Surwit, & Pilon, 1981). At 2-year follow-up, this subject reported about one third the number of Raynaud's attacks as during baseline. Surwit, Allen, Gilgor, and Duvic (1982) treated 18 women and 2 men exhibiting Raynaud's phenomenon as a consequence of progressive systemic sclerosis. Subjects were randomly assigned to receive either 8 weeks of prazosin (an adrenergic blocking agent associated with peripheral vasodilation) or placebo medication. Midway through drug treatment, all subjects were introduced to taped AT. Cold challenge tests at pre, mid, and posttreatment revealed that neither prazosin or AT alone affected finger temperature but that their combination produced significant finger warming. The failure of AT alone to produce thermal effects in these subjects was attributed to the more severe nature of Raynaud's phenomenon versus Raynaud's disease. Unfortunately, the clinical effects of these treatments were not reported.

Adding to the existing high level of rigor in the AT for Raynaud's literature, the most recent contribution to this area is exemplary. Freedman, Ianni, and Wenig (1983) contrasted 10 sessions of taped AT, finger skin temperature biofeedback (ST), ST training while under a cold stress challenge (ST-CS), and frontalis electromyographic biofeedback (EMG) for 32 individuals with Raynaud's disease. Half the subjects in each condition also received cognitive stress management after Meichenbaum (1977). The ST-CS condition is unique and particularly interesting. Cold stress was applied to the finger of the dominant hand from which the skin temperature biofeedback was derived to give the subject practice in hand warming under conditions that simulated the primary, naturally occurring Raynaud's trigger.

All subjects submitted to two laboratory assessment sessions testing their voluntary skin temperature control and response to cold stress at pretreatment, posttreatment, and 1-year follow-up. For 2 days at pretreatment and follow-up, subjects wore an ambulatory recording apparatus that tracked finger and ambient temperature and heart rate. Finally, clinical effects were evaluated by self-reports of emotional stress and Raynaud's episodes.

The AT subjects failed to raise their finger skin temperature during the training sessions, the posttest assessment, and the follow-up assessment. On most of these temperature measures, the ST-CS group exhibited superior performance (skin temperature increases) and the remaining two groups fell in the intermediary range. Ambulatory temperature readings during Raynaud's attacks revealed that the finger temperature of the AT and EMG subjects combined dropped only 1.3° C from ambient temperature, compared to a drop of 4.7° C for the two ST groups, indicating a greater vulnerability to Raynaud's attacks by the AT and EMG subjects.

During training and posttreatment assessments, muscle tension decreases were more pronounced in the AT and EMG groups than in the two ST groups, demonstrating a good relaxation effect in the former pair. Further, the AT and EMG groups showed within-training-session reductions in stress ratings and, to a lesser extent, heart rate, but the two ST groups did not. Respiration rate and skin conductance level did not distinguish the groups during training or posttreatment. The follow-up laboratory assessment did not reveal significant findings on any of these measures.

The frequency of Raynaud's attacks was of primary importance in this study. The posttreatment percent reduction for the EMG, AT, ST, and ST-CS groups were 17.0 percent, 32.6 percent, 66.8 percent, and 92.5 percent, respectively. At 1-year follow-up, the two ST groups showed excellent maintenance of gains, while the AT and EMG groups reverted to their baseline levels. Daily stress ratings did not distinguish the groups. Analyses of the contribution of cognitive stress management were negative.

In sum, this study indicated that AT and EMG indirectly affect Raynaud's disease by inducing a general relaxation effect, whereas the ST treatments directly altered peripheral blood flow. As a consequence, the ST treatments, particularly ST-CS, produced larger and more enduring treatment effects.

Other Relaxation Techniques

Uncontrolled trials with Quieting Response training (Ford, Stroebel, Strong, & Szarek, 1983a) achieved success with 18 of 23 Raynaud's disease patients (for further details, see *Other Relaxation Techniques, Muscle-Contraction Headache* section). Success decreased to 9 of 15 if other psychophysiologic symptoms were present in addition to Raynaud's disease, and decreased further in 4 of 10 cases of Raynaud's phenomenon.

Relaxation Comparisons

The only entry in this section (Keefe, Surwit, & Pilon, 1980) contrasted autogenic training (AT), progressive relaxation, and AT/skin temperature biofeedback combined with females suffering from Raynaud's disease. All groups registered equally significant symptomatic improvement and performed equally well in laboratory cold stress tests.

Final Comments on Relaxation Therapy for Raynaud's Disease

Interesting, but inconsistent trends emerge in this literature. Autogenics (AT), with its emphasis on warmth in the extremities, is well suited for Raynaud's application. Therefore, it is not surprising that the Surwit-Keefe group found AT to be effective. It is particularly noteworthy that AT was an effective treatment independent of skin temperature biofeedback, with which it is so often paired.

In sharp contrast to these findings, Freedman et al. (1983) demonstrated AT ineffectualness in their thoughtful and meticulous study. This group also documented the advantages of training biofeedback under stressful conditions, and by implication, relaxation training under adverse circumstances promises more robust therapeutic effects as well. This latter strategy deserves vigorous research initiatives with this and other target symptoms.

The positive findings of Surwit and Keefe for AT cannot be denied, despite the failure to replicate in another laboratory. The negative findings of Freedman et al. (1983) are particularly puzzling, since they employed the same AT tape recording that Surwit, Pilon, and Fenton (1978) used, and administered 10 training sessions compared to six in the Surwit et al. study. Future research will write the concluding decision on AT for Raynaud's disease.

DIABETES

Diabetes is a disease of depressed glucose metabolism secondary to inadequate insulin production or function (Bradley, 1982; Surwit, Feinglos, & Scovern, 1983). Even when well managed, diabetes commands major life-style accommodations and shortens life. As the above authors and others (Cox et al., 1984) have indicated, one important factor that regulates bodily stores of glucose is arousal of the autonomic nervous system, and modulation therein, by formal relaxation or other avenues, may be a beneficial component in a program for diabetes care.

Progressive Relaxation (PR)

Bradley (1982) presented pilot data suggesting that three men with insulin-dependent diabetes could exert a small lowering effect on blood glucose level by practicing PR, in comparison to three nonpracticing diabetics.

A more sophisticated report of PR for non-insulin-dependent diabetes has since been reported (Surwit & Feinglos, 1983). Twelve subjects, claiming a history of stress reactive diabetes, were treated as inpatients with standardized diets. Prior to and following treatment, subjects submitted to a 3-hour oral glucose tolerance test and a 30-minute intravenous insulin tolerance test. Half the patients received treatment consisting of 10 taped PR and 5 electromyographic biofeedback sessions, all within 1 week. During the posttreatment assessment, treated subjects practiced PR. Treated subjects registered significant improvement in glucose tolerance, and untreated subjects did not. Two other measures, insulin sensitivity and insulin secretory activity were not influenced by treatment. A subsequent report (Surwit & Feinglos, 1984) revealed that significant reductions in plasma cortisol materialized for the treated subjects only, but epinephrine and norepinephrine were unaffected in both groups.

Self-control Relaxation (SCR)

There is one example of SCR for diabetes (Lammers, Naliboff, & Straatmeyer, 1984). Four male outpatients, all insulin-dependent, were trained in PR and gradually converted to SCR. Treatment effects were evaluated in a single subject, reversal design distributed over about 3 months. Two subjects achieved lower glucose levels, though this was independent of self-rated stress.

Autogenics (AT)

Daniels (1939) briefly summarized a 1935 article by Bauch published in German, in which seven diabetics were trained in relaxation; the method was not described, but it was said to be similar to AT and progressive relaxation. There occurred decreased insulin consumption and improvement in mood, insomnia, etc.

Final Comments on Relaxation Therapy for Diabetes

Sound theory and encouraging data stand in support of relaxation for diabetes, but this area is clinically immature. Short-term trials with small numbers of subjects leave clinically salient issues untouched.

Is it feasible for insulin-dependent diabetics to consume lower levels of insulin over a long period of time in cooperation with a sustained relaxation regimen, and what increment in health benefits would these individuals derive? Research has yet to address questions such as these, thus precluding judgment at the present time on the clinical utility of relaxation for diabetes. In light of the seriousness of the disease and Surwit's encouraging data, this area begs for vigorous research efforts. Relaxation is potentially a potent factor in the overall, complex self-care program of diabetics (Wing, Epstein, Nowalk, & Lamparski, 1986).

HEMOPHILIA

A congenital disorder appearing in males only, hemophilia is characterized by frequent bleeding secondary to inadequate clotting (Hilgartner, 1976). Over time, arthritis typically develops in the joints where bleeding has most often occurred.

Physical insult is sure to instigate bleeding, but internal hemorrhaging also may occur spontaneously. Some have reasoned that autonomic arousal triggers spontaneous bleeding episodes (Lichstein & Eakin, 1985), thus providing a rationale for relaxation application. Further, relaxation has been employed to diminish arthritic pain that is common among hemophiliacs.

Progressive Relaxation (PR)

Varni has been the main contributor in this area. All of his studies involve small numbers of hemophiliacs and present a relaxation package composed of progressive relaxation, a secular version of meditation having breath and mantra components, and pleasant imagery.

His first publication (Varni, 1980) relieved the insomnia difficulties of a hemophiliac, but effectuated no improvement in bleeding frequency or associated discomfort. Three subsequent publications (Varni, 1981a, 1981b; Varni & Gilbert, 1982) reported consistent, positive effects on arthritic pain in a total of six young adults. Perceived arthritic pain was reduced by more than half in these individuals with correlated skin temperature increases in the affected joints. Decreased pain medication consumption and other benefits, such as less morning stiffness and improved sleep, also occurred. Follow-ups documented excellent therapeutic longevity up to 1 year. Unfortunately, bleeding frequency and acute pain during bleeds were unaffected.

Autogenic Training (AT)

Case history data (Luthe & Schultz, 1969a, pp. 131–136) recommend the use of AT for hemophilia in alleviating pain and associated symptomatology, such as anxiety and insomnia. Systematic, controlled evaluations of AT for hemophilia have not been conducted.

Relaxation Comparisons

We (Lichstein & Eakin, 1985) conducted a comparison of progressive relaxation and self-control relaxation with seven young adult hemophiliacs using a multiple baseline, partial crossover design. Neither treatment proved effective. We found, as Varni did, that bleeding was unresponsive to treatment, but we were also unable to replicate arthritic pain reduction. These disappointing results prevailed despite high relaxation practice compliance (by significant other report) and physiological evidence of successful relaxation.

Final Comments on Relaxation Therapy for Hemophilia

Based upon the strength of Varni's data, relaxation therapy for hemophilia is best conceived of as a form of pain management. Available data condemn relaxation as a means of arresting the primary hemophilia problem, bleeding. Our (Lichstein & Eakin, 1985) inability to replicate Varni's pain management successes may be due to the presence of multiple strategies and cognitive restructuring elements in the latter.

MUSCLE-CONTRACTION HEADACHE

Muscle-contraction headache (also known as tension headache) is characterized by mild to moderate bilateral pain typically focused in the frontal or suboccipital regions, and is presumably due to chronic contracture of the muscles in the affected zones (Dalessio, 1972). However, the label "muscle-contraction" headache may be a misnomer. Serious doubt has been cast on the assumption that there is a muscular etiology for the symptomology labeled muscle-contraction headache. With increasing frequency, recent findings fail to observe correlations between muscular tension and headache pain (e.g., Epstein & Abel, 1977; Harper & Steger, 1978) or distinctions in cranial muscle tension levels between muscle-contraction headache sufferers and headache-free individuals (e.g., Andrasik, Blanchard, Arena, Saunders, & Barron, 1982; Bakal & Kaganov, 1977). Some have speculated on a vascular basis for this disorder (Cohen, 1978; Drummond & Lance, 1981; Pikoff, 1984b; Williamson, 1981), but compelling supportive evidence for this alternative view is also wanting. Nevertheless, the most frequently offered rationales for relaxation therapy for this disorder claim muscular relaxation and, to a lesser extent, general stress reduction as the guiding principle. The reader is referred to recent comprehensive reviews of psychosocial approaches with this disorder (Haynes, 1981; Nuechterlein & Holroyd, 1980).

Progressive Relaxation (PR)

Early individual case reports recommended the use of PR for muscle-contraction headache (Epstein, Webster, & Abel, 1976; Jacobson, 1970; Todd & Kelley, 1970). Treating six subjects in uncontrolled trials, Tasto and Hinkle (1973) reported substantial reductions in the frequency and duration of headaches.

Many of the current studies in this section pitted PR against one of the most common psychological treatments for this disorder: electromyographic (EMG) biofeedback. In most cases (Chesney & Shelton, 1976; Gray, Lyle, McGuire, & Peck, 1980; Martin & Mathews, 1978), PR produced significant reductions in headache symptomatology and was at least as effective as EMG biofeedback. PR also proved superior to no treatment in the one study of this group that included such a comparison (Chesney & Shelton, 1976).

PR, in combination with autogenic training, was ineffective with tension headache sufferers and inferior to EMG biofeedback in one study (Hutchings & Reinking, 1976). At 1-year follow-up (Reinking & Hutchings, 1981), treatment differences had washed out. Long-term benefits were associated with perseverance in relaxation practice and ability to relax forehead muscle tension. Another group (Daly, Donn, Galliher, & Zimmerman, 1983; Daly, Zimmerman, Donn, & Galliher, 1985) did find PR to be effective for tension headaches, but not as effective as biofeedback.

Philips and Hunter (1981) found that PR produced significant improvement on several headache and pain behavior indices in a selected group of tension headache sufferers who did not display elevated EMG levels. The addition of pleasant imagery did not result in incremental treatment effects beyond PR. Another group (Jacob, Turner, Szekely, & Eidelman, 1983) observed an average 34 percent headache improvement in their sample, and outcome was inversely correlated with pretreatment level of depression.

Self-control Relaxation (SCR)

The first application of SCR to muscle-contraction headache was surprisingly sophisticated in its design. Cox, Freundlich, and Meyer (1975) contrasted eight sessions of EMG biofeedback/cue-controlled relaxation (CCR) combined, differential relaxation/CCR combined, and placebo medication with headache sufferers recruited through a newspaper announcement. At posttreatment, self-reported headache activity did not distinguish the three groups, although the trend favored the two treatment groups over the placebo group. Frontalis EMG levels, psychosomatic complaints, and medication consumption were significantly lower in the two treatment groups, which did not differ from each other, than in the placebo group. By 4-month follow-up, headache benefits had progressed in the two treated groups, so that they were now equally superior to the placebo group.

One year after the Cox et al. study, Mitchell and White (1976) published a case study of a young woman whose headaches responded well to a broad-spectrum SCR program. A similar treatment regimen has since been employed successfully in a case of posttraumatic head injury headache, which presents in much the same way as muscle-contraction headache (Smith & Denney, 1983).

The next major study in this area was that of Holroyd and Andrasik (1978). Attempting to evaluate the role of cognitive self-control strategies, they assigned muscle-contraction headache sufferers to treatments consisting of (a) cognitive restructuring, (b) cognitive restructuring/SCR combined, (c) psychodynamic group therapy, or (d) only self-monitoring of headaches. Analyses of four self-reported headache measures and medication consumption revealed significant improvement for groups *a, b,* and *c,* but not *d* at posttreatment and 6-week follow-up. Two therapists treated half the subjects in each condition, and the headache levels reported by those subjects in groups *a, b,* and *c,* treated by the more experienced therapist, were significantly lower than those treated by the less experienced therapist. Changes in frontalis muscle tension and headache activity were uncorrelated. The results of this study suggest that neither specific cognitive coping strategies (group *a*) nor SCR (group *b*) are any more effective than discussion about the causes and characteristics of individuals' headaches (group *c*), which may relieve headaches by inadvertently aiding individuals in adopting more constructive attitudes.

In what is probably the largest prospective psychological treatment of headache study yet conducted, Blanchard and his associates reported in partial (Blanchard, Andrasik, Neff, Teders, et al., 1982) and more complete (Blanchard, Andrasik, Evans, Neff, et al., 1985; Blanchard, Andrasik, Neff, Arena, et al., 1982) form on SCR, biofeedback, and biofeedback/autogenics treatments for several headache types. I will describe the relevant portions of these studies in several sections of this chapter.

Blanchard, Andrasik, Neff, Arena, et al. (1982) administered 10 relaxation sessions to 33 muscle-contraction headache sufferers. The relaxation course began with PR and gradually converted to differential and cue-controlled relaxation, as described by Bernstein and Borkovec (1973). Subjects' self-reported headache data revealed significant pre-post reductions on all parameters measured: headache index (a blend of severity and duration), peak headache intensity, and number of headache-free days. Seventeen of these subjects (52 percent) attained at least a 50 percent reduction in headache index. Treatment was ineffective with elderly subjects (Blanchard, Andrasik, Evans, & Hillhouse, 1985). Medication consumption was unaltered. The poor responders were subsequently offered electromyographic biofeedback, but these results will not be presented herein. More recently, Blanchard, Andrasik, Evans, Neff, et al. (1985) reported a 41.5 percent success rate using only SCR with 94 muscle-contraction headache sufferers.

Comparable treatment gains were obtained by delivering these same services with less than half the therapist contact, relying mainly on cost-effective manuals and tapes (Teders et al., 1984). Williamson et al. (1984) have also observed headache relief with self-help relaxation, but less than that attained with therapist-delivered relaxation therapy.

Successfully treated subjects returned to the clinic once per month for 6 months posttreatment (Andrasik, Blanchard, Neff, & Rodichok, 1984). At these meetings, subjects received either brief contact, comprised mainly of encouragement to continue practicing, or formal booster treatments. At 1-year posttreatment, there was excellent maintenance of therapy gains in both these groups, suggesting that the more costly booster strategy was unnecessary. However, the utility of the brief contact strategy cannot be determined, as a no-contact follow-up group was not included.

In these and related studies, this research group conducted correlational analyses to identify predictor variables of successful SCR treatment of muscle-contraction headache. Some of the stronger predictor variables were low scores on the social introversion scale of the MMPI (Blanchard, Andrasik, Neff, Arena, et al., 1982), small frontalis muscle and hand temperature responses during cognitive stress, and high skin resistance levels during initial relaxation exposure (Blanchard, Andrasik, Arena, Neff, Jurish, et al., 1983), amount of self-reported home relaxation practice (Blanchard, Andrasik, Arena, Neff, Saunders, et al., 1983), and accuracy of forearm muscle tension discrimination (Blanchard, Jurish, Andrasik, & Epstein, 1981). Multivariate analyses (Blanchard, Andrasik, Arena, Neff, Jurish, et al., 1983) identified muscle-contraction headache clients who also exhibited the vascular symptoms of unilateral, throbbing pain as good SCR responders. In their recent summary publication, Blanchard, Andrasik, Evans, Neff, et al. (1985) provided additional data linking indicators with improved outcome. Some of these indicators are age below 40 and low trait anxiety.

The identification of several factors that might plausibly be expected to predict positive outcome, but failed to do so, is also noteworthy. Falling into this category were therapist experience, clients' perceptions of therapist competence, warmth, or helpfulness (Blanchard, Andrasik, Arena, Neff, Saunders, et al., 1983), depression as measured by the Beck Depression Inventory of Beck, Ward, Mendelsohn, Mock, and Erbaugh (1961) (Blanchard, Andrasik, Neff, Arena, et al., 1982), and high capacity for absorption as described by Tellegen and Atkinson (1974) (Neff, Blanchard, & Andrasik, 1983).

Passive Relaxation

Warner and Lance (1975) applied passive relaxation to 17 muscle-contraction headache sufferers in uncontrolled trials. Six months hence, 14 of these individuals claimed significant headache relief, and most reduced associated medications. In the same year, Haynes, Griffin, Mooney, and Parise (1975) conducted a controlled trial comparing passive relaxation, electromyographic biofeedback, and no treatment. The treated groups responded very well and by 6-month follow-up, headache activity was near zero among relaxation and biofeedback subjects, but not far removed from baseline level in control subjects.

Autogenics (AT)

Autogenic feedback training (AFT), combining skin temperature biofeedback and AT, was introduced primarily to treat migraineurs (Sargent, Green, & Walters, 1972, 1973), but it also was applied to tension headache sufferers. Scanty anecdotal data in these early reports suggested that this approach was helpful with about half of these patients. More recently, AFT was again applied to individuals with this type headache (Sargent, Solbach, & Coyne, 1980), but outcome data were not reported. Other encouraging uncontrolled data on AFT for muscle-contraction headache are available (Diamond & Franklin, 1977a; Werder & Sargent, 1984).

Investigating AT in isolation, eight tension headache sufferers were equally divided between eight sessions of AT or AT combined with frontal electromyographic biofeedback (Cott, Goldman, Pavloski, Kirschberg, & Fabich, 1981). Equivalently significant reductions in headaches and medication consumption obtained for these two groups at posttreatment, and treatment gains were maintained at 1-year follow-up. Controls to defend against multiple threats to internal validity were not included in this otherwise interesting study. Anderson, Lawrence, and Olson (1981) also tested AT alone and contrasted this with cognitive coping skills or both treatments combined in a within-subject analysis. The two treatments taken independently did appear to be effective, but less so than their joint presentation.

Two other studies pitted AT against biofeedback, and AT fared poorly. Steger and Harper (1980) assigned relaxation tapes (mainly composed of AT) to one group of muscle-contraction headache sufferers, and these individuals practiced relaxation at home with little professional contact. The second group received eight treatment sessions comprised of electromyographic (EMG) biofeedback and coping skills training. The AT subjects achieved significant pre-post reductions on frontalis EMG measures, but not on any of three self-reported headache indices. Between group tests revealed the biofeedback/coping skills group attained greater improvement on headache intensity and frequency of severe headaches. Juenet, Cottraux, and Collet (1983) contrasted taped AT with electrodermal biofeedback. Both groups received 10 treatment sessions. At pre, post, and 4-month follow-up, only the biofeedback group obtained headache gains.

Other Relaxation Techniques

Eufemia and Wesolowski (1983) presented rigorous case history data on a recently conceived method of relaxation called *behavioral relaxation training*. (For further information on this technique, see discussion of the Behavioral Relaxation Scale, Chapter 4, and the *Anxiety* and *Children's Problems* sections, this chapter.) Relaxation is induced by assuming a series of relaxed postures, and in this case, a sharp reduction in tension headaches and muscle activity followed. Fichtler and Zimmermann (1973) also presented positive case study data on 10 muscle-contraction headache sufferers using an unspecified method of taped relaxation.

Stroebel developed a method he calls Quieting Response (QR) training and he first publicized a description of the method in an audio cassette (Stroebel, 1978). QR (described in Stroebel, 1982) begins with a blend of electromyographic and skin temperature biofeedback, deep breathing, progressive relaxation, and autogenic training. It culminates in a 6 to 10-second, four step self-scan—(a) recognize anxiety cue, (b) inward smile, (c) relaxed breath, and (d) limp mouth and shoulders—which may then be employed to promote relaxation in the natural environment. Compared to other relaxation approaches presented in this book, there is a paucity of data available on QR.

Stroebel and his colleagues (Ford, Stroebel, Strong, & Szarek, 1982) reported on the application of QR training with 37 psychiatric inpatients diagnosed as psychotic, neurotic, or personality disorder. This report is included in this section because the most common target symptom was headaches (65 percent, mixture of headache types), followed by sundry psychophysiologic disorders such as irritable colon, hypertension, insomnia, and the like. QR training was delivered in eight weekly, 1-hour sessions.

Clinical outcome was determined by a multifactor rating system that led to a successful/unsuccessful judgment. Overall, 51 percent of these patients were considered successful, and this outcome was unrelated to psychiatric diagnosis. QR training had no effect on general psychiatric condition at time of discharge, state or trait (Spielberger, Gorsuch, & Lushene, 1970) anxiety, or length of hospital stay. Older and less depressed patients exhibited the best treatment response.

A subsequent report (Ford, Stroebel, Strong, & Szarek, 1983a) evaluated the identical treatment protocol with 340 nonpsychiatric outpatients presenting a distribution of psychophysiologic symptoms similar to those of the inpatients reported above. This article reported outcomes at follow-ups varying up to 2 years, specific to each symptom; the results will be related in the separate sections of this chapter. Thirteen of 33 (39 percent) of muscle-contraction headache sufferers were judged successful. For this and the other target symptoms, a host of descriptors were correlated with outcome (Ford, Stroebel, Strong, & Szarek, 1983b), but robust predictor variables did not emerge.

Relaxation Comparisons

The only entry in this section pitted progressive relaxation (PR) against a near orthodox rendition of autogenic training (AT), with clients diagnosed as muscle-contraction, migraine, or mixed headache (Janssen & Neutgens, 1986). I will present the muscle-contraction headache results herein, and the outcome with the other two groups in the *Migraine* section, which follows.

PR was highly effective with the muscle-contraction headache clients, but AT exerted no therapeutic impact with this group. These differences were demonstrative and stable at 3-month follow-up. It is interesting to note that similar differences did not arise with the other two symptom groups.

Final Comments on Relaxation Therapy for Muscle-contraction Headache

Progressive relaxation and self-control relaxation have proved to be effective interventions for this type of headache, but data on autogenic training do not recommend this third procedure. Follow-up data, ranging up to a year, evince good maintenance of therapeutic gains.

The mechanisms of relaxation therapy efficacy in this domain remain unclear. Illustrative of this point are studies that find credible placebo treatments approximate the headache relief attained by relaxation (Cox et al., 1975; Holroyd & Andrasik, 1978). Recent data (e.g., Andrasik, Blanchard, Arena, Teders, et al., 1982) support traditional notions that individuals claiming muscle-contraction headaches also exhibit elevated stress symptomatology. Thus, relaxation and stress management (discussed in Chapter 6) may operate either directly on contracted muscles or on other physiological irritants, or indirectly on personality factors to achieve headache relief.

Blanchard, Jaccard, Andrasik, Guarnieri, and Jurish (1985) explored the rarely invoked question of financial effects of relaxation therapy. Combining treatments (relaxation and biofeedback) and headache types (muscle-contraction, migraine, and mixed), pretreatment headache treatment costs (mainly hospital, physician, and medication expenses) were reduced up to 80 percent following relaxation therapy. These remarkable data speak to the efficacy of treatment and merit the serious attention of health providers.

MIGRAINE HEADACHE

Migraine headache and related vascular headache disorders are usually more painful than muscle-contraction headache, and are usually marked by one or more other distinctive characteristics: preheadache aura, nausea, unilateral pain, and a pulsatile sensation (Dalessio, 1972). Most migraine researchers agree that the disorder is due to dilation of the extracranial arteries, in combination with neurochemical anomalies (Dalessio, 1978). Further, there is mounting evidence that there is cephalic muscle tension involvement, perhaps even to a greater degree than in muscle-contraction headache (Bakal & Kaganov, 1977). The most common psychological treatments for this disorder involve some form of biofeedback (see reviews by Adams, Feuerstein, & Fowler, 1980; Blanchard, Andrasik, Ahles, Teders, & O'Keefe, 1980), although the present review will focus on relaxation therapy. Child migraine has attracted increasing interest of late (Hoelscher & Lichstein, 1984), and some data bearing on children also will be presented.

Progressive Relaxation (PR)

Some studies presented PR jointly with the popular approach of skin temperature biofeedback, thus frustrating the intent of this review to isolate the influences of PR (Drury, DeRisi, & Liberman, 1979; Kohlenberg & Cahn, 1981; Lashley & Elder, 1982). All of these studies found significant migraine improvement subsequent to treatment. Drury et al. (1979) also included autogenic phrases in the treatment package. Kohlenberg and Cahn (1981) found a home treatment package to be more effective than a headache information book, which served as a placebo control.

Early on, Wolff (1963) cited PR as a helpful component in migraine management, but trials of PR as an independent intervention have produced mixed results. Two individual case studies (Campbell, O'Brien, Bickett, & Lutzker, 1983; Lutker, 1971) described successful treatments of migraineurs, including positive follow-up data, but two others (Houts, 1982; Stambaugh & House, 1977) reported weak or negative effects for PR.

Mitchell and Mitchell (1971; also reported in K. R. Mitchell, 1971) conducted a rigorous test and obtained negative results. PR was compared with no treatment and a treatment that combined systematic desensitization and assertiveness training. At 4-month follow-up, significant reductions in the frequency and duration of migraine attacks occurred only in the systematic desensitization/assertiveness training group. Olness and MacDonald (1981) presented some encouraging case histories treating child migraine with a mixture of PR and relaxing imagery.

One group (Daly, Donn, Galliher, & Zimmerman, 1983; Daly, Zimmerman, Donn, & Galliher, 1985) contrasted PR, electromyographic biofeedback, and skin temperature biofeedback with migraineurs, and obtained 1-year follow-up data. PR proved effective (55 percent of subjects made significant gains) and improvement was well maintained over time, but the two biofeedback groups were superior. A similar pattern obtained with muscle-contraction headache subjects as reported above.

Self-control Relaxation (SCR)

The Blanchard treatment protocol (Blanchard, Andrasik, Evans, Neff, et al., 1985; Blanchard, Andrasik, Neff, Arena, et al., 1982; Blanchard, Andrasik, Neff, Teders, et al., 1982), described under SCR for muscle-contraction headache, was applied to two additional diagnostic groups: migraine headache (n = 30) and mixed migraine and muscle-contraction headache (n = 28). Both of these groups also manifested significant reductions on headache index, peak headache intensity, and number of headache-free days, but a smaller proportion of migraine (30 percent) and mixed (21 percent) clients surpassed the 50 percent improvement criterion with SCR treatment than did the muscle-contraction headache clients (52 percent). Medication consumption was also unchanged in these two groups. There was excellent maintenance of therapy gains at 1-year follow-up, as per the follow-up procedure described above in the *Muscle-contraction Headache* section (Andrasik, Blanchard, Neff, & Rodichok, 1984).

The poor responders were exposed next to a course of skin temperature biofeedback/autogenic training combined, and these data are presented in the autogenics section below. Jurish et al. (1983) have found that a largely home-based, self-administered treatment course, composed of SCR and skin temperature biofeedback, was equally as effective as the same treatments presented in the more costly, traditional therapist-administered form. In their recent summary publication, Blanchard, Andrasik, Evans, Neff, et al. (1985) reported a 28.1 percent improvement rate for migraineurs (n = 32) and a 22.6 percent improvement rate for mixed headache types (n = 31).

Separate correlational analyses were conducted to identify predictor variables of successful SCR treatment for (a) the migraine clients and (b) the mixed migraine and muscle-contraction headache clients. Variables predictive of success for the former were low scores on the hysteria scale of the MMPI (Blanchard, Andrasik, Neff, Arena, et al., 1982), and lowered hand temperature during cognitive stress (Blanchard, Andrasik, Arena, Neff, Jurish, et al., 1983); for the latter were low trait anxiety (Blanchard, Andrasik, Neff, Arena, et al., 1982), and small initial frontalis muscle relaxation response (Blanchard, Andrasik, Arena, Neff, Jurish, et al., 1983); and for both groups were amount of home relaxation practice (Blanchard, Andrasik, Arena, Neff, Saunders, et al., 1983), and high capacity for absorption (Neff, Blanchard, & Andrasik, 1983). Blanchard, Andrasik, Evans, Neff, et al. (1985) observed that age under 40 and low trait anxiety were fairly good predictors of successful SCR treatment for migraine, but reported no substantively predictive new data in the case of mixed headaches. Plausible predictive factors that poorly correlated with SCR outcome in both of the vascular groups were therapist experience, and clients' perceptions of therapist competence, warmth, or helpfulness (Blanchard, Andrasik, Arena, Neff, Saunders, et al., 1983), depression (Blanchard, Andrasik, Neff, Arena, et al., 1982), and accuracy of forearm muscle tension discrimination (Blanchard, Jurish, Andrasik, & Epstein, 1981).

The only other data on SCR for adult migraine comes from Mitchell and White (1977a). Six migraineurs received a taped training package similar to that of Blanchard, Andrasik, Neff, Arena, et al. (1982). The combination of cue-controlled relaxation, differential relaxation, and self-desensitization yielded a 45 percent reduction in frequency of migraine episodes. Treatment gains held constant at 3-month follow-up. A component analysis design ruled out the contributions of self-recording and self-monitoring from these results.

Episodic cluster headache is a form of vascular headache distinguished by unilateral pain, tearing, and rhinorrhea, occurring in clusters of brief headache attacks separated by long periods of remission (Kudrow, 1980). Blanchard, Andrasik, Jurish, and Teders (1982) applied their standard 10-session SCR treatment protocol, followed by 12 sessions of skin temperature biofeedback/autogenics combined, to seven clients satisfying the above definition. Only final outcome data were reported, reflecting the summative impact of SCR, biofeedback, and autogenics. For two of these clients, no treatment data were available. There was a complete absence of headache activity during the treatment and follow-up periods for these two individuals, and this was expected due to their history of long remission periods (3 and 7 years). Three of the five remaining clients exhibited decreases on such measures as delay of expected headache episodes, headache intensity, etc. In no case were the headaches eliminated.

Passive Relaxation

In the same uncontrolled trials reported under *Muscle-Contraction Headache,* Warner and Lance (1975) treated 12 migraineurs with passive relaxation. At 6 months posttreatment, eight exhibited at least a 50 percent reduction in headache frequency. Nine patients were on lower medication dosages at follow-up, compared to baseline.

Meditation

Benson, Klemchuk, and Graham (1974) evaluated Transcendental Meditation (TM) with 17 severe migraineurs and 4 cluster headache sufferers. Three of the migraineurs manifested significant headache improvement, one got worse, and thirteen showed no change. One of the cluster headache subjects showed great improvement, which was maintained at a 1-year check, two showed temporary improvement, and one no change. To quote the authors, TM demonstrated "limited usefulness" (p. 51) for severe migraine and cluster headaches.

During the course of her initial hypertension trials, Patel (1973) observed anecdotally that the multielement treatment regimen benefited the migraine headaches of one of her hypertensive subjects.

Autogenics (AT)

In the late 1960s, Sargent and his associates at the Menninger Foundation pioneered the combined use of autogenics and biofeedback for migraine headache. This work was based on the theory that handwarming is accomplished through general suppression of the sympathetic nervous system, which simultaneously counteracts the vascular mechanisms producing migraine (Fahrion, 1978; Sargent, Walters, & Green, 1973). But subsequent research has failed to support the hemodynamic aspects of this view (Sovak, Kunzel, Sternbach, & Dalessio, 1978). Their initial results appeared in three reports (Sargent, Green, & Walters, 1972, 1973; Sargent, Walters, & Green, 1973). Overall, global outcome analyses were provided on 61 migraineurs. Over a period of months, subjects were treated with skin temperature biofeedback, designed to warm the hands, and abbreviated AT (emphasizing total bodily relaxation and hand warmth). The treatment package was termed autogenic feedback training (AFT). Self-report data revealed a 74 percent success rate (criteria not stated). Three health professionals rendered independent clinical ratings on about half the subjects and judged that between 68 percent and 90 percent of the subjects improved.

Other laboratories have also conducted largely uncontrolled clinical trials with the familiar combination of AT and skin temperature biofeedback (Andreychuk & Skriver, 1975; Boller & Flom, 1979; Dalessio, Kunzel, Sternbach, & Sovak, 1979; Diamond & Montrose, 1984; Fahrion, 1978; Mitch, McGrady, & Iannone, 1976) or AT alone (Stambaugh & House, 1977), and have obtained encouraging results with migraineurs. I should add that Mitch et al. (1976) found AFT to be less effective with individuals presenting with mixed migraine and muscle-contraction headache.

Sargent, Solbach, and Coyne (1980) offered AFT in a concentrated format,

10 sessions in 5 days, to accommodate out-of-town patients. Of those who returned follow-up questionnaire data, some two thirds reported headache improvement at 6 months posttreatment.

A more recent entry by this group (Solbach, Sargent, & Coyne, 1984) is also the most sophisticated. They presented data on 136 migraineurs, including 83 women who complained mainly about the common problem of migraines associated with menstruation. Subjects were assigned to four groups, three of which included AT: (a) AT only, (b) AT plus skin temperature biofeedback (or AFT), (c) AT plus electromyographic biofeedback, and (d) no treatment. In the menstrual migraine subset, all four groups (including no treatment) achieved equally significant headache improvement, suggesting potent nonspecific factors were operative with these subjects. For the entire sample, however, group b (AFT) proved most effective, groups a and c equally effective but less so than b, and group d (no treatment) was significantly less effective than the rest. This same group (Sargent, Solbach, Coyne, Spohn, & Segerson, 1986) has since published a migraine treatment study employing an identical design, very similar subject demographics, and near identical results. Due to small discrepancies in subject characteristics and results (e.g., the superiority of the AFT group now approached significance), it is not clear whether this is the same study as Solbach et al. (1984) or not.

Blanchard, Andrasik, and their colleagues (Blanchard, Andrasik, Evans, Neff, et al., 1985; Blanchard, Andrasik, Neff, Arena, et al., 1982; Blanchard, Andrasik, Neff, Teders, et al., 1982) applied Sargent's AFT approach to migraineurs and individuals with mixed migraine and muscle-contraction headache. Scanty data were also obtained on self-control relaxation (SCR) and AFT combined for episodic cluster headache (Blanchard, Andrasik, Jurish, & Teders, 1982), and this information is presented above under SCR.

It is paramount to remember that the Blanchard group first presented SCR to all of their vascular headache clients. Subsequently, AFT was offered only to those who responded poorly to SCR. Therefore, the treatment results reported below may well be nonrepresentative of the general population of vascular headache clients, by virtue of Blanchard's clients' prior exposure to a treatment regimen and their biased response.

Outcome data on 12 sessions of AFT scheduled over 6 to 9 weeks were presented on 16 clients by Blanchard, Andrasik, Neff, Teders, et al. (1982) and on 28 clients by Blanchard, Andrasik, Neff, Arena, et al. (1982). The following results are from the more complete report. There was a significant reduction in headache index, peak headache intensity, and number of headache-free days from post SCR to post AFT for the mixed clients, but not the migraineurs. There were no significant changes in medication consumption for either group. Excellent maintenance of treatment gains over 1 year obtained with the mixed clients, as it did with others treated in the Blanchard et al. program (Andrasik et al., 1984). Six of 14 migraineurs and 9 of 14 mixed clients exceeded the success criterion of 50 percent improvement on the headache index across these same points in time. Thus, somewhat surprisingly, the pure vascular clients did not benefit from AFT, a vascular treatment, as much as did the clients presenting with both vascular and muscular symptomatology. However, updated information from this group (Blanchard, Andrasik, Evans, Neff, et al., 1985) found that this differential response did not continue. There was an overall improvement rate of 52.5 percent in migraineurs ($n = 61$) and 52.1 percent in the combined group ($n = 71$).

Predictor variables of a positive AFT treatment outcome, for both the migraine and the mixed migraine and muscle contraction headache clients, included low scores on the Psychosomatic Symptom Checklist (PSC) of Cox, Freundlich, and Meyer (1975) (Blanchard, Andrasik, Neff, Arena, et al., 1982), low scores on the hysteria scale of the MMPI (Blanchard, Andrasik, Neff, Teders, et al., 1982), small initial frontalis muscle relaxation response (Blanchard, Andrasik, Arena, Neff, Jurish, et al., 1983), and low capacity for absorption (Neff et al., 1983). Recent predictor data (Blanchard, Andrasik, Evans, Neff, et al., 1985) were consistent with the findings above. Some noteworthy factors that poorly correlated with treatment outcome included hand temperature changes during AFT (Blanchard, Andrasik, Arena, Neff, Saunders, et al., 1983; Blanchard, Andrasik, Neff, Teders, et al., 1982), therapist experience, and clients' perceptions of therapist competence, warmth, or helpfulness (Blanchard, Andrasik, Arena, Neff, Saunders, et al., 1983), and depression (Blanchard, Andrasik, Neff, Arena, et al., 1982).

In one of the few studies to test AT only for migraine headaches (Lacroix et al., 1983), AT tapes emphasizing heaviness, warmth, and breath exercises constituted one treatment group, skin temperature biofeedback the second, and electromyographic biofeedback the third. At posttreatment, skin temperature biofeedback was the most effective, but improvement continued to accumulate in the AT group so that it equaled the efficacy of the skin temperature group by 6-month follow-up. Sorbi and Tellegen (1984) also examined AT alone in contrast to skin temperature biofeedback in one stage of a multistage, multicomponent treatment program. On all five measures of headache activity, AT and biofeedback proved comparable, although unlike biofeedback, AT did attain significant within-group improvement on three measures: headache duration, intensity, and discomfort.

There has been increasing interest in AT for child migraine, but much of these efforts have been uncontrolled (Diamond & Franklin, 1977b; Diamond & Montrose, 1984; Werder, 1978; Werder & Sargent, 1984). Recently, two studies (Andrasik, Blanchard, Edlund, & Rosenblum, 1982; Labbe & Williamson, 1983) elevated the methodological rigor in this area by testing AFT for children with multiple baseline across subject designs. In both studies, migraine reduction was substantive and coincided with the staggered introduction of treatment. Labbe and Williamson reported complete absence of headaches for their three children at 2-year follow-up. However, neither study incorporated controls for placebo effects. More recently, Labbe and Williamson (1984) employed autogenic-like warmth imagery with skin temperature biofeedback for migrainous children and obtained very strong treatment effects compared to a no-treatment group.

Imagery

The few studies available in this section are uncontrolled clinical trials. Paulley and Haskell (1975) employed relaxing imagery and advice to moderate "migraine personality" (essentially Type A behavior pattern). About two thirds of 80 migraineurs reported major improvement during follow-up periods ranging up to 8 years. Sim (1980b) combined his (1980a) imagery method with breath meditation. At 6-month follow-up, all but one of 29 migraineurs were headache free.

Other Relaxation Techniques

Uncontrolled trials with Quieting Response training (Ford, Stroebel, Strong, & Szarek, 1983a) achieved success with 29 of 45 (64 percent) classic or common migraine patients (for further details, see *Other Relaxation Techniques, Muscle-Contraction Headache* section). A comparable rate of success, 79 of 131 or 60 percent, occurred with mixed headache sufferers. A second uncontrolled report (Sallade, 1980) observed a 50 percent headache reduction in migrainous children receiving a combination of deep breathing, progressive relaxation, and pleasant imagery.

Relaxation Comparisons

Blanchard, Theobald, Williamson, Silver, and Brown (1978) contrasted progressive relaxation (PR), skin temperature biofeedback/autogenics combined, and no treatment. Significant pre- to posttreatment gains were obtained by the PR group in four of six self-reported headache parameters (e.g., frequency, duration, etc.). Gains made by the PR group exceeded those of the no-treatment group on three of six measures. Posttreatment differences between the PR and biofeedback/autogenics groups washed out by 3-month follow-up, at which time both treated groups exhibited significant headache reductions. Similarly, therapeutic gains held up well at 1-year follow-up for both treatments, with only minor difference between them (Silver, Blanchard, Williamson, Theobald, & Brown, 1979).

In their comparison of PR and autogenic training (AT) with migraineurs, Janssen and Neutgens (1986) obtained results similar to Silver et al. (1979). (See further discussion of Janssen and Neutgens under *Muscle-Contraction Headache.*) Their mixed headache sample profited more from AT than PR at posttreatment, although PR caught up by the 3-month follow-up.

A second study (Friedman & Taub, 1984) treated 66 migraineurs in seven conditions. Of current interest are the Benson meditation, autogenics/skin temperature biofeedback, and no-treatment groups. Both treatment groups produced migraine decrements superior to no treatment, but did not differ from each other at posttreatment or 1-year follow-up. High hypnotic susceptibility aided treatment response.

Brown (1984) conducted an interesting test of Lang's theory of imagery propositions (see Chapter 2). Migraineurs were trained in relaxing imagery emphasizing (a) response propositions (e.g., feeling drowsy, muscles relaxed, breathing slow), (b) stimulus propositions (e.g., warm sun, white sand, gulls flying), or (c) a credible placebo involving subconscious reconditioning. Laboratory cold pressor tests and reported headache activity found both treatment groups (a and b) to be superior to group c. However, the propositional content of the imagery proved extraneous as groups a and b did not differ. The relaxation or cognitive distraction mechanisms that mediated treatment gains were apportioned equally by the two versions of guided imagery.

Final Comments on Relaxation Therapy for Migraine Headache

In his classic text, Wolff (1963) advanced what subsequently became a widely held belief that chronic stress and personality factors (virtually identical to what is now called Type A behavior pattern) play a significant etiological role in vascular headaches. However, the thrust of recent research empirically testing this assertion (e.g., Andrasik, Blanchard, Arena, Teders et al., 1982) has failed to marshall supportive evidence. Thus, we are left to believe that relaxation does not operate at the level of behavioral or personality change (stress management), but rather directly alters pathophysiological processes in vascular headache sufferers.

Reversing the pattern obtained with muscle-contraction headache, now the results of progressive relaxation (PR) and self-control relaxation are marginal, and the results of autogenics (AT) are strong. However, it is surprising to note that the few studies that contain direct PR and AT contrasts fail to demonstrate the superiority of the latter. Several studies (e.g., Andrasik, Blanchard, Edlund, & Rosenblum, 1982; Sargent, Solbach, & Coyne, 1980) documented that treatment gains, having been established, are then lost when relaxation practice is discontinued, a phenomenon not unfamiliar to relaxation therapy.

There has been much activity in the area of AT/skin temperature biofeedback combined (AFT) for migraine, and current reviews endorse this approach (Diamond, 1979; Fahrion, 1978). However, reliable, methodologically rigorous evidence in support of this clinical strategy is not plentiful. Further, most of the data on AT for migraine has this technique paired with biofeedback, successfully concealing the level of AT influence. The few studies that independently evaluated AT did find it to be effective, but generally less so than skin temperature biofeedback. Lastly, treatment cost reductions following relaxation therapy represent a novel and convincing indicator of treatment efficacy in this domain. (See expanded discussion of Blanchard, Jaccard et al., 1985, in final comments of *Muscle-Contraction Headache* section.)

CHRONIC PAIN

The treatment of head pain (headache) represents a special case in pain treatment by virtue of its common occurrence and symptomatic consistency. Other types of pain also invite psychological interventions, particularly when the pain is chronic and unresponsive to routine medical treatment. Chapter 6 discusses the most common psychological approach to pain—treatment packages. Those few studies that employed relaxation only, or relaxation complemented by perhaps one other treatment, will be described next.

Progressive Relaxation (PR)

Sanders (1983) employed a multiple baseline design variant to evaluate PR and three other pain treatment components with four back pain inpatients. Robust dependent measures (pain, up time, and medication use) documented the superiority of PR. This study stands as a well-controlled, convincing demonstration of PR efficacy in this domain.

Turner (1982) provided data consistent with the above. Low back pain outpatients were given PR, stress management (including PR), or no treatment. Following treatment, PR subjects reported significant improvement compared to baseline levels in others' view of their health status, depression (Beck Depression Inventory; Beck et al., 1961), and self-reported pain. During this same period, untreated subjects made no progress. At 2-year follow-up, PR subjects still registered significant improvement over baseline, although some gains had diminished since posttreatment. In contrasts with stress management, PR was competitive although some indices favored the multicomponent intervention (e.g., self-rated pain at 1-month posttreatment).

Self-control Relaxation (SCR)

Treating mostly back and joint pain patients, Linton and Gotestam (1984) compared SCR (method described in Linton, 1982), SCR plus operant conditioning techniques, and no treatment. SCR patients made significant gains on subjective pain and depression, and rated their treatment as highly credible. Untreated subjects showed no change. The operant-enhanced group showed greater improvement than SCR on medication use and on increases in social and physical activity. At about 9 months posttreatment, the SCR only group showed the greatest pain improvement.

Passive Relaxation

Nigl and Fischer-Williams (1980) presented four case histories testifying to the utility of relaxation and electromyographic biofeedback combined for low back pain. Scant details were provided on the relaxation technique, but it appeared to be similar to the method of passive relaxation.

Meditation

There has been one meditation-based pain treatment program, and it was reported in preliminary (Kabat-Zinn, 1982) and final (Kabat-Zinn, Lipworth, & Burney, 1985) form. The method employed was termed *mindfulness meditation,* and it is distinct from most of the methods of meditation reviewed in this book. It involves detached self-observation while quietly sitting or walking, but discourages focal concentration on a word, image, object, etc. The treatment regimen also included Hatha Yoga exercises to stretch and strengthen the musculature.

Ninety outpatients, complaining of intractable pain derived from the back, head, chest, etc., were administered 10 weekly meditation sessions. Several self-report instruments documented an approximate 50 percent pain decrease at posttreatment, as well as improved coping with persistent pain. Most treatment gains were well maintained at about 1-year follow-up.

Other indicators of successful treatment were also reported. There was improvement in associated symptoms and moods. Some 70 percent of medicated patients reduced analgesic consumption by treatment end. Comparisons with a smaller sample of pain patients receiving traditional treatment, namely, physical therapy, nerve blocks, etc., consistently favored the superiority of meditation.

Autogenics (AT)

A small amount of case study data exists in this area. Two arthritic patients received electromyographic biofeedback/AT combined for half a year (Wickramasekera, Truong, Bush, & Orr, 1976). Over the treatment course, there occurred within- and between-session decrements in perceived pain and heightened threshold of induced pain. More importantly, out-of-session arthritic pain decreased about 50 percent and 25 percent in the two patients. Blacker (1980) presented the case history of a woman with refractory shoulder pain secondary to an auto accident. The combination of skin temperature biofeedback and AT eliminated pain, and this was sustained at 3-year follow-up.

Treating a heterogeneous group of patients (e.g., back pain, migraine, and cancer), Hartman and Ainsworth (1980) employed AT during the baseline period of a study designed primarily to contrast the pain management efficacy of biofeedback and stress inoculation. Unfortunately, their analyses do not permit evaluation of AT effects.

Relaxation Comparisons

Linton and Melin (1983), in treating primarily back pain patients, pitted a traditional rehabilitation program that included progressive relaxation against the same program supplemented by self-control relaxation. The primary dependent measure, subjective pain, did not favor either group. However, self-control relaxation subjects attained higher levels of social and physical activity and rated themselves as less impaired than progressive relaxation subjects.

Final Comments on Relaxation Therapy for Chronic Pain

Core pain problems provoke maladaptive physical and cognitive reactions that amplify the pain experience. Relaxation interventions for intractable pain probably exert their primary influence on this reactive component. The available data speak well of the helpfulness of varied relaxation approaches herein, boasting strong, durable effects.

Many questions remain for future research. Successful placebo-controlled trials would strengthen our confidence in the efficacy of relaxation. Identification of relation-responsive subsets within symptomatic categories would be helpful in guiding treatment decisions. Lastly, as multiple disciplines and treatments compete for dominion over pain patients, investigations of the temporal or sequence position of relaxation, relative to the onset of insult or the presentation of other treatments, might yield clinically useful information.

DYSMENORRHEA

Painful menstruation is termed *primary dysmenorrhea,* when the origin of the distress cannot be specified, or *secondary dysmenorrhea,* when the pain is attributed to a known pelvic disorder (Denney & Gerrard, 1981). Some observers (Chesney & Tasto, 1975a; Dalton, 1969) recommend further differentiation within the primary category. The spasmodic type is characterized by the appearance of acute pain, simultaneous with the onset of menstruation or shortly thereafter. The congestive type exhibits depressed mood and less intense pain during the premenstrual period. Premenstrual syndrome (PMS) should not be confused with congestive dysmenorrhea, even though they both occur prior to the onset of menstruation. PMS is distinguished by reports of diffuse pain, marked depression, and irritability (Gannon, 1981; Rose & Abplanalp, 1983). The argument that there is a greater muscular basis for the spasmodic than the congestive type suggests that relaxation therapy may be more useful with the former (Denney & Gerrard, 1981; Tasto & Insel, 1977), although some data (e.g., Cox & Meyer, 1978; Nelson, Sigmon, Amodei, & Jarrett, 1984; Webster, 1980) are inconsistent with this thesis.

Progressive Relaxation (PR)

Tasto and Chesney (1974) provided the first example of relaxation therapy for primary dysmenorrhea, although this was predated by a successful case study using systematic desensitization (Mullen, 1968). Tasto and Chesney (1974) evaluated seven undergraduates complaining of menstrual pain. These authors observed significant improvement on three menstrual questionnaires subsequent to PR treatment supplemented with pleasant imagery associated with menstruation. In a carefully designed follow-up study, Chesney and Tasto (1975b) contrasted PR plus coping imagery associated with the onset of menstruation with unstructured group discussion and no treatment. Only the relaxation treatment proved beneficial, but only with women diagnosed as spasmodic dysmenorrhea. As predicted, women exhibiting congestive type did not profit from psychological intervention. Other successful case study data are also available (Martin, Collins, Hillenberg, Zabin, & Katell, 1981).

Autogenics (AT)

In a case study of a woman diagnosed as spasmodic dysmenorrhea, Dietvorst and Osborne (1978) presented the often combined treatments of skin temperature biofeedback and AT. The patient reported significant pain reduction following treatment. Unlike the progressive relaxation treatments, this intervention did not include imagery related to menstruation, suggesting that the imagery component was not an active therapy ingredient in prior studies. Encouraging data on the mixture of AT and biofeedback for this disorder has been forthcoming from other investigators as well (Balick, Elfner, May, & Moore, 1982). Summarizing across numerous reports, Luthe and Schultz (1969a) estimate 40 to 70 percent of dysmenorrheic patients exhibit a therapeutic response to AT.

Heczey has conducted the most systematic work in this area. Her first effort, completed in 1975 (cited in Heczey, 1980), found that AT/skin temperature biofeedback combined were therapeutically effective, but no more so than false feedback with dysmenorrheic women. However, vaginal temperature increases occurred with the former group only, suggesting relaxation of the uterine muscles occurred in this group. The outcome and temperature results were conflictual, as it was hypothesized that treatment effects were mediated by uterine relaxation.

Her second treatment study (Heczey, 1980) contrasted eight sessions of (a) the combination of progressive relaxation, AT, digital temperature biofeedback, and vaginal temperature biofeedback, (b) individual AT, (c) AT training in groups of four subjects, and (d) no treatment.

The combined group a attained significantly greater improvement on dysmenorrheic symptoms than groups b and c, which in turn surpassed the no-treatment group. While providing encouraging data on AT for this disorder, the potential usefulness of focusing treatment in the affected zone (vaginal biofeedback) appears more promising.

Other Relaxation Techniques

Taped relaxation training (method unspecified) fared poorly in comparison to relaxation combined with electromyographic (EMG) biofeedback derived from the abdominal region, with college students presenting dysmenorrheic complaints (Bennink, Hulst, & Benthem, 1982). Self-reported distress was significantly reduced in the combined group only. This same group also registered significantly lower abdominal EMG than the relaxation group.

In one of the few studies, in this or any other area, pitting relaxation against medication, dysmenorrheic symptomatology responded as well to relaxation (method unspecified) as to prostaglandin synthesis inhibitor (Evans, Lee, & Christoff, 1985). Further details on this study, presented at a convention, are unavailable.

Final Comments on Relaxation Therapy for Dysmenorrhea

Symptomatic women have exhibited positive relaxation treatment responses, but significant ambiguity persists. Positive responses to placebo groups detract from the authenticity of relaxation therapy. The failure of the spasmodic/congestive dichotomy and of local physiological changes to predict treatment outcome consistently further cloud this area.

As other pain syndromes have responded well to relaxation and dysmenorrhea claims some degree of muscular involvement, this disorder seemingly presents a good prognosis for relaxation therapy, but it has received surprisingly little attention. I expect this will be a fruitful area of research in the future. Two avenues that might be worthwhile to pursue concern verifying regular home relaxation practice and establishing adequate levels of minimum therapeutic dosage, for example, 2 months of once daily relaxation practice.

PREPARATION FOR CHILDBIRTH

Reduced health risk for the mother and the child are just some of the factors that have made "natural" childbirth attractive to physicians and parents. The term *natural childbirth* indicates little or no use of anesthesia or analgesic medicine in the birth process. However, the term sometimes serves as a synonym for the most common approach to natural childbirth, that being the Lamaze (1956/1970) method. Herein, I will rely on the first definition, which is not specific to any particular technique.

Originally, the Lamaze technique, which was adapted from methods first popularized in Russia, involved a series of breathing patterns and skeletal muscle relaxation to which visual focusing and the active cooperation of the husband have since been added (Bing, 1969). Although this approach shares many features in common with yoga techniques and progressive relaxation, it is sufficiently distinct so as to preclude its further discussion in the present context. The interested reader is referred to Lamaze's book and scholarly reviews of this and related approaches (Beck & Hall, 1978; Chertok, 1961; Stevens, 1976; Wideman & Singer, 1984).

Progressive Relaxation (PR)

Early in his career, Jacobson showed sufficient interest in the use of PR to attain natural childbirth that he used the occasion of his first child's birth to successfully test the method (Szirmai, 1980). Some 30 years later, Jacobson (1959) published a laymen's guide to natural childbirth with PR. However, there is little supportive data on the utility of this approach. A brief report that tested PR/electromyographic biofeedback combined on pregnant hypertensives found no benefits from relaxation therapy during childbirth (Sherman, Hayashi, Gaarder, Huff, & Williams, 1978). Horan (1973) introduced PR to his wife during labor without prior training, and she found this counterproductive.

In the only relaxation study to do so, Halonen and Passman (1985) employed PR to address a common aspect of childbirth—postpartum depression. At about 2 weeks following childbirth, women armed with PR reported significantly lower Beck Depression Inventory (Beck et al., 1961) scores than women receiving only what little relaxation is usually included in natural childbirth classes.

Autogenics (AT)

Luthe and Schultz (1969a, pp. 149–156) described the work of Prill who trained over 1000 pregnant women to practice AT during labor and delivery. His work, and that of others, suggests that AT can reduce the intensity and duration of labor and facilitate the birth process.

An interesting study pitted "respiratory autogenic training" (RAT) against the traditional Lamaze method (Zimmermann-Tansella et al., 1979). Few details are presented on the method of RAT other than it is a mixture of autogenics and progressive relaxation. Pregnant women, trained in RAT, reported less anxiety and less pain during labor than Lamaze-trained, demographically matched women. No differences emerged on medications received during labor and delivery, doctors' ratings of patients' relaxation during labor, babies' health, and other medical indices. In sum, RAT demonstrated a small advantage.

Imagery

In the same report as above in the progressive relaxation section, Horan (1973) replaced PR with imagery of a pleasant nature scene and cheery activities their child would later enjoy. Labor was easily tolerated with little medication.

Final Comments on Relaxation Therapy for Preparation for Childbirth

In their survey of American hospitals, Wideman and Singer (1984) found that natural childbirth methods are, by now, near universally accepted. Despite the prolificacy of these approaches, there are virtually no experimentally controlled, scientific data attesting to benefits to either mother or child derived from natural childbirth. Mothers who are physically healthier than the norm and avail themselves of high quality prenatal care may be most likely to study and employ natural childbirth. The promise that natural childbirth produces a happier and healthier mother and child may, in part, be due to a self-selection bias. Experimental controls for confounding factors of this sort have yet to be implemented.

Basic (e.g., Stevens & Heide, 1977) and clinical (e.g., Sanders, 1983) research on relaxation for pain control in areas other than childbirth have supported the utility of relaxation therapy. Applications to childbirth seem highly desirable. Besides addressing the global clinical outcome issues raised above, future research must also differentially evaluate the influence of competing explanations of natural childbirth efficacy, such as the benefits of increased medical procedure information and social support (Wideman & Singer, 1984).

PREPARATION FOR MEDICAL AND DENTAL TREATMENT

Routine medical and dental examinations and, to a greater extent, invasive procedures may trigger feelings of anxiety in patients. Emotional distress associated with medical and dental procedures are problematic on several counts: (a) the patient experiences a noxious emotion, (b) the patient's emotional state may be a disruptive influence in the treatment process, (c) emotional turmoil may diminish the patient's treatment response, and (d) emotional turmoil may prolong the recuperative period. Psychological support, information provision, modeling of appropriate conduct, and treatment-relevant skills training are some of the approaches that have been employed to relieve stress and avert the above problems (Anderson & Masur, 1983; Kendall & Watson, 1981).

Progressive Relaxation (PR)

The first test of PR training in this domain involved males undergoing open heart surgery and was reported in duplicate (Aiken, 1972; Aiken & Henrichs, 1971). Fifteen males who practiced PR for 3 days prior to surgery were compared to 15 age-matched males who did not receive PR prior to the same surgery. PR treatment had no effect on mortality rate, but it did significantly reduce the number of patients who manifested postoperative reactions. Similarly, the PR group scored significantly lower on four of five signs of surgical stress: anesthesia time, cardiopulmonary bypass time, total units of blood, and degree of hypothermia.

Wilson (1981) conducted a careful test of taped PR versus provision of information about surgery. Seventy patients hospitalized for elective abdominal surgery were randomly assigned to four groups: (a) normal hospital procedures, (b) a taped message describing the medical procedures and sensations likely to be experienced before, during, and after surgery, (c) taped PR, and (d) PR/information combined. The PR and PR/information groups surpassed the control group on several measures of recovery: a hospital recovery scale, number of pain injections, and postoperative output of epinephrine. Patients receiving the information treatment did not differ from the control group on any measure. Comparisons between treatments were not conducted. Patients exhibiting relatively low preoperative fear particularly benefited from PR, as evidenced by a shortened hospital stay.

This same investigator and his associates (Wilson, Moore, Randolph, & Hanson, 1982) has since replicated the information and PR treatments with gastrointestinal endoscopy patients. A no-treatment control group exposed to normal hospital routines was included. Ratings of distress during the procedure and mood after the procedure revealed an advantage of the PR group over the control. Heart rate increases and objectively quantified problems during the procedure also favored PR in comparison with the control. PR and control subjects were comparable in valium use, resting heart rate during the procedure, and reported response to endoscopy. In contrast to the findings of Wilson (1981), patients reporting high preoperative fear benefited more from PR than those with low fear ratings. Here again, statistical comparisons between the two treatment groups were not conducted.

Kaplan and his colleagues conducted two studies relevant to this section, and both studies employed a combination of PR and slow, deep breathing. The first (Kaplan, Atkins, & Lenhard, 1982) was primarily a test of different cognitive strategies, and half the subjects in each condition also received relaxation. Subjects undergoing sigmoidoscopy, a type of anal exam, experienced less anxiety but perceived the exam as longer when aided by relaxation.

The second study (Kaplan, Metzger, & Jablecki, 1983) tested (*a*) relaxation, (*b*) cognitive restructuring, (*c*) *a* and *b* combined, or (*d*) social attention control, with patients undergoing a painful electromyographic exam. Heart rate, subjective reports, and observational indices evinced the superiority of the treated groups (*a, b,* and *c*) over *d,* but revealed no differential utility among *a, b,* and *c.*

Pickett and Clum (1982) reported an unsuccessful trial with PR. On the day prior to gallbladder surgery, patients were (a) taught PR, (b) given didactic information about PR, (c) trained to use pleasant imagery to distract their attention away from surgery-related thoughts, or (d) given no special preparation. Patients trained in imagery showed diminished postsurgical anxiety. PR did not prove useful on measures of anxiety or pain.

Jacobson (1970, p. 184) incidentally reported that PR aided one of his anxiety-prone patients to better tolerate dental treatment. Studies presenting taped PR (Corah, Gale, & Illig, 1979a, 1979b; Corah, Gale, Pace, & Seyrek, 1981; Lamb & Strand, 1980) and live PR (Miller, Murphy, & Miller, 1978) in the dental office have found this treatment to be helpful in reducing anxiety associated with dental procedures. Miller et al. employed self-control relaxation, and the Corah et al. studies employed passive relaxation. These two lines of research will be discussed in the following sections. Lamb and Strand (1980) randomly assigned patients to treatment or no-treatment groups. Treated individuals received PR immediately before encountering the dentist. Their state anxiety (State-Trait Anxiety Inventory, STAI; Spielberger, Gorsuch, & Lushene, 1970) was markedly reduced and stayed low throughout the dental appointment. Trait anxiety scores on this same questionnaire were unaffected, mirroring the findings of others (Johnson & Spielberger, 1968; Stoudenmire, 1972). Reduced anxiety levels did not occur in the untreated group.

Self-control Relaxation (SCR)

Miller, Murphy, and Miller (1978) invited anxious dental patients to receive relaxation training to diminish dental fears. Subjects were assigned to 10-session courses of either electromyographic (EMG) biofeedback, SCR (after Bernstein & Borkovec, 1973), or self-devised relaxation control. Before and after the treatment course, subjects were assessed in the dental chair while awaiting routine treatment. Most of the dependent measures—frontalis EMG, self-reported dental anxiety (Corah, 1969), and STAI-State anxiety—showed significantly greater improvement in the two treatment groups (which did not differ from each other) than in the control group. STAI-Trait anxiety improved equally in all groups. Beck, Kaul, and Russell (1978) reported similar data with a group of 10 women treated with cue-controlled relaxation (CCR). They also observed that anxiety reduction benefits extended beyond the dental setting.

CCR was also part of a SCR program to aid preschool children in overcoming dental anxiety (Siegel & Peterson, 1980). One session of SCR, which also included breath relaxation, pleasant imagery, and calming self-talk, was contrasted with a sensory information condition and placebo treatment. Both treated groups were equally effective and surpassed the placebo group in diminishing anxious behavior in a dental examination, as measured by the method of Melamed, Weinstein, Hawes, and Katin-Borland (1975). Pulse-rate changes and dentist's ratings of the children's anxiety and cooperation followed a similar pattern. A replication study (Siegel & Peterson, 1981) found that these treatments produced therapeutic effects, which endured at least 1 week to a posttreatment dental examination.

Peterson and Shigetomi (1981) presented the same SCR package as Siegel and Peterson (1980), a film modeling coping, both interventions, or no treatment to children undergoing tonsillectomies. The analyses yielded several marginally significant findings suggestive of the superiority of the SCR treatment.

Passive Relaxation

As mentioned above, Corah and his associates conducted two studies to evaluate taped relaxation for dental anxiety. In the first study (Corah, Gale, & Illig, 1979a), dental patients practiced passive relaxation, played a video game for distraction, or were given a button by which they could signal discomfort to the dentist to prompt his temporarily discontinuing. A fourth group received no special treatment. Treatments were delivered during the second of two dental visits. Patients' anxiety ratings and dentists' ratings of perceived patient anxiety showed significant improvement in the PR and distraction groups only. Electrodermal response revealed significant relaxation effects in the passive relaxation group and, ironically, significant arousal in the distraction group.

In a partial replication, this same research group (1979b) compared passive relaxation, video game distraction, and no treatment in the same basic experimental design. According to dental anxiety self-ratings (Corah, 1969), but not electrodermal indices, patients receiving relaxation (particularly women) derived significantly greater anxiety reduction benefits than patients in the other two groups. Dentists' ratings again found passive relaxation and distraction to be useful anxiety palliatives.

The final study by this group (Corah, Gale, Pace, & Seyrek, 1981) was composed of dental patients receiving (*a*) no special preparation, (*b*) taped passive relaxation delivered in a slow, soothing voice, (*c*) the same content as in *b* delivered in a conversational tone, or (*d*) a travel story delivered in a slow soothing voice. The thrust of four self-report and physiological measures ordered the effectiveness of the conditions in reducing dental treatment aversiveness as *b, c, d,* and lastly *a.* This is one of the few process studies of relaxation, and it supports clinical lore about the importance of a relaxed presentation style.

Meditation

Anecdotal reports have claimed analgesic benefits for TM during periodontal work (Morse & Hildebrand, 1976) and dental surgery (Palmer, 1980). A somewhat more rigorous follow-up by Morse, Schacterle, Furst, and Bose (1981) compared the separate and combined effects of hypnosis, meditation (method unspecified), and anesthesia on endodontic patients' anxiety. The conclusions of this study were seriously hampered by small cell sizes. Nevertheless, it did appear that all the treatments exerted a significant influence in reducing anxiety in pre-post session measures of self-report and salivation.

Wells (1982) combined training in Bensonian relaxation, electromyographic biofeedback, and progressive relaxation to ease the postoperative pain of individuals receiving abdominal surgery. Compared to patients given standard preoperative preparation, the relaxation subjects experienced less postoperative distress due to pain, as indicated on a pain rating scale (Johnson, 1973), but *more* postoperative complications. There were no differences between the groups on all other measures: surgery and recovery room duration, postoperative discomfort, abdominal muscle tension, or focal pain experience. Scott and Clum (1984) tested Bensonian relaxation singly with mixed surgical patients and found that it diminished postsurgical pain, but only among individuals described as sensitizers—overly vigilant and anxious.

Autogenics (AT)

A hypersensitive gag reflex can impair dental treatment, and in one case history (Gerschman, Burrows, & Fitzgerald, 1981) it prevented wearing of dentures. However, this woman responded well to the combination of supportive psychotherapy and AT, and she was symptom-free at 2-year follow-up.

Imagery

Horan, Layng, and Pursell (1976) applied the technique of "in vivo" emotive imagery to dental pain. Women seeking dental treatment submitted to a counterbalanced series of tapes during actual treatment. The tapes presented the featured method of relaxation through imagery of pleasant nature scenes, neutral cognitive material, or blank tape, in a within-subject design. Heart rate did not vary between the tape periods, but self-rated comfort favored the relaxing imagery period over the other two.

In a study designed to analyze aspects of modeling processes (Klingman, Melamed, Cuthbert, & Hermecz, 1984), the combination of pleasant imagery and controlled breathing proved to be an effective coping strategy for dental phobic children. Those who utilized these relaxation devices reported less dental and general fear, and were more cooperative during a dental procedure, than children who were informed of these coping devices but not given encouragement to employ them.

Other Relaxation Techniques

The postoperative response of elective surgery (cholecystectomy, herniorrhaphy, or hemorrhoidectomy) patients was evaluated with self-report measures of discomfort and amount of analgesic medication consumption (Flaherty & Fitzpatrick, 1978). Patients trained in Roon's (1961) simple method of relaxation involving relaxing the jaw, slow breathing, and quieting the mind, did significantly better on these indicators than untrained patients. However, a second study (Fuller, Endress, & Johnson, 1978) found slow abdominal breathing ineffective in reducing stress among women undergoing a routine pelvic examination.

Final Comments on Relaxation Therapy in Preparation for Medical and Dental Treatment

This section marshalls strong evidence that individuals can expect attenuated subjective, behavioral, and/or physiological distress in medical and dental treatment subsequent to relaxation training. Claims for relaxation therapy beyond anxiety relief for such crucial concerns as recuperative course and clinical outcome of medical procedures have received weaker support.

Most of the studies testing relaxation with patients awaiting surgery were able to administer very few training sessions due to the short interval between hospital admission and surgery (Wells, 1982). Thus, patients were hurriedly learning their new relaxation skill while distracted by the anxiety cues of the hospital. With little opportunity to practice, they were soon challenged by the intense stress of surgery. Future research in this area would do well to begin relaxation training on an outpatient basis as soon as the surgery decision is made, and certainly not less than 1 month before surgery.

CANCER

Cancer is among the most feared and devastating diseases. A number of psychological theories have been advanced as to the origin and course of this disease, and a variety of psychotherapeutic approaches have been proferred (Barofsky, 1981; Wellisch, 1981). Herein I will examine relaxation approaches to various aspects of cancer.

Progressive Relaxation (PR)

In most of the research in this section, PR has not targeted the disease process itself, but rather the impact of chemotherapy side effects (Nerenz, Leventhal, & Love, 1982). Some 20 percent of cancer chemotherapy patients suffer nausea and vomiting in anticipation of medication toxicity (Morrow, 1982; Morrow, Arseneau, Asbury, Bennett, & Boros, 1982; Nesse, Carli, Curtis, & Kleinman, 1980; Nicholas, 1982), and PR treatments have attempted to reduce this gastrointestinal distress. Hypnosis, in combination with muscle relaxation and imagery techniques, has registered noteworthy successes in this domain and is reviewed elsewhere (Redd & Andrykowski, 1982; Redd, Rosenberger, & Hendler, 1982–1983).

One of the first reports in this area was a case study of a woman exhibiting chronic gagging and regurgitation, following the removal of a cancerous tumor from her esophagus (Redd, 1980). During the course of a dozen PR sessions immediately preceding meals, the symptomatology gradually disappeared and did not reappear at 9-month follow-up. Cotanch (1983b) has also reported encouraging uncontrolled data of a similar sort on 12 cancer patients. Alternatively, Kaempfer (cited in Cotanch, 1983a) observed anxiety enhancement resulting from PR in four of five treated patients, as PR elevated their awareness of their disease. Also, Morrow (1984) reported that taped PR, but not live PR, induced nausea in his cancer patients.

Burish and his associates have been the major contributors to PR treatment of anticipatory distress related to chemotherapy side effects, and their research program will now be reviewed. Individual case studies suggested that combinations of PR/pleasant imagery (Burish & Lyles, 1979) and PR/electromyographic biofeedback (Burish, Shartner, & Lyles, 1981) can greatly reduce nausea, emesis, anxiety, and depression associated with chemotherapy. In their first group design study (Burish & Lyles, 1981), two sessions of the PR/pleasant imagery combination were contrasted with no treatment. Only the treated group exhibited significant reductions in anxiety, hostility, and depression as measured by the Multiple Affect Adjective Check List (MAACL; Zuckerman, Lubin, Vogel, & Valerius, 1964) during chemotherapy sessions preceded by PR/imagery. Patients' self-ratings and nurses' ratings of patients were in agreement that the treated patients were less anxious and nauseated than the untreated patients. Blood pressure and heart rate measures did not render a definitive advantage for the treatment. Follow-up data strongly indicated that the above benefits persevered after relaxation training was discontinued. Further, treated subjects posted significantly lower heart rates than untreated subjects during follow-up chemotherapy sessions.

More recently, this group attained a high level of methodological rigor (Lyles, Burish, Krozely, & Oldham, 1982). This study replicated most of the design features of their previous two-group study, with the addition of a supportive counseling group to control for social influence and other nonspecific effects. Moreover, patients were equated between groups on the potency of their chemotherapy regimen and on the stage in chemotherapy treatment. The results were very strong and consistent. On a majority of the dependent measures (systolic blood pressure, heart rate, anxiety, depression, and nurses' ratings of patients' anxiety and nausea), patients receiving PR/imagery before chemotherapy sessions attained significantly lower levels compared to the counseling and no-treatment groups, which did not differ from each other. On almost all of the remaining measures (patients' self-ratings of nausea, and the duration and severity of nausea at home following chemotherapy sessions), the PR/imagery group did better than either the counseling or the no-treatment group. Measures taken at a follow-up session after treatment had been completed revealed many of the treatment gains had been maintained, although reversals did occur on a substantial number of measures, particularly depression, nurses' ratings of anxiety and nausea, and duration of nausea at home following the session. A related study (Carey & Burish, 1985) has since obtained the surprising finding of an inverse relationship between pretreatment anxiety and relaxation therapy response in this population.

Morrow (1986) reported an interesting study that distinguished between nausea in anticipation of chemotherapy and nausea resulting from chemotherapy. Cancer patients receiving only chemotherapy treatment and complaining of nausea were assigned to systematic desensitization, PR, supportive counseling, or no treatment. Overall, systematic desensitization was the most effective treatment in pre-post assessments. PR proved more effective in reducing the severity and duration of posttreatment nausea, but not of anticipatory nausea, than counseling and no treatment.

Another group (Campbell, Dixon, Sanderford, & Denicola, 1984) targeted a novel aspect of the cancer syndrome and offered preliminary data. Cancer patients often experience weight loss due to the presence of pain, nausea, etc. In a group of 12 patients who regularly practiced a blend of progressive relaxation, the relaxation response, deep breathing, and guided imagery, 75 percent experienced weight change in a desirable direction.

Self-control Relaxation (SCR)

Hamberger (1982) employed SCR with an individual manifesting a generalized nausea response derived from a course of radiation therapy for bladder cancer 3 years earlier. During a 6-month baseline, the patient was bedridden an average of 4.5 days per month due to gastric distress. The effects of SCR were immediate and, with minor exception, eliminated the gastric attacks through 1-year follow-up.

Addressing questions bearing momentous implications, poorly controlled reports have raised the possibility that hypnotic imagery or visualization can improve immunocompetence (Hall, Longo, & Dixon, 1981; Minning, 1982), and cancer itself can be arrested by psychotherapy/relaxation/visualization (Hall, 1983; Simonton, Matthews-Simonton, & Creighton, 1978; Simonton, Matthews-Simonton, & Sparks, 1980). While discussion of these issues has generated much interest and hope, the substance of these investigations constitutes little more than speculation.

Recently, however, a major breakthrough has been achieved by a multidisciplinary research team headed by Kiecolt-Glaser (1985). Healthy geriatric volunteers were randomly assigned to self-control relaxation training, unstructured social contact, or no treatment. Both treatment groups met three times a week for a month. Immunocompetence impact was assessed by biochemical and questionnaire measures obtained pre, post, and at 1-month follow-up. Although this study may best be categorized as basic research, it is included in this chapter because of its strong link to clinical concerns.

Of primary interest in this investigation were effects on natural killer (NK) cell activity, whose action has been linked to cancer and viral control and to effects on other immune system processes, Herpes antibody titers, and mitogen concentration. The social contact and no-treatment groups produced no biochemical effects. The relaxation group produced significant, desirable change in pre-post assessments on two of the measures: NK cell activity and Herpes antibody titers. Treatment effects were maintained at follow-up for the antibodies, but not for NK cell activity.

Self-rated sleep and a measure of psychological adjustment, the Hopkins Symptom Checklist (Derogatis, Lipman, Rickels, Uhlenhuth, & Covi, 1974), registered gains for the relaxation group only at posttreatment, but not follow-up. Other self-report measures of appetite, life satisfaction, and loneliness were unresponsive to the experimental manipulations.

This same research group (Kiecolt-Glaser et al., 1986) has since evaluated similar dependent measures in testing a multicomponent relaxation program with medical students before and after examinations. Relaxation comprising hypnosis, suggestion, progressive relaxation, autogenic training, and imagery proved moderately helpful in guarding against the psychological and biochemical toll of exams.

The results of these rigorously designed and well-executed studies suggest that the body's natural defenses against cancer and viral diseases can be mobilized by stress reduction via relaxation. The obvious implications of this approach for health maintenance and disease control represent a revolutionary application of relaxation therapy. However, assertions as to the ultimate importance of this research must await equally rigorous demonstrations that psychological manipulations of immunocompetence do in fact alter disease processes.

Meditation

Weddington, Blindt, and McCracken (1983) presented case histories that mirror the antiemetic efforts with progressive relaxation. Relaxation (breath meditation, relaxing cue words, and hand temperature biofeedback) abated nausea related to cancer chemotherapy in two patients.

Ainslie Meares, a major exponent in this area, takes a different approach than most of those who apply progressive relaxation. The goal for this author is to cure the disease itself.

The method is referred to as *intensive meditation,* but the articles on cancer treatment (e.g., Meares, 1979a) give us limited insight into the actual procedures of the technique. An earlier publication (Meares, 1967) described a method of relaxation in detail, and this appears to be the technique subsequently applied to cancer patients. The method is a combination of passive relaxation (i.e., focusing on relaxing body sensations) and an attitude referred to as "regression." Regression involves relinquishing the customary adult cognitive styles of critical and logical thinking in favor of an undisciplined, unfocused set. It strikes me that Meares' notion of regression is a blend of free association from psychoanalysis and a passive attitude from autogenics. Recent comments by Meares (1982–1983) suggest that verbal instruction is deemphasized, relying primarily on nonverbal communication and touch to induce the meditative state.

Meares prescribed intensive meditation for 2 to 4 hours daily, far more meditation than is recommended by other contemporary approaches. Theoretically, the meditation helps mobilize the body's immunological resources (Meares, 1976, 1978a, 1979a). Several case histories (Meares, 1976, 1978b, 1979a, 1979b, 1980, 1981) describe dramatic improvement in terminal cancer cases. In some instances, the malignant process was arrested during the period of meditation, but resumed its course shortly after the patient tired of meditation and discontinued its practice (Meares, 1977a, 1977b).

Many forces other than those specific to meditation could account for Meares' experience with cancer patients. Controlled research would be welcomed to rule out alternative explanations and to develop a maximally effective meditation procedure for cancer. It is possible that there exists a great potential in meditation for aiding the body's ability to combat this and other diseases.

Other Relaxation Techniques

Though details were omitted, one report (Dolgin, Katz, McGinty, & Siegel, 1985) observed that relaxation methods are helpful in reducing anticipatory nausea among children undergoing chemotherapy.

Final Comments on Relaxation Therapy for Cancer

The toxicity of some chemotherapy regimens produces side effects of such catastrophic proportions that their aversiveness rivals that of the cancer itself (Stoudemire, Cotanch, & Laszlo, 1984). As a result, some elect to forego chemotherapy and thereby shorten life. For others, psychogenic emesis develops in association with chemotherapy, serving only to exacerbate an already noxious status. In summarizing explanations advanced to account for relaxation influence on chemotherapy side effects, Burish and Carey (1984) suggest that nausea is a conditioned response controlled by hospital stimuli that have been associated with the intrinsic aversiveness of the chemotherapy. Relaxation may act to moderate sympathetic arousal that would otherwise potentiate gastrointestinal upset. Relaxation may also facilitate the discernment and control of early cues of gastrointestinal upset by enhancing self-awareness. The clinical outcome research in this area is well designed and effective. Relaxation therapy appears to be a satisfactory treatment for this significant problem.

One of the main challenges to relaxation therapy in this domain results from the fact that relaxation therapy is labor intensive. Future efforts to employ indigenous personnel as therapeutic agents and/or encourage self-administration are much needed. Unfortunately, Morrow's (1984) data on this subject are discouraging.

Concerning relaxation treatment of the cancer itself, I do not believe we can take much stock in the existing data. The research of Kiecolt-Glaser and her colleagues is among the most exciting in the relaxation arena, but it is in its infancy with respect to such questions as arresting cancer. Basic research, including animal studies, is more advanced on this subject than clinical research, and it points rather convincingly to stress causing impaired immunocompetence (Jemmott & Locke, 1984). Thus, clinical psychoimmunology, of which relaxation therapy is a subset, remains an exciting and optimistic but as yet unconfirmed territory.

DRUG ABUSE

Many factors contribute to the excessive use of drugs. For example, episodes of anxiety or depression may prompt stress reduction and escapism through drugs. To combat emotional triggers such as these, some relaxation technique is often included in comprehensive treatment packages for drug abuse. This is discussed more fully in Chapter 6.

A slightly different perspective maintains that enduring personality deficits can motivate individuals to compensate with elevated drug consumption. Within the array of relaxation techniques, the meditation approaches have made the strongest claims for promoting general personality enhancement. Consequently, meditation (most notably Transcendental Meditation) researchers have shown the most interest in relaxation effects on drug usage.

Progressive Relaxation (PR)

Relaxation as a unitary intervention could conceivably exert a powerful influence on those smokers for whom anxiety reduction is a major factor. However, the only study to test this hypothesis (Levenberg & Wagner, 1976) failed to observe unequal PR influence on individuals whose smoking was correlated with anxiety versus smoking independent of anxiety. As is typically the case in all smoking treatments, PR was associated with a substantial (about 70 percent) smoking decrease at posttreatment and a near-complete return to baseline smoking level by 4-month follow-up.

The remaining few studies in this domain, though they did not select subjects on anxiety criteria, obtained more encouraging results than Levenberg and Wagner (1976). In a multicondition study, Wagner and Bragg (1970) obtained a 77 percent smoking reduction in seven PR subjects, and they were still 54 percent below baseline at 3-month follow-up. Similarly, a second study of PR subjects found smoking reduced by 43 percent at posttreatment and by 35 percent at 3-month follow-up (Sutherland, Amit, Golden, & Roseberger, 1975).

Brief mention is due a study that found a single session of PR was of no incremental value in fading subjects from caffeine use (James, Stirling, & Hampton, 1985). This negative finding stands in contrast to the uncontrolled, positive results reported by Hyner (1979) in the meditation section below.

Meditation

The bulk of this research studied the effects of Transcendental Meditation on drug consumption. Several case studies reported that TM is helpful in controlling the use of such drugs as marijuana, alcohol, and cigarette smoking (Carrington & Ephron, 1975). The initial group studies (Benson, 1969, 1974a; Benson & Wallace, 1972b; Monahan, 1977; Shafii, Lavely, & Jaffe, 1974, 1975) gathered retrospective accounts from TM practitioners. Katz (1977) has since conducted the same sort of research on a prospective basis. These surveys suggest that the regular practice of TM is accompanied by substantial reductions in the use of a wide range of drugs including alcohol, marijuana, caffeine, hallucinogens, narcotics, etc. Unfortunately, this research is confounded by the subject self-selection bias and other methodological flaws, discussed at length in the Chapter 3 section on TM. Therefore, we cannot conclude that a randomly selected individual would enjoy these same drug reduction benefits, if exposed to TM.

The study reported below (Brautigam, 1977) boasts two features that distinguish it from the above group. It recruited known drug abusers, and it randomly assigned subjects to treatment and no-treatment conditions. Drug abusers (hashish, LSD, amphetamines, or opiates) known to a hospital were invited to take the TM course. Twenty individuals came forth and were then randomly assigned to either TM or group counseling therapy (control group). After 3 months, the control group was also given TM and was followed for another 3 months. During the first 3-month period, TM subjects reduced their hashish use by over 90 percent, while the control subjects reported about a 20 percent reduction. Similarly, "hard" drug use was nearly eliminated among the TM subjects, while the control subjects nearly doubled their consumption of hard drugs. When the control subjects were exposed to TM during the second 3 month period, their drug use dropped off precipitously, replicating the results of the first treatment period. At 2-year follow-up, there was an 80 percent relapse rate. Further analyses revealed that the TM subjects made significantly greater gains than did control subjects on a number of psychological variables (e.g., self-confidence, anxiety, adjustment).

Brautigam clearly presented the strongest evidence to date on TM for drug abuse. However, the study has one serious shortcoming that detracts from its findings. All subjects were invited to participate in a TM study, and all were told that TM would help reduce their drug problem. Control subjects were informed of their group counseling assignment only after they agreed to participate in TM treatment. Surely, many of these individuals reacted with disappointment or resentment to this news. Low attendance at the counseling sessions supports this conclusion. Therefore, we cannot conclude that TM is a more effective drug treatment than counseling. We can conclude that TM (with placebo effects uncontrolled) was a successful aid to short-term reduction in drug abuse.

Anderson (1977) offered TM to 115 servicemen hospitalized for detoxification from mild heroin use. All of the participants voluntarily accepted TM training and practiced enthusiastically during their hospitalization. Upon completing treatment, 26 subjects were discharged from the army, and there is little information on them. Of the 89 subjects remaining in the army, *every one* discontinued TM practice and resumed some form of drug abuse within a month.

One TM study (Kline, Docherty, & Farley, 1982) delivered this treatment to recovering alcoholics and other "emotionally disturbed" individuals. Pre-post assessments, consisting of the Minnesota Multiphasic Personality Inventory (Hathaway & McKinley, 1943) and the Tennessee Self Concept Scale (Fitts, 1964), were administered to this group and a second wave of matched, untreated subjects. No within- or between-group differences emerged.

There is one poorly controlled account of applying Benson's (1975) relaxation approach to control drug consumption. Hyner (1979) employed relaxation and reinforcing reminder cards to assist a female graduate student, who was suffering tachycardia, in reducing her caffeine and nicotine intake. The intervention had an immediate impact and its success was maintained at 1-year follow-up, although the design does not permit assessment of the independent contribution of relaxation to the outcome. Brief mention is due a study by Patel and Carruthers (1977), which is discussed in greater detail under *Essential Hypertension* in this chapter. Treating cigarette smokers with a meditation, biofeedback, and health education program, these authors reported a 60 percent smoking reduction at 6-month follow-up.

Autogenics (AT)

One of the earliest North American applications of AT came from Canada (Orme & Snider, 1964). Alcoholics participating in group AT sessions reported reduced anxiety and improved sleep. Drug consumption effects were not reported. More recently, Roszell and Chaney (1982) reported similar anecdotal data with former heroin and polydrug users. Both of the above studies supplemented AT with intentional formulae (see Chapter 4).

Other Relaxation Techniques

Snowden (1978) compared an unspecified method of relaxation with relaxation-assisted covert sensitization. Relaxation brought no relief from heroin use for individuals exhibiting either an internal or external locus of control (Rotter, 1966).

Schubert (1983) assigned smokers to three conditions: unspecified relaxation, hypnosis, or no treatment. At 4-month posttreatment, 58 percent of the relaxation group was abstinent. This quit rate was equivalent to the hypnosis group and superior to the no-treatment group.

Relaxation Comparisons

Marlatt and his associates tested Benson's (1975) meditation against progressive relaxation with heavy social drinking college students (reported in duplicate: Marlatt & Marques, 1977; Marlatt, Pagano, Rose, & Marques, 1984). Bibliotherapy and no-treatment control groups were also included. The meditation and progressive relaxation groups achieved significant and equivalent reductions in alcohol consumption, as did the bibliotherapy group. Contrary to expectations, the relaxation groups showed decreases in locus of control.

Final Comments on Relaxation Therapy for Drug Abuse

In their review of the TM for drug abuse literature, Aron and Aron (1980) were less concerned than myself regarding the methodological shortcomings cited above, as they drew favorable conclusions on the application of TM for this problem. In the absence of a single well-controlled study in this area, I believe it is premature to draw any conclusions, save for these preliminary results are encouraging. However, as drug abuse is such a tenacious and multi-faceted problem, the comprehensive treatment package approach outlined in Chapter 6 is probably preferable to any single treatment.

Treatment plausibility from the point of view of the consumer is an important concern. In this vein, Hynd and his associates have collected credibility data in relaxation therapy. Both smokers (Hynd, Stratton, & Severson, 1978) and nonsmokers (Hynd, Chambers, Stratton, & Moan, 1977) view relaxation therapy for smoking control as highly credible. Despite this, I cannot recommend relaxation as a unitary intervention for smoking. The thrust of the small amount of available data in this area is only mildly positive. I am also struck by how old the studies in this area are. This suggests that researchers have long abandoned this avenue.

ATHLETIC PERFORMANCE

Mainly two reasons have been advanced to justify teaching athletes relaxation. First, the distracting and debilitating effects of excessive performance anxiety can be reduced. Second, greater concentration and efficiency of effort can be attained.

Progressive Relaxation (PR)

There is one study testing PR in this area (Lanning & Hisanaga, 1983). Female high school volleyball players were trained in PR and breath control or untreated. Reported anxiety was diminished in the treated group only. More impressively, only treated subjects exhibited improved performance in competition.

Meditation

Griffiths, Steel, Vaccaro, and Karpman (1981) randomly assigned neophyte scuba divers to six sessions of electromyographic biofeedback, taped meditation (details of the procedure not given), or listening to a neutral tape. The treated groups manifested less STAI-State anxiety (State-Trait Anxiety Inventory; Spielberger, Gorsuch, & Lushene, 1970) than the control group. Negative results were obtained on STAI-Trait anxiety, several physiological indices, and an underwater performance test.

Autogenics (AT)

The group that tested meditation with scuba trainees (see Griffiths et al., 1981, above) has since assessed the combined treatments of breath regulation, AT, and cognitive rehearsal of performance skills with this same population (Griffiths, Steel, Vaccaro, Allen, & Karpman, 1985). They observed reduced STAI-State anxiety and improved scuba performance in these students, compared to others not given this extra training.

Several authors (Barolin, 1977; Krenz, 1984; Monus, 1977; Schilling, 1980; Tomita, 1977) have recounted their uncontrolled use of AT (at times in conjunction with other treatment modalities) with competitive athletes. Each notes successes and failures. Some have supplemented AT relaxation with intentional formulae (see Chapter 4). Observed benefits include improved performance, decreased anxiety, decreased insomnia, increased enjoyment of practice and competition, and improved general well-being. Some problems noted were decreased strength following deep relaxation and frustration when expected performance enhancement did not occur.

Final Comments on Relaxation Therapy for Athletic Performance

The rationale for training athletes, particularly tense ones, in relaxation is plausible, and the small amount of available data is encouraging. It may well be that future research will carve a valued position for relaxation therapy within the burgeoning field of sports psychology.

INSOMNIA

Insomnia—difficulty initiating and maintaining adequate sleep—affects a large proportion of the population on an occasional or chronic basis (see psychophysiological disorders of initiating and maintaining sleep, Association of Sleep Disorders Centers, 1979). Clinical practitioners routinely distinguish between primary insomnia (psychological causation) and secondary insomnia (an independent disorder such as arthritis or depression, or other sleep problems, such as apnea, that induce sleep disruption). The sequelae of insomnia include daytime irritability, sleepiness, and impaired concentration. The most prominent factors thought to be responsible for primary insomnia are intrusive cognitions, somatic arousal, and incompatible behaviors at bedtime. Relaxation therapy is employed mainly for primary insomnia, but it also may be used in conjunction with other treatments for secondary insomnia. More extensive insomnia reviews focusing on the issues of assessment (Bootzin & Engle-Friedman, 1981; Lichstein & Kelley, 1979) and treatment (Borkovec, 1982; Lichstein & Fischer, 1985) are available for the interested reader.

Progressive Relaxation (PR)

PR has been applied more frequently to insomnia than to any other disorder. In part motivated by his own sleep difficulties (Jacobson, 1938a, p. 111), Jacobson began studying the relationship between relaxation and sleep induction as early as 1908 (Jacobson, 1938b, pp. 232–233). Over the years, Jacobson (1920b, 1921, 1938a, 1970) maintained an active interest in insomnia treatment, including the publication of a book on this subject (Jacobson, 1938b). All of the above data were anecdotal, Jacobson having never conducted a controlled study of PR for insomnia.

More recently, others have also provided uncontrolled accounts of PR effectiveness for insomnia with medical outpatients (Hinkle & Lutker, 1972), and a hemophiliac (Varni, 1980; also included meditation, imagery, and stimulus control). Ascher and Efran (1978) estimated that some 85 percent of insomniacs they have treated were responsive to PR. Attaining somewhat greater experimental control, Mitchell and White (1977b) documented the separate and combined benefits of PR, pleasant imagery, and cognitive restructuring in a combined within- and between-subjects design. PR produced a large sleep latency decrease with one group (29 minutes), the introduction of imagery gained an additional reduction of 13 minutes with this same group, and the combination of PR and imagery was associated with a 21 minute decrease in a second group. As with Jacobson, all of these reports relied on clients' sleep estimates to gauge therapy progress.

Beginning in the early 1970s, largely due to Borkovec's contributions, the PR for insomnia literature witnessed major methodological advances, including the introduction of methodological innovations that have since been embraced by clinical researchers outside the sleep domain. Borkovec's research will now be reviewed.

Borkovec's first published study on insomnia compared three sessions of PR, hypnotic relaxation, self-relaxation control, or no treatment with insomniac college students (Borkovec & Fowles, 1973). Pre/post comparisons of self-reported latency to sleep revealed significant improvement for the PR (46/25 minutes) and hypnosis (43/24 minutes) groups, but not the no-treatment group (44/44 minutes). Similar results prevailed for number of awakenings during the night and feelings of restedness in the morning. PR and hypnosis did not differ on any measure and, surprisingly, they were superior to the self-relaxation control group only on ratings of morning restedness. Within-session physiological changes on skin conductance, muscle tension, and heart and respiration rates failed to correlate with improvement on any sleep index, contrary to predictions based on a physiological arousal theory of insomnia.

Subsequent articles, employing a comparable design, found PR to be equally effective as single item systematic desensitization with home PR practice (Borkovec, Steinmark, & Nau, 1973; Steinmark & Borkovec, 1974) or without home PR practice (Borkovec, Steinmark, & Nau, 1973), and more effective than placebo and no treatment (Steinmark & Borkovec, 1974). Steinmark and Borkovec (1974) collected 5-month follow-up data by telephone. Compared to the last treatment week, the PR and desensitization groups reported significant decreases in latency to sleep, while the placebo group increased nonsignificantly on this measure. This same study is particularly noteworthy in that it introduced two exemplary methodological strategies affording greater confidence in the results. First, following the pilot work of Borkovec and Nau (1972), client credibility ratings of their respective treatments confirmed comparable expectancy for improvement existed between the groups. Second, counterdemand instructions (i.e., expect no improvement) prevailed for the first 3 weeks before positive demand instructions (i.e., sleep improvement should occur about now) were presented in the last week. The PR and desensitization groups improved during the counterdemand period; the placebo group "improved" by self-reports only after the positive demand instruction was invoked.

The last study in this series (Borkovec & Weerts, 1976) challenged the accumulated findings to date. For the first time, electroencephalography supplemented self-report sleep data. Insomniac college students were randomly assigned to four sessions of PR, placebo, or no treatment. Counterdemand instructions prevailed during the first 3 weeks and positive demand during the 4th. All subjects submitted to two consecutive nights in the sleep laboratory during pretreatment, week 3 (counterdemand), and week 4 (positive demand).

Comparisons of latency to sleep in the laboratory at week 3 found no group differences. At week 4, PR was superior to no treatment, but it did not surpass the placebo group. PR subjects went from 29 to 12 minutes latency to sleep in the pretreatment and week 4 assessments. At these same points, the placebo group registered 25 and 21 minutes sleep latency, but the differences between the two groups were nonsignificant. Analyses of self-report data also yielded equivocal results. Credibility ratings were comparable in the PR and placebo groups.

Telephone assessments at 1-year posttreatment indicated that the PR group maintained their self-reported sleep improvement from 40 minutes at baseline, to 28 minutes during treatment week 4, and 27 minutes at follow-up, while the placebo group now reported a 58 minute latency to sleep, exceeding their baseline level by 5 minutes. Although the results of this study favor PR, the margin of superiority over placebo and no treatment was less than that observed in Borkovec's previous studies. Several other sleep studies by Borkovec contrasted PR with passive relaxation and are reported in the relaxation comparisons section below.

Numerous other, mostly well-designed PR for insomnia studies are summarized in Table 7.1. All of these studies employed random assignment to groups, identified latency to sleep as the primary target, and employed self-report estimates to measure sleep parameters. One study (Freedman & Papsdorf, 1976) also obtained sleep laboratory data before and after treatment, which confirmed the utility of PR.

Inspection of Table 7.1 reveals that PR was superior to placebo and no-treatment groups at posttreatment in 8 of 14 studies. Only in one study (Turner & Ascher, 1982) did PR effects surpass those of another bona fide treatment. Follow-up data collected 2 months to 1 year after treatment, although marred

TABLE 7.1. Progressive Relaxation for Sleep-Onset Insomnia Group Design Studies[a]

| Study | Treatment Groups[b] | | | | | | | | | Sleep Latency Improvement | |
	PR	EEG	EMG	MED	SD	SC	PI	PL	NT	Posttreatment	Follow-up
Ascher & Efran, 1978	+				+		+		+	PI>PR/SD=NT	
Bell, 1979	+	+							+	EEG>PR=NT	
Bootzin, 1973	+					+		+	+	SC>PR>PL=NT	
Cannici, Malcolm, & Peek, 1983	+								+	PR>NT	PR>NT
Carr-Kaffashan & Woolfolk, 1979	+			+				+		PR/MED>PL	PR/MED>PL
Freedman & Papsdorf, 1976	+		+					+		PR=EMG>PL	PR=EMG=PL
Gershman & Clouser, 1974	+				+				+	PR=SD>NT	PR=SD>NT
Hughes & Hughes, 1978	+		+			+		+		PR=EMG=SC=PL	PR=EMG=SC=PL
Lacks, Bertelson, Gans, & Kunkel, 1983	+					+	+	+		SC>PR=PI=PL	SC>PR=PI=PL
Lick & Heffler, 1977	+							+	+	PR>PL=NT	
Nicassio, Boylan, & McCabe, 1982	+		+					+	+	PR=EMG=PL>NT	PR=EMG=PL
Toler, 1978	+					+			+	PR=SC=NT	PR=SC
Turner & Ascher, 1979	+					+	+	+	+	PR=SC=PI>PL=NT	
Turner & Ascher, 1982	+					+	+		+	PR=SC>PI=NT	

[a]This table omits Borkovec's research reviewed in the text and studies reviewed in the *Relaxation Comparisons* section. [b]The treatment group abbreviations signify progressive relaxation (PR), electroencephalographic biofeedback (EEG), electromyographic biofeedback (EMG), meditation (MED), systematic desensitization (SD), stimulus control (SC), paradoxical instruction (PI), placebo treatments (PL), and no treatment (NT).

by high attrition rates, mostly indicated good maintenance of sleep improvement.

Averaging across the studies in Table 7.1, PR subjects estimated their latency to sleep to be 75 minutes before treatment and 42 minutes after. However, the importance of these gains is tempered by the fact that the subjects also invested an additional 20 or so minutes to practice PR, a most interesting point raised by Freedman and Papsdorf (1976). Among those studies that reported follow-up data, PR subjects averaged 45 minutes latency to sleep at follow-up.

Some of these studies reported additional PR benefits accruing to middle of the night awakenings (Carr-Kaffashan & Woolfolk, 1979; Gershman & Clouser, 1974; Turner & Ascher, 1979, 1982) and ratings of overall quality of sleep (Carr-Kaffashan & Woolfolk, 1979; Gershman & Clouser, 1974; Lick & Heffler, 1977; Turner & Ascher, 1979, 1982). Studies (Freedman & Papsdorf, 1976; Lick & Heffler, 1977) inquiring into the relationship between physiological changes within training sessions and sleep improvement found no correlation. Lastly, two studies compared experienced and novice PR therapists. One (Turner & Ascher, 1982) found the former to be more effective, and the other (Lick & Heffler, 1977) found no difference.

Although the great majority of insomnia studies were interested primarily in sleep latency disturbances, incidental data on benefits for middle of the night awakenings has also been reported, as noted in the preceding paragraph. One of Jacobson's (1921) earliest publications described the case of a woman who fell "to sleep readily, but awakened at about 2 a.m., then hearing the clock strike for hours" (p. 245). After 11 PR treatments, this problem was largely remediated.

Only two recent studies, both from the same research group, focused on sleep-maintenance insomnia. In their first report, Coates and Thoresen (1979) presented a multifaceted treatment package, including PR, imagery, breath manipulations, cognitive restructuring, and cue-controlled relaxation, to a 58-year-old woman, presenting with a 33-year history of sleep-maintenance insomnia. Sleep laboratory assessments documented large reductions in the frequency and duration of awakenings, particularly during the first third of the night. In their more recent effort (Thoresen, Coates, Kirmil-Gray, & Rosekind, 1981), the efficacy of a similar treatment package in reducing the number and length of awakenings was replicated with three individuals.

Childhood insomnia has been a neglected area of study, probably because of poorly articulated complaints by children and poor detection by parents (Dixon, Monroe, & Jakim, 1981). To date, there are two uncontrolled case studies, concerning an 11-year-old (Weil & Goldfried, 1973) and a 13-year-old (Anderson, 1979), that recommend the use of PR for childhood insomnia. Anderson (1979) also reduced parental attention to sleep complaints, suggesting that the child's insomnia, or insomnia complaints, were under operant control.

Self-control Relaxation (SCR)

As insomnia is highly situation specific and is readily accessible to static forms of relaxation, there has been little interest in SCR for insomnia. The sole study in this area (Mitchell, 1979) tested SCR, SCR/pleasant imagery combined, didactic treatment, and no treatment. The didactic treatment is somewhat novel in the sleep literature and involved educating individuals about variability in sleep needs, scheduling sleep more intelligently, etc. At posttreatment and 6-week follow-up, sleep latency improvement in the SCR/imagery group exceeded all others, and the SCR and didatic groups were equivalently superior to no treatment. Ratings of presleep tension and intrusive cognitions followed a similar pattern. Apparently, imagery was a worthwhile addition to SCR.

Passive Relaxation

Borkovec conducted a series of studies in this area, and these are presented in the *Relaxation Comparisons* section below. French and Tupin (1974) were among the first to apply passive relaxation to insomnia. They combined this with pleasant imagery and reported success in three of five cases.

Haynes and his colleagues have made the most important contribution to this area. In their first study (Haynes, Woodward, Moran, & Alexander, 1974), insomniac college students received six sessions of either passive relaxation or placebo treatment. Although major sleep latency gains were made by the placebo group according to pre/posttreatment self-reports (53/40 minutes to fall asleep), the relaxation group did significantly better (61/34 minutes to fall asleep). The relaxation group also reduced number of awakenings during the night from 2.8 to 0.7, whereas the placebo group went from 2.6 to 1.3.

Haynes, Sides, and Lockwood (1977) replicated the above design and added an electromyographic biofeedback group. Passive relaxation made significant pre/post gains in latency to sleep (51/26 minutes) as did biofeedback (49/23 minutes), but the placebo group did not (48/45 minutes). The identical pattern obtained at 3-month follow-up for latency to sleep (17, 19, and 51 minutes for relaxation, biofeedback, and placebo, respectively), and at posttreatment and 3-month follow-up for awakenings during the night. Scanty data at 1-year follow-up suggested the two active groups maintained their gains well.

Finally, Shealy (1979) contrasted passive relaxation, passive relaxation/stimulus control treatment combined, placebo treatment, self-monitoring only, and no treatment. During the counterdemand period, the combination treatment surpassed passive relaxation alone, which in turn was more effective than the control groups. During the positive demand period and at 6-month follow-up, the two active treatments were equally effective and superior to the control groups in reducing latency to sleep. Chronic insomniacs had a poorer treatment response than individuals whose insomnia developed within the past year. Subsequent analyses (Shealy, Lowe, & Ritzler, 1980) indicated reductions in MMPI (Minnesota Multiphasic Personality Inventory; Hathaway & McKinley, 1943) scales for hysteria, hypochondriasis, and depression accompanied sleep latency reductions.

Meditation

There are relatively little data available here. One study already alluded to in the progressive relaxation section (Carr-Kaffashan & Woolfolk, 1979) presented progressive relaxation and meditation in combination, preventing evaluation of their separate contributions. A second meditation study by this same group (Woolfolk, Carr-Kaffashan, McNulty, & Lehrer, 1976) observed equal efficacy between progressive relaxation and meditation (presented in *Relaxation Comparisons* section below).

In the only insomnia trial of Transcendental Meditation, ten insomniacs went from an average 76 minutes latency to sleep to 15 minutes following treatment in a single group, pre-post design (Miskiman, 1977a). At 1-year follow-up, reported latency to sleep was still at 15 minutes (Miskiman, 1977b).

Alperson and Biglan (1979) conducted an interesting study evaluating a self-administered treatment manual combining Benson's (1975) mantra meditation and stimulus control procedures. Other conditions were (a) a manual of placebo exercises and (b) no treatment, self-monitoring only. Latency to sleep was significantly and equally improved in the treatment and placebo groups at posttreatment, while untreated subjects worsened. This last group was then administered treatment, and by 6 weeks posttreatment, the three groups were indistinguishable. Separate analyses on an elderly (age 55 or older) subset of the treatment group revealed they were unresponsive to treatment and experienced particular difficulties with awakenings during the night.

Autogenics (AT)

Luthe and Schultz (1969b) list some 110 foreign citations of AT for insomnia. This same book (p. 142) described Luthe's successful treatment of sleep maintenance insomnia in 91 out of 100 clients. Additional confirmatory data from uncontrolled studies has appeared in English (Graham, Wright, Toman, & Mark, 1975; Jus & Jus, 1977b; Kahn, Baker, & Weiss, 1968; Traub, Jencks, & Bliss, 1973). The Jus and Jus (1977b) article is noteworthy. These investigators employed only the heaviness and warmth sequences, as their basic research (Jus & Jus, 1977a) revealed that drowsiness accompanies these first two standard exercises, but is replaced by a refreshed feeling if the last four standard exercises follow.

Coursey, Frankel, Gaarder, and Mott (1980) conducted the most rigorous test of AT for insomnia to date, and obtained modest results. Volunteers from the community were randomly assigned to AT, electromyographic biofeedback, or electrosleep therapy. Three of six biofeedback subjects, two of six AT subjects, and none of 10 electrosleep subjects satisfied stringent sleep laboratory and subjective success criteria. Treatment successes also registered gains on sleep efficiency percentage, awakenings during the night, and other indicators.

Other Relaxation Techniques

In Chapter 5, I presented the rationale and procedures of ocular relaxation. There have been two clinical trials of this method for insomnia, and one of these (Lichstein & Blew, 1980) also tested progressive relaxation and may be found in the *Relaxation Comparisons* section below.

Lichstein (1983) treated five student insomniacs with ocular relaxation in a single subject withdrawal design. Averaging latency to sleep across subjects, subjects estimated this to be 70 minutes during baseline I, 34 minutes during ocular relaxation I, 43 minutes during baseline II, and 24 minutes during ocular relaxation II. At about 10 months posttreatment, all subjects except one maintained their improvement very well. The group average was 29 minutes latency to sleep. Ratings of cognitive arousal at bedtime closely tracked changes in latency to sleep.

Relaxation Comparisons

Two studies contrasted progressive relaxation (PR) and autogenic training (Freedman, Hauri, Coursey, & Frankel, 1978; Nicassio & Bootzin, 1974). There were no significant differences between these treatments in either study. Nicassio and Bootzin found both methods to be superior to control groups, but Freedman et al. did not. Other comparative studies of PR found it to be equivalent to two versions of metronome-conditioned relaxation, and all three superior to no treatment (Pendleton & Tasto, 1976), equivalent to an unspecified imagery exercise, and both superior to no treatment (Ribordy, 1976), and equivalent to ocular relaxation, though neither surpassed placebo and no-treatment groups on latency to sleep (Lichstein & Blew, 1980).

Borkovec and his colleagues conducted several tests of PR versus passive relaxation, and in all cases, PR proved superior. In their first study in this series (Borkovec, Kaloupek, & Slama, 1975), insomniac college students showed greater sleep latency reductions with PR than with passive relaxation, placebo treatment, or no treatment, according to self-reported sleep assessments during the counterdemand period. During the positive demand period (last week of treatment), only the PR condition was significantly different from no treatment, with the other two groups falling between them. At 5-month follow-up, only the PR group made further gains since treatment ended, although there were no significant differences between the treated groups at follow-up. A subsequent, similarly designed study (Borkovec, Grayson, O'Brien, & Weerts, 1979) with sleep laboratory evaluations before and after treatment confirmed the superiority of PR over passive relaxation with idiopathic insomniacs (insomnia diagnosis verified in sleep laboratory), but not pseudoinsomniacs (sleep laboratory evaluation did not reveal insomnia). Self-report data indicated PR produced larger sleep latency reductions than passive relaxation in both insomnia types.

Borkovec and Hennings (1978) addressed the same issue as above with a novel approach. They extracted the passive relaxation component (i.e., physiological attention focusing) from PR, leaving a tense-release procedure having no internal focusing component. Student insomniacs were randomly assigned to four sessions of taped PR, taped tense-release relaxation without physiological self-monitoring (subjects' attention was devoted to pleasant images unrelated to the body), or no treatment. Both treated groups made equivalent, significant gains in latency to sleep, and the no-treatment group did not. In summary, Borkovec contends that the main active ingredient in PR is the tension-release component.

Woolfolk and McNulty (1983) recently conducted the first attempt to replicate Borkovec's consistent findings. Insomniac volunteers were randomly assigned to conditions providing a complete factorial exploration of tense-release cycles and imagery. The groups were: (a) tense-release with somatic focusing (PR), (b) somatic focusing without tense-release cycles (passive relaxation), (c) neutral imagery with tense-release cycles (as in Borkovec & Hennings above), and (d) neutral imagery without tense-release cycles. A fifth no-treatment group was included. All four treated groups significantly reduced their latency to sleep from baseline to the third (counterdemand) and fourth (positive demand) weeks, while the no-treatment group was unchanged. However, at week 3, only those change scores from the two imagery groups (c & d) surpassed change scores from the no-treatment group, and at week 4, only the imagery with no tense-release group (d) surpassed no treatment. By 6-month follow-up, the two imagery groups (c & d) surpassed the two somatic focusing groups (a & b), as imagery effects on sleep onset continued to improve, and the somatic focusing groups reverted toward baseline. In sum, this study sharply contrasts with Borkovec's data, in that the tense-release operation did not prove to be important. Data bearing on this question from outside the insomnia area also indicate that the tense-release operation does not serve a key function in PR (see discussion of Haynes, Moseley, & McGowan, 1975, Chapter 3).

The final study in this section also included PR, now contrasted with a meditation technique combining breath awareness with a mantra (Woolfolk, Carr-Kaffashan, McNulty, & Lehrer, 1976). A no-treatment group was also included. From baseline to posttreatment to 6-month follow-up, sleep latency measures were 65, 29, and 27 minutes, respectively, for progressive relaxation, and 74, 34, and 25 minutes for meditation. These changes were significant and equal, and they were greater than the no-treatment group, which did not change.

Final Comments on Relaxation Therapy for Insomnia

There can be no doubt that relaxation relieves insomnia. However, four qualifications do apply.

First, current research trends (discussed in Borkovec, 1982) suggest that sleep suffers more from cognitive than physiological arousal, and that relaxation efficacy may derive from distracting attention away from worries. The development of more effective means of capturing errant thoughts may supplant part of the role that relaxation now plays in insomnia treatment.

Second, relaxation treatments do not ordinarily convert an insomniac into a noninsomniac. Rather, the insomnia problem is lessened.

Third, insomniacs vary along numerous nonorthogonal dimensions: sleep onset versus sleep maintenance, objective (verified in sleep lab) versus pseudo or subjective (disputed in sleep lab), primary versus secondary, and others. Borkovec's research (Borkovec, Grayson, O'Brien, & Weerts, 1979) has begun to isolate which types of insomnia are responsive to relaxation therapy. More research along these lines is strongly indicated.

Fourth, insomnia is most prevalent in the elderly, and this population is least able to tolerate the side effects from the most common treatment for this disorder, sleep medication (Bootzin, Engle-Friedman, & Hazelwood, 1983; Siegal & Lichstein, 1980). To date, there has been surprisingly little investigation of psychological control of geriatric insomnia, particularly in the domain of relaxation therapy. While didactic interventions, which educate the elderly as to their changing sleep needs and attempt to alter sleep goals, appear promising (Lichstein & Fischer, 1985), relaxation therapy certainly warrants thorough trials. To this end, passive relaxation, meditation, autogenics, etc., may be more acceptable than progressive relaxation, due to the latter's strenuousness.

Borkovec's studies consistently found passive relaxation to be a weak intervention, whereas the research of Woolfolk, Haynes, and Shealy found it to be efficacious. As Shealy (1979) pointed out, Borkovec only used four treatment sessions compared to six by himself and Haynes. Passive relaxation may require more treatment exposure than progressive relaxation. However, this conclusion is contradicted by the fact that Woolfolk and McNulty (1983) also used four sessions and obtained a successful outcome with passive relaxation.

Several attempts to relate insomnia severity (Lacks, Bertelson, Gans, & Kunkel, 1983; Shealy, Lowe, & Ritzler, 1980), insomnia chronicity (Shealy et al., 1980), client gender (Shealy et al., 1980), and client psychopathology to relaxation treatment outcome have been unsuccessful. In contrast, some studies have found that females respond to PR better than males (Freedman, Hauri, Coursey, & Frankel, 1978; Nicassio & Bootzin, 1974), and middle-aged subjects respond better than the elderly (Lick & Heffler, 1971; Nicassio & Bootzin, 1974).

MUSCULAR DYSFUNCTION

Chronic contracture, intermittent spiking, and diminished capacity are some of the typical ways in which muscles function improperly. The first two classes of disorders involve muscle overactivity secondary to a variety of instigators, including degenerative diseases of the central nervous system, spontaneous neural discharges, and acute anxiety. The third class, diminished capacity, refers to conditions such as paralysis and atrophy and has received very little attention from relaxation therapists compared to the first two groups. Basmajian (1979) and others pioneered high precision methods of biofeedback to effect neuromuscular reeducation of muscles exhibiting diminished capacity, and this work will not be included in the present discussion. Similarly, electromyographic (EMG) biofeedback frequently has been employed to reduce excessive muscular activity, and this approach has been reviewed elsewhere (Keefe & Surwit, 1978).

Progressive Relaxation (PR)

In one of his earliest publications, Jacobson (1920a) reported a case of PR for head tics. A few years hence, Jacobson (1925b, 1927b) applied his method to treat esophageal spasm and spastic colon. These two studies presented several case histories documenting a positive clinical response. Latimer (1981) applied EMG biofeedback and PR to the same disorder, and obtained positive clinical effects but no alteration in underlying spasm. We (Lichstein, Eakin, & Dunn, 1986) have observed analogous but weaker findings, in combining PR and EMG biofeedback to intervene with a case of oropharyngeal dysphagia (swallowing difficulty due to muscle spasms). Along these same lines, Lashley and Elder (1982) observed marked reduction of spasms of the chest muscle in their client following presentation of a combination of frontalis EMG biofeedback, PR, and social contingencies. Controlled trials have yet to be conducted in this area of upper alimentary canal and thoracic muscle spasms.

A trend in current research has addressed the problems of muscular disability arising from diseases of the central nervous system: Huntington's disease, Parkinson's disease, and cerebral palsy. Two case history accounts (Bannister, 1977; Macpherson, 1967) reported on the usefulness of PR in controlling the choreiform movements (involuntary, rigid, jerky striate muscle action) associated with Huntington's disease. Although these articles described very positive treatment effects and good therapeutic maintenance at long-term follow-up, they both included conjoint treatments and other methodological ills inherent in case histories.

Spoth, Etringer, Gaffney, and Hutzell (1982) incorporated greater methodological rigor in treating two Huntington's patients. The patients received only PR treatment following baselines of dissimilar lengths. Effects were evaluated by unobtrusive behavioral observations of choreiform movements outside of the treatment sessions and peg manipulation tests of muscle coordination. No improvement in choreiform movements occurred in the more severely impaired patient, but he did show significant progress on the muscle coordination tests. The second patient achieved major reductions in choreiform movements, but no benefits in coordination. Follow-up data were collected on the second patient only. At 8 months, these data were encouraging, but difficult to interpret, as a medication increase had been initiated in the interim since posttreatment.

Shumaker (1980) reported disappointing results in testing a combination of PR and EMG biofeedback with Parkinson's disease tremor. Pre-post evaluations of manual dexterity and speed on two pegboard tasks revealed that gains made over 15 weekly treatment sessions did not exceed those changes accruing to a no-treatment group. Ortega (1978) employed similar peg tasks to evaluate taped PR effects on cerebral palsy spasticity. In a multiple baseline design across four subjects, improvements averaging a 24 percent increase in speed closely corresponded to the introduction of treatment. Therapeutic gains were largely maintained at 3-week follow-up.

Shifting to less catastrophic causes of muscular dysfunction, Moss, Garrett, and Chiodo (1982) provided an excellent overview of the complex subject of temporomandibular joint (TMJ) pain. Chronic contracture of various cranial muscles, most notably the masseter, is but one of an array of factors that may lead to the TMJ syndrome, characterized by jaw pain, constricted range of mandibular movement, dizziness, and other symptoms. A closely related disorder, myofascial pain dysfunction syndrome (MPDS), is distinguished by unilateral jaw pain and no detectable organic pathology (Moss et al., 1982).

Gessel and Alderman (1971) were the first to apply PR to disorders of this sort. Eleven individuals diagnosed with MPDS received meticulous training in PR at a pace akin to that recommended by Jacobson (1964b). Treatment results, presented in the form of a clinical narrative, yielded six successful and five unsuccessful cases. The authors concluded that PR treatment failure for this disorder was associated with higher levels of depression among the nonresponders compared to the responders. Others (Reading & Raw, 1976) have also provided successful cases of PR for mandibular pain.

Brooke, Stenn, and Mothersill (1977) offered a combination of PR, autogenics, biofeedback, and coping skills training to 22 MPDS patients who failed to benefit from conservative dental treatment: tranquilizers, occlusal splint, and/or physiotherapy. Twenty-one of these patients exhibited "marked improvement" after eight weekly treatment sessions. In a more detailed, subsequent report (Stenn, Mothersill, & Brooke, 1979), a similar psychological treatment protocol was tested with 11 MPDS patients. All patients received PR and cognitive behavior therapy (e.g., assertiveness training, rational emotive therapy) to combat the assumed etiologic role of stress. In addition, half of the patients also received biofeedback derived from the masseter muscle. Over the 7-week treatment course, all subjects exhibited significant decreases in self-reported pain and objective MPDS symptoms, as revealed in a dental examination, though the biofeedback subjects made greater gains in both measures than the subjects who did not receive biofeedback. Interestingly, there were no differences in masseter muscle tension between these two groups, thus casting ambiguity over the mechanism of MPDS relief. Therapeutic gains were maintained by all subjects at a 3-month follow-up.

In the most carefully conducted study in this area to date (Moss, Wedding, & Sanders, 1983), five TMJ patients received a treatment sequence comprising taped PR and EMG biofeedback in separate, single case experimental designs. Three of these five patients showed TMJ improvement on such measures as jaw pain and tension. Except in the case of persistent shoulder pain in one patient, the effectiveness of PR exceeded that of EMG biofeedback in the three successful patients.

Bruxism refers to teeth grinding (Morse, 1982), and this may also give rise to TMJ dysfunction symptomatology. Dentists (e.g., Zeldow, 1976) acknowledge the role of jaw and facial relaxation in treating this disorder, but little systematic data on this account has been forthcoming. Lashley and Elder (1982) reported on one patient who found relief from this disorder subsequent to biofeedback (from the frontalis and masseter muscles) and PR combined.

Aphasia—impaired speech secondary to brain damage—may result, in part, from excessive tension in the speech musculature. Marshall and Watts (1976) trained 16 aphasic adults in PR and observed significantly improved speech following these sessions, compared to speech following rest control periods.

Self-control Relaxation (SCR)

Turpin and Powell (1984) presented three well-documented case studies of individuals presenting with longstanding multiple tics. Cue-controlled relaxation proved therapeutically viable with only one of these clients.

Passive Relaxation

Temporomandibular joint (TMJ) pain patients were treated with either masseter muscle biofeedback or taped passive relaxation (Funch & Gale, 1984). Both treatments proved effective, and at 2-year follow-up, some 60 percent of passive relaxation subjects evinced significant improvement. Subjects who profited most from relaxation tended to be younger, suffered TMJ pain a shorter period of time, and reported multiple psychosomatic complaints. The main thrust of these results were replicated in a second study (Gale & Funch, 1984).

Although adequate details on the method of relaxation were not provided, it appears that Jackson and Hughes (1978) used a form of taped passive relaxation, in combination with imaginal rehearsal, to help fourth grade students relax their musculature to improve their handwriting. Students selected for their poor handwriting practiced relaxation and were compared, in a pre-posttest design, with two no-treatment groups matched for poor handwriting ability or having normal handwriting skills. Social attention was equated between the three groups by giving the two control groups an amount of didactic instruction equal to the duration of relaxation training given the experimental group. Analyses of handwriting samples revealed that the relaxation group achieved significantly greater improvement on several writing indices (e.g., slant, spacing), compared to both the matched and normal groups, which did not differ from each other. Carter and Synolds (1974) had previously reported on a single group outcome study testing the same relaxation method. Carter and Synolds did not conduct statistical analyses, but their narrative report positively evaluated relaxation effects on the handwriting of children diagnosed as minimally brain injured. More recently, Jackson, Jolly, and Hamilton (1980) demonstrated that relaxation alone was less effective than relaxation combined with instruction in handwriting technique.

Meditation

A case study attempting to gain control over treatment induced dyskinesia (Szekely, Turner, & Jacob, 1982) is in interesting contrast to much of the progressive relaxation literature described above. A Parkinson's disease patient suffered severe head, arm, and leg jerking as side effects of L-dopa therapy. Zen breath meditation appeared effective in diminishing these mannerisms, but other threats to internal validity (placebo effect, marital stress, etc.) could also explain the reduced dyskinesia.

Stuttering is a complex problem often having multiple causes. Tension dysfunction of the speech musculature may be one contributing factor. McIntyre, Silverman, and Trotter (1974) collected some retrospective, anecdotal data on six Transcendental Meditation (TM) practitioners suggesting that TM benefited their stuttering.

Autogenics (AT)

Uchiyama (1965) employed AT relaxation exercises as part of broad-spectrum autogenic therapy (meditative exercises, an organ-specific formula, intentional formulae, and graphomotor retraining) to treat the writer's cramp of two telephone operators. The case study data presented were very positive, but defy determination of the active therapy ingredient(s).

In one of the few relaxation studies to target diminished muscular capacity, Wolf and Binder-Macleod (1983) combined AT, progressive relaxation, and electromyographic biofeedback to improve the walking of stroke victims. Other conditions were biofeedback (both strengthening and relaxing as need be) for relevant muscles, biofeedback for irrelevant muscles, and a no-treatment control. The relevant biofeedback group attained some small gains in range of motion and functional walking ability. The relaxation group (and the other two groups) made no gains.

Other Relaxation Techniques

Sharpe (1974) reported the case history of a 51-year-old male who, for 10 months, suffered blepharospasm: eyelid closure due to local muscle spasm (Faulstich, Carnrike, & Williamson, 1985). After 14 weeks of relaxation practice (method unspecified), symptomatology was virtually eliminated, and therapy gains were maintained at 9-month follow-up.

Relaxation Comparisons

A study by DeAjuriaguerra, Badaracco, Trillat, and Soubiran (cited in Schultz & Luthe, 1959) treated 10 cases of writer's cramp with progressive relaxation (orthodox Jacobsonian style) and nine cases with orthodox autogenic training, and concluded, in their narrative analysis, that autogenics was superior. All 10 subjects receiving autogenics registered some degree of improvement, including four who were symptom free, but only six of nine receiving progressive relaxation exhibited improvement, and none were symptom free.

Final Comments on Relaxation Therapy for Muscular Dysfunction

Muscular dysfunction presents an excellent opportunity for relaxation application, particularly for progressive relaxation with its muscular focus. Surprisingly, this domain has not inspired a great deal of effort by relaxation researchers, and the caliber of experimental methodologies was often weak when interventions were tested.

Spasm and contracture conditions, without organic substrata, are particularly inviting of relaxation therapy. Alimentary spasm, facial tics, TMJ syndrome, bruxism, and writer's cramp are illustrative of psychogenic disorders that promise good relaxation therapy prognosis. In some cases, the wedding of electromyographic biofeedback and relaxation would prove more efficacious than either treatment separately. Single subject experimental designs (Hersen & Barlow, 1976) appear well suited to engineer conservative methodologies for this class of disorders, as muscular dysfunction often manifests in idiosyncratic forms. Control group design studies would, of course, be desirable when adequate numbers of subjects are available.

SEIZURES

Manifesting with one or more attentional, mood, or musculoskeletal symptomatology, seizures are often multidetermined and in some cases stress induced. Basic and clinical research recommend the use of biofeedback for seizure control (reviewed in Lubar & Deering, 1981). A smaller and methodologically weaker literature on relaxation therapy is reviewed below.

Progressive Relaxation (PR)

There is one case history (Mostofsky, 1975) of a 28-year-old woman whose mixed seizure disorder responded well to PR within a 3-week treatment period. These gains were maintained at 1-year follow-up.

Self-control Relaxation (SCR)

Wells, Turner, Bellack, and Hersen (1978) treated a mentally retarded, 22-year-old female with cue-controlled relaxation (CCR) and evaluated treatment influence with a single subject experimental design. Psychomotor seizures averaged about three per day during baseline and were reduced to near zero during CCR. The subsequent phase, treatment withdrawal, witnessed a spike in seizures that exceeded baseline levels. Seizures again diminished substantially with treatment resumption and for about a half year hence. Earlier, Ince (1976) also reported an excellent treatment response in a case study of CCR for a child experiencing grand mal and petit mal seizures.

Autogenics (AT)

There is a small amount of AT data available on this subject. Lubar and Deering (1981, p. 106) observed a decrease from 20 to three myoclonic seizures a month in a patient practicing AT. Sipos and Tomka (1977) studied a woman subject to petit male activity, and observed diminished epileptic discharges during AT, but not fewer than occurred during a mental computation control period, compared to relaxed wakefulness.

In the only controlled study in this section, De Rivera, De Montigny, Remillard, and Andermann (1977) randomly assigned 21 patients with temporal lobe epilepsy to AT or supportive psychotherapy. Psychiatrists, blind to patient treatment, rated greater gains for the AT than the psychotherapy group on several psychological and psychosomatic scales. Only a subset of the AT group, those with high frequency seizures (as many as two per day), exhibited reduced seizures.

Final Comments on Relaxation Therapy for Seizures

Seizure disorder represents a highly heterogeneous population with respect to stress etiology, brain pathology, genetic involvement, form, and frequency. Further, each case of seizure disorder is a result of multiple determinants. In sum, relaxation therapy can likely be useful for only a highly select subset of this population.

Comprehensive baseline assessment should be a major focus of future efforts in this domain, to identify symptom profiles that predict responsivity to relaxation. Similarly, differential diagnosis of negative prognosticators is perhaps even more important. For example, some authors (De Rivera et al., 1977; Lubar & Deering, 1981) have pointed out that slow EEG waves occur in partial-complex and other types of seizures, and that relaxation therapy may *elicit* seizure activity in these individuals. The reader would do well to heed this caution.

SEXUAL DYSFUNCTION

Understandably, most people who suffer from some form of sexual dysfunction will be anxious as a result. However, in their recent review, Norton and

Jehu (1984) articulate evidence of anxiety as a causal factor in this problem. This is particularly true when the anxiety is specific to sexual functioning, rather than of a general nature.

Sexual functioning in both men and women requires a coordinated interplay of parasympathetic and sympathetic autonomic processes during successive phases of arousal and orgasm (Kaplan, 1974). Anxiety mechanisms are incompatible with parasympathetic processes and thereby interfere with initial arousal. The physiology of sexual functioning creates a well-defined need for relaxation therapy, although in many cases, cognitive and interpersonal communication aspects also demand attention.

Progressive Relaxation (PR)

In their highly regarded program for female orgasmic dysfunction, Heiman, LoPiccolo, and LoPiccolo (1976) recommended the use of PR to abate and avoid anxiety in the early stages of expanding self-intimacy. However, data on PR as a unitary intervention or package component for this disorder is unavailable.

Meditation

Delmonte (1984a) presented two brief case studies describing the mantra meditation treatment of retarded ejaculation. However, the treatment protocol also included traditional psychotherapy (psychodynamic, gestalt, and marital) and other relaxation strategies (yoga, progressive relaxation, and autogenic training).

Other Relaxation Techniques

Women seeking treatment for sexual frigidity were randomly assigned to systematic desensitization, videotaped desensitization, or a relaxation (method unspecified) control group (Wincze & Caird, 1976). Unlike the two desensitization groups, the relaxation group did not demonstrate diminished heterosexual anxiety. However, this was not a fair test of relaxation, as these subjects were informed that the "planned" treatment (i.e., desensitization) was being withheld temporarily.

Final Comments on Relaxation Therapy for Sexual Dysfunction

The disruptive influence of anxiety to sexual functioning invites relaxation applications in this domain. However, unitary interventions, be it relaxation, marital therapy, etc., are insufficient in most cases (LoPiccolo & LoPiccolo, 1978). Further, systematic desensitization can target sexual anxiety with greater precision than relaxation alone (as suggested by Norton & Jehu, 1984), and this may be the preferred vehicle for relaxation influence in this area.

Relaxation alone, or relaxation in concert with other techniques, has been underutilized in the treatment of sexual dysfunction. A female disorder, vaginismus, serves to emphasize this point. This disorder involves sharp muscular contractions around the vaginal opening, triggered by attempted intromission. This is a muscular spasm disorder that may include phobic features. LoPiccolo and Stock (1986) recommended relaxation and progressive dilation of the vagina as the standard treatment for vaginismus, but there is not a single controlled trial of this approach. Save for a few case histories that typically employ systematic desensitization and dilation treatment for vaginismus (e.g., Krige, 1985), no data exists as to the usefulness of relaxation for this disorder, which seems well suited for relaxation therapy.

ASTHMA

Asthma is a pulmonary disorder involving smooth muscle spasm and excessive mucous flow in the lungs, with labored breathing the result (Creer, 1982). Most asthma researchers believe asthma episodes arise from a combination of allergic and psychological precipitants. The interested reader is directed to overviews of a variety of psychological approaches to asthma (Alexander, 1981) and biofeedback interventions (Kotses & Glaus, 1981) in particular. As for relaxation therapy, its aim is to mitigate stress factors that provoke, maintain, or exacerbate asthma, and to relieve bronchial muscle spasm.

Progressive Relaxation (PR)

In one of Jacobson's first clinical reports (1921), he provided some anecdotal data on PR for asthma. Additional data of a similar nature appeared subsequently (Jacobson, 1938a).

Moore (1965) published the first evaluation of PR for asthma in the current era. Adult and child asthmatics were assigned to a 2-month treatment course comprising eight sessions of: (a) PR and autogenic training combined, (b) treatment a supplemented by strong therapist suggestions predicting improvement, or (c) systematic desensitization. After the first treatment course, each subject was reassigned to a second treatment to form a partial Latin Square design. All groups reported comparable improvement in the frequency of asthma attacks. The two relaxation groups exhibited statistically significant improvement in peak expiratory flow rate (PEFR), though the magnitude of these changes was small. In contrast, the systematic desensitization group attained large magnitude increases in PEFR (about 200 liters/minute), far exceeding those of the other two groups.

In 1972, Alexander and his associates published two studies testing PR with young adolescents receiving residential treatment for asthma. The first study (Alexander, Miklich, & Hershkoff, 1972) contrasted the effects of small group administrations of PR and quiet activities, such as reading, in a random assignment, between-group design. The PR group surpassed the control group in average within-session improvement on self-ratings of relaxation and PEFR.

The second study (Alexander, 1972) employed a within-group design by exposing one group of children to three to five quiet rest sessions, followed by three to five PR sessions over 2 weeks. The results of this study closely duplicated the first. Again, PEFR increases were greater during the PR sessions. In both studies, the PEFR change associated with PR averaged about 10 percent, and reached about 30 percent in the top third of the PR subjects. State and trait anxiety measures (Spielberger, Gorsuch, & Lushene, 1970), taken in the second study, did not correlate with PEFR performance. However, children who claimed their asthmatic attacks were triggered by emotional factors did achieve significantly greater PEFR gains than those who did not perceive emotionality as relevant to their asthma. Outcome data, roughly comparable to those of the two Alexander outcome studies, have since been reported in trials with the combined treatments of taped PR and electromyographic biofeedback conducted with children attending a summer camp for asthmatics (Scherr, Crawford, Sergent, & Scherr, 1975).

The first negative results on PR for asthma appeared in 1973. Davis, Saunders, Creer, and Chai (1973) recruited from the same population of resident asthmatic children as did Alexander. Subjects were randomly assigned to five sessions of either PR, PR and frontalis electromyographic biofeedback combined, or a quiet-rest control. Each group contained severe and nonsevere asthmatics, and among the former, there were no differential treatment effects between groups. For the nonsevere asthmatics, the combination of PR and biofeedback produced greater PEFR improvement than PR alone, which in turn surpassed the control group. However, it should be pointed out that the PR group showed no pre-post change. Its superiority over the control group was due to deterioration in PEFR performance by the control children. Lastly, PEFR readings, taken during the week following treatment, revealed no differences between the groups, thus adding a discouraging note on therapeutic maintenance.

Two more negative outcome studies appeared in 1979. Alexander, Cropp, and Chai (1979) evaluated inpatient, asthmatic children during three pretreatment sessions, five sessions which combined PR and autogenic training, and three posttreatment sessions. They conducted the most exhaustive pulmonary function assessment to date, evaluating 12 different variables. With minor exception, they did not detect any evidence of treatment effects. Erskine and Schonell (1979) treated 10 adult asthma sufferers with four taped sessions of either PR or PR/pleasant imagery combined. Pulmonary and self-report indices failed to reveal any treatment effects.

Overall, a clear pattern of results has emerged in the PR treatment of asthma. Initial, modest successes have been overshadowed by more recent, consistently negative findings.

A recent study reported in partial (Hock, Bramble, & Kennard, 1977) and more complete (Hock, Rodgers, Reddi, & Kennard, 1978) form is an exception to this discouraging trend. Eight sessions of PR, combined with pleasant imagery, proved effective with male children (mean age 12 years), as measured by forced expiratory volume (FEV) trials and frequency of asthmatic attacks. Relaxation was more effective than assertiveness training or no treatment. FEV gains held at 1-month posttreatment, but frequency of asthmatic attacks reverted to baseline level.

Self-control Relaxation (SCR)

In the only example of SCR for asthma, Sirota and Mahoney (1974) treated a woman whose asthma attacks were at times triggered by anxiety. Also noteworthy was the client's use of a portable timer as a self-relaxation reminder. Within 2 weeks of commencing SCR therapy, the client discontinued use of a portable nebulizer, employed about nine times a day during baseline, to alleviate asthmatic attacks. Medication consumption was also cut substantially. Therapy gains were maintained at 2- and 6-month follow-ups.

Passive Relaxation

Yorkston, McHugh, Brady, Serber, and Sergeant (1974) employed a method of relaxation with adult asthmatics that is closely akin to passive relaxation [see Yorkston and Sergeant (1969) for a description of the technique]. Relaxation was compared with systematic desensitization in a between-subjects design. Measures of forced expiratory volume (FEV) in 1 second, taken before and after each of the six treatment sessions, revealed significant improvement by the desensitization subjects only. Clinical ratings at 2-year follow-up agreed with the initial findings. Similar results have since been reported by this same research group (Yorkston, Eckert, McHugh, Philander, & Blumenthal, 1979) for adult asthmatic patients on steroid treatment. No treatment differences emerged with patients not on steroid protocols, suggesting a treatment by asthmatic severity interaction.

Meditation

A study of Transcendental Meditation (TM) for asthma was reported in preliminary (Honsberger & Wilson, 1973) and then final (Wilson, Honsberger, Chiu, & Novey, 1975) form. Adolescents and adults presenting with stable, uncomplicated asthma were randomly assigned to either (a) TM treatment or (b) only reading about the TM philosophy. After 3 months, the groups reversed roles to complete a crossover design. Dependent measures were collected during baseline, at 3 and 6 months for posttreatment, and at 12 months for follow-up. Self-ratings of asthma attacks favored the treated group a during the first 3 months, but then group b caught up during the second 3 months when it also was treated.

My interpretation of this data is less enthusiastic than that of the authors. Within-group changes might be explained by time-mediated trends, and the differences between groups did not appear significant to me (statistical analyses were not reported for this measure). Group *a* showed significant improvement in three pre-post measures of pulmonary function (PEFR, FEV, and airway resistance), but these gains vanished during the second 3-month period when this group was no longer encouraged to meditate (although about 50 percent continued to do so). As a result of its TM training, group *b* improved only in airway resistance. Medication levels did not exhibit significant change. At posttreatment (6 months) and at 6-month follow-up (12-month point), the majority of subjects and their physicians rated the TM treatment as helpful to their asthma, despite the scant empirical evidence noted above. Moreover, the modest advantage by TM over control in this study could well be due to differential expectations engendered in these two groups. Specifically, the control group knew it was being denied treatment, and the readings they were given promised future relief.

Addressing a condition somewhat related to asthma, Tandon (1978) contrasted yoga (mainly breathing exercises and posturing) and physiotherapy with male adults suffering from severe airway obstruction (chronic bronchitis). Over 9 months of treatment, there were no significant differences between the groups on any measure. Neither group showed improvement on static pulmonary function tests, but the yoga group did improve on some physiological measures of exercise tolerance (heart rate and cycling work load), although not on pulmonary aspects of this assessment. Self-report indicators of symptomatic relief favored the yoga subjects. Here again, we see small but noticeable advantages accruing to relaxation.

Final Comments on Relaxation Therapy for Asthma

Alexander (1981), one of the premier researchers in this area, concluded " . . . that no relaxation method of any kind has a *clinically* significant effect on pulmonary physiology in either childhood or adult asthmatics" (p. 386). Other reviews in the same area (Erskine-Milliss & Schonell, 1981; Kotses & Glaus, 1981; Richter & Dahme, 1982) disagree with Alexander, in that they are somewhat encouraged by the results of autogenic training, meditation, and biofeedback.

Several matters deserve future attention in this area. First, excepting for a few studies (Moore, 1965; Scherr et al., 1975), the treatment protocols for asthma do not usually call for more than five relaxation sessions. As most of these subjects are children, and much less is known about the relaxation response of children compared to adults, this may be a subtherapeutic dosage. Future clinical trials should test the effects of prolonged therapeutic exposure. Second, Alexander (1972; Alexander et al., 1972) clearly demonstrated the presence of high intersubject variability in therapeutic response to relaxation. This being the case, we would expect an unimpressive average group response to mask clinically significant individual responses in group trials of relaxation therapy for asthma. More emphasis needs to be placed on identifying particular individuals within this medically and psychologically heterogeneous group (Kinsman, Dirks, Jones, & Dahlem, 1980), who can benefit from relaxation.

Barber (1984) raised an interesting point. At the outset of asthmatic symptoms, affected individuals may experience conditioned anxiety and attendant sympathetic arousal and thereby exacerbate respiratory distress. Self-control relaxation (and more comprehensive stress management tools) may prove useful, if pressed into service when asthmatic symptoms first appear. This treatment strategy has received little attention heretofore. Lastly, one aspect of the asthmatic syndrome involves the poorly coordinated and inefficient use of the voluntary or accessory muscles of breathing (Goyeche, Ago, & Ikemi, 1980, 1982). This suggests that relaxation techniques emphasizing breath regulation (as in some meditation approaches) would be helpful.

CHILDREN'S PROBLEMS

In contrast to the number of adult applications, relaxation therapy for children has received little attention. An exception to this disparity is relaxation for children and adolescents with asthma reviewed above.

The relaxation techniques taught in Chapters 4 and 5 of this book are intended for adults, and in their present form would be less helpful for some children. Relaxation inductions with emotionally disturbed and intellectually or physically handicapped children often require modifications of customary techniques employed with adults. Excellent discussions of child formats are available elsewhere (Cautela & Groden, 1978; Harvey, 1979; Koeppen, 1974). Examples of modifications that these authors recommend are to: (a) use food reinforcers to encourage relaxation practice; (b) cast procedures in the form of a game; for example "wrinkle your nose as if to rid it of a pesky fly"; (c) keep the training sessions short; and (d) physically guide some of the tensing operations.

The potential for relaxation applications to children appears to be great. Many of the same adult disorders that have been successfully treated by relaxation also manifest during childhood, and affected children might profit from similar treatment. Moreover, the age range of children who can learn relaxation probably extends to the early years. This latter question has not been systematically addressed, but case study data suggest that children as young as 4 years old can master progressive relaxation (Tasto, 1969; Walker, 1979). Luthe and Blumberger (1977) recommended against the use of autogenic training with children younger than 5 years old.

Data presented in this section will be limited to treatments of problems largely peculiar to childhood, as exemplified by hyperactivity and learning disabilities. Treatments of children with such disorders as headache and muscular dysfunction are described in the symptomatic section of this chapter.

Progressive Relaxation (PR)

To begin, it is interesting to note that within the prolificacy of Edmund Jacobson's writings, PR for children is almost entirely ignored. An exception to this is his relatively recent book on the subject of education (Jacobson, 1973b). Here Jacobson presents scanty anecdotal data mostly describing teachers training their own classes, as young as kindergarten age, in PR for such purposes as decreasing overactivity and increasing attention to academic tasks.

Case reports endorse the application of PR to a variety of disorders of children and adolescents. PR appears to have been helpful for children exhibiting a foot fetish (Walker, 1979), a toilet phobia (Walker, 1979), and adolescents manifesting chronic tension (Bergland & Chal, 1972; Elitzur, 1976).

Hyperactivity presents as a likely target for PR, and six studies tested this. Two produced positive findings (Bhatara, Arnold, Lorance, & Gupta, 1979; Braud, 1978) and four negative (Denkowski & Denkowski, 1984; Klein & Deffenbacher, 1977; Luiselli, Steinman, Marholin, & Steinman, 1981; Putre, Loffio, Chorost, Marx, & Gilbert, 1977).

Braud (1978) randomly assigned 15 hyperactive children (ages 6–13 years) to 12 sessions of taped PR or frontalis electromyographic (EMG) biofeedback, or to a no-treatment control group (HC). Measures were also collected from untreated, age-matched nonhyperactive children (NC). At pretreatment, the three groups of hyperactive children registered significantly higher muscle tension readings than the NC. By the end of treatment, the PR and biofeedback subjects manifested lower EMG scores than NC, while HC were still significantly elevated. Skin temperature data produced an analogous pattern. These results appear less impressive when interpreted in light of a similar test conducted by Putre et al. (1977) with hyperactive children (7–13 years old). They compared the EMG effects of a PR tape and a tape of interesting adventure stories. Both groups achieved significant, but equal, EMG reductions. This suggests that the gains of the PR and biofeedback groups in Braud (1978) would not have surpassed those of a credible placebo treatment, had such a condition been included. Similarly, on measures of academic performance, conduct, and locus of control, Denkowski and Denkowski (1984) found taped PR, biofeedback, and placebo equally ineffective.

Other data reported by Braud (1978) are as follows. Parents completed behavioral questionnaires and rating scales (e.g., aggressivenes, happiness, oppositional behavior), revealing greater problems among the three groups of hyperactive children than NC at pretreatment. At posttreatment, these data for HC were significantly higher than that for PR, biofeedback, or NC. Psychological tests of motor coordination, attention span, and memory showed a like pattern, though not as strong. The overall positive results of this study are very encouraging. In agreement with Braud are the data of Bhatara, Arnold, Lorance, and Gupta (1979). They reported improved conduct in the home, but not in school, for hyperkinetic children treated with taped PR combined with EMG biofeedback. However, these gains washed out by 12-week follow-up.

Klein and Deffenbacher (1977) presented only five treatment sessions of either PR or strenuous exercise to third grade boys. The control groups were "placebo" play with clay, hyperactive no treatment (HC), and matched non-hyperactive no treatment (NC). Children in the PR, exercise, and NC groups outperformed the HC children on a card game (Kagan, 1965), but not on a maze tracing (Sykes, Douglas, Weiss, & Minde, 1971) posttest. PR did not surpass the placebo group on either test. The disappointing outcome of this study may be due to insufficient treatment exposure and too little breadth in the dependent measures.

Luiselli et al. (1981) treated four children (ages 12 and 13 years) who exhibited poor attention span, oppositional behavior, and poor academic progress. Daily over a 3-week period, the children were administered PR training or a recreational card game preceding a classroom period, during which observations were taken of several on-task, disruptive, and academic behaviors. Measures taken on days following relaxation, closely matched data from days in which the children only played card games. This study corrected most of the shortcomings of the other studies in this area and strongly argues against the usefulness of PR for this class of children, save for one possible reservation. If relaxation effects persisted across days in which PR was omitted, PR benefits would be attributed to card playing. Unfortunately, this study did not include a no-treatment control that could have addressed this issue. Nevertheless, this study was exemplary in three respects. First, trained observers, supplemented by reliability observers, collected most of the dependent measures and were blind as to which treatment had been delivered on a given day. Second, the experimenters employed a nine-item check list of behavioral indicators of relaxation to verify that a successful relaxation induction had occurred (see Chapter 4 for further description of this check list). Third, this is one of the few studies in this area to assess academic effects of PR.

There have been several attempts to alter the behavior of autistic children and adolescents through PR. Uncontrolled case studies have found PR to be useful with this population in reducing general excitedness (Graziano & Kean, 1968) and stereotypic behavior (Groden, Baron, Cautela, & Groden, 1977).

In the most current and, by far, the most rigorous PR trial with autism (Marholin, Steinman, Luiselli, Schwartz, & Townsend, 1979), PR proved ineffective on several behavioral and academic indices. This study included all of the key design features of the Luiselli et al. (1981) study described above. Five autistic adolescents practiced PR or played Simon Says in a random sequence over a 1–2 month period. During classroom periods that followed these training sessions, observers recorded the occurrence of on-task, disruptive, stereotypic, and academic behaviors. Mean levels of these measures collected on days following PR were virtually identical to mean levels from days following Simon Says. The addition of verbal reminder cues to relax did not improve the effectiveness of PR.

Autogenics (AT)

A capsulated summary (Angers et al., 1977a) of 100 mostly foreign language studies on AT for children cites numerous obtained benefits. The main benefits being: intellectual (e.g., improved attention and memory), social (improved friendships and public speaking), affective (decreased anxiety and depression), psychophysiologic (decreased sleep disturbance and gastrointestinal disorders), and miscellaneous (improved creativity and athletic performance).

Imagery

Carter and Russell (1981) sought to overcome arousal that interferes with academic performance and fosters inappropriate conduct in children with learning disabilities. The treatment package consisted of visual imagery relaxation, electromyographic biofeedback, and passive muscle relaxation.

In the first study reported, elementary age boys diagnosed as learning disabled received 5 weeks of treatment. Pre-post evaluations indicated that they made significantly greater gains than untreated controls on eight of nine dependent measures, including tests of reading, spelling, intelligence, and memory. The second study evaluated conduct changes in 20 learning disabled elementary school boys who received the same treatment. Parents' ratings on the Child Behavior Check List (Cassel, 1962) revealed significant improvement on all six subscales, and children's self-ratings on the Tennessee Self-Concept Scale (Fitts, 1964) evidenced improvement on 9 of 11 subscales. This study did not include a control group. The third study replicated the first in a school setting, with learning disabled children of both sexes, and was administered by the classroom teachers. Again, the treated children made significantly greater academic gains than the controls. Lastly, the treatment package, extended to 6 weeks, was administered to 358 oppositional children seen in an outpatient treatment facility. Diverse academic gains were obtained with this group as well.

Although none of these studies can claim more than minimal methodological controls, the clinical results are impressive. Demonstration of long-term maintenance of these changes would have made the therapeutic effects more meaningful.

Other Relaxation Techniques

Dunn and Howell (1982) presented 10 boys (ages not given) with 10 "neutral" treatment sessions of play therapy as a placebo control, followed by 10 sessions of either taped relaxation (method not specified), frontalis electromyographic (EMG) biofeedback, or relaxation/biofeedback combined. All subjects exhibited substantial EMG reductions over the 20-session course in a gradual pattern, which does not argue for the clear superiority of any of the treatments over the placebo. Psychological test data (e.g., motor coordination, memory), parental ratings, and behavioral observations all registered no change during the placebo phase, but significant improvement during the treatment phase. This study corrected one of the faults of the Braud (1978) effort by using an adequate placebo control.

Two hyperactive, mentally retarded children were trained in one dozen relaxation techniques, including imagery, breath, and progressive relaxation, and contrasted with an untreated, matched control subject (Lessen & McLain, 1980). The sole dependent measure, electrodermal activity, revealed substantial gains only for the treated subjects. The absence of behavioral measures and indications of setting generalization limit the importance of these findings, despite the fact that impressive gains were made with a difficult population.

Raymer and Poppen (1985) applied the method of behavioral relaxation training (see *Relaxation Comparisons* divison of *Anxiety,* this chapter, for further description of the procedure) to three hyperactive boys in a multiple baseline design. Frontalis muscle tension and the behavioral relaxation scale (see Chapter 4) evinced successful relaxation inductions by the therapist in the office and by the mother in the home. Child hyperactivity (as rated by the parents) declined substantially.

Final Comments on Relaxation Therapy for Children's Problems

The literature on relaxation for children is neither extensive nor methodologically mature (Richter, 1984). Despite some positive findings, the bulk of the evidence does not recommend this approach. Important dependent measures, such as academic performance and physiological functioning, have been neglected. Generalization and maintenance of treatment effects remain as big question marks. However, children do present as largely untested ground for developing relaxation therapy.

Differences may obtain in applying relaxation to children as opposed to adults. Some thoughts on this subject were presented in the introductory remarks of this section. Other changes that may prove useful are as follows. Research with adults supports the assertion that live relaxation inductions are more effective than taped. Cost efficient taped inductions have received insufficient trials with children, and it may be misleading to assume these will also prove unsatisfactory with children. Brief training courses on the order of five sessions are the rule with adults. Longer courses may be required by children. Involvement of significant others is uncommon in relaxation training with adults. With children, it may be helpful to incorporate parents, teachers, etc., as relaxation trainers and as allies in encouraging practice.

GENERAL WELL-BEING

Western methods of relaxation usually forecast relatively narrow, symptom-specific benefits accruing to the practitioner. Eastern approaches are not so confined. Methods such as yoga, Zen, and Transcendental Meditation (TM) claim broad personality and spiritual change occur with their disciples, partly due to these systems' emphases on attitude, philosophy of life, and technique (Walsh, 1983; Yogi, 1976). As pointed out in the previous chapter, Western methods usually target individuals with an emotional or physical disability, whereas Eastern methods encompass well-adjusted individuals seeking a growth experience.

Chapter 3 described the results of a large number of studies with normal subjects. Much of that research, particularly in TM, consisted of evaluations of normal individuals seeking growth experiences, and these "studies" might be more appropriately housed in the present section. In any case, I have elected to confine the present discussion to more formal studies, which recruited normal subjects and boasted a preventive emphasis.

Self-control Relaxation (SCR)

Well-adjusted, undergraduate volunteers (Sherman & Plummer, 1973) were given either six SCR sessions or no treatment to determine if the general population would derive benefits from SCR in coping with routine stress challenge. SCR subjects registered significant improvement on the IPAT Anxiety Scale (Cattell, 1957) and the Fear Survey Scale (FSS; Wolpe & Lang, 1964), but not on the Willoughby (Wolpe, 1958) or the Minnesota Multiphasic Personality Inventory (MMPI; Hathaway & McKinley, 1943). The control subjects showed no significant improvement, but between-group comparisons yielded only minor differences. Data collected by mail at 2 years posttreatment (Sherman, 1975), suggested that most of the relaxation subjects were still practicing SCR and deriving anxiety reduction benefits from it.

Meditation

TM theorists claim that their method develops the whole individual and better prepares TM practitioners to cope with life's challenges. Thus, Aron and Aron (1979) speak of immunization to stress following TM and other benefits, such as improved family relationships when all members practice TM, but supportive data are sparse.

Peters, Benson, and Porter (1977) conducted a worksite test of Bensonian meditation with normal volunteers. Pre-post questionnaire analyses documented significantly improved general well-being for the meditation group, compared to an untreated group, on two of five measures. Gains were made on indices of illness symptoms and work performance, but not subjective illness, sociability, or happiness. It is instructive to note, however, that a third group, simply taking daily rest breaks, fared as well as the meditation group on all measures.

Autogenics (AT)

A group of Canadian researchers (Angers et al., 1977a, 1977b) introduced truncated AT (heaviness series only) to teachers and several classes of an elementary school. Their main goals were to determine if organizational obstacles could be overcome, and if beneficial individual changes could be induced.

Some teachers and administrators did in fact contest the wisdom of broad AT exposure, claiming various dangers to health, pragmatic complications, and the like. Nevertheless, the program was implemented, though only sketchy details were provided of the results.

Individual home practice supplemented daily scheduled group practice in school. Home practices were most often done prior to meals. Some negative side effects, such as dizziness and nausea, were reported. Age-adapted training and progress note manuals were found to be useful. The adults reported predictable benefits, such as sleep and mood improvement. The children willingly practiced AT, suggesting enjoyment of it, but these studies did not include other outcome data.

A third report on the same project (Luthe, Trudeau, Mailhot, & Vallieres, 1977) added preliminary data on cardiovascular effects. Pre-post assessments sandwiching 10 weeks of practice yielded unremarkable results. Systolic blood pressure shrunk lower and also grew more variable in the AT students compared to untreated controls. Diastolic pressure and heart rate were unaffected. A few children exhibited paradoxical blood pressure and heart rate responses.

Final Comments on Relaxation Therapy for General Well-being

In coming years, more common use of relaxation to maintain or extend health (as opposed to remediating illness) may result from increased attention to the subject of prevention. Matarazzo (1983) coined the term *behavioral immunogens* in referring to health promoting behaviors, and cited exercise, regular sleep, and the like as examples. Matarazzo did not recommend relaxation, but relaxation could plausibly define a role for itself in this domain. Masek, Epstein, and Russo (1981) focused on health risk behaviors, termed *behavioral pathogens* by Matarazzo (1983). Masek et al. prescribed a substantive role for relaxation as part of treatment packages for Type A behavior, chronic stress, etc., but did not envision relaxation dissemination among asymptomatic individuals. Barrios and Shigetomi (1980) do recommend preventive coping skills (including relaxation), but they fail to articulate the mechanics of their dissemination.

To date, Eastern relaxation techniques have laid nearly exclusive claim on healthy consumers of relaxation. As interest in prevention continues to stir, Western methods may also attract a healthy audience.

SOCIAL FIELD EFFECTS

In the entire realm of relaxation, there are no findings so remarkable as the Transcendental Meditation (TM) social field effects. This phenomenon involves the dissemination of momentous TM benefits throughout a community, when a small but critical percentage of individuals in that community practice TM. Research on TM social field effects has exclusively employed crime level as the dependent measure, as TM theory predicts decreased aggression, this is a socially significant concern, and reliable data are readily available from respected sources.

Borland and Landrith (1977) were the first to present data bearing on this claim, and their approach was sound. They identified 11 United States cities that satisfied the following criteria: (a) population approximately between 25,000 and 50,000, and (b) approximately 1 percent of their population trained in TM. These were labeled the experimental cities and were compared with 11 control cities matched for population, college enrollment, and geographic region. TM practitioners in the control cities comprised less than 1 percent of the population ranging from 0.02 percent to 0.62 percent. The FBI and local police furnished crime data. In the year following attainment of the 1 percent TM criteria, the trend for crime to increase was reversed, as all of the experimental cities showed a decrease in crime rate averaging 8.2 percent. During the same period, the prevailing crime trend continued, as crime increased in 8 of 11 control cities, with the average increase among all 11 being 8.3 percent. The increase, decrease, and difference between the two groups were all statistically significant.

Dillbeck, Landrith, and Orme-Johnson (1981) have since replicated these results in studying the 24 United States cities with population exceeding 10,000 people and 1 percent trained in TM, and 24 matched control cities. A significant decrease in crime rate occurred in the experimental cities, while crime in the control cities continued to increase at the same pace as in previous years.

Aron and Aron (1981) described three experiments on social field effects associated with the presence of TM-Sidhi participants, advanced TM practitioners. These studies involved a TM-Sidhi group entering a new community to practice meditation. The thrust of these results were as follows. Dramatic reductions in crime and violence coincided with their presence, but then returned to the previous level when the TM-Sidhi group departed. These TM-Sidhi studies have the methodological advantage of being experimental in nature, unlike the correlational studies reported above that are more likely subject to the influence of unidentified causal factors.

Borland and Landrith (1977) reviewed the theoretical basis for social field effects. It is explained in terms of a "phase transition model of social change" (p. 645) derived from analogous phenomena occurring in the physical world. Specifically, a disordered array of molecules will begin to cohere when a subset of the molecules are induced to cohere. In other words, when a critical mass is attained, a pervading influence (the exact nature of this energy force is as yet unspecified) encourages a more harmonious organization among all group members. An extended discussion of mathematics and theoretical physics relating to the question of phase transition phenomena is available for the interested reader (Domash, 1977b).

Final Comments on TM for Social Field Effects

The type of assertions TM researchers advance for social field effects is unheard of among other relaxation approaches or among clinical interventions in general. In the past, such claims as extending the influence of a focal manipulation to naive members of the community have been confined within the boundaries of parapsychology. Nevertheless, I am struck by the methodological sophistication of the TM research in this area (which is not characteristic of TM research in general), and the strength and consistency of the published findings. The importance of this work cannot be overstated, as its august implications encompass nothing less than world peace (Orme-Johnson, 1983). Although I am inclined, due to personal biases about the organization of nature, to disbelieve that TM plays a causal role in the social field effects reported above, I can offer no scientific criticism to challenge the validity of this phenomenon.

MISCELLANEOUS APPLICATIONS

This section is comprised of clinical research that does not fit into any of the other sections of this chapter. For the most part, these studies are relaxation applications for disorders on which there is insufficient data to justify creation of a new chapter section.

Progressive Relaxation (PR)

There are a few uncontrolled accounts of the utility of PR in reducing the self-injurious behavior of schizophrenics (Cautela & Baron, 1973; these authors did not specify the method of relaxation, but based on their other publications, it was probably PR) and retarded individuals (Steen & Zuriff, 1977). PR was alleged to exert its influence by (a) serving as an incompatible response, and (b) dispelling eliciting anxiety. Negative outcome data on PR trials with schizophrenics also exist (Weinman, Gelbart, Wallace, & Post, 1972).

Military air crew members, disabled by airsickness, were treated with multimodality biofeedback and relaxation (progressive relaxation, breath meditation, and pleasant imagery) and challenged by nausea induction in Coriolis trials, a rapidly rotating, tilting chair ride (Levy, Jones, & Carlson, 1981). With up to 11 months follow-up available, 16 of 19 participants successfully completed this program and returned to flying duty. These results are consistent with encouraging basic research findings emphasizing autogenics and biofeedback for motion sickness, summarized in Chapter 3.

Several PR studies of single subjects targeted interesting symptomatology. One case study (Gray & Lawlis, 1982) described the successful treatment of pruritic eczema, as evidenced by reduced rash and itching, by the combination of PR, biofeedback, autogenics, and cognitive skills training. Malatesta,

Sutker, and Adams (1980) reported demonstrable but short-lived reductions in tinnitus from PR in their subject. A negative outcome of PR for tinnitus was also reported by another group (Jakes, Hallam, Rachman, & Hinchcliffe, 1986). Mizes and Fleece (1986) reported about a 50 percent reduction in number of bulimic episodes in their client treated with PR. Others (VanderPlate & Kerrick, 1985) have found PR helpful in reducing the recurrence of genital herpes.

Utilizing a clever method of heat-induced hot flashes, Germaine and Freedman (1984) compared PR and alpha biofeedback in controlling this discomfort among symptomatic menopausal women. Laboratory response to heat stimulation and frequency of actual hot flashes showed significant improvement in PR, but not biofeedback subjects.

One study targeted rheumatoid arthritis (Achterberg, McGraw, & Lawlis, 1981). Although only scant details are provided on the relaxation method, it appears to be PR. Driven by the theory that stress and muscle tension exacerbate this disorder (see review by Anderson, Bradley, Young, McDaniel, & Wise, 1985), 24 female arthritic patients received taped PR in 12 sessions over 6 weeks. Additionally, half the subjects received digital skin temperature biofeedback training to promote warmth, and half to increase cooling. With few exceptions, differences were not observed between type of biofeedback training. Over the treatment course, the main benefits were improved sleep and decreased duration and severity of reported pain. A subsequent comparison with patients receiving only conventional physiotherapy suggested that physical functioning effects were comparable in PR versus physiotherapy.

Passive Relaxation

Gunnison and Renick (1985) supplied some case descriptions of a brief relaxation procedure, similar to passive relaxation, successfully applied in six cases of bulimia.

Meditation

There are isolated reports of Transcendental Meditation (TM) benefiting a variety of disorders including psychoses (Glueck & Stroebel, 1975), stress in prisoners (Cox, 1972), multiple dysfunction in a retarded woman (Eyerman, 1981), worksite productivity (Frew, 1974), obesity (Saxena & Saxena, 1977), and emotional control in troubled youth (Kimble, 1975). However, the anecdotal nature of these TM studies renders their conclusions preliminary.

Over a 1 year period, Cooper and Aygen (1979) evaluated self-selected TM practitioners with hypercholesterolemia and matched controls. Significant cholesterol reduction occurred in the TM group only.

Woolfolk (1984) presented an interesting single subject experimental analysis of "self-control" meditation for anger control, one of the very few demonstrations of such an adaptation of meditation. The method of meditation, mixed mantra and breath awareness components, and the mechanics of the self-control orientation mimicked that of self-control versions of progressive relaxation (see Chapter 5). After learning conventional, static meditation, the client was taught to attend to cues of impending anger and to use brief, open-eyed meditation that added visual fixation on an object in such high risk situations.

During successive weeks of baseline and conventional meditation, self-ratings of anger and client ratings submitted by significant others indicated no change. However, the introduction of self-control meditation was associated with clearcut anger suppression, as evidenced by both sources of data. Anger ratings rose sharply when the client was instructed to discontinue all meditation (week 4) and stabilized when conventional meditation was resumed (week 5). Reinstatement of self-control meditation (week 6) again witnessed dramatic improvement. Gains were well maintained at 1- and 3-month follow-ups.

Autogenics (AT)

Individuals with demonstrated food and tree allergies mastered AT and then discussed, imagined, and ate or touched the allergic substance (Ikemi, Nakagawa, Kusano, & Sugita, 1965). Exposure trials were terminated at the first sign of adverse reaction, as in traditional Wolpean desensitization. Treatment response was generally good and inversely correlated with allergy severity. Encouraging case histories on AT for allergies have also been reported by others (Teshima et al., 1982).

There has been one case report on tinnitus, ringing in the ear (Elfner, May, Moore, & Mendelson, 1981). The combination of AT and two biofeedback modalities—electromyography and skin temperature—did not alter tinnitus loudness, but eliminated its perceived noxiousness. Uncontrolled data from Rath and Lohmann (1977) suggested that AT may aid the psychophysiologic functioning and general adjustment of kidney disease patients undergoing hemodialysis, but is less helpful for kidney transplant recipients.

Kawakami, Kuroda, Sasaki, Soma, and Matsunaga (1977) described an interesting test of AT maintenance effects for peptic ulcer. Patients having been successfully medically treated for this disorder were followed for 1-year hence, with or without AT instruction. Patients practicing AT registered a relapse rate of 18 percent, compared to 28 percent in the untrained group, but this difference did not reach statistical significance. As per AT patients' report of home practice, the relapse rate among individuals who discontinued AT because they were symptom free was 38 percent, compared to 9 percent among persistent practitioners. Statistical analyses were not conducted on this comparison.

Shibata and his associates reported, in a series of articles (Shibata & Kuwahara, 1967; Shibata & Motoda, 1967a, 1967b, 1968), a clinical trial of AT for recovering schizophrenics. Most tolerated the relaxation experience well, and manifested such benefits as improved sleep and greater emotional stability. About half the patients exhibited slower brain waves post-AT, corroborating the psychological benefits. Several questionnaires documented improved ego strength and decreased anxiety, but symptomatic flare-ups did occur with some patients, and 27 percent of patients registered deterioration on the Minnesota Multiphasic Personality Inventory (Hathaway & McKinley, 1943). Positive and negative ancillary AT effects, termed *autogenic discharges,* frequently occurred in these patients, but these were not dissimilar to the autogenic discharges observed in samples of psychosomatic patients studied by others. Hoppe (1961) has also reported anecdotal data on the usefulness of AT for schizophrenics.

Other Relaxation Techniques

Shaw and Walker (1979) described a case study in which the foot fetish of an 8-year-old retarded child was eliminated, by substituting an unspecified method of relaxation for sexual responding.

Uncontrolled trials with Quieting Response training (Ford, Stroebel, Strong, & Szarek, 1983a) achieved success with 7 of 13 (54 percent) irritable colon patients (for further details, see *Other Relaxation Techniques, Muscle-Contraction Headache* section). A 50 percent drop in number of attacks was the success criterion.

Final Comments on Miscellaneous Applications of Relaxation Therapy

Most of the studies cited in this section are case reports, and not much can be said of their import until systematic, controlled research confirms their findings. Some of these preliminary studies did, nevertheless, target interesting disorders that might prove reliably responsive to relaxation therapy. Airsickness (and by implication, motionsickness), skin rash, hypercholesterolemia, allergies, and ulcer are examples. Several more methodologically sophisticated studies demonstrated relaxation therapy benefits for menopausal hot flashes, arthritic pain, and anger. Future research in these three areas is strongly warranted.

OVERVIEW OF RELAXATION THERAPY

The great number of disorders to which relaxation therapy has been applied is impressive. This broad applicability prompted one group of observers to call relaxation the "behavioral medicine aspirin" (Russo, Bird, & Masek, 1980, p. 7). Based upon the amount and strength of available research, some symptom domains present a clearly positive prognosis for relaxation therapy, others a clearly negative prognosis, and, of course, ambiguity persists in still others. The areas where one or more methods of relaxation have garnered convincing outcome data are anxiety, phobias, essential hypertension, muscle-contraction headache, chemotherapy side effects, and insomnia. The most discouraging data have arisen in hemophilia, drug abuse, and children's problems.

Several domains have yielded promising results, but may be considered clinically immature due to conflicting or inadequate trials. These areas, which present a high potential for future research, are diabetes, chronic pain, cancer, seizures, and social field effects.

In their discussion of methodological issues in relaxation research, Borkovec, Johnson, and Block (1984) delineate over 30 points of concern, and hardly one is trivial. To sample their recommendations, they discuss such matters as differential attrition in conditions, inclusion of *credible* placebo groups, variations in relaxation technique procedure, adequate follow-up, transfer of therapeutic gains to the natural setting, and the like. I suspect that most areas of psychological inquiry would succumb to such careful methodological scrutiny much more readily than would relaxation therapy.

Uncontrolled case studies are well represented in the relaxation literature. However, the literature is also replete with sterling examples of methodologically sophisticated studies yielding conclusions that warrant our hearty confidence. To name but a few, Blanchard and Andrasik's headache work, Agras and Taylor's hypertension work, Borkovec's insomnia program, Burish's efforts in cancer side effects, and Freedman's research on Raynaud's disease are methodologically competitive with the finest products of any other area of psychological inquiry. In sum, not only has the area of relaxation therapy kept abreast of advances in methodology, but it has pioneered new territory in setting standards of scientific rigor.

The question of treatment integrity (Yeaton & Sechrest, 1981), namely, whether the treatment was received as intended, is perhaps the paramount abiding methodological issue in relaxation therapy, and it manifests in two ways. First, delivery of a relaxation induction does not guarantee that a relaxation effect was produced, reminding us that the term *relaxation* refers to both a procedure and its influence. Unsuccessful relaxation training, for any of a number of reasons, will yield unjustified conclusions of relaxation therapy ineffectualness. Despite the critical need to know if a relaxation effect was successfully induced, some 70 percent of studies employing relaxation (as of a decade ago), obtained no evidence (self-report, behavioral, or physiological) to document a relaxation effect (Luiselli, Marholin, Steinman, & Steinman, 1979). The relatively few clinical trials that have verified the presence of relaxation independent of symptomatic outcome are laudable (e.g., Blake, 1965; Linton & Melin, 1983). Data are not available on current practice, but therapists are probably still lax in determining relaxation extent, and likely assume robust relaxation inductions have occurred more often than is justified. Second, the bulk of relaxation training is designed to be self-administered in the privacy of the client's home. Low levels of home relaxation practice, as is often the case (e.g., Lichstein & Hoelscher, 1986; Taylor, Agras, Schneider, & Allen, 1983), may diminish treatment exposure below therapeutic levels. Chapter 1 contains a more complete discussion of this matter. In sum, treatment integrity must be fully reckoned with by relaxation therapists and researchers before relaxation efficacy can be discounted, or confirmed, with confidence.

Two other clinical issues in relaxation therapy, not altogether unrelated to treatment integrity, are particularly deserving of future research. First, Hillenberg and Collins (1982) observed that half the clinical studies of relaxation therapy employed four or fewer treatment sessions. In light of Eastern yogis acquiring additional meditation benefits after 20 years of practice (reported in Chapter 3), four sessions seem too few. Inadequate regularity and longevity of relaxation practice, subsets of the larger issue of compliance, threaten the initiation and maintenance of therapeutic gains. Based upon Hillenberg and Collins' data, therapists and researchers may be inadvertently encouraging low compliance in recommending so little relaxation exposure. Future investigators need to devote more attention to promoting regular, long-term practice.

Second, approaching life with a relaxed attitude would produce symptomatic relief and enhance global quality of life in many of the individuals who receive relaxation therapy. Yet, development of such an attitude has, to date, rarely been a prominent goal of relaxation therapy.

Consider a typical client, who enters therapy with symptoms evolving from a tense, achievement-oriented approach to life, and then resists taking 15 minutes a day to practice relaxation because he or she is too tense and achievement oriented. Beck (1984) pointed out that relaxation consists of "doing nothing," and seems philosophically alien to those who stand to profit the most from it.

Bernstein and Borkovec (1973, p. 46) identified "distracting, intrusive thoughts" as "perhaps the most disruptive factor the client can present" in practicing relaxation. In Chapter 1, I discussed how such thoughts can be harnessed to help train a relaxed attitude and the importance of generalizing this attitude outside of the relaxation setting. In this and other ways, relaxation presents an opportunity for attitude change that may comprise the most important therapeutic facet of relaxation. The philosophy of relaxation, separate from the method, should receive far more attention in the future than it has heretofore.

References

Achterberg, J., McGraw, P., & Lawlis, G. F. (1981). Rheumatoid arthritis: A study of relaxation and temperature biofeedback training as an adjunctive therapy. *Biofeedback and Self-Regulation, 6,* 207–223.

Adam, G. (1978). Visceroception, awareness, and behavior. In G. E. Schwartz & D. Shapiro (Eds.), *Consciousness and self-regulation: Advances in research and theory* (Vol. 2, pp. 199–214). New York: Plenum Press.

Adams, H. E., Feuerstein, M., & Fowler, J. L. (1980). Migraine headache: Review of parameters, etiology, and intervention *Psychological Bulletin, 87,* 217–237.

Agras, W. S., Horne, M., & Taylor, C. B. (1982). Expectation and the blood-pressure-lowering effects of relaxation. *Psychosomatic Medicine, 44,* 389–395.

Agras, W. S., Kazdin, A. E., & Wilson, G. T. (1979). *Behavior therapy: Toward an applied clinical science.* San Francisco: Freeman.

Agras, W. S., Schneider, J. A., & Taylor, C. B. (1984). Relaxation training in essential hypertension: A failure of retraining in relaxation procedures. *Behavior Therapy, 15,* 191–196.

Agras, W. S., Southam, M. A., & Taylor, C. B. (1983). Long-term persistence of relaxation-induced blood pressure lowering during the working day. *Journal of Consulting and Clinical Psychology, 51,* 792–794.

Agras, W. S., Taylor, C. B., Kraemer, H. C., Allen, R. A., & Schneider, J. A. (1980). Relaxation training: Twenty-four-hour blood pressure reductions. *Archives of General Psychiatry, 37,* 859–863.

Aiken, L. H. (1972, June). Systematic relaxation to reduce preoperative stress. *Canadian Nurse, 68,* 38–42.

Aiken, L. H., & Henrichs, T. F. (1971). Systematic relaxation as a nursing intervention technique with open heart surgery patients. *Nursing Research, 20,* 212–217.

Ajaya, S. (1976). The psychology of breath. In R. M. Ballentine (Ed.), *Science of breath* (pp. 59–80). Glenview, IL: Himalayan International Institute of Yoga Science and Philosophy.

Alexander, A. B. (1972). Systematic relaxation and flow rates in asthmatic children: Relationship to emotional precipitants and anxiety. *Journal of Psychosomatic Research, 16,* 405–410.

Alexander, A. B. (1981). Behavioral approaches in the treatment of bronchial asthma. In C. K. Prokop & L. A. Bradley (Eds.), *Medical psychology: Contributions to behavioral medicine* (pp. 373–394). New York: Academic Press.

Alexander, A. B., Cropp, G. J. A., & Chai, H. (1979). Effects of relaxation training on pulmonary mechanics in children with asthma. *Journal of Applied Behavior Analysis, 12,* 27–35.

Alexander, A. B., Miklich, D. R., & Hershkoff, H. (1972). The immediate effects of systematic relaxation training on peak expiratory flow rates in asthmatic children. *Psychosomatic Medicine, 34,* 388–394.

Alexander, F. (1931). Buddhistic training as an artificial catatonia (M. J. Powers, Trans.). *Psychoanalytic Review, 18,* 129–145. (Original work published 1922)

Alexander, F. (1933). On Ferenczi's relaxation principle. *International Journal of Psychoanalysis, 14,* 183–192.

Allen, G. J. (1973). Treatment of test anxiety by group-administered and self-administered relaxation and study counseling. *Behavior Therapy, 4,* 349–360.

Allison, J. (1970). Respiratory changes during transcendental meditation. *Lancet, 1,* 833–834.

Alperson, J., & Biglan, A. (1979). Self-administered treatment of sleep onset insomnia and the importance of age. *Behavior Therapy, 10,* 347–356.

Alpert, R., & Haber, R. N. (1960). Anxiety in academic situations. *Journal of Abnormal and Social Psychology, 61,* 207–215.

American Psychiatric Association. (1977). Position statement on meditation. *American Journal of Psychiatry, 134,* 720.

American Psychiatric Association. (1980). *Diagnostic and statistical manual of mental disorders* (3rd ed.). Washington, DC: Author.

Anand, B. K., Chhina, G. S., & Singh, B. (1961a). Some aspects of electroencephalographic studies in Yogis. *Electroencephalography and Clinical Neurophysiology, 13,* 452–456.

Anand, B. K., Chhina, G. S., & Singh, B. (1961b). Studies on Shri Ramanand Yogi during his stay in an air-tight box. *Indian Journal of Medical Research, 49,* 82–89.

Anant, S. S. (1968). Treatment of alcoholics and drug addicts by verbal aversion techniques. *International Journal of the Addictions, 3,* 381–388.

Anderson, D. J. (1977). Transcendental Meditation as an alternative to heroin abuse in servicemen. *American Journal of Psychiatry, 134,* 1308–1309.

Anderson, D. R. (1979). Treatment of insomnia in a 13-year-old boy by relaxation training and reduction of parental attention. *Journal of Behavior Therapy and Experimental Psychiatry, 10,* 263–265.

Anderson, K. O., Bradley, L. A., Young, L. D., McDaniel, L. K., & Wise, C. M. (1985). Rheumatoid arthritis: Review of psychological factors related to etiology, effects, and treatment. *Psychological Bulletin, 98,* 358–387.

Anderson, K. O., & Masur, F. T., III. (1983). Psychological preparation for invasive medical and dental procedures. *Journal of Behavioral Medicine, 6,* 1–40.

Anderson, L., Lubetkin, B., Logan, D., & Alpert, M. (1973). Comparison of relaxation methods for alcoholics: Differential relaxation versus sensory awareness [Summary]. *Proceedings of the 81st Annual Convention of the American Psychological Association, 8,* 391–392.

Anderson, M. P., & Borkovec, T. D. (1980). Imagery processing and fear reduction during repeated exposure to two types of phobic imagery. *Behaviour Research and Therapy, 18,* 537–540.

Anderson, N. B., Lawrence, P. S., & Olson, T. W. (1981). Within-subject analysis of autogenic training and cognitive coping training in the treatment of tension headache pain. *Journal of Behavior Therapy and Experimental Psychiatry, 12,* 219–223.

Andrasik, F., Blanchard, E. B., Arena, J. G., Saunders, N. L., & Barron, K. D. (1982). Psychophysiology of recurrent headache: Methodological issues and new empirical findings. *Behavior Therapy, 13,* 407–429.

Andrasik, F., Blanchard, E. B., Arena, J. G., Teders, S. J., Teevan, R. C., & Rodichok, L. D. (1982). Psychological functioning in headache sufferers. *Psychosomatic Medicine, 44,* 171–182.

Andrasik, F., Blanchard, E. B., Edlund, S. R., & Rosenblum, E. L. (1982). Autogenic feedback in the treatment of two children with migraine headache. *Child and Family Behavior Therapy, 4*(4), 13–23.

Andrasik, F., Blanchard, E. B., Neff, D. F., & Rodichok, L. D. (1984). Biofeedback and relaxation training for chronic headache: A controlled comparison of booster treatments and regular contacts for long-term maintenance. *Journal of Consulting and Clinical Psychology, 52,* 609–615.

Andreychuk, T., & Skriver, C. (1975). Hypnosis and biofeedback in the treatment of migraine headache. *International Journal of Clinical and Experimental Hypnosis, 23,* 172–183.

Angers, P., Bilodeau, F., Bouchard, C., Luthe, W., Mailhot, D., Trudeau, M., & Vallieres, G. (1977a). Application of autogenic training in an elementary school. Parts I and II. In W. Luthe & F. Antonelli (Eds.), *Therapy in psychosomatic medicine: Autogenic Therapy* (pp. 246–257). Rome: Edizioni L. Pozzi.

Angers, P., Bilodeau, F., Bouchard, C., Luthe, W., Mailhot, D., Trudeau, M., & Vallieres, G. (1977b). Application of autogenic training in an elementary school. Part III. Conclusions and recommendations. In W. Luthe & F. Antonelli (Eds.), *Therapy in psychosomatic medicine: Autogenic therapy* (pp. 258–262). Rome: Edizioni L. Pozzi.

Appelle, S., & Oswald, L. E. (1974). Simple reaction time as a function of alertness and prior mental activity. *Perceptual and Motor Skills, 38,* 1263–1268.

Arcan, P. (1977). Autogenic group therapy. In W. Luthe & F. Antonelli (Eds.), *Therapy in psychomatic medicine: Autogenic therapy* (pp. 384–386). Rome: Edizioni L. Pozzi.

Aron, A., & Aron, E. N. (1980). The Transcendental Meditation program's effect on addictive behavior. *Addictive Behaviors, 5,* 3–12.

Aron, A., & Aron, E. N. (1981). *Evidence from Transcendental Meditation research for a social field.* Paper presented at the meeting of the Society for General Systems Research, Louisville, KY.

Aron, E. N., & Aron, A. (1979). The Transcendental Meditation program for the reduction of stress-related conditions. *Journal of Chronic Diseases and Therapeutics Research, 3*(9), 11–21.

Aron, E. N., & Aron, A. (1982). Transcendental Meditation program and marital adjustment. *Psychological Reports, 51,* 887–890.

Ascher, L. M., & Efran, J. S. (1978). Use of paradoxical intention in a behavioral program for sleep onset insomnia. *Journal of Consulting and Clinical Psychology, 46,* 547–550.

Aserinsky, E., & Kleitman, N. (1953). Regularly occurring periods of eye motility, and concomitant phenomena, during sleep. *Science, 118,* 273–274.

Ashem, B., & Donner, L. (1968). Covert sensitization with alcoholics: A controlled replication. *Behaviour Research and Therapy, 6,* 7–12.

Ashenberg, Z. S., Morgan, G. D., & Fisher, E. B., Jr. (1984, May). *Psychological stress and smoking recidivism: A prospective assessment.* Paper presented at the meeting of the Society of Behavioral Medicine, Philadelphia.

Association of Sleep Disorders Centers. (1979). Diagnostic classification of sleep and arousal disorders (1st ed.). *Sleep, 2,* 1–137.

Azrin, N. H., & Nunn, R. G. (1974). A rapid method of eliminating stuttering by a regulated breathing approach. *Behaviour Research and Therapy, 12,* 279–286.

Azrin, N. H., & Nunn, R. G. (1977). *Habit control in a day.* New York: Simon & Schuster.

Azrin, N. H., Nunn, R. G., & Frantz, S. E. (1979). Comparison of regulated-breathing versus abbreviated desensitization on reported stuttering episodes. *Journal of Speech and Hearing Disorders, 44,* 331–339.

Bacon, M., & Poppen, R. (1985). A behavioral analysis of diphragmatic breathing and its effects on peripheral temperature. *Journal of Behavior Therapy and Experimental Psychiatry, 16,* 15–21.

Badawi, K., Wallace, R. K., Orme-Johnson, D., & Rouzere, A. M. (1984). Electrophysiologic characteristics of respiratory suspension periods occurring during the practice of the Transcendental Meditation program. *Psychosomatic Medicine, 46,* 267–276.

Bagchi, B. K. (1936). Mental hygiene and the Hindu doctrine of relaxation. *Mental Hygiene, 20,* 424–440.

Bagchi, B. K. (1969). Mysticism and mist in India. *Journal of the American Society of Psychosomatic Dentistry and Medicine, 16,* 73–87, 120–136.

Bagchi, B. K., & Wenger, M. A. (1957). Electro-physiological correlates of some yogi exercises. *Electroencephalography and Clinical Neurophysiology, 9* (Suppl. 7), 132–149.

Bahrke, M. S., & Morgan, W. P. (1978). Anxiety reduction following exercise and meditation. *Cognitive Therapy and Research, 2,* 323–333.

Bailey, R. D. (1984). Autogenic regulation training and sickness absence amongst student nurses in general training. *Training of Advanced Nursing, 9,* 581–587.

Bakal, D. A., & Kaganov, J. A. (1977). Muscle contraction and migraine headache: Psychophysiologic comparison. *Headache, 17,* 208–215.

Bali, L. R. (1979). Long-term effect of relaxation on blood pressure and anxiety levels of essential hypertensive males: A controlled study. *Psychosomatic Medicine, 41,* 637–646.

Balick, L., Elfner, L., May, J., & Moore, J. D. (1982). Biofeedback treatment of dysmenorrhea. *Biofeedback and Self-Regulation, 7,* 499–520.

Ballentine, R. M. (1976). Anatomy and physiology of breath. In R. M. Ballentine (Ed.), *Science of breath* (pp. 23–58). Glenview, IL: Himalayan International Institute of Yoga Science and Philosophy.

Bandura, A. (1969). *Principles of behavior modification.* New York: Holt, Rinehart & Winston.

Bandura, A. (1978). The self system in reciprocal determinism. *American Psychologist, 33,* 344–358.

Bandura, A., Blanchard, E. B., & Ritter, B. (1969). Relative efficacy of desensitization and modeling approaches for inducing behavioral, affective, and attitudinal changes. *Journal of Personality and Social Psychology, 13,* 173–199.

Banner, C. N., & Meadows, W. M. (1983). Examination of the effectiveness of various treatment techniques for reducing tension. *British Journal of Clinical Psychology, 22,* 183–193.

Bannister, G. (1977). Scotch tape as an adjunct to relaxation training in a case of Huntington's chorea. *Journal of Behavior Therapy and Experimental Psychiatry, 8,* 321–324.

Banquet, J. P. (1973). Spectral analysis of the EEG in meditation. *Electroencephalography and Clinical Neurophysiology, 35,* 143–151.

Banquet, J. P., & Lesevre, N. (1980). Event-related potentials in altered states of consciousness. *Motivation, Motor and Sensory Processes of the Brain, Progress in Brain Research, 54,* 447–453.

Banyai, E. I., & Hilgard, E. R. (1976). A comparison of active-alert hypnotic induction with traditional relaxation induction. *Journal of Abnormal Psychology, 85,* 218–224.

Barber, T. X. (1965). Measuring "hypnotic-like" suggestibility with and without "hypnotic induction"; psychometric properties, norms, and variables influencing response to the Barber Suggestibility Scale (BSS). *Psychological Reports, 16,* 809–844.

Barber, T. X. (1969). *Hypnosis: A scientific approach.* New York: Van Nostrand Reinhold.

Barber, T. X. (1970). *LSD, marijuana, yoga, and hypnosis.* Chicago: Aldine.

Barber, T. X. (1976). *Pitfalls in human research: Ten pivotal points.* Elmsford, NY: Pergamon Press.

Barber, T. X. (1978). Hypnosis, suggestions, and psychosomatic phenomena: A new look from the standpoint of recent experimental studies. *American Journal of Clinical Hypnosis, 21,* 13–27.

Barber, T. X. (1984). Hypnosis, deep relaxation, and active relaxation: Data, theory, and clinical applications. In R. L. Woolfolk & P. M. Lehrer (Eds.), *Principles and practice of stress management* (pp. 142–187). New York: Guilford.

Barber, T. X., & Calverley, D. S. (1964). Toward a theory of hypnotic behavior: Effects on suggestibility of defining the situation as hypnosis and defining response to suggestions as easy. *Journal of Abnormal and Social Psychology, 68,* 585–592.

Barber, T. X., & Calverley, D. S. (1965a). Empirical evidence for a theory of hypnotic behavior: Effects on suggestibility of five variables typically included in hypnotic induction procedures. *Journal of Consulting Psychology, 29,* 98–107.

Barber, T. X., & Calverley, D. S. (1965b). Empirical evidence for a theory of "hypnotic" behavior: The suggestibility-enhancing effects of motivational suggestions, relaxation-sleep suggestions, and suggestions that the S will be effectively "hypnotized." *Journal of Personality, 33,* 256–270.

Barber, T. X., & Calverley, D. S. (1969). Multidimensional analysis of "hypnotic" behavior. *Journal of Abnormal Psychology, 74,* 209–220.

Barefoot, J. C., Dahlstrom, W. G., & Williams, R. B., Jr. (1983). Hostility, CHD incidence, and total mortality: A 25-year follow-up study of 255 physicians. *Psychosomatic Medicine, 45,* 59–63.

Barlow, D. H., Cohen, A. S., Waddell, M. T., Vermilyea, B. B., Klosko, J. S., Blanchard, E. B., & DiNardo, P. A. (1984). Panic and generalized anxiety disorders: Nature and treatment. *Behavior Therapy, 15,* 431–449.

Barlow, D. H., Leitenberg, H., & Agras, W. S. (1969). Experimental control of sexual deviation through manipulation of the noxious scene in covert sensitization. *Journal of Abnormal Psychology, 5,* 597–601.

Barlow, D. H., & Wolfe, B. E. (1981). Behavioral approaches to anxiety disorders: A report on the NIMH-SUNY, Albany research conference. *Journal of Consulting and Clinical Psychology, 49,* 448–454.

Barmark, S. M., & Guanitz, S. C. B. (1979). Transcendental meditation and heterohypnosis as altered states of consciousness. *International Journal of Clinical and Experimental Hypnosis, 27,* 227–239.

Barofsky, I. (1981). Issues and approaches to the psychosocial assessment of the cancer patient. In C. K. Prokop & L. A. Bradley (Eds.), *Medical psychology: Contributions to behavioral medicine* (pp. 55–65). New York: Academic Press.

Barolin, G. S. (1977). Autogenic training with athletes. In W. Luthe & F. Antonelli (Eds.), *Therapy in psychosomatic medicine: Autogenic therapy* (pp. 293–295). Rome: Edizioni L. Pozzi.

Barr, B. P., & Benson, H. (1984). The relaxation response and cardiovascular disorders. *Behavioral Medicine Update, 6*(4), 29–30.

Barrios, B. A., Ginter, E. J., Scalise, J. J., & Miller, F. G. (1980). Treatment of test anxiety by applied relaxation and cue-controlled relaxation. *Psychological Reports, 46,* 1287–1296.

Barrios, B. A., & Shigetomi, C. C. (1979). Coping-skills training for the management of anxiety: A critical review. *Behavior Therapy, 10,* 491–522.

Barrios, B. A., & Shigetomi, C. C. (1980). Coping skills training: Potential for prevention of fears and anxieties. *Behavior Therapy, 11,* 431–439.

Bartlett, J. C., Burleson, G., & Santrock, J. W. (1982). Emotional mood and memory in young children. *Journal of Experimental Child Psychology, 34,* 59–76.

Barwood, T. J., Empson, J. A. C., Lister, S. G., & Tilley, A. J. (1978). Auditory evoked potentials and transcendental meditation. *Electroencephalography and Clinical Neurophysiology, 45,* 671–673.

Basler, H. D., Brinkmeier, U., Buser, K., Haehn, K. D., & Molders-Kober, R. (1982). Psychological group treatment of essential hypertension in general practice. *British Journal of Clinical Psychology, 21,* 295–302.

Basmajian, J. V. (Eds.). (1979). *Biofeedback: Principles and practice for clinicians.* Baltimore: Williams & Wilkins.

Bassett, J. E., Blanchard, E. B., & Estes, L. D. (1977). Effects of instructional-expectancy sets on relaxation training with prisoners. *Journal of Community Psychology, 5,* 166–170.

Batey, D. M., Lehrer, P. M., & Woolfolk, R. L. (1984, May). *Self-report of muscle tension using S.S. Stevens' magnitude estimation method: Evaluation of a method of assessing the results of relaxation therapy.* Paper presented at the meeting of the Society of Behavioral Medicine, Philadelphia.

Bauer, R. M., & Craighead, W. E. (1979). Psychophysiological responses to the imagination of fearful and neutral situations: The effects of imagery instructions. *Behavior Therapy, 10,* 389–403.

Beary, J. F., & Benson, H. (1974). A simple psychophysiologic technique which elicits the hypometabolic changes of the relaxation response. *Psychosomatic Medicine, 36,* 115–120.

Beck, A. T. (1984). Cognitive approaches to stress management. In R. L. Woolfolk & P. M. Lehrer (Eds.), *Principles and practice of stress management* (pp. 255–305). New York: Guilford.

Beck, A. T., Ward, C. H., Mendelsohn, M., Mock, J., & Erbaugh, J. (1961). An inventory for measuring depression. *Archives of General Psychiatry, 4,* 561–571.

Beck, F. M. , Kaul, T. J., & Russell, R. K. (1978). Treatment of dental anxiety by cue-controlled relaxation. *Journal of Counseling Psychology, 25,* 591–594.

Beck, N. C., & Hall, D. (1978). Natural childbirth: A review and analysis. *Obstetrics and Gynecology, 52,* 371–379.

Becker, D. E., & Shapiro, D. (1981). Physiological responses to clicks during Zen, Yoga, and TM meditation. *Psychophysiology, 18,* 694–699.

Bedell, J. R. (1976). Systematic desensitization, relaxation-training and suggestion in the treatment of test anxiety. *Behaviour Research and Therapy, 14,* 309–311.

Beiman, I., Graham, L. E., & Ciminero, A. R. (1978a). Self-control progressive relaxation training as an alternative nonpharmacological treatment for essential hypertension: Therapeutic effects in the natural environment. *Behaviour Research and Therapy, 16,* 371–375.

Beiman, I., Graham, L. E., & Ciminero, A. R. (1978b). Setting generality of blood pressure reductions and the psychological treatment of reactive hypertension. *Journal of Behavioral Medicine, 1,* 445–453.

Beiman, I., Israel, E., & Johnson, S. A. (1978). During training and posttraining effects of live and taped extended progressive relaxation, self-relaxation, and electromyogram biofeedback. *Journal of Consulting and Cllinical Psychology, 46,* 314–321.

Beiman, I. H., Johnson, S. A., Puente, A. E., Majestic, H. W., & Graham, L. E. (1984). The relationship of client characteristics to outcome for transcendental meditation, behavior therapy, and self-regulation. In D. H. Shapiro, Jr. & R. N. Walsh (Eds.), *Meditation: Classic and contemporary perspectives* (pp. 565–571). Hawthorne, NY: Aldine.

Bell, J. S. (1979). The use of EEG theta biofeedback in the treatment of a patient with sleep-onset insomnia. *Biofeedback and Self-Regulation, 4,* 229–236.

Bellack, A. (1973). Reciprocal inhibition of a laboratory conditioned fear. *Behaviour Research and Therapy, 11,* 11–18.

Bennett, G., & Millard, M. (1985). Compliance with relaxation training: The effect of providing information. *Behavioural Psychotherapy, 13,* 110–119.

Bennett, J. E. & Trinder, J. (1977). Hemispheric laterality and cognitive style associated with Transcendental Meditation. *Psychophysiology, 14,* 293–296.

Bennink, C. D., Hulst, L. L., & Benthem, J. A. (1982). The effects of EMG biofeed-back and relaxation training on primary dysmenorrhea. *Journal of Behavioral Medicine, 5,* 329–341.

Benson, H. (1969). Yoga for drug abuse. *New England Journal of Medicine, 281,* 1133.

Benson, H. (1974a). Decreased alcohol intake associated with the practice of meditation: A retrospective investigation. *Annals of the New York Academy of Sciences, 233,* 174–177.

Benson, H. (1974b). Your innate asset for combating stress. *Harvard Business Review, 52*(4), 49–60.

Benson, H. (1975). *The relaxation response.* New York: Morrow.

Benson, H. (1977). Systemic hypertension and the relaxation response. *New England Journal of Medicine, 296,* 1152–1156.

Benson, H., Alexander, S., & Feldman, C. L. (1975). Decreased premature ventricular contractions through use of the relaxation response in patients with stable ischaemic heart-disease. *Lancet, 2,* 380–382.

Benson, H., Beary, J. F., & Carol, M. P. (1974). The relaxation response. *Psychiatry, 37,* 37–46.

Benson, H., Dryer, T., & Hartley, L. H. (1978). Decreased VO$_2$ consumption during exercise with elicitation of the relaxation response. *Journal of Human Stress, 4,* 38–42.

Benson, H., Frankel, F. H., Apfel, R., Daniels, M.D., Schniewind, H. E., Nemiah, J. C., Sifneos, P. E., Crassweller, K. D., Greenwood, M. M., Kotch, J. B., Arns, P. A., & Rosner, B. (1978). Treatment of anxiety: A comparison of the usefulness of self-hypnosis and a meditational relaxation technique. An overview. *Psychotherapy and Psychosomatics, 30,* 229–242.

Benson, H., Herd, J. A., Morse, W. H., & Kelleher, R. T. (1969). Behavioral induction of arterial hypertension and its reversal. *American Journal of Physiology, 217,* 30–34.

Benson, H., Klemchuk, H. P., & Graham, J. R. (1974). The usefulness of the relaxation response in the therapy of headache. *Headache, 14,* 49–52.

Benson, H., Kotch, J. B., & Crassweller, K. D. (1978). Stress and hypertension: Interrelations and management. *Cardiovascular Clinics, 9,* 113–124.

Benson, H., Kotch, J. B., Crassweller, K. D., & Greenwood, M. M. (1977). Historical and clinical considerations of the relaxation response. *American Scientist, 65,* 441–445.

Benson, H., Marzetta, B. R., & Rosner, B. A. (1974). Decreased blood pressure associated with the regular elicitation of the relaxation response: A study of hypertensive subjects. In R. S. Eliot (Ed.), *Contemporary problems in cardiology (vol. 1). Stress and the heart* (pp. 293–302). Mt. Kisco, NY: Futura.

Benson, H., Rosner, B. A., Marzetta, B. R., & Klemchuk, H. P. (1974a). Decreased blood pressure in borderline hypertensive subjects who practiced meditation. *Journal of Chronic Diseases, 27,* 163–169.

Benson, H., Rosner, B. A., Marzetta, B. R., & Klemchuk, H. M. (1974b). Decreased blood-pressure in pharmacologically treated hypertensive patients who regularly elicited the relaxation response. *Lancet, 1,* 289–291.

Benson, H., Shapiro, D., Tursky, B., & Schwartz, G. E. (1971). Decreased systolic blood pressure through operant conditioning techniques in patients with essential hypertension. *Science, 173,* 740–742.

Benson, H., Steinert, R. F., Greenwood, M. M., Klemchuk, H. M., & Peterson, N. H. (1975). Continuous measurement of O_2 consumption and CO_2 elimination during a wakeful hypometabolic state. *Journal of Human Stress, 1,* 37–44.

Benson, H., & Wallace, R. K. (1972a). Decreased blood pressure in hypertensive subjects who practiced meditation. *Circulation,* Vols. *45* and *46*(Suppl. 2), 130.

Benson, H., & Wallace, R. K. (1972b). Decreased drug abuse with Transcendental Meditation—A study of 1,862 subjects. In C. J. D. Zarafonetis (Ed.), *Drug abuse: Proceedings of the international conference* (pp. 369–376). Philadelphia: Lea & Febiger.

Bergland, B. W., & Chal, A. H. (1972). Relaxation training and a junior high behavior problem. *School Counselor, 19,* 288–293.

Bernstein, D. A., & Borkovec, T. D. (1973). *Progressive relaxation training: A manual for the helping professions.* Champaign, IL: Research Press.

Bernstein, D. A., & Given, B. A. (1984). Progressive relaxation: Abbreviated methods. In R. L. Woolfolk & P. M. Lehrer (Eds.), *Principles and practice of stress management* (pp. 43–69). New York: Guilford.

Berry, T. (1971). *Religions of India: Hinduism, Yoga, Buddhism.* New York: Bruce.

Bertilson, H. S., Bartz, A. E., & Zimmerman, A. D. (1979). Treatment program for borderline hypertension among college students: Relaxation, finger temperature biofeedback, and generalization. *Psychological Reports, 44,* 107–114.

Best, J. A., Owen, L. E., & Trentadue, L. (1978). Comparison of satiation and rapid smoking in self-managed smoking cessation. *Addictive Behaviors, 3,* 71–78.

Bexton, W. H., Heron, W., & Scott, T. H. (1954). Effects of decreased variation in the sensory environment. *Canadian Journal of Psychology, 8,* 70–76.

Bhatara, V., Arnold, L. E., Lorance, T., & Gupta, D. (1979). Muscle relaxation therapy in hyperkinesis: Is it effective? *Journal of Learning Disabilities, 12,* 182–186.

Bing, E. (1969). *Six practical lessons for an easier childbirth.* New York: Bantam Books.

Birchfield, R. I., Sieker, H. O., & Heyman, A. (1958). Alterations in blood gases during natural sleep and narcolepsy. *Neurology, 8,* 107–112.

Blacker, H. M. (1980). Volitional sympathetic control. *Anesthesia and Analgesia, 59,* 785–788.

Blackwell, B., Hanenson, I., Bloomfield, S., Magenheim, H., Gartside, P., Nidich, S., Robinson, A., & Zigler, R. (1976). Transcendental meditation in hypertension: Individual response patterns. *Lancet, 1,* 223–226.

Blake, B. G. (1965). The application of behaviour therapy to the treatment of alcoholism. *Behaviour Research and Therapy, 3,* 75–85.

Blake, B. G. (1967). A follow-up of alcoholics treated by behaviour therapy. *Behaviour Research and Therapy, 5,* 89–94.

Blanchard, E. B. (1982). Behavioral medicine: Past, present, and future. *Journal of Consulting and Clinical Psychology, 50,* 795–796.

Blanchard, E. B., & Ahles, T. A. (1979). Behavioral treatment of psychophysical disorders. *Behavior Modification, 3,* 518–549.

Blanchard, E. B., Andrasik, F., Ahles, T. A., Teders, S. J., & O'Keefe, D. (1980). Migraine and tension headache: A meta-analytic review. *Behavior Therapy, 11,* 613–631.

Blanchard, E. B., Andrasik, F., Arena, J. G., Neff, D. F., Jurish, S. E., Teders, S. J., Barron, K. D., & Rodichok, L. D. (1983). Nonpharmacologic treatment of chronic headache: Prediction of outcome. *Neurology, 33,* 1596-1603.

Blanchard, E. B., Andrasik, F., Arena, J. G., Neff, D. F., Saunders, N. L., Jurish, S. E., Teders, S. J., & Rodichok, L. D. (1983). Psychophysiological responses as predictors of response to behavioral treatment of chronic headache. *Behavior Therapy, 14,* 357-374.

Blanchard, E. B., Andrasik, F., Evans, D. D., & Hillhouse, J. (1985). Biofeedback and relaxation treatments for headache in the elderly: A caution and a challenge. *Biofeedback and Self-Regulation, 10,* 69-73.

Blanchard, E. B., Andrasik, F., Evans, D. D., Neff, D. F., Appelbaum, K. A., & Rodichok, L. D. (1985). Behavioral treatment of 250 chronic headache patients: A clinical replication series. *Behavior Therapy, 16,* 308-327.

Blanchard, E. B., Andrasik, F., Jurish, S. E., & Teders, S. J. (1982). The treatment of cluster headache with relaxation and thermal biofeedback. *Biofeedback and Self-Regulation, 7,* 185-191.

Blanchard, E. B., Andrasik, F., Neff, D. F., Arena, J. G., Ahles, T. A., Jurish, S. E., Pallmeyer, T. P., Saunders, N. L., Teders, S. J., Barron, K. D., & Rodichok, L. D. (1982). Biofeedback and relaxation training with three kinds of headache: Treatment effects and their prediction. *Journal of Consulting and Clinical Psychology, 50,* 562–575.

Blanchard, E. B., Andrasik, F., Neff, D. F., Saunders, N. L., Arena, J. G., Pallmeyer, T. P., Teders, S. J., Jurish, S. E., & Rodichok, L. D. (1983). Four process studies in the behavioral treatment of chronic headache. *Behaviour Research and Therapy, 21,* 209-220.

Blanchard, E. B., Andrasik, F., Neff, D. F., Teders, S. J., Pallmeyer, T. P., Arena, J. G., Jurish, S. E., Saunders, N. L., Ahles, T. A., & Rodichok, L. D. (1982). Sequential comparisons of relaxation training and biofeedback in the treatment of three kinds of chronic headache or, the machines may be necessary some of the time. *Behaviour Research and Therapy, 20,* 469-481.

Blanchard, E. B., & Epstein, L. H. (1978). *A biofeedback primer.* Reading, MA: Addison-Wesley.

Blanchard, E. B., Jaccard, J., Andrasik, F., Guarnieri, P., & Jurish, S. E. (1985). Reduction in headache patients' medical expenses associated with biofeedback and relaxation treatments. *Biofeedback and Self-Regulation, 10,* 63-68.

Blanchard, E. B., Jurish, S. E., Andrasik, F., & Epstein, L. H. (1981). The relationship between muscle discrimination ability and response to relaxation training in three kinds of headaches. *Biofeedback and Self-Regulation, 6,* 537-545.

Blanchard, E. B., McCoy, G. C., Andrasik, F., Acerra, M., Pallmeyer, T. P., Gerardi, R., Halpern, M., & Musso, A. (1984). Preliminary results from a controlled evaluation of thermal biofeedback as a treatment for essential hypertension. *Biofeedback and Self-Regulation, 9,* 471-495.

Blanchard, E. B., McCoy, G. C., Musso, A., Gerardi, M. A., Pallmeyer, T. P., Gerardi, R., Cotch, P. A., Siracusa, K., & Andrasik, F. (1986). A controlled comparison of thermal biofeedback and relaxation training in the treatment of essential hypertension: I. Short-term and long-term outcome. *Behavior Therapy, 17,* 563–579.

Blanchard, E. B., Theobald, D. E., Williamson, D. A., Silver, B. V., & Brown, D. A. (1978). Temperature biofeedback in the treatment of migraine headaches: A controlled evaluation. *Archives of General Psychiatry, 35,* 581–588.

Blizard, D. A., Cowings, P., & Miller, N. E. (1975). Visceral responses to opposite types of autogenic-training imagery. *Biological Psychology, 3,* 49–55.

Boals, G. F. (1978). Toward a cognitive reconceptualization of meditation. *Journal of Transpersonal Psychology, 10,* 143–182.

Bohachick, P. (1984). Progressive relaxation training in cardiac rehabilitation: Effect on psychologic variables. *Nursing Research, 33,* 283–287.

Boice, R. (1983). Observational skills. *Psychological Bulletin, 93,* 3–29.

Boller, J. D., & Flom, R. P. (1979). Treatment of the common migraine: Systematic application of biofeedback and autogenic training. *American Journal of Clinical Biofeedback, 2,* 63–64.

Bootzin, R. R. (1973, August). *Stimulus control of insomnia.* Paper presented at the meeting of the American Psychological Association, Montreal.

Bootzin, R. R., & Engle-Friedman, M. (1981). The assessment of insomnia. *Behavioral Assessment, 3,* 107–126.

Bootzin, R. R., Engle-Friedman, M., & Hazelwood, L. (1983). Insomnia. In P. M. Lewinsohn & L. Teri (Eds.), *Clinical geropsychology: New directions in assessment and treatment* (pp. 81–115). Elmsford, NY: Pergamon Press.

Borgeat, F., Hade, B., Larouche, L. M., & Bedwani, C. N. (1980). Effect of therapist's active presence on EMG biofeedback training of headache patients. *Biofeedback and Self-Regulation, 5,* 275–282.

Borgeat, F., Stravynski, A., & Chaloult, L. (1983). The influence of two different sets of information and suggestions on the subjective effects of relaxation. *Journal of Human Stress, 9*(3), 40–45.

Borkovec, T. D. (1982). Insomnia. *Journal of Consulting and Clinical Psychology, 50,* 880–895.

Borkovec, T. D., & Fowles, D. C. (1973). Controlled investigation of the effects of progressive and hypnotic relaxation on insomnia. *Journal of Abnormal Psychology, 82,* 153–158.

Borkovec, T. D., Grayson, J. B., & Cooper, K. M. (1978). Treatment of general tension: Subjective and physiological effects of progressive relaxation. *Journal of Consulting and Clinical Psychology, 46,* 518–528.

Borkovec, T. D., Grayson, J. B., O'Brien, G. T., & Weerts, T. C. (1979). Relaxation treatment of pseudoinsomnia and idiopathic insomnia: An electroencephalographic evaluation. *Journal of Applied Behavior Analysis, 12,* 37–54.

Borkovec, T. D., & Hennings, B. L. (1978). The role of physiological attention-focusing in the relaxation treatment of sleep disturbance, general tension, and specific stress reaction. *Behaviour Research and Therapy, 16,* 7–19.

Borkovec, T. D., Johnson, M. C., & Block, D. L. (1984). Evaluating experimental designs in relaxation research. In R. L. Woolfolk & P. M. Lehrer (Eds.), *Principles and practice of stress management* (pp. 368–403.). New York: Guilford.

Borkovec, T. D., Kaloupek, D. G., & Slama, K. M. (1975). The facilitative effect of muscle tension-release in the relaxation treatment of sleep disturbance. *Behavior Therapy, 6,* 301–309.

Borkovec, T. D., & Nau, S. D. (1972). Credibility of analogue therapy rationales. *Journal of Behavior Therapy and Experimental Psychiatry, 3,* 257–260.

Borkovec, T. D., & Sides, J. K. (1979a). The contribution of relaxation and expectancy to fear reduction via graded imaginal exposure to feared stimuli. *Behaviour Research and Therapy, 17,* 529–540.

Borkovec, T. D., & Sides, J. K. (1979b). Critical procedural variables related to the physiological effects of progressive relaxation: A review. *Behaviour Research and Therapy, 17,* 119–125.

Borkovec, T. D., Steinmark, S. W., & Nau, S. D. (1973). Relaxation training and single-item desensitization in the group treatment of insomnia. *Journal of Behavior Therapy and Experimental Psychiatry, 4,* 401–403.

Borkovec, T. D., & Weerts, T. C. (1976). Effects of progressive relaxation on sleep disturbance: An electroencephalographic evaluation. *Psychosomatic Medicine, 38,* 173–180.

Borkovec, T. D., Weerts, T. C., & Bernstein, D. A. (1977). Assessment of anxiety. In A. R. Ciminero, K. S. Calhoun, & H. E. Adams (Eds.), *Handbook of behavioral assessment* (pp. 367–428). New York: Wiley.

Borland, C., & Landrith, G., III. (1977). Improved quality of city life through the Transcendental Meditation program: Decreased crime rate. In D. W. Orme-Johnson & J. T. Farrow (Eds.), *Scientific research on the Transcendental Meditation program: Collected papers* (Vol. 1, 2nd ed., pp. 639–648). Livingston Manor, NY: Maharishi European Research University Press.

Borrie, R. A., & Suedfeld, P. (1980). Restricted environmental stimulation therapy in a weight reduction program. *Journal of Behavioral Medicine, 3,* 147–161.

Boswell, P. C., & Murray, E. J. (1979). Effects of meditation on psychological and physiological measures of anxiety. *Journal of Consulting and Clinical Psychology, 47,* 606–607.

Boudreau, L. (1972). Transcendental meditation and yoga as reciprocal inhibitors. *Journal of Behavior Therapy and Experimental Psychiatry, 3,* 97–98.

Bowles, C., Smith, J., & Parker, K. (1979). EMG biofeedback and progressive relaxation training: A comparative study of two groups of normal subjects. *Western Journal of Nursing Research, 1,* 179–189.

Bradley, B. W., & McCanne, T. R. (1981). Autonomic responses to stress: The effects of progressive relaxation, the relaxation response, and expectancy of relief. *Biofeedback and Self-Regulation, 6,* 235–251.

Bradley, C. (1982). Psychophysiological aspects of the management of diabetes mellitus. *International Journal of Mental Health, 11,* 117–132.

Brady, J. P. (1973). Metronome-conditioned relaxation: A new behavioural procedure. *British Journal of Psychiatry, 122,* 729–730.

Brady, J. P., Luborsky, L., & Kron, R. E. (1974). Blood pressure reduction in patients with essential hypertension through metronome-conditioned relaxation: A preliminary report. *Behavior Therapy, 5,* 203–209.

Braud, L. W. (1978). The effects of frontal EMG biofeedback and progressive relaxation upon hyperactivity and its behavioral concomitants. *Biofeedback and Self-Regulation, 3,* 69–89.

Braud, L. W., & Braud, W. G. (1974). Further studies of relaxation as a psi-conducive state. *Journal of the American Society for Psychical Research, 68,* 229–245.

Braud, W. G. (1981). Psi performance and autonomic nervous system activity. *Journal of the American Society for Psychical Research, 75,* 1–35.

Braud, W. G., & Braud, L. W. (1973). Preliminary explorations of psi-conducive states: Progressive muscular relaxation. *Journal of the American Society for Psychical Research, 67,* 26–46.

Braud, W., & Masters, D. (1980). Electrodermal reactions to opposite types of autogenic training imagery. *Biological Psychology, 10,* 211–218.

Brauer, A. P., Horlick, L., Nelson, E., Farquhar, J. W., & Agras, W. S. (1979). Relaxation therapy for essential hypertension: A veterans administration outpatient study. *Journal of Behavioral Medicine, 2,* 21–29.

Brautigam, E. (1977). Effects of the Transcendental Meditation program on drug abusers: A prospective study. In D. W. Orme-Johnson & J. T. Farrow (Eds.), *Scientific research on the Transcendental Meditation program: Collected papers* (Vol. 1, 2nd ed., pp. 506–514). Livingston Manor, NY: Maharishi European Research University Press.

Bregman, N. J., & McAllister, H. A. (1982). Motivation and skin temperature biofeedback: Yerkes-Dodson revisited. *Psychophysiology, 19,* 282–285.

Brener, J. (1977). Sensory and perceptual determinants of voluntary visceral control. In G. E. Schwartz & J. Beatty (Eds.), *Biofeedback: Theory and research* (pp. 29–66). New York: Academic Press.

Brieland, D. (1977). Historical overview. *Social Work, 22,* 341–346.

Brockway, B. S., Kleinmann, G., Edleson, J., & Gruenewald, K. (1977). Non-aversive procedures and their effect on cigarette smoking. *Addictive Behaviors, 2,* 121–128.

Brodman, K., Erdmann, A. J., Jr., & Wolff, H. G. (1949). *Manual: Cornell Medical Index Health Questionnaire.* New York: Cornell University Medical College.

Brooke, R. I., Stenn, P. G., & Mothersill, K. J. (1977). The diagnosis and conservative treatment of myofascial pain dysfunction syndrome. *Oral Surgery, 44,* 844–852.

Brooks, J. S., & Scarano, T. (1985). Transcendental Meditation in the treatment of post-Vietnam adjustment. *Journal of Counseling and Development, 64,* 212–215.

Brown, D., Forte, M., & Dysart, M. (1984). Visual sensitivity and mindfulness meditation. *Perceptual and Motor Skills, 58,* 775–784.

Brown, D. P., & Engler, J. (1980). The stages of mindfulness meditation: A validation study. *Journal of Transpersonal Psychology, 12,* 143–192.

Brown, J. M. (1984). Imagery coping strategies in the treatment of migraine. *Pain, 18,* 157–167.

Brown, S. D. (1980). Coping skills training: An evaluation of a psychoeducational program in a community mental health setting. *Journal of Counseling Psychology, 27,* 340–345.

Brunson, B. I. (1983). An automated self-paced relaxation training program for students. *Journal of College Student Personnel, 24,* 268.

Budzynski, T. H. (1973). Biofeedback procedures in the clinic. *Seminars in Psychiatry,* *5,* 537–547.

Budzynski, T. H. (1974). *Relaxation training program* (Cassette Recording). New York: Guilford.

Bujatti, M., & Riederer, P. (1976). Serotonin, noradrenaline, dopamine metabolites in Transcendental Meditation-technique. *Journal of Neural Transmission, 39,* 257–267.

Bullard, P. D., & DeCoster, D. T. (1972). The effects of hypnosis, relaxation and reinforcement on hypnotic behaviors and experiences. *American Journal of Clinical Hypnosis, 15,* 93–97.

Bulpitt, C. J., & Dollery, C. T. (1973). Side effects of hypotensive agents evaluated by a self-administered questionnaire. *British Medical Journal, 3,* 485–490.

Burish, T. G., & Carey, M. P. (1984). Conditioned responses to cancer chemotherapy: Etiology and treatment. In B. H. Fox & B. H. Newberry (Eds.), *Impact of psychoendrocrine systems in cancer and immunity* (pp. 147–178). Lewiston, NY: Hogrefe.

Burish, T. G., Hendrix, E. M., & Frost, R. O. (1981). Comparison of frontal EMG biofeedback and several types of relaxation instructions in reducing multiple indices of arousal. *Psychophysiology, 18,* 594–602.

Burish, T. G., & Lyles, J. N. (1979). Effectiveness of relaxation training in reducing the aversiveness of chemotherapy in the treatment of cancer. *Journal of Behavior Therapy and Experimental Psychiatry, 10,* 357–361.

Burish, T. G., & Lyles, J. N. (1981). Effectiveness of relaxation training in reducing adverse reactions to cancer chemotherapy. *Journal of Behavioral Medicine, 4,* 65–78.

Burish, T. G., Shartner, C. D., & Lyles, J. N. (1981). Effectiveness of multiple muscle-site EMG biofeedback and relaxation training in reducing the aversiveness of cancer chemotherapy. *Biofeedback and Self-Regulation, 6,* 523–535.

Butler, G., Cullington, A., Munby, M., Amies, P., & Gelder, M. (1984). Exposure and anxiety management in the treatment of social phobia. *Journal of Consulting and Clinical Psychology, 52,* 642–650.

Cacioppo, J. T. (1982). Social psychophysiology: A classic perspective and contemporary approach. *Psychophysiology, 19,* 241–251.

Cacioppo, J. T., & Petty, R. E. (1981). Electromyograms as measures of extent and affectivity of information processing. *American Psychologist, 36,* 441–456.

Callahan, E. J., & Leitenberg, H. (1973). Aversion therapy for sexual deviation: Contingent shock and covert sensitization. *Journal of Abnormal Psychology, 81,* 60–73.

Campbell, D. F., Dixon, J. K., Sanderford, L. D., & Denicola, M.A. (1984). Relaxation: Its effect on the nutritional status and performance status of clients with cancer. *Journal of the American Dietetic Association, 84,* 201–204.

Campbell, D. T., & Stanley, J. C. (1963). *Experimental and quasi-experimental designs for research.* Chicago: Rand McNally.

Campbell, R. V., O'Brien, S., Bickett, A. D., & Lutzker, J. R. (1983). In-home parent training, treatment of migraine headaches, and marital counseling as an ecobehavioral approach to prevent child abuse. *Journal of Behavior Therapy and Experimental Psychiatry, 14,* 147–154.

Cannici, J., Malcolm, R., & Peek, L. A. (1983). Treatment of insomnia in cancer patients using muscle relaxation training. *Journal of Behavior Therapy and Experimental Psychiatry, 14,* 251–256.

Cannon, W. B. (1929). *Bodily changes in pain, hunger, fear and rage* (2nd ed.). New York: Appleton-Century.

Canter, A., Kondo, C. Y., & Knott, J. R. (1975). A comparison of EMG feedback and progressive muscle relaxation training in anxiety neurosis. *British Journal of Psychiatry, 127,* 470–477.

Cappo, B. M., & Holmes, D. S. (1984). The utility of prolonged respiratory exhalation for reducing physiological and psychological arousal in non-threatening and threatening situations. *Journal of Psychosomatic Research, 28,* 265–273.

Carey, M. P., & Burish, T. G. (1985). Anxiety as a predictor of behavioral therapy outcome for cancer chemotherapy patients. *Journal of Consulting and Clinical Psychology, 53,* 860–865.

Carpenter, J. T. (1977). Meditation, esoteric traditions–Contributions to psychotherapy. *American Journal of Psychotherapy, 31,* 394–404.

Carpenter, M. B. (1972). *Core text of neuroanatomy.* Baltimore: Williams & Wilkins.

Carrington, P. (1978a). *Freedom in meditation.* Garden City, NY: Anchor Press.

Carrington, P. (1978b). The uses of meditation in psychotherapy. In A. A. Sugerman & R. E. Tarter (Eds.), *Expanding dimensions of consciousness* (pp. 81–98). New York: Springer.

Carrington, P. (1984). Modern forms of meditation. In R. L. Woolfolk & P. M. Lehrer (Eds.), *Principles and practice of stress management* (pp. 108–141). New York: Guilford.

Carrington, P., Collings, G. H., Jr., Benson, H., Robinson, H., Wood, L. W., Lehrer, P. M., Woolfolk, R. L., & Cole, J. W. (1980). The use of meditation-relaxation techniques for the management of stress in a working population. *Journal of Occupational Medicine, 22,* 221–231.

Carrington, P., & Ephron, H. S. (1975). Clinical use of meditation. In J. H. Masserman (Ed.), *Current psychiatric therapies* (Vol. 15, pp. 101–108). New York: Grune & Stratton.

Carr-Kaffashan, L., & Woolfolk, R. L. (1979). Active and placebo effects in treatment of moderate and severe insomnia. *Journal of Consulting and Clinical Psychology, 47,* 1072–1080.

Carroll, D., Baker, J., & Preston, M. (1979). Individual differences in visual imaging and the voluntary control of heart rate. *British Journal of Psychology, 70,* 39–49.

Carroll, D., Marzillier, J. S., & Merian, S. (1982). Psychophysiological changes accompanying different types of arousing and relaxing imagery. *Psychophysiology, 19,* 75–82.

Carroll, D., Marzillier, J. S., & Watson, F. (1980). Heart rate and self-report changes accompanying different types of relaxing imagery. *Behaviour Research and Therapy, 18,* 273–279.

Carsello, C. J., & Creaser, J. W. (1978). Does Transcendental Meditation training affect grades? *Journal of Applied Psychology, 63,* 644–645.

Carter, J. L., & Russell, H. L. (1981). *Use of biofeedback/relaxation procedures with learning disabled children.* Unpublished manuscript, University of Houston.

Carter, J. L., & Synolds, D. (1974). Effects of relaxation training upon handwriting quality. *Journal of Learning Disabilities, 7,* 236-238.

Cartwright, R., Butters, E., Weinstein, M., & Kroeker, L. (1977). The effects of pre-sleep stimuli of different sources and types on REM sleep. *Psychophysiology, 14,* 388-392.

Cassel, R. N. (1962). *The Child Behavior Rating Scale.* Beverly Hills, CA: Western Psychological Services.

Cattell, R. B. (1957). *The IPAT Anxiety Scale.* Champaign, IL: Institute for Personality and Ability Testing.

Cattell, R. B., Eber, H. W., & Tatsuoka, M. M. (1970). *Handbook for the Sixteen Personality Factor Questionnaire* (16 PF). Champaign, IL: Institute for Personality and Ability Testing.

Cautela, J. R. (1966a). A behavior therapy approach to pervasive anxiety. *Behaviour Research and Therapy, 4,* 99-109.

Cautela, J. R. (1966b). Treatment of compulsive behavior by covert sensitization. *Psychological Record, 16,* 33-41.

Cautela, J. R. (1967). Covert sensitization. *Psychological Reports, 20,* 459-468.

Cautela, J. R. (1970). Treatment of smoking by covert sensitization. *Psychological Reports, 26,* 415-420.

Cautela, J. R. (1977). The use of covert conditioning in modifying pain behavior. *Journal of Behavior Therapy and Experimental Psychiatry, 8,* 45-52.

Cautela, J. R., & Baron, M. G. (1973). Multifaceted behavior therapy of self-injurious behavior. *Journal of Behavior Therapy and Experimental Psychiatry, 4,* 125-131.

Cautela, J. R., & Baron, M. G. (1977). Covert conditioning: A theoretical analysis. *Behavior Modification, 1,* 351-368.

Cautela, J. R., & Groden, J. (1978). *Relaxation: A comprehensive manual for adults, children, and children with special needs.* Champaign, IL: Research Press.

Cautela, J. R., & McCullough, L. (1978). Covert conditioning: A learning-theory perspective on imagery. In J. L. Singer & K. S. Pope (Eds.), *The power of human imagination: New methods in psychotherapy* (pp. 227-254. New York: Plenum Press.

Cautela, J. R., & Wisocki, P. A. (1971). Covert sensitization for the treatment of sexual deviations. *Psychological Record, 21,* 37-48.

Cautela, J. R., & Wisocki, P. A. (1977). The thought stopping procedure: Description, application, and learning theory interpretations. *Psychological Record, 27,* 255-264.

Cauthen, N. R., & Prymak, C. A. (1977). Meditation versus relaxation: An examination of the physiological effects of relaxation training and of different levels of experience with transcendental meditation. *Journal of Consulting and Clinical Psychology, 45,* 496-497.

Chan, W., Faruqi, I., Kitagawa, J. M., & Raju, P. T. (1969). *The great Asian religions.* London: Macmillan.

Chaney, D. S., & Andreasen, L. (1972). Relaxation and neuromuscular tension control and changes in mental performance under induced tension. *Perceptual and Motor Skills, 34,* 677-678.

Chang, G. C. C. (1959). *The practice of Zen.* New York: Harper & Row.

Chang, G. C. C. (1963). *Teachings of Tibetan Yoga*. New Hyde Park, NY: University Books.

Chang-Liang, R., & Denney, D. R. (1976). Applied relaxation as training in self-control. *Journal of Counseling Psychology, 23,* 183–189.

Chappell, M. N., & Stevenson, T. I. (1936). Group psychological training in some organic conditions. *Mental Hygiene, 20,* 588–597.

Charlesworth, E. A., Murphy, S., & Beutler, L. E. (1981). Stress management skill for nursing students. *Journal of Clinical Psychology, 37,* 284–290.

Charlesworth, E. A., Williams, B. J., & Baer, P. E. (1984). Stress management at the worksite for hypertension: Compliance, cost-benefit, health care and hypertension-related variables. *Psychosomatic Medicine, 46,* 387–397.

Chaudhuri, H. (1975). Yoga psychology. In C. T. Tart (Ed.), *Transpersonal psychologies* (pp. 231–280). New York: Harper & Row.

Chertok, L. (1961). Relaxation and psychosomatic methods of preparation for childbirth. *American Journal of Obstetrics and Gynecology, 82,* 262–267.

Chesney, M. A., & Shelton, J. L. (1976). A comparison of muscle relaxation and electromyogram biofeedback treatments for muscle contraction headache. *Journal of Behavior Therapy and Experimental Psychiatry, 7,* 221–225.

Chesney, M. A., & Tasto, D. L. (1975a). The development of the menstrual symptom questionnaire. *Behaviour Research and Therapy, 13,* 237–244.

Chesney, M. A., & Tasto, D. L. (1975b). The effectiveness of behavior modification with spasmodic and congestive dysmenorrhea. *Behaviour Research and Therapy, 13,* 245–253.

Chesni, Y. (1980). A happy conclusion of a psychoanalytical psychotherapy by progressive relaxation and systematic desensitization. In F. J. McGuigan, W. E. Sime, & J. M. Wallace (Eds.), *Stress and tension control* (pp. 157–162). New York: Plenum Press.

Christoph, P., Luborsky, L., Kron, R., & Fishman, H. (1978). Blood pressure, heart rate and respiratory responses to a single session of relaxation: A partial replication. *Journal of Psychosomatic Research, 22,* 493–501.

Cinciripini, P. M., & Floreen, A. (1982). An evaluation of a behavioral program for chronic pain. *Journal of Behavioral Medicine, 5,* 375–389.

Clark, D. F. (1963). The treatment of monosymptomatic phobia by systematic desensitization. *Behaviour Research and Therapy, 1,* 63–68.

Clark, D. M., Salkovskis, P. M., & Chalkley, A. J. (1985). Respiratory control as a treatment for panic attacks. *Journal of Behavior Therapy and Experimental Psychiatry, 16,* 23–30.

Clark, M. E. (1979). Therapeutic applications of physiological control: The effectiveness of respiratory pacing in reducing autonomic and subjective distress. *Dissertation Abstracts International, 39,* 4571B–4572B. (University Microfilms No. 79-04,796)

Clarke, J. C., & Jackson, J. A. (1983). *Hypnosis and behavior therapy: The treatment of anxiety and phobias*. New York: Springer.

Coates, T. J., & Thoresen, C. E. (1979). Treating arousals during sleep using behavioral self-management. *Journal of Consulting and Clinical Psychology, 47,* 603–605.

Coe, W. C. (1980). Expectations, hypnosis, and suggestion in behavior change. In F.

H. Kanfer & A. P. Goldstein (Eds.), *Helping people change: A textbook of methods* (2nd ed., pp. 423–469). Elmsford, NY: Pergamon Press.

Cogan, R., & Kluthe, K. B. (1980). Effect of relaxation on discriminative sensitivity and ratings of sensory experience. *Journal of Psychosomatic Research, 24,* 29–34.

Cogan, R., & Kluthe, K. B. (1981). The role of learning in pain reduction associated with relaxation and patterned breathing. *Journal of Psychosomatic Research, 25,* 535–539.

Cohen, A. S., Barlow, D. H., & Blanchard, E. B. (1985). Psychophysiology of relaxation-associated panic attacks. *Journal of Abnormal Psychology, 94,* 96–101.

Cohen, J., & Sedlacek, K. (1983). Attention and autonomic self-regulation. *Psychosomatic Medicine, 45,* 243–257.

Cohen, M. J. (1978). Psychophysiological studies of headache: Is there similarity between migraine and muscle contraction headaches? *Headache, 18,* 189–196.

Cohen, W. (1957). Spatial and textural characteristics of the Ganzfeld. *American Journal of Psychology, 70,* 403–410.

Cole, P. A., Maldonado, A. J., Fuqua, R. W., Kent, N. D., Gault, F., Garman, F., & Macken, M. F. (1985, March). *Physiological effects of relaxation training during stressful and non-stressful conditions in Type A and Type B coronary patients.* Paper presented at the meeting of the Society of Behavioral Medicine, New Orleans.

Collins, F. L., Jr., Martin, J. E., & Hillenberg, J. B. (1982). Assessment of compliance with relaxation instructions: A pilot validation study. *Behavioral Assessment, 4,* 219–223.

Compton, W. C., & Becker, G. M. (1983). Self-actualizations and experience with Zen meditation: Is a learning period necessary for meditation? *Journal of Clinical Psychology, 39,* 925–929.

Comroe, J. H., Jr. (1965). *Physiology of respiration.* Chicago: Year Book.

Connor, W. H. (1974). Effects of brief relaxation training on autonomic response to anxiety-evoking stimuli. *Psychophysiology, 11,* 591–599.

Consolazio, C. F., Johnson, R. E., & Pecora, L. J. (1963). *Physiological measurements of metabolic functions in man.* New York: McGraw-Hill.

Conze, E. (1959). *Buddhism: Its essence and development.* New York: Harper & Row.

Cooke, G. (1968). Evaluation of the efficacy of the components of reciprocal inhibition psychotherapy. *Journal of Abnormal Psychology, 73,* 464–467.

Cooper, M. J., & Aygen, M. M. (1979). A relaxation technique in the management of hypercholesterolemia. *Journal of Human Stress, 5*(4), 24–27.

Corah, N. L. (1969). Development of a dental anxiety scale. *Journal of Dental Research, 48,* 596.

Corah, N. L., Gale, E. N., & Illig, S. J. (1979a). Psychological stress reduction during dental procedures. *Journal of Dental Research, 58,* 1347–1351.

Corah, N. L., Gale, E. N., & Illig, S. J. (1979b). The use of relaxation and distraction to reduce psychological stress during dental procedures. *Journal of the American Dental Association, 98,* 390–394.

Corah, N. L., Gale, E. N., Pace, L. F., & Seyrek, S. K. (1981). Evaluation of content and vocal style in relaxation instructions. *Behaviour Research and Therapy, 19,* 458–460.

Corby, J. C., Roth, W. T., Zarcone, V. P., Jr., & Kopell, B. S. (1978). Psychophysio-logical correlates of the practice of Tantric Yoga meditation. *Archives of General Psychiatry, 35,* 571-577.

Cotanch, P. H. (1983a). Relaxation techniques as antiemetic therapy. In J. Laszlo (Ed.), *Antiemetics and cancer chemotherapy* (pp. 164-176). Baltimore: Williams & Wilkins.

Cotanch, P. H. (1983b). Relaxation training for control of nausea and vomiting in patients receiving chemotherapy. *Cancer Nursing, 6,* 277-283.

Cott, A., Goldman, J. A., Pavloski, R. P., Kirschberg, G. J., & Fabich, M. (1981). The long-term therapeutic significance of the addition of electromyographic biofeed-back to relaxation training in the treatment of tension headaches. *Behavior Therapy, 12,* 556-559.

Cottier, C., Shapiro, K., & Julius, S. (1984). Treatment of mild hypertension with progressive muscle relaxation: Predictive value of indexes of sympathetic tone. *Ar-chives of Internal Medicine, 144,* 1954-1958.

Counts, K. D., Hollandsworth, J. G., Jr., & Alcorn, J. D. (1978). Use of electromyo-graphic biofeedback and cue-controlled relaxation in the treatment of test anxiety. *Journal of Consulting and Clinical Psychology, 46,* 990-996.

Coursey, R. D., Frankel, B. L., Gaarder, K. R., & Mott, D. E. (1980). A comparison of relaxation techniques with electrosleep therapy for chronic, sleep-onset insomnia: A sleep-EEG study. *Biofeedback and Self-Regulation, 5,* 57-73.

Cowings, P. S. (1977a). Combined use of autogenic therapy and biofeedback in train-ing effective control of heart rate by humans. In. W. Luthe & F. Antonelli (Eds.), *Therapy in psychosomatic medicine: Autogenic therapy* (pp. 167-173). Rome: Edizi-oni L. Pozzi.

Cowings, P. S. (1977b). Observed differences in learning ability of heart rate self-reg-ulation as a function of hypnotic susceptibility. In W. Luthe & F. Antonelli (Eds.), *Therapy in psychosomatic medicine: Autogenic therapy* (pp. 221-226). Rome: Edizi-oni L. Pozzi.

Cowings, P. S., Billingham, J., & Toscano, W. B. (1977). Learned control of multiple autonomic responses to compensate for the debilitating effects of motion sickness. *Therapy in Psychosomatic Medicine, 4,* 318-323.

Cowings, P. S., & Toscano, W. B. (1977). Psychosomatic health: Simultaneous control of multiple autonomic responses in humans. A training method. *Therapy in Psycho-somatic Medicine, 4,* 184-189.

Cowings, P. S., & Toscano, W. B. (1982). The relationship of motion sickness suscepti-bility to learned autonomic control for symptom suppression. *Aviation, Space, and Environmental Medicine, 53,* 570-575.

Cox, D. J., Freundlich, A., & Meyer, R. G. (1975). Differential effectiveness of electro-myograph feedback, verbal relaxation instructions, and medication placebo with tension headaches. *Journal of Consulting and Clinical Psychology, 43,* 892-898.

Cox, D. J., & Meyer, R. G. (1978). Behavioral treatment parameters with primary dysmenorrhea. *Journal of Behavioral Medicine, 1,* 297-310.

Cox, D. J., Taylor, A. G., Nowacek, G., Holley-Wilcox, P., Pohl, S. L., & Guthrow, E. (1984). The relationship between psychological stress and insulin-dependent diabetic blood glucose control: Preliminary investigations. *Health Psychology, 3,* 63–75.

Cox, S. B. (1972). Transcendental Meditation and the criminal justice system. *Kentucky Law Journal, 60,* 411–418.

Cragan, M. K., & Deffenbacher, J. L. (1984). Anxiety management training and relaxation as self-control in the treatment of generalized anxiety in medical outpatients. *Journal of Counseling Psychology, 31,* 123–131.

Craighead, W. E., Kazdin, A. E., & Mahoney, M. J. (1976). *Behavior modification: Principles, issues and applications.* Boston: Houghton Mifflin.

Credidio, S. G. (1980). Stress management with a psychophysiological profile, biofeedback, and relaxation training techniques. *American Journal of Clinical Biofeedback, 3,* 130–136.

Credidio, S. G. (1982). Comparative effectiveness of patterned biofeedback vs meditation training on EMG and skin temperature changes. *Behaviour Research and Therapy, 20,* 233–241.

Creer, T. L. (1982). Asthma. *Journal of Consulting and Clinical Psychology, 50,* 912–921.

Crits-Christoph, P., & Singer, J. L. (1981). Imagery in cognitive-behavior therapy: Research and application. *Clinical Psychology Review, 1,* 19–32.

Crowther, J. H. (1983). Stress management training and relaxation imagery in the treatment of essential hypertension. *Journal of Behavioral Medicine, 6,* 169–187.

Curtis, W. D., & Wessberg, H. W. (1976). A comparison of heart rate, respiration, and galvanic skin response among meditators, relaxers, and controls. *Journal of Altered States of Consciousness, 2,* 319–324.

Cuthbert, B., Kristeller, J., Simons, R., Hodes, R., & Lang, P. J. (1981). Strategies of arousal control: Biofeedback, meditation, and motivation. *Journal of Experimental Psychology: General, 110,* 518–546.

Dalal, A. S., & Barber, T. X. (1969). Yoga, "yogic feats," and hypnosis in the light of empirical research. *American Journal of Clinical Hypnosis, 11,* 155–166.

Dalessio, D. J. (1972). *Wolff's headache and other head pain* (3rd ed.). New York: Oxford University Press.

Dalessio, D. J. (1978). Mechanisms of headache. *Medical Clinics of North America, 62,* 429–442.

Dalessio, D. J., Kunzel, M., Sternbach, R., & Sovak, M. (1979). Conditioned adaptation-relaxation reflex in migraine therapy. *Journal of the American Medical Association, 242,* 2102–2104.

Dalton, K. (1969). *The menstrual cycle.* New York: Pantheon Books.

Daly, E. J., Donn, P. A., Galliher, M. J., & Zimmerman, J. S. (1983). Biofeedback applications to migraine and tension headaches: A double-blinded outcome study. *Biofeedback and Self-Regulation, 8,* 135–152.

Daly, E. J., Zimmerman, J. S., Donn, P. A., & Galliher, M. J. (1985). Psychophysiological treatment of migraine and tension headaches: A 12-month follow-up. *Rehabilitation Psychology, 30,* 3–10.

Danaher, B. G. (1974). Theoretical foundations and clinical applications of the Premack Principle: Review and critique. *Behavior Therapy, 5,* 307–324.

Danaher, B. G. (1977). Rapid smoking and self-control in the modification of smoking behavior. *Journal of Consulting and Clinical Psychology, 45,* 1068–1075.

Daniels, G. E. (1939). Present trends in the evaluation of psychic factors in diabetes mellitus: A critical review of the experimental, general medical and psychiatric literature of the last five years. *Psychosomatic Medicine, 1,* 527–552.

Daniels, L. K. (1975a). Treatment of grand mal epilepsy by covert and operant conditioning techniques: A case study. *Psychosomatics, 16,* 65–67.

Daniels, L. K. (1975b). The treatment of psychophysiological disorders and severe anxiety by behavior therapy, hypnosis and transcendental meditation. *American Journal of Clinical Hypnosis, 17,* 267–270.

Datey, K. K., Deshmukh, S. N., Dalvi, C. P., & Vinekar, S. L. (1969). "Shavasan": A yogic exercise in the management of hypertension. *Angiology, 20,* 325–333.

Davidson, D. M., Winchester, M. A., Taylor, C. B., Alderman, E. A., & Ingels, N. B., Jr. (1979). Effects of relaxation therapy on cardiac performance and sympathetic activity in patients with organic heart disease. *Psychosomatic Medicine, 41,* 303–309.

Davidson, J. M. (1976). The physiology of meditation and mystical states of consciousness. *Perspectives in Biology and Medicine, 19,* 345–380.

Davidson, P. O., & Hiebert, S. F. (1971). Relaxation training, relaxation instruction, and repeated exposure to a stressor film. *Journal of Abnormal Psychology, 78,* 154–159.

Davidson, R. J. (1978). Specificity and patterning in biobehavioral systems: Implications for behavior change. *American Psychologist, 33,* 430–436.

Davidson, R. J., & Goleman, D. J. (1977). The role of attention in meditation and hypnosis: A psychobiological perspective on transformations of consciousness. *International Journal of Clinical and Experimental Hypnosis, 25,* 291–308.

Davidson, R. J., Goleman, D. J., & Schwartz, G. E. (1976). Attentional and affective concomitants of meditation: A cross-sectional study. *Journal of Abnormal Psychology, 85,* 235–238.

Davidson, R. J., & Schwartz, G. E. (1976). The psychobiology of relaxation and related states: A multi-process theory. In D. I. Mostofsky (Ed.), *Behavior control and modification of physiological activity* (pp. 399–442). Englewood Cliffs, NJ: Prentice-Hall.

Davies, J. (1977). The Transcendental Meditation program and progressive relaxation: Comparative effects on trait anxiety and self-actualization. In D. W. Orme-Johnson & J. T. Farrow (Eds.), *Scientific research on the Transcendental Meditation program: Collected papers* (Vol. 1, 2nd ed., pp. 449–452). Livingston Manor, NY: Maharishi European Research University Press.

Davis, M., Eshelman, E. R., & McKay, M. (1980). *The relaxation and stress reduction workbook.* Richmond, CA: New Harbinger.

Davis, M. H., Saunders, D. R., Creer, T. L., & Chai, H. (1973). Relaxation training facilitated by biofeedback apparatus as a supplemental treatment in bronchial asthma. *Journal of Psychosomatic Research, 17,* 121–128.

Davison, G. C. (1966). Anxiety under total curarization: Implications for the role of muscular relaxation in the desensitization of neurotic fears. *Journal of Nervous and Mental Disease, 143,* 443–448.

Davison, G. C. (1968). Systematic desensitization as a counterconditioning process. *Journal of Abnormal Psychology, 73,* 91–99.

Dawley, H. H., Jr. (1975). Anxiety reduction through self-administered relaxation. *Psychological Reports, 36,* 595–597.

Day, R. C., & Sadek, S. N. (1982). The effect of Benson's relaxation response on the anxiety levels of Lebanese children under stress. *Journal of Experimental Child Psychology, 34,* 350–356.

Deardorff, C. M., Melges, F. T., Hout, C. N., & Savage, D. J. (1975). Situations related to drinking alcohol: A factor analysis of questionnaire responses. *Journal of Studies on Alcohol, 36,* 1184–1195.

Deatherage, G. (1975). The clinical use of "mindfulness" meditation techniques in short-term psychotherapy. *Journal of Transpersonal Psychology, 7,* 133–143.

DeBerry, S. (1981–1982). Evaluation of progressive muscle relaxation on stress related symptoms in a geriatric population. *International Journal of Aging and Human Development, 14,* 255–269.

DeBerry, S. (1982). The effects of meditation-relaxation on anxiety and depression in a geriatric population. *Psychotherapy: Theory, Research and Practice, 19,* 512–521.

Deffenbacher, J. L. (1976). Relaxation *in vivo* in the treatment of test anxiety. *Journal of Behavior Therapy and Experimental Psychiatry, 7,* 289–292.

Deffenbacher, J. L., Demm, P. M., & Brandon, A. D. (1986). High general anger: Correlates and treatment. *Behaviour Research and Therapy, 24,* 481–489.

Deffenbacher, J. L., & Hahnloser, R. M. (1981). Cognitive and relaxation coping skills in stress inoculation. *Cognitive Therapy and Research, 5,* 211–215.

Deffenbacher, J. L., Mathis, H., & Michaels, A. C. (1979). Two self-control procedures in the reduction of targeted and nontargeted anxieties. *Journal of Counseling Psychology, 26,* 120–127.

Deffenbacher, J. L., & Michaels, A. C. (1980). Two self-control procedures in the reduction of targeted and nontargeted anxieties–A year later. *Journal of Counseling Psychology, 27,* 9–15.

Deffenbacher, J. L., Michaels, A. C., Michaels, T., & Daley, P. C. (1980). Comparison of anxiety management training and self-control desensitization. *Journal of Counseling Psychology, 27,* 232–239.

Deffenbacher, J. L., & Payne, D. M. J. (1977). Two procedures for relaxation as self-control in the treatment of communication apprehension. *Journal of Counseling Psychology, 24,* 255–258.

Deffenbacher, J. L., & Rivera, N. (1976). A behavioral self-control treatment of test anxiety in minority populations: Some cases and issues. *Psychological Reports, 39,* 1188–1190.

Deffenbacher, J. L., & Snyder, A. L. (1976). Relaxation as self-control in the treatment of test and other anxieties. *Psychological Reports, 39,* 379–385.

Deffenbacher, J. L., & Suinn, R. M. (1982). The self-control of anxiety. In P. Karoly & F. H. Kanfer (Eds.), *Self-management and behavior change: From theory to practice* (pp. 393–442). Elmsford, NY: Pergamon Press.

Degossely, M., & Bostem, F. (1977). Autogenic training and states of consciousness:

A few methodological problems. In W. Luthe & F. Antonelli (Eds.), *Therapy in psychosomatic medicine: Autogenic therapy* (pp. 18–25). Rome: Edizioni L. Pozzi.

Deikman, A. J. (1963). Experimental meditation. *Journal of Nervous and Mental Disease, 136,* 329–343.

Deikman, A. J. (1966). Implications of experimentally induced contemplative meditation. *Journal of Nervous and Mental Disease, 142,* 101–116.

Delman, R. P., & Johnson, H. J. (1976). Biofeedback and progressive muscle relaxation: A comparison of psychophysiological effects. *Psychophysiology, 13,* 181.

Delmonte, M. M. (1979). Pilot study of conditioned relaxation during simulated meditation. *Psychological Reports, 45,* 169–170.

Delmonte, M. M. (1980). Personality characteristics and regularity of meditation. *Psychological Reports, 46,* 703–712.

Delmonte, M. M. (1981a). Expectation and meditation. *Psychological Reports, 49,* 699–709.

Delmonte, M. M. (1981b). Suggestibility and meditation. *Psychological Reports, 48,* 727–737.

Delmonte, M. M. (1983). Mantras and meditation: A literature review. *Perceptual and Motor Skills, 57,* 64–66.

Delmonte, M. M. (1984a). Case reports on the use of meditative relaxation as an intervention strategy with retarded ejaculation. *Biofeedback and Self-Regulation, 9,* 209–214.

Delmonte, M. M. (1984b). Electrocortical activity and related phenomena associated with meditation practice: A literature review. *International Journal of Neuroscience, 24,* 217–231.

Delmonte, M. M. (1984c). Factors influencing the regularity of meditation practice in a clinical population. *British Journal of Medical Psychology, 57,* 275–278.

DeLongis, A., Coyne, J. C., Dakof, G., Folkman, S., & Lazarus, R. S. (1982). Relationship of daily hassles, uplifts, and major life events to health status. *Health Psychology, 1,* 119–136.

Dembroski, T. M., MacDougall, J. M., Williams, R. B., Haney, T. L., & Blumenthal, J. A. (1985). Components of Type A, hostility, and anger-in: Relationship to angiographic findings. *Psychosomatic Medicine, 47,* 219–233.

Denicola, J. A., Furze, C. T., & O'Keeffe, J. (1982, November). *Group administered relaxation and stress management training with essential hypertensives.* Paper presented at the meeting of the Association for Advancement of Behavior Therapy, Los Angeles.

Denicola, J., & Sandler, J. (1980). Training abusive parents in child management and self-control skills. *Behavior Therapy, 11,* 263–270.

Denkowski, K. M., & Denkowski, G. C. (1984). Is group progressive relaxation training as effective with hyperactive children as individual EMG biofeedback treatment? *Biofeedback and Self-Regulation, 9,* 353–364.

Denney, D. R. (1980). Self-control approaches to the treatment of test anxiety. In I. G. Sarason (Ed.), *Test anxiety: Theory, research, and applications* (pp. 209–243). Hillsdale, NJ: Erlbaum.

Denney, D. R., & Gerrard, M. (1981). Behavioral treatments of primary dysmenorrhea: A review. *Behaviour Research and Therapy, 19,* 303–312.

De Rivera, J. L. G., De Montigny, C., Remillard, G., & Andermann, F. (1977). Autogenic therapy of temporal lobe epilepsy. In W. Luthe & F. Antonelli (Eds.), *Therapy in psychosomatic medicine: Autogenic therapy* (pp. 40–47). Rome: Edizioni L. Pozzi.

Derogatis, L. R., Lipman, R. S., & Covi, L. (1973). SCL-90: An outpatient psychiatric rating scale–Preliminary report. *Psychopharmacology Bulletin, 9*(1), 13–28.

Derogatis, L. R., Lipman, R. S., Rickels, K., Uhlenhuth, E. H., & Covi, L. (1974). The Hopkins Symptom Checklist (HSCL): A measure of primary symptom dimensions. In P. Pichot & R. Olivier-Martin (Eds.), *Modern problems of pharmacopsychiatry: Vol. 7. Psychological measurements in psychopharmacology* (pp. 79–110). Basel, Switzerland: S. Karger.

Devi, I. (1963). *Renew your life through Yoga.* Englewood Cliffs, NJ: Prentice-Hall.

Dhammasudhi, S. (1968). *Insight meditation* (2nd ed.). London: Committee for the Advancement of Buddhism.

Diamond, S. (1979). Biofeedback and headache. *Headache, 19,* 180–184.

Diamond, S., & Franklin, M. (1977a). Autogenic training and biofeedback techniques in the treatment of chronic headache problems. In W. Luthe & F. Antonelli (Eds.), *Therapy in psychosomatic medicine: Autogenic therapy* (pp. 174–179). Rome: Edizioni L. Pozzi.

Diamond, S., & Franklin, M. (1977b). Autogenic training with biofeedback in the treatment of children with migraine. In W. Luthe & F. Antonelli (Eds.), *Therapy in psychosomatic medicine: Autogenic therapy* (pp. 190–192). Rome: Edizioni L. Pozzi.

Diamond, S., & Montrose, D. (1984). The value of biofeedback in the treatment of chronic headache: A four-year retrospective study. *Headache, 24,* 5–18.

Dietvorst, T. F., & Osborne, D. (1978). Biofeedback-assisted relaxation training for primary dysmenorrhea: A case study. *Biofeedback and Self-Regulation, 3,* 301–305.

Dillbeck, M. C. (1977). The effect of the Transcendental Meditation technique on anxiety level. *Journal of Clinical Psychology, 33,* 1076–1078.

Dillbeck, M. C., & Bronson, E. C. (1981). Short-term longitudinal effects of the Transcendental Meditation technique on EEG power and coherence. *International Journal of Neuroscience, 14,* 147–151.

Dillbeck, M. C., Landrith, G., III, & Orme-Johnson, D. W. (1981). The Transcendental Meditation program and crime rate change in a sample of forty-eight cities. *Journal of Crime and Justice, 4,* 25–45.

DiNardo, P. A., & Raymond, J. B. (1979). Locus of control and attention during meditation. *Journal of Consulting and Clinical Psychology, 47,* 1136–1137.

Dixon, K. N., Monroe, L. J., & Jakim, S. (1981). Insomniac children. *Sleep, 4,* 313–318.

Dobbs, S. D., Strickler, D. P., & Maxwell, W. A. (1981). The effects of stress and relaxation in the presence of stress on urinary pH and smoking behaviors. *Addictive Behaviors, 6,* 345–353.

Dobson, K. S. (1985). The relationship between anxiety and depression. *Clinical Psychology Review, 5,* 307–324.

Dolgin, M. J., Katz, E. R., McGinty, K., & Siegel, S. E. (1985). Anticipatory nausea and vomiting in pediatric cancer patients. *Pediatrics, 75,* 547–552.

Domash, L. H. (1977a). Introduction. In D. W. Orme-Johnson & J. T. Farrow (Eds.), *Scientific research on the Transcendental Meditation program: Collected papers* (Vol. 1, 2nd ed., pp. 13–31). Livingston Manor, NY: Maharishi European Research University Press.

Domash, L. H. (1977b). The Transcendental Meditation technique and quantum physics: Is pure consciousness a macroscopic quantum state in the brain? In D. W. Orme-Johnson & J. T. Farrow (Eds.), *Scientific research on the Transcendental Meditation program: Collected papers* (Vol. 1, 2nd ed., pp. 652–670). Livingston Manor, NY: Maharishi European Research University Press.

Domino, G. (1977). Transcendental meditation and creativity: An empirical investigation. *Journal of Applied Psychology, 62,* 358–362.

Douglas, N. (1971). *Tantra Yoga.* New Delhi, India: Munshiram Manoharlal.

Drennen, W., & Chermol, B. (1978). Relaxation and placebo-suggestion as uncontrolled variables in TM research. *Journal of Humanistic Psychology, 18,* 89–93.

Drescher, V. M., Whitehead, W. E., Morrill-Corbin, E. D., & Cataldo, M. F. (1985). Physiological and subjective reactions to being touched. *Psychophysiology, 22,* 96–100.

Drummond, P. D., & Lance, J. W. (1981). Extracranial vascular reactivity in migraine and tension headache. *Cephalalgia, 1,* 149–155.

Drury, R. L., DeRisi, W. J., & Liberman, R. P. (1979). Temperature biofeedback treatment for migraine headache: A controlled multiple baseline study. *Headache, 19,* 278–284.

Dugan, M., & Sheridan, C. (1976). Effects of instructed imagery on temperature of hands. *Perceptual and Motor Skills, 42,* 14.

Dunn, F. M., & Howell, R. J. (1982). Relaxation training and its relationship to hyperactivity in boys. *Journal of Clinical Psychology, 38,* 92–100.

Dwivedi, K. N., Gupta, V. M., & Udupa, K. N. (1977). A preliminary report on some physiological changes due to Vipashyana meditation. *Indian Journal of Medical Sciences, 31,* 51–54.

Dyckman, J. M., & Cowan, P. A. (1978). Imaging vividness and the outcome of in vivo and imagined scene desensitization. *Journal of Consulting and Clinical Psychology, 46,* 1155–1156.

Earle, J. B. B. (1981). Cerebral laterality and meditation: A review of the literature. *Journal of Transpersonal Psychology, 13,* 155–173.

Edelman, R. I. (1970). Effects of progressive relaxation on autonomic processes. *Journal of Clinical Psychology, 26,* 421–425.

Edinger, J. D., & Jacobsen, R. (1982). Incidence and significance of relaxation treatment side effects. *The Behavior Therapist, 5,* 137–138.

Elfner, L. F., May, J. G., Moore, J. D., & Mendelson, J. M. (1981). Effects of EMG and thermal feedback training on tinnitus: A case study. *Biofeedback and Self-Regulation, 6,* 517–521.

Eliade, M. (1969). *Yoga: Immortality and freedom* (2nd ed., W. R. Trask, Trans.). Princeton, NJ: Princeton University Press. (Original work published 1954)

Elitzur, B. (1976). Self-relaxation program for acting-out adolescents. *Adolescence, 11,* 569–572.

Elkins, D., Anchor, K. N., & Sandler, H. M. (1978). Physiological effects of relaxation training. *American Journal of Clinical Biofeedback, 1,* 30.

Elkins, R. L. (1980). Covert sensitization treatment of alcoholism: Contributions of successful conditioning to subsequent abstinence maintenance. *Addictive Behaviors, 5,* 67–89.

Elliott, C. H., & Denney, D. R. (1975). Weight control through covert sensitization and false feedback. *Journal of Consulting and Clinical Psychology, 43,* 842–850.

Elliott, C. H., & Denney, D. R. (1978). A multiple-component treatment approach to smoking reduction. *Journal of Consulting and Clinical Psychology, 46,* 1330–1339.

Ellis, A. (1973). *Humanistic psychotherapy.* New York: McGraw-Hill.

Ellis, A. (1984). The place of meditation in cognitive-behavior therapy and rational-emotive therapy. In D. H. Shapiro, Jr. & R. N. Walsh (Eds.), *Meditation: Classic and contemporary perspectives* (pp. 671–673.). Hawthorne, NY: Aldine.

Elson, B. D., Hauri, P., & Cunis, D. (1977). Physiological changes in Yoga meditation. *Psychophysiology, 14,* 52–57.

Endler, N. S., Hunt, J. M., & Rosenstein, A. J. (1962). An S-R inventory of anxiousness. *Psychological Monographs, 76*(17, Whole No. 536).

Engel, B. T., Glasgow, M. S., & Gaarder, K. R. (1983). Behavioral treatment of high blood pressure: III. Follow-up results and treatment recommendations. *Psychosomatic Medicine, 45,* 23–29.

English, E. H., & Baker, T. B. (1983). Relaxation training and cardiovascular response to experimental stressors. *Health Psychology, 2,* 239–259.

Epstein, L. H., & Abel. G. G. (1977). An analysis of biofeedback training effects for tension headache patients. *Behavior Therapy, 8,* 37–47.

Epstein, L. H., Hersen, M., & Hemphill, D. P. (1974). Music feedback in the treatment of tension headache: An experimental case study. *Journal of Behavior Therapy and Experimental Psychiatry, 5,* 59–63.

Epstein, L. H., Webster, J. S., & Abel, G. G. (1976). Self-managed relaxation in the treatment of tension headaches. In J. D. Krumboltz & C. E. Thoresen (Eds.), *Counseling methods* (pp. 344–348). New York: Holt, Rinehart & Winston.

Erbeck, J. R., Elfner, L. F., & Driggs, D. F. (1983). Reduction of blood pressure by indirect biofeedback. *Biofeedback and Self-Regulation, 8,* 63–72.

Erskine, J., & Schonell, M. (1979). Relaxation therapy in bronchial asthma. *Journal of Psychosomatic Research, 23,* 131–139.

Erskine-Milliss, J., & Schonell, M. (1981). Relaxation therapy in asthma: A critical review. *Psychosomatic Medicine, 43,* 365–372.

Eufemia, R. L., & Wesolowski, M. D. (1983). The use of a new relaxation method in a case of tension headache. *Journal of Behavior Therapy and Experimental Psychiatry, 14,* 355–358.

Evans, T. A., Lee, A. E., & Christoff, K. A. (1985, March). *The treatment of primary dysmenorrhea: A comparison of three methods.* Paper presented at the meeting of the Society of Behavioral Medicine, New Orleans.

Ewing, J. W., & Hughes, H. H. (1978). Cue-controlled relaxation: Its effect on EMG levels during aversive stimulation. *Journal of Behavior Therapy and Experimental Psychiatry, 9,* 39–44.

Eyerman, J. (1981). Transcendental Meditation and mental retardation. *Journal of Clinical Psychiatry, 42,* 35–36.

Eysenck, H. J. (1959). *The manual of the Maudsley Personality Inventory.* London: University of London Press.

Eysenck, H. J. (1963). *The Eysenck Personality Inventory.* San Diego: Educational & Industrial Testing Service.

Eysenck, H. J., & Eysenck, S. B. G. (1975). *Manual for the Eysenck Personality Questionnaire.* San Diego: Educational & Industrial Testing Service.

Fahrion, S. L. (1978). Autogenic biofeedback treatment for migraine. *Research and Clinical Studies in Headache, 5,* 47–71.

Fairbank, J. A., DeGood, D. E., & Jenkins, C. W. (1981). Behavioral treatment of a persistent post-traumatic startle response. *Journal of Behavior Therapy and Experimental Psychiatry, 12,* 321–324.

Farmer, R., & Wright, J. (1971). Muscular reactivity and systematic desensitization. *Behavior Therapy, 2,* 1–10.

Farrow, J. T., & Hebert, J. R. (1982). Breath suspension during the Transcendental Meditation technique. *Psychosomatic Medicine, 44,* 133–153.

Faulstich, M. E., Carnrike, C. L. M., Jr., & Williamson, D. A. (1985). Blepharospasm and Meige syndrome: A review of diagnostic, aetiological and treatment approaches. *Journal of Psychosomatic Research, 29,* 89–94.

Fee, R. A., & Girdano, D. A. (1978). The relative effectiveness of three techniques to induce the trophotropic response. *Biofeedback and Self-Regulation, 3,* 145–157.

Feindler, E. L., Marriott, S. A., & Iwata, M. (1984). Group anger control training for junior high school delinquents. *Cognitive Therapy and Research, 8,* 299–311.

Fenwick, P. B. C., Donaldson, S., Gillis, L., Bushman, J., Fenton, G. W., Perry, I., Tilsley, C., & Serafinowicz, H. (1977). Metabolic and EEG changes during Transcendental Meditation: An explanation. *Biological Psychology, 5,* 101–118.

Fenz, W. D., & Epstein, S. (1965). Manifest anxiety: Unifactorial or multifactorial composition? *Perceptual and Motor Skills, 20,* 773–780.

Ferenczi, S. (1930). The principle of relaxation and neocatharsis. *International Journal of Psychoanalysis, 2,* 428–443.

Ferenczi, S. (1960). *Further contributions to the theory and technique of psycho-analysis.* London: Hogarth. (Original work published 1925)

Ferguson, J. M., Marquis, J. N., & Taylor, C. B. (1977). A script for deep muscle relaxation. *Diseases of the Nervous System, 38,* 703–708.

Ferguson, P., & Gowan, J. (1976). TM: Some preliminary findings. *Journal of Humanistic Psychology, 16,* 51–60.

Feuerstein, G. (1975). *Textbook of Yoga.* London: Rider.

Fewtrell, W. D. (1984). Relaxation and depersonalization. *British Journal of Psychiatry, 145,* 217.

Fey, S. G., & Lindholm, E. (1978). Biofeedback and progressive relaxation: Effects on systolic and diastolic blood pressure and heart rate. *Psychophysiology, 15,* 239–247.

Fichtler, H., & Zimmermann, R. R. (1973). Changes in reported pain from tension headaches. *Perceptual and Motor Skills, 36,* 712.

Fitts, W. H. (1964). *Tennessee Self Concept Scale.* Nashville: Counselor Recordings and Tests.

Flagler, J. M. (1967, August 8). The visions of "Saint Tim." *Look,* pp. 18-21.

Flaherty, G. G., & Fitzpatrick. J. J. (1978). Relaxation technique to increase comfort level of postoperative patients: A preliminary study. *Nursing Research, 27,* 352-355.

Flannery, R. B., Jr. (1972). Covert conditioning in the behavioral treatment of an agoraphobic. *Psychotherapy: Theory, Research and Practice, 9,* 217-220.

Flaxman, J. (1979). Affect-management and habit mechanisms in the modification of smoking behavior. *Addictive Behaviors, 4,* 39-46.

Folkins, C. H., Lawson, K. D., Opton, E. M., Jr., & Lazarus, R. S. (1968). Desensitization and experimental reduction of threat. *Journal of Abnormal Psychology, 73,* 100-113.

Ford, M. R., Stroebel, C. F., Strong, P., & Szarek, B. L. (1982). Quieting Response training: Treatment of psychophysiological disorders in psychiatric inpatients. *Biofeedback and Self-Regulation, 7,* 331-339.

Ford, M. R., Stroebel, C. F., Strong, P., & Szarek, B. L. (1983a). Quieting Response training: Long-term evaluation of a clinical biofeedback practice. *Biofeedback and Self-Regulation, 8,* 265-278.

Ford, M. R., Stroebel, C. F., Strong, P., & Szarek, B. L. (1983b). Quieting Response training: Predictors of long-term outcome. *Biofeedback and Self-Regulation, 8,* 393-408.

Forem, J. (1974). *Transcendental Meditation.* New York: Dutton.

Foreyt, J. P., Mitchell, R. E., Garner, D. T., Gee, M., Scott, L. W., & Gotto, A. M. (1982). Behavioral treatment of obesity: Results and limitations. *Behavior Therapy, 13,* 153-161.

Forman, S. G. (1982). Stress management for teachers: A cognitive-behavioral program. *Journal of School Psychology, 20,* 180-187.

Fowler, J. E., Budzynski, T. H., & VandenBergh, R. L. (1976). Effects of an EMG biofeedback relaxation program on the control of diabetes. *Biofeedback and Self-Regulation, 1,* 105-112.

Fowler, W. S. (1954). Breaking point of breathholding. *Journal of Applied Physiology, 6,* 539-545.

Fox, R., Joy, V. L., & Rotatori, A. F. (1981). Comparison of progressive relaxation training and practice sessions using the adjective generation technique. *Psychological Reports, 49,* 301-302.

Fox, R., & Oitker, D. (1980). Adjective generation technique: Assessment measure for training in progressive relaxation. *Psychological Reports, 47,* 853-854.

Foy, D. W., Nunn, L. B., & Rychtarik, R. G. (1984). Broad-spectrum behavioral treatment for chronic alcoholics: Effects of training controlled drinking skills. *Journal of Consulting and Clinical Psychology, 52,* 218-230.

Frame, C. L., Turner, S. M., Jacob, J. G., & Szekely, B. (1984). Self-exposure treatment of agoraphobia. *Behavior Modification, 8,* 115-122.

Freedman, R., Hauri, P., Coursey, R., & Frankel, B. (1978). Behavioral treatment of insomnia: A collaborative study. *Biofeedback and Self-Regulation, 3,* 208–209.

Freedman, R., & Ianni, P. (1983). Self-control of digital temperature: Physiological factors and transfer effects. *Psychophysiology, 20,* 682–689.

Freedman, R. R., Ianni, P., & Wenig, P. (1983). Behavioral treatment of Raynaud's disease. *Journal of Consulting and Clinical Psychology, 51,* 539–549.

Freedman, R., & Papsdorf, J. D. (1976). Biofeedback and progressive relaxation treatment of sleep-onset insomnia: A controlled, all-night investigation. *Biofeedback and Self-Regulation, 1,* 253–271.

Freeling, N. W., & Shemberg, K. M. (1970). The alleviation of test anxiety by systematic desensitization. *Behaviour Research and Therapy, 8,* 293–299.

Freeman, G. L. (1931). Mental activity and the muscular processes. *Psychological Review, 38,* 428–449.

Freeman, G. L. (1933). The facilitative and inhibitory effects of muscular tension upon performance. *American Journal of Psychology, 45,* 17–52.

Fremouw, W. J., & Harmatz, M. G. (1975). A helper model for behavioral treatment of speech anxiety. *Journal of Consulting and Clinical Psychology, 43,* 652–660.

Fremouw, W. J., & Zitter, R. E. (1978). A comparison of skills training and cognitive restructuring-relaxation for the treatment of speech anxiety. *Behavior Therapy, 9,* 248–259.

French, A. P., Schmid, A. C., & Ingalls, E. (1975). Transcendental meditation, altered reality testing, and behavioral change: A case report. *Journal of Nervous and Mental Disease, 161,* 55–58.

French, A. P., & Tupin, J. P. (1974). Therapeutic application of a simple relaxation method. *American Journal of Psychotherapy, 28,* 282–287.

Frew, D. R. (1974). Transcendental meditation and productivity. *Academy of Management Journal, 17,* 362–368.

Friedman, H., & Taub, H. A. (1984). Brief psychological training procedures in migraine treatment. *American Journal of Clinical Hypnosis, 26,* 187–200.

Friedman, M., & Rosenman, R. H. (1959). Association of specific overt behavior pattern with blood and cardiovascular findings. *Journal of the American Medical Association, 169,* 1286–1296.

Friedman, M., Thoresen, C. E., Gill, J. J., Powell, L. H., Ulmer, D., Thompson, L., Price, V. A., Rabin, D. D., Breall, W. S., Dixon, T., Levy, R., & Bourg, E. (1984). Alteration of type A behavior and reduction in cardiac recurrences in postmyocardial infarction patients. *American Heart Journal, 108,* 237–248.

Friedman, M., Thoresen, C. E., Gill, J. J., Ulmer, D., Thompson, L., Powell, L., Price, V., Elek, S. R., Rabin, D. D., Breall, W. S., Piaget, G., Dixon, T., Bourg, E., Levy, R. A., & Tasto, D. L. (1982). Feasibility of altering type A behavior pattern after myocardial infarction. *Circulation, 66,* 83–92.

Fromm, E. (1963). Psychoanalysis and Zen Buddhism. In D. T. Suzuki, E. Fromm, & R. De Martino (Eds.), *Zen Buddhism and psychoanalysis* (pp. 77–141). New York: Grove Press.

Fromm-Reichmann, F. (1950). *Principles of intensive psychotherapy.* Chicago: University of Chicago Press.

Fromm-Reichmann, F., & Moreno, J. L. (Eds.). (1956). *Progress in psychotherapy, 1956.* New York: Grune & Stratton.

Frumkin, K., Nathan, R. J., Prout, M. F., & Cohen, M. C. (1978). Nonpharmacologic control of essential hypertension in man: A critical review of the experimental literature. *Psychosomatic Medicine, 40,* 294–320.

Frumkin, L. R., & Pagano, R. R. (1979). The effect of transcendental meditation on iconic memory. *Biofeedback and Self-Regulation, 4,* 313–322.

Fuller, S. S., Endress, M. P., & Johnson, J. E. (1978). The effects of cognitive and behavioral control on coping with an aversive health examination. *Journal of Human Stress, 4*(4), 18–25.

Funch, D. P., & Gale, E. N. (1984). Biofeedback and relaxation therapy for chronic temporomandibular joint pain: Predicting successful outcomes. *Journal of Consulting and Clinical Psychology, 52,* 928–935.

Gaarder, K. R., & Montgomery, P. S. (1977). *Clinical biofeedback: A procedural manual.* Baltimore: Williams & Wilkins.

Gaber, L. B., Arieli, O., & Merbaum, M. (1984). Relaxation and assertive training as automated adjunct behaviour therapy administered in a self-control orientation with psychiatric patients. *British Journal of Clinical Psychology, 23,* 301–309.

Gale, E. N., & Funch, D. P. (1984). Factors associated with successful outcome from behavioral therapy for chronic temporomandibular joint (TMJ) pain. *Journal of Psychosomatic Research, 28,* 441–448.

Ganguli, H. C. (1982). Meditation program and modern youth: Dynamics of initiation. *Human Relations, 35,* 903–926.

Gannon, L. (1981). Psychological and physiological factors in the development, maintenance, and treatment of menstrual disorders. In S. N. Haynes & L. Gannon (Eds.), *Psychosomatic disorders: A psychophysiological approach to etiology and treatment* (pp. 79–132). New York: Praeger.

Garmany, G. (1952). *Muscle relaxation as an aid to psychotherapy.* London: Actinic Press.

Gash, A., & Karliner, J. S. (1978). No effect of transcendental meditation on left ventricular function. *Annals of Internal Medicine, 88,* 215–216.

Gatchel, R. J., Hatch, J. P., Watson, P. J., Smith, D., & Gaas, E. (1977). Comparative effectiveness of voluntary heart rate control and muscular relaxation as active coping skills for reducing speech anxiety. *Journal of Consulting and Clinical Psychology, 45,* 1093–1100.

Gatchel, R. J., & Price, K. P. (Eds.). (1979). *Clinical applications of biofeedback: Appraisal and status.* Elmsford, NY: Pergamon Press.

Geer, J. H., & Katkin, E. S. (1966). Treatment of insomnia using a variant of systematic desensitization: A case report. *Journal of Abnormal Psychology, 71,* 161–164.

Gellhorn, E. (1958a). The influence of curare on hypothalamic excitability and the electroencephalogram. *Electroencephalography and Clinical Neurophysiology, 10,* 697–703.

Gellhorn, E. (1958b). The physiological basis of neuromuscular relaxation. *Archives of Internal Medicine, 102,* 392–399.

Gellhorn E. (1964). Motion and emotion: The role of proprioception in the physiology and pathology of the emotions. *Psychological Review, 71,* 457–472.

Gellhorn, E. (1967). *Principles of autonomic-somatic integrations.* Minneapolis: University of Minnesota Press.

Gellhorn, E. (1969). Further studies on the physiology and pathophysiology of the tuning of the central nervous system. *Psychosomatics, 10,* 94–104.

Gellhorn, E. , & Kiely, W. F. (1972). Mystical states of consciousness: Neurophysiological and clinical aspects. *Journal of Nervous and Mental Disease, 154,* 399–405.

Gentry, W. D. (1978). About the *Journal of Behavioral Medicine. Journal of Behavioral Medicine, 1,* 1–2.

Germaine, L. M., & Freedman, R. R. (1984). Behavioral treatment of menopausal hot flashes: Evaluation by objective methods. *Journal of Consulting and Clinical Psychology, 52,* 1072–1079.

Gerschman, J. A., Burrows, G. D., & Fitzgerald, P. J. (1981). Hypnosis in the control of gagging. *Australian Journal of Clinical and Experimental Hypnosis, 9,* 53–59.

Gershman, L., & Clouser, R. A. (1974). Treating insomnia with relaxation and desensitization in a group setting by an automated approach. *Journal of Behavior Therapy and Experimental Psychiatry, 5,* 31–35.

Gersten, D. J. (1978). Meditation as an adjunct to medical and psychiatric treatment. *American Journal of Psychiatry, 135,* 598–599.

Gervino, E. V., & Veazey, A. E. (1984). The physiologic effects of Benson's relaxation response during submaximal aerobic exercise. *Journal of Cardiac Rehabilitation, 4,* 254–259.

Gessel, A. H., & Alderman, M. M. (1971). Management of myofascial pain dysfunction syndrome of the temporomandibular joint by tension control training. *Psychosomatics, 12,* 302–309.

Gilbert, G. S., Parker, J. C., & Claiborn, C. D. (1978). Differential mood changes in alcoholics as a function of anxiety management strategies. *Journal of Clinical Psychology, 34,* 229–232.

Gillan, P., & Rachman, S. (1974). An experimental investigation of desensitization in phobic patients. *British Journal of Psychiatry, 124,* 392–401.

Gillespie, C. R., & Peck, D. F. (1980). The effects of biofeedback and guided imagery on finger temperature. *Biological Psychology, 11,* 235–247.

Girodo, M. (1974). Yoga meditation and flooding in the treatment of anxiety neurosis. *Journal of Behavior Therapy and Experimental Psychiatry, 5,* 157–160.

Glaister, B. (1982). Muscle relaxation training for fear reduction of patients with psychological problems: A review of controlled studies. *Behaviour Research and Therapy, 20,* 493–504.

Glantz, K. (1981). The use of a relaxation exercise in the treatment of borderline personality organization. *Psychotherapy: Theory, Research and Practice, 18,* 379–385.

Glasgow, M. S., Gaarder, K. R., & Engel, B. T. (1982). Behavioral treatment of high blood pressure. II. Acute and sustained effects of relaxation and systolic blood pressure biofeedback. *Psychosomatic Medicine, 44,* 155–170.

Glasgow, R. E. (1978). Effects of a self-control manual, rapid smoking, and amount of therapist contact on smoking reduction. *Journal of Consulting and Clinical Psychology, 46,* 1439–1447.

Glueck, B. C., & Stroebel, C. F. (1975). Biofeedback and meditation in the treatment of psychiatric illnesses. *Comprehensive Psychiatry, 16,* 303–321.

Glueck, B. C., & Stroebel, C. F. (1978). Psychophysiological correlates of relaxation. In A. A. Sugerman & R. E. Tarter (Eds.), *Expanding dimensions of consciousness* (pp. 99–129). New York: Springer.

Gode, J. D., Singh, R. H., Settiwar, R. M., Gode, K. D., & Udupa, K. N. (1974). Increased urinary excretion of testosterone following a course of Yoga in normal young volunteers. *Indian Journal of Medical Sciences, 28,* 212–215.

Godsey, R. L. (1980). Efficacy of response contingent and program contingent progression in live and taped progressive relaxation training. *Dissertation Abstracts International, 40,* 3928B. (University Microfilms No. 80–83,135)

Goebel, M., Viol, G. W., Lorenz, G. J., & Clemente, J. (1980). Relaxation and biofeedback in essential hypertension: A preliminary report of a six-year project. *American Journal of Clinical Biofeedback, 3,* 20–29.

Goldfried, M. R. (1971). Systematic desensitization as training in self-control. *Journal of Consulting and Clinical Psychology, 37,* 228–234.

Goldfried, M. R. (1976). *Behavioral management of anxiety: A clinician's guide* (Cassette Recording). New York: Guilford.

Goldfried, M. R. (1977). The use of relaxation and cognitive relabeling as coping skills. In R. B. Stuart (Ed.), *Behavioral self-management: Strategies, techniques and outcomes* (pp. 82–116). New York: Brunner/Mazel.

Goldfried, M. R. (1980). Toward the delineation of therapeutic change principles. *American Psychologist, 35,* 991–999.

Goldfried, M. R., & Goldfried, A. P. (1977). Importance of hierarchy content in the self-control of anxiety. *Journal of Consulting and Clinical Psychology, 45,* 124–134.

Goldfried, M. R., & Merbaum, M. (1973). A perspective on self-control. In M. R. Goldfried & M. Merbaum (Eds.), *Behavior change through self-control* (pp. 3–34). New York: Holt, Rinehart & Winston.

Goldfried, M. R., & Trier, C. S. (1974). Effectiveness of relaxation as an active coping skill. *Journal of Abnormal Psychology, 83,* 348–355.

Goldiamond, I. (1965). Self-control procedures in personal behavior problems. *Psychological Reports, 17,* 851–868.

Goldman, B. L., Domitor, P. J., & Murray, E. J. (1979). Effects of Zen meditation on anxiety reduction and perceptual functioning. *Journal of Consulting and Clinical Psychology, 47,* 551–556.

Goldring, W., Chasis, H., Schreiner, G. E., & Smith, H. W. (1956). Reassurance in the management of benign hypertensive disease. *Circulation, 14,* 260–264.

Goldstein, A. J., Serber, M., & Piaget, G. (1970). Induced anger as a reciprocal inhibitor of fear. *Journal of Behavior Therapy and Experimental Psychiatry, 1,* 67–70.

Goldstein, I. B., Shapiro, D., & Thananopavarn, C. (1984). Home relaxation techniques for essential hypertension. *Psychosomatic Medicine, 46,* 398–414.

Goldstein, I. B., Shapiro, D., Thananopavarn, C., & Sambhi, M. P. (1982). Comparison of drug and behavioral treatments of essential hypertension. *Health Psychology, 1,* 7–26.

Goleman, D. (1971). Meditation as meta-therapy: Hypotheses toward a proposed fifth state of consciousness. *Journal of Transpersonal Psychology, 3,* 1–25.

Goleman, D. (1972a). The Buddha on meditation and states of consciousness. Part I: The teachings. *Journal of Transpersonal Psychology, 4,* 1–44.

Goleman, D. (1972b). The Buddha on meditation and states of consciousness. Part II: A typology of meditation techniques. *Journal of Transpersonal Psychology, 4,* 151–210.

Goleman, D. (1977). *The varieties of the meditative experience.* New York: Dutton.

Goleman, D., & Epstein, M. (1983). Meditation and well-being: An Eastern model of psychological health. In R. Walsh & D. H. Shapiro, Jr. (Eds.), *Beyond health and normality: Explorations of exceptional psychological well-being* (pp. 229–252). New York: Van Nostrand Reinhold.

Goleman, D. J., & Schwartz, G. E. (1976). Meditation as an intervention in stress reactivity. *Journal of Consulting and Clinical Psychology, 44,* 456–466.

Gopal, K. S., Bhatnagar, O. P., Subramanian, N., & Nishith, S. D. (1973). Effect of yogasanas and pranayamas on blood pressure, pulse rate and some respiratory function. *Indian Journal of Physiology and Pharmacology, 17,* 273–276.

Gordon, R. M. (1976). Effects of volunteering and responsibility on the perceived value and effectiveness of a clinical treatment. *Journal of Consulting and Clinical Psychology, 44,* 799–801.

Govinda, L. A. (1959). *Foundations of Tibetan mysticism.* London: Rider.

Goyeche, J. R. M., Ago, Y., & Ikemi, Y. (1980). Asthma: The yoga perspective. Part I: The somatopsychic imbalance in asthma: Towards a holistic therapy. *Journal of Asthma Research, 17,* 111–121.

Goyeche, J. R. M., Ago, Y., & Ikemi, Y. (1982). Asthma: The yoga perspective. Part II: Yoga therapy in the treatment of asthma. *Journal of Asthma, 19,* 189–201.

Goyeche, J. R. M., Chihara, T., & Shimizu, H. (1972). Two concentration methods: A preliminary comparison. *Psychologia, 15,* 110–111.

Graham, K. R., Wright, G. W., Toman, W. J., & Mark, C. B. (1975). Relaxation and hypnosis in the treatment of insomnia. *American Journal of Clinical Hypnosis, 18,* 39–42.

Graham, L. E., Beiman, I., & Ciminero, A. R. (1977). The generality of the therapeutic effects of progressive relaxation training for essential hypertension. *Journal of Behavior Therapy and Experimental Psychiatry, 8,* 161–164.

Gray, C. L., Lyle, R. C., McGuire, R. J., & Peck, D. F. (1980). Electrode placement, EMG feedback, and relaxation for tension headaches. *Behaviour Research and Therapy, 18,* 19–23.

Gray, S. G., & Lawlis, G. F. (1982). A case study of pruritic eczema treated by relaxation and imagery. *Psychological Reports, 51,* 627–633.

Graybiel, A., Wood, C. D., Miller, E. F., & Cramer, D. B. (1968). Diagnostic criteria for grading the severity of acute motion sickness. *Aerospace Medicine, 39,* 453–455.

Grayson, J. B., & Borkovec, T. D. (1978). The effects of expectancy and imagined response to phobic stimuli on fear reduction. *Cognitive Therapy and Research, 2,* 11–24.

Graziano, A. M., & Kean, J. E. (1968). Programmed relaxation and reciprocal inhibition with psychotic children. *Behaviour Research and Therapy, 6,* 433–437.

Green, E. E., Green, A. M., & Norris, P. A. (1980). Self-regulation training for control of hypertension. *Primary Cardiology, 6,* 126–131; 135–137.

Green, E. E., Green, A. M., & Walters, E. D. (1970). Voluntary control of internal states: Psychological and physiological. *Journal of Transpersonal Psychology, 9,* 1–26.

Green, K. D., Webster, J., Beiman, I., Rosmarin, B., & Holliday, P. (1981). Progressive and self-induced relaxation training: Their relative effects on subjective and autonomic arousal to fearful stimuli. *Journal of Clinical Psychology, 37,* 309–315.

Griez, E., & Van Den Hout, M. A. (1982). Effects of carbon dioxide-oxygen inhalations on subjective anxiety and some neurovegetative parameters. *Journal of Behavior Therapy and Experimental Psychiatry, 13,* 27–32.

Griez, E., & Van Den Hout, M. A. (1983). Carbon dioxide and anxiety: Cardiovascular effects of a single inhalation. *Journal of Behavior Therapy and Experimental Psychiatry, 14,* 297–304.

Griffiths, T. J., Steel, D. H., Vaccaro, P., Allen, R., & Karpman, M. (1985). The effects of relaxation and cognitive rehearsal on the anxiety levels and performance of scuba students. *International Journal of Sport Psychology, 16,* 113–119.

Griffiths, T. J., Steel, D. H., Vaccaro, P., & Karpman, M. B. (1981). The effects of relaxation techniques on anxiety and underwater performance. *International Journal of Sport Psychology, 12,* 176–182.

Grimm, L. G. (1980). The evidence for cue-controlled relaxation. *Behavior Therapy, 11,* 283–293.

Grimm, L., & Kanfer, F. H. (1976). Tolerance of aversive stimulation. *Behavior Therapy, 7,* 593–601.

Grings, W. W., & Uno, T. (1968). Counterconditioning: Fear and relaxation. *Psychophysiology, 4,* 479–485.

Groden, J., Baron, M. G., Cautela, J. R., & Groden, G. (1977, December). *The use of relaxation with retarded and autistic children and adolescents.* Paper presented at the meeting of the Association for Advancement of Behavior Therapy, San Francisco.

Gross, R. T, & Fremouw, W. J. (1982). Cognitive restructuring and progressive relaxation for treatment of empirical subtypes of speech-anxious subjects. *Cognitive Therapy and Research, 6,* 429–436.

Grossberg, J. M. (1965). *The physiological effectiveness of brief training in differential muscle relaxation* (Tech. Rep. No. 9). San Diego: San Diego State College, Department of Psychology.

Gruen, W. (1972). A successful application of systematic self-relaxation and self-suggestions about postoperative reactions in a case of cardiac surgery. *International Journal of Clinical and Experimental Hypnosis, 20,* 143–151.

Gunnison, H., & Renick, T. F. (1985). Bulimia: Using fantasy-imagery and relaxation techniques. *Journal of Counseling and Development, 64,* 79–80.

Gurdjieff, G. (1973). *Views from the real world.* New York: Dutton.

Hackett, G., & Horan, J. J. (1979). Partial component analysis of a comprehensive smoking program. *Addictive Behaviors, 4,* 259–262.

Hackett, G., & Horan, J. J. (1980). Stress inoculation for pain: What's really going on? *Journal of Counseling Psychology, 27,* 107–116.

Hadley, J. M. (1938). Various roles of relaxation in psychotherapeutics. *Journal of General Psychology, 19,* 191–203.

Hafner, R. J. (1982). Psychological treatment of essential hypertension: A controlled comparison of meditation and meditation plus biofeedback. *Biofeedback and Self-Regulation, 7,* 305–316.

Hager, J. L, & Surwit, R. S. (1978). Hypertension self-control with a portable feedback unit or meditation-relaxation. *Biofeedback and Self-Regulation, 3,* 269–276.

Hall, H., Longo, S., & Dixon, R. (1981, October). *Hypnosis and the immune system: The effect of hypnosis on T and B cell function.* Paper presented at the meeting of the Society for Clinical and Experimental Hypnosis, Portland, OR.

Hall, M. D. (1983). Using relaxation imagery with children with malignancies: A developmental perspective. *American Journal of Clinical Hypnosis, 25,* 143–149.

Hall, S. M., Loeb, P. C., & Kushner, M. (1984). Methadone dose decreases and anxiety reduction. *Addictive Behaviors, 9,* 11–19.

Hallam, R. S., & Jakes, S. C. (1985). Tinnitus: Differential effects of therapy in a single case. *Behaviour Research and Therapy, 23,* 691–694.

Halonen, J. S., & Passman, R. H. (1985). Relaxation training and expectation in the treatment of postpartum distress. *Journal of Consulting and Clinical Psychology, 53,* 839–845.

Hamberger, L. K. (1982). Reduction of generalized aversive responding in a post-treatment cancer patient: Relaxation as an active coping skill. *Journal of Behavior Therapy and Experimental Psychiatry, 13,* 229–233.

Hamberger, L. K., & Lohr, J. M. (1980). Relationship of relaxation training to the controllability of imagery. *Perceptual and Motor Skills, 51,* 103–110.

Hamberger, L. K., & Lohr, J. M. (1981). Effect of trainer's presence and response-contingent feedback in biofeedback-relaxation training. *Perceptual and Motor Skills, 53,* 15–24.

Hamberger, L. K., & Lohr, J. M. (1984). *Stress and stress management: Research and applications.* New York: Springer.

Hamberger, L. K., & Schuldt, W. J. (1986). Live and taped relaxation instructions: Effects of procedural variables. *Biofeedback and Self-Regulation, 11,* 31–46.

Hamilton, S. B., & Bornstein, P. H. (1977). Modified induced anxiety: A generalized anxiety reduction procedure. *Journal of Consulting and Clinical Psychology, 45,* 1200–1201.

Haney, J. N., & Euse, F. J. (1976). Skin conductance and heart rate responses to neutral, positive, and negative imagery: Implications for covert behavior therapy procedures. *Behavior Therapy, 7,* 494–503.

Hanley, C. P., & Spates, J. L. (1978). Transcendental Meditation and social psychological attitudes. *Journal of Psychology, 99,* 121–127.

Harano, K., Ogawa, K., & Naruse, G. (1965). A study of plethysmography and skin temperature during active concentration and autogenic exercise. In W. Luthe (Ed.), *Autogenic training: International edition* (pp. 55–58). New York: Grune & Stratton.

Harper, R. G., & Steger, J. C. (1978). Psychological correlates of frontalis EMG and pain in tension headache. *Headache, 18,* 215–218.

Harris, J. K., Maldonado, A. J., Fuqua, R. W., Cole, P., Gault, F., Garman, F., & Macken, M. F. (1984, May). *Physiological effects of relaxation training during stress in Type A and Type B coronary patients.* Paper presented at the meeting of the Society of Behavioral Medicine, Philadelphia.

Harris, V. A., Katkin, E. S., Lick, J. R., & Habberfield, T. (1976). Paced respiration as a technique for the modification of autonomic response to stress. *Psychophysiology, 13,* 386–391.

Harrison, R. F., O'Moore, A. M., O'Moore, R. R., & McSweeney, J. R. (1981). Stress profiles in normal infertile couples: Pharmacological and psychological approaches to therapy. In V. Insler & G. Bettendorf (Eds.), *Advances in diagnosis and treatment of infertility* (pp. 143–157). New York: Elsevier/North Holland.

Hart, K. E. (1984). Anxiety management training and anger control for Type A individuals. *Journal of Behavior Therapy and Experimental Psychiatry, 15,* 133–139.

Hartman, L. M., & Ainsworth, K. D. (1980). Self-regulation of chronic pain: Preliminary empirical findings. *Canadian Journal of Psychiatry, 25,* 38–43.

Hartman, P. E., & Reuter, J. M. (1983, March). *The effects of relaxation therapy and cognitive coping skills training on the control of diabetes mellitus.* Paper presented at the meeting of the Society of Behavioral Medicine, Baltimore.

Harvey, J. R. (1978). Diaphragmatic breathing: A practical technique for breath control. *The Behavior Therapist, 1*(2), 13–14.

Harvey, J. R. (1979). The potential of relaxation training for the mentally retarded. *Mental Retardation, 17,* 71–76.

Haslam, M. T. (1974). The relationship between the effect of lactate infusion on anxiety states, and their amelioration by carbon dioxide inhalation. *British Journal of Psychiatry, 125,* 88–90.

Hatch, J. P., Klatt, K. D., Supik, J. D., Rios, N., Fisher, J. G., Bauer, R. L., & Shimotsu, G. W. (1985). Combined behavioral and pharmacological treatment of essential hypertension. *Biofeedback and Self-Regulation, 10,* 119–138.

Hathaway, S. R., & McKinley, J. C. (1943). *Minnesota Multiphasic Personality Inventory: Manual.* New York: Psychological Corporation.

Haugen, G. B., Dixon, H. H., & Dickel, H. A. (1958). *A therapy for anxiety tension reactions.* New York: MacMillan.

Haward, L. R. C. (1965). Reduction in stress reactivity by autogenic training. In W. Luthe (Ed.), *Autogenic training: International edition* (pp. 96–103). New York: Grune & Stratton.

Hawkins, R. C., II, Doell, S. R., Lindseth, P., Jeffers, V., & Skaggs, S. (1980). Anxiety reduction in hospitalized schizophrenics through thermal biofeedback and relaxation training. *Perceptual and Motor Skills, 51,* 475–482.

Haynes, R. B., Taylor, D. W., & Sackett, D. L. (Eds.). (1979). *Compliance in health care.* Baltimore: Johns Hopkins University Press.

Haynes, S. N. (1981). Muscle-contraction headache: A psychophysiological perspective of etiology and treatment. In S. N. Haynes & L. Gannon (Eds.), *Psychosomatic disorders: A psychophysiological approach to etiology and treatment* (pp. 447–484). New York: Praeger.

Haynes, S. N., Griffin, P., Mooney, D., & Parise, M. (1975). Electromyographic bio-feedback and relaxation instructions in the treatment of muscle contraction headaches. *Behavior Therapy, 6,* 672–678.

Haynes, S. N., Moseley, D., & McGowan, W. T. (1975). Relaxation training and biofeedback in the reduction of frontalis muscle tension. *Psychophysiology, 12,* 547–552.

Haynes, S. N., Sides, H., & Lockwood, G. (1977). Relaxation instructions and frontalis electromyographic feedback intervention with sleep-onset insomnia. *Behavior Therapy, 8,* 644–652.

Haynes, S. N., Woodward, S., Moran, R., & Alexander, D. (1974). Relaxation treatment of insomnia. *Behavior Therapy, 5,* 555–558.

Health and Public Policy Committee, American College of Physicians. (1985). Biofeedback for hypertension. *Annals of Internal Medicine, 102,* 709–715.

Hebert, R., & Lehmann, D. (1977). Theta bursts: An EEG pattern in normal subjects practicing the Transcendental Meditation technique. *Electroencephalography and Clinical Neurophysiology, 42,* 397–405.

Heczey, M. D. (1980). Effects of biofeedback and autogenic training on dysmenorrhea. In A. J. Dan, E. A. Graham, & C. P. Beecher (Eds.), *The menstrual cycle: Vol. 1. A synthesis of interdisciplinary research* (pp. 283–291). New York: Springer.

Heide, F. J. (1986). Psychophysiological responsiveness to auditory stimulation during Transcendental Meditation. *Psychophysiology, 23,* 71–75.

Heide, F. J., & Borkovec, T. D. (1983). Relaxation-induced anxiety: Paradoxical anxiety enhancement due to relaxation training. *Journal of Consulting and Clinical Psychology, 51,* 171–182.

Heide, F. J., & Borkovec, T. D. (1984). Relaxation-induced anxiety: Mechanisms and theoretical implications. *Behaviour Research and Therapy, 22,* 1–12.

Heide, F. J., Wadlington, W. L., & Lundy, R. M. (1980). Hypnotic responsivity as a predictor of outcome in meditation. *International Journal of Clinical and Experimental Hypnosis, 28,* 358–366.

Heiman, J., LoPiccolo, L., & LoPiccolo, J. (1976). *Becoming orgasmic: A sexual growth program for women.* Englewood Cliffs, NJ: Prentice-Hall.

Hendler, C. S., & Redd, W. H. (1986). Fear of hypnosis: The role of labeling in patients' acceptance of behavioral interventions. *Behavior Therapy, 17,* 2–13.

Hendricks, C. G. (1975). Meditation as discrimination training: A theoretical note. *Journal of Transpersonal Psychology, 7,* 144–146.

Hermecz, D. A., & Melamed, B. G. (1984). The assessment of emotional imagery training in fearful children. *Behavior Therapy, 15,* 156–172.

Hersen, M., & Barlow, D. H. (1976). *Single-case experimental designs: Strategies for studying behavior change.* Elmsford, NY: Pergamon Press.

Hershey, M., & Kearns, P. (1979). The effect of guided fantasy on the creative thinking and writing ability of gifted students. *Gifted Child Quarterly, 23,* 71–77.

Herzfeld, G. M., & Taub, E. (1977). Suggestion as an aid to self-regulation of hand temperature. *International Journal of Neuroscience, 8,* 23–26.

Herzfeld, G. M., & Taub, E. (1980). Effect of slide projections and tape-recorded suggestions on thermal biofeedback training. *Biofeedback and Self-Regulation, 5,* 393–405.

Hess, W. R. (1957). *The functional organization of the diencephalon.* New York: Grune & Stratton.

Hiebert, B., Dumka, L., & Cardinal, J. (1983). The validity of self-monitored physiological indices of relaxation. *Canadian Counsellor, 18,* 47–48.

Hiebert, B., & Fox, E. E. (1981). Reactive effects of self-monitoring anxiety. *Journal of Counseling Psychology, 28,* 187–193.

Hilgartner, M. W. (Ed.). (1976). *Hemophilia in children.* Littleton, MA: PSG.

Hillenberg, J. B., & Collins, F. L., Jr. (1982). A procedural analysis and review of relaxation training research. *Behaviour Research and Therapy, 20,* 251–260.

Hillenberg, J. B., & Collins, F. L., Jr. (1983). The importance of home practice for progressive relaxation training. *Behaviour Research and Therapy, 21,* 633–642.

Hillenberg, J. B., & Collins, F. L., Jr. (1986). The contribution of progressive relaxation and cognitive coping training in stress management programs. *The Behavior Therapist, 9,* 147, 149.

Hinkle, J. W., & Lutker, E. R. (1972). Insomnia: A new approach. *Psychotherapy: Theory, Research and Practice, 9,* 236–237.

Hirai, T. (1974). *Psychophysiology of Zen.* Tokyo: Igaku Shoin.

Hirai, T. (1975). *Zen meditation therapy.* Tokyo: Japan Publications.

Hjelle, L. A. (1974). Transcendental Meditation and psychological health. *Perceptual and Motor Skills, 39,* 623–628.

Hochberg, J. E., Triebel, W., & Seaman, G. (1951). Color adaptation under conditions of homogeneous visual stimulation (Ganzfeld). *Journal of Experimental Psychology, 41,* 153–159.

Hock, R. A., Bramble, J., & Kennard, D. W. (1977). A comparison between relaxation and assertive training with asthmatic male children. *Biological Psychiatry, 12,* 593–596.

Hock, R. A., Rodgers, C. H., Reddi, C., & Kennard, D. W. (1978). Medico-psychological interventions in male asthmatic children: An evaluation of physiological change. *Psychosomatic Medicine, 40,* 210–215.

Hodgson, R., & Rachman, S. (1974). II. Desynchrony in measures of fear. *Behaviour Research and Therapy, 12,* 319–326.

Hodgson, R., Rachman, S., & Marks, I. M. (1972). The treatment of chronic obsessive-compulsive neurosis: Follow-up and further findings. *Behaviour Research and Therapy, 10,* 181–189.

Hoefer, P. F. A. (1941). Innervation and "tonus" of striated muscle in man. *Archives of Neurology and Psychiatry, 46,* 947–972.

Hoefer, P. F. A., & Putnam, T. J. (1939). Action potentials of muscles in normal subjects. *Archives of Neurology and Psychiatry, 42,* 201–218.

Hoelscher, T. J., & Lichstein, K. L. (1984). Behavioral assessment and treatment of child migraine: Implications for clinical research and practice. *Headache, 24,* 94–103.

Hoelscher, T. J., Lichstein, K. L., Fischer, S., & Hegarty, T. B. (1987). Relaxation treatment of hypertension: Do home relaxation tapes enhance treatment outcome? *Behavior Therapy, 18,* 33-37.

Hoelscher, T. J., Lichstein, K. L., & Rosenthal, T. L. (1984). Objective vs. subjective assessment of relaxation compliance among anxious individuals. *Behaviour Research and Therapy, 22,* 187-193.

Hoelscher, T. J., Lichstein, K. L., & Rosenthal, T. L. (1986). Home relaxation practice in hypertension treatment: Objective assessment and compliance induction. *Journal of Consulting and Clinical Psychology, 54,* 217-221.

Hoenig, J. (1968). Medical research on Yoga. *Confina Psychiatrica, 11,* 69-89.

Hoffman, J. W., Benson, H., Arns, P. A., Stainbrook, G. L., Landsberg, L., Young, J. B., & Gill, A. (1982). Reduced sympathetic nervous system responsivity associated with the relaxation response. *Science, 215,* 190-192.

Hollandsworth, J. G., Jr., Gintner, G. G., Ellender, B. S., & Rectanus, E. F. (1984). O_2 consumption, heart rate and subjective ratings under conditions of relaxation and active coping. *Behaviour Research and Therapy, 22,* 281-288.

Holmes, D. S. (1984). Meditation and somatic arousal reduction: A review of the experimental evidence. *American Psychologist, 39,* 1-10.

Holmes, D. S., Solomon, S., Cappo, B. M., & Greenberg, J. L. (1983). Effects of Transcendental Meditation versus resting on physiological and subjective arousal. *Journal of Personality and Social Psychology, 44,* 1245-1252.

Holroyd, K. A., & Andrasik, F. (1978). Coping and the self-control of chronic tension headache. *Journal of Consulting and Clinical Psychology, 46,* 1036-1045.

Homme, L. E. (1965). Perspectives in psychology: XXIV. Control of coverants, the operants of the mind. *Psychological Record, 15,* 501-511.

Honsberger, R., & Wilson, A. F. (1973). Transcendental meditation in treating asthma. *Respiratory Therapy, 3,* 79-80, 128.

Hoppe, K. D. (1961). Relaxation through concentration–concentration through relaxation: Autogenic training with neurotic and psychotic patients. *Medical Times, 89,* 254-263.

Horan, J. J. (1973). "In vivo" emotive imagery: A technique for reducing childbirth anxiety and discomfort. *Psychological Reports, 32,* 1328.

Horan, J. J., & Dellinger, J. K. (1974). "In vivo" emotive imagery: A preliminary test. *Perceptual and Motor Skills, 39,* 359-362.

Horan, J. J., Hackett, G., Buchanan, J. D., Stone, C. I., & Demchik-Stone, D. (1977). Coping with pain: A component analysis of stress inoculation. *Cognitive Therapy and Research, 1,* 211-221.

Horan, J. J., Layng, F. C., & Pursell, C. H. (1976). Preliminary study of effects of "in vivo" emotive imagery on dental discomfort. *Perceptual and Motor Skills, 42,* 105-106.

Hoshmand, L. T., Helmes, E., Kazarian, S., & Tekatch, G. (1985). Evaluation of two relaxation training programs under medication and no-medication conditions. *Journal of Clinical Psychology, 41,* 22-29.

Houts, A. C. (1982). Relaxation and thermal feedback treatment of child migraine headache: A case study. *American Journal of Clinical Biofeedback, 5,* 154-157.

Howard, W. A., Murphy, S. M., & Clarke, J. C. (1983). The nature and treatment of fear of flying: A controlled investigation. *Behavior Therapy, 14,* 557–567.

Hugdahl, K. (1981). The three-systems-model of fear and emotion—a critical examination. *Behaviour Research and Therapy, 19,* 75–85.

Hughes, R. C., & Hughes, H. H. (1978). Insomnia: Effects of EMG biofeedback, relaxation training, and stimulus control. *Behavioral Engineering, 5,* 67–72.

Humphreys, C. (1970). *Concentration and meditation.* Baltimore, MD: Penguin Books. (Original work published 1935)

Hunt, W. A., Barnett, L. W., & Branch, L. G. (1971). Relapse rates in addiction programs. *Journal of Clinical Psychology, 27,* 455–456.

Hurley, J. D. (1980). Differential effects of hypnosis, biofeedback training, and trophotropic responses on anxiety, ego strength, and locus of control. *Journal of Clinical Psychology, 36,* 503–507.

Husek, T. R., & Alexander, S. (1963). The effectiveness of the Anxiety Differential in examination situations. *Educational and Psychological Measurement, 23,* 309–318.

Hutchings, D. F., Denney, D. R., Basgall, J., & Houston, B. K. (1980). Anxiety management and applied relaxation in reducing general anxiety. *Behaviour Research and Therapy, 18,* 181–190.

Hutchings, D. F., & Reinking, R. H. (1976). Tension headaches: What form of therapy is most effective? *Biofeedback and Self-Regulation, 1,* 183–190.

Hynd, G. W., Chambers, C., Stratton, T. T., & Moan, E. (1977). Credibility of smoking control strategies in non-smokers: Implications for clinicians. *Psychological Reports, 41,* 503–506.

Hynd, G. W., Stratton, T. T., & Severson, H. H. (1978). Smoking treatment strategies, expectancy outcomes, and credibility in attention-placebo control conditions. *Journal of Clinical Psychology, 34,* 182–186.

Hyner, G. C. (1979). Relaxation as principal treatment for excessive cigarette use and caffeine ingestion by a college female. *Psychological Reports, 45,* 531–534.

Ikemi, Y., Ishikawa, H., Goyeche, J. R. M., & Sasaki, Y. (1978). Positive and negative aspects of the altered states of consciousness induced by autogenic training, Zen and yoga. *Psychotherapy and Psychosomatics, 30,* 170–178.

Ikemi, Y., Nagata, S., Ago, Y., & Ikemi, A. (1982). Self-control over stress. *Journal of Psychosomatic Research, 26,* 51–56.

Ikemi, Y., Nakagawa, S., Kimura, M., Dobeta, H., Ono, Y., & Sugita, M. (1965). Bloodflow change by autogenic training—including observations in a case of gastric fistula. In W. Luthe (Ed.), *Autogenic training: International edition* (pp. 64–68). New York: Grune & Stratton.

Ikemi, Y., Nakagawa, S., Kusano, T., & Sugita, M. (1965). The application of autogenic training to "psychological desensitization" of allergic disorders. In W. Luthe (Ed.), *Autogenic training: International edition* (pp. 228–233). New York: Grune & Stratton.

Ince, L. P. (1976). The use of relaxation training and a conditioned stimulus in the elimination of epileptic seizures in a child: A case study. *Journal of Behavior Therapy and Experimental Psychiatry, 7,* 39–42.

Israel, E., & Beiman, I. (1977). Live versus recorded relaxation training: A controlled investigation. *Behavior Therapy, 8,* 251–254.

Jackson, H. J., & King, N. J. (1981). The emotive imagery treatment of a child's trauma-induced phobia. *Journal of Behavior Therapy and Experimental Psychiatry, 12,* 325–328.

Jackson, K., & Hughes, H. (1978). Effects of relaxation training on cursive handwriting of fourth grade students. *Perceptual and Motor Skills, 47,* 707–712.

Jackson, K. A., Jolly, V., & Hamilton, B. (1980). Comparison of remedial treatments for cursive handwriting of fourth-grade students. *Perceptual and Motor Skills, 51,* 1215–1221.

Jacob, R. G., Beidel, D. C., & Shapiro, A. P. (1984). The relaxation word of the day: A simple technique to measure adherence to relaxation. *Journal of Behavioral Assessment, 6,* 159–165.

Jacob, R. G., Fortmann, S. P., Kraemer, H. C., Farquhar, J. W., & Agras, W. S. (1985). Combining behavioral treatments to reduce blood pressure: A controlled outcome study. *Behavior Modification, 9,* 32–54.

Jacob, R. G., Kraemer, H. C., & Agras, W. S. (1977). Relaxation therapy in the treatment of hypertension. *Archives of General Psychiatry, 34,* 1417–1427.

Jacob, R. G., Shapiro, A. P., McDonald, R. H., & Beidel, D. C. (1984, May). *Biobehavioral approaches to hypertension: Relaxation therapy, pharmacotherapy, and their interaction.* Paper presented at the meeting of the Society of Behavioral Medicine, Philadelphia.

Jacob, R. G., Turner, S. M., Szekely, B. C., & Eidelman, B. H. (1983). Predicting outcome of relaxation therapy in headaches: The role of "depression." *Behavior Therapy, 14,* 457–465.

Jacobs, G. D., Heilbronner, R. L., & Stanley, J. M. (1984). The effects of short term flotation REST on relaxation: A controlled study. *Health Psychology, 3,* 99–112.

Jacobsen, R., & Edinger, J. D. (1982). Side effects of relaxation treatment. *American Journal of Psychiatry, 139,* 952–953.

Jacobson, A. M., Manschreck, T. C., & Silverberg, E. (1979). Behavioral treatment for Raynaud's disease: A comparative study with long-term follow-up. *American Journal of Psychiatry, 136,* 844–846.

Jacobson, E. (1912). Further experiments on the inhibition of sensations. *American Journal of Psychology, 23,* 345–369.

Jacobson, E. (1920a). Reduction of nervous irritability and excitement by progressive relaxation. *Transactions of the Section on Nervous and Mental Diseases, American Medical Association,* 17–29.

Jacobson, E. (1920b). Use of relaxation in hypertensive states. *New York Medical Journal, 111,* 419–422.

Jacobson, E. (1921). Treatment of nervous irritability and excitement. *Illinois Medical Journal, 39,* 243–247.

Jacobson, E. (1924). The technic of progressive relaxation. *Journal of Nervous and Mental Disease, 60,* 568–578.

Jacobson, E. (1925a). Progressive relaxation. *American Journal of Psychology, 36,* 73–87.

Jacobson, E. (1925b). Voluntary relaxation of the esophagus. *American Journal of Physiology, 72,* 387–394.

Jacobson, E. (1927a). Action currents from muscular contractions during conscious processes. *Science, 66,* 403.

Jacobson, E. (1927b). Spastic esophagus and mucous colitis. *Archives of Internal Medicine, 39,* 433–445.

Jacobson, E. (1928). Differential relaxation during reading, writing and other activities as tested by the knee-jerk. *American Journal of Physiology, 86,* 675–693.

Jacobson, E. (1929). *Progressive relaxation.* Chicago: University of Chicago Press.

Jacobson, E. (1930a). Electrical measurements of neuromuscular states during mental activities. I. Imagination of movement involving skeletal muscle. *American Journal of Physiology, 91,* 567–608.

Jacobson, E. (1930b). Electrical measurements of neuromuscular states during mental activities. II. Imagination and recollection of various muscular acts. *American Journal of Physiology, 94,* 22–34.

Jacobson, E. (1930c). Electrical measurements of neuromuscular states during mental activities. III. Visual imagination and recollection. *American Journal of Physiology, 95,* 694–702.

Jacobson, E. (1930d). Electrical measurements of neuromuscular states during mental activities. IV. Evidence of contraction of specific muscles during imagination. *American Journal of Physiology, 95,* 703–712.

Jacobson, E. (1931a). Electrical measurements of neuromuscular states during mental activities. V. Variation of specific muscles contracting during imagination. *American Journal of Physiology, 96,* 115–121.

Jacobson, E. (1931b). Electrical measurements of neuromuscular states during mental activities. VI. A note on mental activities concerning an amputated limb. *American Journal of Physiology, 96,* 122–125.

Jacobson, E. (1931c). Electrical measurements of neuromuscular states during mental activities. VII. Imagination, recollection and abstract thinking involving the speech musculature. *American Journal of Physiology, 97,* 200–209.

Jacobson, E. (1932). Electrophysiology of mental activities. *American Journal of Psychology, 44,* 677–694.

Jacobson, E. (1934a). Electrical measurements concerning muscular contraction (tonus) and the cultivation of relaxation in man: Relaxation-times of individuals. *American Journal of Physiology, 108,* 573–580.

Jacobson, E. (1934b). Electrical measurements concerning muscular contraction (tonus) and the cultivation of relaxation in man: Studies on arm flexors. *American Journal of Physiology, 107,* 230–248.

Jacobson, E. (1934c). *You must relax.* New York: Whittlesey House.

Jacobson, E. (1935). Variations in muscular "tonus." *American Journal of Physiology, 113,* 71.

Jacobson, E. (1936a). The course of relaxation in muscles of athletes. *American Journal of Psychology, 48,* 98–108.

Jacobson, E. (1936b). The influence of skeletal muscle tension and relaxation on blood pressure. *American Journal of Physiology, 116,* 86.

Jacobson, E. (1938a). *Progressive relaxation* (2nd ed.). Chicago: University of Chicago Press.

Jacobson, E. (1938b). *You can sleep well: The abc's of restful sleep for the average person.* New York: Whittlesey House.

Jacobson, E. (1939a). The neurovoltmeter. *American Journal of Psychology, 52,* 620–624.

Jacobson, E. (1939b). Variations in blood pressure with skeletal muscle tension and relaxation. *Annals of Internal Medicine, 12,* 1194–1212.

Jacobson, E. (1939c). Variations in blood pressure with skeletal muscle tension (action-potentials) in man. III. The influence of brief voluntary contractions. *American Journal of Physiology, 126,* 546–547.

Jacobson, E. (1940a). Cultivated relaxation in "essential" hypertension. *Archives of Physical Therapy, 21,* 645–654, 694.

Jacobson, E. (1940b). The direct measurement of nervous and muscular states with the integrating neurovoltmeter (action potential-integrator). *American Journal of Psychiatry, 97,* 513–523.

Jacobson, E. (1940c). An integrating voltmeter for the study of nerve and muscle potentials. *Review of Scientific Instruments, 11,* 415–418.

Jacobson, E. (1940d). Variation of blood pressure with brief voluntary muscular contractions. *Journal of Laboratory and Clinical Medicine, 25,* 1029–1037.

Jacobson, E. (1940e). Variation of blood pressure with skeletal muscle tension and relaxation. II. The heart beat. *Annals of Internal Medicine, 13,* 1619–1625.

Jacobson, E. (1940f). Variations of muscular tension (action-potentials) in man. *American Journal of Physiology, 129,* 388–389.

Jacobson, E. (1941a). The physiological conception and treatment of certain common "psychoneuroses." *American Journal of Psychiatry, 98,* 219–226.

Jacobson, E. (1941b). Recording action-potentials without photography. *American Journal of Psychology, 54,* 266–269.

Jacobson, E. (1942). The effect of daily rest without training to relax on muscular tonus. *American Journal of Psychology, 55,* 248–254.

Jacobson, E. (1943a). Cultivated relaxation for the elimination of "nervous breakdowns." *Archives of Physical Therapy, 24,* 133–143, 176.

Jacobson, E. (1943b). The cultivation of physiological relaxation. *Annals of Internal Medicine, 19,* 965–972.

Jacobson, E. (1943c). Innervation and "tonus" of striated muscle in man. *Journal of Nervous and Mental Disease, 97,* 197–203.

Jacobson, E. (1943d). "Tonus" in striated muscle. *American Journal of Psychology, 56,* 433–437.

Jacobson, E. (1947). The influence of relaxation upon the blood pressure in "essential hypertension." *Federation Proceedings, 6,* 135–136.

Jacobson, E. (1948). Theory of essential hypertension in man. *Transactions of the New York Academy of Sciences, 11,* 49–50.

Jacobson, E. (1955). Principles underlying coronary heart disease. Considerations for a working hypothesis. *Cardiologia, 26,* 83–102.

Jacobson, E. (1957). The tension in hypertension. *Bulletin of the Sangamon County Medical Society,* pp. 147–149.

Jacobson, E. (1959). *How to relax and have your baby.* New York: McGraw-Hill.

Jacobson, E. (1963). *Tension control for businessmen.* New York: McGraw-Hill.

Jacobson, E. (1964a). *Anxiety and tension control.* Philadelphia: Lippincott.

Jacobson, E. (1964b). *Self-operations control: A manual of tension control.* Philadelphia: Lippincott.

Jacobson, E. (1967a). *Biology of emotions: New understanding derived from biological multidisciplinary investigation; First electrophysiological measurements.* Springfield, IL: Thomas.

Jacobson, E. (1967b). Briefer relaxation methods. In E. Jacobson (Ed.), *Tension in medicine* (pp. 128–136). Springfield, IL: Thomas.

Jacobson, E. (Ed.). (1967c). *Tension in medicine.* Springfield, IL: Thomas.

Jacobson, E. (1970). *Modern treatment of tense patients.* Springfield, IL: Thomas.

Jacobson, E. (1973a). Electrophysiology of mental activities and introduction to the psychological process of thinking. In F. J. McGuigan & R. A. Schoonover (Eds.), *The Psychophysiology of thinking: Studies of covert processes* (pp. 3–31). New York: Academic Press.

Jacobson, E. (1973b). *Teaching and learning: New methods for old arts.* Chicago: National Foundation for Progressive Relaxation.

Jacobson, E. (1977). The origins and development of progressive relaxation. *Journal of Behavior Therapy and Experimental Psychiatry, 8,* 119–123.

Jacobson, E. (1979). Some highlights of my life. *Journal of Behavior Therapy and Experimental Psychiatry, 10,* 5–9.

Jacobson, E., & Carlson, A. J. (1925). The influence of relaxation upon the knee jerk. *American Journal of Physiology, 73,* 324–328.

Jacobson, E., & Kraft, F. L. (1942). Contraction potentials (right quadriceps femoris) in man during reading. *American Journal of Physiology, 137,* 1–5.

Jaffe, D. T., & Bresler, D. E. (1980). The use of guided imagery as an adjunct to medical diagnosis and treatment. *Journal of Humanistic Psychology, 20,* 45–59.

Jahn, D. L., & Lichstein, K. L. (1980). The resistive client: A neglected phenomenon in behavior therapy. *Behavior Modification, 4,* 303–320.

Jakes, S. C., Hallam, R. S., Rachman, S., & Hinchcliffe, R. (1986). The effects of reassurance, relaxation training and distraction on chronic tinnitus sufferers. *Behaviour Research and Therapy, 24,* 497–507.

James, J. E., & Hampton, B. A. M. (1982). The relative efficacy of directive and nondirective treatment in behavioral weight control. *Behavior Therapy, 13,* 463–475.

James, J. E., Stirling, K. P., & Hampton, B. A. M. (1985). Caffeine fading: Behavioral treatment of caffeine abuse. *Behavior Therapy, 16,* 15–27.

James, W. (1902). *The varieties of religious experience.* New York: Random House.

Janda, L. H., & Cash, T. F. (1976). Effects of relaxation training upon physiological and self-report indices. *Perceptual and Motor Skills, 42,* 444.

Janda, L. H., & Rimm, D. C. (1972). Covert sensitization in the treatment of obesity. *Journal of Abnormal Psychology, 80,* 37–42.

Jannoun, L., Oppenheimer, C., & Gelder, M. (1982). A self-help treatment program for anxiety state patients. *Behavior Therapy, 13,* 103–111.

Janssen, K., & Neutgens, J. (1986). Autogenic training and progressive relaxation in the treatment of three kinds of headache. *Behaviour Research and Therapy, 24,* 199–208.

Jedrczak, A., Beresford, M., & Clements, G. (1985). The TM-Sidhi program, pure consciousness, creativity and intelligence. *Journal of Creative Behavior, 19,* 270–275.

Jedrczak, A., & Clements, G. (1984). The TM-Sidhi programme and field independence. *Perceptual and Motor Skills, 59,* 999–1000.

Jemmott, J. B., III, & Locke, S. E. (1984). Psychosocial factors, immunologic mediation, and human susceptibility to infectious diseases: How much do we know? *Psychological Bulletin, 95,* 78–109.

Jenkins, C. D., Zyzanski, S. J., & Rosenman, R. H. (1979). *Jenkins Activity Survey.* New York: The Psychological Corporation.

Jerremalm, A., Jansson, L., & Ost, L. G. (1986a). Cognitive and physiological reactivity and the effects of different behavioral methods in the treatment of social phobia. *Behaviour Research and Therapy, 24,* 171–180.

Jerremalm, A., Jansson, L., & Ost, L. G. (1986b). Individual response patterns and the effects of different behavioral methods in the treatment of dental phobia. *Behaviour Research and Therapy, 24,* 587–596.

Jessup, B. A., & Neufeld, R. W. J. (1977). Effects of biofeedback and "autogenic relaxation" techniques on physiological and subjective responses in psychiatric patients: A preliminary analysis. *Behavior Therapy, 8,* 160–167.

Jevning, R., Pirkle, H. C., & Wilson, A. F. (1977). Behavioral alteration of plasma phenylalanine concentration. *Physiology and Behavior, 19,* 611–614.

Jevning, R., Smith, R., Wilson, A. F., & Morton, M. E. (1976). Alterations in blood flow during Transcendental Meditation. *Psychophysiology, 13,* 168.

Jevning, R., Wilson, A. F., & Davidson, J. M. (1978). Adrenocortical activity during meditation. *Hormones and Behavior, 10,* 54–60.

Jevning, R., Wilson, A. F., Smith, W. R., & Morton, M. E. (1978). Redistribution of blood flow in acute hypometabolic behavior. *American Journal of Physiology, 235,* 89–92.

Jevning, R., Wilson, A. F., & VanderLaan, E. F. (1978). Plasma prolactin and growth hormone during meditation. *Psychosomatic Medicine, 40,* 329–333.

Johnson, D. T., & Spielberger, C. D. (1968). The effects of relaxation training and the passage of time on measures of state- and trait-anxiety. *Journal of Clinical Psychology, 24,* 20–23.

Johnson, J. E. (1973). Effects of accurate expectations about sensations on the sensory and distress components of pain. *Journal of Personality and Social Psychology, 27,* 261–275.

Johnson, S. M., & Sechrest, L. (1968). Comparison of desensitization and progressive relaxation in treating test anxiety. *Journal of Consulting and Clinical Psychology, 32,* 280–286.

Jones, H. H. (1953). A review of relaxation. *Physical Therapy Review, 34,* 570–574.

Jourard, S. M. (1968). *Disclosing man to himself.* Princeton, NJ: Van Nostrand.

Juenet, C., Cottraux, J., & Collet, L. (1983, December). *G. S. R. feedback and*

Schultz's relaxation in tension headaches: A comparative study. Paper presented at the meeting of the World Congress on Behavior Therapy, Washington, DC.

Jung, C. G. (1969). *The archetypes and the collective unconscious* (2nd ed., R. F. C. Hull, Trans.). In H. Read, M. Fordham, G. Adler, & W. McGuire (Eds.), *The collected works of C. G. Jung* (Vol. 9, Part 1). Princeton, NJ: Princeton University Press.

Jurish, S. E., Blanchard, E. B., Andrasik, F., Teders, S. J., Neff, D. F., & Arena, J. G. (1983). Home- versus clinic-based treatment of vascular headache. *Journal of Consulting and Clinical Psychology, 51,* 743-751.

Jus, A., & Jus, K. (1965a). The evolution of the respiratory pattern during autogenic training. In W. Luthe (Ed.), *Autogenic training: International edition* (pp. 104-105). New York: Grune & Stratton.

Jus, A., & Jus, K. (1965b). The galvanic skin response during autogenic training. In W. Luthe (Ed.), *Autogenic training: International edition* (pp. 92-93). New York: Grune & Stratton.

Jus, A., & Jus, K. (1965c). The structure and reactivity of the electroencephalogram during autogenic training. In W. Luthe (Ed.), *Autogenic training: International edition* (pp. 12-14). New York: Grune & Stratton.

Jus, A., & Jus, K. (1969). Some remarks on "passive" concentration and on autogenic shift. In L. Chertok (Ed.), *Psychophysiological mechanisms of hypnosis* (pp. 52-57). New York: Springer-Verlag.

Jus, A., & Jus, K. (1977a). EEG studies of full AT (SE.-I to VI) and abbreviated AT (SE.-I, SE-II). In W. Luthe & F. Antonelli (Eds.), *Therapy in psychosomatic medicine: Autogenic therapy* (pp. 12-17). Rome: Edizioni L. Pozzi.

Jus, K., & Jus, A. (1977b). Evening practice of heaviness and warmth exercises as a substitute for hypnotic drugs. In W. Luthe & F. Antonelli (Eds.), *Therapy in psychosomatic medicine: Autogenic therapy* (pp. 86-88). Rome: Edizioni L. Pozzi.

Kabat-Zinn, J. (1982). An outpatient program in behavioral medicine for chronic pain patients based on the practice of mindfulness meditation: Theoretical considerations and preliminary results. *General Hospital Psychiatry, 4,* 33-47.

Kabat-Zinn, J., Lipworth, L., & Burney, R. (1985). The clinical use of mindfulness meditation for the self-regulation of chronic pain. *Journal of Behavioral Medicine, 8,* 163-190.

Kagan, J. (1965). Reflection-impulsivity and reading ability in primary grade children. *Child Development, 36,* 609-628.

Kahn, M., Baker, B. L., & Weiss, J. M. (1968). Treatment of insomnia by relaxation training. *Journal of Abnormal Psychology, 73,* 556-558.

Kanas, N., & Horowitz, M. J. (1977). Reactions of Transcendental Meditators and nonmeditators to stress films. *Archives of General Psychiatry, 34,* 1431-1436.

Kanellakos, D. P., & Lukas, J. S. (1974). *The psychobiology of Transcendental Meditation: A literature review.* Menlo Park, CA: Benjamin.

Kanfer, F. H. (1971). The maintenance of behavior by self-generated stimuli and reinforcement. In A. Jacobs and L. B. Sachs (Eds.), *The psychology of private events: Perspectives on covert response systems* (pp. 39-59). New York: Academic Press.

Kanfer, F. H., & Karoly, P. (1982). The psychology of self-management: Abiding issues and tentative directions. In P. Karoly & F. H. Kanfer (Eds.), *Self-management and behavior change: From theory to practice* (pp. 571–599). Elmsford, NY: Pergamon Press.

Kaplan, H. S. (1974). *The new sex therapy.* New York: Brunner/Mazel.

Kaplan, R. M., Atkins, C. J., & Lenhard, L. (1982). Coping with a stressful sigmoidoscopy: Evaluation of cognitive and relaxation preparations. *Journal of Behavioral Medicine, 5,* 67–82.

Kaplan, R. M., Metzger, G., & Jablecki, C. (1983). Brief cognitive and relaxation training increases tolerance for a painful clinical electromyographic examination. *Psychosomatic Medicine, 45,* 155–162.

Kapleau, P. (Ed.). (1966). *The three pillars of Zen.* New York: Harper & Row.

Karambelkar, P. V., Vinekar, S. L., & Bhole, M. V. (1968). Studies on human subjects staying in an air-tight pit. *Indian Journal of Medical Research, 56,* 1282–1288.

Karoly, P., & Kanfer, F. H. (Eds.). (1982). *Self-management and behavior change: From theory to practice.* Elmsford, NY: Pergamon Press.

Kasamatsu, A., & Hirai, T. (1966). An electroencephalographic study on the Zen meditation (Zazen). *Folia Psychiatrica et Neurologica Japonica, 20,* 315–336.

Kasamatsu, A., Okuma, T., Takenaka, S., Koga, E., Ikeda, K., & Sugiyama, H. (1957). The EEG of "Zen" and "Yoga" practitioners. *Electroencephalography and Clinical Neurophysiology, 9*(Suppl. 9), 51–52.

Katz, D. (1974). Relaxation due to verbal suggestion: A psychophysiological study. *Psychological Record, 24,* 523–532.

Katz, D. (1977). Decreased drug use and prevention of drug use through the Transcendental Meditation program. In D. W. Orme-Johnson & J. T. Farrow (Eds.), *Scientific research on the Transcendental Meditation program: Collected papers* (Vol. 1, 2nd ed., pp. 536–543). Livingston Manor, NY: Maharishi European Research University Press.

Katz, N. W. (1979). Comparative efficacy of behavioral training, training plus relaxation, and a sleep/trance hypnotic induction in increasing hypnotic susceptibility. *Journal of Consulting and Clinical Psychology, 47,* 119–127.

Kawakami, K., Kuroda, M., Sasaki, D., Soma, S., & Matsunaga, F. (1977). Autogenic training in relapsing peptic ulcer. In W. Luthe & F. Antonelli (Eds.), *Therapy in psychosomatic medicine: Autogenic therapy* (pp. 48–53). Rome: Edizioni L. Pozzi.

Kazdin, A. E. (1975). Covert modeling, imagery assessment, and assertive behavior. *Journal of Counseling and Clinical Psychology, 43,* 716–724.

Kazdin, A. E. (1977). Research issues in covert conditioning. *Cognitive Therapy and Research, 1,* 45–58.

Kazdin, A. E. (1978). *History of behavior modification: Experimental foundations of contemporary research.* Baltimore: University Park Press.

Kazdin, A. E., & Smith, G. A. (1979). Covert conditioning: A review and evaluation. *Advances in Behaviour Research and Therapy, 2,* 57–98.

Kazdin, A. E., & Wilcoxon, L. A. (1976). Systematic desensitization and nonspecific treatment effects: A methodological evaluation. *Psychological Bulletin, 83,* 729–758.

Keefe, F. J. (1978). Biofeedback vs. instructional control of skin temperature. *Journal of Behavioral Medicine, 1,* 383–390.

Keefe, F. J., & Surwit, R. S. (1978). Electromyographic biofeedback: Behavioral treatment of neuromuscular disorders. *Journal of Behavioral Medicine, 1,* 13-24.

Keefe, F. J., Surwit, R. S., & Pilon, R. N. (1979). A 1-year follow-up of Raynaud's patients treated with behavioral therapy techniques. *Journal of Behavioral Medicine, 2,* 385-391.

Keefe, F. J., Surwit, R. S., & Pilon, R. N. (1980). Biofeedback, autogenic training, and progressive relaxation in the treatment of Raynaud's disease: A comparative study. *Journal of Applied Behavior Analysis, 13,* 3-11.

Keefe, F. J., Surwit, R. S., & Pilon, R. N. (1981). Collagen vascular disease: Can behavior therapy help? *Journal of Behavior Therapy and Experimental Psychiatry, 12,* 171-175.

Keefe, T. (1975). Meditation and the psychotherapist. *American Journal of Orthopsychiatry, 45,* 484-489.

Kellogg, R. H. (1964). Central chemical regulation of respiration. In W. O. Fenn & H. Rahn (Ed.), *Handbook of physiology. Section III: Respiration* (Vol. 1, pp. 507-534). Washington, DC: American Physiological Society.

Kelton, A., & Belar, C. D. (1983). The relative efficacy of autogenic phrases and autogenic-feedback training in teaching hand warming to children. *Biofeedback and Self-Regulation, 8,* 461-475.

Kendall, B. L. (1967). Clinical relaxation for neuroses and psychoneuroses. In E. Jacobson (Ed.), *Tension in medicine* (pp. 71-84). Springfield, IL: Thomas.

Kendall, K. A. (1982). A sixty-year perspective of social work. *Social Casework, 63,* 424-428.

Kendall, P. C., & Norton-Ford, J. D. (1982). *Clinical psychology: Scientific and professional dimensions.* New York: Wiley.

Kendall, P. C., & Watson, D. (1981). Psychological preparation for stressful medical procedures. In C. K. Prokop & L. A. Bradley (Eds.), *Medical psychology: Contributions to behavioral medicine* (pp. 197-221). New York: Academic Press.

Kennedy, D., Wormith, S., Michaud, J., Marquis, H., & Gendreau, P. (1975). Crisis intervention in a correctional centre. *Journal of Community Psychology, 3,* 93-94.

Kennedy, R. B. (1976). Self-induced depersonalization syndrome. *American Journal of Psychiatry, 133,* 1326-1328.

Kibler, V. E., & Foreman, R. J. (1983). Effects of progressive muscle relaxation training on trait anxiety. *Psychological Reports, 53,* 128-130.

Kiecolt-Glaser, J. K., Glaser, R., Strain, E. C., Stout, J. C., Tarr, K. L., Holliday, J. E., & Speicher, C. E. (1986). Modulation of cellular immunity in medical students. *Journal of Behavioral Medicine, 9,* 5-21.

Kiecolt-Glaser, J. K., Glaser, R., Williger, D., Stout, J., Messick, G., Sheppard, S., Ricker, D., Romisher, S. C., Briner, W., Bonnell, G., & Donnerberg, R. (1985). Psychosocial enhancement of immunocompetence in a geriatric population. *Health Psychology, 4,* 25-41.

Kimble, C. J. (1975). Transcendental Meditation in the youth authority. *Youth Authority Quarterly, 28,* 38-42.

King, N. J. (1980). The therapeutic utility of abbreviated progressive relaxation: A critical review with implications for clinical practice. In M. Hersen, R. M. Eisler, &

P. M. Miller (Eds.), *Progress in behavior modification* (Vol. 10, pp. 147–182). New York: Academic Press.

King, N. J., & Montgomery, R. B. (1980). A component analysis of biofeedback induced self-control of peripheral (finger) temperature. *Biological Psychology, 10,* 139–152.

Kinsman, R. A., Dirks, J. F., Jones, N. F., & Dahlem, N. W. (1980). Anxiety reduction in asthma: Four catches to general application. *Psychosomatic Medicine, 42,* 397–405.

Kinsman, R. A., & Staudenmayer, H. (1978). Baseline levels in muscle relaxation training. *Biofeedback and Self-Regulation, 3,* 97–104.

Kirkland, K., & Hollandsworth, J. G., Jr. (1980). Effective test taking: Skills-acquisition versus anxiety-reduction techniques. *Journal of Consulting and Clinical Psychology, 48,* 431–439.

Kirkley, B. G., Schneider, J. A., Agras, W. S., & Bachman, J. A. (1985). Comparison of two group treatments for bulimia. *Journal of Consulting and Clinical Psychology, 53,* 43–48.

Kirmil-Gray, K., Eagleston, J. R., Thoresen, C. E., & Zarcone, V. P., Jr. (1985). Brief consultation and stress management treatments for drug-dependent insomnia: Effects on sleep quality, self-efficacy, and daytime stress. *Journal of Behavioral Medicine, 8,* 79–99.

Kirsch, I., & Henry, D. (1979). Self-desensitization and meditation in the reduction of public speaking anxiety. *Journal of Consulting and Clinical Psychology, 47,* 536–541.

Kirschenbaum, D. S., Harris, E. S., & Tomarken, A. J. (1984). Effects of parental involvement in behavioral weight loss therapy for preadolescents. *Behavior Therapy, 15,* 485–500.

Klajner, F., Hartman, L. M., & Sobell, M. B. (1984). Treatment of substance abuse by relaxation training: A review of its rationale, efficacy and mechanisms. *Addictive Behaviors, 9,* 41–55.

Klein, M. H., Greist, J. H., Gurman, A. S., Neimeyer, R. A., Lesser, D. P., Bushnell, N. J., & Smith, R. E. (1985). A comparative outcome study of group psychotherapy vs. exercise treatments for depression. *International Journal of Mental Health, 13,* 148–177.

Klein, S. A., & Deffenbacher, J. L. (1977). Relaxation and exercise for hyperactive impulsive children. *Perceptual and Motor Skills, 45,* 1159–1162.

Kleinsorge, H., & Klumbies, G. (1964). *Technique of relaxation: Self-relaxation* (R. L. Walker, Trans.). Baltimore: Williams & Wilkins. (Original work published 1962)

Klepac, R. K., Hauge, G., Dowling, J., & McDonald, M. (1981). Direct and generalized effects of three components of stress inoculation for increased pain tolerance. *Behavior Therapy, 12,* 417–424.

Kline, K. S., Docherty, E. M., & Farley, F. H. (1982). Transcendental Meditation, self/actualization, and global personality. *Journal of General Psychology, 106,* 3–8.

Klinger, E., Gregoire, K. C., & Barta, S. G. (1973). Physiological correlates of mental activity: Eye movements, alpha, and heart rate during imagining, suppression, concentration, search, and choice. *Psychophysiology, 10,* 471–477.

Klingman, A., Melamed, B. G., Cuthbert, M. I., & Hermecz, D. A. (1984). Effects of participant modeling on information acquisition and skill utilization. *Journal of Consulting and Clinical Psychology, 52,* 414–422.

Kluger, M. A., Jamner, L. D., & Tursky, B. (1985). Comparison of the effectiveness of biofeedback and relaxation training on hand warming. *Psychophysiology, 22,* 162–166.

Klumbies, G., & Eberhardt, G. (1966). Results of autogenic training in the treatment of hypertension. In J. J. L. Ibor (Ed.), *VI World Congress of Psychiatry* (pp. 46–47). Amsterdam: Excerpta Medica.

Koeppen, A. S. (1974, October). Relaxation training for children. *Elementary School Guidance and Counseling, 9,* 14–21.

Kohen, D. P., Olness, K. N., Colwell, S. O., & Heimel, A. (1984). The use of relaxation-mental imagery (self-hypnosis) in the management of 505 pediatric behavioral encounters. *Journal of Developmental and Behavioral Pediatrics, 5,* 21–25.

Kohlenberg, R. J., & Cahn, T. (1981). Self-help treatment for migraine headaches: A controlled outcome study. *Headache, 21,* 196–200.

Kohr, R. L. (1977). Dimensionality of meditative experience: A replication. *Journal of Transpersonal Psychology, 9,* 193–203.

Kohr, R. L. (1978). Changes in subjective meditation experience during a short term project. *Journal of Altered States of Consciousness, 3,* 221–234.

Kolsawalla, M. B. (1978). An experimental investigation into the effectiveness of some yogic variables as a mechanism of change in the value-attitude system. *Journal of Indian Psychology, 1,* 59–68.

Kolvin, I. (1967). "Aversive imagery" treatment in adolescents. *Behaviour Research and Therapy, 5,* 245–248.

Kondas, O. (1967). Reduction of examination anxiety and "stage-fright" by group desensitization and relaxation. *Behaviour Research and Therapy, 5,* 275–281.

Kondo, A. (1952). Intuition in Zen Buddhism. *American Journal of Psychoanalysis, 12,* 10–14.

Kondo, A. (1958). Zen in psychotherapy: The virtue of sitting. *Chicago Review, 12,* 57–64.

Korchin, S. J. (1983). The history of clinical psychology: A personal view. In M. Hersen, A. E. Kazdin, & A. S. Bellack (Eds.), *The clinical psychology handbook* (pp. 5–19). Elmsford, NY: Pergamon Press.

Kotses, H., & Glaus, K. D. (1981). Applications of biofeedback to the treatment of asthma: A critical review. *Biofeedback and Self-Regulation, 6,* 573–593.

Krampen, G., & Ohm, D. (1984). Effects of relaxation training during rehabilitation of myocardial infarction patients. *International Journal of Rehabilitation Research, 7,* 68–69.

Krenz, E. W. (1984). Improving competitive performance with hypnotic suggestions and modified autogenic training: Case reports. *American Journal of Clinical Hypnosis, 27,* 58–63.

Kretschmer, W. (1969). Meditative techniques in psychotherapy. In C. T. Tart (Ed.), *Altered states of consciousness* (pp. 219–228). New York: Wiley.

Krige, P. (1985). Vaginismus: A case report. *South African Medical Journal, 67,* 1057–1059.

Krishnamurti, J. (1967). *Commentaries on living: Third series* (D. Rajagopal, Ed.). Wheaton, IL: Quest. (Original work published 1960)

Kubie, L. S. (1943). The use of induced hypnagogic reveries in the recovery of repressed amnesic data. *Bulletin of the Menninger Clinic, 7,* 172–182.

Kubose, S. K. (1976). An experimental investigation of psychological aspects of meditation. *Psychologia, 19,* 1–10.

Kudrow, L. (1980). *Cluster headache: Mechanisms and management.* New York: Oxford University Press.

Kumaraiah, V. (1979). Behavioural treatment of drug addiction: A multiple approach. *Indian Journal of Clinical Psychology, 6,* 43–46.

Kutz, I., Borysenko, J. Z., & Benson, H. (1985). Meditation and psychotherapy: A rationale for the integration of dynamic psychotherapy, the relaxation response, and mindfulness meditation. *American Journal of Psychiatry, 142,* 1–8.

Kutz, I., Leserman, J., Dorrington, C., Morrison, C. H., Borysenko, J. Z., & Benson, H. (1985). Meditation as an adjunct to psychotherapy: An outcome study. *Psychotherapy and Psychosomatics, 43,* 209–218.

LaBaw, W., Holton, C., Tewell, K., & Eccles, D. (1975). The use of self-hypnosis by children with cancer. *American Journal of Clinical Hypnosis, 17,* 233–238.

Labbe, E. E., & Williamson, D. A. (1983). Temperature biofeedback in the treatment of children with migraine headaches. *Journal of Pediatric Psychology, 8,* 317–326.

Labbe, E. E., & Williamson, D. A. (1984). Treatment of childhood migraine using autogenic feedback training. *Journal of Consulting and Clinical Psychology, 52,* 968–976.

Lacks, P., Bertelson, A. D., Gans, L., & Kunkel, J. (1983). The effectiveness of three behavioral treatments for different degrees of sleep onset insomnia. *Behavior Therapy, 14,* 593–605.

Lacroix, J. M., Clarke, M. A., Bock, J. C., Doxey, N., Wood, A., & Lavis, S. (1983). Biofeedback and relaxation in the treatment of migraine headaches: Comparative effectiveness and physiological correlates. *Journal of Neurology, Neurosurgery, and Psychiatry, 46,* 525–532.

Lader, M. H., & Mathews, A. M. (1970). Comparison of methods of relaxation using physiological measures. *Behaviour Research and Therapy, 8,* 331–337.

Ladouceur, R., Boudreau, L., & Theberge, S. (1981). Awareness training and regulated-breathing method in modification of stuttering. *Perceptual and Motor Skills, 53,* 187–194.

Ladouceur, R., Cote, C., Leblond, G., & Bouchard, L. (1982). Evaluation of regulated-breathing method and awareness training in the treatment of stuttering. *Journal of Speech and Hearing Disorders, 47,* 422–426.

Ladouceur, R., & Martineau, G. (1982). Evaluation of regulated-breathing method with and without parental assistance in the treatment of child stutterers. *Journal of Behavior Therapy and Experimental Psychiatry, 13,* 301–306.

LaFemina, R. (1979). Sexual arousal as a sympathetic inhibitor in the treatment of claustrophobia. *Journal of Behavior Therapy and Experimental Psychiatry, 10,* 57–60.

Laman, C., & Evans, R. I. (1980). Behavioral medicine: The history and the past. *National Forum, 60*(1), 13–18.

Lamaze, F. (1970). *Painless childbirth: Psychoprophylactic method* (L. R. Celestin, Trans.). Chicago: Henry Regnery. (Original work published 1956)

Lamb, D. H., & Strand, K. H. (1980). The effect of a brief relaxation treatment for dental anxiety on measures of state and trait anxiety. *Journal of Clinical Psychology, 36,* 270–274.

Lammers, C. A., Naliboff, B. D., & Straatmeyer, A. J. (1984). The effects of progressive relaxation on stress and diabetic control. *Behaviour Research and Therapy, 22,* 641–650.

Lang, P. J. (1977). Imagery in therapy: An information processing analysis of fear. *Behavior Therapy, 8,* 862–886.

Lang, P. J. (1978). Anxiety: Toward a psychophysiological definition. In H. S. Akiskal & W. L. Webb (Eds.), *Psychiatric diagnosis: Exploration of biological predictors* (pp. 365–389). New York: Spectrum.

Lang, P. J. (1979). A bio-informational theory of emotional imagery. *Psychophysiology, 16,* 495–512.

Lang, P. J., Kozak, M. J., Miller, G. A., Levin, D. N., & McLean, A., Jr. (1980). Emotional imagery: Conceptual structure and pattern of somato-visceral response. *Psychophysiology, 17,* 179–192.

Lang, P. J., & Lazovik, A. D. (1963). Experimental desensitization of a phobia. *Journal of Abnormal and Social Psychology, 66,* 519–525.

Lang, P. J., Lazovik, A. D., & Reynolds, D. J. (1965). Desensitization, suggestibility, and pseudotherapy. *Journal of Abnormal Psychology, 70,* 395–402.

Lang, P. J., Levin, D. N., Miller, G. A., & Kozak, M. J. (1983). Fear behavior, fear imagery, and the psychophysiology of emotion: The problem of affective response integration. *Journal of Abnormal Psychology, 92,* 276–306.

Lang, P. J., Melamed, B. G., & Hart, J. (1970). A psychophysiological analysis of fear modification using an automated desensitization procedure. *Journal of Abnormal Psychology, 76,* 220–234.

Lang, R., Dehof, K., Meurer, K. A., & Kaufmann, W. (1979). Sympathetic activity and Transcendental Meditation. *Journal of Neural Transmission, 44,* 117–135.

Lange, A. J., & Jakubowski, P. (1976). *Responsible assertive behavior: Cognitive/behavioral procedures for trainers.* Champaign, IL: Research Press.

Langen, D. (1969). Peripheral changes in blood circulation during autogenic training and hypnosis (results of experimental research). In L. Chertok (Ed.), *Psychophysiological mechanisms of hypnosis* (pp. 58–66). New York: Springer-Verlag.

Langevin, R., Stanford, A., & Block, R. (1975). The effects of relaxation instructions on erotic arousal in homosexual and heterosexual males. *Behavior Therapy, 6,* 453–458.

Langosch, W., Seer, P., Brodner, G., Kallinke, D., Kulick, B., & Heim, F. (1982). Behavior therapy with coronary heart disease patients: Results of a comparative study. *Journal of Psychosomatic Research, 26,* 475–484.

Lanning, W., & Hisanaga, B. (1983). A study of the relation between the reduction of competition anxiety and an increase in athletic performance. *International Journal of Sport Psychology, 14,* 219–227.

Lanphier, E. H., & Rahn, H. (1963). Alveolar gas exchange during breath holding with air. *Journal of Applied Physiology, 18,* 478–482.

Lapierre, J. (1977). The therapeutic object relationship as an active agent in the course of autogenic training. In W. Luthe & F. Antonelli (Eds.), *Therapy in psychosomatic medicine: Autogenic therapy* (pp. 377–383). Rome: Edizioni L. Pozzi.

Lashley, J. K., & Elder, S. T. (1982). Selected case studies in clinical biofeedback. *Journal of Clinical Psychology, 38,* 530–540.

Latimer, P. R. (1981). Biofeedback and self-regulation in the treatment of diffuse esophageal spasm: A single-case study. *Biofeedback and Self-Regulation, 6,* 181–189.

Lawson, D. M., & May, R. B. (1970). Three procedures for the extinction of smoking behavior. *Psychological Record, 20,* 151–157.

Laxer, R. M., Quarter, J., Kooman, A., & Walker, K. (1969). Systematic desensitization and relaxation of high-test-anxious secondary school students. *Journal of Counseling Psychology, 16,* 446–451.

Laxer, R. M., & Walker, K. (1970). Counterconditioning versus relaxation in the desensitization of test anxiety. *Journal of Counseling Psychology, 17,* 431–436.

Layman, E. M. (1976). *Buddhism in America.* Chicago: Nelson-Hall.

Lazarus, A. A. (1961). Group therapy of phobic disorders by systematic desensitization. *Journal of Abnormal and Social Psychology, 63,* 504–510.

Lazarus, A. A. (1971). *Behavior therapy and beyond.* New York: McGraw-Hill.

Lazarus, A. A. (1976). Psychiatric problems precipitated by Transcendental Meditation. *Psychological Reports, 39,* 601–602.

Lazarus, A. A., & Abramovitz, A. (1962). The use of "emotive imagery" in the treatment of children's phobias. *Journal of Mental Science, 108, 191–195.*

Legate, J. J. (1981). Zen and creativity. *Journal of Creative Behavior, 15,* 23–35.

Leger, L. A. (1978). Spurious and actual improvement in the treatment of preoccupying thoughts by thought-stopping. *British Journal of Social and Clinical Psychology, 17,* 373–377.

Lehrer, P. M. (1972). Physiological effects of relaxation in a double-blind analog of desensitization. *Behavior Therapy, 3,* 193–208.

Lehrer, P. M. (1978). Psychophysiological effects of progressive relaxation in anxiety neurotic patients and of progressive relaxation and alpha feedback in nonpatients. *Journal of Consulting and Clinical Psychology, 46,* 389–404.

Lehrer, P. M. (1982). How to relax and how not to relax: A re-evaluation of the work of Edmund Jacobson–I. *Behaviour Research and Therapy, 20,* 417–428.

Lehrer, P. M., Atthowe, J. M., & Weber, B. S. P. (1980). Effects of progressive relaxation and autogenic training on anxiety and physiological measures, with some data on hypnotizability. In F. J. McGuigan, W. E. Sime, & J. M. Wallace (Eds.), *Stress and tension control* (pp. 171–184). New York: Plenum Press.

Lehrer, P. M., Batey, D., Woolfolk, R. L., Remde, A., & Garlick, T. (1983, December). *Does tensing muscles help to relax them? Does thinking about muscle tension increase it? A test of some procedural variables in progressive relaxation therapy.* Paper presented at the meeting of the World Congress on Behavior Therapy, Washington, DC.

Lehrer, P. M., Schoicket, S., Carrington, P. & Woolfolk, R. L. (1980). Psychophysiological and cognitive responses to stressful stimuli in subjects practicing progressive relaxation and Clinically Standardized Meditation. *Behaviour Research and Therapy, 18,* 293–303.

Lehrer, P. M., Woolfolk, R. L., Rooney, A. J., McCann, B., & Carrington, P. (1983). Progressive relaxation and meditation: A study of psychophysiological and therapeutic differences between two techniques. *Behaviour Research and Therapy, 21,* 651–662.

Leischow, S. J., & Chornock, W. (1985, March). *The effect of diaphragmatic and thoracic breathing on cardiovascular arousal.* Paper presented at the meeting of the Society of Behavioral Medicine, New Orleans.

Lesh, T. V. (1970). Zen meditation and the development of empathy in counselors. *Journal of Humanistic Psychology, 10,* 39–74.

Lessen, E. I., & McLain, B. (1980). Relaxation training and GSR used to reduce hyperactivity in intermediate aged EMR children. *Behavioral Engineering, 6,* 117–121.

Lester, D., Leitner, L. A., & Posner, I. (1984). The effects of a stress management training programme on police officers. *International Review of Applied Psychology, 33,* 25–31.

Leuner, H. (1978). Basic principles and therapeutic efficacy of guided affective imagery (GAI). In J. L. Singer & K. S. Pope (Eds.), *The power of human imagination: New methods in psychotherapy* (pp. 125–166). New York: Plenum Press.

Leung, P. (1973). Comparative effects of training in external and internal concentration on two counseling behaviors. *Journal of Counseling Psychology, 20,* 227–234.

Leva, R. A. (1974). Modification of hypnotic susceptibility through audio-tape relaxation training: Preliminary report. *Perceptual and Motor Skills, 39,* 872–874.

Levenberg, S. B., & Wagner, M. K. (1976). Smoking cessation: Long-term irrelevance of mode of treatment. *Journal of Behavior Therapy and Experimental Psychiatry, 7,* 93–95.

Levendusky, P., & Pankratz, L. (1975). Self-control techniques as an alternative to pain medication. *Journal of Abnormal Psychology, 84,* 165–168.

Levenkron, J. C., Cohen, J. D., Mueller, H. S., & Fisher, E. B., Jr. (1983). Modifying the Type A coronary-prone behavior pattern. *Journal of Consulting and Clinical Psychology, 51,* 192–204.

Leventhal, H., & Cleary, P. D. (1980). The smoking problem: A review of the research and theory in behavioral risk modification. *Psychological Bulletin, 88,* 370–405.

Levin, R. B., & Gross, A. M. (1985). The role of relaxation in systematic desensitization. *Behaviour Research and Therapy, 23,* 187–196.

Levy, R. A., Jones, D. R., & Carlson, E. H. (1981). Biofeedback rehabilitation of airsick aircrew. *Aviation, Space, and Environmental Medicine, 52,* 118–121.

Levy, R. L. (1981). Behavioral advances in social work. *Behavioral Counseling Quarterly, 1,* 176–188.

Lewinsohn, P. M., Munoz, R. F., Youngren, M. A., & Zeiss, A. M. (1978). *Control your depression.* Englewood Cliffs, NJ: Prentice-Hall.

Lewis, C. E., Biglan, A., & Steinbock, E. (1978). Self-administered relaxation training and money deposits in the treatment of recurrent anxiety. *Journal of Consulting and Clinical Psychology, 46,* 1274–1283.

Ley, R., & Walker, H. (1973). Effects of carbon dioxide-oxygen inhalation on heart rate, blood pressure, and subjective anxiety. *Journal of Behavior Therapy and Experimental Psychiatry, 4,* 223-228.

Lichstein, K. L. (1983). Ocular relaxation as a treatment for insomnia. *Behavioral Counseling and Community Interventions, 3,* 178-185.

Lichstein, K. L., & Blew, A. (1980, November). *Ocular relaxation and progressive relaxation treatments for insomnia.* Paper presented at the meeting of the Association for Advancement of Behavior Therapy, New York.

Lichstein, K. L., & Eakin, T. L. (1985). Progressive versus self-control relaxation to reduce spontaneous bleeding in hemophiliacs. *Journal of Behavioral Medicine, 8,* 149-162.

Lichstein, K. L., Eakin, T. L., & Dunn, M. E. (1986). Combined psychological and medical treatment of oropharyngeal dysphagia. *Clinical Biofeedback and Health, 9,* 9-14.

Lichstein, K. L., & Fischer, S. M. (1985). Insomnia. In M. Hersen & A. S. Bellack (Eds.), *Handbook of clinical behavior therapy with adults* (pp. 319-352). New York: Plenum Press.

Lichstein, K. L., & Hoelscher, T. J. (1986). A device for unobtrusive surveillance of home relaxation practice. *Behavior Modification, 10,* 219-233.

Lichstein, K. L., & Hung, J. H. F. (1980). Covert sensitization: An examination of covert and overt parameters. *Behavioral Engineering, 6,* 1-18.

Lichstein, K. L., & Kelley, J. E. (1979). Measuring sleep patterns in natural settings. *Behavioral Engineering, 5,* 95-100.

Lichstein, K. L., & Lipshitz, E. (1982). Psychophysiological effects of noxious imagery: Prevalence and prediction. *Behaviour Research and Therapy, 20,* 339-345.

Lichstein, K. L., & Sallis, J. F. (1981). Covert sensitization for smoking: In search of efficacy. *Addictive Behaviors, 6,* 83-91.

Lichstein, K. L., & Sallis, J. F. (1982). Ocular relaxation to reduce eye movements. *Cognitive Therapy and Research, 6,* 113-118.

Lichstein, K. L., Sallis, J. F., Hill, D., & Young, M. C. (1981). Psychophysiological adaptation: An investigation of multiple parameters. *Journal of Behavioral Assessment, 3,* 111-121.

Lichstein, K. L., & Stalgaitis, S. J. (1980). Treatment of cigarette smoking in couples by reciprocal aversion. *Behavior Therapy, 11,* 104-108.

Lichstein, K. L., Wagner, M. T., Krisak, J., & Steinberg, F. (1987). Stress management for acting-out, inpatient adolescents. *Journal of Child and Adolescent Psychotherapy, 4,* 19-31.

Lichtenstein, E., & Danaher, B. G. (1976). Modification of smoking behavior: A critical analysis of theory, research, and practice. In M. Hersen, R. M. Eisler, & P. M. Miller (Eds.), *Progress in behavior modification* (Vol. 3, pp. 79-132). New York: Academic Press.

Lick, J. R., & Heffler, D. (1977). Relaxation training and attention placebo in the treatment of severe insomnia. *Journal of Consulting and Clinical Psychology, 45,* 153-161.

Lilly, J. C. (1956). Mental effects of reduction of ordinary levels of physical stimuli on intact, healthy persons. *Psychiatric Research Reports, 5,* 1-9.

Lilly, J. C. (1977). *The deep self: Profound relaxation and the tank isolation technique.* New York: Simon & Schuster.

Lindemann, H. (1973). *Relieve tension the autogenic way.* New York: Wyden.

Linden, W. (1973). Practicing of meditation by school children and their levels of field dependence-independence, test anxiety, and reading achievement. *Journal of Consulting and Clinical Psychology, 41,* 139–143.

Linder, L. H., & McGlynn, F. D. (1971). Experimental desensitization of mouse-avoidance following two schedules of semi-automated relaxation training. *Behaviour Research and Therapy, 9,* 131–136.

Ling, T. (1973). *The Buddha.* New York: Scribner.

Lintel, A. G., III. (1980). Physiological anxiety responses in Transcendental Meditators and nonmeditators. *Perceptual and Motor Skills, 50,* 295–300.

Linton, S. J. (1982). Applied relaxation as a method of coping with chronic pain: A therapist's guide. *Scandinavian Journal of Behaviour Therapy, 11,* 161–174.

Linton, S. J., & Gotestam, K. G. (1984). A controlled study of the effects of applied relaxation and applied relaxation plus operant procedures in the regulation of chronic pain. *British Journal of Clinical Psychology, 23,* 291–299.

Linton, S. J., & Melin, L. (1983). Applied relaxation in the management of chronic pain. *Behavioural Psychotherapy, 11,* 337–350.

Lipsky, M. J., Kassinove, H., & Miller, N. J. (1980). Effects of rational-emotive therapy, rational role reversal, and rational-emotive imagery on the emotional adjustment of community mental health patients. *Journal of Consulting and Clinical Psychology, 48,* 366–374.

Little, B. C., Hayworth, J., Benson, P., Hall, F., Beard, R. W., Dewhurst, J., & Priest, R. G. (1984). Treatment of hypertension in pregnancy by relaxation and biofeedback. *Lancet, 1,* 865–867.

Lohr, J. M., & Rookey, C. (1982, November). *The effect of relaxation training and level of fear upon controllability of fearful and neutral imagery.* Paper presented at the meeting of the Association for Advancement of Behavior Therapy, Los Angeles.

Lomont, J. F., & Edwards, J. E. (1967). The role of relaxation in systematic desensitization. *Behaviour Research and Therapy, 5,* 11–25.

Longo, D. J., & Vom Saal, W. (1984). Respiratory relief therapy: A new treatment procedure for the reduction of anxiety. *Behavior Modification, 8,* 361–378.

LoPiccolo, J., & LoPiccolo, L. (Eds.). (1978). *Handbook of sex therapy.* New York: Plenum Press.

LoPiccolo, J., & Stock, W. E. (1986). Treatment of sexual dysfunction. *Journal of Consulting and Clinical Psychology, 54,* 158–167.

Lowenstein, T. J., & Robyak, J. E. (1979). Study skills and stress reduction: The radio as a medium for community programming. *Personnel and Guidance Journal, 57,* 553–554.

Lozanov, G. (1978). *Suggestology and outlines of suggestopedy* (M. Hall-Pozharlieva & K. Pashmakova, Trans.). New York: Gordon & Breach. (Original work published 1971)

Lubar, J. F., & Deering, W. M. (1981). *Behavioral approaches to neurology.* New York: Academic Press.

Luborsky, L., Ancona, L., Masoni, A., Scolari, G., & Longoni, A. (1980–1981). Behavioral versus pharmacological treatments for essential hypertension: A pilot study. *International Journal of Psychiatry in Medicine, 10,* 33–40.

Luborsky, L., Brady, J. P., McClintock, M., Kron, R. E., Bortnichak, E., & Levitz, L. (1976). Estimating one's own systolic blood pressure: Effects of feedback training. *Psychosomatic Medicine, 38,* 426–438.

Luborsky, L., Crits-Christoph, P., Brady, J. P., Kron, R. E., Weiss, T., Cohen, M., & Levy, L. (1982). Behavioral versus pharmacological treatments for essential hypertension–A needed comparison. *Psychosomatic Medicine, 44,* 203–213.

Luiselli, J. K. (1980). Relaxation training with the developmentally disabled: A reappraisal. *Behavior Research of Severe Developmental Disabilities, 1,* 191–213.

Luiselli, J. K. (1981). Facilitating transfer of clinical biofeedback training: A review of some procedures. *Behavioral Engineering, 7,* 1–6.

Luiselli, J. K. (1984). Treatment of an assaultive, sensory-impaired adolescent through a multicomponent behavioral program. *Journal of Behavior Therapy and Experimental Psychiatry, 15,* 71–78.

Luiselli, J. K., Marholin, D., II, Steinman, D. L., & Steinman, W. M. (1979). Assessing the effects of relaxation training. *Behavior Therapy, 10,* 663–668.

Luiselli, J. K., Steinman, D. L., Marholin, D., II, & Steinman, W. M. (1981). Evaluation of progressive muscle relaxation with conduct-problem, learning-disabled children. *Child Behavior Therapy, 3,* 41–55.

Luk, C. (1964). *The secrets of Chinese meditation.* London: Rider.

Luthe, W. (1962a). Autogenic training: Method, research and application in psychiatry. *Diseases of the Nervous System, 23,* 383–392.

Luthe, W. (1962b). Method, research and application of autogenic training. *American Journal of Clinical Hypnosis, 5,* 17–23.

Luthe, W. (1962c). The psychophysiologic and clinical significance of autogenic discharges and various forms of autogenic abreaction. *Japanese Journal of Hypnosis, 7,* 3–22.

Luthe, W. (1963). Autogenic training: Method, research and application in medicine. *American Journal of Psychotherapy, 17,* 174–195.

Luthe, W. (Ed.). (1965a). *Autogenic training: International edition.* New York: Grune & Stratton.

Luthe, W. (1965b). Autogenic training in North America. In W. Luthe (Ed.), *Autogenic training: International edition* (pp. 297–302). New York: Grune & Stratton.

Luthe, W. (1965c). Changes of iodine metabolism during autogenic therapy. In W. Luthe (Ed.), *Autogenic training: International edition* (pp. 71–78). New York: Grune & Stratton.

Luthe, W. (1965d). Lowering of serum cholesterol during autogenic therapy. In W. Luthe (Ed.), *Autogenic training: International edition* (pp. 88–91). New York: Grune & Stratton.

Luthe, W. (Ed.). (1969–1973). *Autogenic therapy* (6 vols.) New York: Grune & Stratton.

Luthe, W. (1970a). *Research and theory* (Vol. 4). In W. Luthe (Ed.), *Autogenic therapy.* New York: Grune & Stratton.

Luthe, W. (1970b). *Dynamics of autogenic neutralization* (Vol. 5). In W. Luthe (Ed.), *Autogenic therapy*. New York: Grune & Stratton.

Luthe, W. (1973). *Treatment with autogenic neutralization* (Vol. 6). In W. Luthe (Ed.), *Autogenic therapy*. New York: Grune & Stratton.

Luthe, W., & Blumberger, S. R. (1977). Autogenic therapy. In E. D. Wittkower & H. Warnes (Eds.), *Psychosomatic medicine: Its clinical applications* (pp. 146–165). New York: Harper & Row.

Luthe, W., Jus, A., & Geissmann, P. (1965). Autogenic state and autogenic shift: Psychophysiologic and neurophysiologic aspects. In W. Luthe (Ed.), *Autogenic training: International edition* (pp. 3–11). New York: Grune & Stratton.

Luthe, W., & Schultz, J. H. (1969a). *Medical applications* (Vol. 2). In W. Luthe (Ed.), *Autogenic therapy*. New York: Grune & Stratton.

Luthe, W., & Schultz, J. H. (1969b). *Applications in psychotherapy* (Vol. 3). In W. Luthe (Ed.), *Autogenic therapy*. New York: Grune & Stratton.

Luthe, W., Trudeau, M., Mailhot, D., & Vallieres, G. (1977). Blood pressure and heart rate variations in elementary school children with and without autogenic training. In W. Luthe & F. Antonelli (Eds.), *Therapy in psychosomatic medicine: Autogenic therapy* (pp. 270–275.) Rome: Edizioni L. Pozzi.

Lutker, E. R. (1971). Treatment of migraine headache by conditioned relaxation: A case study. *Behavior Therapy, 2,* 592–593.

Lyles, J. N., Burish, T. G., Krozely, M. G., & Oldham, R. K. (1982). Efficacy of relaxation training and guided imagery in reducing the aversiveness of cancer chemotherapy. *Journal of Consulting and Clinical Psychology, 50,* 509–524.

Macpherson, E. L. R. (1967). Control of involuntary movement. *Behaviour Research and Therapy, 5,* 143–145.

Malatesta, V. J., Sutker, P. B., & Adams, H. E. (1980). Experimental assessment of tinnitus aurium. *Journal of Behavioral Assessment, 2,* 309–317.

Malec, J., & Sipprelle, C. N. (1977). Physiological and subjective effects of Zen meditation and demand characteristics. *Journal of Consulting and Clinical Psychology, 45,* 339–340.

Malhotra, J. C. (1961). Yoga and mental hygiene. *Proceedings of the Third World Congress of Psychiatry* (Vol. 2, pp. 1063–1066). Toronto: University of Toronto Press.

Malhotra, J. C. (1963). Yoga and psychiatry: A review. *Journal of Neuropsychiatry, 4,* 375–385.

Marchetti, A., McGlynn, F. D., & Patterson, A. S. (1977). Effects of cue-controlled relaxation, a placebo treatment, and no treatment on changes in self-reported and psychophysiological indices of test anxiety among college students. *Behavior Modification, 1,* 47–72.

Margolis, H., McLeroy, K. R., Runyan, C. W., & Kaplan, B. H. (1983). Type A behavior: An ecological approach. *Journal of Behavioral Medicine, 6,* 245–258.

Marholin, D., II, Steinman, W. M., Luiselli, J. K., Schwartz, C. S., & Townsend, N. M. (1979). The effects of progressive muscle relaxation on the behavior of autistic adolescents: A preliminary analysis. *Child Behavior Therapy, 1,* 75–84.

Marks, I. M. (1978). *Living with fear*. New York: McGraw-Hill.

Marlatt, G. A., & Gordon, G. R. (Eds.). (1985). *Relapse prevention: Maintenance strategies in the treatment of addictive behaviors.* New York: Guilford.

Marlatt, G. A., & Marques, J. K. (1977). Meditation, self-control and alcohol use. In R. B. Stuart (Ed.), *Behavioral self-management: Strategies, techniques and outcomes* (pp. 117–153). New York: Brunner/Mazel.

Marlatt, G. A., Pagano, R. R., Rose, R. M., & Marques, J. K. (1984). Effects of meditation and relaxation training upon alcohol use in male social drinkers. In D. H. Shapiro, Jr., & R. N. Walsh (Eds.), *Meditation: Classic and contemporary perspectives* (pp.105–120). Hawthorne, NY: Aldine.

Marquis, J. N., Ferguson, J. M., & Taylor, C. B. (1980). Generalization of relaxation skills. *Journal of Behavior Therapy and Experimental Psychiatry, 11,* 95–99.

Marshall, R. C., & Watts, M. T. (1976). Relaxation training: Effects on the communicative ability of aphasic adults. *Archives of Physical Medicine and Rehabilitation, 57,* 464–467.

Marshall, W. L., Boutilier, J., & Minnes, P. (1974). The modification of phobic behavior by covert reinforcement. *Behavior Therapy, 5,* 469–480.

Marston, A. R., & McFall, R. M. (1971). Comparison of behavior modification approaches to smoking reduction. *Journal of Consulting and Clinical Psychology, 36,* 153–162.

Martin, A. R. (1951). The fear of relaxation and leisure. *American Journal of Psychoanalysis, 11,* 42–50.

Martin, I. C. A. (1970). Progressive relaxation facilitated. *Behaviour Research and Therapy, 8,* 217–218.

Martin, J. E., Collins, F. L., Jr., Hillenberg, J. B., Zabin, M. A., & Katell, A. D. (1981). Assessing compliance to home relaxation: A simple technology for a critical problem. *Journal of Behavioral Assessment, 3,* 193–198.

Martin, J. E., & Epstein, L. H. (1980). Evaluating the situational specificity of relaxation in mild essential hypertension. *Perceptual and Motor Skills, 51,* 667–674.

Martin, P. R., & Mathews, A. M. (1978). Tension headaches: Psychophysiological investigation and treatment. *Journal of Psychosomatic Research, 22,* 389–399.

Martinetti, R. F. (1976). Influence of Transcendental Meditation on perceptual illusion: A pilot study. *Perceptual and Motor Skills, 43,* 822.

Masek, B. J., Epstein, L. H., & Russo, D. C. (1981). Behavioral perspectives in preventive medicine. In S. M. Turner, K. S. Calhoun, & H. E. Adams (Eds.), *Handbook of clinical behavior therapy* (pp. 475–499). New York: Wiley.

Masek, B. J., Russo, D. C., & Varni, J. W. (1984). Behavioral approaches to the management of chronic pain in children. *Pediatric Clinics of North America, 31,* 1113–1131.

Maslow, A. H. (1968). *Toward a psychology of being* (2nd ed.). New York: Van Nostrand Reinhold.

Masters, W. H., & Johnson, V. E. (1970). *Human sexual inadequacy.* Boston: Little, Brown.

Matarazzo, J. D. (1983). Graduate education in health psychology, behavioral immunogens, and behavioral pathogens. *Health Psychology, 2*(Suppl.), 53–62.

Mathew, R. J., Ho, B. T., Kralik, P., Weinman, M., & Claghorn, J. L. (1981). Anxiety and platelet MAO levels after relaxation training. *American Journal of Psychiatry, 138,* 371-373.

Mathews, A. M. (1971). Psychophysiological approaches to the investigation of desensitization and related procedures. *Psychological Bulletin, 76,* 73-91.

Mathews, A. M., & Gelder, M. G. (1969). Psycho-physiological investigation of brief relaxation training. *Journal of Psychosomatic Research, 13,* 1-12.

Mathews, A., & Shaw, P. (1977). Cognitions related to anxiety: A pilot study of treatment. *Behaviour Research and Therapy, 15,* 503-505.

Matthews, K. A. (1982). Psychological perspectives on the Type A behavior pattern. *Psychological Bulletin, 91,* 293-323.

Mattsson, P. O. (1960). Communicated anxiety in a two-person situation. *Journal of Consulting Psychology, 24,* 488-495.

Maupin, E. W. (1962). Zen Buddhism: A psychological review. *Journal of Consulting Psychology, 26,* 362-378.

May, E., House, W. C., & Kovacs, K. V. (1982). Group relaxation therapy to improve coping with stress. *Psychotherapy: Theory, Research and Practice, 19,* 102-109.

Mayer, J. A., Frederiksen, L. W., & Scanlon, G. J. (1984, March). *Relaxation training: The effect of take-home audio tapes on frequency of practice.* Paper presented at the meeting of the Southeastern Psychological Association, New Orleans.

McCaul, K. D., Solomon, S., & Holmes, D. S. (1979). Effects of paced respiration and expectations on physiological and psychological responses to threat. *Journal of Personality and Social Psychology, 37,* 564-571.

McClure, C. M. (1959). Cardiac arrest through volition. *California Medicine, 90,* 440-441.

McConaghy, N., Armstrong, M. S., & Blaszczynski, A. (1981). Controlled comparison of aversive therapy and covert sensitization in compulsive homosexuality. *Behaviour Research and Therapy, 19,* 425-434.

McCready, K. F., Berry, F. M., & Kenkel, M. B. (1985). Supervised relaxation training: A model for greater accessibility of behavioral interventions. *Professional Psychology: Research and Practice, 16,* 595-604.

McCullough, J. P., & Powell, P. O. (1972). A technique for measuring clarity of imagery in therapy clients. *Behavior Therapy, 3,* 447-448.

McDonagh, J. M., & McGinnis, M. (1973). Skin temperature increases as a function of base-line temperature, autogenic suggestion, and biofeedback [Summary]. *Proceedings of the 81st Annual Convention of the American Psychological Association, 8,* 547-548.

McEvoy, T. M., Frumkin, L. R., & Harkins, S. W. (1980). Effects of meditation on brainstem auditory evoked potentials. *International Journal of Neuroscience, 10,* 165-170.

McFarlain, R. A., Mielke, D. H., & Gallant, D. M. (1976). Comparison of muscle relaxation with placebo medication for anxiety reduction in alcoholic inpatients. *Current Therapeutic Research, 20,* 173-176.

McGlynn, F. D., Bichajian, C., Giesen, J. M., & Rose, R. L. (1981). Effects of cue-controlled relaxation, a credible placebo treatment and no treatment on shyness among college males. *Journal of Behavior Therapy and Experimental Psychiatry, 12,* 299-306.

McGlynn, F. D., Kinjo, K., & Doherty, G. (1978). Effects of cue-controlled relaxation, a placebo treatment, and no treatment on changes in self-reported test anxiety among college students. *Journal of Clinical Psychology, 34,* 707–714.

McGlynn, F. D., Mealiea, W. L., Jr., & Landau, D. L. (1981). The current status of systematic desensitization. *Clinical Psychology Review, 1,* 149–179.

McGrath, P. (1983). Psychological aspects of recurrent abdominal pain. *Canadian Family Physician, 29,* 1655–1659.

McGuigan, F. J. (1978). Interview with Edmund Jacobson. *Biofeedback and Self-Regulation, 3,* 287–300.

McGuigan, F. J. (1984). Progressive relaxation: Orgins, principles, and clinical applications. In R. L. Woolfolk & P. M. Lehrer (Eds.), *Principles and practice of stress management* (pp. 12–42). New York: Guilford.

McGuigan, F. J. (1986). Edmund Jacobson (1888–1983). *American Psychologist, 41,* 315–316.

McIntyre, M. E., Silverman, F. H., & Trotter, W. D. (1974). Transcendental Meditation and stuttering: A preliminary report. *Perceptual and Motor Skills, 39,* 294.

McKechnie, R. J. (1975). Relief from phantom limb pain by relaxation exercises. *Journal of Behavior Therapy and Experimental Psychiatry, 6,* 262–263.

McNair, D. M., Lorr, M., & Droppleman, L. F. (1971). *Profile of Mood States.* San Diego: Educational & Industrial Testing Service.

McNamara, J. R. (Eds.). (1979). *Behavioral approaches to medicine: Application and analysis.* New York: Plenum Press.

Meares, A. (1967). *Relief without drugs.* New York: Doubleday.

Meares, A. (1976). Regression of cancer after intensive meditation. *Medical Journal of Australia, 2,* 184.

Meares, A. (1977a). Atavistic regression as a factor in the remission of cancer. *Medical Journal of Australia, 2,* 132–133.

Meares, A. (1977b). Regression of cancer after intensive meditation followed by death. *Medical Journal of Australia, 2,* 374–375.

Meares, A. (1978a). The quality of meditation effective in the regression of cancer. *Journal of the American Society of Psychosomatic Dentistry and Medicine, 25,* 129–132.

Meares, A. (1978b). Regression of osteogenic sarcoma metastases associated with intensive meditation. *Medical Journal of Australia, 2,* 433.

Meares, A. (1979a). Meditation: A psychological approach to cancer treatment. *Practitioner, 222,* 119–122.

Meares, A. (1979b). Regression of cancer of the rectum after intensive meditation. *Medical Journal of Australia, 2,* 539–540.

Meares, A. (1980). Remission of massive metastastis from undifferentiated carcinoma of the lung associated with intensive meditation. *Journal of the American Society of Psychosomatic Dentistry and Medicine, 27,* 40–41.

Meares, A. (1981). Regression of recurrence of carcinoma of the breast at mastectomy site associated with intensive meditation. *Australian Family Physician, 10,* 218–219.

Meares, A. (1982–1983). A form of intensive meditation associated with the regression of cancer. *American Journal of Clinical Hypnosis, 25,* 114–121.

Meduna, L. J. (1950). *Carbon dioxide therapy: A neuro-physiological treatment of nervous disorders.* Springfield, IL: Thomas.

Meichenbaum, D. H. (1969). The effects of instructions and reinforcement on thinking and language behavior of schizophrenics. *Behaviour Research and Therapy, 7,* 101–114.

Meichenbaum, D. (1977). *Cognitive-behavior modification: An integrative approach.* New York: Plenum Press.

Meichenbaum, D. & Jaremko, M. E. (Eds.). (1983). *Stress reduction and prevention.* New York: Plenum Press.

Melamed, B. G., Weinstein, D., Hawes, R., & Katin-Borland, M. (1975). Reduction of fear-related dental management problems with use of filmed modeling. *Journal of the American Dental Association, 90,* 822–826.

Meldman, M. J. (1966). PRR study no. 7: Decreased PRR through muscle relaxation. *Diseases of the Nervous System, 27,* 747–749.

Melzack, R. (1971). Phantom limb pain: Implications for treatment of pathologic pain. *Anesthesiology, 35,* 409–419.

Melzack, R., & Loeser, J. D. (1978). Phantom body pain in paraplegics: Evidence for a central "pattern generating mechanism" for pain. *Pain, 4,* 195–210.

Meyers, A. W., & Craighead, W. E. (1978). Adaptation periods in clinical psychophysiological research: A recommendation. *Behavior Therapy, 9,* 355–362.

Michaels, R. R., Huber, M. J., & McCann, D. S. (1976). Evaluation of transcendental meditation as a method of reducing stress. *Science, 192,* 1242–1244.

Michaels, R. R., Parra, J., McCann, D. S., & Vander, A. J. (1979). Renin, cortisol, and aldosterone during transcendental meditation. *Psychosomatic Medicine, 41,* 50–54.

Miles, W. R. (1964). Oxygen consumption during three yoga-type breathing patterns. *Journal of Applied Physiology, 19,* 75–82.

Miller, M. (1926). Changes in the response to electric shock produced by varying muscular conditions. *Journal of Experimental Psychology, 9,* 26–44.

Miller, M. P., Murphy, P. J., & Miller, T. P. (1978). Comparison of electromyographic feedback and progressive relaxation training in treating circumscribed anxiety stress reactions. *Journal of Consulting and Clinical Psychology, 46,* 1291–1298.

Miller, N. E. (1969). Learning of visceral and glandular responses. *Science, 163,* 434–445.

Miller, N. E. (1978). Biofeedback and visceral learning. In M. R. Rosenzweig & L. W. Porter (Eds.), *Annual review of psychology* (pp. 373–404). Palo Alto, CA: Annual Reviews.

Miller, P. M., Hersen, M., Eisler, R. M., & Hilsman, G. (1974). Effects of social stress on operant drinking of alcoholics and social drinkers. *Behaviour Research and Therapy, 12,* 67–72.

Miller, R. K., & Bornstein, P. H. (1977). Thirty-minute relaxation: A comparison of some methods. *Journal of Behavior Therapy and Experimental Psychiatry, 8,* 291–294.

Miller, W. R., & Taylor, C. A. (1980). Relative effectiveness of bibliotherapy, individual and group self-control training in the treatment of problem drinkers. *Addictive Behaviors, 5,* 13-24.

Mills, W. W., & Farrow, J. T. (1981). The Transcendental Meditation technique and acute experimental pain. *Psychosomatic Medicine, 43,* 157-164.

Minning, C. A. (1982). *Correlations between imagery, imagery ratings, personallity factors, and blood neutrophil functions.* Unpublished doctoral dissertation, Michigan State University, East Lansing.

Mishra, R. S. (1959). *Fundamentals of Yoga: A handbook of theory, practice, and application.* New York: Julian.

Miskiman, D. E. (1977a). The treatment of insomnia by the Transcendental Meditation program. In D. W. Orme-Johnson & J. T. Farrow (Eds.), *Scientific research on the Transcendental Meditation program: Collected papers* (Vol. 1, 2nd ed., pp. 296-298). Livingston Manor, NY: Maharishi European Research University Press.

Miskiman, D. E. (1977b). Long-term effects of the Transcendental Meditation program in the treatment of insomnia. In D. W. Orme-Johnson & J. T. Farrow (Eds.), *Scientific research on the Transcendental Meditation program: Collected papers* (Vol. 1, 2nd ed., pp. 299). Livingston Manor, NY: Maharishi European Research University Press.

Mitch, P. S., McGrady, A., & Iannone, A. (1976). Autogenic feedback training in migraine: A treatment report. *Headache, 15,* 267-270.

Mitchell, K. R. (1971). A psychological approach to the treatment of migraine. *British Journal of Psychiatry, 119,* 533-534.

Mitchell, K. R. (1979). Behavioral treatment of presleep tension and intrusive cognitions in patients with severe predormital insomnia. *Journal of Behavioral Medicine, 2,* 57-69.

Mitchell, K. R., & Mitchell, D. M. (1971). Migraine: An exploratory treatment application of programmed behaviour therapy techniques. *Journal of Psychosomatic Research, 15,* 137-157.

Mitchell, K. R., & White, R. G. (1976). Self-management of tension headaches: A case study. *Journal of Behavior Therapy and Experimental Psychiatry, 7,* 387-389.

Mitchell, K. R., & White, R. G. (1977a). Behavioral self-management: An application to the problem of migraine headaches. *Behavior Therapy, 8,* 213-221.

Mitchell, K. R., & White, R. G. (1977b). Self-management of severe predormital insomnia. *Journal of Behavior Therapy and Experimental Psychiatry, 8,* 57-63.

Mizes, J. S., & Fleece, E. L. (1986). On the use of progressive relaxation in the treatment of bulimia: A single-subject design study. *International Journal of Eating Disorders, 5,* 169-176.

Monahan, R. J. (1977). Secondary prevention of drug dependence through the Transcendental Meditation program in metropolitan Philadelphia. *International Journal of the Addictions, 12,* 729-754.

Monus, A. (1977). Autogenic training in the preparation of archers. In W. Luthe & F. Antonelli (Eds.), *Therapy in psychosomatic medicine: Autogenic therapy* (pp. 289-292). Rome: Edizioni L. Pozzi.

Moore, N. (1965). Behaviour therapy in bronchial asthma: A controlled study. *Journal of Psychosomatic Research, 9,* 257-276.

Morgan, K. W. (Ed.). (1953). *The religion of the Hindus.* New York: Ronald Press.

Morrell, E. M., & Hollandsworth, J. G., Jr. (1986). Norepinephrine alterations under stress conditions following the regular practice of meditation. *Psychosomatic Medicine, 48,* 270–277.

Morris, C. L. (1979). Relaxation therapy in a clinic. *American Journal of Nursing, 79,* 1958–1959.

Morris, J. (1977). Autogenic behavior therapy: Treatment of phobias. In W. Luthe & F. Antonelli (Eds.), *Therapy in psychosomatic medicine: Autogenic therapy* (pp. 201–203). Rome: Edizioni L. Pozzi.

Morris, R. J. (1973). Shaping relaxation in the unrelaxed client. *Journal of Behavior Therapy and Experimental Psychiatry, 4,* 353–354.

Morrow, G. R. (1982). Prevalence and correlates of anticipatory nausea and vomiting in chemotherapy patients. *Journal of the National Cancer Institute, 68,* 585–588.

Morrow, G. R. (1984). Appropriateness of taped versus live relaxation in the systematic desensitization of anticipatory nausea and vomiting in cancer patients. *Journal of Consulting and Clinical Psychology, 52,* 1098–1099.

Morrow, G. R. (1986). Effect of the cognitive hierarchy in the systematic desensitization treatment of anticipatory nausea in cancer patients: A component comparison with relaxation only, counseling, and no treatment. *Cognitive Therapy and Research, 10,* 421–446.

Morrow, G. R., Arseneau, J. C., Asbury, R. F., Bennett, J. M., & Boros, L. (1982). Anticipatory nausea and vomiting with chemotherapy. *New England Journal of Medicine, 306,* 431–432.

Morse, D. R. (1982). Stress and bruxism: A critical review and report of cases. *Journal of Human Stress, 8*(1), 43–54.

Morse, D. R., & Furst, M. L. (1982). Meditation: An in-depth study. *Journal of the American Society of Psychosomatic Dentistry and Medicine, 29*(5), 3–96.

Morse, D. R., & Hildebrand, C. N. (1976). Case report: Use of TM in periodontal therapy. *Dental Survey, 52,* 36–37, 39.

Morse, D. R., Martin, J. S., Furst, M. L., & Dubin, L. L. (1977). A physiological and subjective evaluation of meditation, hypnosis, and relaxation. *Psychosomatic Medicine, 39,* 304–324.

Morse, D. R., Martin, J. S., Furst, M. L., & Dubin, L. L. (1979). A physiological and subjective evaluation of neutral and emotionally–charged words for meditation. *Journal of the American Society of Psychosomatic Dentistry and Medicine, 26,* 31–38, 56–62, 106–112.

Morse, D. R., Schacterle, G. R., Furst, M. L., & Bose, K. (1981). Stress, relaxation, and saliva: A pilot study involving endodontic patients. *Oral Surgery, Oral Medicine, Oral Pathology, 52,* 308–313.

Morse, D. R., Schacterle, G. R., Furst, M. L., Brokenshire, J., Butterworth, M., & Cacchio, J. (1981). Examination-induced stress in meditators and non-meditators as measured by salivary protein changes. *Stress, 2*(3), 20–24; *2*(4), 15.

Morse, D. R., Schacterle, G. R., Furst, M. L., Goldberg, J., Greenspan, B., Swiecinski, D., & Susek, J. (1982). The effect of stress and meditation on salivary protein and bacteria: A review and pilot study. *Journal of Human Stress, 8*(4), 31–39.

Moss, R. A., Garrett, J., & Chiodo, J. F. (1982). Temporomandibular joint dysfunction and myofascial pain dysfunction syndromes: Parameters, etiology, and treatment. *Psychological Bulletin, 92,* 331–346.

Moss, R. A., Wedding, D., & Sanders, S. H. (1983). The comparative efficacy of relaxation training and masseter EMG feedback in the treatment of TMJ dysfunction. *Journal of Oral Rehabilitation, 10,* 9–17.

Mostofsky, D. I. (1975). Teaching the nervous system. *New York University Education Quarterly, 6*(3), 8–13.

Mullen, F. G., Jr. (1968). The treatment of a case of dysmenorrhea by behavior therapy techniques. *Journal of Nervous and Mental Disease, 147,* 371–376.

Muskatel, N., Woolfolk, R. L., Carrington, P., Lehrer, P. M., & McCann, B. S. (1984). Effect of meditation training on aspects of coronary-prone behavior. *Perceptual and Motor Skills, 58,* 515–518.

Naifeh, K. H., Kamiya, J., & Sweet, D. M. (1982). Biofeedback of alveolar carbon dioxide tension and levels of arousal. *Biofeedback and Self-Regulation, 7,* 283–299.

Nakagawa, S., Ishida, Y., Dobeta, H., & Kimura, M. (1966). Gastrointestinal changes during autogenic training. In J. J. L. Ibor (Ed.), *VI World Congress of Psychiatry* (p. 47). Amsterdam: Excerpta Medica.

Nakamura, C. Y., & Broen, W. E., Jr. (1965a). Facilitation of competing responses as a function of "subnormal" drive conditions. *Journal of Experimental Psychology, 69,* 180–185.

Nakamura, C. Y., & Broen, W. E., Jr. (1965b). Further study of effects of low drive states on competing responses. *Journal of Experimental Psychology, 70,* 434–436.

Nakano, A. (1971). Eye movements in relation to mental activity of problem-solving. *Psychologia, 14,* 200–207.

Naranjo, C. (1971). Meditation: Its spirit and techniques. In C. Naranjo & R. E. Ornstein (Eds.), *On the psychology of meditation* (pp. 3–132). New York: Viking.

Nath, C., & Rinehart, J. (1979). Effects of individual and group relaxation therapy on blood pressure in essential hypertensives. *Research in Nursing and Health, 2,* 119–126.

Nathan, R. G., Nathan, M. M., Vigen, M. P., & Wellborn, J. G. (1981). Relaxation training tapes: Preferences and effects of gender and background. *Perceptual and Motor Skills, 53,* 927–934.

Neff, D. F., Blanchard, E. B., & Andrasik, F. (1983). The relationship between capacity for absorption and chronic headache patients' response to relaxation and biofeedback treatment. *Biofeedback and Self-Regulation, 8,* 177–183.

Nelson, R. O. (1977). Assessment and therapeutic functions of self-monitoring. In M. Hersen, R. M. Eisler, & P. M. Miller (Eds.), *Progress in behavior modification* (Vol. 5, pp. 263–308). New York: Academic Press.

Nelson, R. O., Sigmon, S., Amodei, N., & Jarrett, R. B. (1984). The Menstrual Symptom Questionnaire: The validity of the distinction between spasmodic and congestive dysmenorrhea. *Behaviour Research and Therapy, 22,* 611–614.

Nerenz, D. R., Leventhal, H., & Love, R. R. (1982). Factors contributing to emotional distress during cancer chemotherapy. *Cancer, 50,* 1020–1027.

Nesse, R. M., Carli, T., Curtis, G. C., & Kleinman, P. D. (1980). Pretreatment nausea in cancer chemotherapy: A conditioned response? *Psychosomatic Medicine, 42,* 33–36.

Neufeld, W. (1951). Relaxation methods in U.S. Navy air schools. *American Journal of Psychiatry, 108,* 132–137.

Nicassio, P., & Bootzin, R. (1974). A comparison of progressive relaxation and autogenic training as treatments for insomnia. *Journal of Abnormal Psychology, 83,* 253–260.

Nicassio, P., Boylan, M. B., & McCabe, T. G. (1982). Progressive relaxation, EMG biofeedback and biofeedback placebo in the treatment of sleep-onset insomnia. *British Journal of Medical Psychology, 55,* 159–166.

Nicholas, D. R. (1982). Prevalence of anticipatory nausea and emesis in cancer chemotherapy patients. *Journal of Behavioral Medicine, 5,* 461–463.

Nidich, S., Seeman, W., & Dreskin, T. (1973). Influence of transcendental meditation: A replication. *Journal of Counseling Psychology, 20,* 565–566.

Nigl, A. J., & Fischer-Williams, M. (1980). Treatment of low back strain with electromyographic biofeedback and relaxation training. *Psychosomatics, 21,* 495–496, 498–499.

Nomellini, S., & Katz, R. C. (1983). Effects of anger control training on abusive parents. *Cognitive Therapy and Research, 7,* 57–68.

Norton, G. R., & Jehu, D. (1984). The role of anxiety in sexual dysfunctions: A review. *Archives of Sexual Behavior, 13,* 165–183.

Norton, G. R., & Johnson, W. E. (1983). A comparison of two relaxation procedures for reducing cognitive and somatic anxiety. *Journal of Behavior Therapy and Experimental Psychiatry, 14,* 209–214.

Novaco, R. W. (1976). Treatment of chronic anger through cognitive and relaxation controls. *Journal of Consulting and Clinical Psychology, 44,* 681.

Novaco, R. W. (1977). Stress inoculation: A cognitive therapy for anger and its application to a case of depression. *Journal of Consulting and Clinical Psychology, 45,* 600–608.

Novaco, R. W. (1980). Training of probation counselors for anger problems. *Journal of Counseling Psychology, 27,* 385–390.

Nowlis, V. (1965). Research with the Mood Adjective Check List. In S. S. Tomkins & C. E. Izard (Eds.), *Affect, cognition, and personality: Empirical studies* (pp. 352–389). New York: Springer.

Nuechterlein, K. H., & Holroyd, J. C. (1980). Biofeedback in the treatment of tension headache: Current status. *Archives of General Psychiatry, 37,* 866–873.

Nurnberg, H. G. (1978). Meditation and psychotherapy. *World Journal of Psychosynthesis, 10,* 37–40.

Nystul, M. S., & Garde, M. (1977). Comparison of self-concepts of Transcendental Meditators and nonmeditators. *Psychological Reports, 41,* 303–306.

Nystul, M. S., & Garde, M. (1979). The self-concepts of regular Transcendental Meditators, dropout meditators, and nonmeditators. *Journal of Psychology, 103,* 15–18.

O'Brien, J. S. (1979). A modified thought stopping procedure for the treatment of agoraphobia. *Journal of Behavior Therapy and Experimental Psychiatry, 10,* 121–124.

O'Brien, J. S., Raynes, A. E., & Patch, V. D. (1972). Treatment of heroin addiction with aversion therapy, relaxation training and systematic desensitization. *Behaviour Research and Therapy, 10,* 77-80.

Ohno, Y., Takeya, T., & Matsubara, H. (1977). Autogenic behavior therapy. In W. Luthe & F. Antonelli (Eds.), *Therapy in psychosomatic medicine: Autogenic therapy* (pp. 195-200). Rome: Edizioni L. Pozzi.

Oken, D. (1983). In memoriam: Edmund Jacobson, M. D., Ph.D.: 1888-1983. *Psychosomatic Medicine, 45,* 93.

O'Leary, K. D., & Borkovec, T. D. (1978). Conceptual, methodological, and ethical problems of placebo groups in psychotherapy research. *American Psychologist, 33,* 821-830.

Ollendick, T. H., & Nettle, M. D. (1977). An evaluation of the relaxation component of induced anxiety. *Behavior Therapy, 8,* 561-566.

Olness, K., & MacDonald, J. (1981). Self-hypnosis and biofeedback in the management of juvenile migraine. *Developmental and Behavioral Pediatrics, 2,* 168-170.

Olson, R. E., & Malow, R. M. (1985, March). *Effects of relaxation training on psychophysiological facial pain patients.* Paper presented at the meeting of the Society of Behavioral Medicine, New Orleans.

O'Moore, A. M., O'Moore, R. R., Harrison, R. F., Murphy, G., & Carruthers, M. E. (1983). Psychosomatic aspects in idiopathic infertility: Effects of treatment with autogenic training. *Journal of Psychosomatic Research, 27,* 145-151.

Onda, A. (1967). Zen, autogenic training and hypnotism. *Psychologia, 10,* 133-136.

O'Neill, G. W., & Schafer, L. (1982, November). *A comparison of progressive muscle relaxation and Benson's relaxation response in the management of hypertension.* Paper presented at the meeting of the Association for Advancement of Behavior Therapy, Los Angeles.

Orme, M. E. J., & Snider, J. G. (1964). Autogenic training in the treatment of alcoholism. *Quarterly Journal of Studies on Alcohol, 25,* 547-550.

Orme-Johnson, D. W. (1973). Autonomic stability and Transcendental Meditation. *Psychosomatic Medicine, 35,* 341-349.

Orme-Johnson, D. W. (1977). The dawn of the age of enlightenment: Experimental evidence that the Transcendental Meditation technique produces a fourth and fifth state of consciousness in the individual and a profound influence of orderliness in society. In D. W. Orme-Johnson & J. T. Farrow (Eds.), *Scientific research on the Transcendental Meditation program: Collected papers* (Vol. 1, 2nd ed., pp. 671-691). Livingston Manor, NY: Maharishi European Research University Press.

Orme-Johnson, D. W. (1983). *The world peace project: An experimental analysis of achieving world peace through the TM-Sidhi program.* Unpublished manuscript, Maharishi International University, Fairfield, IA.

Orme-Johnson, D. W., & Farrow, J. T. (Eds.). (1977). *Scientific research on the Transcendental Meditation program: Collected papers* (Vol. 1, 2nd ed.). Livingston Manor, NY: Maharishi European Research University Press.

Orme-Johnson, D. W., & Haynes, C. T. (1981). EEG phase coherence, pure consciousness, creativity, and TM-Sidhi experiences. *Neuroscience, 13,* 211-217.

Ornish, D., Scherwitz, L. W., Doody, R. S., Kesten, D., McLanahan, S. M., Brown, S. E., DePuey, E. G., Sonnemaker, R., Haynes, C., Lester, J., McAllister, G. K., Hall, R. J., Burdine, J. A., & Gotto, A. M., Jr. (1983). Effects of stress management training and dietary changes in treating ischemic heart disease. *Journal of the American Medical Association, 247,* 54–59.

Ornstein, R. E. (1971). The techniques of meditation and their implications for modern psychology. In C. Naranjo & R. E. Ornstein (Eds.), *On the psychology of meditation* (pp. 137–232). New York: Viking.

Ortega, D. F. (1978). Relaxation exercise with cerebral palsied adults showing spasticity. *Journal of Applied Behavior Analysis, 11,* 447–451.

Osberg, J. W., III. (1981). The effectiveness of applied relaxation in the treatment of speech anxiety. *Behavior Therapy, 12,* 723–729.

Osipow, S. H., & Kreinbring, I. (1971). Temporal stability of an inventory to measure test anxiety. *Journal of Counseling Psychology, 18,* 152–154.

Osis, K., Bokert, E., & Carlson, M. L. (1973). Dimensions of the meditative experience. *Journal of Transpersonal Psychology, 5,* 109–135.

Ost, L. G., Jerremalm, A., & Jansson, L. (1984). Individual response patterns and the effects of different behavioral methods in the treatment of agoraphobia. *Behaviour Research and Therapy, 22,* 697–707.

Ost, L. G., Jerremalm, A., & Johansson, J. (1981). Individual response patterns and the effects of different behavioral methods in the treatment of social phobia. *Behaviour Research and Therapy, 19,* 1–16.

Ost, L. G., Johansson, J., & Jerremalm, A. (1982). Individual response patterns and the effects of different behavioral methods in the treatment of claustrophobia. *Behaviour Research and Therapy, 20,* 445–460.

Ost, L. G., Lindahl, I. L., Sterner, U., & Jerremalm, A. (1984). Exposure in vivo vs applied relaxation in the treatment of blood phobia. *Behaviour Research and Therapy, 22,* 205–216.

Otis, A. B. (1964). Quantitative relationships in steady-state gas exchange. In W. O. Fenn & H. Rahn (Eds.), *Handbook of physiology. Section III: Respiration* (Vol. 1, pp. 681–698). Washington, DC: American Physiological Society.

Otis, A. S., & Lennon, R. T. (1967). *Otis–Lennon Mental Ability Test.* New York: Harcourt, Brace & World.

Otis, L. S. (1974, April). If well-integrated but anxious, try TM. *Psychology Today,* pp. 45–46.

Ouspensky, P. D. (1957). *The fourth way.* New York: Knopf.

Owens, C. M. (1975). Zen Buddhism. In C. T. Tart (Ed.), *Transpersonal psychologies* (pp. 153–202). New York: Harper & Row.

Pagano, R. R., & Frumkin, L. R. (1977). The effect of transcendental meditation on right hemispheric functioning. *Biofeedback and Self-Regulation, 2,* 407–415.

Pagano, R. R., Rose, R. M., Stivers, R. M., & Warrenburg, S. (1976). Sleep during transcendental meditation. *Science, 191,* 308–310.

Pagano, R. R., & Warrenburg, S. (1983). Meditation: In search of a unique effect. In R. J. Davidson, G. E. Schwartz, & D. Shapiro (Eds.), *Consciousness and self-regulation: Advances in research and theory* (Vol. 3, pp. 153–210). New York: Plenum Press.

Page, R. D., & Schaub, L. H. (1978). EMG biofeedback applicability for differing personality types. *Journal of Clinical Psychology, 34,* 1014–1020.

Palmer, D. K. (1980). Inspired analgesia through transcendental meditation. *New Zealand Dental Journal, 76,* 61–64.

Parker, J. C., Gilbert, G. S., & Thoreson, R. W. (1978a). Anxiety management in alcoholics: A study of generalized effects of relaxation techniques. *Addictive Behaviors, 3,* 123–127.

Parker, J. C., Gilbert, G. S., & Thoreson, R. W. (1978b). Reduction of autonomic arousal in alcoholics: A comparison of relaxation and meditation techniques. *Journal of Consulting and Clinical Psychology, 16,* 879–886.

Pascal, G. R. (1947). The use of relaxation in short-term psychotherapy. *Journal of Abnormal and Social Psychology, 42,* 226–242.

Pascal, G. R. (1949). The effect of relaxation upon recall. *American Journal of Psychology, 62,* 32–47.

Patel, C. H. (1973). Yoga and bio-feedback in the management of hypertension. *Lancet, 2,* 1053–1055.

Patel, C. (1975a). 12-month follow-up of yoga and bio-feedback in the management of hypertension. *Lancet, 1,* 62–64.

Patel, C. (1975b). Yoga and biofeedback in the management of hypertension. *Journal of Psychosomatic Research, 19,* 355–360.

Patel, C. (1976). Reduction of serum cholesterol and blood pressure in hypertensive patients by behaviour modification. *Journal of the Royal College of General Practitioners, 26,* 211–215.

Patel, C. H. (1977). Biofeedback-aided relaxation and meditation in the management of hypertension. *Biofeedback and Self-Regulation, 2,* 1–41.

Patel, C., & Carruthers, M. (1977). Coronary risk factor reduction through biofeedback-aided relaxation and meditation. *Journal of the Royal College of General Practitioners, 27,* 401–405.

Patel, C., Marmot, M. G., & Terry, D. J. (1981). Controlled trial of biofeedback-aided behavioural methods in reducing mild hypertension. *British Medical Journal, 282,* 2005–2008.

Patel, C., Marmot, M. G., Terry, D. J., Carruthers, M., Hunt, B., & Patel, M. (1985). Trial of relaxation in reducing coronary risk: Four year follow up. *British Medical Journal, 290,* 1103–1106.

Patel, C., & North, W. R. S. (1975). Randomized controlled trial of yoga and biofeedback in management of hypertension. *Lancet, 2,* 93–95.

Paul, G. L. (1966a). *Insight vs. desensitization in psychotherapy.* Stanford, CA: Stanford University Press.

Paul, G. L. (1966b, September). The specific control of anxiety: "Hypnosis" and "Conditioning." In L. Oseas (Chair), *Innovations in therapeutic interactions.* Symposium presented at the meeting of the American Psychological Association, New York.

Paul, G. L. (1969a). Extraversion, emotionality, and physiological response to relaxation training and hypnotic suggestion. *International Journal of Clinical and Experimental Hypnosis, 17,* 89–98.

Paul, G. L. (1969b). Inhibition of physiological response to stressful imagery by relaxation training and hypnotically suggested relaxation. *Behaviour Research and Therapy, 7,* 249–256.

Paul, G. L. (1969c). Physiological effects of relaxation training and hypnotic suggestion. *Journal of Abnormal Psychology, 74,* 425-437.

Paul, G. L., & Shannon, D. T. (1966). Treatment of anxiety through systematic desensitization in therapy groups. *Journal of Abnormal Psychology, 71,* 124-135.

Paul, G. L., & Trimble, R. W. (1970). Recorded vs. "live" relaxation training and hypnotic suggestion: Comparative effectiveness for reducing physiological arousal and inhibiting stress response. *Behavior Therapy, 1,* 285-302.

Paulley, J. W., & Haskell, D. A. L. (1975). The treatment of migraine without drugs. *Journal of Psychosomatic Research, 19,* 367-374.

Peerbolte, M. L. (1967). Meditation for school children. *Main Currents in Modern Thought, 24,* 19-21.

Pelletier, K. R. (1974). Influence of Transcendental Meditation upon autokinetic perception. *Perceptual and Motor Skills, 39,* 1031-1034.

Pelletier, K. R., & Peper, E. (1977). Developing a biofeedback model: Alpha EEG feedback as a means for pain control. *International Journal of Clinical and Experimental Hypnosis, 25,* 361-371.

Pendleton, L. R., & Tasto, D. L. (1976). Effects of metronome-conditioned relaxation, metronome-induced relaxation, and progressive muscle relaxation in insomnia. *Behaviour Research and Therapy, 14,* 165-166.

Pennebaker, J. W., & Skelton, J. A. (1981). Selective monitoring of physical sensations. *Journal of Personality and Social Psychology, 41,* 213-223.

Pensinger, W. L., & Paine, D. A. (1977-1978). Deautomatization and the autogenic discharge. *Journal of Altered States of Consciousness, 3,* 325-335.

Perri, M. G., Shapiro, R. M., Ludwig, W. W., Twentyman, C. T., & McAdoo, W. G. (1984). Maintenance strategies for the treatment of obesity: An evaluation of relapse prevention training and posttreatment contact by mail and telephone. *Journal of Consulting and Clinical Psychology, 52,* 404-413.

Peters, R. K., Benson, H., & Peters, J. M. (1977). Daily relaxation response breaks in a working population: II. Effects on blood pressure. *American Journal of Public Health, 67,* 954-959.

Peters, R. K., Benson, H., & Porter, D. (1977). Daily relaxation response breaks in a working population: I. Effects on self-reported measures of health, performance, and well-being. *American Journal of Public Health, 67,* 946-953.

Peterson, L., & Greathouse, A. (1983). Study skills training: The need for exam skills training versus arousal altering treatment. *Behavioral Counseling and Community Interventions, 3,* 108-121.

Peterson, L., & Shigetomi, C. (1981). The use of coping techniques to minimize anxiety in hospitalized children. *Behavior Therapy, 12,* 1-14.

Philipp, R. L., Wilde, G. J. S., & Day, J. H. (1972). Suggestion and relaxation in asthmatics. *Journal of Psychosomatic Research, 16,* 193-204.

Philips, C., & Hunter, M. (1981). The treatment of tension headache-II. EMG "normality" and relaxation. *Behaviour Research and Therapy, 19,* 499-507.

Phillips, B. (Ed.). (1973). *The essentials of Zen Buddhism.* Westport, CT: Greenwood Press.

Phillips, L. W. (1971). Training of sensory and imaginal responses in behavior therapy.

In R. D. Rubin, H. Fensterheim, A. A. Lazarus, & C. M. Franks (Eds.), *Advances in behavior therapy* (pp. 111–122). New York: Academic Press.

Pickett, C., & Clum, G. A. (1982). Comparative treatment strategies and their interaction with locus of control in the reduction of postsurgical pain and anxiety. *Journal of Consulting and Clinical Psychology, 50,* 439–441.

Piggins, D., & Morgan, D. (1977). Note upon steady visual fixation and repeated auditory stimulation in meditation and the laboratory. *Perceptual and Motor Skills, 44,* 357–358.

Piggins, D., & Morgan, D. (1978). Perceptual phenomena resulting from steady visual fixation and repeated auditory input under experimental conditions and in meditation. *Journal of Altered States of Consciousness, 3,* 197–203.

Pikoff, H. (1984a). A critical review of autogenic training in America. *Clinical Psychology Review, 4,* 619–639.

Pikoff, H. (1984b). Is the muscular model of headache still viable? A review of conflicting data. *Headache, 24,* 186–198.

Pollack, A. A., Weber, M. A., Case, D. B., & Laragh, J. H. (1977). Limitations of transcendental meditation in the treatment of essential hypertension. *Lancet, 1,* 71–73.

Pomerleau, O. F. (1979). Behavioral medicine: The contribution of the experimental analysis of behavior to medical care. *American Psychologist, 34,* 654–663.

Pomerleau, O., Adkins, D., & Pertschuk, M. (1978). Predictors of outcome and recidivism in smoking cessation treatment. *Addictive Behaviors, 3,* 65–70.

Pomerleau, O. F., & Brady, J. P. (Eds.). (1979). *Behavioral medicine: Theory and practice.* Baltimore: Williams & Wilkins.

Poole, A. D., Sanson-Fisher, R. W., & German, G. A. (1981). The rapid-smoking technique: Therapeutic effectiveness. *Behaviour Research and Therapy, 19,* 389–397.

Poppen, R., & Maurer, J. P. (1982). Electromyographic analysis of relaxed postures. *Biofeedback and Self-Regulation, 7,* 491–498.

Pratap, V., Berrettini, W. H., & Smith, C. (1978). Arterial blood gases in Pranayama practice. *Perceptual and Motor Skills, 46,* 171–174.

Price, H. L. (1960). Effects of carbon dioxide on the cardiovascular system. *Anesthesiology, 21,* 652–663.

Prince, R. (1978). Meditation: Some psychological speculations. *Psychiatric Journal of the University of Ottawa, 3,* 202–209.

Prokop, C. K., & Bradley, L. A. (Eds.). (1981). *Medical psychology: Contributions to behavioral medicine.* New York: Academic Press.

Puente, A. E. (1981). Psychophysiological investigations on transcendental meditation. *Biofeedback and Self-Regulation, 6,* 327–342.

Puente, A. E., & Beiman, I. (1980). The effects of behavior therapy, self-relaxation, and transcendental meditation on cardiovascular stress response. *Journal of Clinical Psychology, 36,* 291–295.

Puryear, H. B., Cayce, C. T., & Thurston, M. A. (1976). Anxiety reduction associated with meditation: Home study. *Perceptual and Motor Skills, 43,* 527–531.

Putre, W., Loffio, K., Chorost, S., Marx, V., & Gilbert, C. (1977). An effectiveness study of a relaxation training tape with hyperactive children. *Behavior Therapy, 8,* 355–359.

Qualls, P. J., & Sheehan, P. W. (1981). Imagery encouragement, absorption capacity, and relaxation during electromyograph biofeedback. *Journal of Personality and Social Psychology, 41,* 370–379.

Quayle, C. M. (1980). The relative effectiveness of audio-taped relaxation and live-therapist presented relaxation in terms of physiological parameters. *Dissertation Abstracts International, 40,* 3961B. (University Microfilms No. 80–05,114)

Quider, R. (1981). The "Lozanov method" as a psi-conducive state: The effect of relaxation suggestion, and music on ESP test scores. *Research Letter, 11,* 43–54.

Quider, R. P. F. (1984). The effect of relaxation/suggestion and music on forced-choice ESP scoring. *Journal of the American Society for Psychical Research, 78,* 241–262.

Rachman, A. W. (1981). Clinical meditation in groups. *Psychotherapy: Theory, Research and Practice, 18,* 252–258.

Rachman, S. (1965). Studies in desensitization-I: The separate effects of relaxation and desensitization. *Behaviour Research and Therapy, 3,* 245–251.

Rachman, S. (1968). The role of muscular relaxation in desensitization therapy. *Behaviour Research and Therapy, 6,* 159–166.

Radtke, H. L., Spanos, N. P., Armstrong, L. A., Dillman, N., & Boisvenue, M. E. (1983). Effects of electromyographic feedback and progressive relaxation training on hypnotic susceptibility: Disconfirming results. *International Journal of Clinical and Experimental Hypnosis, 31,* 98–106.

Raikov, V. L. (1978). Specific features of suggested anesthesia in some forms of hypnosis in which the subject is active. *International Journal of Clinical and Experimental Hypnosis, 26,* 158–166.

Rama, S. (1979). *Lectures on yoga* (6th ed.). Honesdale, PA: Himalayan International Institute of Yoga Science and Philosophy.

Ram Dass, B. (1971). *Be here now.* New York: Crown.

Ram Dass. (1978). *Journey of awakening: A meditator's guidebook.* New York: Bantam Books.

Rao, S. (1968). Oxygen consumption during yoga-type breathing at altitudes of 520 m. and 3,800 m. *Indian Journal of Medical Research, 56,* 701–705.

Rapee, R. M. (1985). A case of panic disorder treated with breathing retraining. *Journal of Behavior Therapy and Experimental psychiatry, 16,* 63–65.

Raskin, M., Bali, L. R., Peeke, H. V. (1980). Muscle biofeedback and transcendental meditation: A controlled evaluation of efficacy in the treatment of chronic anxiety. *Archives of General Psychiatry, 37,* 93–97.

Rath, K. U., & Lohmann, R. (1977). Changes in psychological test performance before and after autogenic therapy in dialysis and kidney transplant patients. In W. Luthe & F. Antonelli (Eds.), *Therapy in psychosomatic medicine: Autogenic therapy* (pp. 342–349). Rome: Edizioni L. Pozzi.

Raymer, R., & Poppen, R. (1985). Behavioral relaxation training with hyperactive children. *Journal of Behavior Therapy and Experimental Psychiatry, 16,* 309–316.

Read, G. D. (1944). *Childbirth without fear.* New York: Harper & Brothers.

Reading, A., & Raw, M. (1976). The treatment of mandibular dysfunction pain. *British Dental Journal, 140,* 201–205.

Redd, W. H. (1980). In vivo desensitization in the treatment of chronic emesis following gastrointestinal surgery. *Behavior Therapy, 11,* 421–427.

Redd, W. H., & Andrykowski, M. A. (1982). Behavioral intervention in cancer treatment: Controlling aversion reactions to chemotherapy. *Journal of Consulting and Clinical Psychology, 50,* 1018–1029.

Redd, W. H., Rosenberger, P. H., & Hendler, C. S. (1982–1983). Controlling chemotherapy side effects. *American Journal of Clinical Hypnosis, 25,* 161–172.

Redmond, D. P., Gaylor, M. S., McDonald, R. H., Jr., & Shapiro, A. P. (1974). Blood pressure and heart-rate response to verbal instruction and relaxation in hypertension. *Psychosomatic Medicine, 36,* 285–297.

Reed, H. (1978). Improved dream recall associated with meditation. *Journal of Clinical Psychology, 34,* 150–156.

Reed, M., & Saslow, C. (1980). The effects of relaxation instructions and EMG biofeedback on test anxiety, general anxiety, and locus of control. *Journal of Clinical Psychology, 36,* 683–690.

Reed, R., & Meyer, R. G. (1974). Reduction of test anxiety via autogenic therapy. *Psychological Reports, 35,* 649–650.

Rehm, L. P., Mattei, M. L., Potts, S., & Skolnick, M. (1974, December). *Effects of practice, emotional content, and relaxation on vividness and latency of imagery.* Paper presented at the meeting of the Association for Advancement of Behavior Therapy, Chicago.

Reinking, R. H., & Hutchings, D. (1981). Follow-up to: "Tension headaches: What form of therapy is most effective?" *Biofeedback and Self-Regulation, 6,* 57–62.

Reinking, R. H., & Kohl, M. L. (1975). Effects of various forms of relaxation training on physiological and self-report measures of relaxation. *Journal of Consulting and Clinical Psychology, 43,* 595–600.

Reisman, J. M. (1976). *A history of clinical psychology.* New York: Irvington.

Reynolds, S. B. (1984). Biofeedback, relaxation training, and music: Homeostasis for coping with stress. *Biofeedback and Self-Regulation, 9,* 169–179.

Reynolds, W. M., & Coats, K. I. (1986). A comparison of cognitive-behavioral therapy and relaxation training for the treatment of depression in adolescents. *Journal of Consulting and Clinical Psychology, 54,* 653–660.

Ribordy, S. C. (1976). The behavioral treatment of insomnia. *Dissertation Abstracts International, 37,* 477B. (University Microfilms No. 76-16,769)

Richardson, A. (1969). *Mental imagery.* London: Routledge & Kegan Paul.

Richter, N. C. (1984). The efficacy of relaxation training with children. *Journal of Abnormal Child Psychology, 12,* 319–344.

Richter, R., & Dahme, B. (1982). Bronchial asthma in adults: There is little evidence for the effectiveness of behavioral therapy and relaxation. *Journal of Psychosomatic Research, 26,* 533–540.

Rickard, H. C., Crist, D. A., & Barker, H. (1985). The effects of suggestibility on relaxation. *Journal of Clinical Psychology, 41,* 466–468.

Riddick, C., & Meyer, R. G. (1973). The efficacy of automated relaxation training with response contingent feedback. *Behavior Therapy, 4,* 331–337.

Rieker, H. U. (1971). *The Yoga of light* (E. Becherer, Trans.). New York: Herder & Herder.

Riley, W. T., Berry, S. L., & Kennedy, W. A. (1986). Rationale exposure and compliance to relaxation training. *Psychological Reports, 58,* 499–502.

Rimm, D. C., & Masters, J. C. (1979). *Behavior Therapy: Techniques and empirical findings* (2nd ed.). New York: Academic Press.

Rimm, D. C., & Medeiros, D. C. (1970). The role of muscle relaxation in participant modeling. *Behaviour Research and Therapy, 8,* 127–132.

Rivers, S. M., & Spanos, N. P. (1981). Personal variables predicting voluntary participation in and attrition from a meditation program. *Psychological Reports, 49,* 795–801.

Roberts, B. W., & Forester, W. E. (1979). Group relaxation–acute and chronic effects on essential hypertension. *Cardiovascular Medicine, 5,* 575–576, 579–580.

Rogers, C. A., & Livingston, D. D. (1977). Accumulative effects of periodic relaxation. *Perceptual and Motor Skills, 44,* 690.

Romanczyk, R. G., Tracey, D. A., Wilson, G. T., & Thorpe, G. L. (1973). Behavioral techniques in the treatment of obesity: A comparative analysis. *Behaviour Research and Therapy, 11,* 629–640.

Roon, K. (1961). *Karin Roon's new way to relax* (2nd ed.). New York: Greystone Press.

Rose, J. E., Ananda, S., & Jarvik, M. E. (1983). Cigarette smoking during anxiety-provoking and monotonous tasks. *Addictive Behaviors, 8,* 353–359.

Rose, M. I., Firestone, P., Heick, H. M. C., & Faught, A. K. (1983). The effects of anxiety management training on the control of juvenile diabetes mellitus. *Journal of Behavioral Medicine, 6,* 381–395.

Rose, R. M., & Abplanalp, J. M. (1983). The premenstrual syndrome. *Hospital Practice, 18*(6), 129–134, 136, 139–141.

Rosen, G. M. (1976). A manual for self-administered progressive relaxation. In J. P. Flanders (Ed.), *Practical psychology* (pp. 261–267). New York: Harper & Row.

Rosen, G. M. (1977). *The relaxation book.* Englewood Cliffs, NJ: Prentice-Hall.

Rosenbaum, M. S., & Ayllon, T. (1981). Treating bruxism with the habit-reversal technique. *Behaviour Research and Therapy, 19,* 87–96.

Rosenstiel, A. K., & Scott, D. S. (1977). Four considerations in using imagery techniques with children. *Journal of Behavior Therapy and Experimental Psychiatry, 8,* 287–290.

Rosenthal, R. (1966). *Experimenter effects in behavioral research.* New York: Appleton-Century-Crofts.

Rosenthal, T. L. (1980). Social cueing processes. In M. Hersen, R. M. Eisler, & P. M. Miller (Eds.), *Progress in behavior modification* (Vol. 10, pp. 111–146). New York: Academic Press.

Rosenthal, T. L., & Rosenthal, R. H. (1983). Stress: Causes, measurement, and management. In K. D. Craig & R. J. McMahon (Eds.), *Advances in clinical behavior therapy* (pp. 3–26). New York: Brunner/Mazel.

Roskies, E., Kearney, H., Spevack, M., Surkis, A., Cohen, C., & Gilman, S. (1979).

Generalizability and durability of treatment effects in an intervention program for coronary-prone (type A) managers. *Journal of Behavioral Medicine, 2,* 195–207.

Roskies, E., Spevack, M., Surkis, A., Cohen, C., & Gilman, S. (1978). Changing the coronary-prone (type A) behavior pattern in a nonclinical population. *Journal of Behavioral Medicine, 1,* 201–216.

Roszell, D. K., & Chaney, E. F. (1982). Autogenic training in a drug abuse program. *International Journal of the Addictions, 17,* 1337–1349.

Rothman, G. (1961). Psychodrama and autogenic relaxation. *Group Psychotherapy, 14,* 26–29.

Rotter, J. B. (1966). Generalized expectancies for internal versus external control of reinforcement. *Psychological Monographs, 80*(1, Whole No. 609).

Roughton, F. J. W. (1964). Transport of oxygen and carbon dioxide. In W. O. Fenn & H. Rahn (Eds.), *Handbook of physiology. Section III: Respiration* (Vol. 1, pp. 767–825). Washington, DC: American Physiological Society.

Ruggieri, V., & Mazza, P. (1980). Effects of muscle tone and changes in autonomic balance on cognitive style. *Psychological Reports, 46,* 916–918.

Russell, R. K., & Matthews, C. O. (1975). Cue-controlled relaxation in *in vivo* desensitization of a snake phobia. *Journal of Behavior Therapy and Experimental Psychiatry, 6,* 49–51.

Russell, R. K., Miller, D. E., & June, L. N. (1974). Group cue-controlled relaxation in the treatment of test anxiety. *Behavior Therapy, 5,* 571–573.

Russell, R. K., Miller, D. E., & June, L. N. (1975). A comparison between group systematic desensitization and cue-controlled relaxation in the treatment of test anxiety. *Behavior Therapy, 6,* 172–177.

Russell, R. K., & Sipich, J. F. (1973). Cue-controlled relaxation in the treatment of test anxiety. *Journal of Behavior Therapy and Experimental Psychiatry, 4,* 47–49.

Russell, R. K., & Sipich, J. F. (1974). Treatment of test anxiety by cue-controlled relaxation. *Behavior Therapy, 5,* 673–676.

Russell, R. K., Sipich, J. F., & Knipe, J. (1976). Progressive relaxation training: A procedural note. *Behavior Therapy, 7,* 566–568.

Russell, R. K., & Wise, F. (1976). Treatment of speech anxiety by cue-controlled relaxation and desensitization with professional and paraprofessional counselors. *Journal of Counseling Psychology, 23,* 583–586.

Russell, R. K., Wise, F., & Stratoudakis, J. P. (1976). Treatment of test anxiety by cue-controlled relaxation and systematic desensitization. *Journal of Counseling Psychology, 23,* 563–566.

Russo, D. C., Bird, B. L., & Masek, B. J. (1980). Assessment issues in behavioral medicine. *Behavioral Assessment, 2,* 1–18.

Ryan, V. L., Krall, C. A., & Hodges, W. F. (1976). Self-concept change in behavior modification. *Journal of Consulting and Clinical Psychology, 44,* 638–645.

Sabel, B. A. (1980). Transcendental Meditation and concentration ability. *Perceptual and Motor Skills, 50,* 799–802.

Sackner, M. A. (1975). Diaphragmatic breathing exercises: Therapy in chronic obstructive pulmonary disease. *Journal of the American Medical Association, 231,* 295–296.

Sallade, J. B. (1980). Group counseling with children who have migraine headaches. *Elementary School Guidance and Counseling, 15,* 87–89.

Sallis, J. F. (1980). *Issues in the therapeutic use of meditation.* Memphis, TN: Memphis State University. (ERIC Document Reproduction Service No. ED 181358)

Sallis, J. F. (1982). Meditation and self-actualization: A theoretical comparison. *Psychologia, 25,* 59–64.

Sallis, J. F., & Lichstein, K. L. (1979). The frontal electromyographic adaptation response: A potential source of confounding. *Biofeedback and Self-Regulation, 4,* 337–339.

Sallis, J. F., & Lichstein, K. L. (1982). Analysis and management of geriatric anxiety. *International Journal of Aging and Human Development, 15,* 197–211.

Sallis, J. F., Lichstein, K. L., Clarkson, A. D., Stalgaitis, S., & Campbell, M. (1983). Anxiety and depression management for the elderly. *International Journal of Behavioral Geriatrics, 1,* 3–12.

Sanders, S. H. (1983). Component analysis of a behavioral treatment program for chronic low-back pain. *Behavior Therapy, 14,* 697–705.

Saraceni, C., Ruggeri, G., & Cagossi, M. (1977). Experimental study of psychodynamic processes involved in A.T. A preliminary report. In W. Luthe & F. Antonelli (Eds.), *Therapy in psychosomatic medicine: Autogenic therapy* (pp. 359–363). Rome: Edizioni L. Pozzi.

Sarason, I. G. (1972). Experimental approaches to test anxiety: Attention and the uses of information. In C. D. Spielberger (Ed.), *Anxiety: Current trends in theory and research* (Vol. 2, pp. 381–403). New York: Academic Press.

Sarason, I. G., Johnson, J. H., Berberich, J. P., & Siegel, J. M. (1979). Helping police officers to cope with stress: A cognitive-behavioral approach. *American Journal of Community Psychology, 7,* 593–603.

Sargent, J. D., Green, E. E., & Walters, E. D. (1972). The use of autogenic feedback training in a pilot study of migraine and tension headaches. *Headache, 12,* 120–124.

Sargent, J. D., Green, E. E., & Walters, E. D. (1973). Preliminary report on the use of autogenic feedback training in the treatment of migraine and tension headaches. *Psychosomatic Medicine, 35,* 129–135.

Sargent, J. D., Solbach, P., & Coyne, L. (1980). Evaluation of a 5-day non-drug training program for headache at the Menninger Foundation. *Headache, 20,* 32–41.

Sargent, J., Solbach, P., Coyne, L., Spohn, H., & Segerson, J. (1986). Results of a controlled, experimental, outcome study of nondrug treatments for the control of migraine headaches. *Journal of Behavioral Medicine, 9,* 291–323.

Sargent, J. D., Walters, E. D. & Green, E. E. (1973). Psychosomatic self-regulation of migraine headaches. *Seminars in Psychiatry, 5,* 415–428.

Sato, K. (1958). Psychotherapeutic implications of Zen. *Psychologia, 1,* 213–218.

Saxena, R. P., & Saxena, U. (1977). Loss of weight in obese patients who regularly elicited the relaxation response. *Journal of Chronic Diseases and Therapeutics Research, 1*(1), 32–34.

Schandler, S. L., & Dana, E. R. (1983). Cognitive imagery and physiological feedback relaxation protocols applied to clinically tense young adults: A comparison of state, trait, and physiological effects. *Journal of Clinical Psychology, 39,* 672–681.

Schandler, S. L., & Grings, W. W. (1976). An examination of methods for producing relaxation during short-term laboratory sessions. *Behaviour Research and Therapy, 14,* 419–426.

Scherr, M. S., Crawford, P. L., Sergent, C. B., & Scherr, C. A. (1975). Effect of bio-feedback techniques on chronic asthma in a summer camp environment. *Annals of Allergy, 35,* 289–295.

Schilling, D. J., & Poppen, R. (1983). Behavioral relaxation training and assessment. *Journal of Behavior Therapy and Experimental Psychiatry, 14,* 99–107.

Schilling, G. (1980). Psycho-regulative procedure in Swiss sport—more as an alibi or fire-brigade? Reports on experiences had. *International Journal of Sport Psychology, 11,* 189–201.

Schinke, S. P. (Ed.). (1981). *Behavioral methods in social welfare.* Hawthorne, NY: Aldine.

Schinke, S. P., Blythe, B. J., & Doueck, H. J. (1978). Reducing cigarette smoking: Evaluation of a multifaceted interventive program. *Behavioral Engineering, 4,* 107–112.

Schlichter, K. J., & Horan, J. J. (1981). Effects of stress inoculation on the anger and aggression management skills of institutionalized juvenile delinquents. *Cognitive Therapy and Research, 5,* 359–365.

Schubert, D. K. (1983). Comparison of hypnotherapy with systematic relaxation in the treatment of cigarette habituation. *Journal of Clinical Psychology, 39,* 198–202.

Schulte, H. J., & Abhyanker, V. V. (1979). Yogic breathing and psychologic states. *Arizona Medicine, 36,* 681–683.

Schultz, J. H. (1926). Uber selbsttatige (autogene) umstellungen der warmestrahlung der menschlichen haut im autosuggestiven training. *Dtsch. Med. Wschrft., 14,* 571–572.

Schultz, J. H. (1932). *Das autogene training.* Leipzig: Verlag.

Schultz, J. H. (1954–1955). Autogenic training. *British Journal of Medical Hypnotism, 6*(2), 33–35.

Schultz, J. H. (1957). Autogenous training. In J. H. Masserman & J. L. Moreno (Eds.), *Progress in pschotherapy* (Vol. 2, pp. 173–176). New York: Grune & Stratton.

Schultz, J. H., & Luthe, W. (1959). *Autogenic training: A psychophysiologic approach in psychotherapy.* New York: Grune & Stratton.

Schultz, J. H., & Luthe, W. (1961). Autogenic training. *Proceedings of the Third World Congress of Psychiatry* (Vol. 1, pp. 191–200). Toronto: University of Toronto Press.

Schultz, J. H., & Luthe, W. (1969). *Autogenic methods* (Vol. 1). In W. Luthe (Ed.), *Autogenic therapy.* New York: Grune & Stratton.

Schultz, W. C. (1967). *Joy: Expanding human awareness.* New York: Grove Press.

Schuster, R. (1979). Empathy and mindfulness. *Journal of Humanistic Psychology, 19*(1), 71–77.

Schwartz, G. E. (1980). Stress management in occupational settings. *Public Health Reports, 95,* 99–108.

Schwartz, G. E., Davidson, R. J., & Goleman, D. J. (1978). Patterning of cognitive and somatic processes in the self-regulation of anxiety: Effects of meditation versus exercise. *Psychosomatic Medicine, 40,* 321–328.

Schwartz, G. E., & Weiss, S. M. (1978). Yale Conference on Behavioral Medicine: A proposed definition and statement of goals. *Journal of Behavioral Medicine, 1,* 3–12.

Scott, L. E., & Clum, G. A. (1984). Examining the interaction effects of coping style and brief interventions in the treatment of postsurgical pain. *Pain, 20,* 279–291.

Seeburg, K. N., & DeBoer, K. F. (1980). Effects of EMG biofeedback on diabetes. *Biofeedback and Self-Regulation, 5,* 289–293.

Seeman, W., Nidich, S., & Banta, T. (1972). Influence of transcendental meditation on a measure of self-actualization. *Journal of Counseling Psychology, 19,* 184–187.

Seer, P. (1979). Psychological control of essential hypertension: Review of the literature and methodological critique. *Psychological Bulletin, 86,* 1015–1043.

Seer, P., & Raeburn, J. M. (1980). Meditation training and essential hypertension: A methodological study. *Journal of Behavioral Medicine, 3,* 59–71.

Segreto-Bures, J., & Kotses, H. (1982). Experimenter expectancy effects in frontal EMG conditioning. *Psychophysiology, 19,* 467–471.

Shafii, M. (1973a). Adaptive and therapeutic aspects of meditation. *International Journal of Psychoanalytic Psychotherapy, 2,* 364–382.

Shafii, M. (1973b). Silence in the service of ego: Psychoanalytic study of meditation. *International Journal of Psychoanalysis, 54,* 431–443.

Shafii, M., Lavely, R., & Jaffe, R. (1974). Meditation and marijuana. *American Journal of Psychiatry, 131,* 60–63.

Shafii, M., Lavely, R., & Jaffe, R. (1975). Meditation and the prevention of alcohol abuse. *American Journal of Psychiatry, 132,* 942–945.

Shapiro, A. P., Redmond, D. P., McDonald, R. H., Jr., & Gaylor, M. (1975). Relationships of perception, cognition, suggestion and operant conditioning in essential hypertension. *Progress in Brain Research, 42,* 299–312.

Shapiro, D. (1979). Biofeedback and behavioral medicine in perspective. *Biofeedback and Self-Regulation, 4,* 371–381.

Shapiro, D., & Goldstein, I. B. (1982). Biobehavioral perspectives on hypertension. *Journal of Consulting and Clinical Psychology, 50,* 841–858.

Shapiro, D. H., Jr. (1978a). Behavioral and attitudinal changes resulting from a "Zen experience" workshop in Zen meditation. *Journal of Humanistic Psychology, 18,* 21–29.

Shapiro, D. H., Jr. (1978b). Instructions for a training package combining formal and informal Zen meditation with behavioral self-control strategies. *Psychologia, 21,* 70–76.

Shapiro, D. H., Jr. (1978c). *Precision nirvana.* Englewood Cliffs, NJ: Prentice-Hall.

Shapiro, D. H., Jr. (1980). *Meditation: Self-regulation strategy and altered state of consciousness.* Hawthorne, NY: Aldine.

Shapiro, D. H., Jr. (1982). Overview: Clinical and physiological comparison of meditation with other self-control strategies. *American Journal of Psychiatry, 139,* 267–274.

Shapiro, D. H., Jr. (1983a). A content analysis of views of self-control: Relation to positive and negative valence, and implications for a working definition. *Biofeedback and Self-Regulation, 8,* 73–86.

Shapiro, D. H., Jr. (1983b). Meditation as an altered state of consciousness: Contributions of Western behavioral science. *Journal of Transpersonal Psychology, 15,* 61–81.

Shapiro, D. H., Jr., Shapiro, J., Walsh, R. N., & Brown, D. (1982). Effects of intensive meditation on sex-role identification: Implications for a control model of psychological health. *Psychological Reports, 51,* 44–46.

Shapiro, S., & Lehrer, P. M. (1980). Psychophysiological effects of autogenic training and progressive relaxation. *Biofeedback and Self-Regulation, 5,* 249–255.

Sharpe, R. (1974). Behaviour therapy in a case of blepharospasm. *British Journal of Psychiatry, 124,* 603–604.

Sharpley, C. F., & Rogers, H. J. (1984). A meta-analysis of frontalis EMG levels with biofeedback and alternative procedures. *Biofeedback and Self-Regulation, 9,* 385–393.

Shaw, E. R., & Blanchard, E. B. (1983). The effects of instructional set on the outcome of a stress management program. *Biofeedback and Self-Regulation, 8,* 555–565.

Shaw, W. A. (1940). The relation of muscular action potentials to imaginal weight lifting. *Archives of Psychology, No. 247,* 1–50.

Shaw, W. J., & Walker, C. E. (1979). Use of relaxation in the short-term treatment of fetishistic behavior: An exploratory case study. *Journal of Pediatric Psychology, 4,* 403–407.

Shealy, R. C. (1979). The effectiveness of various treatment techniques on different degrees and durations of sleep-onset insomnia. *Behaviour Research and Therapy, 17,* 541–546.

Shealy, R. C., Lowe, J. D., & Ritzler, B. A. (1980). Sleep onset insomina: Personality characteristics and treatment outcome. *Journal of Consulting and Clinical Psychology, 48,* 659–661.

Sheikh, A. A. (Ed.). (1983). *Imagery: Current theory, research, and application.* New York: Wiley.

Shelton, J. L. (1973). Murder strikes and panic follows–Can behavior modification help? *Behavior Therapy, 4,* 706–708.

Sheridan, C. L., Boehm, M. B., Ward, L. B., & Justesen, D. R. (1976). Autogenic-biofeedback, autogenic phrases, and biofeedback compared [Summary]. *Proceedings of the Biofeedback Research Society Seventh Annual Meeting,* 68.

Sherman, A. R. (1975). Two-year follow-up of training in relaxation as a behavioral self-management skill. *Behavior Therapy, 6,* 419–420.

Sherman, A. R., Mulac, A., & McCann, M. J. (1974). Synergistic effect of self-relaxation and rehearsal feedback in the treatment of subjective and behavioral dimensions of speech anxiety. *Journal of Consulting and Clinical Psychology, 42,* 819–827.

Sherman, A. R., & Plummer, I. L. (1973). Training in relaxation as a behavioral self-management skill: An exploratory investigation. *Behavior Therapy, 4,* 543–550.

Sherman, R., Hayashi, R., Gaarder, K., Huff, R., & Williams, M. (1978). Failure of intensive short term relaxation training to reduce blood pressure of pregnant hypertensives or preeclaptics. *Psychophysiology, 15,* 277.

Sherman, R. A. (1976). Case reports of treatment of phantom limb pain with a combination of electromyographic biofeedback and verbal relaxation techniques. *Biofeedback and Self-Regulation, 1,* 353.

Sherman, R. A. (1980). Published treatments of phantom limb pain. *American Journal of Physical Medicine, 59,* 232-244.

Sherman, R. A. (1982). Home use of tape-recorded relaxation exercises as initial treatment for stress-related disorders. *Military Medicine, 147,* 1062, 1065-1066.

Sherman, R. A., Gall, N., & Gormly, J. (1979). Treatment of phantom limb pain with muscular relaxation training to disrupt the pain-anxiety-tension cycle. *Pain, 6,* 47-55.

Sherman, R. A., Sherman, C. J., & Gall, N. G. (1980). A survey of current phantom limb pain treatment in the United States. *Pain, 8,* 85-99.

Sherman, R. A., & Tippens, J. K. (1982). Suggested guidelines for treatment of phantom limb pain. *Orthopedics, 5,* 1595-1600.

Shibata, J. I., & Kuwahara, M. (1967). Electroencephalographic studies of schizophrenic patients treated with autogenic training. *American Journal of Clinical Hypnosis, 10,* 25-29.

Shibata, J. I., & Motoda, K. (1967a). The application of autogenic training to a group of schizophrenic patients. *American Journal of Clinical Hypnosis, 10,* 15-19.

Shibata, J. I., & Motoda, K. (1967b). Clinical evaluation with psychological tests of schizophrenic patients treated with autogenic training. *American Journal of Clinical Hypnosis, 10,* 20-24.

Shibata, J. I., & Motoda, K. (1968). A study of autogenic discharges in schizophrenic patients. *American Journal of Clinical Hypnosis, 10,* 249-254.

Shiffman, S. (1982). Relapse following smoking cessation: A situational analysis. *Journal of Consulting and Clinical Psychology, 50,* 71-86.

Shiffman, S. (1984). Coping with temptations to smoke. *Journal of Consulting and Clinical Psychology, 52,* 261-267.

Shimano, E. T., & Douglas, D. B. (1975). On research in Zen. *American Journal of Psychiatry, 132,* 1300-1302.

Shipley, R. H. (1979). Implosive therapy: The technique. *Psychotherapy: Theory, Research and Practice, 16,* 140-147.

Shipley, R. H. (1981). Maintenance of smoking cessation: Effect of follow-up letters, smoking motivation, muscle tension, and health locus of control. *Journal of Consulting and Clinical Psychology, 49,* 982-984.

Shoemaker, J. E., & Tasto, D. L. (1975). The effects of muscle relaxation on blood pressure of essential hypertensives. *Behaviour Research and Therapy, 13,* 29-43.

Shor, R. E., & Orne, E. C. (1962). Harvard Group Scale of Hypnotic Susceptibility, Form A. Palo Alto, CA: Consulting Psychologists Press.

Shore, R. E., Orne, M. T., & O'Connell, D. N. (1962). Validation and cross-validation of a scale of self-reported personal experiences which predicts hypnotizability. *Journal of Psychology, 53,* 55-75.

Shostrom, E. L. (1966). *Personal Orientation Inventory: An inventory for the measurement of self-actualization.* San Diego: Education and Industrial Testing Service.

Shumaker, R. G. (1980). The response of manual motor functioning in Parkinsonians to frontal EMG biofeedback and progressive relaxation. *Biofeedback and Self-Regulation, 5,* 229–234.

Siegal, G. S., & Lichstein, K. L. (1980). The treatment of gerontologic insomnia. *Canadian Counsellor, 14,* 121–126.

Siegal, L. J., & Peterson, L. (1980). Stress reduction in young dental patients through coping skills and sensory information. *Journal of Consulting and Clinical Psychology, 48,* 785–787.

Siegal, L. J., & Peterson, L. (1981). Maintenance effects of coping skills and sensory information on young children's response to repeated dental procedures. *Behavior Therapy, 12,* 530–535.

Sigman, M., & Amit, Z. (1982). Progressive relaxation exercises and human gastric acid output–A study using telemetric measurements. *Behaviour Research and Therapy, 20,* 605–612.

Sigman, M., & Amit, Z. (1983). Cognitive inhibition of human gastric acid output–Studies using telemetric measurement. *Journal of Behavioral Medicine, 6,* 233–244.

Silver, B. V., & Blanchard, E. B. (1978). Biofeedback and relaxation training in the treatment of psychophysiological disorders: Or are the machines really necessary? *Journal of Behavioral Medicine, 1,* 217–239.

Silver, B. V., Blanchard, E. B., Williamson, D. A., Theobald, D. E., & Brown, D. A. (1979). Temperature biofeedback and relaxation training in the treatment of migraine headaches: One-year follow-up. *Biofeedback and Self-Regulation, 4,* 359–366.

Sim, M. K. (1980a). Treatment of disease without the use of drugs. II.–The relationship between thought control and galvanic skin resistance. *Singapore Medical Journal, 21,* 479–482.

Sim, M. K. (1980b). Treatment of disease without the use of drugs. III. Self-treatment of migraine by thought control. *Singapore Medical Journal, 21,* 522–524.

Sime, W. E. (1977). A comparison of exercise and meditation in reducing physiological response to stress. *Medicine and Science in Sports, 9,* 55.

Sime, W. E., & DeGood, D. E. (1977). Effect of EMG biofeedback and progressive muscle relaxation training on awareness of frontalis muscle tension. *Psychophysiology, 14,* 522–530.

Simon, M. J., & Salzberg, H. C. (1981). Electromyographic feedback and taped relaxation instructions to modify hypnotic susceptibility and amnesia. *American Journal of Clinical Hypnosis, 24,* 14–21.

Simonton, O. C., Matthews-Simonton, S., & Creighton, J. (1978). *Getting well again.* Los Angeles: Tarcher.

Simonton, O. C., Matthews-Simonton, S., & Sparks, T. F. (1980). Psychological intervention in the treatment of cancer. *Psychosomatics, 21,* 226–227, 231–233.

Simpson, D. D., Dansereau, D. F., & Giles, G. J. (1972). A preliminary evaluation of physiological and behavioral effects of self-directed relaxation. *JSAS: Catalog of Selected Documents in Psychology, 2,* 59. (Ms. No. 141)

Singer, J. L. (1974). *Imagery and daydream methods in psychotherapy and behavior modification.* New York: Academic Press.

Singer, J. L. (1975). *The inner world of daydreaming.* New York: Harper & Row.

Singer, J. L., Greenberg, S., & Antrobus, J. S. (1971). Looking with the mind's eye: Experimental studies of ocular motility during daydreaming and mental arithmetic. *Transactions of the New York Academy of Sciences, 33,* 694–709.

Singer, J. L., & Pope, K. S. (Eds.). (1978). *The power of human imagination: New methods in psychotherapy.* New York: Plenum Press.

Singh, K. (1970). *The crown of life (3rd ed.).* Delhi, India: Ruhani Satsang.

Sinha, S. N., Prasad, S. C., & Sharma, K. N. (1978). An experimental study of cognitive control and arousal processes during meditation. *Psychologia, 21,* 227–230.

Sipich, J. F., Russell, R. K., & Tobias, L. L. (1974). A comparison of covert sensitization and "nonspecific" treatment in the modification of smoking behavior. *Journal of Behavior Therapy and Experimental Psychiatry, 5,* 201–203.

Sipos, K., & Tomka, I. (1977). A comparative study of electrical and clinical manifestations of petit mal epilepsy during various levels of vigilance and under the influence of autogenic training. In W. Luthe & F. Antonelli (Eds.), *Therapy in psychosomatic medicine: Autogenic therapy* (pp. 29–39). Rome: Edizioni L. Pozzi.

Sipprelle, C. N. (1967). Induced anxiety. *Psychotherapy: Theory, Research and Practice, 4,* 36–40.

Sirota, A. D., & Mahoney, M. J. (1974). Relaxing on cue: The self regulation of asthma. *Journal of Behavior Therapy and Experimental Psychiatry, 5,* 65–66.

Sivananda, S. S. (1971). *Kundalini Yoga.* Himalayas, India: Divine Life Society.

Slater, S. L., & Leavy, A. (1966). The effects of inhaling a 35 percent CO_2–65 percent O_2 mixture upon anxiety level in neurotic patients. *Behaviour Research and Therapy, 4,* 309–316.

Slonim, N. B., & Hamilton, L. H. (1976). *Respiratory physiology* (3rd ed.). St. Louis: Mosby.

Small, L. (1971). *The briefer psychotherapies.* New York: Brunner/Mazel.

Smith, J. C. (1975). Meditation as psychotherapy: A review of the literature. *Psychological Bulletin, 82,* 558–564.

Smith, J. C. (1976). Psychotherapeutic effects of transcendental meditation with controls for expectation of relief and daily sitting. *Journal of Consulting and Clinical Psychology, 44,* 630–637.

Smith, J. C. (1978). Personality correlates of continuation and outcome in meditation and erect sitting control treatments. *Journal of Consulting and Clinical Psychology, 46,* 272–279.

Smith, J. C. (1985). *Relaxation dynamics.* Champaign, IL: Research Press.

Smith, J. C., & Seidel, J. M. (1982). The factor structure of self-reported physical stress reactions. *Biofeedback and Self-Regulation, 7,* 35–47.

Smith, T. W., & Denney, D. R. (1983). Relaxation training in the reduction of traumatic headaches: A case study. *Behavioural Psychotherapy, 11,* 109–115.

Snider, J. G., & Oetting, E. R. (1966). Autogenic training and the treatment of examination anxiety in students. *Journal of Clinical Psychology, 22,* 111–114.

Snow, W. G. (1977). The physiological and subjective effects of several brief relaxation training procedures. *Dissertation Abstracts International, 38,* 3417B.

Snowden, L. R. (1978). Personality tailored covert sensitization of heroin abuse. *Addictive Behaviors, 3,* 43–49.

Snyder, A. L., & Deffenbacher, J. L. (1977). Comparison of relaxation as self-control and systematic desensitization in the treatment of test anxiety. *Journal of Consulting and Clinical Psychology, 45,* 1202–1203.

Sokoloff, L. (1960). The effects of carbon dioxide on the cerebral circulation. *Anesthesiology, 21,* 664–673.

Solbach, P., Sargent, J., & Coyne, L. (1984). Menstrual migraine headache: Results of a controlled, experimental, outcome study of non-drug treatments. *Headache, 24,* 75–78.

Sorbi, M., & Tellegen, B. (1984). Multimodel migraine treatment: Does thermal feedback add to the outcome? *Headache, 24,* 249–255.

Southam, M. A., Agras, W. S., Taylor, C. B., & Kraemer, H. C. (1982). Relaxation training: Blood pressure lowering during the working day. *Archives of General Psychiatry, 39,* 715–717.

Sovak, M., Kunzel, M., Sternbach, R. S., & Dalessio, D. J. (1978). Is volitional manipulation of hemodynamics a valid rationale for biofeedback therapy of migraine? *Headache, 18,* 197–202.

Spanos, N. P., Gottlieb, J., & Rivers, S. M. (1980). The effects of short-term meditation practice on hypnotic responsivity. *Psychological Record, 30,* 343–348.

Spanos, N. P., Radtke-Bodorik, H. L., & Stam, H. J. (1980). Disorganized recall during suggested amnesia: Fact not artifact. *Journal of Abnormal Psychology, 89,* 1–19.

Spanos, N. P., Rivers, S. M., & Gottlieb, J. (1978). Hypnotic responsivity, meditation, and laterality of eye movements. *Journal of Abnormal Psychology, 87,* 566–569.

Spanos, N. P., Steggles, S., Radtke-Bodorik, H. L., & Rivers, S. M. (1979). Nonanalytic attending, hypnotic susceptibility, and psychological well-being in trained meditators and nonmeditators. *Journal of Abnormal Psychology, 88,* 85–87.

Spence, K. W. (1956). *Behavior theory and conditioning.* New Haven: Yale University Press.

Spiegler, M. D., Liebert, R. M., McMains, M. J., & Fernandez, L. E. (1969). Experimental development of a modeling treatment to extinguish persistent avoidance behavior. In R. D. Rubin & C. M. Franks (Eds.), *Advances in behavior therapy, 1968* (pp. 45–51). New York: Academic Press.

Spielberger, C. D., Gorsuch, R. L., & Lushene, R. E. (1970). *State-Trait Anxiety Inventory.* Palo Alto, CA: Consulting Psychologists Press.

Spittell, J. A., Jr. (1972). Raynaud's phenomenon and allied vasospastic conditions. In J. F. Fairbairn, II, J. L. Juergens, & J. A. Spitttell, Jr. (Eds.), *Peripheral vascular diseases* (4th ed., pp. 387–419). Philadelphia: Saunders.

Spoth, R. (1980). Using a differential stress reduction model with substance abusers: Matching treatment presentation with locus of control. *Behavioural Analysis and Modification, 4,* 188–200.

Spoth, R., Etringer, B., Gaffney, J. M., & Hutzell, R. R. (1982). Effects of progressive relaxation on Huntington's disease patients' choreiform movements and coordination: An exploratory study. *The Behavior Therapist, 5,* 176, 182.

Spoth, R., & Meade, C. (1981). Differential application of cue-controlled relaxation in the reduction of general anxiety. *Journal of Behavior Therapy and Experimental Psychiatry, 12,* 57–61.

Springer, C. J., Sachs, L. B., & Morrow, J. E. (1977). Group methods of increasing hypnotic susceptibility. *International Journal of Clinical and Experimental Hypnosis, 25,* 184–191.

Stam, H. J., McGrath, P. A., & Brooke, R. I. (1984). The effects of a cognitive-behavioral treatment program on temporo-mandibular pain and dysfunction syndrome. *Psychosomatic Medicine, 46,* 534–545.

Stambaugh, E. E., II, & House, A. E. (1977). Multimodality treatment of migraine headache: A case study utilizing biofeedback, relaxation, autogenic and hypnotic treatments. *American Journal of Clinical Hypnosis, 19,* 235–240.

Stanescu, D. C., Nemery, B., Veriter, C., & Marechal, C. (1981). Pattern of breathing and ventilatory response to CO_2 in subjects practicing hatha-yoga. *Journal of Applied Physiology, 51,* 1625–1629.

Stanford, R. G., & Mayer, B. (1974). Relaxation as a psi-conducive state: A replication and exploration of parameters. *Journal of the American Society for Psychical Research, 68,* 182–191.

Staples, R., Coursey, R., & Smith, B. (1975, October). *A comparison of EMG biofeedback, progressive relaxation and autogenic training as relaxation techniques.* Paper presented at the meeting of the Biofeedback Research Society, Monterey, CA.

Steen, P. L., & Zuriff, G. E. (1977). The use of relaxation in the treatment of self-injurious behavior. *Journal of Behavior Therapy and Experimental Psychiatry, 8,* 447–448.

Stefanek, M. E., & Hodes, R. L. (1986). Expectancy effects on relaxation instructions: Physiological and self-report indices. *Biofeedback and Self-Regulation, 11,* 21–29.

Steger, J. C., & Harper, R. G. (1980). Comprehensive biofeedback versus self-monitored relaxation in the treatment of tension headache. *Headache, 20,* 137–142.

Steinmark, S. W., & Borkovec, T. D. (1974). Active and placebo treatment effects on moderate insomnia under counterdemand and positive demand instructions. *Journal of Abnormal Psychology, 83,* 157–163.

Steinmetz, J. L., Lewinsohn, P. M., & Antonuccio, D. O. (1983). Prediction of individual outcome in a group intervention for depression. *Journal of Consulting and Clinical Psychology, 51,* 331–337.

Stenn, P. G., Mothersill, K. J., & Brooke, R. I. (1979). Biofeedback and a cognitive behavioral approach to treatment of myofascial pain dysfunction syndrome. *Behavior Therapy, 10,* 29–36.

Stephanos, S., Biebl, W., & Plaum, F. G. (1976). Ambulatory analytical psychotherapy for the treatment of psychosomatic patients: A report on the method of 'relaxation analytique.' *British Journal of Medical Psychology, 49,* 305–313.

Steptoe, A., & Greer, K. (1980). Relaxation and skin conductance feedback in the control of reactions to cognitive tasks. *Biological Psychology, 10,* 127–138.

Steptoe, A., & Ross, A. (1982). Voluntary control of cardiovascular reactions to demanding tasks. *Biofeedback and Self-Regulation, 7,* 149–166.

Stevens, R. J. (1976). Psychological strategies for management of pain in prepared childbirth I: A review of the research. *Birth and the Family Journal, 3,* 157–164, 177.

Stevens, R. J. (1977). Psychological strategies for management of pain in prepared childbirth II: A study of psychoanalgesia in prepared childbirth. *Birth and the Family Journal, 4,* 4–9.

Stevens, R. J., & Heide, F. (1977). Analgesic characteristics of prepared childbirth techniques: Attention focusing and systematic relaxation. *Journal of Psychosomatic Research, 21,* 429–438.

Stone, R. A., & DeLeo, J. (1976). Psychotherapeutic control of hypertension. *New England Journal of Medicine, 294,* 80–84.

Stoudemire, A., Cotanch, P., & Laszlo, J. (1984). Recent advances in the pharmacologic and behavioral management of chemotherapy-induced emesis. *Archives of Internal Medicine, 144,* 1029–1033.

Stoudenmire, J. (1972). Effects of muscle relaxation training on state and trait anxiety in introverts and extraverts. *Journal of Personality and Social Psychology, 24,* 273–275.

Stoudenmire, J. (1973). The effect of length of sessions and spacing of sessions on muscle relaxation training. *Journal of Community Psychology, 1,* 235–236.

Stoudenmire, J. (1975). A comparison of muscle relaxation training and music in the reduction of state and trait anxiety. *Journal of Clinical Psychology, 31,* 490–492.

Stout, C. C., Thornton, B., & Russell, H. L. (1980). Effect of relaxation training on students' persistence and academic performance. *Psychological Reports, 47,* 189–190.

Stoyva, J. (1973). The discussion of Dr. Jacobson's paper. In F. J. McGuigan & R. A. Schoonover (Eds.), *The psychophysiology of thinking: Studies of covert processes* (pp. 24–25). New York: Academic Press.

Straughan, J. H., & Dufort, W. H. (1969). Task difficulty, relaxation, and anxiety level during verbal learning and recall. *Journal of Abnormal Psychology, 74,* 621–624.

Strickler, D., Bigelow, G., Wells, D., & Liebson, I. (1977). Effects of relaxation instructions on the electromyographic responses of abstinent alcoholics to drinking-related stimuli. *Behaviour Research and Therapy, 15,* 500–502.

Strickler, D. P., Tomaszewski, R., Maxwell, W. A., & Suib, M. R. (1979). The effects of relaxation instructions on drinking behavior in the presence of stress. *Behaviour Research and Therapy, 17,* 45–51.

Stroebel, C. F. (1978). *Quieting Response training* (Cassette Recording). New York: Guilford.

Stroebel, C. F. (1982). *QR: The Quieting Reflex.* New York: Putnam.

Stroebel, C. F., & Glueck, B. C. (1978). Passive meditation: Subjective, clinical, and electrographic comparison with biofeedback. In G. E. Schwartz & D. Shapiro (Eds.), *Consciousness and self-regulation: Advances in research and theory* (Vol. 2, pp. 401–428). New York: Plenum Press.

Stuart, R. B. (1967). Behavioral control of overeating. *Behaviour Research and Therapy, 5,* 357–365.

Suedfeld, P. (1980). *Restricted environmental stimulation: Research and clinical applications.* New York: Wiley.

Suedfeld, P., & Borrie, R. A. (1978). Altering states of consciousness through sensory deprivation. In A. A. Sugerman & R. E. Tarter (Eds.), *Expanding dimensions of consciousness* (pp. 226–252). New York: Springer.

Suedfeld, P., & Kristeller, J. L. (1982). Stimulus reduction as a technique in health psychology. *Health Psychology, 1,* 337–357.

Suedfeld, P., Roy, C., & Landon, P. B. (1982). Restricted environmental stimulation therapy in the treatment of essential hypertension. *Behaviour Research and Therapy, 20,* 553–559.

Suess, W. M., Alexander, A. B., Smith, D. D., Sweeney, H. W., & Marion, R. J. (1980). The effects of psychological stress on respiration: A preliminary study of anxiety and hyperventilation. *Psychophysiology, 17,* 535–540.

Sugano, H., & Takeya, T. (1970). Measurement of body movement and its clinical application. *Japanese Journal of Physiology, 20,* 296–308.

Suinn, R. M. (1972a). Behavior rehearsal training for ski racers. *Behavior Therapy, 3,* 519–520.

Suinn, R. M. (1972b). Removing emotional obstacles to learning and performance by visuo-motor behavior rehearsal. *Behavior Therapy, 3,* 308–310.

Suinn, R. M. (1975). The cardiac stress management program for Type A patients. *Cardiac Rehabilitation, 5*(4), 13–15.

Suinn, R. M. (1976). Visuo-motor behavior rehearsal for adaptive behavior. In J. Krumboltz & C. Thoresen (Eds.), *Counseling methods* (pp. 360–366). New York: Holt, Rinehart & Winston.

Suinn, R. M., & Bloom, L. J. (1978). Anxiety management training for pattern A behavior. *Journal of Behavioral Medicine, 1,* 25–35.

Suinn, R. M., & Richardson, F. (1971). Anxiety management training: A nonspecific behavior therapy program for anxiety control. *Behavior Therapy, 2,* 498–510.

Sullivan, H. S. (1953). *The interpersonal theory of psychiatry.* New York: Norton.

Sultana, M., & Siddiqui, A. Q. (1983). Efficacy of relaxation therapy in the treatment of neurotic ailments. *Journal of the Royal Society of Health, 103,* 97–98.

Surwit, R. S. (1973). Biofeedback: A possible treatment for Raynaud's disease. In L. Birk (Ed.), *Biofeedback: Behavioral medicine* (pp. 123–130). New York: Grune & Stratton.

Surwit, R. S. (1981). Behavioral approaches to Raynaud's disease. *Psychotherapy and Psychosomatics, 36,* 224–245.

Surwit, R. S. (1982). Behavioral treatment of Raynaud's syndrome in peripheral vascular disease. *Journal of Consulting and Clinical Psychology, 50,* 922–932.

Surwit, R. S., Allen, L. M., III, Gilgor, R. S., & Duvic, M. (1982). The combined effect of prazosin and autogenic training on cold reactivity in Raynaud's phenomenon. *Biofeedback and Self-Regulation, 7,* 537–544.

Surwit, R. S., Bradner, M. N., Fenton, C. H., & Pilon, R. N. (1979). Individual differences in response to the behavioral treatment of Raynaud's disease. *Journal of Consulting and Clinical Psychology, 47,* 363–367.

Surwit, R. S., & Feinglos, M. N. (1983). The effects of relaxation on glucose tolerance in non-insulin-dependent diabetes. *Diabetes Care, 6,* 176–179.

Surwit, R. S., & Feinglos, M. N. (1984). Relaxation-induced improvement in glucose tolerance is associated with decreased plasma cortisol. *Diabetes Care, 7,* 203–204.

Surwit, R. S., Feinglos, M. N., & Scovern, A. W. (1983). Diabetes and behavior: A paradigm for health psychology. *American Psychologist, 38,* 255–262.

Surwit, R. S., & Fenton, C. H. (1980). Feedback and instructions in the control of digital skin temperature. *Psychophysiology, 17,* 129–132.

Surwit, R. S., Pilon, R. N. & Fenton, C. H. (1978). Behavioral treatment of Raynaud's disease. *Journal of Behavioral Medicine, 1,* 323–335.

Surwit, R. S., Shapiro, D., & Good, M. I. (1978). Comparison of cardiovascular biofeedback, neuromuscular biofeedback, and meditation in the treatment of borderline essential hypertension. *Journal of Consulting and Clinical Psychology, 46,* 252–263.

Surwit, R. S., Williams, R. B., Jr., & Shapiro, D. (1982). *Behavioral approaches to cardiovascular disease.* New York: Academic Press.

Sutherland, A., Amit, Z., Golden, M., & Roseberger, Z. (1975). Comparison of three behavioral techniques in the modification of smoking behavior. *Journal of Consulting and Clinical Psychology, 43,* 443–447.

Suzuki, D. T. (1963). Lectures on Zen Buddhism. In D. T. Suzuki, E. Fromm, & R. De Martino (Eds.), *Zen Buddhism and psychoanalysis* (pp. 1–76). New York: Grove Press.

Swanson, D. W., Maruta, T., & Swenson, W. M. (1979). Results of behavior modification in the treatment of chronic pain. *Psychosomatic Medicine, 41,* 55–61.

Swanson, D. W., Swenson, W. M., Maruta, T., & McPhee, M. C. (1976). Program for managing chronic pain. I. Program description and characteristics of patients. *Mayo Clinic Proceedings, 51,* 401–408.

Swearer, D. K. (Ed.). (1971). *Secrets of the lotus: Studies in Buddhist meditation.* New York: Macmillan.

Sweeney, G. A., & Horan, J. J. (1982). Separate and combined effects of cue-controlled relaxation and cognitive restructuring in the treatment of musical performance anxiety. *Journal of Counseling Psychology, 29,* 486–497.

Sykes, D. H., Douglas, V. I., Weiss, G., & Minde, K. K. (1971). Attention in hyperactive children and the effect of methylphenidate (Ritalin). *Journal of Child Psychology and Psychiatry, 12,* 129–139.

Szekely, B. C., Turner, S. M., & Jacob, R. G. (1982). Behavioral control of L-dopa induced dyskinesia in Parkinsonism. *Biofeedback and Self-Regulation, 7,* 443–447.

Szirmai, E. (1980). Edmund Jacobson–pioneer and "father" of tension control and progressive relaxation. In F. J. McGuigan, W. E. Sime, & J. M. Wallace (Eds.), *Stress and tension control* (pp. 303–311). New York: Plenum Press.

Tandon, M. K. (1978). Adjunct treatment with yoga in chronic severe airways obstruction. *Thorax, 33,* 514–517.

Tarler-Benlolo, L. (1978). The role of relaxation in biofeedback training: A critical review of the literature. *Psychological Bulletin, 85,* 727–755.

Tasto, D. L. (1969). Systematic desensitization, muscle relaxation and visual imagery in the counterconditioning of four-year-old phobic child. *Behaviour Research and Therapy, 7,* 409–411.

Tasto, D. L., & Chesney, M. A. (1974). Muscle relaxation treatment for primary dysmenorrhea. *Behavior Therapy, 5,* 668–672.

Tasto, D. L., & Hinkle, J. E. (1973). Muscle relaxation treatment for tension headaches. *Behaviour Research and Therapy, 11,* 347–349.

Tasto, D. L., & Huebner, L. A. (1976). The effects of muscle relaxation and stress on the blood pressure levels of normotensives. *Behaviour Research and Therapy, 14,* 89–91.

Tasto, D. L., & Insel, P. M. (1977). The premenstrual and menstrual syndromes–A psychological approach. In S. Rachman (Ed.), *Contributions to medical psychology* (Vol. 1, pp. 153–166). Oxford: Pergamon Press.

Taylor, C. B. (1978). Relaxation training and related techniques. In W. S. Agras (Ed.), *Behavior modification: Principles and clinical applications* (2nd ed., pp. 134–162). Boston: Little, Brown.

Taylor, C. B., Agras, W. S., Schneider, J. A., & Allen, R. A. (1983). Adherence to instructions to practice relaxation exercises. *Journal of Consulting and Clinical Psychology, 51,* 952–953.

Taylor, C. B., Farquhar, J. W., Nelson, E., & Agras, W. S. (1977). Relaxation therapy and high blood pressure. *Archives of General Psychiatry, 34,* 339–342.

Taylor, C. B., Kenigsberg, M. L., & Robinson, J. M. (1982). A controlled comparison of relaxation and diazepam in panic disorder. *Journal of Clinical Psychiatry, 43,* 423–425.

Taylor, J. A. (1953). A personality scale of manifest anxiety. *Journal of Abnormal and Social Psychology, 48,* 285–290.

Tebecis, A. K., Ohno, Y., Matsubara, H., Sugano, H., Takeya, T., Ikemi, Y., & Takasaki, M. (1977). A longitudinal study of some physiological parameters and autogenic training. *Psychotherapy and Psychosomatics, 27,* 8–17.

Tebecis, A. K., Ohno, Y., Takeya, T., Sugano, H., Matsubara, H., Tanaka, Y., Ikemi, Y., & Takasaki, M. (1977). Fine body movement during autogenic training: Longitudinal and short-term changes. *Biofeedback and Self-Regulation, 2,* 417–426.

Teders, S. J., Blanchard, E. B., Andrasik, F., Jurish, S. E., Neff, D. F., & Arena, J. G. (1984). Relaxation training for tension headache: Comparative efficacy and cost-effectiveness of a minimal therapist contact versus a therapist-delivered procedure. *Behavior Therapy, 15,* 59–70.

Tellegen, A., & Atkinson, G. (1974). Openness to absorbing and self-altering experiences ("absorption"), a trait related to hypnotic susceptibility. *Journal of Abnormal Psychology, 83,* 268–277.

Tenney, S. M., & Lamb, T. W. (1965). Physiological consequences of hypoventilation and hyperventilation. In W. O. Fenn & H. Rahn (Eds.), *Handbook of physiology. Section 3: Respiration* (Vol. II, pp. 979–1010). Washington, DC: American Physiological Society.

Teshima, H., Kubo, C., Kihara, H., Imada, Y., Nagata, S., Ago, Y., & Ikemi, Y. (1982). Psychosomatic aspects of skin diseases from the standpoint of immunology. *Psychotherapy and Psychosomatics, 37,* 165–175.

Thomas, D., & Abbas, K. A. (1978). Comparison of transcendental meditation and progressive relaxation in reducing anxiety. *British Medical Journal, 2,* 1749.

Thompson, J. G., Griebstein, M. G., & Kuhlenschmidt, S. L. (1980). Effects of EMG biofeedback and relaxation training in the prevention of academic underachievement. *Journal of Counseling Psychology, 27,* 97–106.

Thoresen, C. E., Coates, T. J., Kirmil-Gray, K., & Rosekind, M. R. (1981). Behavioral self-management in treating sleep-maintenance insomnia. *Journal of Behavioral Medicine, 4,* 41–52.

Thoresen, C. E., & Mahoney, M. J. (1974). *Behavioral self-control.* New York: Holt, Rinehart & Winston.

Throll, D. A. (1981). Transcendental Meditation and progressive relaxation: Their psychological effects. *Journal of Clinical Psychology, 37,* 776–781.

Throll, D. A. (1982). Transcendental Meditation and progressive relaxation: Their physiological effects. *Journal of Clinical Psychology, 38,* 522–530.

Thyer, B. A. (1983). Behavior modification in social work practice. In M. Hersen, R. M. Eisler, & P. M. Miller (Eds.), *Progress in behavior modification* (Vol. 15, pp. 173–216). New York: Academic Press.

Thyer, B. A., Papsdorf, J. D., Himle, D. P., McCann, B. S., Caldwell, S., & Wickert, M. (1981). In vivo distraction-coping in the treatment of test anxiety. *Journal of Clinical Psychology, 37,* 754–764.

Todd, F. J., & Kelley, R. J. (1970). The use of hypnosis to facilitate conditioned relaxation responses: A report of three cases. *Journal of Behavior Therapy and Experimental Psychiatry, 1,* 295–298.

Toler, H. C. (1978). The treatment of insomnia with relaxation and stimulus-control instructions among incarcerated males. *Criminal Justice and Behavior, 5,* 117–130.

Tomita, Z. (1977). Studies of AT applied to groups of Japanese athletes. In W. Luthe & F. Antonelli (Eds.), *Therapy in psychosomatic medicine: Autogenic therapy* (pp. 296–300). Rome: Edizioni L. Pozzi.

Torrey, E. F. (1972). *The mind game: Witchdoctors and psychiatrists.* New York: Emerson Hall.

Toscano, W. B., & Cowings, P. S. (1982). Reducing motion sickness: A comparison of autogenic-feedback training and an alternative cognitive task. *Aviation, Space, and Environmental Medicine, 53,* 449–453.

Tosi, D. J., & Reardon, J. P. (1976). The treatment of guilt through rational stage-directed therapy. *Rational Living, 11,* 8–11.

Townsend, R. E., House, J. F., & Addario, D. (1975). A comparison of biofeedback-mediated relaxation and group therapy in the treatment of chronic anxiety. *American Journal of Psychiatry, 132,* 598–601.

Traub, A. C., Jencks, B., & Bliss, E. L. (1973). Effects of relaxation training on chronic insomnia. *Sleep Research, 3,* 164.

Traut, E. F. (1932). Progressive relaxation in the management of hypertension. *Medical Clinics of North America, 16,* 347–349.

Travis, F. (1979). The Transcendental Meditation technique and creativity: A longitudinal study of Cornell University undergraduates. *Journal of Creative Behavior, 13,* 169–180.

Travis, T. A., Kondo, C. Y., & Knot, J. R. (1976). Heart rate, muscle tension, and alpha production of transcendental meditators and relaxation controls. *Biofeedback and Self-Regulation, 1,* 387–394.

Treichel, M., Clinch, N., & Cran, M. (1973). The metabolic effects of Transcendental Meditation. *The Physiologist, 16,* 472.

Trexler, L. D., & Karst, T. O. (1972). Rational-emotive therapy, placebo, and no-treatment effects on public-speaking anxiety. *Journal of Abnormal Psychology, 79,* 60–67.

Turin, A., Nirenberg, J., & Mattingly, M. (1979). Effects of comprehensive relaxation training (CRT) on mood: A preliminary report on relaxation training plus caffeine cessation. *The Behavior Therapist, 2*(4), 20–21.

Turk, D. C., Meichenbaum, D., & Genest, M. (1983). *Pain and behavioral medicine: A cognitive-behavioral perspective.* New York: Guilford.

Turner, J. A. (1982). Comparison of group progressive-relaxation training and cognitive-behavioral group therapy for chronic low back pain. *Journal of Consulting and Clinical Psychology, 50,* 757–765.

Turner, J. W., Jr., & Fine, T. H. (1983). Effects of relaxation associated with brief restricted environmental stimulation therapy (REST) on plasma cortisol, ACTH, and LH. *Biofeedback and Self-Regulation, 8,* 115–126.

Turner, P. E. (1978). A psychophysiological assessment of selected relaxation strategies. *Dissertation Abstracts International, 39,* 3010B. (University Microfilms No. 7824063)

Turner, R. M., & Ascher, L. M. (1979). Controlled comparison of progressive relaxation, stimulus control, and paradoxical intention therapies for insomnia. *Journal of Consulting and Clinical Psychology, 47,* 500–508.

Turner, R. M., & Ascher, L. M. (1982). Therapist factor in the treatment of insomnia. *Behaviour Research and Therapy, 20,* 33–40.

Turpin, G., & Powell, G. E. (1984). Effects of massed practice and cue-controlled relaxation on tic frequency in Gilles de la Tourette's syndrome. *Behaviour Research and Therapy, 22,* 165–178.

Tuttle, W. W. (1924). The effect of sleep upon the patellar tendon reflex. *American Journal of Physiology, 68,* 345–347.

Uchiyama, K. (1965). Some clinical considerations concerning the effects of autogenic training on writer's cramp. In W. Luthe (Ed.), *Autogenic training: International edition* (pp. 133–137). New York: Grune & Stratton.

Udupa, K. N., Singh, R. H., & Settiwar, R. M. (1972). Studies on physiological, endocrine and metabolic response to the practice of Yoga in young normal volunteers. *Journal of Research in Indian Medicine, 6,* 345–353.

Udupa, K. N., Singh, R. H., & Settiwar, R. M. (1975). Studies on the effect of some yogic breathing exercises (Pranayams) in normal persons. *Indian Journal of Medical Research, 63,* 1062–1065.

Udupa, K. N., Singh, R. H., & Yadav, R. A. (1973). Certain studies on psychological and biochemical responses to the practice of Hatha Yoga in young normal volunteers. *Indian Journal of Medical Research, 61,* 237–244.

Uherik, A., & Sebej, F. (1978). Effect of autogenic training on lateral differences in bioelectrical skin reactivity. *Studia Psychologica, 20,* 294–299.

Upper, D., & Cautela, J. R. (Eds). (1979). *Covert conditioning.* Elmsford, NY: Pergamon Press.

Upper, D., & Ross, S. M. (Eds.). (1979). *Behavioral group therapy, 1979.* Champaign, IL: Research Press.

Vahia, N. S., Doongaji, D. R., Deshmukh, D. K., Vinekar, S. L., Parekh, H. C., &

Kapoor, S. N. (1972). A deconditioning therapy based upon concepts of Patanjali. *International Journal of Social Psychiatry, 18,* 61–66.

Vahia, N. S., Doongaji, D. R., Jeste, D. V., Kapoor, S. N., Ardhapurkar, I., & Nath, S. R. (1973). Further experience with the therapy based upon concepts of Patanjali in the treatment of psychiatric disorders. *Indian Journal of Psychiatry, 15,* 32–37.

Vajiranana, P. M. (1962). *Buddhist meditation in theory and practice.* Colombo, Ceylon: M. D. Gunasena.

Vakil, R. J. (1950). Remarkable feat of endurance by a yogi priest. *Lancet, 2,* 871.

Van Den Hout, M. A., & Griez, E. (1982a). Cardiovascular and subjective responses to inhalation of carbon dioxide: A controlled test with anxious patients. *Psychotherapy and Psychosomatics, 37,* 75–82.

Van Den Hout, M. A., & Griez, E. (1982b). Cognitive factors in carbon dioxide therapy. *Journal of Psychosomatic Research, 26,* 209–214.

VanderPlate, C., & Kerrick, G. (1985). Stress reduction treatment of severe recurrent genital herpes virus. *Biofeedback and Self-Regulation, 10,* 181–188.

Van Egeren, L. F., Feather, B. W., & Hein, P. L. (1971). Desensitization of phobias: Some psychophysiological propositions. *Psychophysiology, 8,* 213–228.

Van Nuys, D. (1973). Meditation, attention, and hypnotic susceptibility: A correlational study. *International Journal of Clinical and Experimental Hypnosis, 21,* 59–69.

Varni, J. W. (1980). Behavioral treatment of disease-related chronic insomnia in a hemophiliac. *Journal of Behavior Therapy and Experimental Psychiatry, 11,* 143–145.

Varni, J. W. (1981a). Behavioral medicine in hemophilia arthritic pain management: Two case studies. *Archives of Physical Medicine and Rehabilitation, 62,* 183–187.

Varni, J. W. (1981b). Self-regulation techniques in the management of chronic arthritic pain in hemophilia. *Behavior Therapy, 12,* 185–194.

Varni, J. W., & Gilbert, A. (1982). Self-regulation of chronic arthritic pain and long-term analgesic dependence in a haemophiliac. *Rheumatology and Rehabilitation, 21,* 171–174.

Vasilos, J. G., & Hughes, H. (1979). Skin temperature control: A comparison of direct instruction, autogenic suggestion, relaxation, and biofeedback training in male prisoners. *Corrective and Social Psychiatry and Journal of Behavior Technology, Methods and Therapy, 25,* 119–124.

Ventis, W. L. (1973). Case history: The use of laughter as an alternative response in systematic desensitization. *Behavior Therapy, 4,* 120–122.

Voukydis, P. C., & Forwand, S. A. (1977). The effect of elicitation of the relaxation response in patients with intractable ventricular arrhythmias. *Circulation, 56*(4), 157.

Waddell, M. T., Barlow, D. H., & O'Brien, G. T. (1984). A preliminary investigation of cognitive and relaxation treatment of panic disorder: Effects on intense anxiety vs "background" anxiety. *Behaviour Research and Therapy, 22,* 393–402.

Wadden, T. A. (1983). Predicting treatment response to relaxation therapy for essential hypertension. *Journal of Nervous and Mental Disease, 171,* 683–689.

Wadden, T. A. (1984). Relaxation therapy for essential hypertension: Specific or nonspecific effects? *Journal of Psychosomatic Research, 28,* 53–61.

Wadden, T. A., Luborsky, L., Greer, S., & Crits-Christoph, P. (1984). The behavioral treatment of essential hypertension: An update and comparison with pharmacological treatment. *Clinical Psychology Review, 4,* 403–429.

Wagner, M. K., & Bragg, R. A. (1970). Comparing behavior modification approaches to habit decrement-smoking. *Journal of Consulting and Clinical Psychology, 34,* 258–263.

Walker, C. E. (1979). Treatment of children's disorders by relaxation training: The poor man's biofeedback. *Journal of Clinical Child Psychology, 8,* 22–25.

Wallace, R. K. (1970). Physiological effects of Transcendental Meditation. *Science, 167,* 1751–1754.

Wallace, R. K., & Benson, H. (1972). The physiology of meditation. *Scientific American, 226,* 84–90.

Wallace, R. K., Benson, H., & Wilson, A. F. (1971). A wakeful hypometabolic physiologic state. *American Journal of Physiology, 221,* 795–799.

Wallace, R. K., Dillbeck, M., Jacobe, E., & Harrington, B. (1982). The effects of the Transcendental Meditation and TM-Sidhi program on the aging process. *International Journal of Neuroscience, 16,* 53–58.

Wallace, R. K., Silver, J., Mills, P. J., Dillbeck, M. C., & Wagoner, D. E. (1983). Systolic blood pressure and long-term practice of the Transcendental Meditation and TM-Sidhi program: Effects of TM on systolic blood pressure. *Psychosomatic Medicine, 45,* 41–46.

Walrath, L. C., & Hamilton, D. W. (1975). Autonomic correlates of meditation and hypnosis. *American Journal of Clinical Hypnosis, 17,* 190–196.

Walsh, P., Dale, A., & Anderson, D. E. (1977). Comparison of biofeedback pulse wave velocity and progressive relaxation in essential hypertensives. *Perceptual and Motor Skills, 44,* 839–843.

Walsh, R. N. (1976). Reflections on psychotherapy. *Journal of Transpersonal Psychology, 8,* 100–111.

Walsh, R. (1977). Initial meditative experiences: Part I. *Journal of Transpersonal Psychology, 9,* 151–192.

Walsh, R. N. (1978). Initial meditative experiences: Part II. *Journal of Transpersonal Psychology, 10,* 1–28.

Walsh, R. N. (1979). Meditation research: An introduction and review. *Journal of Transpersonal Psychology, 11,* 161–174.

Walsh, R. (1980). The consciousness disciplines and the behavioral sciences: Questions of comparison and assessment. *American Journal of Psychiatry, 137,* 663–673.

Walsh, R. (1983). Meditation practice and research. *Journal of Humanistic Psychology, 23,* 18–50.

Walsh, R. N., Goleman, D., Kornfield, J., Pensa, C., & Shapiro, D. (1978). Meditation: Aspects of research and practice. *Journal of Transpersonal Psychology, 10,* 113–133.

Walsh, R., & Roche, L. (1979). Precipitation of acute psychotic episodes by intensive meditation in individuals with a history of schizophrenia. *American Journal of Psychiatry, 136,* 1085–1086.

Warner, G., & Lance, J. W. (1975). Relaxation therapy in migraine and chronic tension headache. *Medical Journal of Australia, 1,* 298–301.

Warrenburg, S., & Pagano, R. (1982–1983). Meditation and hemispheric specialization I: Absorbed attention in long-term adherence. *Imagination, Cognition and Personality, 2,* 211–229.

Warrenburg, S., Pagano, R. R., Woods, M., & Hlastala, M. (1980). A comparison of somatic relaxation and EEG activity in classical progressive relaxation and Transcendental Meditation. *Journal of Behavioral Medicine, 3,* 73–93.

Washburn, M. C. (1978). Observations relevant to a unified theory of meditation. *Journal of Transpersonal Psychology, 10,* 45–66.

Watts, A. W. (1957). *The way of Zen.* New York: Random House.

Webster, J. S., Ahles, T. A., Thompson, J. K., & Raczynski, J. M. (1984). The assessment of subjective tension levels among several muscle groups: The tension mannequin. *Journal of Behavior Therapy and Experimental Psychiatry, 15,* 323–328.

Webster, S. K. (1980). Problems for diagnosis of spasmodic and congestive dysmenorrhea. In A. J. Dan, E. A. Graham, & C. P. Beecher (Eds.), *The menstrual cycle: Vol 1. A synthesis of interdisciplinary research* (pp. 292–304). New York: Springer.

Weddington, W. W., Jr., Blindt, K. A., & McCracken, S. G. (1983). Relaxation training for anticipatory nausea associated with chemotherapy. *Psychosomatics, 24,* 281–283.

Weerts, T. C., & Lang, P. J. (1978). Psychophysiology of fear imagery: Differences between focal phobia and social performance anxiety. *Journal of Consulting and Clinical Psychology, 46,* 1157–1159.

Weil, A. T. (1963, November 5). The strange case of the Harvard drug scandal. *Look,* pp. 38, 43–44, 46, 48.

Weil, G., & Goldfried, M. R. (1973). Treatment of insomnia in an eleven-year-old child through self-relaxation. *Behavior Therapy, 4,* 282–284.

Weiner, S. L., & Ehrlichman, H. (1976). Ocular motility and cognitive process. *Cognition, 4,* 31–43.

Weinman, B., Gelbart, P., Wallace, M., & Post, M. (1972). Inducing assertive behavior in chronic schizophrenics: A comparison of socioenvironmental, desensitization, and relaxation therapies. *Journal of Consulting and Clinical Psychology, 39,* 246–252.

Weinstein, D. J. (1976). Imagery and relaxation with a burn patient. *Behaviour Research and Therapy, 14,* 481.

Weiss, S. M. (1980). Behavioral medicine in the United States: Research, clinical, and training opportunities. *International Journal of Mental Health, 9,* 182–196.

Weiss, T., Cheatle, M. D., Rubin, S. I., Reichek, N., & Brady, J. P. (1985). Effects of repeated ambulatory ECG monitoring and relaxation practice on premature ventricular contractions. *Psychosomatic Medicine, 47,* 446–450.

Weissberg, M. (1975). Anxiety-inhibiting statements and relaxation combined in two cases of speech anxiety. *Journal of Behavior Therapy and Experimental Psychiatry, 6,* 163–164.

Weitzenhoffer, A. M., & Hilgard, E. R. (1959). *Stanford Hypnotic Susceptibility Scale, Forms A and B.* Palo Alto, CA: Consulting Psychologists Press.

Weitzenhoffer, A. M., & Hilgard, E. R. (1962). *Stanford Hypnotic Susceptibility Scale, Form C.* Palo Alto, CA: Consulting Psychologists Press.

Wellisch, D. K. (1981). Intervention with the cancer patient. In C. K. Prokop & L. A. Bradley (Eds.), *Medical psychology: Contributions to behavioral medicine* (pp. 223–240). New York: Academic Press.

Wells, K. C., Turner, S. M., Bellack, A. S., & Hersen, M. (1978). Effects of cue-controlled relaxation on psychomotor seizures: An experimental analysis. *Behaviour Research and Therapy, 16,* 51–53.

Wells, N. (1982). The effect of relaxation on postoperative muscle tension and pain. *Nursing Research, 31,* 236–238.

Welwood, J. (1980). Reflections on psychotherapy, focusing, and meditation. *Journal of Transpersonal Psychology, 12,* 127–141.

Wenger, M. A., & Bagchi, B. K. (1961). Studies of autonomic functions in practitioners of Yoga in India. *Behavioral Science, 6,* 312–323.

Wenger, M. A., Bagchi, B. K., & Anand, B. K. (1961). Experiments in India on "voluntary" control of the heart and pulse. *Circulation, 24,* 1319–1325.

Werder, D. S. (1978). An exploratory study of childhood migraine using thermal biofeedback as a treatment alternative. *Biofeedback and Self-Regulation, 3,* 242–243.

Werder, D. S., & Sargent, J. D. (1984). A study of childhood headache using biofeedback as a treatment alternative. *Headache, 24,* 122–126.

Werner, O. R., Wallace, R. K., Charles, B., Janssen, G., Stryker, T., & Chalmers, R. A. (1986). Long-term endocrinologic changes in subjects practicing the Transcendental Meditation and TM-Sidhi program. *Psychosomatic Medicine, 48,* 59–66.

West, M. (1979a). Meditation. *British Journal of Psychiatry, 135,* 457–467.

West, M. A. (1979b). Physiological effects of meditation: A longitudinal study. *British Journal of Social and Clinical Psychology, 18,* 219–226.

West, M. A. (1980). Meditation, personality and arousal. *Personality and Individual Differences, 1,* 135–142.

Westcott, M. R., & Huttenlocher, J. (1961). Cardiac conditioning: The effects and implications of controlled and uncontrolled respiration. *Journal of Experimental Psychology, 61,* 353–359.

White, J. (1976). *Everything you want to know about TM—Including how to do it.* New York: Pocket Books.

White, P. D., Gilner, F. H., Handal, P. J., & Napoli, J. G. (1983). A behavioral intervention for death anxiety in nurses. *Omega, 14,* 33–42.

Whybrow, P. C., Akiskal, H. S., & McKinney, W. T. (1984). *Mood disorders: Toward a new psychobiology.* New York: Plenum Press.

Wickramasekera, I., Truong, X. T., Bush, M., & Orr, C. (1976). The management of rheumatoid arthritic pain: Preliminary observations. In I. Wickramasekera (Ed.), *Biofeedback, behavior therapy and hypnosis: Potentiating the verbal control of behavior for clinicians* (pp. 47–55). Chicago: Nelson-Hall.

Wideman, M. V., & Singer, J. E. (1984). The role of psychological mechanisms in preparation for childbirth. *American Psychologist, 39,* 1357–1371.

Wilder, J. (1957). The law of initial value in neurology and psychiatry: Facts and problems. *Journal of Nervous and Mental Disease, 125,* 73–86.

Williams, L. R. T., & Herbert, P. G. (1976). Transcendental Meditation and fine perceptual-motor skill. *Perceptual and Motor Skills, 43,* 303–309.

Williams, L. R. T., & Vickerman, B. L. (1976). Effects of Transcendental Meditation on fine motor skill. *Perceptual and Motor Skills, 43,* 607–613.

Williams, P., Francis, A., & Durham, R. (1976). Personality and meditation. *Perceptual and Motor Skills, 43,* 787–792.

Williams, P., & West, M. (1975). EEG responses to photic stimulation in persons experienced at meditation. *Electroencephalography and Clinical Neurophysiology, 39,* 519–522.

Williamson, D. A. (1981). Behavioral treatment of migraine and muscle-contraction headaches: Outcome and theoretical explanations. In M. Hersen, R. M. Eisler, & P. M. Miller (Eds.), *Progress in behavior modification* (Vol. 11, pp. 163–201). New York: Academic Press.

Williamson, D. A., Monguillot, J. E., Jarrell, M. P., Cohen, R. A., Pratt, J. M., & Blouin, D. C. (1984). Relaxation for the treatment of headache: Controlled evaluation of two group programs. *Behavior Modification, 8,* 407–424.

Wilson, A., & Smith, F. J. (1968). Counterconditioning therapy using free association: A pilot study. *Journal of Abnormal Psychology, 73,* 474–478.

Wilson, A., & Wilson, A. S. (1970). Psychophysiological and learning correlates of anxiety and induced muscle relaxation. *Psychophysiology, 6,* 740–748.

Wilson, A. F., Honsberger, R., Chiu, J. T., & Novey, H. S. (1975). Transcendental meditation and asthma. *Respiration, 32,* 74–80.

Wilson, G. T., & O'Leary, K. D. (1980). *Principles of behavior therapy.* Englewood Cliffs, NJ: Prentice-Hall.

Wilson, J. F. (1981). Behavioral preparation for surgery: Benefit or harm? *Journal of Behavioral Medicine, 4,* 79–102.

Wilson, J. F., Moore, R. W., Randolph, S., & Hanson, B. J. (1982). Behavioral preparation of patients for gastrointestinal endoscopy: Information, relaxation, and coping style. *Journal of Human Stress, 8*(4), 13–23.

Wilson, M. (1985). The effects of relaxation and cognitive expectancy on attraction in a social interaction. *Journal of Social and Clinical Psychology, 3,* 293–306.

Wincze, J. P., & Caird, W. K. (1976). The effects of systematic desensitization and video desensitization in the treatment of essential sexual dysfunction in women. *Behavior Therapy, 7,* 335–342.

Wing, R. R., Epstein, L. H., Nowalk, M. P., & Lamparski, D. M. (1986). Behavioral self-regulation in the treatment of patients with diabetes mellitus. *Psychological Bulletin, 99,* 78–89.

Witkin, H. A. (1950). Individual differences in ease of perception of embedded figures. *Journal of Personality, 19,* 1–15.

Wodarski, J. S., & Bagarozzi, D. A. (1979). *Behavioral social work.* New York: Human Sciences Press.

Wolberg, L. R. (1954). *The technique of psychotherapy.* New York: Grune & Stratton.

Wolf, S. L., & Binder-Macleod, S. A. (1983). Electromyographic biofeedback applications to the hemiplegic patient: Changes in lower extremity neuromuscular and functional status. *Physical Therapy, 63,* 1404–1413.

Wolfe, D. A., Sandler, J., & Kaufman, K. (1981). A competency-based parent training program for child abusers. *Journal of Consulting and Clinical Psychology, 49,* 633–640.

Wolfe, R. L. (1977). A comparison of self- versus therapist-administered biofeedback relaxation training and desensitization. *Dissertation Abstracts International, 38,* 923B–924B. (University Microfilms No. 77-16,258)

Wolff, H. G. (1963). *Headache and other head pain* (2nd ed.). New York: Oxford University Press.

Wolkove, N., Kreisman, H., Darragh, D., Cohen, C., & Frank, H. (1984). Effect of transcendental meditation on breathing and respiratory control. *Journal of Applied Physiology, 56,* 607–612.

Wollersheim, J. P. (1970). Effectiveness of group therapy based upon learning principles in the treatment of overweight women. *Journal of Abnormal Psychology, 76,* 462–474.

Wolpe, J. (1958). *Psychotherapy by reciprocal inhibition.* Stanford, CA: Stanford University Press.

Wolpe, J. (1973). *The practice of behavior therapy* (2nd ed.). Elmsford, NY: Pergamon Press.

Wolpe, J. (1982). *The practice of behavior therapy* (3rd ed.). Elmsford, NY: Pergamon Press.

Wolpe, J. (1984). Deconditioning and ad hoc uses of relaxation: An overview. *Journal of Behavior Therapy and Experimental Psychiatry, 15,* 299–304.

Wolpe, J., & Lang, P. J. (1964). A fear survey schedule for use in behaviour therapy. *Behaviour Research and Therapy, 2,* 27–30.

Wood, C. J. (1986). Evaluation of meditation and relaxation on physiological response during the performance of fine motor and gross motor tasks. *Perceptual and Motor Skills, 62,* 91–98.

Woodbury, D. M., & Karler, R. (1960). The role of carbon dioxide in the nervous system. *Anesthesiology, 21,* 686–703.

Woolfolk, R. L. (1975). Psychophysiological correlates of meditation. *Archives of General Psychiatry, 32,* 1326–1333.

Woolfolk, R. L. (1984). Self-control meditation and the treatment of chronic anger. In D. H. Shapiro, Jr. & R. N. Walsh (Eds.), *Meditation: Classic and contemporary perspectives* (pp. 550–554). Hawthorne, NY: Aldine.

Woolfolk, R. L., Carr-Kaffashan, L., McNulty, T. F., & Lehrer, P. M. (1976). Meditation training as a treatment for insomnia. *Behavior Therapy, 7,* 359–365.

Woolfolk, R. L., & Lehrer, P. M. (Eds.). (1984). *Principles and practice of stress management.* New York: Guilford.

Woolfolk, R. L., Lehrer, P. M., McCann, B. S., & Rooney, A. J. (1982). Effects of progressive relaxation and meditation on cognitive and somatic manifestations of daily stress. *Behaviour Research and Therapy, 20,* 461–467.

Woolfolk, R. L., & McNulty, T. F. (1983). Relaxation treatment for insomnia: A component analysis. *Journal of Consulting and Clinical Psychology, 51,* 495–503.

Woolfolk, R. L., & Rooney, A. J. (1981). The effect of explicit expectations on initial meditation experiences. *Biofeedback and Self-Regulation, 6,* 483–491.

Worthington, E. L., Jr. (1978). The effects of imagery content, choice of imagery content, and self-verbalization on the self-control of pain. *Cognitive Therapy and Research, 2,* 225–240.

Worthington, E. L., Jr., & Feldman, D. A. (1981). Presentational style of therapeutic directive and response to cold pressor pain. *Perceptual and Motor Skills, 53,* 506.

Worthington, E. L., Jr., & Martin, G. A. (1980). A laboratory analysis of response to pain after training in three Lamaze techniques. *Journal of Psychosomatic Research, 24,* 109–116.

Worthington, E. L., Jr., & Shumate, M. (1981). Imagery and verbal counseling methods in stress inoculation training for pain control. *Journal of Counseling Psychology, 28,* 1–6.

Wroblewski, P. F., Jacob, T., & Rehm, L. P. (1977). The contribution of relaxation to symbolic modeling in the modification of dental fears. *Behaviour Research and Therapy, 15,* 113–115.

Yates, A. J., & Sambrailo, F. (1984). Bulimia nervosa: A descriptive and therapeutic study. *Behaviour Research and Therapy, 22,* 503–517.

Yates, D. H. (1946). Relaxation in psychotherapy. *Journal of General Psychology, 34,* 213–238.

Yeaton, W. H., & Sechrest, L. (1981). Critical dimensions in the choice and maintenance of successful treatments: Strength, integrity, and effectiveness. *Journal of Consulting and Clinical Psychology, 49,* 156–167.

Yesavage, J. A. (1984). Relaxation and memory training in 39 elderly patients. *American Journal of Psychiatry, 141,* 778–781.

Yesavage, J. A., Rose, T. L., & Spiegel, D. (1982). Relaxation training and memory improvement in elderly normals: Correlation of anxiety ratings and recall improvement. *Experimental Aging Research, 8,* 195–198.

Yogi, M. M. (1975). *Transcendental Meditation.* New York: Plume.

Yogi, M. M. (1976). *Creating an ideal society.* West Germany: Maharishi European Research University Press.

Yorkston, N. J., Eckert, E., McHugh, R. B., Philander, D. A., & Blumenthal, M. N. (1979). Bronchial asthma: Improved lung function after behaviour modification. *Psychosomatics, 20,* 325–327, 330–331.

Yorkston, N. J., McHugh, R. B., Brady, R., Serber, M., & Sergeant, H. G. S. (1974). Verbal desensitization in bronchial asthma. *Journal of Psychosomatic Research, 18,* 371–376.

Yorkston, N. J., & Sergeant, H. G. S. (1969). A simple method of relaxation. *Lancet, 2,* 1319–1321.

Younger, J., Adriance, W., & Berger, R. J. (1975). Sleep during Transcendental Meditation. *Perceptual and Motor Skills, 40,* 953–954.

Yuille, J. C., & Sereda, L. (1980). Positive effects of meditation: A limited generalization? *Journal of Applied Psychology, 65,* 333–340.

Yulis, S., Brahm, F., Charnes, G., Jacard, L. M., Picota, E., & Rutman, F. (1975). The extinction of phobic behavior as a function of attention shifts. *Behaviour Research and Therapy, 13,* 173–176.

Zaichkowsky, L. D., & Kamen, R. (1978). Biofeedback and meditation: Effects on muscle tension and locus of control. *Perceptual and Motor Skills, 46,* 955–958.

Zamarra, J. W., Besseghini, I., & Wittenberg, S. (1977). The effects of the Transcendental Meditation program on the exercise performance of patients with angina pectoris. In D. W. Orme-Johnson & J. T. Farrow (Eds.), *Scientific research on the Transcendental Meditation program: Collected papers* (Vol. 1, 2nd ed., pp. 270–278). Livingston Manor, NY: Maharishi European Research University Press.

Zeisset, R. M. (1968). Desensitization and relaxation in the modification of psychiatric patients' interview behavior. *Journal of Abnormal Psychology, 73,* 18–24.

Zeldow, L. L. (1976). Treating clenching and bruxing by habit change. *Journal of the American Dental Association, 93,* 31–33.

Zimmermann-Tansella, C., Dolcetta, G., Azzini, V., Zacche, G., Bertagni, P., Siani, R., & Tansella, M. (1979). Preparation courses for childbirth in primipara. A comparison. *Journal of Psychosomatic Research, 23,* 227–233.

Zubek, J. P. (1973). Behavioral and physiological effects of prolonged sensory and perceptual deprivation: A review. In J. E. Rasmussen (Ed.), *Man in isolation and confinement* (pp. 9–83). Chicago: Aldine.

Zuckerman, M. (1960). The development of an affect adjective check list for the measurement of anxiety. *Journal of Consulting Psychology, 24,* 457–462.

Zuckerman, M., Lubin, B., Vogel, L., & Valerius, E. (1964). Measurement of experimentally induced affects. *Journal of Consulting Psychology, 28,* 418–425.

Zuroff, D. C., & Schwarz, J. C. (1978). Effects of transcendental meditation and muscle relaxation on trait anxiety, maladjustment, locus of control, and drug use. *Journal of Consulting and Clinical Psychology, 46,* 264–271.

Zuroff, D. C., & Schwarz, J. C. (1980). Transcendental meditation versus muscle relaxation: A two-year follow-up of a controlled experiment. *American Journal of Psychiatry, 137,* 1229–1231.

Author Index

Subject Index